THE ART OF BEING HUMAN THE HUMANITIES AS A TECHNIQUE FOR LIVING

CUSTOM EDITION FOR KAPLAN UNIVERSITY

Richard Paul Janaro • Thelma C. Altshuler

Taken from:
The Art of Being Human: The Humanities as a Technique for Living, Ninth Edition
by Richard Paul Janaro · Thelma C. Altshuler

Custom Publishing

New York   Boston   San Francisco
London   Toronto   Sydney   Tokyo   Singapore   Madrid
Mexico City   Munich   Paris   Cape Town   Hong Kong   Montreal

Cover Art: *Rainforest Leaves*, by Alisa Harding Stein; *Mask Performer Bali*, by Angela Sciaraffa; *SS4-1*, by Eugenie Lewalski Berg; *Inside Piano*, by S. Olsen/K. Mirza

Taken from:

The Art of Being Human: The Humanities as a Technique for Living, Ninth Edition
by Richard Paul Janaro and Thelma C. Altshuler
Copyright © 2009 by Pearson Education, Inc.
Published by Longman
New York, New York 10036

Printed in the United States of America

10 9 8 7 6 5 4

2008361186

RG

Pearson
Custom Publishing
is a division of

PEARSON

www.pearsonhighered.com

ISBN 10: 0-558-10877-6
ISBN 13: 978-0-558-10877-9

Detailed Contents

1 The Humanities: Still Vital

Overview of This Book

Some believe that in the twenty-first century, humans must adapt to the rapid, almost daily, advances in technology—to what Alvin Toffler more than thirty years ago called "future shock"—and that those who don't will be lost in a bewildering world of iPods, BlackBerries, and even computers being developed not only to think as efficiently as the human brain (or more so) but to experience emotion as well. New television screens as thin as sheets of paper; remote controls so powerful that you can start your dinner cooking while you are driving home; robots performing a brain operation in Fort Wayne, Indiana, controlled by a surgeon in Rangoon—and the list goes on and on.

Toffler predicted that the rate at which advances are made would accelerate to dizzying proportions, but perhaps only an Einstein could have imagined the speed. Some are wondering whether this technological takeover will eventually leave humanity behind in the dust, as if to say "All right, you invented us, but you've done your job, and now we don't need you."

Not only humanity but the *humanities*, the subject of this book, could be left in the dust unless we realize that those who love the humanities are often people who know how to use technology not for its own sake but for the betterment of human life. Poets of today may use a computer to give us memorable words and images. Visual artists may use not only computers but video, even fax machines, to express themselves and add new shapes to the world around us. In short, there is still a place for humanity. Machines can assist composers, but they can't come up with the music. Well, maybe they can, but they will be using notes and scales programmed by human beings. And if a composer doesn't like what a machine is turning out, there is always the delete button.

While we are marveling at the infinite potential of Google and the rest of the Internet, let us not forget that human beings created them. If we relax our minds and let them rust from lack of use, we are forgetting that the people who have given us the machines to work for us have not relaxed *their* minds. Let us use the creators and the innovators as our role models, not just use the amazing products of their intellectual labors. Yet one could wish they had thought to paste labels advising us, for example, "In addition to downloading Bon Jovi, you might also download Beethoven's Eroica Symphony."

◉ The goal of this book is to show you there is a wonderful, magical world of human devising that has existed as long as humanity has existed.

Source: © Fotosearch.

3

The goal of this book is to show you there is a wonderful, magical world of human devising that has existed for as long as humanity has existed, and that it is still here, waiting each day to be discovered anew. It is the world of the humanities. The humanities are just outside your door, waiting. They are also inside *you* if you know where to look. All you have to do is open that door or get in touch with your creative self and extend a welcoming hand. If you do, your life will be changed very much for the better. And you will want to run out into the street and share the wonder with everyone you meet!

Defining the Humanities

The humanities can no longer be defined in a simple statement. At one time they were said to be the best products of the best minds. The word **humanities** grew out of the term **humanism**, which did indeed once mean the study of what great artists, writers, and philosophers had accomplished. During the Renaissance, that huge artistic and political revolution that swept over Western Europe beginning in the fifteenth century, there was a revival of interest in the culture of ancient Greece and Rome—a culture that had been left largely unexamined during the thousand-year span following the fall of Rome. (Actually, *renaissance* means "rebirth.") The intelligentsia of the Renaissance believed that only through a study of classical art, literature, and philosophy could a person become *fully* human. Thus these **disciplines** became known as the humanities. In time, the term had to be extended beyond the study of Greek and Roman culture to include that of major Western European countries: first Italy, then France and Spain, then Britain, and finally Germany. As cultures multiplied, so did the disciplines people needed to study in pursuit of humanness. Music, theater, and dance began to flourish during the Renaissance, and scholars realized that these disciplines were also part of the ancient world's legacy.

The term *humanities* must now be broadened still further. Yes, we still need to pay attention to extraordinary artistic and intellectual achievements that have been singled out for special praise and that now represent what is sometimes called the "humanistic tradition." All of us belong to the human race and should want to know as much as possible about the distinguished contributions of those who have gone before. Yet we also need to recognize that the "humanistic tradition" usually was limited to the contributions made by *men* of the classical and then the Western European worlds. Plato and Michelangelo and Shakespeare continue to deserve our admiration and reward our study, but think of those persons, both male and female, past and present, who may be little known or not known at all but nevertheless left behind or now offer a myriad of wonderful songs, poems, and provocative thoughts waiting to be appreciated.

The humanities are also the creative and intellectual expressions of each of us in moments of inspiration, whether they happen in the shower or just walking down the street on a balmy day when our spirits are lifted by the sheer joy of being alive. In these times of global fears and a future of uncertainty, in these times of dizzying technological advances that can be both marvelous and bewildering, when it can be hard to pinpoint our identity in time and space, the humanities offer a safe haven, a quiet harbor where we can moor our vessels and, at least for a time, confirm who we are.

Each of us is more than a gender, an age, an address, an occupation. Each of us is thoughts, expressed or not, the capacity to be moved, the need to laugh or cry, longings for things just beyond our reach. The humanities give us stories to stimulate our imagination, ideas to stimulate our intellect, musical sounds to excite our passions. Exposure to the humanities helps us foster our ability to respond to the creativity and thought of others and to look inwardly to see what *we* think and what creative impulses lie dormant and cry out to be released. All of this helps us confront our true identity. A major aim of this book is to show how a study of the humanities can be the starting point for the journey into self-knowledge.

The humanities are inspiring achievements in themselves, but we also find value in the *study* of those achievements, in the *critical process* by which scholars and critics interpret the humanities and communicate their findings to others so that these achievements will never be forgotten. This is also the critical process by which we ourselves look squarely at and come to appreciate what is there for us to read, see, or hear. This process, often called *critical thinking*, is essential to being effectively human, the more so as the world's tempo increases. In fact, so crucial is critical thought and so important are the humanities in developing it that Chapter 2 is devoted solely to the subject.

The humanities can also be called a technique for living, accessible to every human being who wants to do more with life. They offer a way of life filled with moments of critical thought and aesthetic pleasure, and they are urgently needed in our world.

The humanities are addictive. Once you let song and story, music and dance, words and ideas into your life, you can never live without them. And you should never *have* to. The humanities are best appreciated in our quiet moments, and quiet is also addictive in a noisy world. *If only everyone on Earth would insist on these quiet moments, wouldn't the world be a happier (and a safer) place?*

In a world that has become a global village, in a world with all its hovering threats of terror attacks and dirty bombs, with so many who are more than willing to sacrifice their own lives to kill others, in a world of environmental woes, a world in which cynics wonder about the value of living—in such a world there are always the humanities to lift our spirits. Art and music and literature, stories and songs, all the marvels of the human mind, the architectural and engineering achievements—or just noticing the first robin of the year—they keep reminding us that, as American novelist William Faulkner said when he accepted the Nobel Prize for Literature in 1949, humanity will not only survive, "it will prevail."

But humanity will not prevail just because we are living longer. Genetic scientists expect to replace the gene responsible for aging and promise life expectancies that were once found only in literary fables. (Perhaps some of us may live to celebrate our "eleventy-first birthday," like Bilbo Baggins of *The Hobbit*.) Existing on and on without coming to terms with who we are and without knowing how to reach a safe haven inside when the world gets maddeningly chaotic about us—maybe that wouldn't be the best technique for living. The humanities help make longer life spans abundantly richer.

The key to the richer life is to be as open-minded as possible. One of the dangers of living longer is becoming too firmly enclosed by the values many of us have held since our earliest days. The humanities cannot fail to inspire open-mindedness. The literature of other cultures, not to mention their music, art, and patterns of thought—becoming aware of the problems they face and *their* way of prevailing—are indispensable to our own development. Why? The answer

We are healthy only to the extent that our ideas are humane.

—Kurt Vonnegut

is simple: the world has grown too small for us not to care what is happening all around us. And the world is just that—all around us. So we need to balance a sharper awareness of who we are with a broader understanding of who *they* are, for they are part of us, and we of them.

The cultural history of Western civilization as traditionally presented will no longer suffice. During the time of the ancient Greeks, for example, were there not many women who thought great thoughts and wrote great poems, even if unknown today? While the much heralded early civilizations, like those of Egypt, China, Japan, Rome, and Greece, have received abundant attention and been the subject of countless critical and historical studies, they do not tell the whole story of human genius. Rich cultures flourished in Africa, South and Central America, the North America that was inhabited long before Columbus "discovered" it, and in the lands that produced Islamic art, science, and philosophy—lands once thought too mysterious for the Western mind to understand. We find vestiges of rich cultures as well in Stonehenge in England and in the thirty-foot statues that stand in eternal attention on Easter Island. In our more recent history, while some were sipping juleps on plantation verandas in the American South, slaves in their humble shanties were weaving elaborate tales and singing complex songs to keep their heritage alive.

The traditional humanistic disciplines have been art, music, literature, and drama, and these are discussed in Part Two, along with the musical stage (opera, musical theater, and dance) and the cinema, because each has by now contributed works that are considered of lasting excellence or, at the very least, represent steps in the direction of art—works that are also valuable in our quest for self-knowledge. Part Three deals with issues and themes that cross disciplinary and cultural boundaries: religion, morality, love, happiness, death, and subjects and art forms that have caused much controversy.

The book concludes with a chapter on freedom—how it can be defined and how it can be achieved and held. The life enriched by the humanities presupposes freedom of choice. We cannot know who we really are if someone else determines who that shall be.

> *The ancient Greeks . . . were convinced that an explanation of, and definition for, Beauty was as concrete and discoverable as the answer to why the days got shorter in winter . . .*
>
> —Bruce Maddox

Gifts of the Humanities

Economics tells us that the wants of people are insatiable, but resources are limited. Because almost everything is scarcer than we would like, treasured possessions, as well as basics like food and shelter, come with a price tag. Do we have enough money to buy everything we want? The answer is usually NO!

With the humanities the problem is reversed. *The resources of the humanities are unlimited*, but all too often our wants are meager. In the economic world you can't always be rich by choice, but in the world of the humanities you can be poor by choice.

Several years ago, when the U.S. economy was in a severe recession, banks attracted savings deposits by offering gifts to those who would forgo spending and open CD accounts instead. People were walking out with new toasters, blenders, steam irons, and luggage, and of course bank reserves swelled. Such incentives are cyclical in nature, but the humanities always have gifts that are there for us regardless of what the economy is doing. Here are some of them.

Beauty

The shiny new car stands in the driveway, attracting envious glances from the neighbors. The owner glows with pride. Is it that the newly acquired possession is a sign of the buyer's apparent prosperity? Is it simply that people are genetically prone to owning things and the more the better? Although the answer may be yes, isn't something else involved? Is it something we call **beauty**?

Ever since philosophy began, ever since thoughtful people started inquiring into the meaning and purpose of life, the question of the beautiful has arisen. Its close connection with pleasure has always seemed apparent. It is pleasant and desirable to see beautiful things and beautiful people. People prefer to live amid beauty than amid ugliness.

Though people may debate whether a particular person or piece of music is beautiful, there is widespread agreement that something deserves to be called beautiful if the arrangement of the parts is pleasing, if it seems *right*. The rightness of the arrangement determines the pleasure that it gives us. When there is something in an arrangement that seems *not* right, we are less attracted, possibly even repelled.

Is judging an arrangement—of a painting, a person's face, a story, a dramatic moment—as right or not right entirely subjective? Yes and no. There is widespread agreement about the rightness of *certain* arrangements. Leonardo da Vinci's *La Gioconda*, more popularly known as the *Mona Lisa* (Color Plate 1), has earned the reputation as the world's most famous painting. Each week thousands flock to the Louvre Museum in Paris to see the portrait of the lady with the enigmatic smile. Yet in the centuries since it was created (1503–1505), innumerable art historians and critics have given their opinions of what makes this a great work. They often differ in the specific elements they praise—such as the haunting face or the ambiguity of the gaze—but they tend to agree that the way the artist has assembled the various elements has turned a flat canvas into the illusion of a living, breathing, three-dimensional human being. They tend to agree that *Mona Lisa* is a beautiful work of art.

The pleasure that beauty inspires in us is called **aesthetic**. Yet what kind of pleasure is it? One answer is that the beautiful inspires within us *a feeling of well-being that is its own justification*. True, the attraction of a shiny new car may have less to do with its pure beauty than with the pride we feel in owning it or, if it belongs to someone else, by the envy we feel. When a beautiful face passes by, we might long for closer contact with it, but we would not have such a desire if we did not first make an aesthetic judgment. Even if we are denied closer contact, we probably won't change our opinion of its beauty. The critics who have written volumes about the "secret" of the *Mona Lisa* have already made an aesthetic judgment and are now trying to find the words to describe why the arrangement of the parts is right. A universal definition of beauty that fits every example may be impossible to find, but few of us would deny that the beautiful does indeed exist.

The humanities are, *in part*, a catalogue of works that have tallied a host of positive votes from people who have spent their lives in pursuit of the beautiful and who hold up road signs for us in our own quest. Be advised, however, that the pursuit is endless, the catalogue needs almost daily updating, and the road signs often vary from one culture to another. If we are to expand our capacity for aesthetic pleasure, we need to experience many versions of the beautiful and try to see them from other points of view.

Sharply differing portraits of women considered beautiful in widely separated times and places.

Source: Left: Halle Berry. Credit: Reuters/Corbis. Right: Kitigawa Utamaro, *The Beauty*. Credit: Burstein Collection/Corbis.

Though we travel the world over to find the beautiful, we must carry it with us or we find it not.

—**Ralph Waldo Emerson**

Study the two portraits of women on this page. The photo on the left is that of Halle Berry, a popular Hollywood star, famous not only as an award-winning actress but as an acknowledged beauty. The image on the right is from a woodblock engraving by Japanese artist Kitagawa Utamaro (1753–1806), representing a late eighteenth-century Japanese popular trend in which artists celebrated the beauty of women. Utamaro is known for his 1794 collection called *Physiognomies of Ten Women*. Definitions of what constitutes true female beauty are clearly different here, but each woman, for her time and culture, can be said to illustrate what many have agreed to call beautiful.

In the Asian Wing of New York's Metropolitan Museum of Art, tucked away in a corner that the visitor can easily miss, is a sculpture called *Water Stone* (see photo) by the Japanese artist Isamu Noguchi (1904–1988). It is a gray stone fountain of uneven shape with a perpetual flow of water that, at first glance, appears to be a sheet of clear glass sitting motionless on top but, in reality, trickles slowly down the side so that the escaping water is always equal to the new supply being pumped up from below. The trickle creates a soft sound that soothes and mesmerizes the visitor who takes the time to sit on the bench provided. One woman reported that she sat there, entranced, for nearly an hour.

The arrangement of parts in *Water Stone* includes the shape and texture of the stone, the varying shades created by the falling water, and most important, the

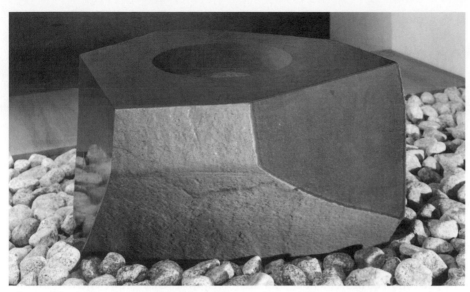

A beautiful arrangement of parts: the shape of the sculpture, the serenity of the water, and its soothing sound as it slowly trickles down the sides.

Source: Isamu Noguchi, *Water Stone,* 1986. Credit: The Metropolitan Museum of Art, Purchase, Anonymous Gift, 1987. (1987.222).

sound itself. But you don't have to be in a museum to experience the beauty of similar arrangements. A woodland stream, flowing over rocks of different shapes, will create varied shadings, and if you shut your eyes and really listen to the water, you will discover that it has a variety of sounds, depending on wind and the different rocks over which it flows.

All you need to do to experience in full how the humanities can take you to that quiet oasis we mentioned is find a stream in the woods, or study closely the different colors in rainwater gushing alongside a curb. When you search for the beautiful, you will be astonished to realize how close it is.

Let's say you go to a popular movie on a Friday night. Sitting there with your popcorn and soda, you might be hoping for nothing more than a few hours of escapist entertainment—just something to whisk you away from worrying about a job or school or a troublesome relationship. Perhaps you are watching (or half-watching) the usual slam-bang car chase while enduring the ear-splitting sound of a spray of bullets magnified by gigantic speakers. Then a car suddenly blasts its way through a huge glass window and divebombs straight into the river below. Just as suddenly, the music stops, and the car falls in slow motion, gracefully contradicting the expected explosiveness that often leaves you indifferent. The moment is justified for its own sake. It is a sudden moment of aesthetic beauty, sometimes employed by an artistic director to soften the horror of the death that will happen within the car. Both movie and television history are filled with unanticipated beautiful moments, most of them soon forgotten. Perhaps you can think of some you have experienced recently. Really noticing is a first step in appreciating the humanities.

Of course, the arts can do more for us than providing an aesthetic moment. Sometimes they may convey a message the artist believes is imperative that we understand. In fact, some take the position that meaning is what we primarily look for in any work. Yet it does a disservice both to the artist and to us the viewers if we always insist on looking for a message. (After all, what is the message in a car diving in slow motion?) Many graphic artists, poets, and novelists object to critics evaluating a work solely in terms of the important—or unimportant—meanings they find.

The painting *Mississippi Monday* (Color Plate 2) by the American artist Romare Bearden (1912–1988) illustrates how an artist's intent can be misunderstood. By his own admission, Bearden was interested primarily in creating aesthetic pleasure. Here he recreates a familiar scene: women hanging up laundry. What appears to be central to the painting is the color and design of the clothes themselves: that is the *arrangement* of the parts. Doubtless the artist would say, "If you want to talk about what the standing woman is tossing from the bag or what the seated woman is doing with her hands, or to ask whether the painting is a commentary on the subservient role of women, go right ahead, but that's not what I'm up to."

The humanities can be enjoyed for both their aesthetic and communicative function. Learning to distinguish one from the other is an important part of *critical thinking*, the subject of Chapter 2.

Beautiful Movement

The best art always seems effortless. . .

—**Stephen Sondheim**

The perfection of movement cannot fail to inspire a sense of awe and admiration. Movement is as much a part of being human as breathing. Few of us move in perfect synchrony, but almost all of us experience joy when we see it done right. Even though our own movements may lack the coordination of, say, the skilled dancer, we find aesthetic pleasure in not just watching others but in getting up and swaying, gliding, or shaking to a rhythm. We have patterned our lives to meeting deadlines and reaching destinations. Perhaps that's why people like, for a change, to be on the dance floor and simply move in rhythm. Are they trying to get somewhere in particular? No. The pleasure of the movement is its own reason for existing.

The French artist Edgar Degas (1834–1917) loved to paint dancers. He seems to have had no message to convey beyond the beauty of the women and the elegance of their movements. Ballerinas gave him aesthetic pleasure. His paintings give that same pleasure to us.

So do the graceful leaps of a figure skater such as the young Japanese star Fumie Suguri. Like all great skaters and dancers, Suguri makes her body do what bodies seem never meant to do. In her leaps she defies gravity. In her spins she defies analysis. To the non-skater (most of us) it becomes nearly impossible to see how two rigid blades attached to her shoes can seem to disappear as she twirls. In this respect, figure skaters are akin to great magicians like David Copperfield. The arrangement of the parts in a given trick seem right if we don't see their function. If the rest of the world were not more often clumsy than otherwise, if our feet didn't get in each other's way from time to time, if we didn't drop things conspicuously, then the art of the figure skater or the magician would perhaps seem less than beautiful.

Language

Words in varied combinations are the means by which we communicate to ourselves and with each other. Through language we make ourselves understood to others, and we are able to understand what we read and what others are saying. The need for language becomes apparent at an early age, and we develop a love of language if we are fortunate enough to be around adults who talk to us (but not in baby-talk), who enjoy reading, and who read to us.

Children develop through recognizable and documented stages. Most children between the ages of two and three become word-conscious. The need to attach

Ballet performances provided the artist with aesthetic pleasure, and the painting can offer us the same experience.

Source: Edgar Degas, *Rehearsal on Stage,* 1876. Credit: Giraudon/Art Resource, NY.

a name to everything in sight appears to be an inborn instinct. Parents as well as older siblings can be annoyed at hearing the persistent "What's that?" throughout the day, even as they are happy that the insatiable demand for words is proceeding as it should. At this stage, children like to repeat sentences and phrases they hear in their surroundings, even if they have no idea what the words mean. Children like the sound and the "taste" of words. Nature supplies the need to acquire words, for the ability to think and to communicate are strategies for our survival.

How or when some of us lose the need for more words is a complex mystery. Unraveling it is perhaps less important than the awareness that *it does not have to happen.* That's where the humanities come in. Through reading, and through listening to great language on the stage or screen, we acquire models of how to say things in ways that make others sit up and take notice. People experienced in using the humanities as a technique for living sometimes make a point by directly quoting well-known lines, assured that their friends will catch the reference.

One of the most famous lines in all of drama is the beginning of Hamlet's third soliloquy: *To be or not to be: that is the question.* When people on similar wavelengths are discussing whether, for example, to stay home and watch television or go downtown for a costly evening of eating out and seeing a movie, the comment "Ah, that is the question" communicates instantly that the speaker is not leaning one way or the other but is wide open to suggestions. Directly quoting or providing variations on famous lines that you know others will recognize is not only fun, but it cuts down on the need for details and circular discussions.

True wit is Nature to advantage dressed:
What oft was thought, but ne'er so well expressed.

—**Alexander Pope**

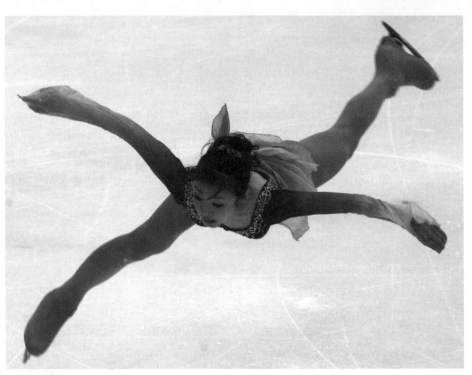

Great dancers and skaters like Fumie Suguri seem to transcend the role that nature has given to the human body.

Source: Ng Han Guan/AP Photo.

Reading is to the mind what exercise is to the body.
—**Joseph Addison**

The most popular work of the medieval English poet Geoffrey Chaucer (1340–1400), *The Canterbury Tales*, contains not only a collection of unforgettable stories but also famous descriptions of the people who tell them. Chaucer was a master at capturing the essence of his characters with swift strokes of his pen, many of which are part of the reservoir of language in the minds of people who read. One of the characters is a lawyer who is always in a hurry and apparently so busy that he could easily have been the envy of lazy people. After describing the man and his behavior in detail, Chaucer adds: "Yet he seemed busier than he was." Who knows how many thousands of readers over the last 600 years have used this line as a reference to people who display feverish but essentially meaningless activity? A high school student is asked why he is not doing his homework. His reply: "I'm very busy with other things." One parent then tells the other, "He seems busier than he is."

The sixth century B.C.E. Greek philosopher Heraclitus is famous for having said: "You cannot step twice into the same river." By this he meant that life is constant change, that the only thing stable in the entire universe is the fact of change itself. A contemporary environmental expert, addressing a college graduating class and wishing to underscore the growing dangers of water pollution, echoed Heraclitus and remarked: "You cannot step *once* into the same river." Clearly, the versatile language derived from the humanities even increases the chance that an urgent cause may win more supporters.

The humanities help us to appreciate a variety of ingenious phrasing and offer us models of how language can be expertly manipulated. One of the greatest comedies ever written, Oscar Wilde's 1895 *The Importance of Being Earnest* (discussed in Chapter 7), is a storehouse of witty lines illustrating that one way of saying something is not necessarily as good as another. In one scene the hero, Jack Worthing, is being interviewed by his fiancé's mother, a social lioness with biting wit, who investigates his credentials as a suitor. At one point she asks the nervous young man whether he smokes. Sheepishly he admits that well yes, he does smoke. Her unexpected reply: "I'm glad to hear it. A man should always have an occupation of some sort." Not only is the lady staying one step ahead of him with her wit, but she is making an indirect statement about the indolence and lack of purpose of the upper classes.

Playing with language has evolved into a high art. Like the beautiful, good language needs no further justification. A person characterized by others as someone with "a way with words" or "a flair for language" generally earns respect (unless, of course, it turns out that the person never has anything else to offer *except* words).

Yet just as a novel or play or movie can be spoiled when authors use words and idioms that have become so commonplace they are no longer effective, so too is the everyday language of most people littered with terminology employed over and over. "I'm so tired I could die" belongs in the category of the no-longer-usable. Yet such hackneyed language keeps slipping from our tongues without our even noticing. "Like" has become the most frequently spoken word in our language, whether used appropriately or not. "I felt like a worn-out dishrag" no longer makes any kind of impression but is at least grammatically sound. What, however, are we to make of "After she said she decided not to go to the dance with me, I was, like, this can't be happening"?

In addition to "like," ordinary speech is now littered with "y'know" and "go" in place of "said"—as in "I go . . . and then he goes . . ." Hollywood and television perpetuate the idea that lines of dialogue are good if they reproduce the way people actually speak. But do we listen closely to that speech, whether it's in real life or on a screen? Does it startle us with its cleverness or a memorable turn of phrase? Does it help us grow? Listen carefully to the speech patterns of people with whom you are conversing. If their language tends to be fresh and interesting, chances are they spend a lot of time reading. Perhaps your own language reflects the same habit. We hope so.

Ideas

Language is not only the vehicle through which we can display our savvy in everyday dealings with others; it is also the means by which we formulate ideas. Still, all of us have flashes of ideas that we can't quite catch hold of because the words aren't there. A philosopher once said, "If you can't say it, you don't know it." When someone explains a complicated idea such as the theory of relativity and we nod to signify understanding, we are more or less guaranteeing that we would be able to deliver the identical explanation in our own words. Very often we cannot do this.

Words are the means by which we think. If we have no words, we cannot have ideas. We can have *intuitions* without words, but they are not the same as ideas. Intuitions are, of course, vital human resources. We don't need words to find a piece of music exciting. Intuitions are necessary for a full appreciation of much that the humanities have to offer. But through our philosophers, novelists, and poets, we derive a love for exciting ideas. After reading a stimulating book that makes an explosive point, one may say: "Oh! I wish I'd thought of that!" And don't we glow with pride when we advance an idea that meets with approval, even admiration?

The most beautiful thing we can experience is the mysterious. It is the source of science.

—Albert Einstein

Difficult things of the world can only be tackled when they are easy. Big things of the world can only be achieved by attending to their small beginnings.

—**Lao-tzu**

When people talk about "the mind," they are really talking about a supposed place inside the brain where ideas are formulated and stored. It is probably better to refer to the formulation and storing of ideas as "thinking." This capacity, once thought to be unique to human beings but now a matter open to question, remains nonetheless the cornerstone of humanity.

Thinking helps us keep our sanity—even in our world of rapidly accelerating change and technological marvels that are said to think *for* us. Fortunately, the brain can still be what makes us want to do more than just survive. Thinking keeps us in touch with ourselves and the world around us. Thinking comes in a variety of forms. Rigorous studies like mathematics, physics, and economics provide powerful exercise for the brain, but not all of us are adept at these disciplines. Yet happily, we have the humanities, which widen both our emotional range and our understanding of many things: the past, the present, human behavior, the workings of the creative mind, and the many unanswered questions that philosophers, scientists, and theologians have asked for centuries. A recently founded movement, the Society for Philosophical Inquiry, is the brainchild of Christopher Phillips, author of *Socrates' Cafe* (2003). In various venues, all with the name Socrates' Cafe, members gather to discuss and share ideas. The format for the meetings is inspired by the teaching methods of Socrates (469–399 B.C.E.), mentor of Plato (427–347 B.C.E.).

Socrates and his young students would gather in an Athenian grove called Academe and discuss specific questions, such as "What is justice?" As recorded by Plato—since the master himself, as far as we know, wrote nothing down—the discussions took this form:

> *The question is posed by Socrates. One student says "Justice is whatever is in the best interest of the ruling party."*
>
> *Socrates answers: "Can the ruling party ever pass a law that is for some reason* not *in its best interest?"*
>
> *Student: "I suppose it could happen."*
>
> *Socrates: "If it* did *happen, would the people be justified in breaking that law?"*
>
> *Student: "I don't think so. A law is a law."*
>
> *Socrates: "In other words, it would be wrong to break a law just because somebody thought it was not in the best interest of the ruling party."*
>
> *Student: "Well . . . maybe it* could *be broken."*
>
> *Socrates: "If you* thought *the law could be broken and I said it couldn't, which of us is right?"*
>
> *Student: "I guess in that case we're both right."*
>
> *Socrates: "Is this your idea of a just society—one in which anyone can decide whether to obey a law or not? Would you want to live in such a society?"*
>
> *Student: "I . . . suppose I wouldn't."*
>
> *Socrates: "Then justice really has to be defined as something that is absolute and not only in the best interest of the ruling party or the individual who decides not to obey a certain law."*

The point of a discussion at a Socrates' Cafe is not to solve all the problems of the world. It is to adapt the technique of the ancient philosopher as well as those of other thinkers to puzzling questions of the past and present. Clearly "justice" is one. It has never been defined to everyone's satisfaction. Whether one agrees or not that justice is absolute and unchanging or that there is no applicable principle other than "might makes right," the discussion and defense of ideas are ways of strengthening our mental faculties. Like dancing, thinking needs no further justification.

Deeper Sense of the Past

The humanities allow us to see more than our personal past. Through the humanities we may immerse ourselves in the firsthand experiences of those who actually lived and often struggled in the past, lived and struggled with many of the problems that face us today. These experiences help each of us to better understand what living is all about. *The realized human being is an accumulation of what has gone before and how that affects the present.*

If birds of a feather flock together, they don't learn enough.
                    —Robert Hall

Becoming familiar with treasures of the past inspires in us the pride of belonging to the community of our species.

Source: Venus de Milo, second century B.C.E. Credit: Erich Lessing/Art Resource, NY.

Through the humanities we can live more than once: here and now, and yesterday as well. Those who refuse to browse among the cumulative treasures of human expression have only themselves to blame if they find themselves trapped in one solitary existence.

Like all of us, the past has its right to be heard. It did not, we know, allow for the *full* representation of its genius, for the contributions of both men and women from a variety of cultures. Still, the past has its own glory, even as it stands. The *Venus de Milo* statue has been around for many hundreds of years. It no longer has arms, but gazing at it, we cannot help seeing the idealism, the adoration of the female form that must have motivated the unknown classical artist. Becoming familiar with treasures of the past not only brings us closer to those who came before us but also inspires in us the pride of belonging to the continuity of our species. The love of beauty is timeless and universal, and the past, as reflected in the humanities, has more than its share of beauty, not to mention ideas and great language.

Some treasures from the past embody issues that still face us. *The Oresteia*, an epic tragedy by the Greek dramatist Aeschylus (525–456 B.C.E.), is based on a very ancient myth about the murder of a mother and her lover by a son seeking revenge for his father's death at their hands. In the final segment of the work, the playwright creates the world's first courtroom drama, in which the hero is acquitted on the grounds that his mother's crime had been greater than his. She had killed a man who was a great warrior and leader of his people. He had killed an adulterous woman and her lover. The decision to acquit the hero was made nearly 2,500 years ago and delivered from the stage at the Theater of Dionysus; it is still discussed today. Teachers of theater history often point out that the acquittal does not sit well with everyone. Feminist scholars, for example, argue that it discriminates against the gender of the victim and ignores the fact that the murdered husband had a mistress. Nevertheless, the work is a milestone in the early history of democracy. There was, after all, a trial. Reading or watching a performance of *The Oresteia* can generate a discussion of whether the law, even in a democracy, judges all persons equally.

Developing a profound respect for the work of Socrates, Plato, Aeschylus, the sculptor of the *Venus de Milo*, and others from the past does not mean that we choose to ignore the achievements of everyone else, including many contemporaries. At the same time, having profound respect for today and a wider vision of tomorrow does not mean that we ought to ignore what can be justly celebrated from yesterday.

Becoming an Infinite Person

By sharpening our awareness of the present—the issues, the important themes and varied ways of presenting them—and by linking us to the past, the humanities widen our view of life. As this book unfolds, you will be learning much more about the humanities and what the various disciplines are and how they can deeply affect your life. Your view of the humanities and the world will continue to expand.

Developing this perspective is of crucial importance in the twenty-first century, a time of amazing technology that changes almost daily. Every day the world grows smaller and the lives of the diverse populations become more interconnected. In such a world we must resist the temptation to concern ourselves exclusively with our own interests and the limited time we have to pursue them. To study the humanities requires time, time that could be spent doing other things. For some, pausing to reflect on art, music, literature, and drama might at first seem like *wasting* time. Who wants to stay inside and read a book when there is so much pulsating life out there? A cellphone call away? A mouse click away?

To answer those questions, let us consider the very model of humanism, the very essence of the infinite person, Leonardo da Vinci (1452–1519). So broad was the range of his curiosity and creative genius that history has accorded him that rarest of titles: *uomo universale*, universal man. He is also called a **Renaissance man**, meaning a man of the broadest possible learning and a widely diverse range of interests and achievements. Since Leonardo's time, that label has been given to many people, both famous and not-so-famous, who refused to be limited to just one field of endeavor, though it is doubtful that many will ever match what Leonardo accomplished: plans for early versions of the airplane and submarine; speculating about the human circulatory system long before William Harvey "officially" discovered the circulation of the blood; building the first hydrometer to measure the displacement of water; inventing the science of meteorology long before there were the proper instruments to make accurate predictions. And on top of all the scientific and technological contributions there are the works of art, including the world's most famous painting, the *Mona Lisa*.

The example of Leonardo da Vinci suggests that, while few may hope to approach his genius, all of us can do more with our lives than we are

History has accorded Leonardo da Vinci that rarest of titles, *uomo universale*. *Source:* Biblioteca Reale, Turin, Italy. Credit: Alinari/Art Resource, NY.

doing at this very moment. There are so many books to be read, so much music to hear, so many plays to see, so many great films that line the shelves of the video stores, orphans silently begging to be taken home. We may not become Renaissance persons, but infinite choices await us. The more we absorb from the humanities, the more we expand our knowledge, our capacity for understanding both ourselves and others. In a sense, we become infinite, intertwining with innumerable lives in myriad combinations.

Some of us rush through life, and some of us saunter through life. Mrs. Vesey sat through life.

—Wilkie Collins

There are many advantages to becoming an infinite person. Here are just three:

- The infinite person commits no crimes against humanity. He or she is no longer narrowly preoccupied with the self and its immediate needs, its sense of having been unfairly used, its desire to avenge wrongs against itself.

- The infinite person is free of rigid prejudices and never works consciously to restrict others from exercising their right to assemble, speak their minds openly, practice their own religion, and follow their own preferences, as long as, in being free, they do not themselves limit the freedom of others.

- The infinite person does not jump to quick conclusions but looks at all sides of an issue before making a judgment, recognizes that no judgment is final, and is always willing to reconsider in the light of new data. This person is therefore not constrained by family and social traditions and willingly seeks out the source of imposed or inherited beliefs so as to reevaluate them. "That's how we've always done it around here" is not the mark of the infinite person.

The book you are about to read is thus not only a visit to the treasure house of the humanities, the stupendous creative and intellectual achievements of human beings. It has the underlying purpose of convincing you that you cannot fail to want to expand your life, to fill every moment with art and thought, once you realize that all it takes is the willingness to do it.

Key Terms

aesthetic an experience in the arts or in life, such as watching a sunset, that we value for no reason beyond itself.

beauty a pleasing arrangement of parts that affects us aesthetically.

discipline in the humanities, a given art form—literature, visual art, music, drama, dance, cinema—as well as a field of academic study, such as "literary theory" or "history of dance."

humanism a movement begun in the early Renaissance that extolled and studied the creative and intellectual legacies of Greece and Rome, leading to the conviction that only through such study could one become fully human; the term *humanism* is now expanded to include the study of contributions from all cultures.

humanities once limited to "the best products of the best minds," narrowly defined as Greek or Roman, but later expanded to include Western European achievements and, more recently, the creative expressions of men and women around the world.

Renaissance man a label often applied to Leonardo da Vinci, indicating his display of genius in many areas from art to science; now used as high praise for anyone who has earned a reputation for high achievement in several fields.

Topics for
Writing and Discussion

1. The text states: "Each of us is more than a gender, an age, an address, an occupation." Explain what this means and how it relates to the study of the humanities.

2. How do you define *beauty*? Give two examples, citing how you would use the term to describe a person and an object.

3. Reread carefully the section called "Ideas." Then restate Socrates' definition of justice in your own words.

4. What does it mean to be an "infinite" person? Describe either someone you know personally or a famous person in the news who seems to fit the label.

5. Briefly give a profile of someone for whom the humanities function as a technique for living. Or do a profile of someone who has no interest in the humanities.

2 Profile of the Critical Thinker

Overview

In the introductory chapter we said that the study of the humanities includes understanding the critical process by which professional critics and scholars interpret and evaluate cultural achievements and communicate their thoughts to others. In this chapter we will elaborate on the elements of professional criticism, presenting examples of what the critic notices when he or she is reviewing a given humanities event. But we will also be dealing with ways in which most of us who are not professional critics can enrich our lives by using some of the same techniques: becoming objective in how we evaluate what we see, read, or hear; separating rational and emotional responses; delaying a final judgment until we have all the data. The critical skill has a strong carryover into everyday life as well. We should find ourselves not making snap judgments about other people or blindly accepting opinions expressed in the media just because we like the commentator. And, of vital importance to the conduct of our own lives, we should find that we are listening carefully to what others tell us before we make up our minds. All too often we are guilty of deciding something is true or that other thing is poppycock, or he is not to be trusted but she always knows what she is talking about. Worse, we often place people in the wax museum of our mind, attaching labels that never change: liar, cheat, double-crosser, tightwad.

Critical thinking sharpens the mind. If we start early enough in life and continue to exercise our critical faculties throughout our lives, chances are good that our mind will not desert us late in life. Toward the end of William Wharton's novel *Dad* (1981), the main character, en route to his father's funeral, has a sudden glimpse of his own aging. "I'll become a bore to others, a drag in conversation, repeat myself, be slow at comprehension, quick at misunderstanding, have lapses in conceptual sequences. All this will probably be invisible to me. I won't even be aware of my own decline."[1]

The older one gets, the more precious does the mind become. Many, early on, seek what they term "altered states," achieved through substance or alcohol abuse. A reason often given is that life is too complex; one has too

21

many responsibilities—school, parental problems, relationship problems—so escape is not only pleasant but absolutely necessary. Even if the use of such escape mechanisms is relatively moderate and there are no lasting effects, the mind, that most fragile and wonderful instrument, is not being used. The danger here is that when one finally is old enough to make important decisions, the critical faculties, so necessary for those decisions, won't be there. Those who miss the chance to develop critical thought can be called *non-critical thinkers*. They do think, of course, but most of the time they are narrowly concerned with the specific details of their everyday life. Decisions are based on what seems most personally important at the moment: for example, *What shall I wear to the party?* The critical thinker might wonder about the purpose of going to a party: in other words, might move from the particular moment to finding a general principle at work. *My acquaintances seem to like parties because . . . Am I just blindly following because . . . ? Why are there so many parties in our society?*

This chapter is dedicated both to those who believe there will be plenty of time in the future to think about weightier matters and those who believe in thinking now.

Apollonian and Dionysian Responses to the Humanities

You miss all the fun if you obey all the rules.

—Katharine Hepburn

Music does not depict scenes or describe objects or tell stories, but it mysteriously embodies the continuous motion and emotion that we experience at the sight of objects and scenes and events.

—Jacques Barzun

The German philosopher Friedrich Nietzsche (1844–1900) wrote a book in 1872 titled *The Birth of Tragedy from the Spirit of Music*, in which he revisits the great age of drama in fifth century (B.C.E.) Athens. He points out that the art form began as choral music and dance, without spoken dialogue. As it evolved, certain soloists became distinct from the Chorus, and through their dialogue they told stories based on ancient myths. *The Oresteia* by Aeschylus, discussed in the previous chapter, is one such story. Most popular were the tragic myths, stories of powerful and rich men (often rulers) who, because of a fatal flaw of character, would fall from the heights, would in fact reach the depths of despair and ruination. Not all of the tragedies, including *The Oresteia*, fit this description exactly, but they are all filled with horror, suffering, and the extremes of human pain. They have scenes that are among the most shattering ever devised.

What bothered Nietzsche was that, in lecturing or writing about tragedy, teachers and critics sometimes forgot that the roots of the art form were in dance and music. He believed the proper response to viewing a tragedy was to allow oneself to respond emotionally, the way we respond to music. He found that viewers and critics alike were focusing on the central characters' moral failings, on the breaking of moral law as the cause of their tragic fall. As a result, Greek tragedies were evaluated and taught in terms of their moral messages, not their strong emotional impact. Nietzsche believed it was wrong to encourage people to view tragedy through reason rather than emotion—wrong to insist on the moral philosophy behind a play at the expense of appreciating the force and the fury that drive it.

He then made a famous distinction between two ways of responding not only to drama but to events in real life. He identified as **Apollonian** that side of the human personality dominated by disciplined, analytical, rational, and coherent thought: in short, the side that responds to Greek tragedy by seeking

Apollo, god of the sun, and Dionysus, god of the vibrant energy of the earth.

Source: Left: Villa Valmarana, Vicenza, Italy. Credit: Scala/Art Resource, NY. Right: Uffizi/Florence, Italy. Credit: The Bridgeman Art Library.

its meaning. He dubbed as **Dionysian** that side of the human personality dominated by emotion, intuition, and freedom from limits: the side that responds emotionally to music as well as the force and fury of tragedy.

These opposing terms are derived from Greek mythology. Apollo was the god of the sun (hence of light and truth) and Dionysus was the god of the vibrant energy of the earth (hence of emotion, spontaneity, and intuition). Nietzsche believed the goal of life was to achieve a balance between reason and emotion: to be able to think clearly, to be steady, reliable, and responsible for one's actions, AND be able to feel, to enjoy the fruits of the vine (so to speak), to express both love and hate (when necessary), unguided by a concern for rules.

Throughout this book we will refer many times to Apollonian and Dionysian elements in the humanities. If critical thinking is a major goal of studying the humanities, the distinction between the two sides of our personality is always the starting point. It is *impossible* to study the humanities without seeing how one or the other or sometimes both together inform a given work.

The Apollonian response means looking at a work objectively before evaluating it. Critical thinking begins on the Apollonian side; writing a critical analysis is always Apollonian, even though a strong emotional response may have inspired the analysis. One can be enraptured by a musical performance *without* wanting to analyze it further. If this is the case, however, the comment "It was great; I was carried away by it" must not be confused with a full critical statement. It has to be recognized for what it is: a statement of a personal experience. "I liked it" is personal and Dionysian. "I liked it because it had . . ." may be introducing an Apollonian evaluation. Both are valid, but they must not be mistaken for each other.

Real knowledge is knowing the extent of one's ignorance.
—**Confucius**

The Popcorn Syndrome

A word of caution. It is all too easy to give the critical mind a vacation, to surrender to the Dionysian excitement of the moment and decide that further considerations are not important. But doing so will not stretch our mental capacities. However, sometimes a given work clearly does not warrant time and mental energy. More seductive is the popcorn experience, usually at the movies. "This is strictly a popcorn movie" means that one should be able to sit back, munch on popcorn, and be entertained without having to think. A huge number of films and television shows belong to this category, as indeed do many novels called "good reads."

Dan Brown's *The Da Vinci Code* (2002), one of the most widely read novels ever written, topped the best-seller list for almost two years and sold well into the millions of copies. The story of a secret organization, oppressed by religious authorities because it can supposedly prove that Jesus was married and sired a family, is told in such fast-moving, cinematic prose that the reader cannot wait to turn the page. Exciting? Yes. Suspenseful? Indeed. A great novel? Here one must pause and reflect. Is the story totally believable? Is there any depth to the main characters? Does the novel leave the reader with what we may call "residual thoughts"? Or is it, like many others, just popcorn fun? Perhaps. Yet one may also decide that any novel *so* entertaining to read is certainly worthwhile. Popular music, films, novels, cartoons in newspapers and magazines, the "funnies"—all that entertains and amuses us for even a short time can be called, at the very least, the "temporary humanities." Like all emotional responses, fun is a legitimate way to spend some time. Nobody gets hurt, nobody dies.

Dionysian enjoyment may also lead to a morning-after headache, what we can call the "popcorn hangover." The night before at the movies, the big bucket of popcorn, the pleasant company, the fast-moving, car-chase plot, the nerve-jangling soundtrack that brings one into a la-la land of no stress. "What a great evening. What a terrific movie!" Then tomorrow dawns. Subliminal replay of the movie on the semiconscious screen of the half-awake mind. The sudden sitting up. The flash of truth. "*How could I possibly have liked that awful film?*" This often happens, and it is a perfectly valid response. The difference between popcorn fun and critical thinking, however, is that, engaging in the latter, determining why the film does not remain in the museum of one's fondest aesthetic experiences, provides a far different sort of pleasure (now that the big bucket of popcorn is empty).

The critical thinker eventually finds a deeper, more satisfying definition of "entertainment." Having enjoyed *The Da Vinci Code* as a good read, you might have looked forward to the 2006 film version, expecting to find not a work of high screen art but at the very least an engrossing, fast-moving thriller. Instead, let us say, you emerge from the theater *without* a popcorn hangover, without any sense of having been involved. You can let it go at that or, preferably, spend a little time pondering why the transference of the novel to the screen did not work for you, especially since the author's prose had been more than once praised as "cinematic." The story line was the same. But wasn't the action slower than you expected it to be? Didn't it lack the pulsating rhythm of popcorn movies you usually enjoy?

The critical mind, perceiving that a response has been largely Dionysian, looks further. After hearing a thrilling interpretation of Beethoven's Ninth Symphony in a concert hall, the critical mind seeks, in the later tranquility of musing on the exciting experience, to consider those elements which caused the response: the beauty of the singers' voices? the unexpected shifts in tempo?

the alternation between the majesty of the musical crescendos and the sudden silences that follow? No two analyses will be exactly the same. Nor need they be. Critical thinking is valid as an ongoing process, not as the road to absolute determination of good or bad. The important thing is that the unexamined Dionysian response may be limited to "Gee, that was terrific!"—okay as far as it goes, but not likely to contribute much toward balancing the two forces in our lives. At best, the unexamined response ought to be restricted to experiences that defy words.

Empathy and Alienation

Empathy, the process by which we identify with a character or a performer so that for a short time we believe we are that person, is a Dionysian trick of our nature. On the one hand, it lures us away from our problems and therefore offers a valuable escape from stress. Empathy is crucial to the entertainment process. If you, for example, should arrive late for a circus performance, sitting down just as the tightrope-walker's act has begun, what you would see is not only the death-defying stunter higher up than you might ever care to be but hundreds of seated patrons swaying back and forth. They would be projecting themselves into the precarious journey, gasping each time the performer (as part of the act) appears about to fall. In similar fashion, you and your fellow audience members in a movie theater may be in a car careening wildly out of control and dodging oncoming traffic in the streets of New York. Filmmakers know about Dionysian empathy and readily design opportunities for indulging in it. If the main character, trapped in a mountain ravine with floodwaters inching upward, attempts to scale the rock wall, she has to be successful at first and then *must* slip when she is halfway up and appear to be doomed. You give free reign to your empathetic imagination because deep down you know all will be well in the end—but you will feel cheated if all is well from the start.

It is the rediscovery of the world of which I have the joy of being a part. It fills me with awareness of the wonder of life, with a feeling of the incredible marvel of being a human being. The music is never the same for me, never! Each day it is something new, fantastic and unbelievable. That is Bach, like nature, a miracle!

—**Pablo Casals**

Just why empathizing with near-death experiences should qualify as entertainment has been debated for centuries. It may be traceable to the eighteenth-century shift away from the onstage blood and gore of popular tragedies, including many of Shakespeare's, which featured hands being chopped off, tongues and eyes being ripped out, horrors that could rival the bloodiest slasher movie of today. The eighteenth century on both sides of the Atlantic introduced a more genteel way of life for the upper classes and those who imitated them. The works of Shakespeare and his contemporaries went into a period of decline, or else were revised with all the horrors eliminated. But little by little, as society became more and more "respectable," stage entertainment began reintroducing melodramatic elements for audiences that enjoyed escape from their morally upright lives. In the late-eighteenth century the circus was born, with its empathy-inducing trapeze and highwire acts and its wild animal

The bloodier the scene, the more many in the audience may feel they are being royally entertained.

Source: Celador/Crawlspace Productions/The Kobal Collection.

encounters. All of this led inevitably to the current Dionysian orgies on film and television, and to circuses with ever more dangerous acts.

The flip side of the Dionysian coin, when it comes to such entertainment, can be called Apollonian alienation. The term **alienation** was coined by Bertolt Brecht, a major German playwright of the early twentieth century, about whom much more will be said in Chapter 7. Brecht wanted to make sure audiences did not become so emotionally involved in plot and character that they failed to heed his messages. He often injected vaudeville slapstick, songs, and dances into very serious material. In this way he hoped to prevent empathetic responses.

As critical thinkers, we are not so restricted. Attending a play or film with strong emotional undercurrents or reading a powerful novel filled with moving, tragic moments, we may appreciate the feelings evoked but can also sit back and look objectively at the work. Questions raised might be: *Why is the hero's downfall so terrifying when he is not a very good person? How does the author make us care about what is happening to him?* When the author's technique becomes transparent, the viewing or reading experience becomes that much richer. And we have seized the opportunity to expand our mind. Critical thinkers tend to retain stronger memories of their experiences and find enjoyment in discussing works with other critical thinkers who may have the same or sharply differing views. Mutual agreement doesn't matter. The process of building "brain muscle" does.

What is written without effort is in general read without pleasure.
—**Samuel Johnson**

When a Purely Emotional Response Is Appropriate

We are not insisting that it is always better to analyze, Apollonian fashion. To enter the Sistine Chapel at the Vatican and see Michelangelo's ornate fresco ceiling is, quite literally, to be bereft of words. None are necessary. Something inside tells us that these artistic arrangements are right, magnificently right. It is to experience what Plato would have called "pure beauty." Time stops for the viewer. Practical concerns disappear. The experience doesn't have to be explained or analyzed. It is the quiet joy of being conscious at the highest level. When you get to a summit like this, you *know* it!

Great works like the *Venus de Milo*, the *David*, the symphonies of Beethoven, or the tragedies of Shakespeare have powerful emotional effects on us long before we begin to exercise sober critical judgment. Even professional critics, whom we shall be discussing presently, no doubt allow themselves to be so affected before they stand back and begin a rational analysis of a work. Often there is no point to the rational analysis if the emotions have not first been stirred. What is unfortunate is that, in writing about or teaching the humanities, many fail to mention emotional appeal.

Here is a poem by the American e.e. cummings (1894–1962), famous for dismantling standard English grammar and finding alternate ways to express feelings and ideas. In this poem, "may my heart always," he delivers

Seeing these famous works may well defy words and make analysis irrelevant.

Source: Sistene Chapel, Vatican Palace. Credit: Erich Lessing, Art Resource, NY.

a clear Dionysian message but in off-the-wall language that can be intuitively understood without requiring further analysis.[2]

> *may my heart always be open to little*
> *birds who are the secrets of living*
> *whatever they sing is better than to know*
> *and if men should not hear them men are old*
>
> *may my mind stroll about hungry*
> *and fearless and thirsty and supple*
> *and even if it's sunday may i be wrong*
> *for whenever men are right they are not young*
>
> *and may myself do nothing usefully*
> *and love yourself so more than truly*
> *there's never been quite such a fool who could fail*
> *pulling all the sky over him with one smile*

Analysis here is not only irrelevant but unfair to the poet. What cummings is expressing all of us can feel. Does he not awaken the Dionysian impulse to "do nothing useful" and believe truly and deeply that being in love is all that really matters? Don't we know, without having to be directly told, that it's better to do what your instinct tells you even if you're wrong than to be self-righteously "right" all of the time? Is cummings irresponsible? Perhaps, but if we find ourselves joyously agreeing with him, then he's allowing us to express—along *with* him— feelings that we usually have to hide. And isn't it better to be a little irresponsible in *art* and save our responsibility for society, where it's needed?

The Importance of Responding Critically

Critical thinking carefully defines, describes, and analyzes something: an election, an important decision, a question that has puzzled or intrigued philosophers for centuries, a new electronic invention, a movie, a novel, the Number One song on the Top 40, or a determination to move into your own apartment. Critical responses, as we have said, build our mental strength. They usually involve the following steps:

Take each man's censure but reserve thy judgment.

—William Shakespeare

1. Defining what it is we want to determine. Example: *Why did this film work for me?*
2. Putting aside instinctive, emotional responses.
3. Collecting and analyzing all pertinent factors.
4. Evaluating the work or the topic in its proper context.
5. Forgetting how it relates only to you. Example: *I know it's good because the main character is young like me.*
6. Having an informed opinion.

Developing the skill of analysis and objective evaluation helps us to deepen our appreciation of the humanities and also to have a better sense of who we are and what seems to be truly worth our time.

Exercising the Mind

Most of us get up and go when we feel the need to exercise our bodies, especially when something has prevented our moving about (such as being cramped for three hours in an airplane seat). Those who have suffered illnesses charged to a lack of exercise may be encouraged to alter the way they live, urged to run, walk, do basketball layups, a host of activities to avoid that sluggish feeling well known to non-exercisers, who usually experience guilt even if they cannot bring themselves to engage in even the briefest of workouts. Yet far too many of us experience no guilt while allowing our minds to be sluggish. The critical responses discussed in the previous section come much easier to minds that are trim and fit. And getting there doesn't even involve a diet!

Critical thinking is enhanced as we engage in three important activities: solving problems, challenging assumptions, and recognizing contexts.

Solving Problems

Problems are only opportunities in work clothes.

—**Henry J. Kaiser**

Critical thinkers are always solving problems, even hypothetical ones. One day the late American philosopher Richard Rorty was relaxing in a backyard hammock, hazily listening to the radio. A DJ announced he was going to play "that golden oldie 'Everybody Loves My Baby,'" which begins with these lines:

> *Everybody loves my baby*
> *But my baby don't love nobody but me*

Suddenly the philosopher's active brain, which had been allowed to float in a reverie, snapped to attention. It knew that something was wrong with the lines, something that did not make sense. He quickly solved the problem. The next day he repeated the lines to a class of philosophy majors and asked them to determine why the lines made no sense. We suggest you cover the following paragraph and try first to find the answer yourself.

Here's Rorty's answer. Since the first line states that *everybody* loves the singer's baby, that baby is logically included in the totality of everybody. It is then permissible to change the line to read *My baby loves my baby*. But if, regardless of the double negative, it is also true that the "me" is the only one loved by the baby, then the second line can be changed to read *My baby loves only me*, and thus baby = me. Professor Rorty, whose active brain was very sharp indeed, realized in a flash that the song was saying "I am my baby," which he assumed was unintentional.

Exercises like Rorty's are the stuff of critical thinking. To solve such problems helps strengthen the brain for times when real problems confront us. Having developed the habit of critical analysis, we are prepared to confront a real problem in our own life. The family member who needs help is a problem thousands face each day. Suppose you have a brother who constantly overspends, is heavily in debt, and cannot curb this extravagance. One reason is that he always counts on being rescued by responsible relatives—for example, *you*.

The first step in solving such a problem is to determine whether a problem actually exists. Whether or not to pay off your brother's debts may not be a problem if you decide not to assume ownership of it. Whose problem is it? It's yours if you wish to avoid the pain of guilt you think you'll experience if you turn your back. But the problem belongs to your brother or to other family members if you decide to withdraw with a clear conscience. If the rest of the family also declines, with a clear conscience, then only your brother has something to solve.

Family bonds are likely to be pretty strong, but you have to weigh all the factors. Does your brother overspend very often? Is your brother capable of earning enough money to pay the debts? If not, will he listen to a rational argument in favor of spending within his limits? Merely to pay off the debts to "avoid the hassle" may send the wrong signal.

No ultimate answer will be found here, but we have just engaged in the act of reasoning. Sometimes easy solutions evade us and we must finally settle on one, hoping for the best. Yet we are less likely to find a successful answer if we have not fully analyzed the problem—if we have not been critical thinkers.

Challenging Assumptions

Assumptions are a fact of everyday communication. They are the beliefs on which opinions are based and conclusions drawn. Often these are *buried*: that is, they lie underneath what people are saying without being acknowledged as assumptions, and often they are the real message that is being communicated. The critical thinker listens carefully, always seeking what is actually being said.

Suppose a newspaper reader turns to you and says that a convicted murderer has been released after being confined to a mental hospital for ten years. In the opinion of the medical staff, that person is no longer a menace to society. The reader then observes, "There ought to be a law against letting people escape the death penalty with a plea of insanity and then releasing them so they can kill again."

The above statement makes no pretense to be factual. It is understood that the speaker is expressing an opinion. The buried assumptions behind the opinion, however, may not be recognized. Here are some possibilities:

1. The question of insanity should have no bearing on a court case.
2. The defendant was not really insane anyway.
3. The state or federal legislature should control how defendants plead.
4. Once a murderer, always a murderer.
5. Those in charge of mental hospitals are not qualified to make accurate judgments about the future behavior of a released patient.

Non-critical listeners are likely to nod in agreement with the reader's observation, because careful debate in this instance involves careful analysis of the buried assumptions. Many do not wish to invest the time needed for making this analysis.

Now suppose that the newspaper reader and the listener in the above example are both seasoned critical thinkers, people who are knowledgeable about the humanities and who exercise their mental faculties as often as possible, knowing how to balance their inner Apollo and Dionysus. A critically thinking reader would no doubt communicate a different version of the newspaper story, such as "Abel Parsons has been released from the mental hospital where he has spent the last ten years. If you remember, his lawyer pleaded not guilty by reason of insanity."

The critically thinking listener might then respond: "Does the article cite any reasons for his release?"

"One. The psychiatrist who has observed him for the whole time called in three consultants, and they all agreed that Parsons appears to be totally rehabilitated."

"Have they provided any sort of monitoring system to keep tabs on what he does at least for a while?"

"It doesn't say."

"They'd *have* to set something up, don't you think?"

The two critical thinkers have not solved a thorny legal problem. What they *have* done in this hypothetical conversation is exercise critical thinking to get at the objective facts of the newspaper story rather than make assumptions about it.

Recognizing Contexts

Each of us lives within contexts: family, circle of friends, religious affiliation, political allegiances. . .

Everyone and everything exist in a **context**, a framework of circumstances and relationships. A sentence is a context, a relationship among words, their individual meanings, and how they come together to express a thought. A forest fire threatening nearby homes is a context for those living in the homes and for those fighting the fire. The Great Depression of the 1930s was a huge context enveloping the entire population of the United States, as well as the countries that depended on the health of the American economy. A college course is a context, and the circumstances of it involve the professor, the syllabus, grading policies, and the grade point average of you and your classmates. Each of us lives within many contexts: family, circle of friends, religious affiliation, political allegiances, and so on and so on.

Knowing that nothing exists independent of one or more contexts, critical thinkers try to avoid making large-scale generalizations and absolute evaluations. Even so, like many others, they are at times not above simplifying, distilling contexts down to something manageable. This is likeliest to be true when past events are recalled and related. *Selective memory* is a universal trait. People, including critical thinkers, can obscure the truth, not only of the past but of what happened just yesterday when the full context of an event is unpleasant or embarrassing to relate. Using the well-practiced skill of **rationalization**, they tell others (as well as themselves) a convenient and palatable version of an event—say, a bitter argument with a sibling. In this version, the absent family member is usually the culprit and the speaker is the victim. By the time the speaker is finished, the context within which the argument took place has become fixed in the speaker's mind exactly as it has been described, and chances are that it doesn't come close to what *really* happened. While dedicated critical thinkers are not immune to reinventing contexts or selecting those that can be comfortably dealt with, they are less likely, upon reflection, to feel good about substituting imagination for reality.

One of the gifts of the humanities we described earlier is a sense of the past, which provides us with *historical context*. A casual browser in a secondhand store filled with attic discards might grow impatient because none of the items belongs to today. Those with a sense of the past, however, would be interested in examining a phonograph, a doll, or a pair of shoes that reveal much about bygone periods. Examining pictorial records from publications of the past increases our interest in and knowledge of earlier times.

Turn to Color Plate 3 and study the 1945 cover for the *Saturday Evening Post*, once among the most popular magazines in the United States. Norman Rockwell (1894–1978), the artist, achieved fame as an interpreter of middle-class life. To see his work is to gain invaluable knowledge of how a large segment of the population lived in twentieth-century America. Notice the way the people are dressed. Look closely at the various objects in what appears to be a repair shop of some kind. Which are hard to recognize now? Why are the flags important? Which have been replaced by updated versions? If nothing else, spending some time with old pictures like this adds to our critical thinking skills.

The more we learn to recognize historical contexts, the less likely are we to evaluate everything in terms of today. In reading books or watching movies from the past, the critical thinker knows better than to judge them in terms of the present. *Gone with the Wind* (1939) is still recognized by professional critics as a milestone in movie making, even though a contemporary viewer may find some of it sentimental and dated. Without overlooking these failings, the critical thinker tries to view the film in the context of 1939 and enjoys what is still to be enjoyed, such as the marvelously advanced (for its time) use of color, the sweeping symphonic score, and the still believable performance of Vivien Leigh as Scarlett O'Hara. Whether a given work belongs to the past *or* the present, we can appreciate its positive achievements without endorsing all of its ideas or techniques.

The ability to appreciate historical context makes one more tolerant of art forms in unfamiliar styles: for example, most operas. Viewers who are visiting an opera house for the first time might easily lose patience with a three-hour performance in which every word is sung in a foreign language and performers are chosen for the power of their voice, not their physical appearance or acting ability. Opera companies throughout the world try to update some classic works, such as Mozart's *The Abduction from the Seraglio*, in order to accommodate modern tastes, but even though a recent production changed the setting from a Turkish harem to a trans-European railroad, the cast still sang in German. In times past, English-speaking audiences did not base their operagoing pleasure on whether or not they could understand the language, and informed audiences of today are still expected to watch most operas in their original language.

The plots of even the most celebrated operas are likely to seem ridiculous. Critical viewers concentrate on the glorious music, the quality of the voices delivering it, the ingenuity of the staging, the imaginative use of scenery, the visual effect of the costumes, and the appropriateness of whatever updating the director has chosen.

Occasionally a work from the past is staged or even totally rewritten in a modern context. One of the most enduringly popular operas is *La Bohème* by Giacomo Puccini (1858–1924). Since its 1896 premiere, it has been performed hundreds of times throughout the world. Audiences seem never to tire of its lush romantic score and its touching, tragic tale of the love between Rodolfo, a poet, and Mimi, a seamstress, living in the shabby bohemian section of Paris along with a number of friends, most of them artists, all of them poor but always hopeful of selling a poem or a painting. The story captures for all time the myth of starving artists living in a garret; and its main characters are, like Romeo and Juliet, doomed to be separated. The final scene in which the fragile Mimi dies from consumption in Rodolfo's bitterly cold attic room has probably brought even the most alienated Apollonian viewer close to tears.

The free lifestyle of the bohemian artist is not, however, limited to the context of 1830 Paris. There continue to be rebellious young people dedicated to innovations in music, art, and theater. New York, in particular, is home to thousands of young hopefuls, often living in cramped, shabby apartments, often without much food, but always trying, like the characters in *La Bohème*, to sell their work or to get work in the theater.

In 1996 what appeared to be a modest, low-budget, rock-musical retelling of *La Bohème* called *Rent* opened in a tiny off-Broadway theater. It was the brainchild of Jonathan Larson, who wrote the book and lyrics and composed the music. Larson died suddenly of an aortic aneurysm after the final dress rehearsal, thus never living to enjoy his show's phenomenal success. To accommodate the crowds, it moved to a large theater on Broadway and later became a successful film.

The ability to appreciate historical context makes one more tolerant of art forms in unfamiliar styles: for example, most operas.

Similar story but vastly different music in startlingly contrasted historical periods.

Source: Left: Perrin/Sygma-Corbis. Right: Sony Pictures/The Kobal Collection.

With an infectious and unrelenting rock beat and its twenty-first-century cast of characters, *Rent* would have bewildered Puccini's original audiences. In the modern version, Rodolfo is transformed into Roger, an HIV-positive rocker determined to write a great song before he dies. Mimi keeps her name, but now she is a drug addict, also HIV-positive. Their friends include a gay couple, a lesbian couple, and a transvestite. Like the bohemians of Puccini's Paris, Larson's characters live together in blissful poverty, singing wildly joyous songs pulsating with hope for the future, though the shadow of death is slowly encroaching.

If one could view both *La Bohème* and *Rent* on successive nights, one would need no further lesson to understand two startlingly contrasted historical periods. Arguments have been raised about which version is more enjoyable. This in itself is one of the pleasures offered by the humanities: the ability to contrast two versions of the same story and defend a preference for one or the other. Yet those who slip easily into different historical contexts will probably find the strong points of both.

Critical Viewing

Before moving on to explore the humanities in greater depth, we will examine the skill of critical viewing. Though professional critics are people who devote much time to the analysis and evaluation of the work of others, we do not have to be professional critics to engage in their art.

How the Professional Critic Responds

The best critics have widely respected opinions. Their work can be found in the pages of leading newspapers like the *New York Times* or *San Francisco Chronicle*, magazines like the *New Yorker*, *Film Comment*, or *Opera News*, as well as Internet sites such as *Prodigy* and *Slate*. What professional critics have to say about something can help us decide among the many choices open to us. In the world of the humanities, with so much that is Dionysian to stir the emotions and, sometimes, to cloud our judgment, the professional critic is an Apollonian voice that can serve as a model for our own growing critical skills.

In 2007 the director Michael Winterbottom made a widely anticipated film version of the book *A Mighty Heart* by Mariane Pearl, widow of Daniel Pearl, the correspondent who in 2002 was kidnapped and gruesomely executed in Pakistan. There had been widespread speculation about which actress would be chosen and have the credentials to play the woman who was in the news on an almost daily basis and whose face and mannerisms were already familiar to millions. When it was learned that most-hounded and photographed celebrity couple in the world, skeptics shook their heads at what they immediately decided was gross miscasting before the first scene was ever shot.

So it is not surprising that Anthony Lane, a highly respected film critic for *The New Yorker*, should begin his **review** of the film with an indictment of contemporary media-directed mass culture, in which preconceived opinions of celebrities such as Jolie make open-minded critical viewing difficult indeed. Lane, in other words, stacks the cards against Jolie at the outset, and we fully expect his review to be a quotable pan.

> *We brace ourselves for a star turn, a hundred minutes of vanity project, but here's the thing: it never happens. Jolie slips into the part, ducks in and out of the action, and generally plays second string to the onrush of events.*[3]

Lane marvels that a superstar allows herself to play second string to what is most important, the violent events in Pakistan. In this way, Lane skillfully paves the way for what will surely be a favorable notice, one that will no doubt impress readers who, like him, had previously made their minds up about the casting. He sees a bright future for someone who had never been taken seriously as an actress.

In the popular press, as well as on the quickie reviews of morning show critics, whose job it is to deliver a fast-talking, two-minute "analysis," such superstars may be praised or panned, but never given minute scrutiny of the kind offered by Anthony Lane. This is the reason the critical viewer seeks the guidance of intelligent opinion and knows how to recognize it.

Howard Cohen, pop music critic for the *Miami Herald*, regularly reviews the latest rock, rap, country, jazz, and rhythm and blues CDs. Since so much music is released each week and since we could not possibly sample every CD in order to decide which ones to buy, Cohen's informed opinions are a service the paper offers. His mini-reviews appear on a weekly basis, and they are loaded with catchy evaluations his readers have learned to trust. He has

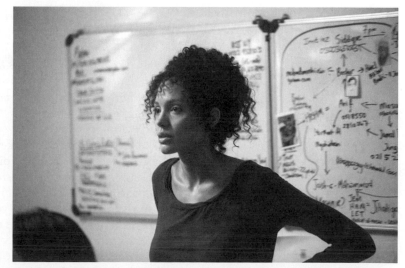

A professional, widely read film critic decides that a superstar can also be an actress.

Source: Plan B/Revolution Films/The Kobal Collection.

paid his dues and is saying in so many words: "I am a professional critic. I can be forthright about my likes and dislikes. That's what I'm paid for, and will be so long as I retain your trust."

In reviewing a CD called *Zeitgeist* (a term employed by philosophers as a reference to the soul or guiding spirit of an age), Cohen brings his dissenting fist down immediately: "With a gift for pretension that always overshadowed his musical ability, leader Billy Corgan hasn't mellowed with age."[4] Cohen handles prose expertly and, as we can see, with a vocabulary that is neither pretentious nor condescending. It tells us his readership includes genuine lovers of rock music who are accustomed to thinking about what they listen to and what critics say about it. But he also backs up his general indictments with some specific details—always the mark of the professional. He is sorry to announce that several former musicians "who helped temper Corgan's excesses . . . are gone." And "there's no finesse in his playing the way . . . Jack White brings textured noise to The White Stripes. Corgan's nasal whine remains one of rock's most annoying sounds."

The type of music reviewed by Cohen and other such critics is presumably well known to many readers. Reviews of an unfamiliar work can also be rewarding because it expands our knowledge of the vast range of musical offerings. Alex Ross, for example, music critic for the *New Yorker*, reviewed the premier performance by the Boston Symphony Orchestra of a work called *La Pasión según San Marcos* (*The Passion of Jesus Christ According to Saint Mark*) by an Argentine composer named Osvaldo Golijov. Ross begins by describing the wild ovation, something rarely seen at a concert featuring a new and avant-garde work. "This level of euphoria is sometimes encountered at the Met, when a favorite singer has an exceptional night. It is not found at concerts of new music."[5] Very probably, not many readers knew much about Golijov at the time of the performance. Mention of the ovation sends a signal: *Pay attention; here is somebody who's going to be very important.* Then Ross adds that the ovation lasted for twenty minutes at the first performance of the work in Stuttgart, Germany, the year before. He also shares his delight in rediscovering Latino concert music:

> *this Latino passion carries two messages: one is that Golijov is a huge talent . . . and the second is that Latino America has a fabulously rich tradition, one that will become a dominant force in coming decades. "Pasión" drops like a bomb on the belief that classical music is an exclusively European art. It has a revolutionary air, as if musical history were starting over, with new, sensuous materials and in a new, affirmative tone.*

The professional critic is likely to bestow extravagant praise on something he or she considers to be a masterpiece, and such praise raises our level of interest.

The professional critic is likely to bestow extravagant praise on something he or she considers to be a masterpiece, and such praise raises our level of interest. In this case one asks: *How tolerant am I of new music? How much do I really know about new music, especially from South America?* Reading this review can excite our curiosity about what young composers, especially from other cultures, are doing, and it should enhance our awareness of the "rich tradition" from which their work springs.

Ross does his homework. He follows his enthusiastic opening comments with a detailed biography of the young composer. We learn that Golijov composed a choral work called *Oceana*, a musical setting of poems by the Chilean poet Pablo Neruda, the 1971 Nobel laureate, and that *La Pasión* was commissioned by the orchestra of Stuttgart—high recognition for an artist not in the European mainstream.

Last, and perhaps most important, Ross dissects the work in detail, explaining what makes it so special. He comments that Bach might have written like this had he been born in Latin America at the end of the twentieth century. The descriptions are enough to entice us into downloading the album. "Brazilian shakers and musical bows, conjuring an ancient world; eerie moans from the accordion, representing the voice of God; then the entry of the chorus, braying in Africanized Spanish over *bata* drums. The listener is thrown into the middle of a Lenten street festival, with three processions of singers, converging into an antiphonal clamor."

Ross describes a "Bachian-Brazilian aria," sung near the end of the work, "and the piece moves for a long spell into the interior world of Jesus's suffering. At the very end, Kaddish is sung for the man on the cross, and the music undergoes an even more mysterious metamorphosis: the language is now Aramaic, the cantillation is Jewish, and the centuries have slipped away like sand."

When confronted with the unfamiliar, those who are new to critical viewing and listening are tempted to think that modern composers go out of their way to sound bizarre. Thus it is reassuring to note that Ross finds a timeless quality in great art. Though some artists, composers, and writers do indeed deliberately seek out novelty, this review reminds us that great works always arise from the passionate need to express something of huge importance, something geniuses have in common, even if their language seems bizarre and unfamiliar in the beginning.

Notice that Ross exhibits considerable knowledge about the elements of music. He hears more than those of us without substantial musical backgrounds. The best critics display their credentials in everything they write and thus they earn our trust.

One could say that professional criticism is an art form in itself. As authors and composers as well as actors and visual artists put themselves on the line whenever they come forth with new work, so too is the critic exposed to the applause or condemnation of the public. The seeming arrogance we often detect in critics' writing may well mask their own vulnerability. If we understand that they are human beings like all of us, we can read them with better understanding and can profit by what they have to teach us.

The Personal Critical Response

One does not have to be a professional critic to engage in the process of evaluation after a careful and fair viewing, listening, or reading. Here is "The world is too much with us," a poem by William Wordsworth (1770–1850), who lived in England's lake country at a time when the Industrial Revolution was beginning to have an impact and many people were moving from the country to the cities seeking a more lucrative lifestyle.[6] Though Wordsworth preferred to live amid the wonders of nature, he was aware of the dangers posed by the promise of economic gain.

> *The world is too much with us; late and soon,*
> *Getting and spending, we lay waste our powers:*
> *Little we see in Nature that is ours;*
> *We have given our hearts away, a sordid boon!*

This Sea that bares her bosom to the moon;
The winds that will be howling at all hours,
And are up-gathered now like sleeping flowers;
For this, for everything, we are out of tune,
It moves us not.—Great God! I'd rather be
A Pagan suckled in a creed outworn;
So might I, standing on this pleasant lea,
Have glimpses that would make me less forlorn;
Have sight of Proteus rising from the sea;
Or hear old Triton blow his wreathed horn.

The first step in becoming an informed critic is not to jump to hasty conclusions.

The first step in becoming an informed critic is *not to jump to a hasty conclusion.* "I don't like it" or "I love this poem" is an irrelevant remark at this early stage in the process of critical thinking.

The next step is to determine what it is you have just read. Describe the poem as clearly and objectively as possible. A possibility: The poem contains (or appears to contain, which might be a more cautious approach, at least in the beginning) a regretful realization that, in a concern for material welfare, we no longer live on close terms with nature. It reminds us that the natural world is a place of wondrous beauty and should be a source of inspiration.

Beauty, of course, is its own justification. To spend all day working for economic gain is to deny oneself one of the major aesthetic joys in life: intimacy with nature. Noticing how the seasons affect the landscape, how plants and flowers will grow and bloom wherever they are given space, costs nothing and yields treasures that money cannot buy.

Wordsworth could not have known about *environmentalism*, but he is already aware that the commerce of everyday life, the "getting and spending," is creating a danger that the natural world will be ignored, uncared for. And so he thinks of an ancient time when mythology turned nature into a wondrous force that we are to be dazzled by and always respect.

If you are adventurous and enjoy probing a little deeper, you can obtain information about the poet's life from the library or Internet. You would learn that, as Wordsworth grew older, he feared he was losing the inspiration he used to feel when he was out in nature. You would also learn that this poem was written in 1804, perhaps during a transitional phase in the poet's development—that is, at a time when, in reaching full maturity, he might have begun to fear that, though he was profiting from writing, he was doing so at the cost of his inspiration. If you wanted to advance this idea, you would do well to tread softly, however. Though many literary scholars take the plunge and read autobiography into every work by an author, the poet in this case might have been making a general statement applicable to all people.

In any case, speculation about ideas in a work sharpens our critical faculties, even if it doesn't say the last word about what we are reading. The important thing is to separate probability from possibility. It is

A modern artist is seeing a world that would probably have appalled Wordsworth.

Source: Philadelphia Museum of Art/Art Resource, NY. © 2008 Estate of Fernand Leger, Artists Rights Society (ARS), NY.

virtually certain that Wordsworth is upset about the pursuit of material gain, and it is possible that, at the age of thirty-four, he fears he might be losing the passion that fired his youth.

The next stage in the critical process is to look at the poet's *craft*—that is, the handling of language and **imagery** (the pictures in your mind that the poem communicates). What makes poetry different from prose is that poets are able to compress a great deal into fewer words than prose requires. They do this by taking shortcuts—sneaking past our commonsense barriers and heading directly into the Dionysian region of intuition, where we understand something without having to be directly told, or without going through an extended process of reasoning. When we grasp something intuitively, we "catch on" right away. One of poetry's gifts to us is thus to sharpen our intuitive faculties.

In this poem Wordsworth does considerable direct talking, as in "Getting and spending, we lay waste our powers." But he also communicates through intuition, as in the famous final lines, beginning with the explosive "Great God!" (which forces us to sit up and pay closer attention). Instead of talking directly about ancient times when people, through their myths, endowed nature with electric super-forces, the poet says he wishes he could have lived back then and shared the imagination of these people as well as the awe and respect they felt in the presence of nature. Instead of mentioning mythology directly, he invokes the names of two mythological sea gods, Proteus and Triton. The old religion made nature come alive and filled believers with inspiration, something sadly lacking in an age of restless commerce and profit-seeking, when nature has been abandoned.

Wordsworth's poem is a **sonnet**, a demanding literary form in which the poet is restricted to fourteen lines. In Wordsworth's time, poets also challenged themselves by using rhyming lines and writing in a definite rhythm. One way of identifying a good poem is to determine whether the rhythm and the rhyme are forced, whether they are deliberately imposed by the poet to meet the requirements, or whether they seem to be the only possible way of expressing the thought.

If you read the poem aloud to find the rhythmic pattern, you discover that unaccented syllables are followed by accented ones, that there never are two accented or unaccented syllables side by side. At the same time, when you read it without stressing the rhythm, the words flow naturally and manage to keep the rhythm unnoticed. The rhyming pattern is also quite regular (the first and fourth lines rhyme, as do the second and third, the fifth and eighth, the sixth and seventh, and finally, the ninth, eleventh, and thirteenth, and the tenth, twelfth, and fourteenth). Yet in reading the poem aloud, following the natural progression of it, you don't find the rhymes jumping out of their context. (There will be much more about the craft of poetry in Chapter 4.)

Being aware that the poet has carefully concealed the artistry behind the poem happens to be one of the pleasures of responding critically. When a pianist performs a complicated jazz solo or a sonata by Mozart, we should not have to think about the years of practicing eight hours a day. When the ice skater glides across the arena in perfect sync with Debussy's "Clair de Lune," we should believe that we can strap on a pair of skates and do the same thing. *Art is the illusion that there is no art.* Only when the skater attempts a triple axel and falls do we then watch future leaps with apprehension, painfully aware of the difficulty involved.

In the critical thinking process, you can now make your personal assessment of the poem as a worthwhile or non-worthwhile experience for the reader. In the case of Wordsworth's sonnet, you are dealing with a poem that is 200 years old. You might want to comment on whether the thought it expresses

I do not feel obliged to believe that the same God who has endowed us with sense, reason, and intellect has intended us to forego their use.

　　　　　　　　—**Galileo**

Track

is relevant to our times. You can ask yourself, "Do the sentiments expressed by the poet have anything to do with me, with the twenty-first century?" Perhaps it is fair to say that humanity's estrangement from the natural world has only increased as time moved on.

Yet, granted that the poem does indeed have contemporary relevance, does it hold any personal value for you? In this last stage of the critical process you are free to make your own assessment. Perhaps you are most taken by the language or the imagery. Perhaps you have become more inclined to look for concealed artistry. Perhaps what is most important is that it made you think about such pressing concerns as global warming and the industrial pollution of air and water. Perhaps you have read other things that you thought spoke with greater force to the modern reader. Or perhaps you have always wanted to try your hand at writing, and Wordsworth's poem made you wish you could spend more time exercising your imagination. *Your personal assessment is your own business.* But remember: it should not get mixed in with the way you describe what you have read. That is not being fair to the work. In a sense, you the reader are part of a jury, expected to be open-minded about the work you are evaluating.

Literalists and Figuratists

How, then, does involvement in the humanities lead to critical thinking? The answer is that it may not if one's responses are limited to the emotions, if one *never* wants to be analytical. Yet it is difficult to believe that there would not come a time when a clash of opinion occurs and when the generally intuitive viewer is asked to defend a positive or negative view. After a time "I didn't like it; I know what I like, and I didn't like this" becomes inadequate. Continued experience in the humanities inevitably broadens our perspective, and we become increasingly skillful in defending our likes or dislikes as well as listening carefully and critically to others.

If you start chatting with a stranger in a theater lobby, and your casual chit-chat leads to comments about the movie you've just seen, you can usually tell whether you're conversing with a critical or a non-critical thinker *by that person's use of language.* The non-critical often relate all experience, whether at the movies or in real life, to themselves. "The movie was too gory for me. I prefer a nice love story." Or it could go the other way: "I hate gooey love stories; give me good old-fashioned horror any time." The critical, however, speak in or imply general principles. This comes from seeing, listening, or reading a great deal and thinking about what has been absorbed.

The non-critical may also be called **literalists**, a term derived from their habitual way of *not* seeing general principles. They are tuned into what is happening at the moment, and their opinions are often shaped by popular views expressed by friends who are just like them or by what a favorite commentator has been saying about global warming, homeland security, the state of the economy, and so on. They prefer supermarket-type, plastic-wrapped ideas that can be taken in whole and never analyzed. For their part, the critical may be termed **figuratists**, a term derived from the fact that their language is colorful and suggests wide experiences in many fields, including the humanities. If they are talking about the present moment, the likelihood is that they will see it in broader terms. There is a vast difference between "The cream in my coffee looks sour" and "Looks as if the world was too much with this cow."

Responding to the literalist's "I know what I like," the figuratist in the lobby may begin with "This movie's dialogue was riddled with clichés," and then give a list of them. The general principle, which is implied and easily defensible, is: *Cliché-riddled dialogue is not the sign of talent; it is visiting familiar territory, which is not worth the viewer's time.* An answer like "Well, I don't have anything else to do, so I don't mind what you call clichés" quickly identifies the speaker as a non-critical literalist.

Literalist Speech

Literalists are limited to what we may call the "everyday concrete." They are also likely to listen haphazardly to what a figuratist is *generally* saying, latching on to the very last thing that was mentioned.

> F: *So many of the so-called professionals I run into don't seem to be what I would call experts. I'd love to meet one who could give me sound answers to important questions: where to live, whether to change jobs, what suntan lotion is most effective, where my children could get the best education.*
>
> L: *I didn't know you had children.*
>
> F: *I don't.*
>
> *(Blank stare)*

One must be able to transcend the narrow confines of a self-centered existence and believe that one will make a significant contribution to life . . .

—Bruno Bettelheim

The figuratist may not be personally involved in *any* of the examples mentioned in the list given. They are meant to introduce the general subject of incompetence in areas where you would expect to find the opposite. The figuratist is also implying that there is no certainty—that in a philosophical sense we are all alone to stumble our way through the world. The figuratist uses specific experiences to arrive at general principles. Friends of "F" may have children, but not necessarily. Being broadly interested in what's happening in the world, "F" knows a good deal about educational systems, has read widely on the subject, has viewed panel discussions, and so on. In the same way, a novelist may begin by writing about her own childhood memories, but if she is a good novelist, she will impart some wisdom that will help all readers make sense out of life, wisdom that comes not necessarily from her own life but from being immersed in reality. Literalists generally don't write books.

> F: *I think my students don't know the difference between the classroom and their bedroom.*
>
> L: *My neighbor says her son likes to sleep in class.*
>
> F: *The least their parents could do is send them to school with pillows.*
>
> L: *I don't think that would be wise.*

Figuratist Speech

Figuratists, especially those who devote considerable time to reading great literature, use fanciful, often metaphoric language—that is, language that means something other than what is being directly said. Effective ways of communicating occur more naturally to them than to people who have spent less time in libraries. For example, at a recent opening of a bad play, a figuratist, talking to friends afterward in the lobby, was overheard commenting: "Watching this, I thought I was giving CPR to a statue." Somehow, "The play was boring" just doesn't have the same *zing*.

Figuratists are adept at twisting words that in their original context were just mildly clever, making them shine with brilliance. Many years ago the celebrated

In this world there are only two tragedies. One is not getting what you want, and the other is getting it.

—Oscar Wilde

Put all your eggs in one basket and--WATCH THAT BASKET.

—Mark Twain

(and somewhat arrogant) British dramatist Noel Coward wrote a personal note to then prime minister Winston Churchill, who was famous for cleverness and quick wit, inviting him to the opening night of his play. He ended the note this way: "Oh, and feel free to bring a friend if you have one." Not one to take an insult lying down, Churchill replied: "I won't be able to make the opening, but I will come the second night if there is one."

An added bonus for the avid reader of great writers is that clever remarks like Churchill's are in the public domain. They can be absorbed into one's own repertoire of shining comments. It is also fun for the figuratist to converse with other widely read friends and either quote from instantly recognizable sources or, even better, come up with a personal variation. Shakespeare has probably penned more frequently quoted lines than any other writer in the English-speaking world, so many in fact that the figuratist feels obliged to allude to but not to repeat them verbatim one more time. The queen in *Hamlet*, tossing flower petals into the heroine's grave, cries "Sweets to the sweet: farewell!" A figuratist, much addicted to chocolates, was heard to say, just before giving in to the temptation of one more delectable piece: "Sweets to the sweet: farewell, teeth!"

The most often repeated of the great lines are those which contain wisdom behind the wit, so that the critical thinker is quick to claim ownership of them, knowing there is no way to improve upon them. The legendary Yogi Berra is credited with many now famous, if not always grammatically respectable, remarks. Much of his wisdom sprang from the observations of a folk philosopher, thinking about his beloved game of baseball. "It ain't over till it's over" is now, despite the grammatical lapse, *the* best way to imply that there is always hope. There is, after all, always a ninth inning, with three outs.

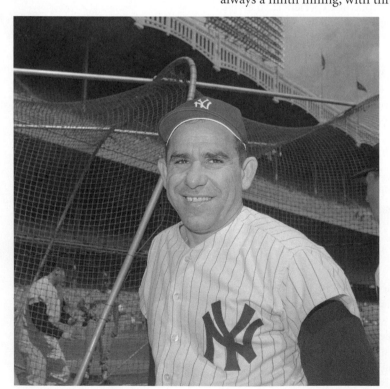

"It ain't over till it's over" just seems more effective than "There's always hope."

Source: Bettmann/Corbis.

Nor is every saying attributed to Yogi Berra the mark of an untutored philosopher with bad grammar. One suspects that, as he grew older and realized his comments were becoming famous, he gave them more depth and an entirely original style. "In theory there is no difference between theory and practice. In practice there is." This sly bit of wisdom sneaks up on us. It could be rephrased like this: "People who spend their lives talking theories really need to see what's out there." But it wouldn't have the *zing* of the seasoned figuratist that Yogi Berra really was. And the critical thinker is always looking for clever uses of language, whether from the libraries or from the baseball stadium.

Critical thinking is indispensable to the art of being human, though the critical thinker is always going to run into an uncritical acquaintance who insists, "I'd rather not think about what I read or see; I'd rather just enjoy myself." Is there no way to convince the acquaintance that it's possible to both think and enjoy—that, in fact, thinking just *might* be the ultimate way to enjoy living? Those who think well speak well, and those who do both will remain avid lovers of the humanities, a perennial reservoir of inspiration that sharpens our critical faculties.

Key Terms

alienation the term used by Bertolt Brecht to describe the ideal, non-emotional state in which the viewer is best able to derive the author's message.

Apollonian a term derived from the Greek god of light and truth; used to describe something or someone that is orderly and rational.

context as used in this chapter, the environment, background, or special circumstances in terms of which a given work is best understood; historical context is the influence that the ideas, values, and styles of a particular time have on a society, work of art, or philosophy.

critical thinking the faculty of rational and logical analysis; looking at subjects objectively, gathering all information, and then drawing conclusions about the subject based on evidence; the opposite of jumping to hasty conclusions based on a purely emotional response.

Dionysian a term derived from the Greek god of wine and vegetation; used to describe spontaneity as well as a lack of order and structure, signifying the passionate and creative (often impulsive) aspects of art, society, or an individual.

empathy the quality of identifying with another (an actual person or a character in a book, film, or play), becoming, in a sense, that person and being involved in his or her problems.

figuratist a critical thinker whose use of language is characteristically colorful, often playful, filled with metaphors that suggest a greater interest in the general than in just the particular.

imagery found especially in poetry, the pictures that the words create in your mind and communicate what ordinary prose cannot, or at least not as economically.

literalist the non-critical person whose language reflects a concern for the immediate moment, especially as what is happening or being viewed relates to the self.

sonnet a fourteen-line poem that originally imposed on poets tight rules of length, rhythm, and rhyming pattern.

rationalizing often mistaken for critical thinking, it is justifying something we have done that our conscience may disapprove of, or explaining away something others do or say that would otherwise damage our ego.

review a careful evaluation of a work of literature, drama, visual art, music, or cinema by a professional or non-professional critic, the former earning a salary for his or her opinions because of demonstrated knowledge of a particular field.

Topics for
Writing and Discussion

1. The evaluation of both the novel and film version of *The Da Vinci Code* in this chapter is that of a hypothetical critical viewer. You may have a different, equally valid opinion. Defend it.

2. May we say that the critical person is Apollonian and the non-critical person is Dionysian? Why or why not? Explain.

3. It has been said: "Wisdom is rooted in the figurative." Explain what this might mean.

4. Take stock of your personality as it is right now, in terms of Apollo and Dionysus. Do you think you have achieved a balance between the two? Does one side predominate? Does one side need work?

5. What made Richard Rorty realize that "My baby don't love nobody but me" didn't make sense?

6. Give an example of a "popcorn hangover" you have experienced.

7. Explain, in Brechtian terms, how you may be alienated while watching a movie.

8. How do you recognize when someone is giving an informed opinion?

9. Briefly indicate and describe the steps in the personal critical process.

10. Write an imaginary conversation between a literalist and a figuratist.

3 Myth and the Origin of the Humanities

Overview

Long before there was print, before the formal arts existed, there were the humanities in the form of **mythology**. Music and dance probably began as rhythmic accompaniments to stylized movements in which people honored and appeased the gods and observed certain stages of life, such as the transition from youth to adulthood. Early forms of the drama occurred when people pretended to be hunting wild animals needed for their survival or heroic warriors battling evil spirits. In Neolithic cave drawings, such as those found in Lascaux, France, our ancestors depicted both the animals on which their survival depended and themselves in the act of hunting those animals. In reimagining the hunt, they endowed their deeds unwittingly with mythic significance.

Early people, in societies that were of necessity closely knit, preserved their history by weaving stories of their past—stories about where they may have originated and their relationship to the gods; stories about great hunters, warriors, and leaders; and eventually, stories designed to illustrate the difference between right and wrong.

Mythology underlies much of the work created in *all* disciplines of the humanities. Literature, visual art, music, drama, cinema—all may have roots in **myths** that are sometimes unique to a given culture but in many instances are universal, found in one version or another in most cultures. For this reason, mythology is an appropriate starting place for our study of the humanities.

What, then, *is* mythology? Webster gives us two ways of defining it. One is "the science or study of myths." The other is "a collection of all the myths of a specific people or about a specific being." Myth can also be defined as "a traditional story of unknown authorship, ostensibly with a historical basis, but serving usually to explain some phenomenon of nature, the origin of humanity, or the customs, religious rites, etc., of a people." Thus we can speak about the mythology of a Native American nation or the mythology of a specific figure such as King Arthur.

In this chapter we discuss the role mythology played in shaping the humanities. We'll conclude by sampling mythic elements in some famous literary works. We also discuss the fact that all of us have our own personal

◉ The 1959 Brazilian film *Black Orpheus*, a modern retelling of the Greek myth, shows the enduring relevance of ancient tales.

Source: The Everett Collection, Inc.

mythology, beginning in early childhood when we objectify our fears and our secret longings, when we divide the world into good and evil and have our heroes and, for the most part, identify with them. Our myths stay with us for life and grow up with us, fulfilling psychological needs at every stage of our development.

We need, at the outset, to demolish some common misconceptions about myth. It has become a deceptively simple four-letter word used in a variety of ways not necessarily related to the humanities, though closely tied to our personal needs. In popular usage, myth is *something erroneous yet widely believed*— something to be refuted by rational adults, such as "The Myth of Mental Illness," or "Myth of calories exposed; eat all you want and get thin!" Another misuse of the word is patronizing, in the sense of "old stories once believed by naive people in a prescientific age that didn't know better."

If myths could be thus dismissed as just false and outmoded beliefs, they would not be the subject of this chapter. But mythology belongs to and affects large numbers of people. Knowledge of myth is basic to cultural literacy. Writers assume that readers will understand mythic references. For example, *romance*, love that goes far deeper than just sexual attraction, is an archetype we can date back to the Middle Ages. In describing *Eternal Sunshine of the Spotless Mind* (2004) as "romantic," *New Yorker* film critic Anthony Lane says that the film suggests "every one of us harbors an inextinguishable need, and that we helplessly swing back toward our soulmates."[1] Intrinsic to the romantic love archetype is the belief that each of us is destined to meet the right person eventually.

That humankind is the mythmaking species is not saying too much. Myths are as necessary for survival as breathing and eating. In addition to influencing both the humanities and, as we shall see, psychology, myth affects the behavior of people all over the world. This chapter examines basic myths about creation, birth, death, the afterlife, love, power, magic numbers, the importance of circles, the arduous journey, and the unspoiled garden. Some of these myths date back to very early people, but all of them recur in many forms. They are symbols in our culture and in our unconscious minds that help to shape the way we view ourselves and our world. They are vital to the study of the humanities.

Myths are clues to the spiritual potentiality of the human life.
—**Joseph Campbell**

Archetypes in Mythology

Even if myths were only a collection of stories about recognizable families, feuds, passion and revenge, they would be enjoyable as literature. Reading them, we are struck by similarities in stories and characters. We might ask ourselves why certain of these are found again and again and often influence the way we ourselves think and react to what others do. Scholars expect even more. They seek in myth a common thread, a chance to learn if the stories tell us something important about the human condition. For this they turn to a theory of psychologist-philosopher Carl Jung (1875–1961), who maintained that all persons are born with an instinctive knowledge of certain **archetypes**, the models by which people comprehend experience and cope with the enormous and often baffling task of being human. Jung believed these models are shared by societies all over the world, though they may take different forms. Archetypes are mythic characters, events, symbols, and buried assumptions transmitted from one generation to another through what Jung labeled the **collective unconscious**.

From the unconscious emanate determining influences which, independently of tradition, guarantee in every single individual a similarity and even a sameness of experience, and also of the way it is represented imaginatively. One of the main proofs of this is the almost universal parallelism between mythological motifs.[2]

Jung's theory is not accepted by all psychologists or scholars of myth, but without it or another comprehensive theory to replace it, we have a difficult time accounting for the continued appearance of certain myths and myth elements: tales of a terrible flood and the salvation of one good man; the stories about dangerous journeys into the land of death and darkness; and above all, tales about the major stages in the life of a singular human being—sometimes partly divine—known as the *hero*. There are, however, some alternative explanations.

One is the *external* theory, the most scientific of the possibilities. According to this theory, stories were spread along migratory routes. Myths originated in specific places and then were transported as people warred, traded, and intermarried with each other. In general, we do find myth similarities among certain cultures whose migrations can be traced.

An example of the migratory spread of old stories is the way the myths of the African Yoruba tribe were transported to Cuba, where they were modified and adopted by a whole new body of listeners. These stories gradually became systematized into both a religion and a philosophy known as *Santeria*, which offers an explanation of universal origins that combines Catholic monotheism with an African belief in multiple deities. Santeria continues to be practiced in Cuba, and its pantheon of heavenly protectors includes both African gods and Christian saints.

Yet another explanation for the universality of myth is the predictable one that human beings share common needs, regardless of geography and level of cultural sophistication, and thus certain elements found in all myths must play their part in helping people cope with the conditions in which they find themselves. Similar needs do not necessarily imply contacts between cultures or a mandatory belief in a collective unconscious. If human needs are very much the same everywhere, why shouldn't myths be?

> *These heavenly archetypes were felt to be true in the same way as the events and forms that inhabit our imaginations often seem more real and significant to us than our mundane existence.*
>
> **—Karen Armstrong**

The Hero as World Myth

In examining the mythic roots of many works in the formal disciplines of the humanities, we can see that Shakespeare's portrait of King Henry V is one of a nearly perfect hero, the champion and defender of a people, the one who seems indestructible. But so is Frodo, the tiny hobbit of *The Lord of the Rings*, who sacrifices home and security and ultimately his very life to save Middle Earth from the terrible Sauron. And the term *hero* applies to women as well as men. Think Sigourney Weaver in the *Alien* trilogy. The Chinese film *Crouching Tiger, Hidden Dragon* (2000) featured a woman who was almost supernaturally adept at the martial arts and could even fly.

The hero is an archetype found in almost every culture—hence the label *world myth*. The Irish novelist James Joyce used the term **monomyth** to convey his belief that the concept of the hero is the same everywhere. (There *are* similarities, of course, from one culture to another, but there are also significant differences.) Regardless of how each culture views existence and its particular survival needs,

> *The hero is an archetype found in almost every culture–hence the label world myth.*

stories of heroes seem to be essential. As early as 1909, Otto Rank, a disciple of Freud, indicated the characteristics of the hero in Western mythology.

> *The hero is the son of parents of the highest station. His conception takes place under difficulty. There is a portent in a dream or oracle connected with the child's birth. The child is then sent away, or exposed to extreme danger. He is rescued by people of humble station, or by humble animals, and reared by them. When grown, he discovers his noble parentage after many adventures, and, over-coming all obstacles in his path, becomes at last recognized as the hero and attains fame and greatness.[3]*

The human passions transform man from a mere thing into a hero, into a being that in spite of tremendous handicaps tries to make sense of life.

—Erich Fromm

Freud, a pioneer in the psychological interpretation of mythology, maintained that the two families in the monomyth—the noble and the common—represent the parents as they appear at different stages of the child's development. But Jung went beyond this interpretation, arguing that the components, or motifs, of this pervasive myth were primordial images, "or—as I have named them—archetypes." For Jung, they were not narrowly connected to individual children but were a profound part of universal expectations of life. In short, *everyone* is prone to believe in and await the coming of a hero.

Birth of the Hero. The hero's birth occurs under wondrous circumstances: bowing trees; a shower of gold penetrating the ceiling of a room in which a young girl has been confined; the visit of a god in the guise of some other creature, animal or human; mysterious prophecies. Usually the hero has been sired by a supernatural being.

From the beginning of human awareness, the phenomenon of birth has preoccupied and baffled people. Eventually they came to know the causal sequence that led to reproduction. But they must have marveled over the sequence, that such a miracle could be possible! Even for "ordinary" mortals, the birth of a child is a glorious event; announcements are mailed, friends offer congratulations, and a birthday remains a special day throughout life. In a real-life version of the prophecy that attends the birth of a hero, the parents are offered best wishes, a way of urging providence to take note of the infant, to destine the child for love and success. Those whose glorious future does not materialize may even believe themselves to have been cursed by fate.

The ultimate meaning of these stories is psychological rather than concrete, and the stories themselves serve only as metaphors for the myth, expressing something that is deeply felt but not easily said.

—David Leeming

Early Recognition of the Hero. The hero destined for greatness must be recognized early in life, often after accomplishing a spectacular physical deed—such as the young Arthur's removal of the sword Excalibur from the stone that had held it until the rightful owner should come along, or the superhuman ability of Theseus to lift a heavy stone that covered a golden sword and sandals, evidence that he was a king's lost son. (One version of the myth, however, credits him not so much with strength as with ingenuity in lifting the stone by devising a lever.) Sometimes recognition comes through fulfillment of a prophecy, as when Jason arrives in the kingdom wearing only one sandal.

The theory behind the monomyth is that the theme of early recognition identifies a universal need for acceptance. In the painful stages of early adolescence, the child asks, "Who am I?" and fears that the answer will be, "You're nobody." Children are so small compared to the adults around them that it's no wonder they lack a sense of worth.

Many of us later admit that in childhood we harbored fantasies of secretly being children of a prominent, even royal, family, stolen from the cradle by gypsies or given away by our true parents. This unknown identity allows the extraordinary child to live with such average people and to perform dreary domestic tasks unsuited for noble beings. One day, the child-turned-adolescent feels, the recognition of special status will surely arrive. One only has to look at the popularity of the Harry Potter books for proof of the widespread appeal of such fantasies.

The Hero's Great Deed. It always occurs in young adulthood, at a time when the hero has left home and is separated from the parents. It is a mythical version of the universal rite of passage: the attainment of adult status at puberty. All mythologies recognize the importance of the transition to adulthood.

Almost every early culture required the accomplishment of an arduous task to signify the end of childhood: enduring bitter cold, surviving in the wilderness, recovering a magic item from a ferocious guardian, conquering a predatory beast. Theseus destroyed the Minotaur of Crete, a creature with the head of a bull and the body of a man, which had demanded the regular sacrifice of the finest Athenian young men and maidens. In order to kill the Minotaur—an extraordinary feat in itself—Theseus had first to find him by making his way through the labyrinth, a series of deceptive passages, which Freud-oriented myth commentators have viewed as the journey through the maze of childhood sexual stages. According to Freudian interpretation, the ultimate discovery and killing of the Minotaur thus becomes the young adult's arrival into sexual maturity.

Many of the great deeds in mythology are physical, but others are purely mental. Oedipus, the protagonist of the great Sophoclean tragedy, achieved greatness by solving the riddle of the Sphinx—half monstrous bird, half woman—who devoured anyone unable to give the correct answer to this question: *What creature goes on four feet in the morning, two feet at midday, and three feet at twilight, and goes slowest when on the most feet?* When Oedipus arrived, Thebes was in a chaotic state of panic, for no one could solve the riddle. But Oedipus did. The answer is *man, who crawls on all fours as a child and therefore goes slowest, walks upright as an adult, and uses a cane near the end of life.* The furious Sphinx kills herself, and Oedipus is made king, only to suffer disastrous consequences.

The celebration of a hero's successful and wondrous feat is a need that stays with us through life. We love to watch and empathize with milestone achievements: the inauguration of the new president; the Academy Award ceremonies; the placing of a ribboned gold medal around the neck of an Olympic champion. We mark the milestones in our personal lives: birthdays; graduation; the first date; the first kiss; a letter of acceptance; getting the desired job; marrying.

The Hero's Loss of Power. Myths of the West seldom end when the heroes are happy and successful. Fairy tales do. (After Cinderella marries, we never hear a word about her relationship with her family, in-laws, or children.) In adult mythology, however, the hero, like Oedipus, usually falls from greatness. King Arthur must live on to see Camelot destroyed, his noble kingdom shattered. In the West, the story of the hero tends to be tragic.

If heroes lose their power, a possible compensation is that their death is usually glorious and their former greatness acknowledged. When Oedipus, who blinds himself so that he might never again look upon his misbegotten children, says, "I am the unclean one who has defiled this land" and makes his way to exile in the desert, the Chorus asks the fearful question: Why does this happen? Why

The first condition that any mythology must fulfill is that of cleaning the doors of perception to the wonder of ourselves and the universe of which we are the ears and eyes and the mind.

—**Joseph Campbell**

When the best leader's work is done, the people say, "We did it ourselves."

—**Lao-tzu**

is Oedipus guilty of patricide and incest when he was doomed by a prophecy to perform these deeds? Why not blame the gods for his unkind fate? Yet, in accepting full responsibility for his deeds, he retains his noble status. In Sophocles' play, the doomed hero walks *unbowed* from the city. The grieving citizens make a respectful path for him. A vast presence is departing, and he will be mourned for many years to come.

After the fall of Camelot, the body of King Arthur is placed on a ship that will sail to the mystic land of Avalon. Great heroes fail, but their failures only testify to the bigness of their lives. It's almost as though mythology is saying "You can't have it both ways. You are either uncelebrated but perhaps content, or you take the risk of greatness, knowing that it doesn't last."

Recognition of the hero's nobility is seldom there during his or her lifetime. In fact, there is sometimes outright hostility toward the hero. Before he undergoes a violent death, Theseus is blamed by his once loyal subjects for the Spartan invasion of Athens at a time when he was gone from the kingdom. They even drive him out of the city, forcing him to seek the hospitality of the rival king who eventually kills him. But later the citizens realize the mistake they have made and erect an enormous tomb to honor his memory.

The history of Western civilization has recorded many instances of actual heroes, rejected or highly controversial during their lifetime but revered after death: Joan of Arc, Galileo, John F. Kennedy, to name a few.

The Hero in Non-Western Mythology. Asian and Middle Eastern cultures have hero stories, but they seldom concern the exploits of a singular mortal who is to be revered and celebrated to the exclusion of ordinary human beings. The Buddha (by birth, a prince named Siddhartha) achieved great humility, never sought power, and discouraged his followers from looking upon him as a deity of some sort.

Joseph Campbell has pointed out that whereas

> *the typical Occidental hero is a personality, and . . . necessarily tragic . . . the Oriental hero is the monad [a simple indivisible unit]: in essence without character . . . untouched by . . . the delusory involvements of the mortal sphere. And just as in the West the orientation to personality is reflected in the concept and experience even of God as a personality, so in the Orient, in perfect contrast, the overpowering sense of an . . . impersonal law . . . harmonizing all things reduces to a mere blot the accident of an individual life.*[4]

Judaic and Islamic traditions contain many stories of Moses and Mohammed, respectively, and their feats of leadership, but both prophets are regarded as spiritual forces, not as mighty conquerors. Before his death, Moses asked that his burial site be concealed so that no elaborate memorial could be built in his memory. The Islamic laws taught by Mohammed assume "the brotherhood of man . . . [the] equality of all believers . . . and absolute submission to the will of God [Allah]."[5]

In Chinese mythology, great dynastic rulers are cited for their virtue and their social achievements, such as in the case of Huang Ti, the "Yellow Emperor," who made agriculture possible and encouraged the development of a musical scale. He is celebrated for having driven out the barbarians, but his success came not from his unique superhuman valor but from the help of the gods, who looked with favor on his virtuous character. Confucius occupied himself not with metaphysical beliefs about the spirit behind the universe but with practical advice for those who would rule: walk the straight and narrow and live for the good of society. In Western mythology, King Arthur comes close to the Confucian ideal, but he was also a brave warrior of consummate fighting skill and would have been less revered if he had not been. He certainly meets the Western "requirement" that the hero be a singular individual capable of astonishing physical feats.

The Hero Today

The archetype of the hero is still very much with us. Celebrities, today's demigods, may not be the literal progeny of deities and mortals, but they are as vivid in the public mind as their bygone counterparts. Their exploits are followed in magazines, gossip columns, and television interviews, and they set the trend in clothes, hair styles, and language.

There are still those who perform Herculean tasks and win admiration: the new home-run king; the world's fastest runner; the first astronauts in space; the first woman to walk the length of Tibet on foot; the first blind climber to reach the top of Everest; actors who receive Oscars for their first screen roles; and Nobel prize winners, often unknown before their achievements catapulted them to celebrity status.

We keep looking for that special someone who solves all problems. The archetype of the mysterious stranger has been important in American mythology because of the early dangers encountered in settling so vast a land and the democratic structure of frontier societies in which leaders were not born into their roles but had to prove themselves. That they often failed to do so made the myth that much more intense.

A classic example of the "special someone" hero myth can be found in George Stevens's 1952 film version of Max Brand's popular Western novel *Shane*. The film

Dreams are private myths. Myths are public dreams.

—Joseph Campbell

We keep looking for that special someone who solves all problems.

Alan Ladd as the mysterious stranger in *Shane* who rides out of the hills and rescues a peaceful community of homesteaders from a ruthless killer hired to drive them from their land.

Source: The Everett Collection, Inc.

features a retired gunfighter who rides out of the Wyoming hills on a white horse, rescues a group of peaceful farmers from the lawless cattlemen intent on driving them off their land, shoots the leader of the bad guys, and then rides back into the misty land of his origin.

Today we still long for that wonderful presidential candidate with precisely the right qualifications, honest to the marrow, who will suddenly materialize at the Iowa caucuses, untainted by past political compromises, and be instantly recognized as the new political messiah. On the other hand, we can quickly desert charismatic orators who announce their candidacy, then are forced to withdraw when they are found to be error prone like the rest of us.

Magic

Almost always present in myths, especially but not exclusively those of the West, is the archetype of magic. Myths the world over are filled with objects like magical rings and weapons of supernatural power when wielded by a hero. Wizards, witches, and sorcerers appear and disappear at will, cast spells, and become close allies of mortals with righteous causes, endowing them with the strength and courage to accomplish their marvelous feats. The hero often has a magic sword with which to conquer opponents. King Arthur has Excalibur and Shu Lien in *Crouching Tiger, Hidden Dragon* has her Green Destiny.

One interpretation of magic-as-archetype may be the need to believe that the resources for coping with life are, like the magic sword, virtually at hand. Another is that only singular individuals can do the big tasks, and since they have magic on their side, the rest of us should not feel ashamed if we cannot live up to their example. In our mythology, magicians like King Arthur's Merlin or Gandalf in *Lord of the Rings* reassure us that, though many tasks appear to be impossible, someone is always there who has the resources to accomplish them.

The Power of Words

Language of a special kind is another recurrent archetype. "In the beginning was the Word," so begins the Gospel of John. "It is written . . . " is found in speech the world over to represent absolute authority. Cultural anthropologists theorize that our male ancestors, in jealous awe of women's reproductive powers, believed that language was literally man-made and that words uttered by men were more miraculous than birth itself. In early cultures, when birth was considered a magical event, men may well have sought ways to match or even surpass this phenomenon in which they seemed to play so small a part. In many myths, the male hero is able to move heaven and earth because he knows secret words. Perhaps this myth helps explain the male tendency to insist on having the last say in all matters.

The words *Open Sesame!* yielded wonders for Ali Baba, even as *Sesame Street* serves as a modern archetype—the thoroughfare that takes children from ignorance to knowledge through the magic of letters and the fantasy creatures that attend them. Rumpelstiltskin was an elf whose magic name had to be guessed to save the queen's firstborn

One interpretation of word significance is male jealousy over female reproductive powers. In myth, the power of the uttered word could be supreme. Men could talk. Perhaps that is why men have traditionally insisted on having the last word.

Magic still captivates audiences, as in the 2004 film *King Arthur.*

Source: © Orion/The Everett Collection, Inc.

child. Special words also have their uses in real-world settings. For example, unless you are told "Simon says," you may not imitate the leader in the child's verson of that game. A sneeze often receives the blessing "Gesundheit!" from well-wishers. When two people happen to say the same thing at the same time, each might immediately exclaim "Jinx!" Presumably, bad luck will attend those who fail to carry out the verbal ritual.

For thousands of years, the world of human affairs has counted on the reliability of someone's word, as when a pact is made over a handshake and the inevitable "I give you my word" is uttered. There are still places in which insisting upon a written contract instead of accepting a spoken promise is greeted with suspicion and hostility. Most of us have yet to dismiss as insignificant the giving of our word, or to minimize the disappointment when others break theirs. In fact, *break* is an interesting verb to use in conjunction with *word*. In myth, a broken magic wand can be disastrous.

Sesame Street is the long-running television show that shows children the magic of words.

Source: Yoshikazu Tsuno/AFP/Getty Images.

The Power of Numbers

The belief in the magic of words is closely associated with the magic of numbers. Humanity long ago discovered that numerical units were basic to the design of both the earthly and the heavenly universe. In *The Divine Comedy*, Dante makes abundant use of the number 3, representing the Trinity. The poem is divided into three parts—*Inferno, Purgatory*, and *Paradise*. The last two parts contain 33 cantos, or chapters, corresponding to the age at which Jesus died; the first part has one extra canto to bring the total to what was considered the perfect number, 100.

In Hebrew tradition, there are mystic numbers. The letters of the Hebrew alphabet have number equivalents, and certain combinations of numbers are believed by some to hold the secrets of the universe. A school of Hebrew mysticism called Kabbalah studies the numerical complexities of Hebrew scripture. For example, some scholars have determined that there are 620, not just 10, commandments: 613 that were present in the five books attributed to Moses and 7 that were added later by rabbis. Not by coincidence, these scholars observe, is the fact that the 10 commandments contain 620 letters.

People still have mystic feelings about numbers and sequences, expecting, for example, that the news of two deaths will lead inevitably to news of a third. The Golden Gate Bridge in San Francisco was a popular place for suicides, and when authorities discovered that the 999th person had leaped to a watery grave, they quickly announced the 1000th suicide as having already occurred, gave the person a fictitious name and occupation, and said services would be private. They knew all too well that a real 1000th would have shown up in no time—so powerful can numbers be.

When the 999th person jumped off the Golden Gate Bridge, the authorities quickly announced that a mythical 1000th had followed suit right away.

The ancient symbol of the mandala may have suggested completeness and order in the universe. For Jung, it suggested the organization of the mind.

Source: The Newark Museum/Art Resource, NY.

Tomorrow, and tomorrow, and tomorrow,
Creeps in this petty pace from day to day,
To the last syllable of recorded time;
And all our yesterdays have lighted fools
The way to dusty death.

—William Shakespeare

The Circle

The circle is an archetype that affects our lives profoundly. Because the circle is an unbroken line without beginning or end that encloses a uniform space, people have used it to symbolize oneness, completeness, and eternity. In myth, it appears as a shield, a ring, a pendant, the sun, and the moon, as well as in markings on cave walls or on stones. Countless circular structures, some dating back many millennia, are found throughout the world: temples, stone circles, and that most intriguing of all round monuments to ancient humanity: Stonehenge, a large circle of heavy stones on Salisbury Plain in southwest England, once thought to have been a place of human sacrifice but now known to have almost certainly been the means of identifying the seasons of the year by the changing positions of the sun.

One universal form of the circle archetype is the *mandala*, found in the art of almost every period and every culture. It is an enclosed circle, often with an intricate design representing the organization of the universe and the various deities that control it. The exact nature of the design is perhaps less significant than the implications of the circular shape. It told people that the universe is an entity—one thing—as indeed the word itself—*universe*—suggested. It told them that, if it could be viewed from an alternate universe, it would be an enormous round object, something like a gigantic crystal ball, self-contained and distinguishable from anything else hovering in space.

Eastern and Western minds apparently came to similar conclusions about the universe. Both decided on the circular, geometrically perfect shape, which made the universe seem somehow *manageable*—that is, within the scope of human comprehension, if not control. Contemporary science continues to debate the nature and extent of the universe, and indeed whether the word does or does not really apply. Is it a random collection of planets and suns formed in the aftermath of an original explosion? Does it extend infinitely? At the same time, physicists continue to seek uniformity in physical laws. Einstein's general theory of relativity maintains that space is both infinite and *curved* and that gravity so warps space that no object can travel in a straight line forever.

Carl Jung saw in the mandala a universal symbol of not only cosmic but psychic organization. He believed that, just as humanity appears unwilling to exist within a shapeless, infinite universe, we also resist disorder in human existence. We reject the idea of discontinuous sensations, a hodgepodge of sensory reports, emotions, and thoughts. The circular shapes in myths, according to Jung, are projections of an inner need to identify a coherent self, a shaped self, one that can be thought about and discussed. In a sense, even our concern with memory is related to the mandala symbol. When we forget a name, for example, we sometimes ransack our minds as if the elusive words were hiding there, as if the mind were a self-contained circle preserving every memory. On this point, East and West have different opinions.

For the East, the circle has traditionally been a symbol of the order behind *nature*. The *yin* and *yang* of Taoist philosophy, which represent the attraction of opposite forces that keep the universe in balance, are artistically depicted as a black and white mandala. But in this philosophy, the human mind is not a self-contained circle. The boundaries between the mind and the outside world are not distinct, as they are in much Western thought. Consciousness is like a flowing river. Thoughts and feelings come and go. Human intelligence is something inherent in the order of nature. It is there when a problem needs to be solved or when a sustained thought process focusing on a particular thing is required. The Western idea of the personal ego as a walled city is a strange concept to the traditional Eastern mind.

In the East, the circle is often a symbol of the oneness of nature and the living beings who inhabit it. In the West, the vocabulary of circles is often narrowly related to self. We have "holistic" medicine that treats the "whole person." When we feel unsure of where we want to go with our lives, we speak of trying to "get it together," and if we feel that we are losing control, friends might offer to help us "pick up the pieces."

Except for different images of the mind, East and West seem to have always liked the idea that everything makes sense; the circle does not suggest chaos. Universal humanity does not want to think of itself as adrift and abandoned in an existence that cannot be comprehended.

The circle also represents immortality. The Hindu and Buddhist concepts of reincarnation and the cycles of existence, shared by many Westerners, are obvious examples. And what is the belief in an afterlife, found the world over, but the concept that existence has no end—like a circle?

The Journey

One of the major archetypes in Western mythology offers a non-circular view of the meaning of existence. The difficult journey is another way of depicting the course of human life. Life-as-a-journey implies both purpose and a final destination, as opposed to a random series of disconnected happenings. We think of life as moving from one stage or "phase" to another; again, this implies that we can make sense of it. The French educator Jean Piaget is famous for having set forth the stages of child development, and his ideas form the basis for much educational theory.

The mythic hero usually sets out on a journey fraught with danger and has a challenging task that must be performed at the conclusion. Fearful obstacles usually threaten the hero along the way: dense, maze-like forests; dangerous beasts; magical potions that induce slumber and prevent motion. But sooner or later, the journey continues.

Life as a journey implies both purpose and a final destination, as opposed to a random series of disconnected happenings.

Our expectations thus formed by the myth, we look for progress in our own lives and in those of others. We expect the obstacles. We say, "No pain, no gain." We are sure the journey will prove worth the effort. Accomplishing the big task will mean recognition and approval. When others seem not to succeed in their journey, we say, "He is stuck in adolescence" or "She's still at the same old job!"

The mythical journey is also a quest. The hero searches for his or her homeland, a buried treasure, the Holy Grail. Attainment of the goal gives shape and purpose to life. And here we note a conflict in the two key symbols. Whereas the circle guarantees life without end, the journey is supposed to yield important results. We don't mind applying the circle to universal order or to the shape of the mind as a self-contained whole, but we resist thinking of life as just one thing after another without purpose, without direction. We hate to think of ourselves as "going around in circles." We like to think that, regardless of life's continual changes, its ups and downs (there are always mythical mountains to cross), life *does* come to something after all.

The journey in Eastern mythology, on the other hand, is a series of happenings, not necessarily in a sequence and without a necessary final task. In the myth of Bodhidharma, the monk who supposedly brought Buddhism from India to China, the hero stops to meditate on a mountain top for nine years, during which his legs fall off. But the story merely points out that this is what occurred. It does not call it a tragedy. For the East, life is indeed one thing after another, and each day has to be accepted for what it is. For the West, a journey without a successful destination is worthless. "She died before her time" is a Western mythic observation. So is "Here he is, thirty-five years old, and what has he done with his life?"

The Garden

In the West, as we have said, journeys are supposed to have successful destinations, but related myths question these destinations. Some myths say we are heading down the "wrong path." Some myths look back to the past and say: "Would that we had never embarked on this journey; we have lost too much."

Myths of a Golden Age, when things were better, extend far back in the Western tradition. In fact, the usual downfall of the hero implies that what was once good is now gone. With the death of King Arthur went all hope of another Camelot. Many myth scholars believe that the archetype of the Golden Age had its origins in the Hebrew Bible's account of the Garden, the earthly paradise Adam and Eve called home until they were cast out for eating the forbidden fruit from the Tree of Knowledge.

The Hebrew Bible also contains a countermyth with a countersymbol to the Garden. Adam and Eve are expelled from *their* Garden, but Abraham and his descendants are offered the hope for a Promised Land, Canaan, the fertile land of milk and honey. Moses leads the Children of Israel out of captivity in Egypt, but he does not live to reach his destination. His followers, however, find that Canaan is anything but a joyful paradise where they can live happily ever after. It is constantly attacked, conquered, and occupied. Yet the promise made by God to Abraham projects the Garden into the future. The Golden Age has yet to come, but come it will.

In the eighteenth century, writers in Europe and America revived the Garden myth as they mourned the shift from rural to urban living. They lamented the wretched lives of the urban poor, densely packed into crime-ridden, filthy slums. The teeming cities represented for these writers the antithesis of the Garden, and they celebrated the unspoiled countryside and the happy, unschooled innocents who lived there, uncorrupted by the greed and arrogance of cosmopolitan life. Literature and drama began to cast their eyes far afield, imagining the paradise of remote lands, where the sun shines warmly all year long, food is abundant, and inhabitants live in perpetual harmony.

This literary movement was inspired by the philosophy of *primitivism*, which held that those who lived far from cities in what was called the "state of nature" were happier, less apt to commit crime, and more willing to share the fruits of the land than their educated and wealthier counterparts. The key spokesperson for primitivism was the French philosopher Jean-Jacques Rousseau (1712–1768), whose contributions to the idea of freedom are discussed in the final chapter of

We must tend our own gardens.
—Voltaire

this book. For now, we need to know that Rousseau restated the myth of the Garden, blaming government and social controls, both products of so-called civilization, for the corruption of humanity. In doing so, he created the archetype of the *noble savage*—untutored but astute in the ways of nature, infinitely resourceful, and able to provide food and shelter for the family.

Primitivism led to the popularity on the stage and in fiction of this new mythic figure. Robinson Crusoe's "man Friday" was far more adept at living without the comforts of civilization than the shipwrecked British gentleman who depends on him for survival. Mark Twain (1835–1910) created Huck Finn and his wonderful raft, and sent them floating down the Mississippi River—a way of life representing a perpetual escape from civilization, its moral codes, its social demands, and its unhappy inhabitants. James M. Barrie gave the world Peter Pan, who eludes the aging process and lives a boy's carefree existence in Never-Never-Land. More recently, Steven Spielberg gave us E.T., the extraterrestrial, an adorable, unspoiled being from outer space who manages to escape the clutches of humanity, which is—except for one tender and understanding little boy—unworthy of his purity. He waits somewhere "up there" for a true believer who will find a way out of the mess we humans have made of the once beautiful Earth.

The "discovery" of America in 1492 gave rise to a new version of the Garden archetype—*the New World*—which continues to influence us today. First came the explorers, proudly planting their nations' flags on the "virgin" soil (while Native Americans watched). Then came boatloads of pilgrims seeking a new start in life. Then by the thousands came immigrants seeking prosperity in streets supposedly paved with gold. As the eastern half of the United States became densely populated and the dream of prosperity gave way to the reality of long hours of work and crowded tenements, the archetype of the Garden was moved out to the frontier, the wide-open American West. Pioneers left their homes by the thousands, seeking a new Canaan. Some prospered, many did not. The promise of the New World still holds out hope for millions throughout the globe.

When they come to a promised land, modern immigrants, like their predecessors, bring with them a strong archetype—the family—as well as the customs, traditional beliefs, and rituals that hold families together. Sometimes the newcomers are received with enthusiasm, and sometimes they are rejected. Often, members of the younger generation drift away, become part of the new culture. The elders sometimes intensify the traditional rituals, hold even more tightly to their customs, close themselves in for fear of losing their identity, self-respect, dignity. Disenchanted by the New World, they remember the old country, where things were better, where people were nicer and the streets safer. Like Dorothy in the Land of Oz, they discover that maybe their original home wasn't so bad after all. The Garden always seems to be somewhere else. But if this archetype can cause disillusionment, it can also be the source of hope.

Gods as Human Beings

As an archetype, the Greek god is written about and depicted in statuary as a larger-than-life mortal. Unlike most other early cultures, the Greeks had ambivalent feelings about their deities. They feared them because of their enormous power and because they could be unpredictable, striking down anyone they chose, at any time, and for any reason. They also resented them. The Greeks believed that nothing in the universe was as important as human beings. If there were to be

> *I am pessimistic about the human race because it is too ingenious for its own good. Our approach to nature is to beat it into submission. We would stand a better chance of survival if we accommodated ourselves to the planet. . .*
>
> —**E. B. White**

gods, why, they must be made in the image of humanity (not the other way around as in Judaism, Christianity, and Islam).

The archetypal term *Greek god*, used to describe a very handsome man, usually refers to Apollo, who was always portrayed as the epitome of physical perfection and whose name itself has become an archetype of male beauty. *Greek goddess*, or just *goddess*, used to describe a woman of surpassing beauty, usually means Aphrodite or the Roman Venus. Although we don't run into an Apollo or a Venus every day, the enduring myth is that such physical perfection, though godlike, *is* attainable by certain mortals.

The Greek deities were thought of as residing on Mount Olympus, which is a very real place, in much the same way that our own deities of the entertainment world live high up in the Hollywood Hills or on the slopes of Aspen or along the Grande Corniche, the topmost road on the French Riviera and home to the wealthy (*and* "beautiful") people of this world. Zeus and Hera, the king and queen of the other Greek deities, were married celebrities who fought bitterly and held grudges against each other. Many human woes were ascribed to the "fact" that Zeus and Hera were often on opposite sides in a war, with each plotting against the other. *In humanizing their gods, the Greeks in effect deified themselves!*

In humanizing their gods, the Greeks in effect deified themselves.

Myth as Explanation

Mythology consists of much more than the archetypes that shape the way we interpret our world and what happens to us in it. For our ancestors, two major aspects of being alive must have been very baffling. One was the mystery of natural phenomena. The other was how to account for all the trouble that seemed to be part of life. Mythology was their way of understanding the mystery of the universe and the pain and hardships of living in it.

If science had been at the disposal of our early ancestors, they might have turned away from mythmaking in favor of observation and experimentation. Lacking science, they created stories to account for what they could not otherwise explain. We should be grateful that they did, for these ancient stories, along with the music and dances that must surely have accompanied group ceremonies, became the foundation on which the humanities now rest securely. The myths they wove made the natural world and its amazing phenomena seem less remote and frightening and helped remove the fear that life was innately evil, that bad things happened without cause.

The need for acceptable explanations for life's tragedies remains with the humanities. Often these explanations are at odds with scientific evidence. For example, in 1927 the American author Thornton Wilder, most well known for his innovative play *Our Town*, published the novel *The Bridge of San Luis Rey*. Significantly, the book appeared just ten years after the outbreak of World War I, while people were still searching for reasons for that conflict.

The bridge in the novel is a footbridge built across a steep gorge in the Andes Mountains of Peru. Thousands traveled across it for years, but on one particular day the bridge collapses, and five travelers are hurled to their deaths. The novel then presents the story of each victim and poses the question "Why this person?" Although scientific explanations are abundant, the author prefers to leave the door open for the possibility that divine intervention was responsible. Is it more comforting to believe everything happens for a reason instead of believing that life is a series of random, senseless occurrences? Our ancestors must have thought so and may have left explanatory myths as their legacy to us.

Creation

Even the greatest scientists and philosophers have wrestled with complex questions about life and our beginnings. Why is there something when there might have been nothing? Is there an essential principle that requires existence to exist? Or did it spring accidentally from nothing? And if so, how and why? Why are *we* here? Why haven't we discovered intelligent life anywhere else in the universe—at least so far? Mythology supplies a number of different answers, and the quest continues.

Accounts of creation are present in almost every early culture. One myth, as recounted in the *Upanishads*, sacred books of India, begins: "At first he was lonely and afraid but, above all, he lacked delight (therefore, we lack delight when alone) and desired a second . . . . This Self then divided itself into two parts; and with that, there were a master and a mistress."[6] But this first woman was afraid to be touched and so hid from her male Self. She turned into various animals, but he pursued her and mated with each of her manifestations—until the natural world, as we know it, was formed. The story does not explain where the Self came from, but once that is accepted, everything else follows in a cause-and-effect sequence.

Most Asian mythologies have no clear-cut story of creation. The Buddhist *dharma* constitutes the orderly principle that guides the universe, and it had no beginning. Therefore, the natural world, which is the outer garment of this order, must have always existed. Confucianism, a major Chinese philosophy, stresses the social world and one's duties within it and avoids the question of how it began, which does not matter as much as how life is lived. However, in another major Chinese philosophy, Taoism (or Dowism), we find a creation story that resembles those of non-Asian cultures, giving further credence to Jung's theory that early cultures developed similar myths without traceable communication with each other. In this story, the universe, as in the Hebrew Bible, was at first a dark, formless void. Within this void, a single egg came into being, inside of which was the fetus of what would eventually become the giant Pan-Gu. After attaining colossal size, Pan-Gu stretched his arms, the egg broke, and the lighter half floated upward to become the sky, while the heavier part sank downward to become the earth. Ever since, the operation of the universe has depended on the attraction of opposites—astonishingly prophetic of the modern electromagnetic theory of nature!

In Greek mythology, precreation is depicted in a similar fashion. It is called the "formless confusion of Chaos," existing only in darkness. Chaos in some mysterious way gave birth to children: one was Gaea, or Mother Earth. Others were Night and Erebus, or Death. Night placed an egg in the depths of Erebus, and from it was born Love (though we are not sure how this love was defined). Love's first act was to create Light and Day.

Greek myths tell us that the gods came after the creation, but this order is not surprising when we consider that, in the Greek myths, the power of Fate appears to be greater than that of the gods. For the Greeks, the power of Fate always existed, was responsible for the coming of Night and Death, and must therefore be reckoned as *the* divine force.[7]

According to an Aztec myth, before the universe was formed, there were gods. A fight developed over who would create which part of the world. Eventually a snake divided in half—one half to create the upper part, the other half to create the lower part. The half that created the earth felt she was less important and began to quarrel with the half that made the heavens. As compensation for her inferior position, the gods added to her importance by allowing different parts of her body to be the source of important elements—the rivers and streams coming from her eyes, for instance.

Many other cultures attribute the origin of the natural world to a divinity that preceded its existence. Judaism, Christianity, and Islam share a common belief that the world was brought into existence by an all-powerful and singular creator. Working within this tradition, the English poet John Milton (1608–1674), in his epic poem *Paradise Lost*, assumes the preexistence of both God and a chaotic universe, which was then transformed into the orderly cosmos the poet knew. According to Milton's interpretation, in the beginning there was

> *the vast immeasurable Abyss,*
> *Outrageous as a Sea, dark, wasteful, wild,*
> *Up from the bottom turn'd by furious winds*
> *And surging waves, as Mountains to assault*
> *Heav'n's highth, and with the centre mix the Pole.*
> *Silence, ye troubl'd waves, and thou Deep, peace,*
> *Said then th' Omnific Word, your discord end.*[8]

In the modern world, a debate continues between those who believe the universe had no known beginning and those who believe it cannot have always existed. Modern science is deeply committed to the law of cause and effect, yet when it comes to the question of whether there was a *first* cause, a deep division of opinion remains. The theory that the origins of the universe can be traced to a big bang, a huge explosion of perhaps a single particle, is widely held. Once this explanation is accepted, the theory manages to explain all that followed. But where, some ask, did the single particle come from? One answer has been that it came from nothing, and that we need not assume "nothing" is empty.

It is interesting to note that one of the crucial unsolved questions about our existence is remarkably similar to those asked by our earliest ancestors.

The Natural World

Once believed to be an ancient site of human sacrifice, Stonehenge—that remarkable stone circle on the Salisbury Plain in southwestern England—is now believed to have been erected as a means of predicting the seasons according to the position of the sun with respect to the stones at various times of the year. When the sun shone directly through the archway formed by the prominent pair of stones in the center, this regular occurrence was taken as the beginning of summer. Yet Stonehenge could not explain why there *were* seasons. Why was it not always summer? Why the bitter cold, when people could freeze to death and food was scarce?

Nature was surely something to inspire wonder, apprehension, and worship. Many early myths sought to explain nature, and early rituals—ceremonial dances as well as animal and human sacrifice—were efforts to control it.

Every part of the earth is sacred to my people. Every single pine needle, every sandy shore, every mist in the dark woods, every meadow, every humming insect. All are holy in the memory and experience of my people.

—Chief Seattle

Stonehenge has stood on the Salisbury Plain in southwestern England for thousand of years; believed to have been an early means of predicting the seasons, it could not explain why there had to be seasons.

Source: Bob Krist/Corbis.

In Scandinavian communities, for example, the fertility deity was Freyr, who was thought to bring rich harvests to the earth. He did so by wooing a maiden symbolizing the union of earth and sky. Rituals that honored Freyr and the abundance he gave were, Scandinavians thought, essential to survival. In almost all early cultures, help from the gods was needed if crops should fail or were insufficient. If the weather did not cooperate, food could be found in the sea if the storm god could be appeased.

In Greek mythology, Apollo, the sun god, drove his chariot across the sky each day, thus accounting for the rising and setting of the sun. Apollo's sister Artemis presided over the moon at night. The king of gods, Zeus, was responsible for hurling thunderbolts, and Poseidon controlled the sea. But these phenomena could be altered at the whim of the gods. Thus the sea might be made so calm that no ships could move when Poseidon wished to punish a fleet that failed to honor him. Or a sea monster might appear, sent by Poseidon in response to the prayer of a mortal to whom he owed a favor, as when Theseus prayed for the destruction of his son, who he believed had committed adultery with his stepmother.

Early peoples performed what was called "sympathetic magic," the acting out of ceremonies designed to affect the behavior of the gods. Thus during the winter solstice, the longest night of the year, people in countries throughout the world attempted to evoke the return of the sun through lighting candles, as if the sun—or the powers in charge of light—would imitate the lesser light below. Similarly, the Native American rain dance is a ritual designed to bring an end to drought.

A Greek explanation for the seasons was the love of Demeter, goddess of the earth, for her daughter Persephone. So joyful was Demeter at the very thought of her daughter that she provided a superabundance of all the good things the earth could yield. One day, however, the girl was glimpsed by Hades, lord of the underworld, who captured her and took her to be his bride. Demeter so mourned her loss that the earth came to be covered with the ice and snow of perpetual winter. If Zeus had not intervened, all human life would have ended, but he was so touched by Demeter's grief that he arranged for Persephone to live with her mother for all but four months of the year, those she owed to her husband. When Persephone is in the underworld, the earth freezes over, and when she returns, her happy mother allows the earth once again to bloom.

Another explanation occurs in the myth of Dionysus, the deity who governed the abundance of the earth. Winter came about because he died and, in the underworld, was torn to pieces and eaten. Still, when he was somehow resurrected and became whole again, spring returned—but only temporarily, for each year Dionysus met his terrible fate again.

The descent into the underworld of both Persephone and Dionysus can be regarded as sacrifices that ensured rebirth. This idea, that without sorrow or death there can be no springtime joy, was an early belief that has captured the minds of writers and philosophers ever since.

For the Greeks, vegetation could be connected to the involvement of gods with beautiful mortals. The blooms of the hyacinth and the narcissus celebrated the transformation of their namesakes from death to eternal life in nature. Hyacinthus was a beautiful young mortal dearly loved by Apollo, who accidentally killed him while they were playing a game of discus throwing. (Note that once again the Greeks attributed human failings to their gods.) Apollo then transformed the dead body into the hyacinth. The narcissus commemorated the death of another beautiful young man, who saw his own reflection in a pool, fell madly in love with it, and pined away from sorrow because he could never possess it.

Mythologist Edith Hamilton interprets such transformation stories in a somewhat ominous way. They are, she speculates, vestiges of ancient human sacrifice rather than of accidental death. Ancient people did offer a select number of handsome young people in sacrificial rituals designed to appease the gods. According to Hamilton, when the Greeks told their myths in later years, they revised the stories to rid themselves of this violent era in their past:

> It might happen, if the fields around a village were not fruitful, if the corn did not spring up as it should, that one of the villagers would be killed and his—or her—blood sprinkled over the barren land. . . . What more natural then, if a beautiful boy had thus been killed, than to think when later the ground blossomed with narcissus or hyacinths that the flowers were his very self, changed and yet living again? So they would tell each other it had happened, a lovely miracle which made the cruel death seem less cruel.[9]

The sacrifice of animals was probably performed each year at the spring festivals honoring Dionysus to ensure the god's return and the renewal of the growing

What more natural than if a beautiful boy had thus been killed, than to think when later the round blossomed with Narcissus or hyacinths that the flowers were his very self?

—Edith Hamilton

season. At the drama festivals, when the tragic protagonist fell from his high position, he became a kind of symbolic sacrifice so order could return to the state.

From what is now Ghana, in West Africa, comes a story of how the country flourished and was prosperous because each year a beautiful young woman was given to a devouring serpent. One year, however, when the woman was led to the pit where the serpent waited, rescue came in the form of a brave young man engaged to marry her. He stood by while the serpent appeared and twice spat venom on the woman, because he knew that only on the third try could the reptile be destroyed. At the appropriate moment, the young man beheaded the serpent, only to find that it kept growing new heads—seven in all. The young woman was saved, but the serpent had its revenge. As the last head was cut off, it flew away, saying, "For seven years, seven months, and seven days, Ghana will receive neither water nor rains of gold." A drought ensued, destroying the populace and a once great empire. In this myth we do not find the cycle motif of Persephone and Dionysus but rather an unhappy explanation for a catastrophe that must have actually taken place.

In Native American mythology, human sacrifice was needed in order to make the heavens work properly. After four worlds failed, a fifth world was revealed. It was discovered that the sun and moon could be set in their courses only by the death of a Navajo each day and another each night. Later, when human beings claimed credit for the prosperity of the world, they were punished by plagues and monsters.

Human Suffering

Sometimes known as the *problem of evil*, suffering caused by natural catastrophes (such as the devastating tsunamis of 2004 that took more than 200,000 lives in southeast Asia) and by the inhumanity of regimes (such as that of the Nazis in the early twentieth century) continues to be analyzed by philosophers, theologians, and creative writers. Our ancestors asked the same questions we hear now. Why are some people consumed with hatred, envy, and greed? Why are there famines, plagues, and wars? Like many contemporaries, they wanted to believe there were reasons for the suffering people had to endure. The idea that terrible things happened without cause was unacceptable because it suggested a universe ruled by chaos, a universe in which humankind was powerless. In creating stories that explained suffering, our ancestors were able to reassure themselves that order did indeed prevail in the universe and that, if they acted in an appropriate manner, they might escape misfortune.

A common explanation for suffering was an early act of transgression against divine law—offending a god or disobeying a command. The Greek myth of Pandora explains how human misfortune came about because of curiosity. Beloved by Zeus, Pandora was given a magical box in which all of the gods had placed something, but she did not know what the contents were, and she was not supposed to open the box. Frustrated by the gnawing desire to discover what treasures were concealed inside, she disobeyed Zeus and opened the box, out of which flew death, sorrow, plagues, war, and every other calamity visited upon mortals ever since. Alarmed, Pandora slammed the box shut, not knowing that trapped inside was the gift of hope.

Color Plates 4 and 5 show two visual interpretations of trouble's origin. In the portrait of Pandora by the nineteenth-century English artist Dante Gabriel

Evil enters like a needle and spreads like an oak tree.

—Ethiopian proverb

Rossetti (1828–1882), the mythical Greek woman appears strong-willed and determined to have her own way, whatever the cost. In *Food for the Spirit*, Haitian artist Gabriel Alix (b. 1930) shows Adam and Eve as equal partners in sin. Given the colorful lusciousness of the fruit hanging over their heads, the viewer may find it hard to blame the first man and woman for failing to obey God's command.

In the Judeo-Christian tradition, God commands Adam and Eve not to eat the forbidden fruit growing on the Tree of Knowledge. (The fruit, often depicted as an apple, is not identified in Genesis, and apples are not native to the Middle East.) Tempted by the serpent, Eve eats the fruit, and Adam does the same. Genesis does not say that Eve prevailed upon Adam to follow her into sin, though later versions turned the story into a myth of woman's weakness. In Milton's *Paradise Lost*, God judges Adam more harshly than he does Eve because, even though Eve has sinned first, Adam, being a man, should have known better.

In an African myth of the Burundi tribe, a woman is again blamed for bringing about human suffering. In the long-ago time in which the myth is set, human beings are not touched by Death because divine dogs protect them. One day Death approaches a woman and promises to give her and her family special protection. When the woman opens her mouth to speak, Death jumps in. Questioned by the chief of the gods concerning the whereabouts of Death, the woman lies and says she has not seen him. The chief of the gods, being all mighty and all knowing, recognizes that the woman is lying and allows Death to dwell inside the woman and all of her descendants.

According to another tale found in the oral tradition of many African cultures, Kintu, the first man, and his wife Nambi are hurrying to leave the land of the sky in order to flee Death. They have been warned not to delay their escape, but Nambi decides to go back for grain. Death follows her as she attempts to rejoin her husband. As a result, death becomes the punishment for all future generations, a motif notably similar to that found in Genesis.

The traditions of the East do not speak of human suffering as caused by disobedience to a divine command; rather, they blame selfish acts by individuals for the world's ills. In Hindu belief, what happens to a person is the result of **karma**, a summation at death of how one's life has been conducted. If it has been less than morally satisfactory, the spirit is reborn into a new body and a less fortunate social position in which hunger and poverty dominate. If it has been mainly satisfactory but not perfect, the spirit is reborn with a chance to live a better life. Thus Hindus speak of "good karma," which means a life blessed by good deeds in a past existence, while "bad karma" is just the opposite.

A legend found in Mexico and in Central and South America is that of *La Llorona* ("The Weeping Woman"). So popular is this figure in oral storytelling that numerous versions of her persist. In one version, she is a phantom, never seen, but heard weeping at night, mourning her children, for whose deaths she is responsible. In another version, she is a spirit doomed to wander forever in search of the children she neglected during her lifetime. Still another version shows her to be blatantly evil, a woman who lures men to follow her only to suffer violent death. In this telling, the woman resembles the Sirens of Greek mythology, the sea maidens whose seductive singing lures sailors to their doom, and the Lorelei in Germanic myth, a lovely maiden who sits on a rock, combing her hair and singing so beautifully that sailors wreck their ships trying to reach her. The tales of

La Llorona are often told as a warning to unmarried pregnant women who, finding themselves abandoned, have no recourse but to give up their babies. Presumably, repeating the story of a mother mourning her lost children reminds young women of what can happen when they indulge in practices forbidden by religion and family.[10]

The tragic results of curiosity and disobedience are also found in two other famous myths, one from the Greeks and the other from the Hebrew Bible. Both illustrate a universal belief that some things are better left unknown. In the Greek myth, an extraordinary musician named Orpheus, later the subject of the operas we discuss in Chapter 8, is in love with the beautiful Eurydice, who dies and is taken to the underworld. Orpheus follows her down and uses the gorgeous strains of his lute to convince the king of the underworld that Eurydice should be returned to the land of the living. His request is granted, with one condition: Orpheus must walk straight up the path without turning around to make sure that Eurydice is following. He almost keeps the pact, but at the last minute, unable to bear the suspense, he turns around, only to see his beloved being reclaimed by the powers of darkness, lost to him forever.

The prizewinning 1959 Brazilian film *Black Orpheus* (see the opening image in this chapter) tells essentially the same tale, set during the night of Carnivale in Rio de Janeiro. A figure wearing the mask of Death pursues the modern Eurydice through a crowded street, finally seizing her and carrying her into an empty building and down an endless spiral staircase. The modern Orpheus follows them, but instead of being given the chance to return to life with her, he dies also. The morning finds the two lovers, together, impaled on the sharp spikes of an aloe plant. In this modern retelling, death is not the result of curiosity or disobedience, but—more tragically—something that occurs without any purpose at all.

The Orpheus and Eurydice story continues to fascinate writers and public alike. In 2000 there was Mary Zimmerman's fanciful stage adaptation of the Roman poet Ovid's *Metamorphoses*, itself an updating of Greek myths. Eurydice is now a modern, liberated woman who decides she is *not* going to follow meekly behind her lord and master, Orpheus. She pays the price, but the assumption is that her independence is worth it.

In a biblical tale, Lot and his family are allowed to escape the destruction of Sodom and Gomorrah, with one condition—that they flee the city without turning around to see what is happening. Lot's wife, however, cannot resist the temptation, and when she turns around, she is transformed into a pillar of salt.

Cursed by Fate

The Greeks introduced another way of accounting for human woes, and that was Fate. It was visually represented as three sisters: one wove the thread of life, another stretched it out, and the third cut it. In addition to having a person's lifespan determined by the whim of Fate, Greek mythology also developed the concept that many people were followed throughout their lives by the unkindness of Fate because of a transgression they had committed in the past, or one that was committed by an ancestor for which they were paying the price. Two of the greatest Greek tragedies are trilogies about noble families cursed by Fate because of past sins.

The Oresteia by Aeschylus (525–456 B.C.E.) consists of three plays about the doomed family of Atreus, who killed his brother's children and then served them

The Greeks personified Fate as three sisters, one of whom wove the thread of life, another stretched it, and the third cut it–presumably on a whim.

to him as food. He committed this atrocity as an act of vengeance against the brother for having forced his wife into adultery. The two sons of Atreus, who must bear the consequences of their father's sin, are Menelaus, king of Sparta, and Agamemnon, a Greek warrior. Menelaus marries the beautiful Helen, who runs off with the Trojan prince Paris, thus precipitating the Trojan War. Agamemnon fights the ten-year war on his brother's side, returning home only to be lured to his death by his wife, whose lover stabs him. The two adulterers are in turn murdered by Agamemnon's son Orestes with the assistance of his sister Electra. The Furies, ferocious mythic women whose duty it is to haunt and terrify evil-doers, pursue Orestes, taunting him demonically day and night until he is exonerated by the goddess Athena in the world's first known trial scene.

The doomed family of Cadmus includes his descendant Oedipus and the four children borne to Oedipus and his wife Jocasta, who was also his natural mother. Cadmus had been a wealthy citizen who offended the gods by bragging that, because of his business success, he was just as powerful as those deities. The disasters visited upon his descendants were punishments for his arrogance.

Greek myths and tragedies are of enduring relevance because the question of whether any of us really has free will is still very much alive.

The tragedy of the doomed Oedipus is told in three plays by Sophocles: *Oedipus the King* (or *Oedipus Rex*), *Antigone*, and *Oedipus at Colonus*. By the fifth century B.C.E., Athenians had developed a highly sophisticated urban civilization, and though the old myths still formed the basis for many plays of the period, they were subject to question. In particular, the Oedipus plays dealt with the issue of whether the protagonist, suffering because he had long ago killed his father and then married his mother without knowing the truth of his parentage, should accept responsibility for his actions when he was doomed by Fate to commit them. Sophocles resolves the issue by having his protagonist willingly accept responsibility as a means of maintaining his dignity. "The gods willed that I should slay the man I didn't know was my father," he says, "but the hand that struck the blow was mine."

Greek myths and the tragedies they inspired remain of enduring relevance because the question of whether any of us really has free will is still very much alive. Free will is at the core of many a court case involving dilemmas of responsibility. Inherited traits, family abuse, poverty, and a bad environment frequently enter into arguments for the defense. In Chapter 10, Freedom, the reader will find much more about this problem, which crops up continually in literature and film.

Myths of Childhood

Our earliest encounters with literature, the stories told or read to us, probably influenced our expectations of later life. Childhood tales—despite their frequent violence and terror—usually satisfy the child's (or even the parent's) need for security by bringing the action to a happy conclusion. How often did we hear "And they all lived happily ever after"?

Adults like to escape from the demands of everyday life by giving in to their childhood love of magical kingdoms, witches, wizards, and perils that are inevitably overcome. The Harry Potter books seem to be as widely read by the adult population as they are by the young. Fables from distant childhood have been kept alive, particularly by the Disney company. Both the young and the not so young have made huge box-office successes of *Snow White*, *The Little Mermaid*,

Beauty and the Beast, Aladdin, and *The Lion King.* This section deals with some childhood tales that are too important not to be considered as valid introductions to the humanities.

The Need for Reassurance

Children who hear about the Three Little Pigs learn that hard work and diligence, not fun and frivolity, pay off in the long run. And Red Riding Hood's journey to Granny's house would certainly have been a lot safer if she had heeded the advice about not speaking to strangers. Similarly, the mother goat in "The Wolf and the Seven Kids" goes off, leaving her children home alone with the admonition not to open the door to anyone. Most of the seven goats pay for disobeying this instruction by being eaten. Of course, as often happens in fairy-tale land, they are rescued, none the worse for their ordeal. Sleeping Beauty, threatened with awful consequences if she pricks her finger on a spindle, cannot resist the temptation to explore a hidden spinning wheel and so suffers the inevitable wound. But like so many childhood myths, that of Sleeping Beauty contains not only dire warnings about disobedience but also the reassurance that nothing *really* bad is ever going to happen.

The Harry Potter stories offer a combination of myths. Harry, the orphan kept under lock and key by relatives who do not understand him, is a modern version of Cinderella. Though neglected and consigned to a bleak future, he has magical powers that will eventually make a difference. In this respect, he also resembles the young King Arthur, the only person able to pull the sword Excalibur from the stone. Both myths appeal to our secret desire for hidden powers that make us superior to others.

Modern children's mythology tends to be less blatantly optimistic than popular myths of the past. Perhaps the stress of modern life filters down into bedtime stories. Or perhaps modern readers (or listeners) have developed a higher tolerance for conflict. Characters can face very real dangers and frightening villains. Sauron, who guards Mount Doom in J.R.R. Tolkien's *Lord of the Rings*, is evil incarnate and ultimately conquered, but only after a furious battle sequence. Maurice Sendak, also known for his imaginative stage and opera sets, has written a number of children's stories, such as *Where the Wild Things Are*, in which a little boy, sent to his room without supper, flies out of his bedroom (without adult permission, of course) and encounters weird, fantastic, sometimes frightening creatures, all vividly illustrated by the author. But, despite the odds, the boy manages to return safely—and to find his supper waiting for him. The myth appeals to the need for escape from humdrum—sometimes burdensome—reality, as well as the need for reassuring safety and love.

The Importance of Being Attractive and Rich

The old fairy tales reinforce stereotypical gender roles, class distinctions, and the notion that good and evil are based on physical appearance. People named Charming, Beauty, and Snow White are beautiful to look at and morally pure. The names Wicked Witch and Stepmother are given to unattractive characters who are up to no good. Cinderella is both breathtakingly beautiful and hard working. By contrast, her stepsisters are selfish, ugly, and possessed of unfortunately large feet. Old people seldom fare well in fairy tales, and critics point to this fact to explain why children often shy away from close contact with the elderly and the wrinkled, who resemble fairy-tale witches.

The fairy tale takes a child's anxieties and dilemmas very seriously and addresses itself directly to them: the need to be loved and the fear that one is thought worthless; the love of life and the fear of death.

—**Bruno Bettelheim**

Red Riding Hood's journey would have been safer if she had heeded the advice about not speaking to strangers.

Source: Gustave Doré, *Little Red Riding Hood.* Credit: Archivo Iconograpico, S. A.Corbis.

Fairy tales take place in magic kingdoms dominated by a class system, for, after all, they originated in a time when it was believed that nobility was inborn. People may not have believed literally in the blue blood of one small segment of the populace, but they were reminded time and again that "class will tell." The heroine of "The Princess and the Pea" is so innately sensitive—so clearly a member of the upper class—that she spends a sleepless night because one pea is under the pile of mattresses on which she has been lying. The pea has been deliberately placed there as a test of her true aristocracy.

The Importance of Names

In one folk tale, a lower-class heroine, a miller's daughter, marries a prince on the strength of a false promise—that she can transform flax into gold. She is locked in a room and told to fill it with the precious metal, but of course she doesn't know how. Help comes from a little man who tells her he can perform the magic, provided she promise to give him her firstborn child. Since the poor girl is not yet married and is in danger of losing her life if she doesn't perform the task before morning, she agrees. The gold appears, the marriage takes place, and in due time a child is born. When reminded of her agreement, she begs for another chance, which she gets! The condition is that she must tell the little man his name. Her first guesses are not even close, but she eventually is victorious when she overhears him boasting, "Rumpelstiltskin is my name."

The myth probably appeals to children of an age when language is becoming important. During dramatic presentations of the story, young audiences continually scream the name to the actress playing the heroine. Perhaps it helps children affirm their own identities, for they too have names, and names, as they are learning, are all-important, especially unusual names that make one unique.

The Dark Side

Though modern childhood mythology does not shy away from confronting real dangers, even the time-honored fairy tales must have evoked multiple responses. As well as magic kingdoms and beautiful characters, there are dangerous forests where lurk goblins, bats, and skulls. Through these and other dark elements, children learn that life is not always sunny.

The beautiful Snow White appears to die from biting into a poisonous apple given to her by her jealous stepmother. She is placed in a glass coffin, though in real life, children are often shielded from close contact with death. Of course, the kiss of a prince restores Snow White to life and leads to the usual proposal of a royal marriage.

In fairy tales, much emphasis is placed on the threat of being eaten. In *Hansel and Gretel*, still popular as children's theater and as opera, the wicked woman in the tempting gingerbread house warms her oven in dreadful preparation for roasting the two children. In the nick of time they are rescued and the wicked woman is consigned to a painful death.

In his 1983 musical play *Into the Woods*, Stephen Sondheim brings together all of the major characters from the fairy tales and puts them into small houses on the edge of the woods, a symbol of the true dangers in the world. Mythical illusion is continually shattered in the play. After their marriage, Cinderella discovers that Prince Charming is having many affairs. When confronted, he explains: "I was raised to be charming, not faithful." Jack's excursion up the magical beanstalk nets no fortune, and the hand of the dead giant falls on and kills the baker's wife. Traditional myths help the makers of the humanities to communicate dark messages.

Roald Dahl's *Charlie and the Chocolate Factory* has been filmed twice in recent times: as the 1971 *Willy Wonka and the Chocolate Factory* and director Tim Burton's 2005 *Charlie and the Chocolate Factory*. Neither version is precisely the wholesome entertainment the title appears to promise. The fable about a wondrous world of unbelievable candy was turned it into a dark story of how greed destroys. The children who can't resist the many temptations drown in a chocolate river or are crushed in mixing machines. The purity and common sense of the young hero, however, are recognized by the factory's proprietor, and he is allowed to ride a magic elevator into a land free of greed and corruption.

Some parents seek to avoid frightening their children (especially at bedtime) by eliminating all threatening motifs, by making sure that hungry wolves are not allowed to eat either little pigs or old ladies. One mother was distressed, however, when her child burst into tears at the end of a bland retelling of "Red Riding Hood" by demanding to know whether the wolf was still hungry!

Is it important for each generation of children to be taught the old fables? Writer Leonard Courier apparently believes so. His 1961 short story "A Christmas Morning" concerns a science-minded father who decides to eliminate all fairy-tale illusions in order to make sure his son will be able to face a harsh world. "The story of Santa Claus is nonsense," he says, and forces the child to stay awake all night so that he will observe the true source of his presents. The child, rubbing his eyes, watches as his parents assemble the gifts under the tree. At dawn he pleads to be allowed to sleep, but his father insists that he have breakfast and then play with his toys.

Before he may eat, however, the boy is required to show that he has learned his lesson. "Finish this sentence," says his father, "There is no—." When the boy keeps silent, the father becomes angry and threatens to beat the child if the correct answer does not come forth. "Well, what is it?" he repeats. "There is no what?"

Wearily, the little boy looks up and says, "There is no father."

There must be more to life than having everything.

—**Maurice Sendak**

Popular Mythology

Much of what we say and how we react to certain situations have roots in mythology, both past and present. Whether we know it or not, we keep creating and perpetuating myths. The fables of the Greek writer Aesop (sixth century B.C.E.) contain many stories and morals that stay with humanity from age to age. There is the story of the tortoise who wins a race against the swifter hare, proving that slow and steady can win a race. And there is a fox who decides that the grapes he is unable to reach are probably sour anyway—hence the continued use of "sour grapes" applied to anyone claiming "I didn't want it anyway." Aesop gave practical advice, but it was often contradictory. "Look before you leap" is the opposite of "He who hesitates is lost." Still, either can contain wisdom, depending on the situation.

Many popular beliefs are quoted without regard to their origins. Discovering the roots of popular mythology is not a plea for being more realistic. Its purpose is to encourage the *habit* of identifying certain thought and emotional patterns so they can be more readily evaluated as either still vital or no longer useful. In a sense, it is also an introduction to the critical appreciation of the humanities.

Common Sayings

Truth is one, the sages speak it by many names.

—**The Vedas**

All of us hear them; nearly everyone uses them. Life would be different without them. They are expressions of beliefs that may have originated in ancient stories, religious teachings, or frequently repeated slogans. They may be considered misconceptions by some, but indeed most of them are not challenged at all. Even those who scoff, however, may not be analyzing why the belief has found such wide acceptance. The following is a selective listing of some common beliefs that constitute our everyday mythology.

"What goes around comes around." In Hindu and Buddhist belief, as we have pointed out, *karma* is connected to a past life. People who have not led exemplary lives must continue to live in a new incarnation, as repayment for past deeds. As commonly used, the expression explains and approves of justice, as when the criminal who seemed beyond the law is discovered and punished, thus "getting what was coming." The saying also helps many of us account for bad things that happen. Apparently it is easier to believe that bad things are not random like a lightning strike but are the logical result of a misdeed. Thus, if we avoid such misdeeds in the future, all will be well.

The other side of the coin is how this belief helps us cope when good deeds are not recognized. Everyone likes to be given credit when it is due, and the popular myth assures people that eventually a reward will come.

"Leave it to Mother Nature." If nothing else, this saying supports the notion that nature is warm, caring, and nurturing. Mother Nature, or Mother Earth, is important in many cultures. Mongolian mythology, for example, has a Mother Earth who is gentle, in contrast to Father Sky, a stern disciplinarian who uses lightning to show his displeasure. In Greek mythology the goddess Gaea, who became Mother Earth, was the daughter of Chaos and mother and wife of both Uranus (the sky) and Pontus (the sea). In early myths, she is a monster, but over the centuries she evolved into a benevolent force. She lives on as the mother of all things, and as Gaia she is often featured by environmentalists on Earth Day to emphasize the need to love and protect the planet.

We like to think that Nature, like a good mother, will somehow forgive her children for pollution, overcrowding, and global warning. Indeed the myth of Mother Nature is the myth of motherhood in general, influencing how many women view their role in life and the expectations of their children. Mother is supposed to look after people's needs, and if she does not do so to their satisfaction, she will be accused of behaving unnaturally.

"They'll think of something." The ending of some Greek plays resolved terrible problems by having an actor dressed as a god come down to the stage. The device was known as a *deus ex machina*, and it has become a standard critical term for plot contrivance. In popular mythology, the *deus* is sometimes medical research. Like the cavalry riding to the rescue, like the mysterious stranger who appears just in time, science will solve every problem, find a cure for every disease in the nick of time. Because "they" have helped so often before, they can be expected to help every time. If rescue is inevitable, every rule of good health can be violated for our bodies or our cities while we wait for our rescuers.

"What do THEY know?" This popular expression is the opposite of expecting miracles from science. Disrespect for, even ridicule of, professional authority is the source of continual tension in the world. It is the Dionysian component in many people that makes them shout down speakers, hurl cream pies, and defy those who are said to know better. Literature and films have often endorsed the hero who is shown to be right by defying rules, while the person in authority has been depicted as unrealistically rigid and deserving of overthrow. This popular myth suggests that a healthy dose of skepticism is important. The sentiment can indeed fuel beneficial social change but, when applied indiscriminately, can lead to anarchy.

"All you need is love." Whether love is defined as the sweetest thing, whether it makes the world go round, or whether it's all you need, a popular belief is that love is as important as breathable air. Even the high divorce rate has not interfered with the widespread belief that living alone is unnatural or that there is no happiness outside commitment to one other person. A first mistake requires the search for the right choice next time, and a newly single person's claim of being happy is met with disbelief and offers of matchmaking. The myth is not only that there is someone for everyone, but that love and talk of love can substitute for any other human concern.

Just as the universe is filled with positive and negative particles, myths frequently have their own negative counterparts. In this case, the popular belief in love at all costs is often rejected by those who believe that love is a delusion or that the search for love will always fail and leave one bereft and miserable. If successive attempts have produced unhappy results, there may be comfort in thinking that love itself is to blame for what happened, that it is wiser never to expect a relationship to succeed.

"It must be fate." Also called destiny, fate plays an important role in Greek mythology and is one of its major legacies. It is still present in the way people react to events. The idea of destiny can offer comfort, relief, and freedom from responsibility because, if something is "meant to be," it will certainly happen, and no one is to blame. There is a positive side as well. If destiny can bring disasters, it can also bring good fortune, love, and happiness. It can be the source of perpetual hope.

In the popular film *Somewhere in Time* (1980), two lovers, separated by a century, finally meet because it is their destiny. The man, who is of the modern world, is at first restless and brooding, as if he knows that his life is incomplete. As soon as he finds himself in another part of time and sees the beautiful woman who seems to be waiting for him, he knows that all is as it should be.

To believe that one is meant for better things, that the answer to prayers is just around the corner, can be uplifting to the spirits, but of course if nothing turns that corner, the result can be a quick flip of the coin, back to "facing the fact" that life is *never* under one's control; life means just waiting for "what will be." The myth can also trap people in defeatist attitudes.

"Just deserts." *Deserts* in this saying is related to *deserve* rather than an after-dinner sweet. Early on, we learn that Santa Claus rewards only good children, while naughty ones receive a piece of coal, getting what they deserve. Life without the myth of deserving is unimaginable. It underlies our whole system of justice, for example. It probably acts as a deterrent to untold numbers of people who might otherwise commit crimes, or even provides secret comfort to people who are serving long sentences in prison: "After all, I *deserve* this."

On the other hand, this belief can be the source of much personal unhappiness. "What did I do to deserve this?" is a question frequently asked in the midst of a crisis. The answer might be that "it was destined" or that somehow the system has broken down and an innocent victim unjustly treated. This is a myth of entitlement, and it's particularly strong among those who expect payment for good deeds. The myth of the red-suited jolly man with the white beard is as pervasive as a myth can be. A wise course might be to ask ourselves *why* we are doing something. Is it for the implicit rightness of the deed or an expected full stocking on the mantelpiece?

"Us versus them." The desire to be part of a group and therefore at odds with people in another group is well established. It may encourage school spirit and often promotes family unity, but it can also lead to wars, mob violence, and a life-long distrust and hatred of "the other." Coaches and army sergeants urge their charges to fight more ferociously by reinforcing the "us/them" distinction, and in time of war it can help to bring about both national unity and inflexible mistrust of the enemy.

The us/them distinction can also be seen in zoning disputes, laws about immigration, and matters of territorial boundaries. It can be found in stories, plays, and novels about children in prominent families who disappoint their parents by failing to realize how lucky they are to be privileged. It underlies the racism implicit in films of the early twentieth century in which ethnic minorities are treated as stupid, bungling, or endearingly childlike. The belief presupposes the superiority of one group over the inferiority or even non-humanness of another.

"There's always room at the top." Belief that unlimited success should be possible for everyone is a spur to ambition as well as a cause for major disappointment in those who never achieve wealth or fame. The very word *top* is loaded with preconceptions and expectations. At the top are star entertainers, athletes, corporation executives, and political leaders. The pervasiveness of the belief is indicated by sales of how-to books and enrollment in seminars promising a quick and guaranteed road up. Of course if the *top* is to have any meaning, there must be a lot of people *below*.

Literature abounds with tales of those who buy into the mythology of upward mobility. The Horatio Alger novels of the early twentieth century all have heroes who start off poor and become wealthy either by hard work or accident. They are success novels, and their counterparts are films about aspiring performers who inevitably became stars after their early disappointments. The myth is so deeply ingrained in Western culture that many believe it is their *duty* to move up.

"Isn't that just like a man/woman?" **Gender roles**—models of appropriate behavior and functions for men and women—were for a long time codified and

unchanging. In many cultures these have been religiously defined, and failure to observe the rules can have serious consequences. Even among those who consider themselves enlightened, old myths that men are this and women are that often lurk in the background.

Gender reversals are not uncommon in mythology and literature, usually as a source of amusement. In one story, the Greek hero Achilles, dressed as a woman to avoid being drafted into military service, reveals his masculine identity when he brings his knees together to catch something thrown to him instead of catching it in his lap by spreading his skirt as a woman would have done. In Shakespeare's *Twelfth Night*, a shipwrecked woman disguises herself as her twin brother so she can safely travel alone. The duke who hires "him" as a servant becomes inexplicably attracted to "him." A modern update of *Twelfth Night* was the 1968 off-Broadway musical *Your Own Thing*, which advocated that it doesn't matter whether a man loves a woman or another man, as long as both are happy.

Still, many popular myths continue about gender. Men are expected to like adventure films, while films about love and betrayal are called chick flicks. Men are thought to never ask directions when lost. Women are not supposed to pass a clothing store without examining the window display. In 2004 business mogul Martha Stewart, called the queen of the domestic divas, was arrested, tried, and convicted in an insider-trading scandal. Her supporters argued that she had been the victim of the masculine cultural mythology that resents a woman's success. In this mythology, the woman who gets ahead is called "pushy" and "unfeminine," while a successful man is called "assertive."

"*Nice guys finish last.* The equation that goodness equals weakness accounts for the perhaps cynical acceptance of cheating, or at least "cutting corners," as an understandably human practice at all ages and places: on the playground, in class, in a courtroom or personnel office. Using test answers dishonestly acquired is only one example, and "everybody does it" furnishes the rationale. It is, after all, the way of the world. To the victor belong the spoils, presumably, regardless of how the spoils are obtained. A bumper sticker reads: "Do unto others before they do unto you."

Does anybody think mythology has no relevance to ordinary living?

How Myths Influence the Humanities

Throughout the rest of this book, especially in Part Two, which introduces you to the formal disciplines, you will see that myths and archetypes underlie a given work. In this final section of Chapter 3, we want to offer some prominent uses of myth found in literature, the theater, and film. You will see how a knowledge of mythology greatly enhances the appreciation of what is read or seen.

A reading of the poem "Leda and the Swan," for example, by the Irish poet William Butler Yeats (1865–1939) is more meaningful if we know the myth of how a woman named Leda was raped by the all-powerful god Zeus, disguised as a swan. Leda bore him two daughters, one of whom was Helen, whose adulterous love for the Trojan prince Paris led, mythically at least, to the Trojan War.

I've always preferred mythology to history. History is truth that becomes an illusion. Mythology is an illusion that becomes reality.

—**Jean Cocteau**

Literature comes alive through our understanding of how Venus, goddess of love, became obsessed with a handsome mortal, Adonis, and begged him not to go hunting, or how the young man disregarded her plea and was mortally wounded, leaving Venus to mourn. Shakespeare was inspired by their story and made it the subject of one of the world's great love poems.

We can read *Endymion* by the English poet John Keats (1795–1821) more easily if we know the fable about the handsome shepherd who, while sleeping on a hill, so arouses the moon goddess with love for him that she casts a spell causing him to sleep forever. He will never wake up, but he will never grow old. The myth of eternal youth is universal—and for obvious reasons.

A reading of the poem *Prometheus Unbound* by the English poet Percy Bysshe Shelley (1792–1822) is enhanced by knowing the story of the mythical Titan who stole fire from the gods and gave it to mortals. Prometheus was punished for his transgression by being shackled to a gigantic rock; every day thereafter a huge vulture ate his liver, which would grow back the following day while the vulture waited to devour it once again, the cycle of torture repeated without end.

Even when death comes in mythology, there is always the question of what comes afterward. Two major kinds of afterlife are described: one sometimes known as paradise, the other a dark, often dismal—and in many stories, eternally painful—place.

In Greek mythology the souls of brave warriors were believed to reside in an eternal paradise called the Elysian Fields after having been spared the pain of death. When it came time for them to die in battle, a benevolent god lifted them up and escorted them to a place of peace. In the medieval legends, after King Arthur is slain in battle, his body is placed on a magical ship that bears him to the far-off land of Avalon, where he will presumably live on forever. In the modern mythic trilogy *Lord of the Rings*, Frodo, the hobbit hero, embarks on a long and treacherous journey to destroy the magic ring that has caused so much pain and death. After bringing peace to Middle Earth, his world, he must leave. In an ending that resembles Arthur's fate, the author J.R.R. Tolkien describes Frodo's final seaward journey in unforgettable terms:

> *Then Frodo . . . went aboard; and the sails were drawn up, and the wind blew, and slowly the ship slipped away down the long dark firth; and . . . went out into the High Sea and passed on into the West, until at last on a night of rain Frodo smelled a sweet fragrance and heard the sound of singing that came over the water. And then . . . the grey rain-curtain turned all to silver glass and was rolled back, and he beheld white shores and beyond them a far green country under a swift sunrise.[11]*

In view of today's environmental concerns, the myth of a green afterlife has much appeal.

The Greeks also had Hades, or the Underworld, where the souls of non-warriors had to live after crossing the River Styx, which led from the land of the living to the land of the dead. Although the Underworld was dark and cheerless, it was not a place of torment.

The Divine Comedy by the Italian poet Dante Alighieri (1265–1321) has given us the popular image of the inferno, or hell, where souls must suffer for their sins. The narrator is led through descending levels by his guide, the Roman poet Virgil. After describing in vivid detail the punishments for various sinners, the poet comes to the place reserved for the greatest sinner of all: Satan. Instead of fire, the archenemy of humankind is fixed for all time in a frozen lake, which symbolizes pure hate. Purgatory, the place where lesser offenders are allowed to do penance for their sins, is described as a a mountain that eventually leads to paradise in the upper regions of the sky. It should be noted, by the way, that Dante's view of the next world came from his extensive grounding in Islamic mystic writings.

John Milton's *Paradise Lost* (1670–1672) begins in heaven, from which the devil, here called Lucifer, again the archetype of pure evil, is evicted after rebelling against God. After declaring that he would rather reign in hell than serve in heaven, he inhabits the palace of Pandemonium, where he, his followers, and all who will die without redemption are granted asylum. Then Lucifer enviously observes the Garden of Eden, which has been created as a paradise of unending beauty and tranquility, the abode of the newly formed Adam and Eve. Disguised as a serpent, he manages to entice them into disobeying God's commandment that they not eat from the Tree of Knowledge and thus bring about their downfall.

Christian writers have probably done the most to make hell an enduringly vivid concept, yet even those who dispute the theological view are apt to use *hell* in their everyday vocabulary, if only as a convenient way to describe a bad day at school or the office, or the frustration of plane delays, reservations lost in a computer malfunction, or luggage sent to an airport a thousand miles away.

Yet what would literature be without the principal resident of hell in all of his villainous manifestations? The medieval legend of the person who sells his soul to the devil in exchange for unlimited knowledge or special skills or non-stop sexual pleasures (depending on the version of the story) appears over and over. The classic use of the legend is *Dr. Faustus* by the tragically short-lived Christopher Marlowe (1564–1593), but it became the toast of Broadway in the 1955 musical comedy *Damn Yankees*, in which a loyal fan of the worst team in baseball history (the now defunct Washington Senators) sells his soul to Mr. Applegate, secretly known as Satan, in exchange for vigorous, athletic youth, allowing him to become a star player and help the Senators win the World Series, beating, of course, the perennial winners, the New York Yankees of the title. In everyday parlance, people speak about selling their souls in the workplace, often meaning they play up to their superiors in hopes of higher pay or a more prestigious title.

Conversely, stories about the triumph of good over evil keep that mythology alive in innumerable forms: movies, television, plays and musicals, children's stories, romance novels, and detective fiction. Usually the victory is predictable and not quite believable, but readers and viewers enjoy the feel-good experience anyway.

All cultures do not have the equivalent of Satan, though most of them *do* have stories illustrating goodness, as in this deceptively simple Buddhist fable:

> *Once there was a monk named Ryokan living a simple life of poverty*
> *and meditation. One night a thief enters the monk's little hut and steals*
> *his food as well as the clothes off his back. Instead of being angry,*
> *Ryokan says: "I only wish I could give you the moonlight on my floor."*[12]

As we have seen, myths, originating in the depths of the unconscious, in the primordial prehistory of our species, and in common beliefs, can become part of

"Goodbye," said the fox. "And now here is my secret. It is only with the heart that one can see rightly; what is essential is invisible to the eye."

—Antoine de Saint-Exupery

our everyday awareness. We can find mythology in films, television shows, literature—even comic strips. Myths, ancient and modern, are tales about characters and events that help to define who we are and where we want to go. Unearthing underlying myths is a vital aspect of critical appreciation, for even if a given work fails for some reason to satisfy us aesthetically, it may still contribute to our expanding knowledge of ourselves and the kind of world we inhabit.

Psychologists studying the phenomenon of the Harry Potter books and the film adaptations point out that children become engrossed in the tales, which represent for them victory over the authority and control of the adult world through magical powers. They agree that children need to identify with heroic figures. Nor do adults ever outgrow their ties with mythology. Fortunately, the humanities are always there to rekindle the magic fires.

Surely we know, in our lucid moments, that no myth contains the full truth. Some mythology interferes with our judgment, and some is downright superstition. Even so, there are those dazzling mazes and those magic rings and the wonderful stranger we keep expecting to arrive.

Key Terms

archetype a model (e.g., the hero, the circle, the journey) that, through mythology, becomes part of our subconscious and an addition to the way we organize our thinking about ourselves, human beings in general, and the nature of the universe.

collective unconscious Jung's phrase for the universality of many myths and archetypes among cultures, some of which could not possibly have had any contact with each other.

gender roles the way acceptable male and female behavior and functions are defined in a given culture.

karma in Hindu and some Buddhist belief, a tabulation of people's deeds throughout their lifetime such that, if they have been mostly good, they are reincarnated into a better existence, and if mostly bad, into a worse existence.

monomyth James Joyce's term for a fundamental myth of all cultures (e.g.,

that of the hero). Also known as a *world myth*.

mythology (1) the collective myths of a specific culture or group of cultures; (2) the organized study of myths, either those of world cultures or of a specific culture.

myths tales and beliefs transmitted from generation to generation, or springing up as part of the popular mind in a current generation, many containing psychological truth or fulfilling some deep-rooted need.

Topics for
Writing and Discussion

1. The purpose of this chapter has been to encourage you to seek out myths that may underlie works in the humanities. It could be argued that the enjoyment of a given work should not depend on knowing its mythic roots. What argument can you give in *favor* of it?

2. Write a short paper about three myths from your early childhood that helped shape your expectations of life. Do you still have them? If so, what role do they play in your life? If not, what happened to make you discard them?

3. Write a short fable about an animal hero who must undertake a dangerous journey to accomplish a task. Share it with the class and see whether they can grasp your meaning or perhaps recognize some contemporary issue in it.

4. Some myths have environmental subjects. In the stories of Demeter, grieving for her daughter Persephone, and Dionysus, descending annually into the underworld, we have an explanation of winter and the return of spring. Make up a fable to explain what happened to the ozone layer, the rain forests, the polar ice caps, or the planet's non-renewable resources.

5. Discuss a recent public figure whose life fits the pattern of the rise and fall of the hero, as described in the chapter.

6. Like the ancient Greeks, we know that the lives of prominent personalities often are filled with tragedies or, at any rate, many troubles. In many of the old myths, troubles beset those who offend the gods. What do you think accounts for the problems of celebrities now?

7. The chapter discusses the myths of the wizard and the mysterious stranger. Are these outmoded now? Still relevant? Found but in different forms?

8. Briefly write your autobiography in mythic terms. Describe your birth, your mission in life, the villains you must outwit, and your magic powers.

9. Take an old fairy tale and rewrite it (seriously or comically) in terms of how it might fill a psychological need of today.

10. The section on "Common Sayings" is not exhaustive. Think of at least two others not mentioned, and explain their purpose as myth.

4 Literature

Overview

The child, resisting bedtime and not wishing just yet to be left alone in a dark-ened room, makes a frequent request: *Tell me a story*. The parent obligingly sits down and says, "All right, but just one. Close your eyes and listen. Once upon a time . . ." The child has a need. It may be inconvenient for the parent at the moment, but the parent knows the need must be met.

The child also will tell stories. Perhaps they will be tales of ghosts and witches, told to other children happily scared and huddled together on Halloween. Perhaps they will be tales told to the parent: "I was trick-or-treat-ing, and this giant with only one eye came to the door, and he tried to steal my candy, but I was too fast for him." Both parents and child know this is fiction. We are all creators of literature at one time or another. Who has not greatly elaborated on an incident that occurred, "jazzing" it up by giving it more drama than it had?

How did it all start? What was the first kind of literature? Our guess is that the literary impulse was being felt long before there were written lan-guages to preserve the earliest expressions of it. In the visual arts, there are cave drawings that date back thousands of years prior to the beginning of written history. Using our imaginations, we can suppose that early (*very* early) people were dancing, chanting, and pounding away with stones and sticks. And there they were: music and dance! It is hard to imagine, however, that some form of literature did not happen along with these other arts.

Let's assume that people are natural-born poets and storytellers (and by natural progression, readers) and therefore there is no good reason to look upon literature as something locked away in libraries. We'll look at a few exam-ples of the major types, or **genres**, of literature: the poem, the novel, and the short story. We'll see how they might have evolved, and the needs they may have served.

Some of the works we shall study are **classics**, in the sense that they have outlived their time and continue to be relevant. Some have earned the right to be called **masterpieces**. A masterpiece is a work that in style, execution, and resonance far exceeds what other writers were doing at the same time. For example, though many sonnets were successful in Shakespeare's time, many of

We are storytelling animals—who we are, what we are, and why. When we die we become part of other stories. This residue is our immortality.

—Salman Rushdie

 Imagination taking flight.

Source: © Fotosearch RF.

77

his sonnets tower above those of his contemporaries in profundity, sophistication of technique (handling of meter and rhyme), and the intricate use of words. Many classics are also masterpieces, but they don't always have to be. Time and circumstances give continuing relevance to a classic. A masterpiece can always stand on its own, and it will find admirers in any age.

This chapter addresses itself to literature of the past and present that springs from the soul of human beings and through which we come to understand ourselves and others with whom we share the amazing condition of being alive. We are going to discuss a few representative works that have achieved literary distinction, some well known, others less familiar but with much to offer.

Literature as History

At some point many thousands of years ago, groups must have felt the need to identify, to *define* themselves. They knew they had common bonds that came from their strivings. Imagine how you would feel if you suddenly developed amnesia and had no clue about your past. Wouldn't you become obsessed with the desire to locate yourself in time and space?

The Basic Literary Impulse: Identity

Literature transmits incontrovertible condensed experience. . . from generation to generation. In this way literature becomes the living memory of a nation.

—Alexander Solzhenitsyn

Early in *The Grapes of Wrath* (1939), by American novelist John Steinbeck (1902–1968), a simple incident illustrates how important it is that people leave behind a record of themselves.[1] Steinbeck saw the westward migration of dispossessed Oklahoma farmers of the 1930s as an example of how human society developed. Trying to get to California, the longed-for promised land of abundant work and prosperity, they were despised nobodies robbed of their roots and their identity and given the collective designation *Okies.* When a family pulled into a large orchard looking for work, the question was always "How many hands for picking?"—never "What is your name?"

During the arduous journey, Grampa Joad, patriarch of the novel's central family, dies and has to be buried by the side of the road in some desolate and nameless place. Tom Joad, a grandson, writes a brief note and puts it on the body. It says with all the simplicity of a folk poem:

> *This here is William James Joad, dyed of a stroke, old, old man. His fokes bured him becaws they got no money to pay for funerls. Nobody kilt him. Just a stroke an he dyed.*

Leaving the body unidentified was unthinkable. If Tom had had a literary bent, he might have wanted to say more.

The pharaohs of ancient Egypt spent most of their adult lives designing their own monumental tombs, which survive to this day. The great pyramids identify not only the rulers, but the culture that bore them. Egypt established its past and present identity through art and architecture. Other cultures did it through literature, usually in oral form, and in some cases their efforts can be traced back thousands of years. The literary impulse was originally the same thing as the need to establish identity and a history.

The First Epic: *Gilgamesh*

The **epic** is a genre that can be found in the literary heritage of most early societies. An epic is a long narrative poem recounting the actions and adventures of a hero who exemplifies strength, courage, and cunning, but not necessarily moral virtue. When survival was the predominant concern of a people, their myth heroes had to seem unconquerable.

One of the oldest of literary works is the epic *Gilgamesh*, the story of a tyrannical king who lived around 4,000 years ago in a land that is now Iraq. Inscribed on twelve tablets, dating from the seventh century B.C.E it was discovered in the ruins of an Assyrian library. Classical scholars believe the story has its origins in a cycle of songs and poems created to celebrate the deeds of a real person, Gilgamesh, a king in the city of Uruk in 2750 B.C.E. Over the course of a thousand years, the songs and poems became popular throughout Mesopotamia, and eventually Babylonian poets transformed them into a singular epic poem. It is believed the definitive version of the epic was compiled by a Babylonian priest named Shin-eqi-unninni.

Central to the poem are the swashbuckling exploits of a superman. So formidable did Gilgamesh become, so devastating to all who stood in his way, that even the gods were intimidated. So they created a gentler, more compassionate counterpart named Enkidu. Some scholars have interpreted Enkidu as Gilgamesh's other self, the side with humane principles. The climax of the epic is a tremendous wrestling match between the two superheroes, ending in a tie, suggesting that both aggressiveness and kindness are necessary for human existence.

Enkidu finally dies in the story, but Gilgamesh lives on, undefeated, and still a mortal problem for the immortal gods. Was the author saying that, even though kindness is a necessary element in the human personality, it is less likely to outlast aggressiveness?

The Iliad, which we consider next, marks a considerable change in the nature and purpose of the genre. It does indeed, like *Gilgamesh*, have a climactic showdown between two supermen, but in this case the one who dies is the central character. His opponent, with far less likeable traits, lives on. It is a work intended, as usual, to provide its audience with a history and an identity. It did just that, but it also extolled the glory and the virtue of an enemy.

Gilgamesh is one of the oldest of literary works, discovered in the 7th century B.C.E. but probably much older than that.

An Early Masterpiece: Homer's *Iliad*

The Iliad is not only a prime example of early literature but one of the treasures of human culture. It has been traditionally attributed to Homer, who may have lived any time between 1200 and 850 B.C.E. For a long time classical scholarship tended to believe that the poem was composed over several centuries and therefore cannot be attributed to one poet. More recent scholarship suggests the poem is too unified *not* to have been the work of a single genius. Nothing is definitively known about the poet, except that, according to legend, he may have been blind.

The Iliad was an ambitious effort to give the nation of Greece a cultural history, a sense of continuity. It was probably not composed before the unification of related but often warring tribes that finally settled in the Greek peninsula, the nearby islands, and along the coast of what is now Turkey. You can see why a country made up of so many different strands of people would want to think of itself as having a definite, single history; otherwise, how would anybody have been able to talk about a heritage? *The Iliad* describes the events leading up to and then

Homer is new and fresh this morning, and nothing perhaps is as old and tired as today's newspaper.
—**Charles Peguy**

Track 2

the waging of the ten-year Greek war against Troy, a city known to Homer as Ilion. Hence the poem's title, which means "The Song of Ilion."

Why song? The answer may be that those who performed the poem could remember the lines better if they were sung. Most of us learned the alphabet because it was set to a simple tune and had the added advantage of rhyme. The absence of written languages is therefore a most important point to remember about much early literature. A minstrel—or rhapsodist—was a professional performer hired by powerful rulers and their court to present their "history." Naturally that history was about the exploits of ancestral rulers who were also brave warriors. Common people don't enter the literary scene in any major way for more than 2,000 years. Homer not only relates his audience to a proud tradition of rulers but relates those rulers to the gods themselves. The war against Troy was fought as part of the expansion and unification of Greece, but Homer tells it as if it were the consequence of a conflict among gods on Mount Olympus.

Three goddesses get into an argument over who is the most beautiful: Athena, goddess of wisdom; Aphrodite, goddess of love; and Hera, queen of the gods and wife of Zeus, the power of the universe. They ask Paris, a Trojan prince, to make the determination and present a golden apple to the winner. Each goddess appears to him privately and offers him a bribe: Athena promises him glory in battle; Hera, money and power. But Paris cannot resist Aphrodite's offer to make the most beautiful woman in the world his wife. Presenting Aphrodite with the apple, he infuriates the other two goddesses.

Unfortunately, the most beautiful woman turns out to be married to King Menelaus, a Greek. Aphrodite causes the wife, Helen, to fall in love with Paris and run away with him to Troy. Both Menelaus and his brother Agamemnon lead the Greek army in pursuit of the adulterous pair, and thus the Trojan War begins. This and other Greek myths were in circulation long before Homer, and as in most cultures, little distinction was made between mythology and history.

Myth/history indicates that the Greeks had a difficult time defeating Troy, waging a decade-long siege. According to legend, to end this stalemate, the Greeks offered the Trojans a huge wooden horse as a peacemaking gift. Hidden inside were Greek soldiers, who crept out in the middle of the night, slaughtering everyone they could find. Historians believe that the story of the horse is totally fictional, but that the war itself actually took place during the twelfth century B.C.E.

Interestingly, the story of the Trojan horse is not included in *The Iliad*, and it is only alluded to in the other epic attributed to Homer, *The Odyssey*. Only much later was the story part of a great literary work, the Roman epic *The Aeneid* by Virgil (70–19 B.C.E.), which attributes the founding of Rome to Aeneas, a Trojan prince who manages to escape the slaughter. A Roman writer would have been only too delighted to depict the Greeks as devious, dishonorable warriors. If the seeds of the Roman empire were in Troy and Troy had been conquered, it is in the spirit of literature-as-history to show that the conquest was an inglorious one.

Why leave out the story of the Trojan horse? Perhaps Homer believed the Greek victory was anything but heroic or flattering to the Greek side. After all, his purpose was to create a nationalistic epic, *right*? Throughout *The Iliad*, Homer establishes Achilles as a Greek hero of titanic proportions, giving his prowess in battle ample treatment. The disarray into which the Greek army fell, perhaps necessitating the trickery of the horse, is explained in terms of Achilles' resentment toward what he considered unfair treatment by Agamemnon. That Achilles is characterized as a brave but strong-willed individual would not in itself have

---

When power narrows the area of man's concern, poetry reminds him of the richness and diversity of his experience.

—**John F. Kennedy**

made him less heroic to the listeners. Epic characters, as we have seen, are braver than they are virtuous. Gilgamesh was hardly a model human being. Had the victory over Troy been accomplished by Greek superiority on the field of battle, *The Iliad* might have been a prime example of literature meant to glorify a nation's past. And Homer may have intended it as such. However, it can also be read as a tragedy of the losing side.

Hector, a prince and Troy's most important defender, is treated so sympathetically that the true climax of the epic is Hector's death at the hands of Achilles, who ties the body of the slain warrior to his chariot and drags it ignominiously around the walls of Troy, afterward selling it back to the Trojans. *The Iliad*, while rooted in Greek history, is essentially a tragic poem about a fallen hero—a hero who was not Greek! In contrast, *The Aeneid* portrays its hero, Aeneas, as the perfect hero—strong, brave, and intelligent. Troy is shown to have fallen because the destiny of Aeneas was to found a city much greater than Troy. Virgil's *Aeneid* is a nationalistic poem. *The Iliad* is not. And although *The Aeneid* is as thrilling and as wondrous as an epic should be, it is the human drama of *The Iliad* that grips the reader.

Engraving on a Greek jug, c. 510 B.C.E., showing a relaxed Achilles receiving payment for Hector's body.

Source: Erich Lessing/Art Resource, NY.

There exists, of course, the possibility that *The Iliad* went through several centuries of change as a memorized poem, sung generation after generation by unknown minstrels. It may have been gradually altered to become a tragic epic. The Greeks, after all, developed the art of tragic theater, indicating that as a nation they loved to be moved by stories of noble people who suffer a downfall. In the plays, the fall of the hero comes about because of a fatal flaw in an otherwise good person. *The Iliad*, as we have it today, anticipates the age of Greek tragedy.

Does Hector have a tragic flaw? In a sense, he does. He is characterized as a brave warrior who goes beyond what is expected of him because, like all warriors, he wants to be remembered for great deeds of valor. The ambition to be known for bravery is characteristic of a hero, to be sure, but it can also be a fatal weakness. Pride would become the major theme of the Greek—and indeed many later—tragedies. *The Iliad* may be said to be the first major work in the literature of the Western world, not only for its soaring poetry, but for the humanization of its major characters, Hector in particular.

Humanization in this sense explains what makes certain literary characters stand apart from others. It is very close to a term that actors often use to define what they are looking for in a character they're going to play: *polarity*, or the binary extremes that exist in our natures. In playing a role, the actor first determines major characteristics defined by the playwright—for example, *he is a jealous husband*; *she is a faithful wife*. Then the actor tries to locate the opposite of these characteristics—*he loves his wife very much and doesn't want to lose her*; *though faithful, she resents his jealousy and secretly wishes she could have a fling*. Great writers have always known that human beings are never just one thing. If characters are given certain unwavering traits instead of the contradictory natures we all share, the result is melodrama rather than tragedy.

The Iliad *deserves its place of honor as the first literary masterpiece of the Western world because*
- *the poet goes beyond strict nationalism, whatever may have been his original intent*

- *the poet establishes a fundamental principle of great literature: life is not a simple struggle between good and evil.*

Like all tragic heroes, Hector has a blind side. Several times before his mortal combat with his archenemy Achilles, he has been warned that he almost certainly will die. His wife, Andromache, pleads with him not to leave her and their son, but Hector is resolute. He firmly believes that he and he alone has the strength and courage to defeat Achilles.

> *Go home, attend to your own handiwork*
> *at loom and spindle, and command the maids*
> *to busy themselves, too. As for the war,*
> *that is for men, all who were born at Ilion,*
> *to put their minds on—most of all for me.²*

"Most of all for me." This is not only courage but pride as well. Here is the polarity in Hector's character; here is Homer's humanization of him. Hector *assumes* he is the only one who can save Troy, just as so many human beings close their minds to the possibility that someone else might be able to perform a difficult task better than they can. His supreme self-confidence causes Hector to fight with reckless abandon against overwhelming odds—and to fail, weakening his city's defenses as well.

To create a great tragic figure like Hector is to create an ironic contradiction. The very thing that destroys Hector (and Troy) is his bravery, but bravery is also the source of human greatness. The suggestion—to be echoed over and over in many enduring literary works—is that *to be great is to be tragic.* If this is a truth of existence, then the question is whether it is better to have failed at something tremendous than to have stayed within limitations and won trivial successes. Great literature inspires big, unanswerable questions like this.

The Iliad deserves its place of honor as the first literary masterpiece of the Western world for a number of reasons. First, the poet goes beyond strict nationalism, whatever may have been his original intent. If that intent had been to inspire the listener with a love of country, the poet became far more concerned with what drives human behavior, how humans interact, and the consequences of those actions. Homer is a born tragic dramatist, though the theater as we know it did not exist in his time.

Second, the poet establishes a fundamental principle of much great literature: *real life is not a simple struggle between good and evil.* If Hector is the hero of *The Iliad*, Achilles is not the villain. The subtitle of the poem is "The Wrath of Achilles," and the warrior's outrage against Agamemnon over a certain prisoner Achilles did not wish to return is indeed the force that drives the plot. Homer as historian presents, without judgment, the story of Achilles' anger. If the author is less compassionate toward the Greek warrior than toward Hector, he duly recognizes the man's strength and courage as well as his place in Greek history.

What makes *The Iliad* not only a great epic but also a great tragedy, however, is the struggle inside Hector between his desire for glory and his understanding of his wife's anguish, his sensitivity to her ardent pleas, born out of his deep love for her. As a reader, you will find that the impact of many masterpieces arises from conflict *within* the characters, not *between* them.

The Russian playwright Anton Chekhov (1860–1904) observed: "Evil flows *through* people, not *from* them." Hector's pride leads him into a violent battle in which not only he but many others are slain. Achilles' refusal to fight costs the Greeks many lives and a more honorable victory. Both men believed their cause was righteous. Neither man could be described as evil, yet their actions had disastrous consequences. That is the way of tragedy and, as the great writers such as Homer knew, the tragic way of humanity.

If Homer had lived in the modern world, how might he have responded to the Holocaust, the My Lai massacre during the Vietnam War, the September 11 terrorist attacks, or the bitter fighting in Iraq? Big questions, difficult answers. Great literature, whether from the past or the present, makes us feel, makes us think, and inevitably we are changed.

Evil flows through men, not from them.

—Anton Chekhov

Poetry

Though classified in this chapter as a form of history, the epic is also narrative poetry, telling a story in rhythmic language. Narrative, as found in *Gilgamesh* and *The Iliad*, was probably the earliest genre of poetry. But as early societies grew in sophistication and produced artists who could be identified by their style, technique, and typical themes, poetry evolved into numerous forms. By the time of the Greek poet Sappho in the sixth century B.C.E., poets were highly trained and respected members of society. They worked in a written language expected to be elevated above everyday talk—that is to say, above *prose*.

Lyrical Poetry

The Romans inherited from the Greeks the desire to cultivate the arts of civilization. Especially popular among the Romans was **lyrical poetry**, so named because it was usually sung to the accompaniment of a *lyre*, a stringed instrument similar to a small harp.

Lyrical Greek poetry is found in the work of Sappho, who may have been the first poet on record to write about deeply personal feelings, even referring to herself by name in prayers to the gods. Sappho is known to have accompanied herself on a lyre and may have composed most of the music as well. She would have used the kind of musical notation that we know existed at the time, but so far none of the music has survived.

Among Sappho's favorite subjects are the joys and the sorrows of being in love. Apparently a woman of strong physical needs, she introduced into literature one of its most enduring themes: unrequited passion—a theme that, as we shall see, became wildly popular during the Renaissance and can still be found in contemporary popular songs.

In one of her most famous poems, *Ode to Aphrodite*, Sappho implores the goddess of love to have pity on her as she languishes in the agony of romantic frustration:

The stars about the lovely moon hiding their shining forms when it lights up the earth at its fullest.

—Sappho

> *Then didst thou, Divine one,*
> *Laugh a bright laugh from lips and eyes immortal,*
> *Ask me, What ailed me—wherefore out of heaven*
> *Thus had I called thee?*
> *What it was made me madden in my heart so?*
> *Question me, smiling—say to me, "My Sappho,*
> *"Who is it wrongs thee? Tell me who refuses*

"Thee, vainly sighing.
"Be it who it may be, he that flies shall follow;
"He that rejects gifts, he shall bring thee many;
"He that hates now shall love thee dearly, madly—
"Aye, though thou wouldst not."[3]

Other writers, especially William Shakespeare, would carry this theme to greater heights, but Sappho will always be remembered as a distinguished pioneer in poetic art (as well as the founder of the first known school for women).

Lyrical poetry flourished in Rome, and again the primary subject was love, a popular Roman pastime. Much of the poetry is highly artificial: high-flown words that professional poets knew would please their public. Since, in Roman society, upper-class women acquired power and independence, the theme of unrequited passion was often expressed from the male point of view, as in this poem by Catullus (87–54 B.C.E.), one of many written to and about a lady named Lesbia.

TRUE OR FALSE

None could ever say that she,
Lesbia! was so loved by me.
Never all the world around
Faith so true as mine was found.
If no longer it endures
(Would it did!) the fault is yours.
I can never think again
Well of you: I try in vain.
But . . . be false . . . do what you will.—
Lesbia! I must love you still.[4]

To the theme of unrequited passion, Catullus and other Romans added that of betrayal and infidelity, of a sworn lover's being false. Instead of swearing vengeance and wishing harm to befall his lady, however, Catullus merely suffers.

The lyric poetry of Greece and Rome was forgotten during the early and late Middle Ages. Poetry became for Christians a way of expressing the mystic experiences of the devout as they tried to escape from worldly temptations and find God. But the classical themes of love were revived during the Renaissance (beginning in the fourteenth century) when women of the aristocracy again attained stature and claimed the right to reject men's pleas for their favors. The pain of scorned love reemerged as a popular subject.

The Sonnet

The **sonnet** is a fourteen-line poetic form invented by the Italians in the early Renaissance, during the revival of interest in classical art and literature. Although the form was new, the usual subject—the pain caused by unsatisfied love—was of classical origin. The poet Francesco Petrarca (1304–1374), known to the English-speaking world as Petrarch, played a large part in the classical revival. He recognized the genius of *The Iliad* and had it translated into Latin. He is best known, however, for having developed the sonnet. The demands of the form, the discipline of having to put all his thoughts and feelings into fourteen rhymed and rhythmic lines, challenged him, as it has challenged poets ever since.

Over the centuries a number of variations on the sonnet have emerged, but the basic form is the Petrarchan. The rhythm, called **iambic pentameter**, also became the fundamental rhythm of English poetry, closely identified with the sonnets and plays of William Shakespeare, who was heavily influenced by Petrarch.

In *iambic pentameter*, each line has five repetitions of an unstressed followed by a stressed syllable. Each pair of syllables is called a *foot*, similar to a bar of music. The word *decide* is an iambic foot. The line "Decide on when to go or not, my dear" has five repetitions of the pattern and is therefore an example of iambic pentameter. Read aloud, the line heavily accents every other syllable. The poet has the difficult task of writing fourteen lines in this pattern without letting the rhythm or rhyme seem heavily forced or obvious. (A listener would soon grow very tired of rigid repetition!) In good sonnets, the lines have a sense of inevitability about them and give no suggestion that the poet was straining to keep the rhythm going or to seek rhymes. When read aloud, the poem should not sound overly rhythmic. Instead, the meter should strike the listener as a happy discovery. In the following lines from an obscure poem, the rhythm (not to mention the rhyme) hits you squarely in the face.

> *He writes to us most every day, and how his letters thrill us!*
> *I can't describe the joys with which his quaint expressions fill us.*

The English language falls easily into iambic patterns. (Ordinary speech tends to be iambic.) Great poets in the language, like Shakespeare, know that rhythm has an emotional effect (as it does in music), but they don't want it to overwhelm the words. Compare the above lines of poetry with the opening lines from one of Shakespeare's most famous sonnets (XVIII). Note that to discover the iambic meter, you have to distort the natural flow of the words.

> *Shall I compare thee to a summer's day?*
> *Thou art more lovely and more temperate*

The challenge to the writer of a Petrarchan sonnet grows more rigorous still. Not only must each line fit the rhythmic pattern, but the poet must find five or seven line-endings that rhyme. Though rhyme may have originated as an aid to memory, it remains an essential ingredient of poetry, still employed by many poets who like the musical resonance that rhyme can create, as well as the challenge of having the rhymes not seem forced. In Petrarchan and Shakespearean sonnets, rhymes are placed in certain sequences and cannot be varied. The great poets are somehow able to stay within the bounds of the rhyme scheme and still find freedom of thought.

Two of Petrarch's schemes can be outlined as follows, using letters of the alphabet to represent the rhyming line-endings: the first is *abba abba cddcee*; the second is *abab cdcd efef gg*. In other words, a poet writing in the first scheme must rhyme the final sound of the first line with that of the fourth, fifth, and eighth lines (*a*), the final sound of the second line with that of the third, sixth, and seventh lines (*b*), while there are two new rhymes for the remaining six lines, represented as *cddcee*.

Shakespeare's own favorite was the second scheme, perhaps because it allows more rhyming options. In Spanish or Italian, for example, many words have the same endings, making rhyme that much easier. In English, however, fewer words

Scorn not the sonnet: critic, you have frowned,
Mindful of its honors; with this key Shakespeare unlocked his heart.
    —William Wordsworth

have multiple rhymes. Perhaps for this very reason, much English and American poetry—most of the speeches in the plays of Shakespeare, for example—abandon rhyme altogether. **Blank verse** is poetic language that has rhythm but not rhyme. You probably wouldn't want to listen to a play in which the dialogue rhymed like an Italian sonnet. But one of the marvels of the Shakespearean play is that the rhythm is there underneath the dialogue—like a faint drum—but it too is seldom obvious.

Here is one of the famous sonnets written by Petrarch to the love of his life, a young married woman he called Laura. "Love's Inconsistency," translated by Thomas Wyatt, captures the mixture of pain and joy well known to everyone who has fallen deeply into a love that is not returned.

> *I find no peace, and all my war is done;*
> *I fear and hope, I burn and freeze likewise;*
> *I fly above the wind, yet cannot rise;*
> *And nought I have, yet all the world I seize on;*
> *That looseth, nor locketh, holdeth me in prison,*
> *And holds me not, yet can I 'scape no wise;*
> *Nor lets me live, nor die, at my devise,*
> *And yet of death it giveth none occasion.*
> *Without eyes I see, and without tongue I plain;*
> *I wish to perish, yet I ask for health;*
> *I love another, and yet I hate myself;*
> *I feed in sorrow, and laugh in all my pain;*
> *Lo, thus displeaseth me both death and life,*
> *And my delight is causer of my grief.*

Many of the rhymes are not exact, but we may assume the translator had a difficult time being faithful to Petrarch's original words in Italian. "Done" and "seize on" are stretching verse conventions quite a bit, as are "prison" and "occasion" and "life" and "grief" in the concluding couplet.

To read literature in translation is often to lose the essence of the work. The content is there, but some subtleties can fall by the wayside. This is not to say that the experience is useless. Without translations, many of us could not read *The Iliad* or *Don Quixote*, to name just two great works in the humanities. The problems of translation, however, are particularly acute for poetry, which is so dependent on the music of the words.

Even if you can't understand Spanish, for example, you can first read a Spanish poem in an English translation to get some idea of what the words mean, and then you can read the original aloud to get some sense of the music. Such an experience is richer than ignoring the original language altogether. Here, first in translation and then in the original Spanish, is a sonnet by Federico Garcia Lorca (1898–1936), one of the greatest Spanish poets. The subject is similar to that of the Petrarchan sonnet, and even in English the directness of Lorca's passion is intense and startling.

Wounds of Love

> *This light, this fire that devours,*
> *this gray landscape that surrounds me,*
> *this pain that comes from one idea,*
> *this anguish of the sky, the earth, the hour,*

and this lament of blood that decorates
a pulseless lyre, a lascivious torch,
this burden of the sea that beats upon me,
this scorpion that beats within my breast

are all a wreath of love, bed of one wounded,
where, sleepless, I dream of your presence
amid the ruins of my fallen breast.

And though I seek the summit of discretion,
your heart gives me a valley spread below
with hemlock and passion of bitter wisdom.

Llagas de amor

Esta luz, esta fuego que devora,
este paisaje gris que me rodea,
este dolor por una sola idea,
este angusta de cielo, mundo y hora,

este llanto de sangre que decora
lira sin pulso ya, lúbrica tea,
este peso del mar que me golpea,
este alacran que por mi pecho mora

son guirnalda de amor, cama de herido,
donde sin sueño, sueño tu presencia
entre las ruinas de mi pecho hundido.

Y aunque busco la cumbre de prudencia
me da tu corazón valle tendido
con cicuta y pasión de amarga ciencia.[5]

Lorca's sonnet has a rhyme scheme: *abba abba cdcdcd*. There is none in the translation, because the translator's goal is to convey the poet's meaning without imposing English rhymes that might distort it.

Among the glories of literature in our language are the 154 sonnets penned by William Shakespeare (1564–1616), universally acknowledged as the master of English verse, not only for the complexity of his thought but for the unsurpassed manner in which he handles both rhythm and rhyme.

Shakespeare's plays are written for the most part in blank verse: unrhymed iambic pentameter. When Shakespeare ends a scene with a **couplet**, two lines that rhyme, he is using a poetic scheme that might seem obvious and undramatic in lesser hands, but he manages to make the rhymes seem perfectly natural. Here is Hamlet's famous couplet spoken after he learns that his uncle murdered his father, whose ghost has demanded vengeance, a violent crime that the young man is afraid he may not have the will to commit:

The time is out of joint: O cursed spite,
That ever I was born to set it right!

Though Shakespeare takes rhyming liberties in his sonnets from time to time, one aspect of his genius certainly has to be an extraordinary vocabulary (said to have included over 30,000 words) from which he was able to draw forth words that perfectly fit rhythm, rhyme, and meaning. The sonnets are generally expressions of love, sometimes obsessive adoration, which is not always returned.

The identity of the person (or persons) to whom these poems are addressed has aroused considerable debate among Shakespearean scholars. However, poetry was popular during the Elizabethan age (sixteenth century), and the subject matter was generally love in both its positive and negative guises. In this respect Elizabethan poetry is similar to today's rhythm and blues ballads, with lyrics that either extol the beauty of the beloved or the heartbreak of a broken romance. Like present-day songwriters, Elizabethan poets did not always write from personal experience. Writing good poetry was a profitable business, and the youthful Shakespeare, who came to the big city of London from the small town of Stratford-upon-Avon without a great deal of money, realized he might be able to support himself with his skills as a writer of plays and poems.

Here, in Sonnet XXIX, he speaks of the joy that love can bring.

Track 3

Shakespeare, with his open candid nature, laid bare his soul.

—A. L. Rowse

> *When, in disgrace with fortune and men's eyes,*
> *I all alone beweep my outcast state*
> *And trouble deaf heaven with my bootless cries*
> *And look upon myself and curse my fate,*
> *Wishing me like to one more rich in hope,*
> *Featured like him, like him with friends possess'd,*
> *Desiring this man's art and that man's scope,*
> *With what I most enjoy contented least;*
> *Yet in these thoughts myself almost despising,*
> *Haply I think on thee, and then my state,*
> *Like to the lark at break of day arising*
> *From sullen earth, sings hymns at heaven's gate;*
> *For thy sweet love remember'd such wealth brings*
> *That then I scorn to change my state with kings.*

His vocabulary was large–almost 30,000 words–but he usually chose small, common words–although in shocking juxtaposition, to describe Juliet, Harriet, or anything else important.

—Jaronde Lanier

The meter of the poem eases only here and there. "And trouble," for example, is an iambic foot with an extra, unstressed syllable, but the rest of the line follows the rhythmic pattern. Often the rhythm of a poem is apparent only through **scanning**: marking a line's syllables as stressed or unstressed, and counting them to determine the pattern. Sometimes you can determine the pattern only by exaggerating the meter as you read a line. Shakespeare does not want his lines to sound *overly* rhythmic. The secret of Shakespearean verse is to read it as if it were prose. Meter and rhyme are often only quietly there. They function like subtle background music in a well-directed film. The genius of the poet is his ability to merge form and content into a unified whole.

Shakespeare uses only two semicolons in Sonnet XXIX. Other lines (except for the final line, of course) use either commas or no punctuation at all. In either case, the thought extends beyond the rhyming word, as in lines 9–12. The rhyming of "despising" and "arising" is glossed over, because there is no pause after "arising." Shakespeare writes prose while adhering to the rules of poetry. He does, as we have said, take liberties here and there, as in "myself almost despising," because clearly a rhyme for "myself" would have posed more of a challenge than a rhyme for "despising." For the most part, however, his fertile mind was able to make rhythmic and rhymed lines fit together logically and inevitably. Larks *do* arise!

Metaphors and Conceits

A **metaphor** is a form of expression in which something is explained in terms of something else. An abstraction such as justice, for example, or a feeling that can only be vaguely expressed, such as love, might be described in terms of something else that is concrete and visual. To say "There is no justice" fails to communicate very much. Saying "Justice for some defendants is the blind lady dropping her scales" is much more effective.

Shakespeare, as we have said, possessed an enormous vocabulary. The linguistic resources stored in his brain gave him the power to express and investigate complex ideas, and often the reader is surrounded by abstractions. So Shakespeare also experimented with metaphor, to create a more visual and concretized way of saying something for which there were no satisfying abstractions. His *Romeo and Juliet*, arguably the world's most enduring romance, cried out for a rich linguistic expression of love in all its complex facets: as lust, as a spiritual bond between two people, as a sweet sensation that does not last, and much more—too much, in fact, for lesser writers to handle as effectively.

Discover magazine columnist Jaron Lanier made use of recent scientific research concerning metaphor to examine one particular metaphor in *Romeo and Juliet*. His example centers on the famous balcony scene, in which the two young people declare their devotion in unforgettable metaphors. When Juliet emerges from her bedchamber, Romeo wonders "what light through yonder window breaks?" Then he answers his own question: "It is the east, and Juliet is the sun." In his column, Lanier considers the appropriateness of comparing a young woman to the sun, and how such a metaphor relates to our ability to make connections across our various senses.[6]

Later on in the scene, Juliet indicates that she is not altogether happy about the feelings she and Romeo are expressing. She is afraid that their infatuation with each other is "too swift, too like the lightning / Which doth cease to be ere one can say it lightens." But there is no going back. They are committed to each other. They must part for the moment, yet "parting is such sweet sorrow / That I shall say good-night till it be morrow." "Sweet" has become a time-honored metaphoric alternate to "nice," but it was Shakespeare who used it in an unexpected context and gave the metaphor a complexity that casual usage rarely captures.

A generation younger than Shakespeare, John Donne (1572–1631), is famous for a special kind of metaphor called the **conceit**, an extremely elaborate and extended association between two dissimilar things. The varied life Donne led helps to explain his unique manner of communicating complex feelings and ideas with references to widely separate human experiences. In his youth, he served as a soldier in English expeditions against the Spanish. In later life, he became an Anglican priest and eventually the dean of St. Paul's Cathedral in

Lauren Ambrose and Oscar Isaac speaking great metaphors in the Public Theatre's 2007 outdoor production of *Romeo and Juliet*.

Source: Sara Krulwich/*The New York Times*, June 25, 2007/Redux Pictures.

London. The development of his poetic works reflects his contrasting modes of living. The poems of his youth express sensuality, cynicism, and a humorous approach to life, while those of his later years exhibit a fervent spirituality. The deeply religious older man, however, retained a strong undercurrent of the younger man's sexual urges, and in the following sonnet, one of his most celebrated, the two sides of his nature merge. The struggle to achieve mystic exaltation and free the self from sin is described in sexually explicit terms.

> Batter my heart, three person'd God; for you
> As yet but knock, breathe, shine, and seek to mend;
> That I may rise, and stand, o'erthrow me, and bend
> Your force, to break, blow, burn, and make me new.
> I, like an usurpt town, to another due,
> Labor to admit you, but Oh, to no end,
> Reason your viceroy in me, me should defend,
> But is captiv'd, and proves weak or untrue.
> Yet dearly I love you, and would be loved fain
> But am betroth'd unto your enemy:
> Divorce me, untie, or break that knot again,
> Take me to you, imprison me, for I
> Except you' enthrall me, never shall be free,
> Nor ever chaste, except you ravish me.

Donne's poems furnish a curious record of his emotional, intellectual, and spiritual progress through life. He brings all the resources of a mind rich in learning to a focus in his poetry.

—Alexander M. Witherspoon

Donne expands his conceit to include not only a violent sexual encounter ("except you ravish me") but a startling plea to God to divorce him from Satan or else to "untie" him, suggesting a kind of mystical adultery. Donne seems to have been deeply in love with his wife, perhaps explaining why it may have been natural for him to associate the sexual and spiritual bonds between two people. But only a great poet would have had the creative audacity to make God one of those people.

John Donne has fascinated critics and scholars for centuries as a writer of great complexity with a hidden self that may never be completely understood apart from what he wrote. Poetry is the key that unlocks the door to the hidden self, which has no language until a poet finds a way to liberate it.

A Modern Love Sonnet

Shakespeare's sonnets may or may not be personal. Donne's certainly are, and as the sonnet form has continued to develop over the years, the content has become almost always an expression of a poet's deepest feelings. At least such expression is characteristic of sonnets by Edna St. Vincent Millay (1892–1950), an American poet who lived a free-spirited life in Greenwich Village. Many of her sonnets are about lost love. Here is one of them:

After her graduation, Miss Millay became a resident of Greenwich Village and symbol of "flaming youth."

—Norman Foerster

> Time does not bring relief; you all have lied
> Who told me time would ease me of my pain!
> I miss him in the weeping of the rain;
> I want him at the shrinking of the tide;
> The old snows melt from every mountain-side,
> And last year's leaves are smoke in every lane;

And last year's bitter loving must remain
Heaped on my heart, and my old thoughts abide,
There are a hundred places where I fear
To go,—so with his memory they brim.
And entering with relief some quiet place
Where never fell his foot or shone his face
I say, "There is no memory of him here!"
And so stand stricken, so remembering him.[7]

Note that the poet adheres closely to iambic pentameter and has a definite rhyme scheme: *abbaabbacdeecd*. Note also that, here again, meaning comes first. The first sentence of the second stanza is five lines long, not stopping to punctuate the rhymes. And as is true of the Shakespearean sonnet, the strict rhythm does not intrude on the thought.

Haiku

The Japanese **haiku** is founded on oneness with the natural world. It is a short poem of seventeen syllables, distributed over three lines—five, seven, five—in which the writer captures an incisive thought or an image derived from direct observation of nature, but in words that ordinary language cannot match. The thought or the image becomes fixed forever in the reader's memory. Its nearest counterpart is Zen painting, in which the artist captures the essence of an object in a few brushstrokes.

Much of this poetry springs from the Buddhist tradition which discourages lengthy rational sequences in favor of sudden intuitive insights. Many poets use haiku as a vehicle for exploring their inner self, and for bringing them into closer contact with nature. Haiku also delights children, many of whom learn to love poetry from the apparent simplicity of the form.

Almost a contemporary of John Donne was Matsuo Basho (1644–1694), who pioneered in the development of haiku.

> *Detestable crow!*
> *Today alone you please me—*
> *black against the snow.[8]*

Here is a haiku by a later poet, Kobayashi Issa (1763–1827):

> *Oh, don't strike the fly!*
> *See? With knees bent and hands clasped*
> *he prays for his life.[9]*

The first poem illustrates the Japanese art of capturing both an image and a thought at the same time, and the second imparts a moral admonition to understand, not harm the natural world.

Parallels to haiku are abundant in the world of visual art, especially among artists who like to create a scene or express a thought using as few details as possible. In the painting shown here, *Shrike*, by the Japanese artist Miyamoto Masashi (pseudonym, Niten), a Samurai and Zen

Much Japanese art is, like haiku, apparently simple but conveying a depth of meaning.

Source: Miyamoto Niten, detail from *Shrike*. Credit: Burstein Collection/Corbis.

Buddhist (1585–1645), the focus is on just two central objects, a bird and a cater-pillar crawling up the tree branch, apparently unaware that the shrike perched atop the branch will soon end its life. Like many haiku, the painting says more about life than a great abundance of words could match.

Simple Forms, Profound Meaning: William Blake

In the centuries that followed the tremendous literary and dramatic achievements of Shakespeare's age, many different poetic forms became popular. William Blake (1757–1827) was fascinated by what a serious writer might do with nursery rhymes. Blake, who was both an artist and a poet, shows in some of his verse how a simple, popular form becomes, in the hands of a master, an unforgettable way of expressing a truth that is both personal and universal.

Unlike today, when modern poets can set down their thoughts and feelings in whatever form they deem suitable, in Blake's time it was customary for a poet to choose among available verse models and adhere closely to their requirements. In two of his most famous achievements, collections known as *Songs of Innocence* (1789) and *Songs of Experience* (1794), Blake met the challenge of simple, childlike verse, heavily rhythmic and forcefully rhymed (unlike the Shakespearean sonnet). But underneath their sing-songy music lies Blake's sorrow over the inevitable loss of childhood innocence and the adult's unavoidable confrontation of what life holds.

The most famous poem in *Songs of Innocence* is "The Lamb," and it is paral-leled in *Songs of Experience* by another, equally famous poem, "The Tiger." Taken together, they make a powerful statement. Both poems speak to religious themes, but their contrasts could not be greater.

The Lamb

Little Lamb, who made thee?
Does thou know who made thee?
Gave thee life and bid thee feed,
By the stream and o'er the mead;
Gave thee clothing of delight,
Softest clothing, wooly, bright;
Gave thee such a tender voice,
Making all the vales rejoice.
Little Lamb, who made thee?
Dost thou know who made thee?

Little Lamb, I'll tell thee,
Little Lamb, I'll tell thee.
He is called by thy name,
For he calls himself a Lamb.
He is meek, and he is mild;
He became a little child.
I a child, and thou a lamb,
We are called by his name.
Little Lamb, God bless thee!
Little Lamb, God bless thee!

Even though the poem suggests a nursery rhyme and is written in a childlike style, lurking behind the surface innocence of the poem is the knowledge that lambs

To see a world in a grain of sand
And heaven in a wild flower,
Hold infinity in the palm of your hand
And eternity in an hour.

—**William Blake**

were sacrificial animals and also that Christ, who "calls himself a Lamb," was himself a sacrifice. The poem suggests the darker world of experience that is to come.

In the *Songs of Experience* Blake uses the same childlike style but expresses emotions that come to us as we grow and begin to experience the world's evil. Here is the companion piece to "The Lamb."

THE TIGER

Tiger! Tiger! burning bright
In the forests of the night:
What immortal hand or eye,
Could frame thy fearful symmetry?

In what distant deeps or skies
Burnt the fire of thine eyes?
On what wings dare he aspire?
What the hand dare seize the fire?

And what shoulder, and what art,
Could twist the sinews of thy heart?
And when thy heart began to beat,
What dread hand? and what dread feet?

What the hammer? what the chain?
In what furnace was thy brain?
What the anvil? what dread grasp
Dare its deadly terrors clasp?

Did he who made the Lamb make thee?

Source: Henri Rousseau, *Tiger in a Tropical Storm (Surprise!)*. Credit: © National Gallery Collection; By kind permission of the Trustees of the National Gallery, London/Corbis.

When the stars threw down their spears,
And water'd heaven with their tears,
Did he smile his work to see?
Did he who made the Lamb make thee?

Tiger! Tiger! burning bright
In the forests of the night:
What immortal hand or eye,
Dare frame thy fearful symmetry?

The poem combines simple language, childlike patter, and *huge questions*. Blake was thirty-seven when he wrote this poem. The child's narrative viewpoint of "The Lamb" is now that of a grown-up, sobered by the world. "Did he who made the Lamb make thee?" is as electrifying a line as exists in the entire range of the humanities and will always speak deeply to anyone who has ever asked the awful question: "If God is good, why is there evil in the world?" Philosophers have pondered this question, and millions of words in complex prose have been written in answer to it. But it took poetic genius to ask it in eight short words that echo through time, defying an answer.

As with all great literature, explanations only scratch the surface. Just as the innocence of "The Lamb" is tempered by the dark reminder of sacrifice, so too is the fearfulness of "The Tiger" tempered by the recognition of the animal's magnificence: "burning bright." Is this a compensation? Does evil fascinate even as it terrifies? Or do the two poems, taken collectively, hint at a divine order behind the universe that is beyond our ability to understand? Great literature unsettles, disturbs, makes us wonder, even as it thrills us with its power.

Religious Poetry

Religious rituals with their rhythmic chantings provided the foundation for much poetry.

The urge to communicate with and sing the praises of a deity is as old as humanity itself and, like dance and music, an early component of the humanities. The key word here is "sing," for much prayer was and continues to be sung or at least *intoned* (expressed as a prolonged monotone or chant). The precise kind of intonation varies from religion to religion as well as among the different sects within a particular faith. Buddhist monks, Roman Catholic clerics during Mass, the cantor in a synagogue, priests in a tribal ceremony, worshippers in a mosque—all chant in their own styles.

What is chanting but intoning words in rhythm and often in rhyme: in short, poetry? Protestant believers singing a hymn are putting poetry to music. Great composers like Mozart and Beethoven adapted prayers and chants into enormous symphonic works requiring full orchestras and large choirs. Words in rhythm, the building blocks of poetry, are integral to human religious experience.

The psalms in the Hebrew Bible, attributed to King David, contain many personal expressions of joy in God's creation and faith in the transcendent power of God's love. Here is one of the most enduring of the psalms in the 1611 King James version of the Bible:

Psalm 23

The Lord is my shepherd; I shall not want.
He maketh me to lie down in green pastures;
He leadeth me beside the still waters.
He restoreth my soul:
He leadeth me in the paths of righteousness for his name's sake.

Yea, though I walk through the valley of the shadow of death,
I will fear no evil: for thou art with me;
Thy rod and thy staff they comfort me.
Thou preparest a table before me in the presence of mine enemies:
Thou anointest my head with oil; my cup runneth over.
Surely goodness and mercy shall follow me all the days of my life:
And I will dwell in the house of the Lord for ever.

This psalm has achieved immortal status. It has been translated into just about every language in the world, as well as rewritten from the perspective of particular cultures. Here is a Native American version.[10]

The Great Father above is a Shepherd Chief.
I am His and with Him I want not.
He throws out to me a rope
and the name of the rope is Love
and he draws me to where the grass is green
and the water not dangerous
and I eat and am satisfied.

Sometimes my heart is very weak
and falls down
but He lifts me up again
and draws me into a good road
His name is Wonderful.

Sometime, and it may be very soon,
it may be very long, long in time
He will draw me into a valley.
It is dark there, but I'll be afraid not,
for it is in between those mountains
that the Shepherd Creator will meet me
and the hunger that I have in my heart
all through this life will be satisfied.

He gives me a staff to lean upon.
He spreads a table before me
with all kinds of food.
He puts His hand upon my head
and all the "tired" is gone.
My cup He fills till it runs over.
What I tell is true.
I lie not.

These roads that are way ahead
will stay with me through life and after,
and afterwards I will go to live
in the Big Tepee and sit down
with the Shepherd Chief forever.

The Native American version of the familiar psalm shows the universality of the theme as well as its simple power.

Though this version is easily recognizable as the 23rd Psalm, notice that the poet has not followed the more well-known King James translation exactly. The poem is localized. God, who is a Shepherd Chief, throws out a rope. The water is not dangerous—neither to drink nor flood the land, perhaps. The valley of death lies between two mountains, but in this case the poet doesn't have to fear an ambush or a sudden rockslide. In the King James translation, God is carrying the staff; but in the Native American version God gives the staff to the narrator, who is presumably old and "tired." The House of the Lord is now the big Tepee. The heartfelt simplicity of this version is touching, illustrating the human need to attain through poetry a higher spiritual consciousness.

Beginnings of Modernism: Emily Dickinson

If I feel physically as if the top of my head were taken off, I know that is poetry.

—**Emily Dickinson**

Poetry is often called *modern* if it has been written within the last hundred years or so. *Modern* can also imply "less accessible than poetry used to be." The fear for many is that modern poetry, like modern art and music, will prove too difficult for the average person to understand. Though some modern poems may be obscure on first reading, most of them *are* approachable if the reader is patient—and, above all, if the work is read aloud. Many modern poets, abandoning traditional forms such as the sonnet, do not use strict rhythm and rhyme. Some, like e.e. cummings (discussed in Chapter 1), distort standard grammar. We need, however, to grant poets the right to create their own forms and their own way of using language.

The American poet Emily Dickinson (1830–1886), an introverted, reclusive woman, found in poetry an outlet for the thoughts and feelings she kept locked away inside her. She wrote for herself. Few of her poems were published during her lifetime, but many of them were found, after her death, in little packets hidden away in a drawer. She is now considered one of the greatest poets of the nineteenth century.

Dickinson had the uncanny ability to take simple, universal experiences and translate them into poetic form:

> After great pain a formal feeling comes—
> The nerves sit ceremonious like tombs;
> The stiff Heart questions—was it He that bore?
> And yesterday—or centuries before?
> The feet mechanical
> Go round a wooden way
> Of ground or air or Ought, regardless grown,
> A quartz contentment like a stone.
> This is the hour of lead
> Remembered if outlived,
> As freezing persons recollect the snow—
> First chill, then stupor, then the letting go.[11]

Dickinson is on the very threshold of modern poetry, except that she, unlike some of our contemporaries, anchors her feelings in traditional iambic meter, and with half of the lines rhyming in couplets. Her *premodernism* is suggested by the fact that the other lines do not rhyme and there is no consistent pattern. The poem begins with two consecutive rhyming couplets, followed by a non-rhyming couplet, followed by a rhyming, followed by a non-rhyming, concluding with a rhyming couplet. To have a pattern, Dickinson could have alternated rhyming with non-rhyming, but there is something magical about the coupling of "snow" and "go." "Letting go" so obviously follows after chill and stupor that it seems almost by accident that "go" should be a rhyme. Try thinking of a non-rhyme that would work as the final line. As we have said before, art is the illusion that there is no art. The words of a great poem just seem to have fallen into place by their own accord. Behind a bad poem we can often detect a poet's hard work.

We might call Dickinson a transition poet. She has one foot in the world of the lyrical poem and the other in the coming world of modern poetry, in which rhythm and rhyme schemes, if they exist at all, are not allowed to get in the way of what the poet wishes to express. Many modern poets turn increasingly to an almost proselike sentence structure, but they can suddenly do a grammatical about-face, as Dickinson does in "The feet mechanical / Go round a wooden way / Of ground or air or Ought, regardless grown." Here the old Apollonian-Dionysian split is evident. The sentence has a standard grammatical structure of subject and verb, but note that the poet uses the adjective "mechanical" instead of the expected adverb form "mechanically." And then we have the three nouns, "ground," "air," and "Ought"—the latter usually a verb but here used as a noun and then strangely capitalized, perhaps to make us focus on its underlying meaning: no matter how much great pain has numbed us, there are duties we have to perform whether we want to or not. The poem is both simple and complex, proselike and poetic in the highest sense of the word. The pairings are Dickinson's signature style, making much of her work instantly recognizable as hers.

To move beyond the strangeness of some of the words is to realize that the poet is crystallizing the universal experience of grief. Anyone who has felt the pain of losing a loved one or the agony of rejection or defeat knows about the numbness that follows the shock. Dickinson makes the numbness seem normal, reassuring those who share her thoughts that they are part of the human fellowship. Here we join forces with a poet who is sharing her very soul.

Poetry of the Harlem Renaissance

From time to time there emerge conscious literary movements, brainchildren of people drawn together by the common aim of bringing their culture, their statements, to the attention of a wider audience. One such movement was the Irish Renaissance of the early twentieth century. Another was the Harlem Renaissance, which, from the mid-1920s to the mid-1930s, launched the careers of dozens of African American artists, including a number of poets. African American poets, for the most part, had been writing in traditional forms, using rhythm and rhyme. The poets who ushered in the Harlem Renaissance often wrote in traditional forms, but the content of their poems was anything but traditional.

On the night of March 21, 1924, Charles S. Johnson, editor of the literary magazine *Opportunity*, invited a number of distinguished white literary figures, including playwright Eugene O'Neill, to attend a celebration of African American literature. Also present to read some of their work were about a dozen relatively unknown poets. Word spread rapidly, and soon Manhattan was buzzing about the astonishing array of talent that had been assembled. Through newspaper articles and radio interviews, many hitherto obscure personalities began to make their presence felt.

Georgia Douglas Johnson (1886–1966) was one such presence. Now considered the first major female African American poet of the twentieth century, she adapted the traditional style of the lyric poem, while communicating anything but lyrical images of the painful hardships endured by a neglected but crucial sector of America. "Black Woman" illustrates how a modern poet makes the reader see life with a different set of eyes.

After you read the poem, look at the painting by Romare Bearden reproduced here. (Bearden also gave us "Mississippi Monday," Color Plate 2.) The two artists complement each other: the painting intensifies our understanding of the poem mother's sorrow.

"Black Woman" shows us that a good modern poem is never over until we reach the final, enlightening line.

BLACK WOMAN

Don't knock at my door, little child,
I cannot let you in,
You know not what a world this is
Of cruelty and sin.
Wait in the still eternity
Until I come to you,
The world is cruel, cruel, child,
I cannot let you in!
Don't knock at my heart, little one,
I cannot bear the pain
Of turning deaf-ear to your call
Time and time again!
You do not know the monster men
Inhabiting the earth,
Be still, be still, my precious child,
I must not give you birth![12]

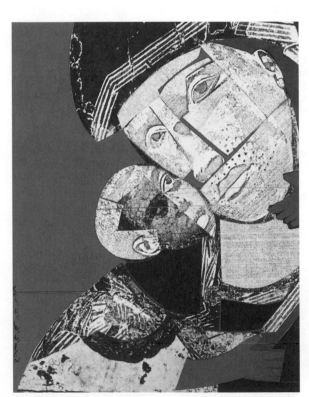

A modern version of the madonna and child theme. Here the face of the mother suggests the hardship of their life, and that of the child shows a sad wisdom beyond his years.

Source: Romare Bearden, *Black Mother and Child.* Credit: Art © Romare Bearden Foundation. Licensed by VAGA, New York, NY. Founders Society Dr. Lula Belle Robinson African Art Fund. Photograph © 1986 The Detroit Institute of Arts.

Although Johnson gives her theme away early in the piece, the poem is not really complete until the shock of the final line, in which she suddenly abandons the metaphor of someone knocking and confronts us with the reality of the woman's plight. Johnson's structure almost defines modern poetry, which is intended to move, startle, and give sudden insight. And it does so with ever increasing complexity. Having to compete with other linear media and, more particularly, with visual media requiring little thought, a good many modern poets go their own way, knowing they will reach a small, understanding audience, one that is accustomed to seeing with new eyes and will work, if need be, to grasp what can be the mystery of that last line.

Johnson's poem is a direct appeal for greater understanding of the pain many women endure. Much modern poetry is far less direct (sometimes maddeningly so!), and poets might be asked why, if the audience for poetry is small anyway, their work is so inaccessible. The answer, we suspect, is that, except for some isolated cases of deliberate obscurity, most modern poets do not consider their poems inaccessible. They are looking for new ways to speak, otherwise why should they write at all? It is our job as readers to broaden our expectations of what a poem should be.

Poetry in Our Time

Great poetry is still being written. In its storehouse is the wisdom accumulated in the process of living. Much of this wisdom is familiar, at least once we get past the barriers, because most readers will find they have had the same experiences as the poet. But unlike the poet, they do not store it away in a memorable form. A great poem is a reminder and, because of a fine poet's genius for language, often an unforgettable one. Carefully reading a poem, we are likely to discover a shared humanity.

Though some poets, such as John Ciardi (1916–1986), have argued for a return to the days when people read poems aloud, the fact is that poetry has become a largely silent art. For this very reason modern poetry need not be grasped immediately; it can be read and reread, studied, thought about, and returned to days later. It occupies its own space, its own corner of the world, into which the reader is invited, a space where a private dialogue takes place between the poet's thoughts and the reader's mind. Such dialogue creates a special kind of bond that exists nowhere else but in the humanities.

Because they consider their work accessible to the patient reader, modern poets usually prefer that their work not be analyzed and translated into a prose equivalent that cannot do justice to the whole. The American poet Archibald MacLeish (1892–1982) wrote his own manifesto for poetry.

While with an eye made quiet by the power
Of harmony, and the deep power of joy,
We see into the life of things.
—**William Wordsworth**

Ars Poetica

A poem should be palpable and mute
As a globed fruit
Dumb
As old medallions to the thumb
Silent as the sleeve-worn stone
Of casement ledges where the moss has grown—
A poem should be wordless
As the flight of birds

A poem should be motionless in time
As the moon climbs
Leaving, as the moon releases
Twig by twig the night-entangled trees,
Leaving, as the moon behind the winter leaves,
Memory by memory the mind
A poem should be motionless in time
As the moon climbs
A poem should be equal to:
Not true
For all the history of grief
An empty doorway and a maple leaf
For love
The leaning grasses and two lights above the sea—
A poem should not mean
But be[13]

Reading this poem out loud, slowly, tasting the words, leads to an immediate understanding of why a poem is a "globed fruit." Here's a prose translation: *Poetry is an experience; it is not reducible to its prose meaning.* How's that? Does that do justice to the poem? We hope the answer is NO!

What is amazing about this poem is that it becomes the very thing it talks about: a poem that is equal to itself and nothing else. Analyzing it further is like asking what a bird means, or a sunset, or a Louis Armstrong jazz improvisation. The American philosopher Ralph Waldo Emerson anticipated modern poetry in the early nineteenth century when he said that the function of the poet is to adorn nature with a "new thing." You can ask, "What is it?"—not "What does it mean?" There is a difference.

In a sense "Ars Poetica" is simplicity itself, the kind of simplicity that is found only in great art. Here, "simple" means "indivisible." Physicists speculate that all matter may have erupted from a simple cell, but what have you said when you've said *that*? A cell that contained everything that could ever be is hardly simple in the ordinary meaning of the term, yet its enormous potential would not have been evident, even if there *had* been someone around to see it! A good many poems are something like that simple cell—maybe the best ones.

Another poet whose work illustrates the complex simplicity that sometimes makes modern poetry seem "difficult" is Billy Collins (b. 1941), who served in 2001 as Poet Laureate of the United States. He is fond of using colloquial American idiom—the language of everyday speech—as a way of inviting the reader in. Once there, however, we realize we are not reading straightforward prose after all, and we have to adjust our consciousness, precisely what the modern poet wants.

MY NUMBER

Is Death miles away from this house,
reaching for a widow in Cincinnati
or breathing down the neck of a lost hiker
in British Columbia?

Is he too busy making arrangements,
tampering with air brakes,
scattering cancer cells like seeds,
loosening the wooden beams of roller coasters

to bother with my hidden cottage
that visitors find so hard to find?

Or is he stepping from a black car
parked at the dark end of the lane,
shaking open the familiar cloak,
its hood raised like the head of a crow,
and removing the scythe from the trunk?

Did you have any trouble with the directions?
I will ask, as I start talking my way out of this.[14]

In addition to its colloquial style, the poem is filled with details drawn from a world we are all familiar with: a hiker, car brakes, garden seeds, a roller coaster, and the death figure so common in Halloween decorations. The final two lines also suggest a familiar situation: trying to persuade the nice police officer not to write a ticket. Billy Collins is one of us, isn't he? Not some lofty genius perched inaccessibly above our heads. Oh, and the title. Straight out of the colloquial way of talking about death, with its suggestion of a lottery. In a lottery only a few people win, most lose, except that *perhaps* in this case it's turned around. Most of the time we win, and only a few don't. There is hope after all. But on the other hand, the random nature of death cautions us against overconfidence. The tendency is to think always that it happens to that widow in Cincinnati or that hiker in Canada, who had no business hiking alone anyway. Still, there's always the chance, slim though it may be, that the car at the end of the lane is *not* there by mistake.

What, then, is the final answer? Shall we go through life, worrying that any moment might be our last? Or do we keep a sense of humor, as in trying to talk our way out of a ticket? Chances are, when your number is up, there's not much you can do about it. But look! Maybe the driver of that black car *will* realize he's got the wrong house. On the other hand . . . we don't need to say it. Billy Collins already has.

We close this section with a poem by Michael Blumenthal (b. 1949), former director of the Creative Writing Center at Harvard and now a resident of Budapest. Though his name is unfamiliar to a large segment of the population, he has attracted a small circle of followers. Like almost every poet, Blumenthal relies on metaphor to communicate thoughts and feelings both to himself and to his readers. As we would expect from a contemporary writer, he seeks to avoid poetic clichés and tired metaphors that have been used so often they have become abstractions themselves.

Like many modern poets, Blumenthal withholds the full statement of his theme until the very last lines, and we discover, to no surprise, that defining and understanding the complexity of love is still an important concern. A goodly number of the poems we have chosen to illustrate the art of poetry do in fact ask variants of the same question he asks in his final four lines: *Is there such a thing as love?*

The poet is the priest of the invisible.

—**Wallace Stevens**

THE TIP OF THE ICEBERG

*Say language really does
what it says it does:
That the bird in your hand
is really a bird, that it takes two
to tango, that whoever digs
his own grave will have to sleep in it.
Say you have a fool for a friend,
feckless and dissipated and greedy
beneath the stars, and that it takes one
to know one. Say that might
makes right, that the best offense
is a good defense, that fools rush in
where trepid angels stammer
in front of the doormats. Say
that life's unfair, that that's
the way it is, that someone tells you
"have a nice day" and really means it.
What would it be like: the word,
reticent and calm, urged out
once again toward its true meaning—
"the worst" really the worst,
"the best" the best, the sum of all
your "everythings" really, now,
everything, even the blurbs*

on the back of your own books
as true as their good intentions?
What would it mean if "until death
do us part" really meant until all breath
leaves me, love, *if "forever" meant*
until the tides cease? *What would signify*
if "love" could only mean love *once again,*
not just the tip of the iceberg, sinking
and in all sincerity.[15]

I have this image.
It's not a generator
It's not a power plant.
But it's like they have
these different points in between.
So it's a place,
it's a poem, like a globular,
like a circle with center points all
over.
All poems are like that.
They have circuits.

—**Joy Harjo**

The poem's title gives us a clue, but it isn't until the final three lines that we understand the relationship between an iceberg and love. Both the word and the emotion are the tip of the iceberg, and underneath, undetected at first, are the dark if not sinister aspects, so that once we have a picture of the iceberg's enormous size, we realize, to our sorrow, that the word and the emotion are relics of an old and tired romanticism. But oh! the poet would so like to go back to a time when one could believe in them and not be disillusioned.

As you explore modern poetry, you will find that analysis and interpretation are less and less necessary. Your Dionysus—your intuitive grasp—will take over, and you will "know" what you are reading. Investigate some more. Go to the library or bookstores, browse, and select a collection of contemporary poems that intrigue you. Some of them will be poems that, when you turn the page to continue reading, have already ended without your knowledge. Okay, so you missed something. Go back and read the poem again and again, out loud. Give it a fair shot. The communication is there, waiting for you. Above all, never ask why the poets don't come right out and say what they have on their mind. After all, if there were another, simpler way of saying what they feel, they wouldn't have had to write the poem in the first place.

The Novel

The emergence of the *novel* as a literary form was inevitable. The novel is essentially a long narrative, and the great epics discussed above are long narratives of adventures, battles, conquests, and complicated human relationships—all the stuff of fiction. In this respect, *The Iliad* and *The Aeneid* could be considered forerunners of the novel, and they certainly are not the only examples. Throughout the world, every culture has produced stories, either written or communicated orally. Much of the Hebrew Bible contains long narratives: for example, the story of Moses leading the people of Israel out of bondage, and the story of the patient Job whose faith is put to a severe test.

Between 400 B.C.E. and 400 C.E., India produced its great Sanskrit epic *The Mahabharata*, a vast tale of family struggles over inherited lands and fortunes, with more episodes than any novel that can be precisely dated. The 800 years of its development tell us that an enormous number of writers were involved. Similarly, both China and Japan have literary traditions that preceded Homer, indicating that the storytelling instinct developed along with human communication skills.

Many literary historians believe that the world's first novel was *The Tale of Genji*, written by a Japanese aristocrat, Lady Murasaki Shikibu, over a thousand years ago. Like the great epics of Homer and Virgil, it is filled with brave deeds and heroes, but it is written in prose.

France in the late Middle Ages produced a number of prose tales called **romances**. These were stories of knighthood, chivalry, and love affairs between brave knights and fair ladies (often married to other men). From England came the tales of King Arthur and the knights of the Round Table. Not only were they artful narratives but they created a whole mythology that continues to influence the human dream. In addition to Camelot, these tales gave prominence to the search for the Holy Grail, which has become a lasting symbol of the elusive prize for which human beings keep searching.

In Western literary history, the word *novel* comes from the Latin *novellus*, meaning new and unfamiliar. Early in the Italian Renaissance, the author Giovanni Boccaccio (1313–1375) used the Italian word **novella** to describe the short prose narratives he wrote. It is very possible that the sense of "novelty" contained in the term was intended to distinguish fictional stories from those that, like the epics, supposedly had a basis in truth.

Early Western Novels

During the sixteenth century, literature flourished in Spain, especially the *picaresque* tale, often quite long, which narrated the adventures of a carefree soldier of fortune, living the free life on the open road and getting involved in all sorts of intrigues and love affairs. The Spanish also had tales similar to the King Arthur legends, dealing with the adventures on the road of brave and dashing knights, who were superheroes, tremendous in battle and noble and chivalrous toward their true loves.

The first known major novelist of the Western world was Miguel de Cervantes Saavedra (1547–1616), whose lifespan closely parallels Shakespeare's. His *Don Quixote* (written between 1612 and 1615) remains one of the most popular and beloved of all novels. The central character is an old man who has read so many stories of brave knights that he has gone mad and believes himself to be one of them. Riding a broken-down old horse named Rocinante and attended by his faithful squire Sancho Panza, he goes off in search of glorious adventure. Intended originally as a satire on the ridiculous excesses of the wandering knight story, *Don Quixote* became, in the opinion of many, a tragic tale of an idealist who sees the world not as it is, but as it ought to be: a world in which people are driven by the noblest of motives, chivalry prevails, and love means forever. *Don Quixote* influenced the work of many novelists who followed, setting the pattern for long, loosely structured adventure yarns, which would find a home in the magazine serials of the eighteenth and nineteenth centuries. The serial was a publishing gimmick, each episode ending with the main character in a perilous strait, and thus keeping the reader coming back to purchase more issues.

The English novel had its true beginnings in the eighteenth century. The coming of the magazine fostered a passion for fiction that had potential novelists busily scribbling. But the period was also one of a passion for science and its search for truth. Those who dictated the taste of the reading public insisted that a lengthy published work, to be worth the time spent in reading it, must be a true story. Consequently, much fiction was passed off as biography or autobiography,

Many credit Lady Murasaki with writing the world's first true novel, *The Tale of Genji*, some 1,000 years ago in Japan.

Source: Ogata Körin, *Portrait of Murasaki Shikibu.* Credit: Private Collection, Paris/Dagli Orti/The Art Archive.

The storyteller takes over to recount the event, and this is the one who survives, who outlives all the others. It is the storyteller in fact that makes us what we are.

—Chinua Achebe

and this meant that the author's real name was often omitted. For example, *Gulliver's Travels* by Jonathan Swift (1667–1745) and *Robinson Crusoe* by Daniel Defoe (1659–1731), two enduringly popular works of fiction, pretended to be nonfictional accounts of actual adventures.

The Novel in America

American writers were slow to gain recognition and respect abroad. In the early nineteenth century, a British critic asked, "Who reads an American book or goes to see an American play?" The question incurred the wrath of native authors, who promptly responded. There was Washington Irving (1783–1859) and his satiric novel masquerading as nonfiction, *A History of New York, by Dietrich Knickerbocker* (1809), which took an irreverent swing at Thomas Jefferson's democratic ideology. Irving may be considered the first American writer to win the long-awaited praise abroad. His achievement was followed closely by that of James Fenimore Cooper (1789–1851), who romanticized the American wilderness in such novels as *The Last of the Mohicans* (1826) and *The Deerslayer* (1841). Then came Nathaniel Hawthorne (1804–1864), who, with *The Scarlet Letter* (1850) and *The House of the Seven Gables* (1851), won almost unanimous praise in England. Herman Melville's *Moby Dick* appeared in 1851, though Melville was not hailed as a great novelist until many years after his death in 1891.

By the end of the nineteenth century, American novelists William Dean Howells and Henry James were making their presence felt on both sides of the Atlantic. Mark Twain had already written *Huckleberry Finn*. American writers no longer had to play catch-up with their European counterparts. Important novels could return a publisher's investment. That's why an eager young writer named F. Scott Fitzgerald (1896–1940) could sit down with great deliberation and resolve to write "the great American novel." We are all familiar with that phrase, which has become for many the great American myth, something to be aspired to but never quite realized. In fact, the pursuit of the great American novel became itself a theme for many American writers, whose heroes usually shed their youthful idealism, confront a harsh world, and realize that the perfect novel can never be written. Yet there was also the influence of the icon created by James Fenimore Cooper: the rugged individualist, not intellectual but schooled in the realities of life, someone who stood head and shoulders above the genteel heroes of European fiction.

Two novelists of the early twentieth century, F. Scott Fitzgerald and Ernest Hemingway, exemplify two kinds of writers, different in their style and themes, but both representatively American nonetheless. Fitzgerald wrote in rich, complex prose, evoking a still classic portrait of the 1920s: the Jazz Age of short-skirted flappers, bathtub gin, sleek roadsters, and endless rounds of wild parties—a carefree period that would come to a crashing end in 1929, when the stock market dropped through the floor and countless investors jumped out of windows.

Fitzgerald was an observer and critic of this careening culture, and in *The Great Gatsby* (1925) he wrote a tragic story of a man who dedicates his life to the pursuit of wealth (though the source of his money is probably outside the law), seems to have achieved the American dream, gives lavish parties which are the talk of affluent Long Island society, makes love to a woman he knows is married, and meets his own predictably violent death.

The Great Gatsby does not proclaim the nobility of the human spirit; it is not politically correct; it does not reveal how to solve the problems of life; it delivers no fashionable or comfortable messages. It is just a masterpiece.
—Matthew J. Broccoli

The final passage of the novel illustrates Fitzgerald's frequently imitated, never duplicated style, and it provides a glimpse into Jay Gatsby, one of the few truly tragic figures in American literature:

> *He had come a long way to this blue lawn and his dream must have seemed so close that he could hardly fail to grasp it. He did not know that it was already behind him, somewhere back in that vast obscurity beyond the city, where the dark fields of the republic rolled on under the night.*[16]

Vastly different from Fitzgerald but of equal stature is Ernest Hemingway (1899–1961), who recreates the rugged individualist hero of earlier times but places him in a number of different locales where he is tested for courage. In *A Farewell to Arms* (1929) he appears as Frederic Henry, an ambulance driver in World War I, who falls in love with a nurse only to see her die. Bitter and angry at the civilization that has ruined his life, not to mention the world, he deserts the army and thus becomes the first in a long line of alienated American heroes who drop out of society.

As Hemingway grew older, however, his sensibilities and values changed. Some Hemingway scholars believe that he became obsessed with maintaining his physical conditioning as well as his magnetic appeal to women. His heroes were transformed into a strong, silent, intensely masculine figure, stoically able to experience and conquer extreme dangers, always falling in love with, then losing, strong women. Biographers see the Hemingway hero as a portrait of the man he longed to be. A *New Yorker* cartoon showed a hairy, muscular arm with its hand holding a rose. The caption read: "*The soul of Ernest Hemingway.*"

Perhaps the alienation of Frederick Henry in *A Farewell to Arms* weighed heavily on Hemingway's conscience. The death of Catherine as well as the futility of war motivate his running away, but to the later Hemingway, it would have been an act of cowardice. The theme of the mature Hemingway novels and stories is the attainment of a courageous stand against not only war but all of life's brutalities.

Hemingway's 1940 novel about the Spanish Civil War, *For Whom the Bell Tolls*, offers the author's most memorable portrait of the stoical, courageous hero, one who is willing to die for a cause that is not his own. The American Robert Jordan joins a band of Spanish guerrillas battling a repressive government. When the superior forces seem to have them trapped in the mountain, Jordan orders them to escape while he mans a machine gun to hold off the advancing army long enough to ensure the guerrillas' safe exit. The scene includes a moving farewell to Maria, a woman with whom he would have gladly lived for the rest of his life. Like all of Hemingway fiction, this novel cannot have a traditional happy ending, yet it does have his characteristic take on what constitutes happiness. For Ernest Hemingway, happiness is having conquered the coward who lives inside each of us. One literary historian has observed that Robert Jordan is Frederick Henry redeemed. Henry saves himself when he deserts the army; Jordan, who might have saved himself, chooses not to.

Archetypes in This Chapter
Icons and Symbols in Literature

American Dream	The belief that anyone, even the poor and new immigrants, can become wealthy and successful in the United States if they apply themselves with sufficient drive and ambition. F. Scott Fitzgerald's character Jay Gatsby represents a tragic interpretation of the American dream.
Sacrificial lamb	The lamb was an animal frequently sacrificed in religious rites throughout the ancient world. In time, the lamb became a symbol of all sacrificial victims. As a symbol, the lamb is also associated with Christ, with his crucifixion and death often interpreted as a form of sacrifice. Explicit references to this archetype can be found in William Blake's poem "The Lamb."
Superhero	An extreme version of a hero who transcends regular human limitations and may be endowed with a supernatural special power. Gilgamesh, Achilles, and Hector are all ancient versions of the superhero.
Trojan horse	A mythical ruse by which the Greeks finally conquered Troy. Greek soldiers hid inside a massive wooden horse, which was taken inside Troy as a gift; the soldiers emerged at night when the city slept. Today, a tactic by which a person, thing, or even a computer virus gains entry to a site through voluntary admission by those protecting it.

The next novel we consider also has a central character seeking to redeem himself, but his choices are more subtle and complicated by the once unknown horror of modern warfare.

An Afghan-Born Novelist

Early in the nineteenth century, when American fiction was young and American writers were trying to shake off their inferiority complexes, their focus was almost exclusively on their own culture. The rest of the world seemed not to exist. Today, however, with television and the Internet, what happens in far-off lands is reported immediately. You can be in your living room and on a street in Baghdad at the same time. Of course, as soon as you shut down the computer or turn off the television, you may, if you choose, return to your own little corner of the world, involved only in your own daily tasks and problems.

One writer, born in Kabul, Afghanistan, has brought the Mideast to startling life in a work of fiction that renders it impossible for a reader to be only sporadically concerned with devastating upheaval in far-off places. Once you become engrossed in this novel by Khaled Hosseini (b. 1966), your understanding of his native country and the turmoil that has engulfed it for three decades deepens and expands, and you will finally close the book a much wiser person. We have chosen to end this section of the chapter by discussing *The Kite Runner* (2003), the book that first brought Hosseini to the attention of the American public.

Hosseini lived in Kabul for the first eight years of his life. In 1974 his father moved the family to Paris, because of better employment opportunities. When communist insurgents overthrew the Afghan monarchy, his family decided against returning to Kabul. Granted political asylum in the United States, the family arrived here with only the clothes on their backs, and they were so poor they relied on welfare and food stamps to survive. Eventually Hosseini was able to put himself through college and medical school. Then, this brilliant refugee from an embattled nation abandoned the profession that was guaranteeing him a comfortable income for life to pursue his writing. Why?

The answer lies in the fact that, in addition to developing a careful scientific eye, Hosseini sprang from a culture of born storytellers. When he was growing up, fiction was his escape from poverty. He knew there was a book locked inside him that had to be written. Life was good in his adopted country, but there were the memories of his boyhood in Kabul, where he must have seen kite runners, and he remembered what life was like before the communist coup. The writer's imagination could readily piece together the fragments of memory and link them into a narrative thread.

Hosseini's central character is Amir, a sensitive, bookish, motherless youth and the despair of his father, who wants a stronger, more athletic son, able to protect himself against bullies. The two, Sunni Muslims, live in relative luxury compared to the Shi'ites. The Sunnis and the Shi'ites form the two main branches of Muslim faith. Each traces itself to a different patriarch and claims to represent the one true religion. They have been enemies for centuries. (For further discussion, see Chapter 10, Religion.) In Amir's Afghanistan, those who owe their allegiance to the Sunnis are the privileged class, while Shi'ites are regarded as second-class citizens. Amir's only friend is Hassan, the housekeeper's son. Their close ties earn the disapproval of the class-conscious society. Hassan and his father are Hazaras, Shi'ite Muslims who work mainly as farmhands and, in cities, as domestics; they are social outcasts, deprived of even the most basic skills such as reading and writing.

Both boys want to become adept in the kite-flying competitions that, next to soccer, are the principal sport in Afghanistan. As hundreds of kites flood the sky, the

It was by far the hottest day of the year. The mountains trapped the bonescorching heat, stifled the city like smoke. Power had been out for days. All over Kabul, electric fans sat idle, almost mockingly so.

—**Khaled Hosseini**

object is to get your kite to force as many of the others out of competition as you can. This goes on until there is one kite left and its owner is crowned champion. But there is another competition, kite *running*, the object of which is to chase down the fallen kites and collect as many as possible. This of course involves pushing and tripping your opponents. Hassan, much to the disapproval of the Sunni boys, becomes a star kite runner. It would seem at this point in the story that the two boys, despite the difference in their class, are leading an idyllic existence. Then the novel turns tragic.

As in many celebrated novels, what drives *The Kite Runner* is a mistake that will cast a shadow over everything that happens afterward. The mistake stems from tragic weaknesses in Amir, both cowardice and the tendency to put himself down at every opportunity, like Hamlet, perpetually analyzing what he is doing wrong, self-criticism that paralyzes his will. When Hassan is raped by a local bully, Amir hides helplessly and watches.

To ease his inner torment, Amir decides to do away with the visual embodiment of his guilt by forcing Hassan to leave. He hides an expensive wristwatch and money under Hassan's mattress so that his friend will be blamed for theft and disgraced.

These lapses haunt Amir throughout his life. And paralleling the torment inside him is what happens to Afghanistan. The monarchy is overthrown in a communist coup, and the class-protected Sunnis no longer dominate. The Taliban take over through violent struggle and impose a repressive society. When Amir, who has been living in America, eventually returns to Afghanistan to try to make things right between himself and Hassan, he arrives to a devastated homeland. Hassan, he discovers, has been massacred, along with his wife, while his son, Sohrab, lives amid squalor in a run-down orphanage. With great difficulty, Amir finds Sohrab, who is deeply scarred by his troubled upbringing in Kabul, and cannot adjust to the comfortable life Amir provides for him in America.

The novel ends on a note that is remotely upbeat. Hosseini does not tie the complex strands together into a neat package. There is no author-manipulated happy outcome, no gift to the reader that says, "I know you want me to show you how their new life in America makes up for the past." Amir, approaching middle-age by now, is still able to beat some children in a kite-flying competition, noting that his adopted son, Sohrab, is showing a little interest. And the boy smiles!

The Kite Runner ends on a note that is remotely upbeat. It is comforting to know that out of upheaval and devastation there can emerge a work of such beauty, showing us the humanities survive even while some cynics are predicting the end of civilization.

Kabul, Afghanistan, before and after the devastation of war, parallels the psychological path of Amir's life in *The Kite Runner*.

Source: Left: Time and Life Pictures/Getty Images. Right: Cheng W. Lee/*The New York Times*/Redux Pictures.

It was only a smile, nothing more. It didn't make everything all right. It didn't make anything all right. Only a smile. A tiny thing. A leaf in the woods, shaking in the wake of a startled bird's flight. But I'll take it. With open arms. Because when spring comes, it melts the snow one flake at a time, and maybe I just witnessed the first flake melting.[17]

As you noticed, the author is also a poet, who uses his scientifically trained observations of the smallest detail to express himself, not only in traditional narrative, but in metaphors as well. It's hard to imagine a more effective way to say that there is always some hope, even if it's "one flake at a time."

It is comforting to know that out of upheaval and devastation there can emerge a work of such beauty, showing us that the humanities survive even while some cynics are predicting the end of civilization.

The Short Story

A case could be made—in fact, *has* been made—that the short story is essentially an American invention, along with jazz, which we discuss in Chapter 6. We have to be cautious, however, because much depends on what we mean by the short story. If we simply mean a brief tale featuring one central action, then we'd have to concede that the Bible got there long before there *was* an America. The stories of Cain and Abel, Joseph and his brothers, Ruth, Abraham's near sacrifice of Isaac, not to mention the Garden of Eden, must be considered literary masterpieces as well as religious writings, models of tales that waste few words. That is precisely what great short stories do.

Magazine Fiction

The short story form gained recognition and respectability early in the nineteenth century with the growing popularity of the magazine. Along with weekly or monthly installments of long novels, magazines printed pieces of short fiction that could be read in one sitting, presumably because writers could not produce lengthy fiction fast enough to meet the demand. Besides, large sums of money awaited those who could devise a fantastic story, especially one involving murder and ghosts in eerie castles and building to a shattering climax. Financial returns on a novel came much more slowly.

When we think of such stories, the name Edgar Allan Poe (1809–1849) immediately comes to mind. With his dark and brooding atmosphere, his old castles with their locked doors and cobwebs, his ghostly voices echoing down dark hallways, Poe made enough money to support his two tragic habits, substance abuse and gambling. Though he appears never to have been very happy in his brief lifetime—something that may explain the fantastic world of the imagination into which he continually escaped—he left behind a treasury of short fiction that clearly established American preeminence in this field.

Later, in France, the short story became swept up with a literary trend known as *realism*—a strong reaction against the earlier novels and stories of sheer fantasy. Character became as important as plot, if not more important, and the short story was expected to climax in a revelation, offering an insight into some aspect of human nature or life itself. The revelation was often an ironic one.

A woman is sitting in her old, shuttered house. She knows that she is alone in the whole world; every other thing is dead. The doorbell rings.

Source: A short tale of horror attributed to Thomas Bailey Aldrich

Epiphany

The sudden insight into life or human nature which short stories often give us is called an **epiphany**, a term borrowed by Irish novelist James Joyce from its biblical meaning: the sudden appearance of Jesus to his disciples after his resurrection. Joyce and subsequent literary critics used the term to mean an action or a line of dialogue that reveals a truth.

A literary epiphany is an action or line of dialogue that reveals a truth.

One story that has achieved international renown, largely because of its shattering epiphany, is "The Lottery" by Shirley Jackson (1919–1965), who often combines the chilling aspects of Poe with climactic meaningfulness. "The Lottery" exists on a number of levels. While it rewards the discerning reader with an epiphany that deepens with each reading, it also offers a suspenseful and realistic surface tale of an annual prize-drawing ceremony in a typical, peaceful small town, with the nature of the "prize" carefully withheld until the horrifying climax. As townspeople gather for the drawing, each one takes from a black box a small scrap of paper. All of the scraps are blank except one, which has a black mark on it. The one who draws this is declared the winner, and the person is then stoned to death by all the others.

Early in the story, the symbolic nature of the events is hinted at. There are rumors being discussed that some towns are thinking of abandoning the lottery. Then an elderly denizen comments that this is a bad idea: "Lottery in June, corn be heavy soon." After the horrifying revelation and the first stone is hurled at the victim, we realize that the author is showing us the survival of an ancient sacrificial ritual in which one person is slain so that the gods will provide an abundant harvest. Yet why write such a story? *That* ritual is no longer practiced in the civilized world. We think about it, discuss it, then realize that the story is not about an agricultural ritual. It is about the survival of many primitive instincts we believe are long buried. Why, for example, does traffic slow to a crawl so drivers can gawk at police cars and an ambulance on the side of the road, the signal of a dreadful accident? Why are disaster films so popular?

Many stories published in recent years have dispensed with the once required epiphany. The modern short story can be just that—a *story*—a brief narrative that doesn't have to lead anywhere. It can be about people and their relationships, not requiring the reader to wonder what it *means*. Modern short story writers are often fond of ending their pieces in a puzzling manner. They write the kind of thing that, according to one professor of literature, "when you turn the page, you find out it's over." They claim the same right granted to modern poets—the right not to be analyzed. But there are still readers who think analysis is an art form in itself and enjoy the added pleasure of thinking about and discussing what they have read. And there are still writers who want to share their insights with readers and want their stories to offer some understanding of life.

A Master of Style and Meaning

Not only is epiphany not "out," but some of the most celebrated contemporary short story writers combine meaning with elegance of language and complexity of character, demonstrating the literary heights which this art form can reach. One such writer is Nobel laureate Nadine Gordimer (b. 1923), one of the most recognized names in the literature of South Africa, with numerous novels and short story collections to her credit. One of Gordimer's recent stories, published in the *New Yorker*, enables us to say with considerable pleasure that the form is still thriving in the hands of masters.

"A Beneficiary" shares with *The Kite Runner* a theme that runs through much literature of both past and present: *the search for one's roots, for a true family.* The theme ties in with that of the alienation and loneliness which are inevitable effects of a rapidly changing world. Charlotte, the main character in Gordimer's story, does not live in a war-torn country like Afghanistan or confront the inhumanity that ancient hostilities continue to breed. In her late twenties, she lives in a comfortable urban environment. Her mother, Laila de Morne, was a self-centered stage actress who never quite achieved the recognition she thought she deserved. Charlotte was raised untraditionally, her irresponsible mother having divorced her neurologist husband and been far too busy to attend to the duties of motherhood. After Laila's death, the neurologist comes back into Charlotte's life, and the two develop the family relationship Charlotte has never known.

Then Gordimer makes use of a classic literary device: the discovery of an old letter that contains a startling revelation. Written by the neurologist to his attorney after Charlotte's birth, it indicates that Laila had told him the child was not his, that the true father was the leading actor of her theater company. But the neurologist, believing the exact paternity could not be proved, wanted to sue for custody. The suit had obviously been unsuccessful.

Charlotte is in a quandary: how does she find her true father? The story couldn't have gone anywhere at this point had Gordimer not availed herself of an author's license to impose a happy coincidence. The actor in question is to appear in a season of plays at a local theater. Charlotte attends each performance, swept away by the man's genius for embodying himself in a host of very different characters. In a certain sense, she falls in love with him, and we naturally expect the inevitable meeting, the finding of the real parent, the traditional happy ending. After all, the family is a sacred unit, is it not? But Gordimer is far too serious an artist to bow to convention. Charlotte is at a loss as to how to proceed. Or should she proceed at all? Must she really have a biological parent?

In fact, the neurologist, meeting the actor, sets up the climax. The neurologist tells the actor that he remembers his powerful performance in the play *Marat/Sade* and that "Laila de Morne was Charlotte Corday." The time has come to please the reader with Charlotte's long-awaited "Laila de Morne was my mother." But the actor's only response is to remind Charlotte that, while Corday was the knife-wielding assassin of Marat, "you're not a Charlotte to carry a knife, spoil your beautiful aura with that, frighten off the men around you." A compliment, nothing more, and not a trace of a guilty conscience, or even a slight memory of the night spent with her mother.

And what has Charlotte learned? What have *we* learned? In an exquisitely wrought final scene, Charlotte drives the neurologist home and, at his doorstep, she "went to him and he saw, without understanding, that he should take her in his arms. She held him. He kissed her cheek, and she pressed it against his. Nothing to do with DNA."[18]

This is the stuff great fiction is made of. In this scene Gordimer captures the subtleties and ambiguities of human consciousness and behavior. What exactly is Charlotte feeling at this moment? Is it an inner joy that she has at last found

. . . and I joked, 'Lucky she doesn't look like me'....my wife picked her up, away from me, and told me, 'She's not your child.'
—**Nadine Gordimer**

a father? Is there a sexual current here as well? There is surely something we could call "love," but it's a long way from the standard, abstract way we define the word. And what matters in the long run? To say that one is no longer an orphan? Or perhaps that finding a nest, a place where one belongs is the only thing that matters, regardless of who is tending that nest?

Maybe the story is really not about finding a parent, at least not primarily. Maybe it's about the difficulty of understanding our true selves, our wants and needs, and the complexity of our longing. Is it enough to have located one's biological parentage? What does one expect from a parent anyway? Is a deep feeling for another better than to tell the world that one is not an orphan? Like her colleagues at the highest literary levels, Gordimer is not satisfied with easy answers. She knows that life doesn't provide them.

Aside from its many layers of possible meanings, "A Beneficiary" offers rich examples of a major writer's literary style and insights that come at us so fast we have a hard time absorbing them in a first reading. In the hands of a lesser writer, Charlotte's response to reading the letter to the attorney could have been factual and bland. "She was overcome by feelings of anger toward her mother. She deserved to know who her real father was." But Gordimer frankly can't find the words that belong in this situation, so she asks the question: "How do you recognize something that is not in the known vocabulary of your emotions?" Instead of glossing over the moment, she makes us wonder and perhaps feel a little guilty over our own tendencies to gloss.

Much of the time, however, Gordimer's sentences are long and complicated, forcing the reader to go very slowly, deliberately, so as not to miss the point. Here is Charlotte's reaction to her first meeting with the man who may or may not have been her natural father: "He was wittily critical at other people's expense, and so with him she was free to think—say—what she found ponderous in those she worked with: the predictability among her set of friends, which she usually tolerated without stirring them up."

The casual reader is likely to be one who wearies of prose that doesn't flow rapidly and superficially toward answering the only important question: well, what happens? The Gordimer reader is as interested in the flow as in the destination. Her highly literate style, like that of other major writers, gives evidence of wisdom behind the words. She knows what she is doing. We know we are in good hands.

A tip-off comes to us from the title itself: Charlotte is *a*, not *the*, beneficiary. The latter is someone named in a will, the one with all the legal rights, but not necessarily the one most loved. To be *a* beneficiary without legal, but only voluntarily granted, rights may in the long run be better than to inherit an estate, especially if *the* beneficiary lucked into the role purely by accident of birth.

This chapter has offered an introduction to a very complex subject by focusing on particular examples from major genres of literature. It makes no claim to being an exhaustive study. We have sampled a few important works by way of encouraging you to make the reading of fiction an ongoing part of your life. We hope you will take it from there. Once you open the pages of literature, short or long, prose or poetry, you will discover infinite worlds and dimensions of reality that can carry you to a place only the humanities know about: your own private island of imagination.

The consequences of slavery only artists can deal with. There are certain things only artists can deal with, and it's our job.

—**Toni Morrison**

Key Terms

blank verse poetry that has an iambic pentameter rhythm but does not rhyme.

classic a literary work that continues to be read even centuries after its initial appearance because it is still relevant.

conceit an elaborate, extended description of something in terms of something else; e.g., in Donne's sonnet "Batter my heart," mystical exaltation is expressed in sexually charged language.

couplet two consecutive lines of poetry that rhyme; often used by Shakespeare to conclude a sonnet.

epic a genre of literature; a long narrative poem recounting the actions of a hero who exemplifies strength, courage, and cunning, but not necessarily moral virtue.

epiphany a sudden insight into life or human nature that often serves as the climax in a work of fiction, particularly a short story. The author James Joyce adapted this term from its original religious context.

genre any distinct category within a discipline such as, in literature, the epic, poetry, the novel, the short story; a genre generally imposes certain requirements on the writer: e.g., a sonnet must have fourteen lines; a haiku must have seventeen syllables.

haiku Japanese poetic form that presents one image, usually derived from an observation of nature, with an underlying thought; usually limited to three lines totalling 17 syllables in the pattern 5, 7, 5.

iambic pentameter classical rhythmic scheme, widely used in English verse, consisting of five repetitions in a poetic line of an unstressed syllable followed by a stressed syllable, as in the line "Shall I compare thee to a summer's day?"

lyrical poetry rhythmic, often rhymed verse, musical in nature, usually dealing with the poet's feelings, especially of love. *Lyric* means "of a lyre," an ancient musical instrument, indicating words sung to music.

masterpiece here, a literary work acknowledged to tower above others of its time in its style, execution, memorable characters, or profound meaning; not necessarily recognized in its time

metaphor widely used literary device in which something abstract is described in terms of something that is more concrete.

novella a work of fiction that is shorter than a novel but longer than a short story.

romance a literary genre popular in the Middle Ages, revolving around the exploits of a brave knight and his love for a beautiful lady, often married to someone else.

scanning marking a line's syllables as stressed or unstressed, and counting them to determine the pattern, sometimes exaggerating the rhythm to do so.

sonnet a fourteen-line verse form controlled by a strict rhythm and rhyme scheme; invented by Renaissance Italian poets and adapted by Shakespeare and later poets.

Topics for
Writing and Discussion

1. Achilles and Hector are the heroes of the *Iliad*, but they couldn't be more different. Describe the characteristics of each one, then indicate why each is a hero in the context of the age that produced the epic.

2. Write a sonnet using iambic pentameter and the rhyme scheme of Shakespeare's "When in disgrace with fortune and men's eyes." Try to make your sentences flow from line to line rather than stop at the end of each line. In other words, try to make your rhyme scheme as low-key as possible.

3. Write a poem, not necessarily observing strict rules of rhythm or rhyme, using one of the following themes:
   a. a romantic involvement you want to break off
   b. a romantic involvement you would like to have
   c. advice to someone who is depressed over a lost love
   d. a verse letter to someone who has stolen your love
   e. a verse letter to the loved one who has been stolen

   It would be interesting to have the poems read aloud to the class by people other than the poets, then ask the class whether the writer was male or female.

4. Reread Blake's "The Lamb" and "The Tiger." With or without rhythm and rhyme, write a short poem about another animal, using it as a symbol for something else you should not name directly. Share the poem with the class and see whether your audience catches your meaning.

5. Traditional haiku presented an image derived from an observation of nature, but modern poets often have fun with the genre. Write some haiku of your own on one or more of these subjects: pollution; a rock concert; an after-school job; a shopping mall. Or choose your own subject. Your poem must be written in three lines and observe the 5/7/5 syllable format.

   As an example, here is a contemporary haiku by poet Fred Witkoff.

   > *The bird sings because*
   > *it has a song, not because*
   > *it has a message.*

6. What do we mean when we say that in good poetry the rhymes seem to be there by chance? Illustrate, using Shakespeare's "When in disgrace with fortune and men's eyes." Be sure you make it clear what you mean by "chance."

7. Reread the material on the *conceit*. Write a short poem in which you describe something (falling in love, breaking up with someone, wishing you had not made a promise that you do not want to keep but feel you must), using an extended metaphor. Hint: The entire poem should focus on one situation or action that is clearly something else.

8. Explain the original religious context of *epiphany*, then indicate why James Joyce thought it an appropriate way to define the most important element in a short story.

9. From what you read about *The Kite Runner* in this chapter, would you say that Amir has found redemption for the tragic mistakes he made early in life? Explain your answer.

10. From what you learned about "A Beneficiary" in this chapter, why do you think many readers might be dissatisfied with the ending?

5 Art

Overview

What makes a true artist? Who decides?

At an exhibition of works by the modern Russian abstract painter Wassily Kandinsky (Color Plate 8), two friends were staring in confusion at one of the pieces. One of them asked the other, "What is that supposed to be?" His friend replied, "I think it's two electric light bulbs." The first man stared some more, then finally nodded in agreement. "You're right. It's two light bulbs, and it's very good, don't you think?" If the artist had been standing by, he might well have thought: *Whatever they see is just fine as far as I'm concerned.* On the other hand, he might have hoped that, with increasing exposure to visual art, these visitors would come to view a work on its own terms.

Most of us share a definite bias toward realism, defined as *that which copies or at least approximates the appearance of objects and persons*. Comic strips, while exaggerations of reality, are nonetheless recognizable facsimiles of the real thing. Animated cartoons may take us to fantasy lands, but there, however distorted, animals are still animals, people are people, and trees are trees.

Yet even the most meticulous efforts to imitate the appearance of the real world are just that: **imitations**. A photograph is not the real thing. Greek and Roman statues *resemble* real people, but their bodies are often perfectly proportioned, as most people's bodies are *not*. Photographic realism—art that so closely imitates real scenes that we feel we could walk right into the canvas—was perfected during the seventeenth and eighteenth centuries. For artists of today, photographic realism may be a starting point from which they depart as they find new ways to express themselves. Nevertheless, many people still judge art in terms of how real it looks.

What makes a true artist? Who decides? Sometimes the judgment of history decides, as in the case of Vincent van Gogh, who died obscure and penniless but whose work has since been acknowledged all over the world. Sometimes acclaim comes during the artist's lifetime: witness Michelangelo, Leonardo, and Picasso. Sometimes judgments vary both during and after an artist's lifetime. The jury is still out when it comes to Andy Warhol, a pop artist who stirred up a controversy when he unveiled a painting of one hundred cans of Campbell's soup. They look so real that we might think they

◗ At its first showing, viewers were disgruntled because *Nude Descending a Staircase* did not seem to show what its title promised.

Source: Marcel Duchamp, *Nude Descending a Staircase #2* (1912). Philadelphia Museum of Art, Pennsylvania. Credit: © 2005 Artists Rights Society (ARS), New York/ADAGP, Paris/Succession Marcel Duchamp/Superstock.

came right off the supermarket shelf, but many viewers asked, "Why would anyone want to paint cans of soup?"

A recent play named, simply, *Art* concerns a man who pays an exorbitant sum for a stark, white canvas with nothing depicted on it. One friend, a cynic, decides he has gone mad. The purchaser is secretly not confident he has made a wise decision but vehemently defends the painting. In a gripping climactic scene, he gives the cynic a Magic Marker and dares him to put something on the canvas he seems to think is so worthless. Without changing his evaluation of the painting, the cynic is nonetheless intimidated and at first hesitates to deface it. Is it the price tag that stops him? Is it the possibility that maybe it *is* art? Whatever the considerations, the cynic has his honor to defend and draws a stick figure skiing down a mountain. The whiteness becomes snow, becomes a recognizable *thing*. The play ends in a minor key. What is art after all?

This chapter offers a brief introduction to the visual arts: painting, sculpture, and architecture. We encourage you to approach the chapter without bias, without defined expectations. Be open to what may at first seem unfamiliar and, in some cases, downright crazy. Above all, do not expect a basic definition of visual art that can apply to every work by every artist. The world of art should be entered with open-ended expectations and an understanding that not every work will look like something recognizable. Consider, instead, the artist's intention. If you can do that, you have made a connection between the artist and yourself. Anyone seeking clear guidelines of taste can find them in any number of excellent resource books. Since the present text aims at offering insight into the use of the humanities as a means of enhancing the quality of life, the emphasis will be on looking into the wondrous variety of things that art can do for us.

> *Art is what the artist does.*
> —**Robert Thiele**

The Need to Imitate

Astonishing cave paintings dating back to the days of primitive cultures teach us that even the earliest humans expressed themselves through art. While the artistic technique is hardly polished, we can recognize the subject—usually animals, such as a wild horse, familiar to the cave dwellers. The exact motivation of the artists cannot be known, but one thing about the work speaks for itself: *the early artists developed a technique for imitating what they saw.* Some of the paintings seem to express feelings as well: perhaps fear of the animal's power, or perhaps a sense of mastery over that power. A good bet, however, is that early artists enjoyed imitation, because they had an instinctive knowledge of how to do it. *They liked to transfer to a two-dimensional surface what they saw in their three-dimensional world.* All visual art is imitation. Some of it—and *only* some of it—strives for a **likeness** of the world out there—the familiar world. Some of it imitates the world of imagination inside the artist, and often it is rejected because it is *not* familiar.

Imitation is also a key factor in music and dramatic art. Music can imitate the sound of birds chirping, the wind whistling through a forest, or waves crashing against a shore, though we know that these effects are created by instruments. Aristotle called the art of acting *mimesis*—or imitation—even though Greek actors wearing masks and walking on stilts could not have *looked* like real people. The actor's art of imitation, from the Greeks to the present, involves the truth, not necessarily the appearance, of human beings.

Very early cave drawings show a basic need to imitate the three-dimensional world.

Source: Gianni Dagli Orti/Corbis.

Imitation, therefore, needs to be broadly defined and understood. The term does not refer exclusively to what looks absolutely real and authentic. In the humanities, imitation means that the artist uses reality as a starting but not necessarily an ending point. Sometimes, though a work of art has the external appearance of reality, it may actually be making a comment about life. Yet we need to be cautious if we find we like a certain work because we know what it is saying.

The painting *The Bar at the Folies Bergère* by the French artist Édouard Manet (1832–1883), whom we discuss later in the chapter, does not represent photographic realism, but its likeness to reality is clear. The expression on the barmaid's face suggests either boredom with her necessary job or quiet despair over the disparity between her own circumstances and those of her affluent customers. One *could* therefore say that the painting is making a social comment, but that is probably not the intent of this artist, who was primarily interested in imitating the shapes, colors, and the light of the world around him. At any rate, social commentary is unlikely to be the reason for the work's enduring fame.

Sometimes artists want to reproduce the sort of scene that catches the fancy of others. They enjoy meeting the challenge of making a two-dimensional canvas look three-dimensional. Sometimes the sheer difficulty of making the canvas seem to have depth, rather than the scene itself, is what motivates the artist. Imitating is such a universal human need that, when it is done well, critical viewers admire without demanding more.

In the 1874 painting *The Ball on Shipboard* by French artist James Tissot (1836–1902), the photographic likeness was probably a strong reason for its appeal. Tissot spent much of his life in England, and in this work he depicts a group of upper-class Victorians on a yachting pleasure cruise. The work is

A good spectator also creates.
—**Swiss proverb**

Social commentary is probably not the primary interest of the artist in this work.

Source: Edouard Manet, *The Bar at the Folies Bergères*. Credit: Fotomarburg/Art Resource, NY.

a meticulous imitation of reality, filled with many details, including the intricate designs on the flags. The painter gives the illusion that he has just happened along at a particular moment and caught the scene with an instantaneous click of his camera. Photography was in its infancy at the time, and the pictures taken may not have been much sharper than the artist's brushwork. At any rate, the painting is so true to life we can almost believe we are standing on that deck, observing those people.

Those who insist on assigning specific meaning to works of art might see a critical attitude on the part of the artist toward the leisurely idleness of Victorian society, but, even if such an attitude existed, it would hardly account for the picture's success. The technique of the artist does that.

On the other hand, we miss out on a great deal if we demand strict realism in every work we view. The artist may be imitating things we have never seen and never will see except on that canvas or in a bronze shape. Visual art, as Ralph Waldo Emerson said of poetry, "adorns nature with a new thing." In all its myriad forms, realistic or not, art enhances our world.

A painting so true to life that we can believe we are stanting on that deck, observing those people.

Source: Tate Gallery, London. Credit: Art Resource, NY.

Let Me See!

It's dangerous to generalize, but it's a safe assumption that most people who are born to be artists felt the urge to imitate. An artist's need to imitate grows out of a particular way of seeing: seeing intensely, noticing details, shapes, and colors. Unfortunately, most of us tend to see selectively, except in isolated moments when a landscape or a sunset calls us sharply to attention. Children tend to see as the artist sees, and perhaps that is why Picasso urged people not to grow up, to come to the world each day as the child does.

The poet Walt Whitman captures the child's—and we could add the young artist's—relationship to the world in these lines:

> *There was a child went forth every day,*
> *And the first object he look'd upon, that object he became,*
> *And that object became part of him for the day or a certain part of the day,*
> *Or for many years or stretching cycles of years.*[1]

Why do children in cars, buses, or trains demand to sit by the window? For that matter, why do they make this demand on planes, when there is often nothing to look at but clouds? What is out there doesn't matter. Children are new to the world, and instinctively they want to see everything, if only clouds. Older people confined in apartments along crowded streets like to look out the window for hours on end. Integral to the experience of being alive is looking at things. Those without sight substitute touching or close listening, but they will frequently describe these actions as "seeing." The point is that we spend much of our lives just looking around for no practical reason, except one: *we have to.*

Though we saw more intensely as children than as adults, most of us probably did not imitate what we looked at—at least not very accurately. Remember what you did when the elementary school teacher asked you to draw a house? Unless you were an instinctive artist, you were content to make the generic two-dimensional house (three rectangles and a triangle), just as you made stick figures to represent people. You made the *symbol* of a house because by now you were acquiring language, and the inner world of symbolism was taking over your life.

If asked to draw the sunrise, the true artist will imitate what he or she has seen many times: a sun that has radiance, depth, and color shadings. The rest of us draw something that could just as easily be a porcupine peeking from behind a fence.

The generic house and the stick figure got the job done for most of us. We assumed everyone knew what we meant when we drew that skeleton of a house, but we were drawing the *idea* of the house. We couldn't be bothered to imitate a real house. Isn't that what cameras are for?

The artist bent on directly imitating something can produce an astonishing likeness of the original. The Dutch masters of the seventeenth century were so good at faithful rendering that many artists who came later decided it was unwise to compete and began to experiment with other techniques and other goals.

What are such goals? One is the imitation of inner reality. Just think of your dreams. Every object, every location is made up of bits and pieces of other things. If you could hold onto a moment of a dream long enough to draw it, you would be, at least for a time, a modern artist. In a sense, the imitation factor is still there, except that a strange new world is being imitated. When the artist's production

Every child is an artist. The problem is how to remain an artist once he grows up.

　　　　　　　—Pablo Picasso

offers unfamiliar stimuli to us, we need to look at it non-judgmentally, trying to absorb all that is there to behold.

The artist who emerges from the childlike wonder at seeing is, ultimately, a creator, not a copy machine. Even the most rigorous attempt to create an absolute likeness is selective. For example, when painting a portrait, the artist may ask the subject to look serious, or perhaps to adopt a coy smile because this is more indicative of the subject's personality. Yet any portrait presents only one, often posed and artificial, reality. We know Leonardo da Vinci's Mona Lisa through her mysterious smile, but we will never know her fully as she was.

The treasure of art, however, is that *its* reality lives on after its subjects change or die. The final product is an addition to reality, not simply a way of reproducing it. The artist always contributes something new, something that never before was put together in precisely that way. Leonardo's *Mona Lisa* is not Mona Lisa. The latter left the earth long ago; the former will never die. Even though it seems to be slowly fading, it is still there, awaiting only a painstaking restoration.

Styles and Media

Now that we know all visual art is imitation but that imitation does not always mean creating a direct likeness, we can talk about the varied styles and methods—or **media**—of imitation.

Imagine a school where everyone else is drawing rectangles and stick figures, except for one pupil who wants to be different, to make a drawing that looks like the real thing. Already we have a *style* decision. The young artist feels confined by the sheet of paper handed out for the assignment. A two-dimensional surface does not offer enough freedom or originality, so the artist brings a bar of soap to school and proceeds to carve a tiny three-dimensional model of a real house. Not only is this a departure from the *style* of the others, but soap is a different *medium* from paper. The medium of imitation can be just as exciting as the act of imitating itself. Standing close to Michelangelo's statue of David or Moses, we are astounded at how lifelike the artist was able to make the marble seem. A painting of David is not the same as the statue, even though we might recognize that both imitate the same character. The medium enters strongly into the experience of art.

If the basic urge of the artist is to imitate the appearance of people, places, and things, the basic style is therefore *art as likeness*: The intention of the artist is to reproduce the appearance of the real world, though artists differ widely on how they define and create that world. Though a myriad of artists claim to be reproducing reality, we nonetheless find in their work a variety of styles and approaches.

Creating Likeness in Different Styles

There may be as many styles of art as there are artists. After all, we are told that no two thumbprints are exactly alike. Such an approach to an introductory study of the visual arts, however, could never establish broad enough categories to explain major developments or to recognize what different styles or "schools" of art are attempting to do. General principles or characteristics that identify a number of artists as belonging to a school or style are valuable tools of learning, even though any given artist can be an exception to the very rules that make such a thing as art history possible.

Even when the ultimate aim is to create something that looks very much like the real thing, artists can greatly differ in the kind of likeness transferred from the external world to a medium, especially if they are widely separated in time or come from very different cultures. The head of a man sculpted in marble by an Athenian artist of the fifth century B.C.E. might in no way resemble the head of a man molded in clay by a contemporary artist living in Fiji. But we would be able to recognize that both artists were creating the likeness of a man. The key is the word "likeness" itself and the myriad ways in which its meaning is understood.

Artwork in earlier civilizations was both decorative and imitative of the real world. Statues of the Egyptian pharaohs were intended to reproduce their appearance as a way of making them immortal. The decorative scrollwork on Greek columns sprang from the artist's imagination and was thus another form of imitation. In London's Westminster Abbey, the tops of stone sepulchers have faithful renderings of the persons entombed below, but the stained-glass windows of the abbey can also be considered art, even though they do not imitate the external world.

Without attempting to comprehend the intricacies of art history, we can, however, begin with the broad generalization that for thousands of years, beginning with the earliest known artistic products (such as cave drawings), a major purpose of art was *indeed* to transfer the real world to a given medium. In this section we investigate Art as Likeness, looking at major achievements and styles in its long history. We shall then be prepared to understand when and why artists began to consider other possibilities of artistic expression.

Art is essentially the affirmation, the blessing, and the deification of existence.

—**Friedrich Nietzsche**

Classical Art

Early in the history of Art as Likeness is the **classicism** of Greece and Rome. But first, let us look again at the term "classic," as defined in Chapter 4, and then consider *classicism* as the style of a specific era in the history of the humanities.

A classic is a work of literature, drama, film, or song that continues to be read, performed, seen, or sung long after its creation. Critics will sometimes become so enthusiastic about a new work that they label it an "instant classic." The implication is usually that the work will endure, will still be relevant many years from now. Of course, when that label is given to a recent work, no one can really know how long it will survive. Generally it is safer, before applying the label "classic," to glance backward and make sure that a given work has indeed outlived its time. The irony is that the creators of acknowledged classics seldom knew their works would live on. History is also filled with would-be artists who were confident they had created a "classic," only to have their work forgotten.

In Western civilization the phrase "classical music" refers primarily to works composed in the West from the middle of the seventeenth to near the end of the eighteenth century. Sometimes the phrase is loosely, if confusingly, applied to *all* concert music composed before the twentieth century, or even more confusingly, to any music heard in concert halls as opposed to that heard on pop radio stations. Chapter 6 discusses classical music in the primary sense of the term. It is associated with the musical style of composers like Haydn and the early Mozart.

In the visual arts, classical refers to a historical period when a culture's distinct artistic styles and media first flowered. Because cultures evolve on their own timelines, their classical periods date to different historical eras. Classical Islamic art, for example, generally dates from the time of the prophet Mohammed (570–612 C.E.) through the eleventh century. It is highly abstract and geometrical in nature, imitative not of the familiar world but of the artist's vision of the spiritual world. Art was used primarily to decorate tapestries, rugs, holy buildings, and the residences of high-ranking persons.

Classical art of India roughly spans the sixth through second centuries B.C.E. Some of it is, like Islamic art, abstract, but much Indian art is amazingly lifelike. Sculptures of nude males show painstaking effort to duplicate in stone the soft textures and muscles of the human body.

Classical Chinese art dates from around 500 B.C.E. to the fall of the Han empire in 220 C.E. Ancient pottery displays lifelike figures of men and animals, similar to those in the cave drawings, suggesting the central importance of the successful hunt. There are also many fantastic masks meant to depict the faces of gods, who of course could not resemble human beings.

Ancient Japanese art has the oldest history, for there is evidence of human settlements in Japan 30,000 years ago. Pottery and household utensils unearthed by archeologists cannot be precisely dated but are assumed to be older than almost any other comparable artifacts. Findings suggest that ceramic art was highly advanced, combining form and function. Jugs and plates served not only for practical household needs but for aesthetic pleasure as well. They tend to have unusual shapes and are often elaborately decorated with abstract designs, indicative of a style of living that required the beautiful as well as the useful.

In Western culture, classical art means the sculpture, wall carvings, **frescoes** (wall paintings), mosaics, and architecture of Greece and Rome. It spans the sixth century B.C.E. through the fifth century C.E. Although the statues and buildings of many tourist-visited ruins are white or gray, the popular image of this art is of stone shapes that lack color. In fact, classical artists were fond of color and had methods for making paints, which have, unfortunately, faded over the centuries. Most of the gleaming white columns found on the Acropolis of Athens, for example, were originally painted in bright colors.

Stone and marble were abundant in this classical world, and artists made generous use of these media. The artists responsible for decorating the city of Athens in the fifth century B.C.E. liked to work in marble, but they left it for the most part in an unpolished state. The Romans, who incorporated Athens into their empire in 146 B.C.E., were intent on rivaling or, if possible, eclipsing that city's monumental achievements in art. Hence Roman sculptors vigorously polished their marble, establishing the process that has been followed ever since.

Much Greek art, including the Parthenon, has been attributed to Phidias, a painter, sculptor, and architect greatly admired during the fifth century. The ruler Pericles hired Phidias as superintendent of public works, commissioning him to create monumental buildings and works of art that would glorify Athens, ensure its immortality, and remind the world that the Athenians were descendants of the gods.

This statue of Poseidon, god of the sea, shows a deity as the perfection of a human being.

Source: Poseidon of Artemision. Credit: Foto Marburg/Art Resource, NY.

Classical Athenian buildings were designed and constructed with mathematical precision, in keeping with the Greek love of numerical and geometric harmony. The statues were mainly depictions of gods and goddesses cast in human forms. They were likenesses of noble, heroic beings, larger than life and thus not direct likenesses of particular human beings. In this sense they represented the perfection of *humanness*, which the artists apparently considered the appropriate way to imitate the appearance of the divine. By depicting their deities as human beings, the artists were also elevating humanity to a godlike level.

Most of the statuary art survives in fragments: torsos, arms, legs, and heads. The faces share a generic look; almost all wear a smile of inner satisfaction. There are probably two reasons for this sameness of expression. One is that divine beings were expected to be happy. The other is that the Athenians, in seeking to tie themselves to the gods, believed that the goal of life was to achieve physical and moral perfection, which entitled them to wear a smile of contentment.

The best preserved of all the statues from the fifth century is *The Charioteer*. Cast in bronze, it shows that classical Greek artists could also imitate real people. The likeness is that of a young man, a chariot driver, who was certainly not a god. Yet his features are without flaw. His face is noble. He could well be a god, even as the Poseidon of Artemision could well be a perfect human.

The idealization is of course deliberate, but by studying this work, we can tell that *The Charioteer* is the work of a sculptor who knew anatomy. The veins of the young man's right arm (the left is missing) as well as his feet are rendered with painstaking fidelity to life, and the folds of his garment are so believable that they suggest the genius of Renaissance artists.

Beginning in the fourth century B.C.E. there was a movement in Greek art toward greater realism and less idealization. Whereas the chariot driver is an ordinary mortal with the appearance of a god, many of the new period's statues depict gods with the more defining features of mortals. There is less geometry and more genuine likeness, suggesting that actual models may have been used. By the third century, classicism gave way to even more ambitious attempts at realism.

The new artists chose subjects that were far less serene than those of their predecessors, more dynamic, with strong appeal to the passions. They often captured moments of sensuality and the agony of death throes for a new kind of public, one that demanded excitement from art. The *Laocoön* is a first-century sculpture, depicting in graphic detail the anguish of a father and his two sons as they are being strangled by sea serpents. The figures are not idealized, unless we were to say that their agony represents the "perfection" of pain! The Romans would imitate the quieter classicism of the fifth century, but they were also heavily influenced by the vivid realism of the later periods.

Greek and Roman art, however, leaves the general impression of a civilization that valued balance and harmony, and for many people "classicism" will continue to mean *that which reflects the love of order*. In fact, the classical music that emerged in the seventeenth century was linked to a revival of interest in that aspect of the classical world demonstrating such order.

This best preserved of all fifth-century Athenian statues shows us that classical artists knew how to imitate real people.

Source: The Charioteer. Credit: Nimatallah/Art Resource, NY.

Man is the measure of all things.

—**Protagoras**

The statue of the *Laocoön*, a father and his sons battling serpents, is a fine example of late classical art. Note that the serene formalism of the earlier period is gone.

Source: Nimatallah/Art Resource, NY.

The classical world is typified by the Parthenon, built as a temple for the goddess Athena. But it also represents the Athenians' passion for the ordered world of mathematics. The floor of the Parthenon was for a long time believed to embody a particular formula discovered and expressed mathematically by Euclid (c. 300 B.C.E.), one of the early founders of geometry. Legend has it that Euclid was fond of handing friends a stick and asking them to indicate where they would divide it that was aesthetically satisfying to them. He found that nearly everybody divided the stick in about the same place, which was not the center. So he began to measure the ratio between the two sections and discovered that it tended to be 1 to 1.68. Expressed verbally, Euclid's law states that the most pleasing relationship between two connecting sections is such that the smaller is to the larger what the larger is to the sum of the two. Euclid called it the law of the **Golden Section**. Fascinated by the theory, mathematicians and art historians have sought—and claim to have found—the Golden Section in a variety of places, including, in addition to the floor of the Parthenon, the foundations of many Roman ruins, the floor plan of medieval cathedrals, the pages of medieval illuminated manuscripts, and in much Renaissance art and architecture. There is some doubt that the exact Euclidean ratio exists in all the places claimed for it, but researchers say many come astoundingly close.

The ratio of the Golden Section, found all over the world, is 1 to 1.68. No one knows how it originated beyond the fact that Euclid was fond of asking people to divide a stick at the most pleasing point and the relationship of the two divisions was often 1 to 1.68.

The floor of this great symbol of Athenian glory seems to exemplify the Golden Section: a ratio of 1 to 1.68 between the shorter and longer sides.

Source: The Parthenon. Credit: Bettmann/Corbis.

Medieval Art

Christianity, which dominated Western civilization from the fifth to the fifteenth centuries, turned its back on what it considered the pagan world of classical art. Visual art mainly had one purpose: to remind the faithful of the life and death of Jesus, Mary, the saints, and the disciples. Artists who were selected by the church devoted their talents to the sacred adornment of church interiors. With a limited number of available paints (often made from the juice of berries), they created art on wood, in stained glass, and on church walls. Sculptors made marble statues of saints and members of the Holy Family. Like the Greeks and Romans centuries before them, medieval artists imagined spiritual beings in human terms, though their work is not completely lifelike. Medieval art generally presents the *idea*, not a faithful imitation, of its subjects. Some of it, however, such as the famous Bayeux tapestry of the eleventh century, does indeed indicate that, when dealing with earthbound subjects, medieval artists attempted to be realistic.

Nearly all of the professional art was done by males. One exception was the art of embroidery, which flourished in both France and England during the period. The Bayeux tapestry is not really a tapestry at all but a series of panels embroidered in colored yarn on a linen background. It stretches 203 feet and tells the story of the Battle of Hastings in 1066, in which Normans under William the Conqueror defeated the Saxon army of King Harold. The tapestry is believed to have been commissioned by William's half-brother and was once attributed to Queen

A panel from the 1886 English replica of the medieval Bayeux tapestry, an example of medieval art made by women.

Source: Nick Wheeler, Corbis.

Portrait of the Madonna, once attributed to St. Luke, but probably painted during the twelfth century. Note how mature the child looks.

Source: Alinari/Art Resource, NY.

Matilda, William's wife. But it was more likely made years later by English embroiderers.

In the twelfth-century painting of the Madonna reproduced here, the artist has made an effort to duplicate the look of a real woman, but the nose is improbably extended, and there is a definite masculinity about the face. The face of the baby Jesus in no way suggests that of an actual infant. It belongs to an adolescent, as it does in nearly all such paintings. Medieval artists thought of the infant Jesus as being already wise. We see the *idea* of the divine child, not the appearance of a real-life baby.

Classicism was, however, by no means completely dormant during the Middle Ages. Medieval cathedrals, generally built during the eleventh and twelfth centuries, utilized classical principles of mathematical order. They were, of course, strongly reflective of the Christian religion, and their floor plan—a central aisle called the *nave* and a smaller chapel on each side—was shaped like the cross. They are considered the finest examples of the **Gothic** style. A sixteenth-century Italian art historian named the style after the "barbarian" Goths, the Teutonic invaders who had conquered Rome. The label was meant to connote a barbaric departure from classicism, perhaps because of the demonic looking gargoyles, statues of ugly, evil monsters designed to frighten away malevolent spirits. But there was nothing barbaric about the plan of construction. With their soaring towers reaching up to heaven and their stone buttresses, the cathedrals were so finely engineered that no mortar was originally used to attach the stones to each other.

Entrance to the cathedral of Notre Dame in Paris, constructed beginning in the twelfth century. If you look carefully, you can see the gargoyles squatting on the ledge beneath the two towers.

Source: David Sailors/Corbis.

Giotto

The work of a thirteenth-century Florentine artist, Giotto di Bondone (1266/67 –1337), introduced revolutionary new techniques and prepared the way for the greater artistic realism of the Renaissance. Along with a number of colleagues, Giotto sought to bring new life to what had become the workmanlike craft of decorating church interiors.

St. Francis of Assisi had been canonized in 1228, just two years after his death, and even though he had taken a vow of poverty and urged his followers to divest themselves of worldly possessions, the decision was made to honor him by erecting a great church. For a number of years after its completion, it lacked interior decorations, but finally Giotto and his assistants were commissioned to do a series of wall paintings depicting incidents in the life of the saint.

As did many Greek and Roman artists, Giotto experimented with *fresco,* an art that would not be perfected until a century after his death. Art scholar William Fleming explains the nature of the art:

> *The artist must first make his drawing on the dry plaster of the wall. Then, taking an area he can finish in a single day, he spreads a thin coat of wet plaster over the dry, making it necessary to retrace the lines underneath. Earth pigments are then mixed with water, combined with white of egg as a binder, and applied directly to the fresh plaster—hence the term* fresco. *The pigments and wet plaster combine chemically to produce a surface as permanent as that of any medium in painting.*[2]

Artists of the Renaissance, influenced by Giotto, experimented with an imitation of how the eye actually sees.

Fresco illustrating the later style of Giotto, when he had begun to master the art of perspective.

Source: Cappella Bardi, S. Croce, Florence, Italy. Credit: Scala/Art Resource, NY.

The fresco *Death of St. Francis* (c. 1320), reproduced here, was not part of the St. Francis cycle painted for the church in Assisi, but is possibly by young artists influenced by the master. This fresco can be found in the cathedral of Santa Croce in Florence and bears the unmistakable mark of Giotto's later style, which had evolved from earlier, more naive attempts at realism. In this work we see a greater mastery of **perspective**, a technique that was just beginning to emerge, with Giotto leading the way.

Artists of the early Italian **Renaissance** were beginning to experiment with efforts to transfer to their medium an imitation of how the eye actually sees. They recognized that if art were to attain true likeness, it would have to seem three-dimensional. Perspective in art is now taken for granted, and viewers new to the work of Giotto may fail to appreciate how revolutionary this technique was. If you look back at the painting of the medieval Madonna, you will note that the infant Jesus, besides having an improbably mature face, is also much larger than we would expect. Perspective is the art of varying the size of figures and objects to approximate how we see. The priests on either side of the saint's bier in the Giotto fresco are larger than the figures standing behind it. The brain then supplies the knowledge that the room has depth.

As a medieval artist, Giotto was still interested in the religious ideas embodied in his work, but as an artist of the emerging Renaissance, he was also interested in fidelity to real life.

Renaissance Art

The *Renaissance*, meaning "rebirth," began in Italy as early as the fourteenth century, then spread throughout western Europe, finally reaching the British Isles late in the sixteenth century. At first an art movement, it led to a political and social revolution against the tight controls of religion. It deemphasized the next world as the sole concern of human beings and began to focus on leading the good life in *this* world. It reinstated science as a legitimate source of knowledge and held a greater respect for individual achievement. In the humanities, the term *renaissance* signifies a renewed interest in the knowledge and art of the classical world—in part because that world had been ignored for so many centuries, but also because classical artists and thinkers were concerned with making sense of and bringing beauty to the only life they believed they were given to live. Renaissance artists combined classical discipline with something new: the demand for freedom of individual expression. The Renaissance constitutes the greatest single revolution in the history of Western art and thought, though centuries earlier the Arab world had kept alive the teachings of Greek philosophy, especially those of Aristotle, with his desire to analyze the human condition and his anticipation of the scientific method.

At first the artistic revolution was a quiet one: artists experimenting with more lifelike representations of the human form. As the years went by, however, the revolutionary fires grew more intense. Artists began to react boldly against religious traditionalism and demand the right to practice their craft without constraints and fear of censorship.

Fillippo Lippi (1406?–1469) typifies the Renaissance spirit. Forced into monastic orders at the age of eight, he had a hard time suppressing his desire to escape from the confines of his cell. Finally he lost the battle and begin to sneak out at night, roaming the countryside, drawing people and objects that caught his eye.

A forerunner of the great Italian Renaissance artists of the sixteenth century, Lippi (better known as Fra Lippo Lippi) was recognized for his genius at a very young age and commissioned to paint biblical scenes in the chapel. So astonishingly real were his figures that he was accused of using forbidden human models. There were even rumors that he hired prostitutes to pose for his depiction of the Virgin Mary.

Of particular interest to the artists of the Italian Renaissance was that in classicism the human body was often depicted in the nude—something prohibited by the church. True, the nude human form as displayed in ancient times had customarily been geometrically perfect and thus not truly lifelike, but classical art set in motion the interest of the new artists in realistic anatomy.

One theory of the near-perfect classicism of Michelangelo's *David* is that the young artist had only classical statues to work from and knew little about the actual human body. *David* is a work in the purely classical style, depicting a human being in heroic, godlike terms, physically perfect in every respect. A widespread belief is that there must have been a model for the sculpture, but even if the suspicion is well founded, Michelangelo still idealized his model in classical style. Eventually, however, he and many of his colleagues *would* work directly and realistically from models, causing considerable scandal among the clergy and political conservatives.

(a) A Dionysian David, showing the Renaissance desire to create lifelike, individualized works of art. (b) By contrast, the Apollonian David of the young Michelangelo is a classical idealization of the human body.

Source: (Right and left) Alinari/Art Resource, NY.

The new art had two dominant characteristics. First, continuing in Giotto's tradition, it tried to make the eye of the viewer see things and people as they appeared in real life, continuing to use perspective to achieve the illusion of three dimensions. Second, it invited an *emotional response* from the viewer. Compare the *David* of Michelangelo, which is the epitome of the Apollonian in art, to the *David* of Italian Renaissance artist Donatello (1386?–1466), which depicts, in Dionysian style, a young man who is surely not idealized, a young man who typifies the respect for individualism and personal differences that would be fundamental in the Renaissance. The sensuality of Donatello, who died a century before Michelangelo, anticipates a new emotional style that is a long way from suggesting classical repose. Yet despite the classicism of Michelangelo's *David*, the Florentines did, after all, react emotionally to it. It is Renaissance in subject if not in form. The subject—the boy about to take on the giant Goliath—was not only biblical but also contemporary and political. The townspeople saw David as a symbol of relatively tiny Florence challenging mightier Italian cities such as Venice or Rome for supremacy in religion, art, and urban sophistication, and perhaps challenging the Vatican itself in the name of individual freedom.

The obsession of Renaissance artists with imitating life as precisely as possible owes something to the general spirit of the age. The new realism, with its charged emotions, its sense of the dramatic, and its introduction of new ways of seeing and imitating life, brought together an astonishing array of great artists, most of them located in or near Florence. Many of these artists have achieved places of honor in the history of the humanities, but Leonardo, Michelangelo, and Raphael were accorded almost instant immortality. Each is generally referred to by his first name only, an honor bestowed on them in their lifetime and retained ever since.

Leonardo

The oldest of the three, Leonardo, came to Florence from the nearby town of Vinci. He excelled in so many fields—as a painter, sculptor, architect, inventor, and at least *conceiver* of such astounding marvels as the submarine and the airplane—that he richly deserves the label "Renaissance man," which is an integral part of the human vocabulary, still used as a reference to those who achieve excellence in many fields of study, such as Einstein, who was not only the greatest scientist of the twentieth century but a writer and accomplished violinist as well.

At least two of Leonardo's works stand out as definitive examples of their respective genres: the mural *The Last Supper* (Color Plate 6), and the portrait *Mona Lisa* (Color Plate 1). Commissioned in 1494 as a sacred fresco for the refectory (dining hall) of Santa Maria del Grazie in Milan, *The Last Supper*, which shows the final gathering of Jesus and his twelve disciples before his arrest and crucifixion, took three years to complete. *The Last Supper* is celebrated for a number of reasons. First, it is a triumph of perspective. Designed to occupy the entire far wall of the dining room, the mural presents to the astonished spectator the illusion that the room actually extends into the painting, continuing on into the natural world glimpsed through the windows behind Jesus and the disciples.

Second, Leonardo introduced a technique known as **chiaroscuro**, in which the contrast between light and shadow deepens the imitation of how people and things

Iron rusts from disuse; stagnant water loses its purity and in cold weather becomes frozen; even so does inaction sap the vigor of the mind.

—Leonardo

look to us in the real world. The technique of blending light and shadow was quickly copied by other artists, but except for Rembrandt, the great seventeenth-century Dutch master, Leonardo's handling of the technique has not been equaled or surpassed. The artist wanted his two-dimensional canvases to come closer to representing how the eye actually sees. Perspective contributed to the illusion of reality, but the interplay of dark and light was necessary for a totally authentic experience of vision. The chiaroscuro effect in *The Last Supper* is among the most dramatic ever captured by an artist, for the shadows in the foreground are in striking contrast to the light coming from the windows, perhaps suggesting the difference between the human world of betrayal and sorrow and a heavenly world of eternal peace.

Third, the mural is a notable example of Leonardo's genius for capturing the endless complexity of human beings, reproducing not just physical but *psychological* likeness. Jesus has just said: "One of you which eateth with me shall betray me" (Mark: 14:18). While he remains the calm center of the group, his pronouncement creates an emotional storm among the others. Most of the disciples are desperate to know if they are the betrayer. Most of the faces show also elements of anger—that one of them might commit so hideous a crime—and fear—that any one of them might be guilty. Only one knows that the betrayal has already taken place.

Does the painting show which one is Judas, the betrayer? Look carefully. From the viewer's perspective, Judas is third to the left of Jesus, his arm leaning on the table, and he appears to be holding the bag of coins he has received for pointing Jesus out to the Romans. The magic of Leonardo is nowhere better illustrated than in the fact that we do not need to see the bag to identify Judas. He is not looking directly toward Jesus.

The figure to the immediate left became the center of a huge controversy ever since the 2002 publication of Dan Brown's bestseller *The Da Vinci Code*, in which the suggestion is made (actually it is stated as a fact) that this person is Mary Magdalene, the only female disciple. In any case, this person is also not looking at Jesus, but the difference is that this person is in deep sorrow.

Leonardo is like a stage director. By his placement of the characters and the direction of their eyes, he controls the manner in which the viewer watches the scene. And *watch* is a more appropriate word than *see*, because though a painting is a static object, depicting a moment frozen in time, *The Last Supper* unfolds as a drama being witnessed on a stage. It overcomes the limitation of having no real movement or sound. Also in the style of the stage director, Leonardo lights the scene, using the chiaroscuro effect to highlight the unspoken drama transpiring between Jesus and Judas.

Leonardo's complex faces, especially that of Jesus, are the parallel in visual art to what the modern theater calls *subtext*, a technique whereby the playwright lets the audience know what is happening below the surface by having a character remain silent or else speak a very few words. Great performers on the stage can provoke thoughts and pique the curiosity by a slight glance or by the silences that precede or follow their words. Similarly, a great artist like Leonardo is able somehow to show what is happening inside a subject. Leonardo is almost without peer in the ability to

Archetypes in This Chapter	
Judas	has become a generic term for "betrayer," especially among close acquaintances when one suspects that the other has betrayed a confidence.
Medieval	adjective for someone or something that is out of date, such as a person with old-fashioned views or a regulation considered outmoded.
Renaissance man	a person of extraordinary accomplishments in many fields, such as Leonardo da Vinci or Albert Einstein.
Starving artist	stereotype of an artist who lives in a garret, with little money or food, but willing to give up everything for art.
Surreal	adjective for a person, object, or event that seems too weird to be part of the familiar world.

Leonardo is also master of subtext, a way of showing what may be happening behind a human face, though just what it is can be debated.

capture emotional complexity behind a face that shows little of it. In Christ's face we can read sorrow, because he knows who the betrayer is and knows that the deed cannot be undone. There is resignation to his imminent death on the cross. And, astonishingly, we see understanding and forgiveness too.

Through both the placement of his figures—Judas and Jesus, for example—and his ability to suggest the inner life, Leonardo greatly influenced the development of dramatic art. Max Reinhardt, one of the great theater directors of the last century, counseled his students and apprentices to study Leonardo if they wanted to learn how best to stage a scene. Stanislavsky, who founded the modern school of truthful acting, was known to have spent many hours in his classes analyzing the dramatic qualities in works like *The Last Supper*.

To better appreciate Leonardo's use of subtext in painting, compare the face of Christ in his version of the Last Supper with that in a modern version (1927) by Gustave van der Woestyne (Color Plate 7). The latter painting, while striking, uses the well-known scene for the purpose of demonstrating a bold new technique. The artist does not attempt to improve upon Leonardo's subtlety. Rather, he appears to want to shock the viewer with strongly outlined faces of both Christ and the disciples that belong to the world of modern art, not that of Renaissance realism. He offers far less subtext for the viewer to ponder. There are probably good reasons for the difference. One is that the modern artist needs to recreate the occasion in his own style. Another is that the artist obviously believes that a real Christ would not have been able to conceal the knowledge of the painful death he was about to endure. Van der Woestyne's *Last Supper* is in keeping with the modern tendency to depict Christ as a human being tragically betrayed.

Leonardo also goes far beyond surface realism in another masterpiece, the *Mona Lisa* (1503–1505). The work has become the most famous single work of art in the world, still attracting huge numbers of visitors each day to the Louvre Museum in Paris (Color Plate 1).

What is all the fuss about? How do we account for the extraordinary stature of this relatively small canvas in the world of the humanities? A reason, of course, may be that widely discussed mysterious smile. One does not find many complexities in portrait paintings, because artists customarily are hired to render both a realistic likeness *and* an idealization in the classical mode. Her famous, and still mysterious, smile particularizes Mona Lisa Gioconda, whom Leonardo was commissioned to paint. She is not only idealized in the traditional manner of portraiture, but she is also an individual woman captured in a particular inner action at a particular time.

A close look at the painting, however, reveals that the mouth is shown with only the faintest trace of a smile. Just as interesting is the fact that Signora Gioconda is looking at something not shown in the painting—just *what* we can never know. But this adds to the mystery.

The following experiment, suggested by one art critic, can be performed right at this moment. Cover the left side of Mona Lisa's face, using your hand or an index card. Presumably you will see a warm, sensuous woman, gazing provocatively—at *you*! Now cover the right side, and presumably you will see an aristocrat who finds something (not you, of course) mildly amusing. Many have said that Leonardo in this work has revealed the essential ambiguity of all human faces and personalities. If we agree, then we could say that the *Mona Lisa* accomplishes a goal many artists rarely achieve: its creator has both particularized and generalized his subject. What should stand out in our mind, however, is that the portrait is a supreme example of the Renaissance movement toward individualism, an organic part of the rebellion against the medieval emphasis on the oneness of all people in the eyes of heaven and the promise of everlasting life in the hereafter rather than on the rich diversity of life in this world.

Michelangelo

What Shakespeare is to theater and Beethoven is to music, Michelangelo is to sculpture. Before he came upon the scene, sculpture was thought to be a skill at best, ordinary decoration at its least. Michelangelo helped to change the reputation of sculpture, making it an art form of the highest order. He did it through an effort of will and physical strength that is almost unimaginable.

As a youth, Michelangelo learned from masters of the classical style, but the artist soon realized he wanted more than what they were teaching. He wanted to create figures that were totally his, that bore his unmistakable mark. In fact, he was so confident that no one would confuse his style with another artist's that he signed his name to a work only once—and that was the *Pietà* in St. Peter's at the Vatican, created when he was just twenty-two and perhaps somewhat less self-assured than he would become in a short time.

No one has mastery before he is at the end of his art and his life.

—**Michelangelo**

(a) In contrast to his later work, this sculpture by Michelangelo has an uplifting serenity about it: clearly the work of a youthful genius who has not yet experienced the pain of living. (b) A very different version by Michelangelo of the *Pietà*.

Source: Left: Michelangelo, *Pietà*. Credit: Scala/Art Resource, NY. Right: Castello Sforesco, Milan, Italy. Credit: Scala/Art Resource, NY.

As Michelangelo matured, his work shows a tension between classicism and the expression of passion. The Vatican *Pietà*, however, viewed by the thousands who daily visit St. Peter's, shows the crucified son, lying across the lap of his grieving mother. Since its creator had come so recently from the studio where he first learned his craft, a craft that was essentially classical, the sculpture, as we should expect, contains more of the *idea* of pain than the *essence* of it. There is a serenity about the work that is uplifting indeed, but a little removed from an effort to capture in marble a most extreme human emotion.

In contrast is the *Pietà Rondanini*, created when the artist was in his eighties. The sculptor attempted to destroy the work before anyone could see it, so convinced was he that it was unworthy of his most severe critic, whom he believed to be God. Presumably it was originally intended for his own tomb, but now we are left with only fragments. Most clearly seen is the face of Mary, on which Michelangelo indelibly chiseled the pain missing in the youthful work. This is intensely personal art, a personal statement by a genius who is not happy with what he has done, a genius who has felt the sorrow unknown to most human beings: the sorrow of having not quite ascended to the very highest level possible for a mortal. Of course, the judgment of the ages has been that Michelangelo did indeed attain this level, but he never enjoyed the knowledge of what he had achieved. A story repeated over and over in the humanities!

Michelangelo's restless, unceasing quest for perfection helps explain why he was not content to stay only with the art of sculpture. He also aspired to be the greatest painter the world had ever known. His biggest challenge—even greater than that of the seventeen-foot block of marble that became *David*—was a task given him by Pope Julius II: to paint the ceiling of the Sistine Chapel inside the Vatican. Michelangelo's imagination was immediately stirred. There was the height itself, as close to heaven as his art was ever likely to take him. There was the huge expanse of the ceiling, allowing for a series of paintings on religious themes that would at the same time present to the viewer a totally unified effect. And there was the challenge that fresco posed, for the plaster had to be applied to the ceiling and painted before it was completely dry. Legend has it that the artist worked almost single-handedly for four long years, lying on his back for hours at a time while plaster continually dripped down on his face. But Michelangelo was both passionate and businesslike in his work. He had assistants, and the project was carefully planned—and kept secret even from the pope until the gasp-filled unveiling. Never for a moment did the artist fear that the pontiff would be disappointed, but Michelangelo may still have harbored the gnawing belief that God was not satisfied.

That Michelangelo not only sought perfection but did so in such challenging media as marble and fresco tells us why he has come to symbolize the Renaissance itself. The unending—and apparently unsatisfied—quest for greatness is surely a sign of an enormous human ego, quite consistent with the period's stress on individualism and human achievement. At the same time, to offer up that ego in the service of God was to renounce the self and worldly fame.

Sometimes losing the struggle against ego added further to his anguish. He was adored by a huge public. Prospective patrons offered incredible sums for his services. How could he not have felt a measure of pride when he saw on all sides confirmation of his greatness? His letters reveal someone who was always at odds with himself, always fighting to suppress his ego. On the other hand, some critics have suggested that to believe God was the only audience suitable for one's work constitutes arrogance of cosmic scope.

His style—sometimes referred to by the word *terribilità*, which means "awfulness" in its fundamental sense of "awesomeness"—reflects the need to challenge the medium in the way that the matador challenges the bull. But Michelangelo cannot be the only artist whose creative process was inspired by the difficulty of the medium. All artists—to *be* artists—have overcome obstacles that would stop most of us in our tracks. The medium cannot surrender willingly; otherwise it is not worth conquering. Referring to the permissiveness in modern poetry and modern theater, where great liberties are allowed in language and structure, one critic has made the telling observation: *Where everything is possible, nothing matters.*

Yet great art must hide the effort that goes into it. Try never to sit in the front row at a ballet. You should not hear the heavy breathing or see the drops of perspiration falling to the stage. Likewise, the blank screen on the computer dares the would-be writer to find just the right words in the right order. And ivory keys coldly reflect overhead stage lights—so still, and offering no help at all to the pianist. Still, we have to know that the passionate striving is there, underneath it all. We've said it before, but it bears repeating: *Art is the illusion that there is no art.*

Raphael

The youngest of the three great artists of the Florentine Renaissance, Raphael died only a year after Leonardo and nearly half a century before Michelangelo. This fact is important to remember, for when we consider how much Raphael achieved in a relatively short lifespan, we can only speculate on what he might have done had he lived longer. Raphael had the advantage of observing the techniques of his two predecessors, and his work clearly shows their influence. Moving to Florence in 1504, when both artists were already being celebrated, he observed Leonardo's characteristic interplay of light and shadow, a technique he borrowed for the *Alba Madonna* of 1510.

The painting illustrates how far the techniques of realism and perspective had progressed from the time of Giotto. The hills in the distance, painted near the top, are much smaller than the figures of the infant Jesus and his playmate. Moreover, the Virgin Mary looks like a real woman, while the playmates look reasonably as children should. The divine nature of mother and child is suggested by the adoring, almost worshipful look on the face of the other child; otherwise this could be a moment in real life.

The chiaroscuro effect comes from the light Raphael gives to his sky and from the dark interior of the cloak from which the Virgin Mary's arm extends, as well as her right sleeve. The background also shows a contrast between light and shadow, and there is shade in the very foreground, suggesting that the figures may be near a tree.

In 1508 Raphael, already famous, had been called to Rome by Pope Julius II, who commissioned him to paint four frescoes for the Vatican Palace, illustrating theology, philosophy, poetry, and justice. The most famous of these is the fresco celebrating philosophy, *The School of Athens* (Color Plate 9). In the painting we see, again, a highly sophisticated use of perspective, with the many, many figures all painted in accurate proportion relative to the two arches in the background and the two statues that tower over the participants. In addition, each figure is painstakingly detailed, despite the fact that, in order to recreate so large a scene, the artist had to paint with extremely minute strokes on the wet plaster.

The work of Raphael and the other great artists of the Italian Renaissance has made Florence and Rome places in which millions, through the magic of the Internet, can observe the humanities coming to vibrant life. These cities provide a good introduction to Internet art tours, and from there you can visit the scores of other

I know an artist who spent a dreadful morning comparing himself to Raphael.
—**Bertrand Russell**

In contrast to the medieval Madonna on page 126, this Virgin Mary looks more like a real woman and the children more lifelike.

Source: Raphael, *The Alba Madonna,* © 1999 Board of Trustees, National Gallery of Art, Washington DC.

magnificent locations in which yesterday is hard to distinguish from today. Eventually you will want to see the originals up close. Life offers few comparable experiences.

Two Women of the Post-Renaissance

Overlooked in art histories for centuries, the works of Sophonisba Anguissola and Artimisia Gentileschi are now being recognized, not just because they were done by women, but because of their brilliance.

Until relatively modern times—say, the last hundred years—women were largely excluded from artistic production by the societies in which they lived. Unfortunately, this was true during both the Renaissance and the *post-Renaissance*, a term sometimes used to describe the art of the late sixteenth century. A few women, however, defied the conventions of their time and managed to produce great art. Two of the most renowned of these women are Sophonisba Anguissola and Artemisia Gentileschi.

Sophonisba Anguissola (c. 1532–1626) and her five sisters were all trained artists, but she was the first female to achieve an international reputation for her art. So precocious was her talent for realistic portraiture that the great Michelangelo agreed to teach her and later expressed admiration for her work.

Georgio Vasari, the first major critic and art historian of the Italian Renaissance, author of the male-oriented *Lives of the Artists*, credited Anguissola with having produced "rare and beautiful" work and placed her above all other female artists. This tells us that she not only held her own in a field dominated by men but that she was probably one of many women who practiced the art of painting.

Several generations younger was Artemisia Gentileschi (1592–1652), whose reputation has eclipsed Anguissola's. Art historians now consider her the most important female artist of the post-Renaissance. She was quite prolific, though only thirty-four of her works have survived. In her time, however, she was scorned by both critics and male colleagues as too aggressive—that is, "unfeminine"—in promoting her work. As a youth she showed as much promise as Anguissola had shown years earlier, but she was denied the chance to study with an established painter.

Scorn for her spread to the public sector when she was involved in a sex scandal that became the topic of gossip in Florence. She accused a fellow artist, Agostino Tassi, of raping her and demanded that he be arrested and brought to justice. The trial lasted seven months, during which several of Tassi's male friends testified that she was generally known as promiscuous. Another witness saved the day by testifying that Tassi had, in his presence, openly boasted of the rape. Her reputation somewhat restored (though still a bit tarnished from all the negative publicity), Gentileschi nonetheless persevered. Feminists and art historians have debated the effect of the trial on her paintings, citing in particular their frequently violent themes. One of her most acclaimed works, *Judith Slaying Holofernes* (Color Plate 10), depicts the biblical heroine Judith, who seduced the Assyrian general Holofernes, then beheaded him with his own sword in order to protect her community from invasion.

Rembrandt: The Perfection of Likeness

From Leonardo on, the demand for portraiture increased in Europe. As years passed, rich and powerful households began to decorate their halls with the watchful eyes of departed ancestors. Perfect likenesses, which might also doctor up an unattractive wrinkle here or a weak chin there, brought newfound riches to artists who could master the skill of faithful—or nearly so—imitation.

The master painters of the **Dutch school** of the seventeenth century were able to reproduce faces, figures, and landscapes with the greatest accuracy possible until the invention of photography two centuries later. In fact, many casual and infrequent visitors to museums still respond most favorably to their work, because of its startling realism. A Dutch **still life**—such as apples, pears, a loaf of bread, and a bottle of wine on a table—can look so real you might imagine all you had to do was reach inside the frame for food and drink.

Of all the Dutch masters, none surpassed Rembrandt Harmenszoon van Rijn (1606–1669) in either quality or quantity of work. Like the great Italian masters, history has accorded Rembrandt the honor of being known by his first name. In a lifetime much shorter than that of Michelangelo, he was able to produce so many works of art that a precise count has yet to be made. While he can be said to have mastered the art of perfect likenesses, he was also, like Leonardo, interested in what we may call **psychological realism**. Like many artists, Rembrandt often worked on commission, but he almost always looked for the challenge in his subject: the character behind the face, the pain suffered (even if he didn't know the cause), the longing for something else that might have compensated for a disappointing life. He was fond of

Art does not reproduce the visible; rather, it makes visible.

—**Paul Klee**

Rembrandt's many self-portraits give us an autobiography without words.

Source: Rembrandt van Rijn, *Self Portrait*, © 1999 Board of Trustees, National Gallery of Art, Washington, DC.

painting old people, whose faces bore the marks and burdens of many years of hardship and loss.

In seeking ways to further the technique of intense inner realism, Rembrandt was aided by the chiaroscuro effect that Leonardo had used so eloquently. So painstakingly did Rembrandt practice the effect that he, rather than Leonardo, has come to be identified with it. In the *Self-Portrait* reproduced here, only the face matters, bathed in light, while almost nothing else about the figure is visible, except for the hand, which is partially in darkness. To look at many paintings by Rembrandt is to see such a contrast between light and darkness that it is tempting to believe the source of light must be external to the painting. Though the amazing light dominates this picture, we must not suppose that the darkness is unimportant to the total effect; for the artist uses it to enhance the aura of quiet wisdom that age and experience in life have given.

A visit to a major museum will afford you the opportunity to look at many conventional portraits, which have their nearly perfect likenesses, but *only* of surface realism. Expressions seem devoid of emotion. They offer not a sign of what sort of life the person has led. It is not an exaggeration to say that Rembrandt's series of self-portraits, painted at various ages and points in his career, give us an autobiography without words.

A Rebellion against Perfect Likeness

The art world was well aware that the Dutch masters had taken the imitative aspect of visual art about as far as it could go. So, as one would expect, new generations of artists would attempt to emulate their work. Well into the eighteenth century, on both sides of the Atlantic, landscape and portrait painting tended to be technically proficient—and, with rare exception, generally unexciting. One of the chief characteristics of art, however, is novelty, so sooner or later this trend had to run its course. Someone was bound to come along and rebel against the tradition of perfect likeness. Could art be anything more than expensive decoration? Francisco Goya (1746–1828), Spain's major artist of the late eighteenth century, answered a resounding Yes! and set about to lead a decisive rebellion.

Goya

His early work, it is true, is characterized by realistic landscapes depicting the natural beauty of the Aragon countryside in which he was nurtured, as well as portraits of considerable vitality, with finely detailed, nearly photographic likenesses of his subjects. The young Goya proved he could do what the Dutch had done—well, almost. Though he was little known when he came to Madrid, the cultural center of Spain, he quickly became a star, gaining great favor among the aristocracy because of his talent for portraiture.

Then something happened he had not counted on: The lifestyle of Madrid's fashionable elite became unbearable to him. He was appalled by the greed, hypocrisy, and constant jockeying for social position, realizing that, if his success were to continue, he would have to race through life churning out portraits for the aristocracy. Fortunately for posterity, the demands of artistic integrity were too great for Goya. Instead of doing the hack work of a money-grubbing portrait painter, he wanted to paint what he *felt* about this society. He wanted to put his negative feelings on canvas, often in a style that mocked the pretentiousness of the lazy, unproductive, yet arrogant aristocracy. The negativity may have been partly influenced by a serious illness which left him totally deaf in 1792.

The artist became a thorough-going cynic, developing a hatred for privileged upper classes and the things they did to hold their power. His "portrait" of royalty, *The Family of Charles IV* (Color Plate 11), completed in 1800, is outrageously satiric in nature and intent. Instead of surface or psychological realism, it is something approaching caricature.

The family is shown standing in a gallery: the king, the queen, and the rest, of varying ages and sizes. In Rembrandtian style, there is light coming into the gallery from some undefined source beyond the canvas, just enough light to illuminate the faces. They are far from the idealization of royalty that artists were normally paid to create. The youngest children have bizarre, almost paranoid expressions. Perhaps for the very first time an artist captured the less-than-enviable lives of children who are not so much spoiled and pampered as enslaved to certain behaviors. The queen seems insensitive to them—and indeed, to just about everything. She is posing foolishly, as though she has a naive conception of what regal bearing is all about. The king is just as silly-looking, but there is also a trace of sadness in his face, a fleeting memory of happy times long ago? We know that the children will grow up to be like their parents.

The fact that the royal family must have been pleased with the portrait—after all, they did accept it and did not throw the artist out of the palace—remains one of the ironies of art history. Were the king and queen so vain or so blind to reality that they never noticed Goya's insulting approach? If so, then Goya was probably right in his assessment of the Madrid court. At any rate, his style became even darker, more pessimistic.

The invasion of Spain by Napoleon during the first decade of the nineteenth century did not help Goya's disposition. The ravages of war, the inhumanities human beings were capable of inflicting on each other, depressed him further. In two of his masterpieces, *The Second of May* and *The Third of May*, Goya used art to make an intense statement about social and political issues by dramatizing the theme of war's cruelty. In the latter work, reproduced here, we see the execution of several Spaniards by Napoleon's firing squad. The artist's focus is on the pleading looks in the faces of the condemned and frightened men. Nothing in the painting detracts from its bitter theme. Anger at the inhumanity of a species that once prided itself on its benevolence and rationality has usurped the desire for perfect likeness. The figures are recognizable as men, but the artist's powerful statement is what we remember. Notice, too, Goya's superb handling of chiaroscuro.

Anger has overcome realism in this famous work from the older, cynical Goya.

Source: Goya, *The Third of May*. Credit: A.K.G., Berlin/Superstock.

A modern perspective is that art by virtue of its activity is beautiful, no matter what the subject matter or technique.

Many of Goya's later works, especially *Saturn Devouring His Children* (Color Plate 12), completed when he was seventy-seven, seem downright unpleasant, if not hideous, to many viewers. They raise even now, as they surely did then, questions about the legitimacy of art that is intended to disturb, to externalize its creator's dismal view of existence—art that seems anything but aesthetic, and provokes feelings of outrage and horror.

Contemporary art that intentionally disturbs the viewer is so commonplace that many of Goya's descendants would regard as impertinent the question of whether art always has to be beautiful. Or they would contend that art by virtue of its artistry always *is* beautiful regardless of subject matter. If one of the criteria for determining that a given work should be labeled as "art" is that the artist has conquered a challenging medium, breaking through steel-like limitations, then Goya's astonishing feat of capturing humanity's elusive passions must be called beautiful.

Impressionism

While Goya opened the door for the intensely personal in art, realistic landscapes and portraits continued to be popular. Although in some countries there were rumblings among younger artists that the days of perfect likeness had run their course, in art meccas such as France and England, art had come to mean "the imitation of likeness in fine detail." Would-be artists were judged on how proficiently they abided by the rules. In Paris, particularly, new artists aspired to have their work exhibited at the annual Salon, a vast exhibition held at the Champs-Élysées Palace. The jurors who selected the works to be shown were by and large drawn from the ranks of so-called experts who had governed popular taste for decades. Paintings in unfamiliar styles were seldom welcome, and the few that slipped by were generally crucified by the critics.

One such regularly rejected artist was Édouard Manet (1832–1883), who was intent on painting in a style that was wholly his own, not following the strict guidelines established by the panel of experts who selected the pieces for Salon showing. Accustomed to rejection, Manet nonetheless went ahead, convinced that eventually his methods would be recognized as legitimate. In 1862 he submitted the work that is now acknowledged as an early masterpiece of the Impressionist movement but was at the time the subject of scorn and derision: *Le Déjeuner sur l'Herbe* (*Picnic on the Lawn*), which features three figures seated on grass: two well-dressed men and a nude woman (Color Plate 42).

Manet advanced a comprehensive rationale for a wholly new style. A painting, he said, should not imitate the superficial appearance of things. Nor should it be valued because it makes a statement. Instead, a painting should be an event, equal to nothing but itself, existing for itself—not for an issue and not as a souvenir of how someone looked. It should be an experience of color and light. The familiar world is the starting point for Manet, as it would be for many who followed in his footsteps, but it becomes a world transformed by some of the most brilliant colors ever applied to canvas, a world in which the outlines of human beings and natural shapes are softened, less boldly distinguished one from the other, but each playing an integral part in the total unity that is a subjective vision of the world at each moment.

Those who were affected by Manet's rationale were also greatly influenced by the science of optics, which had originated during the Middle Ages in Islamic countries, notably Egypt, investigating the phenomenon of sight. The new artists wanted to go further than their Renaissance predecessors in the attempt to recreate true visual experience. They wanted to experiment with how color strikes the eye. Philosophers were beginning to ask questions like "Is color inherent in objects, or is it something that happens within the viewer?" Such questions parallel the traditional "Is beauty in the eye of the beholder?"

The artist, for example, sees a family enjoying a picnic by a lake and decides to paint the event. But what is seen and must therefore be duplicated on canvas is a rush of light falling upon the eye in various hues and shadings, blending in with each other, and with brightness blending in with shadows. Rembrandt and Leonardo had done wonders with the effect of light on their subjects, but their technique was a way of giving drama to those subjects. For the French artists, light *itself* should now be central to art: the colors of the world carried to the marveling eyes of an artist by the amazing phenomenon of light. It would be many years before physicists would discover that light was made up of tiny particles call photons, but Impressionism revolutionized art by instinctively perceiving that light wasn't just *there*: it was somehow a physical thing. Like all physical things, it affected each person differently.

The new style found its name in a haphazard manner. Claude Monet (1840–1926), whose name was often confused with that of Manet, had also been rejected for years by the experts, but he began to sell after many of his contemporaries, working in similar styles, gained recognition. Edmond Renoir, son of another Impressionist, Auguste Renoir, was in Monet's studio one day, browsing through some of Monet's new works, when he came upon an intriguing scene of

Right now a moment of time is fleeting by! Capture its reality in paint! To do that we must put all else out of our minds. We must become the moment.

—Paul Cezanne

fishing boats in the harbor at Le Havre. What attracted him was the vibrant color of sunrise flooding the canvas and the hazy indistinctness of the boats, the entire scene forming a subjective experience capturing a glorious moment in time. He asked Monet what he was going to title the painting. The artist merely shrugged and said, "Oh, you can just call it *Impression*." Renoir, thinking the work deserved a less generic label, wrote *Impression: Sunrise* (Color Plate 13). From then on, Monet and all of his close allies were identified (and not always with a positive connotation) as the *Impressionists*.

The Impressionist revolution in visual art fostered the careers of two major female artists of the nineteenth century: Berthe Morisot (1841–1895), Manet's sister-in-law, and the American Mary Cassatt (1845–1926). Morisot was the first woman admitted to the tight circle of French Impressionists, and her work, like theirs, shows an intense concern with the way light is seen. But, like Manet, she is also interested in creating true likenesses and remained throughout her life on the outer rim of the circle. In *The Psyche* (Color Plate 14), the figure of the woman dominates the work. Morisot takes great care to transfer to the canvas a faithful depiction of the woman and her reflection in the mirror. At the same time, muted light and shadow give the painting the soft glow characteristic of Impressionism. Morisot combines domestic realism with Impressionist techniques.

Impressionism in America

Mary Cassatt was influenced by the Impressionist use of light and by the Impressionist philosophy that, in painting, content is subordinate to the artist's technique. Because of her affluence, she was instrumental in keeping the movement alive and gaining acceptance for it in the United States. Her father, a wealthy businessman of French ancestry, who recognized his daughter's artistic talent, sent her to the Pennsylvania Academy of Fine Art and, after graduation, to live in Paris. There the young woman met many of the important artists of the Impressionist movement and fell under their influence.

In the softness of its colors and its handling of light, her work, on the whole, is tied to that movement, but Cassatt had an agenda of her own. Unlike most of her French colleagues, she was more interested in domestic than in natural scenes as the starting point for a painting. The majority of her paintings focus on people—in particular, mothers and children in close, loving relationships. *The Bath*, shown here, depicts a mother bathing a young girl, and though love and tenderness are masterfully captured by the artist, the figures and their relationship form part of a total design and total effect. All of the details are equally important: the furniture in the background, the mother's dress, the towel wrapped around the child, the bowl of water, the pitcher, and finally, the rug. The Dutch portrait painters of the seventeenth century focused on reproducing an exact likeness of the subject's face. Cassatt is adroit at likeness, but the figures also form part of the entire design. In times past, the details in the room would have formed a visual framework for the subjects. They would have *accentuated* the subject. Here, the figures and their

Though the artist is adroit at imitating likeness, the figures in this painting are part of the entire design.

Source: Mary Cassatt, American, 1844–1926. *The Childs Bath*, 1893, oil on canvas, 39½ × 26 in. Robert A. Waller Fund, 1910. 2. Photograph © 1999 The Art Institute of Chicago. All rights reserved.

surroundings form a continuous flow of experience. In real life, all of us are linked to our surroundings in this way, but we seldom know it unless an Impressionist happens to be standing by.

For *The Bath*, Cassatt paints from a vantage point above the scene, instead of directly in front of it. Perhaps her wish is to disengage the viewer from the normal way of seeing. She forces viewers to look with their right brains (the right brain sees things as they are, without interpretation, while the left brain sees selectively, processing and making sense out of what is seen). From this elevated perspective all of the objects in the scene acquire a visual meaningfulness they might not have in direct head-on observation, which is the normal way of visually connecting with our world. Since most people see selectively, head-on observation tends to invite abstracting—*really* seeing what seems most important—in this case, only the human figures.

The title of the work, *The Bath*, does not indicate whether the woman is the mother or the maid, nor does it prompt us to ask: "What is the artist trying to communicate about these people?" The appropriate questions are: "What happens on the canvas?" and "What is the effect, and how does the artist achieve it?"

Cassatt's *Mother and Child against a Green Background* (Color Plate 15) spells out the relationship in the title, and here the vantage point is direct. But the title also includes the word "background," the color of which seems to matter more than any specific details. This particular piece shows the French influence on Cassatt: the figures flow into streams of color and light. At the same time, the mother-child relationship is clearly evident, a signature characteristic of Cassatt's work.

Another American exponent of Impressionism was James McNeill Whistler (1834–1903), who painted the famous portrait of his mother in 1871. Though the work is universally admired for the subject matter, and though reproductions have sold in the millions, many are unaware that the painting is NOT called "Whistler's Mother" but *Arrangement in Black and Gray*, and the title indicates the artist's purpose. Whistler uses his mother as a woman in a particular moment of time, in a complex of light and shadow which evokes feelings that cannot be quite named. The way she sits, the expression on her face, the folds of her garment—all come together as a total visual experience that says more than "This is my mother." In fact, the portrait, in which the subject is sitting sideways instead of facing forward, is a reminder that Impressionism seeks to imitate visual consciousness, not to abstract from an event a meaning such as "motherhood."

For us artists there waits the joyous compromise through art with all that wounded us in daily life.

—Lawrence Durrell

Not just a portrait of Whistler's mother, but a unified duplication of a total visual design in which the seated woman is just a component.

Source: Musée d'Orsay, Paris, France. Credit: Reunion des Musees Nationaux/Art Resource, NY.

Post-Impressionism

The Impressionist movement took hold so strongly on both sides of the Atlantic that it eventually became as authoritative as the traditions it replaced. Newer artists emerged who began to resist slavish imitation and go their own ways. The label **post-impressionism** has been coined by art historians as a convenient way to refer to the work of the artists who came after the heyday of Impressionism and whose work, though influenced by it, does not clearly belong to the earlier school. Of this group, Vincent van Gogh (1853–1890) was surely the most original and the most intense. He differs from the Impressionists in a major respect. He had no real theory of art. He simply loved color, especially yellow. He had no interest in consulting the science of optics so that he could accurately imitate the experience of seeing. For him, imitating the bright colors of the world was his way of expressing the uninhibited feelings of pleasure they aroused in him. And if he were painting a scene that had less yellow than he liked, he would splash yellow onto the canvas without restraint. No one gives us as much yellow in a starry night as van Gogh does.

Van Gogh is the prototype of the artist who creates entirely for himself. His style was so strange in its time that the few critics who ever took notice of his work were generally baffled, having nothing with which to compare it. If his devoted brother Theo had not handled most of his expenses, chances are he would have been hungry and homeless most of the time. But Theo believed in his genius and stood by him even when his paintings were denounced and ridiculed. Only one of the artist's paintings was sold during his lifetime. Tragically, he committed suicide before he reached the age of thirty-eight.

Van Gogh's life reinforces the romantic concept of the starving artist for whom art is the last outpost of being. Totally alienated, totally misunderstood by almost everyone except his brother, rejected twice as a suitor (once with a vehement cry of "No, never, never!"), hovering much of the time on the thin borderline between functional rationality and insanity (eventually to cross the border, never to return), he survived as long as he did only because of an often childlike delight in his private way of seeing and imitating the world. What obligation did the artist feel to communicate with an everyday world through which he passed as a stranger?

Works such as *Sunflowers, The Potato Eaters*, and *The Starry Night* (Color Plate 16) have become priceless since van Gogh's death. (His work can bring $30 million or more.) These and his many other paintings show a brushstroke method that has become utterly identified with its creator: a short, stabbing technique, as opposed to a flowing line, that makes the entire canvas seem to be throbbing with energy. Despite the indifference of the art world, van Gogh abandoned himself to the sensuous impact of life's forms and colors, absorbing them fully and converting them into a heightened reality—an explosion of pure feeling transferred to color, shapes, and paint textures. Van Gogh's lines and bright colors virtually scream from the canvas.

Van Gogh, unappreciated in his lifetime, nonetheless continued to paint in the style that must have seemed the true expression of his inner being. As we move into our own time, we find less innocence and more conscious, calculated insistence from artists that they be granted license to express themselves in any way they deem fit, to use any medium that suits their purpose, and to be recognized on their own ground. Van Gogh in retrospect is seen to have defied tradition, but he did not do so loudly and rebelliously or with a planned rationale. The twentieth century of the visual arts is one of "artist's rights," a worldwide movement that sometimes has met with bewilderment, confusion, critical scorn, critical praise, even angry denunciation

Flowers bursting with energy against a background of van Gogh's favorite color.

Source: Vincent van Gogh, *Sunflowers.* Credit: Art Resource, NY.

from hostile governments and censors—but also much cheering on the part of humanists who believe that the artist is an endangered species, to be treasured and supported at all costs.

Art as Alteration

Neither van Gogh nor the Impressionists rendered perfect likenesses, nor were they trying to. Unlike Rembrandt, who even with his psychological probing felt responsible to imitate a world the viewer would recognize, they were compelled to transfer to canvas the world as *they* saw it. They never denied that their subjects were themselves, their subjective experience of color and form. Even so, their work does not represent so startling a departure that we cannot recognize on their canvases any trace of the familiar world. What we see is that world drastically changed. Looking at van Gogh's *The Starry Night*, we *still* recognize a sky. At the same time, his work is moving in the direction of what has come to be called **modernism**. Many schools, movements, and techniques dating from about the last quarter of the nineteenth century to roughly the last quarter of the twentieth century have been linked by critics and art historians under that broad term. The style of the literature and visual arts from the late twentieth century to the present is often called **postmodernism**. What unifies modern and postmodern artists and makes them different from, say, van Gogh is *intention*.

Both van Gogh and the Impressionists start with the familiar world and then paint it as they wish. They give us the familiar world as altered by the emotions and the subjective experiences of light, color, and form. But when we speak of the later art as **alteration**, we are speaking of artists *who do not even start with the familiar world*. They want to impose something new on that world, some secret part of themselves. With such an intent, they have no reason to be bound by an artistic tradition unless it suits their personality, unless it can be adapted to their imagination.

Entering the world of modern art can be confusing at first. There may seem to be no rationale at all, no clear overall purpose, no rules. All of this is at least partially true. Rationales, if they are expressed at all, belong to the individual artist, who may deny having any purpose other than to do something on canvas or in stone. When Marcel Duchamp bought a urinal and submitted it, untouched, for an exhibition in 1917, he challenged all definitions of art. Critics of such **found art** ask: "How much work does an artist have to do? What is off-limits for an artist?" Modern artists impose their own rules upon their own work. They may even be the least forgiving of their critics. After all, they are out there creating new traditions, and most of the time they feel alone. Small wonder that they sometimes, like Duchamp, develop a sense of humor.

Some modern art—in fact, a good deal of it—does in fact resemble people, places, and things. But that is usually where its traditionalism ends. Francis Bacon (1909–1992), for example, offers canvases with recognizable reality, but that reality might be somebody sitting on the toilet, or a slab of meat bleeding. You know what it *represents*, but you may ask: "Why would anybody want to paint *that*?"

Art comes to you proposing frankly to give nothing but the highest quality to your moments as they pass.

—Walter Pater

Famous urinal submitted in 1917 to an exhibition sponsored by the American Society of Independent Artists. The artist did not sign his own name but one that closely resembled that of the manufacturer.

Source: Marcel Duchamp, *Fountain.* Credit: © 2005 Artists Rights Society (ARS), New York/ADAGP, Paris/Succession Marcel Duchamp. Tate Gallery, London/Art Resource, NY.

The true function of art is to edit nature and so make it coherent and lovely. The artist is an impassioned proofreader.

—**H. L. Mencken**

The Sixty-ninth Regiment Armory Show, 1913

Some people want to know when modern art actually began. Are we talking about last week or a hundred years ago? Assigning approximate dates also depends on geography. New stirrings in the art world were happening in Europe before the dawn of the twentieth century, long before word reached this side of the Atlantic, much in the same way that the Renaissance was happening in Florence long before it traveled to northern Europe.

Modern art made its way to the United States at the tail end of the *Gilded Age*, a name given to the last two decades of the nineteenth century. Some Americans who had made their fortunes in railroads, coal, or steel, for example, were becoming intensely art conscious. This was the time of elaborate mansions, incredibly luxurious ocean voyages, and the accumulation of what became priceless art collections. New York in particular had a burning need to be respected as a hub of modernism in art. It wanted to see all that was new and exciting. It had already opened its arms to the Impressionists, long before they were fully respected in Europe.

In 1913, the Sixty-ninth Regiment Armory in Manhattan was the site of an exhibition of new works by European artists that is still considered the most important single art show ever held in this country. Many American viewers saw for the first time the startling paintings of van Gogh, as well as the work of other artists whose styles seemed downright puzzling, if not laughable.

One of these artists was Wassily Kandinsky (1866–1944), whom we mentioned at the beginning of this chapter and whose work provides an excellent introduction to modern art. Though as a young artist he achieved technical competence in drawing the human figure, he set his eyes on other goals. Kandinsky came to believe that what mattered in a work of art was *form*: a pleasing arrangement of lines and color, existing for no purpose other than aesthetic experience. In other words, a painting should provide an experience of the beautiful. Kandinsky delved into his imagination, found a new world of pure shapes and forms, and imitated those in a style that came to be known as **abstract art**. However, "What's that supposed to be?" is often the first question viewers ask. (Remember the two viewers who turned a Kandinsky into two light bulbs.)

Having abandoned the study of law for that of art, the young Kandinsky came under the heavy influence of van Gogh and his friend Paul Gauguin (1848–1903), who had made his reputation by painting the lush vegetation and exotic natives of Tahiti. But Gauguin unknowingly took some steps toward abstractionism in that his work presents a few key shapes in bold outline and bold colors (with no pretense at an illusion of depth in them) while eliminating minute, realistic details. When van Gogh turns the familiar world into throbbing symphonies of bold brush strokes and riots of color, his work also leans more toward the abstract than the real. Both of these artists seemed to belong with Kandinsky in the Armory show.

Like many other modern artists, Kandinsky distinguished between beauty and anything else one might see in a painting such as his *Black Lines*: "He argued that in order to speak directly to the soul and avoid materialistic distractions, it was preferable to use an art based solely on the language of color. Free from references to a specific reality, color could become like music, beautiful for its interrelationships of tones and intensities."[3]

Kandinsky's rationale made perfect sense to him, as well as to other exhibited artists, but not to all of the art critics and potential collectors who came to the Armory show in droves, hoping to pick up some real bargains. In fact, not much of the show was received with open arms by either critics or public. The shock of so much alteration was simply too devastating, confined as it was to one building. Canvases by Picasso, who would become the century's most celebrated artist, were widely denounced. The room in which they were displayed was nicknamed the Chamber of Horrors.

The work that caused the biggest uproar and controversy, however, bringing instant notoriety to its creator, was Duchamp's *Nude Descending a Staircase.* One critic called him "the biggest transgressor" in modern art. Duchamp could not have expected to be warmly welcomed after a newspaper published his observation that "the only works of art America has given are her plumbing and her bridges."

For this painting Duchamp had developed his own brand of abstractionism by which he moved from an actual model through successive stages of reduction until all that was left from reality was the sense of descending movement and the hint of a human figure. Duchamp, in other words, abstracted from a real scene only those elements that interested him as an artist, excluding everything else because he had signed away his responsibility and obligation to make his work resemble something a viewer could instantly recognize. The controversy might have been less heated had the painting's title not promised disappointed viewers an interesting reality that was virtually invisible. Abstract art remains a popular form of expression among contemporary artists. Sometimes we can gain subject matter clues from the title, but more often the artist will be altogether casual and call the painting or sculpture *Study*, or *Untitled*, or *Line and Color.*

Piet Mondrian (1872–1944), a Dutch artist who helped establish abstractionism, was already at the peak of his career at the time of the Armory show. His work departs from reality much more radically than does Duchamp's. In it there is not even the suggestion of the familiar world. *Composition*, with its characteristically bland title, is a painting of austere and absolute simplicity in which all dynamic motion is absent; colors, shapes, and lines sit serenely in geometric relationships that defy all need to interpret them. Mondrian can be called a

Art Movements and Styles

Cubism	movement in modern art, epitomized by Picasso, in which the artist breaks down the field of vision into discontinuous segments or in which the artist shows a number of visual events taking place simultaneously (as in *Guernica*).
Dutch school	group of painters producing intensely realistic art, centered in Holland during the seventeenth century, with Rembrandt the outstanding example.
Impressionism	mid-nineteenth-century art movement wherein the attempt to be realistic is abandoned, and instead, the artist projects onto the canvas a subjective experience of the world as color and light. In Impressionist art, forms tend to be less sharply divided from each other than they are in, say, landscape painting.
Gothic	an architectural style of the late Middle Ages, featuring high pointed spires and pointed arches; label coined by a critic of the style who called it barbaric "like the Goths who destroyed the Roman Empire."
performance art	art as an event that generally exists only for the time it takes for the presentation or installation. The wrapped buildings, surrounded islands, and other installations of Christo may be kept for longer periods of time, but not indefinitely.
Pop Art	style of mid-twentieth-century art influenced by comic books, movies, television commercials, and billboard advertising; can be just plain fun or satiric.
post-impressionism	broad term used by art historians for art of the late nineteenth and early twentieth centuries that resembles but is not strict Impressionism; it is neither realistic nor abstract. The work of van Gogh belongs to this category.
superrealism	modern style made famous by sculptures of Duane Hanson that are so lifelike they seem about to move; this art form also can make biting social commentary.
surrealism	modern style associated with work of Salvador Dalí, among others, in which recognizable objects are put together in bizarre contexts that seem like visualizations of dreams.

"classic abstractionist" in that his beautifully ordered designs are meant to evoke the same sort of serenity found in classical art.

Cubism: Picasso and Braque

The enduring fame of the Armory show owes much to its having introduced America to the work of the most baffling, the most controversial, yet easily the most innovative of all modern artists. His work, displayed in the "Chamber of Horrors," drew thousands who came to laugh, but many came away in admiration. He exercised more influence on a whole century of artists than any other we can think of, and he transcended his age so completely that some art historians rank him among the three or four greatest artists of all time.

Pablo Picasso (1881–1973) lived the entire length of the modernist movement in art. Anyone seeing only his work and none by his contemporaries would nonetheless know what modernism is all about. In his youth, he came under the heavy influence of the Impressionists and their decision that, with the emergence of photography, imitative realism was dead. During the incredible span of his artistic existence, he worked steadily and impeccably in more modern styles than any other artist of his time. Classically trained, he could bring to the canvas a lifelike portrait, but he could also duplicate subjective visual experience, or create a wholly new style that was neither realistic nor abstract (in the sense that Mondrian and Kandinsky are abstract) but derived from yet another way of seeing the world. This style, which Picasso invented with strong help from a fellow artist named Georges Braque, was **Cubism**.

Picasso, whose father taught painting, grew up surrounded by art. He was just nineteen when he visited Paris for the first time and there saw and marveled at the colors of the Impressionists. He was particularly drawn to the color blue (as van Gogh was to yellow) and quickly developed extraordinary skill at both imitation and alteration by painting mostly indigent types—such as prostitutes and homeless wanderers—all in distinctly blue tones.

From the outset, Picasso wanted to show more than a "mere" talent for perfect likeness, which he possessed in abundance. As he intended to mark the world with the stamp of his unique genius, so too did Picasso want to alter its reality. And indeed he did, working not only on two-dimensional flat surfaces but in sculpture, architecture, and scenic design for the theater. (He also wrote poems and plays in his spare time!)

His joy in using colors has something of the child about it, the child who refuses to grow up; as a matter of fact, as he aged, he was fond of advising young artists to do everything possible to avoid growing up. Retain your childlike delight in all things, he would say. Don't be suffocated by the adult world of rules and regulations, of schedules and timelines, to the point where you stop hearing the voice of your intuition, where you stop feeling the compulsion to try new things that will shock the society of dull, convention-bound folk.

The child in Picasso led him into an obsession with the circus, where—still in his twenties—he embarked on a new period dominated by pink, orange, yellow, and gray and did portraits of clowns, trapeze artists, and other performers—portraits lifelike enough to be recognizable, but beginning to show the distortions of real forms that would characterize most of his mature work.

At an exhibition of African masks in Paris, he became excited by their colors and distortions of the human face. The influence of these masks was overpower-

Painting isn't an aesthetic operation; it's a form of magic designed as a mediator between this strange hostile world and us; a way of seizing the power by giving form to our terrors as well as our desires.
—**Pablo Picasso**

ing and immediate, leading him to his first major triumph, *Les Demoiselles d'Avignon* (1907), a portrait of five young women in which features and body parts form a geometric design. Early viewers found the painting startling if not amusing, because while pure geometric design might have been a *little* acceptable, designs made from figures that were *supposed* to look like people would have been not only radical but smile provoking (Color Plate 20).

Picasso, in fact, began his career showing intense interest in the art of portraiture. Despite the innovative techniques of the Impressionists and post-impressionists, the assumption still held that making a living as an artist required big commissions from patrons who wanted their likenesses to survive them. At the same time the new discipline known as psychology was making its presence felt, though many refused to call it a science. Picasso was fascinated by descriptions of the unconscious mind and the often huge difference between what people looked like on the outside and what they were really like on the inside. So even when he worked on portraits, distortions began to invade his canvas—sometimes close to caricature. In this he was a descendant of his countryman, Goya. As his new style evolved, his distortions turned into a total revision of reality, while he and Georges Braque created the theory behind Cubism.

Braque (1882–1963), a year younger than Picasso, saw *Les Demoiselles* in its initial showing and admitted that it changed his life and his artistic plans for the future. He made it his business to meet the genius who had opened his eyes to a wholly new way not only of painting but of *seeing*. Acting on advice from his "older" mentor, Braque began working in a new style. He would look at a scene that appealed to him for some reason, then leave it, allowing himself to forget

> *Art is meant to disturb. Science reassures.*
>
> —**Georges Braque**

Supreme example of Cubism, turning the bombing victims into fragmentary and horrifying images of atrocities.

Source: Pablo Picasso, *Guernica*. Credit: © 1999 Estate of Pablo Picasso/Artists Rights Society (ARS), New York.

the realistic details until he was ready to *deconstruct* it in his memory and then *reconstruct* it on the canvas as geometric blocks in bold, unshaded colors. He did a series of landscapes in this style, causing one critic to complain that Braque had taken beautiful subjects and reduced them "to cubes." After the critical article appeared, the label *Cubism* was applied to the work of both Braque and Picasso. In 1909 the two artists formed a close association and consciously devised a Cubism movement, providing for it a clearly articulated rationale.

In thinking critically about their art, the two friends discovered that nobody ever really sees an object or a figure. Rather, what is seen is an event extending over a period of time, no matter how rapidly. The eye, moreover, is in continual motion and observes from continually shifting viewpoints. From where we sit or stand, we *think* we are looking from a particular and fixed vantage point. Both realistic paintings and photographs foster the misconception that such a thing exists as an observer with a stable field of vision. Our language suggests that we see reality, but in truth what we really see is fragments, reassembled by the mind.

Looking at Braque's *The Musician* (1917) (Color Plate 17), we would need to know the title of the painting to have a clue as to the artist's subject. We can make out what looks vaguely like a hand holding a cigarette, and across from it a shape that suggests a musical instrument.

Picasso and Braque did not turn away from realism just to be rebels; they believed **realism**—that is, art as likeness—could not show the world as it is. The world is made up of shapes and colors that swirl before our consciousness as if seen in a kaleidoscope, and if we could slow down our vision, the world would actually look like one of their paintings. We would see pieces of things and pieces of people (as in Picasso's *Seated Bather*, Color Plate 18).

In 1937 Picasso was invited to do a large mural for the Spanish Pavilion at the Paris World's Fair. Instead of choosing a visual event and breaking it into geometric shapes in his customary style, which was based on an intellectual theory of vision and was on the whole non-emotional, the artist used his style to make an impassioned statement against war. *Guernica* is now considered not only Picasso's masterpiece but one of the great artworks of all time. Among other things, it silenced critics who were saying that modern artists were too wrapped up in their technique and their innovations to pay attention to what was happening in the world.

With Cubism, Picasso was able to deliver a message with one swift visual impact, a message that required thousands of words from reporters and innumerable pictures from photographers. The mural describes an event that caused worldwide revulsion: the German air force's infamous saturation bombing of Guernica, the cultural center of the Basque region in northern Spain and a stronghold of the Republican Army fighting against insurgent forces, who would ultimately win the Spanish Civil War. Francisco Franco, leader of the antigovernment army, had appealed to both Germany and Italy for support. The United States backed the Republican government that had been duly elected, while Hitler sided with Franco. The bombing of Guernica was also a way for Germany to demonstrate its military strength to the world.

The bombing took place on April 26, 1937, and numbered among its casualties not only hundreds of Republican soldiers but 2,500 civilians, including hundreds of children. Newspapers around the world published graphic images of the dead. Picasso, who had been undecided about whether he wanted to do a mural

The cubist wished to present the total reality of forms in space, and since objects appear not only as they are seen from one viewpoint at a time, it became necessary to introduce multiple angles of vision and simultaneous presentation of discontinuous planes. This of course shatters the old continuity of composition imposed by the Renaissance single viewpoint.

—Helen Gardner

for the Spanish Pavilion, saw the pictures and was so moved that he rushed home and immediately began sketching out what would become his masterpiece.

When it was unveiled at the World's Fair, *Guernica* received nearly unanimous critical acclaim and established Picasso's supremacy among living artists. There were, of course, detractors. The Marxist government in Russia said that only realistic art could bring about significant social change, and the Nazi regime, as expected, denounced it as "degenerate art".

Without Cubism, a style that can present simultaneously things that happen over a period of time, how could an artist have captured such a scene of total devastation? Few artists have attempted anything of the scope Picasso was able to achieve, for most paintings are essentially static, freezing a single moment in time. What Cubism does in *Guernica* is to place on a two-dimensional plane the dynamic motion generally found only in films.

Like a true masterpiece, *Guernica* continues to be frighteningly relevant. Wars like those in Vietnam and Iraq, which also scarred national and world consciousness, come to mind whenever one looks closely at Picasso's mural. It is not a historical record of an event long past, but a living conscience. As such, it continues to generate profound emotional responses. The United Nations headquarters in Manhattan has on display a tapestry reproduction of the mural. When in 2003 Colin Powell, then the U.S. secretary of state, addressed the UN Security Council to advocate military action against Iraq, the tapestry, which would have been in full view, was covered.

Picasso's work became simpler in his later years, reflecting a childlike innocence that makes as strong a statement in its own way as *Guernica* does. This is a statement of hope for the future in a world tamed by peace and love, a statement that will be needed as long as the horrors of a Guernica repeat themselves. The artist painted childlike doves on the ceiling of a tiny chapel in the southern French town of Valauris, near his home in Nice. With his friend and neighbor Henri Matisse, he developed **collage** into an art form, spending hundreds of hours cutting out tiny designs and pasting them onto large and colorful backgrounds. The ninety-year-old Picasso was not "losing it"—as has been suggested by a few cynics—but was showing that he had managed to do what few of us can: he had kept alive the child inside him. The art of being human needs the spirit of children.

Unreal Realism

One reason for any artist's huge critical reputation is the degree to which the work influences other artists. Future artists viewed Picasso as a revolutionary leader, encouraging others to follow their own bent, regardless of how the public might react. In this section we look at the work of several other modern artists who carry banners of revolution, however different each flag may be.

Surrealism, a popular style during the first half of the twentieth century, employs recognizable shapes and forms put together in unrecognizable contexts. The best way to define it is to say that it claims to imitate the world of dreams and the unconscious mind. It owes much to the psychological studies of Freud and Jung. Their explorations into the strange regions below consciousness excited visual artists, writers, and philosophers. Inner space was proving to be just as fascinating as recent discoveries regarding the physical universe.

The surrealists wanted to imitate the geography of inner space, to make the unconscious mind a tangible part of the external world. At least this was the stated purpose of the movement, the major exponent of which was the Spanish painter Salvador Dalí (1904–1989). Unlike Picasso, who gives us fragments of things, Dalí creates a dream world made up of recognizable images that do not fit rationally together.

Dalí became as famous for his neurotic behavior as for the bizarre world of his canvas. His paintings are objects of fascination for psychiatrists and art critics who interpret an artist's work in terms of psychological disorders. Some cite the artist's maladjusted childhood as responsible for both his behavior and his art. Some call him as mad an artist as ever lived, but add that madness is often the price of genius. This observation may well be made of van Gogh, and future generations of critics may confirm that it applies to Dalí. Yet many will argue that surrealism as practiced by Dalí was a highly commercial, carefully calculated artistic oddity, designed from the outset to capitalize on the popularity of Freud, to make the artist a center of widely publicized controversy, and thus to increase the price of his paintings.

If nothing else, we can say that there is little subtlety in Dalí's style, which is sometimes so obviously Freudian that students of Psychology 101 would have no trouble with it. Dalí seems especially obsessed with the popular Freudian belief that many of our actions are a result of two drives: the constant need for sex, which we are forced to hide, and the death wish, which comes from the pain of our neuroses. A good example is his *Inventions of the Monsters* (Color Plate 19), with its naked upper torso, its disembodied bare buttocks, and its skeletal death figures, all suggesting wicked thoughts and death longings that have been repressed and filed away, thus rekindling the neuroses which caused the misery in the first place.

Was Dalí lost in the maze of the subconscious—or was he giving the public what it wanted?

Source: Salvador Dalí. (Spanish, 1904–1989). *The Persistence of Memory*. 1931. Oil on canvas, 9½ × 13" (24.1 × 33 cm). The Museum of Modern Art, New York. Given anonymously. © 2008 Salvador Dalí, Gala-Salvador Dalí Foundation/Artists Rights Society (ARS), New York.

Dalí's most famous work is *The Persistence of Memory* (1931), a completely Freudian title. It shows a tree branch over which hangs a wristwatch distorted because it is made of a soft, rubbery material. Another rubbery watch hangs limply from a table on which rests a pocket watch that is not rubbery. Yet another limp watch is draped over what ought to be, but is not, a wrist. Those who insist on a Freudian interpretation, as Dalí perhaps hoped they would, may recognize the limp watches as symbols of unresponsive male sex organs, and the non-distorted pocket watch as a symbol of a happier sexual past. Was the artist forced to hide his sexual attitudes? Or was he deliberately giving his public the controversy he thought it wanted?

Even if we grant the possibility that Dalí was giving the public what it wanted—*shock*—and doing it for the money, we still have to ask ourselves where his strange images, figures, and landscapes *came* from if not from his innermost self. And granting that they are emanations from the artist's true unconscious, do they make us aware of anything except the artist's suppressed self? Do they adorn the world with a new kind of beauty?

The paintings of Georgia O'Keeffe (1887–1986) present another form of unreal realism: likeness that is also abstraction. The artist appears to have worked from deep impulses inside her which led her to reinterpret the familiar world. When asked what she was intending to show in her paintings, she answered, "Do you think I know what art is?" Nor was she one bit apologetic. She added, "Do you think I'd care what anybody thought?" Her attitude typifies that of the modern artist insisting on the right to follow the demands of intuition. She maintained resolutely that all art can be analyzed only in terms of what is happening on the canvas, of what the artist is *doing*, not saying.

What O'Keeffe *does*, then, is usually to imitate one or two striking and colorful forms in the familiar world and transfer them to canvas with many details left out. O'Keeffe sees the world not as the Cubists did—broken down into geometric shapes—but as a place in which certain shapes leap out at the artist for whatever reason: the colors, the aesthetic appeal of the form itself, the textures, or as some critics have said, the unconscious significance to the artist of the form—what it *looks* like or *suggests*.

It has been said that O'Keeffe, like many other women conditioned in youth to be proper Victorian wives, was obsessed with sex and often turned real shapes into sexual organs—somewhat akin to Dalí, except that O'Keeffe's images are not placed together in bizarre contexts. She is neither a realist—though she works from real things—nor an abstractionist—though she simplifies reality. She is her own style.

In 1905, eighteen years of age, O'Keeffe left her home in Sun Prairie, Wisconsin, to study at the famous Art Institute of Chicago. Like other young artists at the turn of a new century, she was brimming with exciting ideas about what constitutes art and what an artist has the right to do. Today young people from a later generation of artists may be standing exactly where O'Keeffe stood. Perhaps one or two of them will be thinking it is time to rebel against "traditionalists" like O'Keeffe.

"She brought to the big city her love for simple shapes and extremely bright colors," one biographer notes; "she recalls seeing light on a red, white, and black patterned quilt before she could walk, and, as a toddler, the soft, smooth shapes made by buggy wheels in the dust—they looked good enough to eat!"[4] When she was twenty, O'Keeffe moved to New York. There she met the most fashionable artists of the day, whose work was shown in the studio of photographer Alfred Stieglitz, whom she was eventually to marry. But Stieglitz and his sophisticated circle were not able to influence the maturing artist as much as did the simplicity and sensuous beauty of Asian art.

Where I was born, and where and how I lived is unimportant. It is what I have done and where I have been that should be of interest.

—**Georgia O'Keeffe**

In Asian art O'Keeffe found a style she could immediately understand, respond to, and imitate. The simplicity of a painting such as *Azaleas* (Color Plate 21) by the Japanese artist Ogata Korin (1658–1716) appealed to her love of color and shapes that convey an instantaneous image. Asian influence is clearly evident in *Purple Petunias* (Color Plate 22). Later, when her aesthetic and emotional differences with Stieglitz made their marriage seem less idyllic than it had once been, O'Keeffe moved to New Mexico, a land of bright color and bold shape. In the undulating hills, the orange craggy rocks, the snow-tipped mountains, and the exotic flowers, she found a constant visual stimulation she had never experienced in drab (by comparison) New York.

Her most famous works date from after this move, as she developed her unique style: flowers bursting from their stems; mountains, canyons, the infinite sky with its continually changing colors; the bleached skull of a dead animal. All of these forms she transferred to canvases that were first painted stark white so that the electric colors and the proud shapes would stand out in sharp relief. As colorful as the Southwest surely is, O'Keeffe altered the landscape, giving it an electric vibrancy, giving as much as she took from this land, something all artists claim the right to do.

Pronounced though the Asian influence is on her work, it is hard to imagine that O'Keeffe could have been indifferent to the Native American art of the Southwest, especially that of the most famous Navajo artist, R. C. Gorman (b.1931). He is more interested in depicting human figures than O'Keeffe is, but his work is like hers in its simplicity. Navajo women were among his favorite subjects. If you look at his *Navajo Dawn* (Color Plate 23), you will see the recognizable form of a woman, but the desert scene in which she is placed is simplified to a point of near abstraction. Except for the mountains in the background, the landscape is stark save for one small flowering plant. Gorman's strength is his colors: the dark and light shades of sky and the superb chiaroscuro effect in the handling of the mountains. This is clearly a landscape and a treatment of it that O'Keeffe would have appreciated.

Another contemporary of O'Keeffe and exponent of a simplified realism that leaves out unimportant details was Edward Hopper (1882–1967), who emerged out of the Great Depression of the 1930s. Hopper, like so many artists and writers, could not help being touched by the belief among American artists that art should not only appeal to the aesthetic sense but be a strong social commentary as well.

Hopper's forms come from the streets of urban America and the forlorn, despairing souls who walk them: the homeless, the abandoned, the chronic poor, the newly poor, the alienated drifters who move from one place to another, seeking not only decent jobs but meaningful communication with someone else, and people who we suspect came from good backgrounds and now find themselves displaced. Among his lonely, unhappy Americans are the three hunched figures sitting in a late-night diner in one of his best known paintings: *Nighthawks* (see Chapter 9).

Running through most of his works are the common threads of alienation, despair, and the faint rays of hope perhaps misplaced, stamping him as an artist through whose eyes we experience a sense of the Great Depression. In a few bold details Hopper shows us what American writers have devoted hundreds of pages to describing: American loneliness. Hopper does not give us a perfect likeness of a diner in *Nighthawks*, but the few figures are all he needs to tell his sad stories.

While Dalí, O'Keeffe, and Hopper were honing their craft, a young African American artist named Aaron Douglas (1899–1988) was traveling from Kansas

City for a stopover in New York before heading to Paris. During the 1920s and 1930s the French capital was a magnet, luring artists from every country in the world and with every imaginable style. Ever since the heyday of Impressionism it was recognized as *the* place to be for those intending to make a name for themselves in the art world. However, the stopover took far longer than he expected, for while Douglas was in New York, he discovered Harlem.

Chapter 4 described the achievements of Charles S. Johnson and others who created the Harlem Renaissance and insisted that white America listen to artistic voices that had gone unheeded for too long. Johnson's group was also to discover the electric talent of Douglas and draft him for the Harlem movement.

Douglas, born in Kansas of middle-class stock, and a visual arts graduate of the University of Nebraska, at first lacked a sense of connection to African roots. The eventual discovery of an African heritage made a deep impression on a young artist looking for a style and a statement. What Douglas responded to in Africa was something he had not found in the quiet, uneventful life of midwestern America: a sense of being able to express emotion without restraint, whether it was joy and exaltation or bitterness and sorrow. All around him Harlem voices were giving vent to their feelings in poetry, jazz, dance, and drama. Some were seeking an appropriate visual arts language and encouraged Douglas to join them.

Douglas knew he wanted to go beyond art as strict likeness, but he hadn't an idea of *where* he wanted to go—and why. In Harlem and Cubism he found that idea. Douglas liked the fact that Cubist paintings forced the viewer to reconsider how reality was viewed. He also knew that he did not agree with those African American leaders who urged artists and writers to use their talents to make protest statements. He believed passionately that African American art should be its own movement and stand on its own merit. It too could show the world a new way to see.

The art of ancient Egypt gave Douglas his first encounter with Africa. What both shocked and excited him was that ancient Egyptian artists stylized the human figure in a way that he knew Picasso would understand. In the pen-and-ink drawing *Invincible Music, the Spirit of Africa*, an illustration for the February 1926 issue of *Crisis* magazine, an African drummer expresses himself ecstatically; but the figure is drawn in what Douglas called "Egyptian form." The right eye is unnaturally shown in its entirety, not the way it would be seen in real life. In fact, there is far too much of the man's face for the position of the body, while the left hand is disproportionately larger than the right. Douglas explains that if he drew the hand the way you would see it in real life, "you wouldn't understand that that was a hand. It's only when it's done this way, when the fingers spread out that you understand. So you see that I spread the hand out with the fingers out. . . . I used that hand all the time . . . got it from the Egyptians."[5]

Aaron Douglas created his own style, aiming to go beyond the mere appearance of things.

Source: General Research & Reference Division Schomburg Center for Research in Black Culture, The New York Public Library, Astor, Lenox and Tilden Foundations.

Douglas's style is the result of a philosophy, a deep-rooted belief that in trying to imitate the actual world, art as likeness was really falsifying the way we see that world. Figures such as the drummer enabled him to transfer to visual art the excitement he found in the African American spirit, an excitement that was part of the way he saw things. Thus he was an imitator of both reality and his own emotions.

Superrealism

Hanson's superrealism does not exist just to astonish us with its lifelike appearance, but to make a definite statement about our society.

During the last half of the twentieth century, a sculptor named Duane Hanson (1925–1996) took the banner of revolution and turned his back on modernists who had forsaken realism. What he gave the world was **superrealism**—a method of creating life-size figures that look so real you would expect them to answer if you talked to them. Some critics have compared his sculptures to the figures in Madame Tussaud's famous Wax Museum, a comparison that always infuriated the artist.

For one thing, Hanson's "people" are far more lifelike than the wax replicas of famous personalities at Madame Tussaud's. Yet the artist's aim is not solely to render a likeness so perfect it shocks us; he also insists on our seeing the violent, sordid, and comic elements of our society. Hanson is a commentator on what he believes we have become as a nation. His figures are not celebrities we would recognize. They are social (and very often *antisocial*) types. (Look, for example, at his *Supermarket Lady*.) They are super real in order to help us see more clearly, not just to make us marvel at the artist's skill.

Hanson burst upon the art scene several decades ago with a show that almost redefined sculpture. Neither classical nor abstract, his figures offered the somewhat frightened (and relatively few) visitors to his first studio—an old garage—their startling first experience with superrealistic three-dimensional art. Entering the studio through a rusty and squeaking door, which only added to the ghoulish scene inside, the visitor was greeted by the life-size figure of a young woman hanging from a cross, the victim of a savage rape. In an adjoining alcove one gasped at the horrifying sight of a young woman lying nude on a bed, pairs of blood-stained scissors thrust into her stomach, her open eyes still showing the terror she experienced before death came. Across from this sculpture lay the bloody figure of a dead young man, the twisted wreckage of his motorcycle beside him. As if believing the shock of the exhibit was not yet strong enough, Hanson capped off the evening with the piece that brought him to the attention of the Whitney Museum, New York's premier showcase for what is new, controversial, but significant in contemporary art: bloody corpses of young soldiers strewn across a Vietnamese battlefield. A visitor was heard to whisper: "The technique is marvelous, but would you want this in your *house*?" It was clear from the outset that the sculptor was not primarily interested in selling to private collectors. His fame has come from exhibitions the world over.

Superrealism making a biting commentary about middle-class society.

Source: Duane Hanson, *Supermarket Lady*. Credit: Art © Estate of Duane Hanson/Licensed by VAGA, New York, NY.

With Hanson's statement about violence and America, notoriety was instantaneous, and the artist, perhaps believing no more need be said on the subject, embarked on a second phase in which his sculptures were superrealistic but not as frightening—at least not overtly so. The new figures, like the lady in the supermarket, bring us face to face with the dismal life of the American middle class, accurate down to the last detail. Hanson also is thinking of the soulless accuracy with which human-looking robots are constructed in the Disney theme parks, figures that smile vacuously at us and deliver electronic life-affirming platitudes with all the warmth of the computerized phone voice that says, "Sorry, but I did not understand you. Press or say 'one' again."

While O'Keeffe, Gorman, and Hopper simplify reality, Hanson's details tend to overwhelm, as in the real hair curlers, the dangling cigarette, and most of all, the riot of items flung into the shopping cart: the sack of dog food; the frozen dinners (evidence of what has happened to the art of dining); the bargain packages of teabags and toilet paper: startlingly real, yet there for a purpose other than the likenesses themselves. The sculpture encourages the question of whether this is how life should be. Something seems wrong, but what? Art that makes viewers question the life all of us may come dangerously close to living needs no further justification.

In order to achieve such likeness, Hanson covered a live model with wire to form a "dummy," which he then immersed in plaster of Paris, allowing it to harden enough for him to sculpt the lifelike details and apply the many necessary paints. He finished the process by coating the statue with "fixative," a substance that makes paint or dye permanent. Fixative, highly toxic if breathed in an enclosed space, eventually proved fatal to the artist. He was in the process of changing his style and his medium when his life ended, and we can only speculate on the further riches his legacy might have contained.

Camera and Computer Art

With the increasing popularity of photography since its invention in the nineteenth century, the roles of portrait painting and realistic landscape art, beginning in the early twentieth century, were diminished. People argued that if they wanted something that looked like the real thing, why not go to a medium that could better provide it? We should not, however, overlook the fact that creative artists, fascinated by the new invention, would begin to experiment with and greatly expand its possibilities.

One of the finest photographers working in the twentieth century was Alfred Stieglitz (1864–1946), who was obsessed with the desire to establish photography as a distinctly American art form. Some of his most famous works are camera images of his wife, Georgia O'Keeffe. He became famous both for his portraits, in which he was bent on proving that the camera could capture the inner person as well as, if not better than, the eye of the painter, and scenes of big-city life. Although photographic art at the time was far less sophisticated than it is now, Stieglitz nonetheless was able to use camera imagery to affect us emotionally, as well as to make a statement about life in New York, already showing signs of the congestion and frenetic pace that would become signature characteristics. In 1902 he founded *Camera Notes*, the first periodical devoted to studying the art and science of photography.

While there is a province in which the photographer can tell us nothing more than what we see with our own eyes, there is another in which it proves to us how little our eyes permit us to see.

—**Dorothea Lange**

Arthur Stieglitz, in this portrait of his wife, Georgia O'Keeffe, showed that in-depth portraiture was not the sole province of the painter.

Source: Private Collection/Archives Charmet/The Bridgeman Art Library. © 2008 Estate of Alfred Stieglitz/Artists Rights Society (ARS), NY.

It's admirable, I think, to be open to the new, and willing to learn; I submit, however, that once one has adjusted to the new, it must give pleasure or it will not be art.

—**Richard Wilbur**

Jerry Uelsmann (b. 1934) makes full use of new camera technologies that allow the artist to take multiple images, then link them together in the darkroom to create a world akin to surrealism on canvas. Reproduced here is *Homage to Duchamp* (2000), in which two images of the French artist overlap in a frame that overwhelms the strange room in which it is placed. This is truly photography as alteration.

Computer art is a medium that goes far beyond the "Graphics" menu on a toolbar. Maggie Taylor (b. 1961), for example, conjures up images from a variety ofsources, including photos from digital and regular cameras and pictures scanned from newspaper and magazine clippings. Sometimes the result is a computerized collage, and sometimes Taylor creates a surreal picture, like *The Philosopher's Daughter* (Color Plate 24), that could easily have been painted but, astonishingly, is not.

There is also fax art, which can be an ordinary photocopied reproduction of something, acquiring the label of art only after it has gone through the shading process of a fax machine. We are probably not far from "video cellphone art," in which the receiver of a call will not see the person calling but, instead, a surreal person in a non-existent room. Perhaps that genre is already here. And perhaps you can think of other, newer, more dazzling art forms related to today's electronic devices.

Pop Art

Influenced by comic books, movies, television, commercials, and billboard advertising, **Pop Art** arose as a phenomenon of the mid-twentieth century that brought

Using photography to create a surreal world.

Source: Jerry Uelsmann, *Homage to Duchamp.* Credit: Courtesy Jerry Uelsmann.

fame to a few artists. It has been described as "fun" art, for its exponents all seem to have a sense of humor about much of what they do. They are sometimes, like Hanson, making a statement about the endless fads and superficiality of American culture. It has a link with the second phase of Hanson's art in its focus on ordinary objects and sometimes the sly suggestion that American life has nothing more important to offer.

Claes Oldenburg (b. 1929), a Swedish-born, naturalized American exponent of Pop Art, finished a cardboard and wood mural in 1961 called *The Street*, showing people, buildings, automobiles, and other objects seen in everyday life, but drawn in comic-book style, which is his artistic domain. The following year he achieved notoriety with *Giant Ice-Cream Cone* and the first of his soft vinyl sculptures, *Giant Hamburger*. These were followed by *Giant Tooth Brush*, *Soft Toilet*, and *Giant Ice Bag*, which was made for the Osaka World's Fair, a sculpture that inflates and deflates as the viewer watches. With *Soft Toilet*, reproduced on page 161, he may have been thinking whimsically of Duchamp's still notorious urinal.

Probably the biggest name in Pop Art is Andy Warhol (1928–1987), who earned his reputation with a painting mentioned earlier: *100 Cans*, containing stark likenesses of row upon row of Campbell's beef noodle soup. The inspiration for this kind of art is clearly the popular ad, but the excessive repetition of the can is both amusing and frightening. Is Warhol ridiculing the stultifying conformism in American culture and its lack of imagination?

Yet Warhol is also in *love* with our tawdry culture, as we can see from his portrait of glamorous movie star Marilyn Monroe (Color Plate 25), a heightening of what used to grace the covers of tacky movie magazines. The colors are brilliant, suggesting the unreality of "tinsel town." But the artist, like so many others, was unable to resist the flashy sensuality that turned Monroe—once an unremarkable young woman named Norma Jean Baker—into a modern Aphrodite. Yes, Warhol knows that the star was a studio-manufactured product, but he himself was a filmmaker who manufactured a whole bevy of unreal types for his bizarre movies, including a fleshy transvestite named Divine and an entourage that was a walking Pop Art statement.

Warhol's films were central to his art, and *Chelsea Girls* (1966) ushered in a new cinematic phenomenon, the "underground film," popular for a time with young people who opposed almost anything connected with established American culture. The film lasted more than three hours and was shown on two screens that seemed unconnected with each other. The "plot" comprised disconnected,

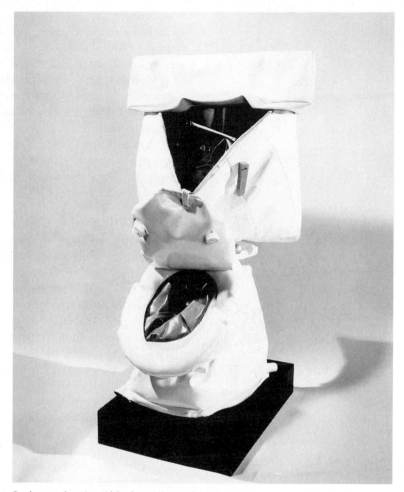

Sculpture showing Oldenburg's love of turning commonplace objects into museum pieces.

Source: Claes Oldenburg, *Soft Toilet*, (1996). Wood, vinyl, kapok, wire, plexiglass; on metal stand and painted wood base. 57 1/16 × 27 5/8 × 28 1/16 in. (144.9 × 70.2 × 71.3 cm) Whitney Museum of American Art, New York. COPYRIGHT Claes Oldenburg and Coosje van Bruggen.

fragmentary sequences but also strangely haunting images. In one five-minute sequence a young woman is shown standing in front of a mirror, cutting her hair. Nothing else happens, yet the intense camera focus on her face and the sound of scissors create a mesmerizing effect.

Warhol's films are occasionally shown on special nights in "art houses"— theaters that cater to "alternative tastes." Most of his film art, however, is hard to track down. Even so, it remains an important link between what we might call "stationary" art that is available in museums and galleries and "impermanent" art that is not meant to last, that occupies a brief moment in time—a new kind of art that may have been an inevitable development in America, a land of short attention spans and people always on the move.

Performance Art

Performance art is art as event. Perhaps performance artists are looking for ways to be different in an art world that changes all the time, a very tall order indeed. Or perhaps they believe that art is more beautiful to the extent that it doesn't stay around very long. Performance artists ignore the goal of one day having their work part of a permanent collection in a prestigious museum; they prefer to do something that will create a momentary stir, even a storm of controversy, and then be seen or heard no more. They may also perform pranks or engineer hoaxes just meant for themselves and a closed circle of friends.

Prank artists often cite Orson Welles, the great film director (more fully discussed in Chapter 7), as the founder of their movement. In the 1930s, Welles and his Mercury Theatre Company performed a radio adaptation of a famous science fiction novel, *The War of the Worlds*, about an army of Martians who invade the United States. Because the radio play was written in the style of a news program, many people—especially those tuning in late—believed the invasion was the real thing. Chaos erupted as people ran from their homes, seeking safe hiding places. Welles insisted the program was not meant as a prank, but some performance artists insist that it *could* have been, and that even if it had been a prank, it would still count as legitimate art.

A great deal of prank art is intended for the sole pleasure of the artists themselves. One artist, for example, purchased a chicken from a supermarket, then brought it to a pet cemetery and conducted a full-scale funeral service. Another entered an alley cat in a prestigious show and, after the lowly entrant had won, greatly enjoyed laughing at the judges. One artist carried bags of horse droppings to Venice, scattering the contents all over the Piazza San Marco, and reported deriving aesthetic pleasure from watching the amazement of tourists, who knew that there were no horses in Venice. Those who refuse to apply the label "art" to such pranks might ask themselves whether art is not supposed to open us to new experiences, and was not the mysterious appearance of the horse droppings indeed a "new" experience? Is there a limit to what qualifies as a legitimate new experience?

A Massachusetts Institute of Technology student is reported to have spent her summer regularly sneaking into Soldiers Field, the Harvard football stadium, wearing a black-and-white striped shirt like that of a referee. On each visit, as she scattered birdseed over the field, she blew a whistle. At the opening football game of the season, when one of the real referees blew his whistle, hundreds of birds swooped into the stadium, ready to eat. Since prank art is necessarily private, the perpetrators might advertise their successes only later on the Internet.

Performance art can also contain social commentary. An instructor at Amherst College, for example, posted bogus signs all over campus, announcing that no more coffee would be sold because it was known to induce caffeine addiction. Then he and his colleagues spread the word that coffee was available from black-market vendors outside the campus. The pranksters posed at the vendors and reported brisk sales. Surely there is a moral here somewhere. During the 1970s at a Miami art gallery, a performance artist destroyed a piano with an axe while his assistant read the names of American soldiers killed in Vietnam.

Superrealist Edward Kienholz (1927–1993) created a computer-generated performance art piece called *Still Live*, which includes an armchair positioned in front of a black box said to contain "a live cartridge and a random timer triggered to fire once within the next 100 years." According to one art critic, "After eight years, it still hasn't gone off. Viewers foolish enough to want to sit in this 'hot seat' must sign a waiver. Kienholz told me, with some scorn and disbelief, that at the opening almost a dozen people did."[6]

No doubt many have sat in the armchair since the work's installation in 1974, but its title, *Still Live*, suggests a possible appeal to hidden Russian roulette impulses. If the artist had expected no one to sit there, why did he compose the piece at all? In any case, the performer here was not the artist, but the actual or potential viewer willing to risk all for a momentary thrill. Perhaps the work existed so that those who sat in the chair could look deep within themselves and ask why they came.

Christo Javacheff (b. 1935), who as an artist uses only his first name, does not imitate or perform; he literally alters the world briefly, creating a huge and highly publicized event. He claims the natural environment as his medium. Among his projects were wrapping over 1 million square feet of Australian coastline in plastic, installing a gigantic curtain between two mountains in Colorado, constructing a twenty-four-mile fence made of twenty-foot-high nylon panels across hills in northern California, and surrounding the islands in Biscayne Bay, Miami, with enormous sheets of flamingo-colored plastic, a feat that struck terror to the hearts of environmentalists, who attempted (unsuccessfully) to halt the proceedings.

Performance art was often considered radically new in the twentieth century, but it can be dated back as far as tribal rituals of many thousand years ago. During the Renaissance, some artists performed little acts to call attention to their work on display. And Will Kemp, the celebrated clown for whom Shakespeare wrote many parts, including the Fool in *King Lear*, was fond of adlibbing and extending a role far beyond what the script allowed, cheered on by his adoring fans.

Architecture as Art

Performance art is transitory by nature, often limited to the time of presentation, and never seen or heard again. This final section is concerned with a more permanent component of society: architecture, which serves a dual purpose. It provides for our many human needs: shelter, work, play, religious worship, and so on. It also gives many of our cities their distinctive look; it adds an aesthetic dimension to life. At its best, architecture is an art form. Major architects Frank Lloyd Wright and Frank O. Gehry have approached the design of buildings as a painter or

Architecture in general is frozen music.

—**Friedrich von Schiller**

sculptor would contemplate beginning a new work: that is, as a contribution to the aesthetic well-being of society.

The fundamental issue in determining whether a given architectural work can be labeled "art" is the interplay of *form* and *function*. The function of a building is to accommodate the needs of the inhabitants. An office building should provide employees with pleasing surroundings that will make working less of a chore, and it should allow employees easy access to spaces they will have to visit throughout the day. It must make doing business there simple and enjoyable, and these days it must be wheelchair accessible. A religious edifice such as a cathedral or a temple should be imposing and awe-inspiring both inside and out, so worshippers or meditators can believe for a time that they have left the familiar world and entered a different, some might say higher, mode of consciousness.

The form of a building—the general impression that it makes as a pleasing presence in a certain space—can be as important as its function. If designed by an architect-as-artist, it can also make a personal statement: *This form is what I consider beautiful, and I offer it for your use and your aesthetic pleasure.* Like all visual artists, architects seek to project themselves into space. They want to know that, because of them, a public area has been altered in some way that reflects their identity and may ensure them lasting honor. They know that architecture is art that alters for very long periods of time, and in some cases forever. The Taj Mahal in India, Saint Peter's basilica in Rome, and the Hagia Sophia in Istanbul have endured for centuries and have become symbols of their culture.

The debate over which is more important, form or function, has continued for centuries and will probably never be resolved. Those who want architecture primarily to serve a useful purpose argue famously that *form follows function.* Others, often called architectural purists, elevate form and the aesthetic experience it provides over what they call "mere utility." Still others ask, "Why can't we have both?"

Religious Architecture

Buildings created for religious worship or meditation are among the finest achievements in world architecture. The Parthenon in Athens, built to honor the goddess Athena, is one of the world's oldest architectural marvels and remains for many the symbol of Western classical civilization. Angkor Wat, the largest of seventy temples in a complex in Cambodia, is not only a place of meditation for thousands of Buddhists but, as one of the wonders of the world, the main tourist attraction in that nation. Each year many thousands come for inspiration and an aesthetic experience that has been described as nearly without parallel. Unlike St. Peter's, which was built to impress upon the visitor the glory of God and the supreme authority of the Roman Catholic church, Angkor Wat is intended as a place in which the visitor can be alone and at peace.

Not many edifices have been cornerstones of two religions, but Angkor Wat, still the world's largest religious building, has been home to both Hinduism and Buddhism. Built originally in honor of the Hindu god Vishnu, it became in 1177 C.E. a Buddhist shrine after the Cambodian king was converted to Buddhism. With five pineapple-shaped towers rising close to 200 feet against the sky, Angkor Wat became the most imposing temple in the holy city of Angkor, spread across 120 miles. The temple contains innumerable passageways and alcoves, the walls of which boast ornate facades depicting both mythic stories and scenes from everyday Cambodian life.

The former Hindu, now Buddhist temple Angkor Wat in Cambodia. It remains one of the world's architectural wonders.

Source: Mark Downey/Masterfile.

Few works of architecture have cast the same sort of spell as Angkor Wat. The English novelist W. Somerset Maugham once observed that the vast temple "needs the glow of sunset or the white brilliance of the moon to give it a loveliness that touches the heart." Many have noted that merely walking its nearly three-mile expanse is a transforming experience, leading to distinct (and for the better) changes in mood and attitude.

Modern cathedrals and other places of worship frequently break with tradition, and the results vary from praise in architectural journals to condemnations by the faithful. St. Louis Catholic Church in Miami looks like a flying saucer about to take off. The Crystal Cathedral in Garden Grove, California, has a neo-Gothic form, except that it is made entirely of glass and, according to some detractors, looks more like a luxury hotel than a church. A Lutheran church in Helsinki, Finland, was carved into the side of a hill and gives the illusion that one is entering a cave rather than a house of prayer.

Secular Architecture

Whenever the desire is to combine function with the form that only a great artist can bring to architecture, conflicts inevitably arise between those who create and those who pay for or use the structure. The architect-as-artist often runs into difficulties with both the general public and the specific person or group that has commissioned a given structure. The artist's irresistible urge to self-expression can be accused of subordinating a building's primary purpose. One notorious example is an office complex in Miami, Florida, built in the shape of a huge snail. Probably reflecting the designer's keen sense of humor, it has provoked much derision over the years.

We shape our buildings: thereafter they shape us.

—**Winston Churchill**

Even where architecture is viewed as a public art, those who finance it can only speculate on how to define the public interest. When a private corporation or city planners underwrite the erection of an expensive building such as a performing arts center, they will expect (for their millions of dollars) an edifice that satisfies both functional and aesthetic needs, but not exclusively the desires of the architect. They know their investment is going to result in an edifice that will be around for a long time, and they are in trouble if it meets with public disapproval! It is going to define their city—for better or worse—as Sydney, Australia, is identified by its daring but internationally admired opera house.

With its gleaming white, sharply pointed gables, looking like monks' hoods, the Sydney Opera House (Color Plate 26) opened in 1973 after sixteen years of construction. The design was to allow for excellent interior acoustics but also to create for the audience a pleasant environment that would heighten the pleasure of the music being heard. The building was also intended to symbolize the city, so that people on ships entering Sydney Harbor for the first time would know they were about to visit a progressive, young metropolitan area very much involved in the arts. An intense contest for the architectural commission resulted in the choice of a celebrated Danish architect, Jorn Utzon, who insisted on being able to express himself as an artist—to shape a certain space so as to embody his vision of the beautiful, not only to obey the functional requirements set forth by the city planners. The opera house, in short, was intended to be a meeting of the civic and the personal.

But not every taxpayer in Sydney agreed that the structure met either practical or aesthetic needs. As always happens when an environment is altered by a forward-looking artist who breaks with established tradition, there were many who decried his efforts and predicted that their city would be a laughingstock. World opinion, however, has been on the side of Utzon; now the Sydney Opera House is often singled out as one of the architectural achievements of the twentieth century, an edifice that perfectly marries form and function.

There is by now widespread agreement, however, over the innovations of a man considered the outstanding American architect of the twentieth century, Frank Lloyd Wright (1867–1959). He was born and raised in the relatively small Wisconsin town of Richmond Center. Accustomed to open spaces, air to breathe, and panoramic landscapes, he must have become aware of a growing urban America with huge buildings beginning to reach for the sky and densely crowded city neighborhoods where residents seldom interacted with nature. The writings of American philosopher Ralph Waldo Emerson and his vehemently anti-city friend Henry David Thoreau also had a strong impact on Wright's architectural vision. Early on, Wright developed a strong rationale for his work: to link the functional demands of large buildings with the environmental demands of his own heart. His mission would be to provide for the practical demands of big business without the claustrophobia of crowded industrial complexes.

At the outset of his career he designed what he called his "prairie house," a rambling one-story structure with plenty of windows and a low, overhanging roof. The idea was that it should blend into its surroundings, unlike the huge nineteenth-century mansions with their ornate external carvings, statues, and stained-glass windows, designed for the blatant display of wealth. Wright's aim was to create a balance among function, form, and the environment.

During the first decade of the twentieth century, Wright designed the Larkin Building in Buffalo, New York, and its distinctively sleek look brought him to the attention of European urban planners. By the 1930s the term "streamlined"

No house should ever be on any hill or anything. It should be of the hill, belonging to it, so hill and house can live together each the happier for the other.

—Frank Lloyd Wright

became fashionable and international in its appeal, and Wright was the acknowledged exponent of the new style, with its use of glass, including glass brick, curved surfaces, spacious interiors, and absence of unnecessary, purely decorative frills. He believed strongly that form follows function. With Wright leading the way, many modern architects said that no building could be considered beautiful if its basic function was impaired by "artistic" aims—such as installing a fountain ringed by statues to block its entrance.

In 1936 Wright designed the administration building and in 1944 the research tower of the Johnson Wax Company in Racine, Wisconsin, an achievement hailed as a masterpieces of modern architecture. One architectural historian proclaimed it "the most profound work of art that America has ever produced."[7]

Money was never Wright's primary consideration. He wanted, first, to shield employees and visitors from the growing ugliness of the urban scene. Although he loved light and made extensive use of glass, he placed windows so that users of the buildings would not have to look out on parking lots and decaying streets. Instead they were enclosed by solid brick walls at street level while light was provided from overhead. He wanted users to feel as though they were "among the pine trees, breathing fresh air and sunlight." Wright was a visionary who helped create the modern world, and he was an archenemy of overbuilding in that world.

Wright's final work—and for many, his crowning achievement—is the Guggenheim Museum on Fifth Avenue in New York. It is admired by some as the best possible example of modern architecture, and scorned by others who say it looks like a parking garage. The building is a series of circular stone ramps, which ascend in great swirls and serve as a thick barrier to the noise of the city. There are

Sometimes scornfully compared to a parking garage, New York's Guggenheim was designed to shut out light and provide visitors with a peaceful environment for viewing art.

Source: Frank Lloyd Wright, Guggenheim Museum, New York. Credit: © Peter Mauss/Esto. All rights reserved.

no windows this time. Instead, light enters through the small spaces between the ramps. Inside, art works are illuminated by soft indirect lighting. The artist's first thought was to shut out as much light as he could and provide visitors with a quiet oasis, another world of human creativity.

Frank O. Gehry (b. 1929) has also taken modern American architecture to new levels. His work tends to put a great deal of emphasis on form without ignoring function. But from the beginning, he approached architectural design with an artist's eye, developing a style that is not only representatively modern but always characteristically *his*. For Gehry, form is paramount, yet his genius lies in the ability to make the form seem an inevitable result of function. Some of his critics call his style impractical, accusing him of subordinating function in the interest of artistic self-expression. A good many artists, however, defend his right to do just that.

Like many of his fellow southern Californians, Gehry enjoys the *funky* in modern art—those elements that incorporate whimsy into serious aims. He is fond of fish, for example, and is apt to put a fish sculpture where one would least expect it—in front of an elevator perhaps. He makes furniture out of corrugated boxes, and he uses chain-link fencing unsparingly and, again, unexpectedly. He will stretch a chain-link fence across a courtyard where it serves no useful purpose except to be an object of art, similar to what Christo might do, except that Gehry's installations are permanent. To those critics who call such installations "frivolous" and "ugly," he replies that he is not sure "what is ugly and what is beautiful." Such a retort, a denial of absolute aesthetic standards in architecture, defends the right of artists to make personal statements with their work.

Yet Gehry is as concerned as Wright about making a space enjoyable to its users. His California roots are evident in the brightness and spaciousness of his interiors. After all, southern California is a land of beaches, where stressed-out workers can go to unwind. In Gehry's buildings, the unwinding process has already begun.

By almost universal consent, Gehry's masterpiece is the Guggenheim Museum in Bilbao, Spain. Here he was commissioned by people who were already on the side of art, people who knew and loved the innovative, however daring and controversial, and people who wanted to call worldwide attention to the city they loved.

The structure stands as a giant work of art in itself, and then the visitor enters to find more and more art, in spacious galleries, lighted for the maximum enjoyment of each work on display. Even more imposing than the Sydney Opera House, the museum has boosted tourism in Bilbao. For those of us who love the humanities, such a financial success is gratifying indeed. And it proves that large segments of the public can respond to what is aesthetically pleasing, if given the chance.

We cannot close this section on architecture as an art form without giving some attention to the hotels that abound in metropolitan areas the world over. Here, the interplay of form and function is especially evident. The great hotels (for those who can afford them) are meant to fulfill every possible comfort need of the guest, but also to provide a pleasing aesthetic environment. In the nineteenth and early twentieth centuries, the greatest care and expense were often lavished on hotel lobbies; but of late the atrium has become a distinctive feature: open corridors built around a fountain or a swimming pool or even a rain forest, affording an instant view of something beautiful as soon as guests step out of their rooms.

I don't think it's very useful to open wide the door for new artists; the ones who break down the door are more interesting.

—Paul Schroeder

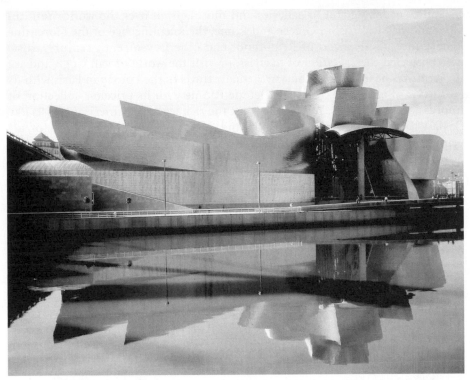

The Guggenheim Museum, Bilbao, Spain, was designed not only to house great art but to be a work of art in itself.

Source: Frank O. Gehry, Guggenheim Museum, Bilbao, Spain. Credit: Ralph Richter/Esto/architekturphoto.

One of the world's most spectacular new edifices is the Burj-al-Arab in Dubai, the capital of the United Arab Emirates. At one time the tallest structure in the world to function exclusively as a hotel, it required three years to build, at a staggering cost that reflects the vast oil wealth behind it. Shaped like a huge schooner mast, it is broad at the base, tapering to a conical tower, with a helipad for the arrival of important guests. The thousand-plus rooms open onto the world's tallest atrium and include a five-bedroom royal suite with a grand piano, a Jacuzzi on the spacious balcony, four bathrooms, and a dining-room table that can accommodate nearly one hundred guests. And it has a restaurant that can be accessed only by submarine!

While abundant praise has been showered on the building as a complex engineering feat, some critics have been put off by what the hotel symbolizes to them: money. One critic said it is a monument "to the triumph of money over practicality." After admitting that the structure was "fabulous," another critic venomously added that it was "the pinnacle of tackiness— like Vegas."

If you never visit Bilbao or spend a night in Burj-al-Arab, you may be fortunate enough to live in a city large enough to support a museum or gallery where traveling exhibits can be shown. Seize the opportunity whenever it presents itself. You will be delighted at how much your range of consciousness will expand and grow. If museums are not available, public libraries and the Internet have the astonishing

The Burj-al-Arab Hotel in Dubai. Las Vegas tackiness or one of the world's architectural splendors?

Source: © George Hammerstein/Solus—Veer/Corbis.

capability of taking you to galleries and museums all over the world. You can relive the classical past in Greece and Rome, the magnificence of the Florentine Renaissance, the Holland of Rembrandt and other seventeenth-century artists who perfected the imitation of likeness, or visit the world of van Gogh and see the treasures he left for us. You can virtually travel to the Louvre in Paris with its multitude of antiquities, or to the Jeu de Paume with its priceless collection of Impressionist paintings. You can discover the rich legacy of American artists like Cassatt, Whistler, Douglas, O'Keeffe, and so many others. The world of art belongs to you, and it is our hope that this chapter has encouraged you to browse in it whenever your spirits need uplifting. Art never fails you if you come to it with an eager curiosity and a willingness to pause. The visual effects can be stunning. Look carefully.

Key Terms

abstract art art that takes from reality only what the artist wants or that renders a visual depiction of concepts in the artist's mind; a work of art that in no way resembles the real world.

alteration how the modern artist changes reality by adding to it shapes, lines, and even colors not found in nature.

chiaroscuro Italian term denoting a way of reproducing in a work of art the interplay of light and shadow in the real world.

classicism the balanced, harmonious, often mathematical characteristics of art and architecture in fifth-century Athens and those aspects of Roman art that were heavily influenced by artists of that period; also used for all subsequent art and architecture created in that style.

collage a work of art in which a variety of materials such as newsprint, magazine pictures, crepe paper, even glass and wood are glued together, forming a new whole, expressive of the artist.

fresco artwork painted on the walls of churches and public buildings, popular in the Renaissance, in which the artist applies paint to wet plaster.

Golden Section an aesthetically pleasing relationship between the two sides of a plane (like a rectangle), such that the shorter is to the longer as the longer is to the sum of both. The ratio is 1 to 1.68.

imitation the transference of what is experienced either outside or inside the artist to a medium of art; it can mean an idealized reproduction (as in classicism), a faithfully realistic one (as in the Dutch school of the seventeenth century), or an externalization of what exists in the artist's mind (as in abstract art).

likeness the reproduction by an artist of a person or landscape with the aim of being as close to reality as possible; popularity began to diminish with the invention of photography in the nineteenth century.

media the particular materials in which a given artist works, such as paint, acrylic, charcoal, stone, or even tires, mufflers, broken pieces of glass, etc.

modernism refers less to a particular art movement than to art produced in the late nineteenth to late twentieth centuries.

perspective technique of rendering, on a plane or curved surface, objects as they appear to natural vision; developed and refined during the early Italian Renaissance.

postmodernism art produced from the late twentieth century to the present; less a specific movement than a broad umbrella term for the many innovative techniques.

psychological realism the manner in which such artists as Leonardo and Rembrandt are able to convey the inner life of their figures.

realism as used in this chapter, art as likeness.

Renaissance the period of artistic, political, and social movement that began in fourteenth-century Italy, then spread throughout western Europe in the fifteenth and sixteenth centuries; characterized by renewed interest in the classical world, and also marking the end of medievalism and the emergence of the modern world.

still life genre of painting in which the artist reproduces the likeness of a particular arrangement of objects, such as a bowl of flowers or fruit or other kinds of food on a table.

Topics for
Writing and Discussion

1. In your own words, explain this statement as it applies to art in general: "Leonardo's *Mona Lisa* is not Mona Lisa."

2. Discuss why the term *terribilitá* (used to describe the passionate qualities in a Michelangelo scupture) is appropriate for Renaissance but not classical sculpture.

3. Go to an art gallery or museum in your area or on the Internet and carefully study a painting that attracts your eye. If none of these sources is available, select one of the illustrations in this chapter or the color inserts. Then describe orally or in writing how you would explain the value of the viewing experience to someone who tends to be uninterested in art.

4. Can you justify the fact that an enormous curtain, stretched by Christo between two mountains, has been called art by its creator and recognized as art by some critics?

5. Write a short paper based on either of the following sentences:
   a. "I would rather be a stable, moderately successful, happy, if obscure, person than a genius like van Gogh."
   b. "I would rather be a genius like van Gogh, even if the price were lack of recognition, than a moderately successful, happy, and obscure person."

6. You and a friend are standing in front of Duchamp's *Nude Descending a Staircase.* Your friend asks, "What is it supposed to be?" You reply that it doesn't matter. Your friend says, "Then how can it be any good?" What is your response?

7. Extravagant praise has been given to Picasso, including the view that he was not only one of the greatest artists who ever lived but one of the most important human beings. Do you find this view justifiable? Explain.

8. The architects studied in this chapter have been concerned with the aesthetic appeal of a building's exterior. The Miami office building that was built to look like a snail has incited both amused approval and critical scorn over the years. Committees have even been formed with the intent to have the building condemned, but so far without success. Other committees have worked diligently to preserve it. Which committee would you join? Explain.

9. At one time, national academies composed of government-subsidized critics and scholars had the power to decide what constituted art. They were like an aesthetic Supreme Court. The French panel keeping the Impressionists out of the prestigious annual Salon maintained they were preserving the integrity of France's artistic traditions.

   If a country refused to have such an academy, would there be any standards? Are standards important? If they don't come from an academy, where *do* they come from? Would it matter if everyone's opinion counted equally? Would it matter if everyone's opinion did *not* count equally? Would it matter if the traditionalists had been replaced by a liberal group who decided that anything anybody said was art could be exhibited?

   Write a short paper focusing on one aspect of this intriguing and ongoing debate.

10. So much of the past is known mainly from the artworks that were its silent witness. Describe the kind of silent witness you would like to leave behind so that people of the future would know what you were like.

6 Music

Overview

We live within an audio environment that is most of the time unplanned. That is, we hear what happens to be around, whether it is a jet taking off, the squeal of auto brakes, a hair dryer, or a train approaching a crossing. There's plenty of unwanted sound, but there is also music: our revenge on random noise. Even the unrelenting beat of the hardest rock music represents somebody's choice, a preference for one sound rather than another. The audio environment can be the sound of a stick being dragged along a wrought-iron fence or the bland tones of supermarket Musak; or it can be U2 at full steam two hours into a concert, or the upbeat country sounds of Martina McBride, or a Beethoven symphony.

Without music, we exist at the mercy of audio pollution as damaging to mental health as air and water pollution are damaging to physical health. Created by instruments or human voices, music can be defined as *the shaped sound between silences*: the better the shape, the richer and more pleasing the sound. Just as visual art offers a wide variety of shapes and forms to provide an enriched visual environment, music has many sounds: Bach, Mozart, Gershwin, Armstrong, Sinatra, the Beatles, Maroon 5. Limiting ourselves to one kind of music is as detrimental to our growth as if we were never to set foot outside our house and discover the unlimited life experiences waiting out there.

Perhaps it seems unnecessary to talk about variety in music. Yet many of us listen only to what we hear on mainstream radio and television stations or at movies, local music venues, and popular concerts. Exploring unfamiliar sounds, finding perhaps the one station (among fifty others) dedicated to music that is new to us, refusing to have our tastes dictated by promoters—these are actions we are free to perform. Yet too often we do not.

We may enjoy the popular music we find on the charts because we hear it all the time. Often we grow up with its sounds filling the house, and some of us come to think there are few musical options we might be overlooking. This is not so. Music has a long and continuing tradition not only in the West but in other parts of the world, dating back hundreds of years—music that is still being played. There are operas, chamber music, symphonies, concerti for

In a world of peace and love music would be the universal language.
—**Henry David Thoreau**

Source: Rome Milan Gallery.

171

orchestra and solo instruments, music to accompany ballets, and music created from non-Western scales.

The difference between the familiar and the unfamiliar in music is not necessarily qualitative. We may place greater value on the familiar music because we are accustomed to it and therefore comfortable with it. We may find lesser value in the unfamiliar because we are *not* comfortable with it, at least at first. This is not the best reason to avoid it. When Elvis Presley and Chuck Berry emerged on the musical scene in the mid-1950s, a good many listeners were horrified, not knowing that a new musical tradition—*rock 'n' roll*—was being born. Now we have rock groups experimenting with such unusual sounds that Elvis Presley and Chuck Berry seem old-fashioned. The purpose of this chapter is to encourage you to explore a wide range of musical sound. Some of it is recognized as part of the world's artistic heritage. Some of it is still very new and may achieve that distinction one day. (It's fun to predict what *will*.)

We will first separate music into its component elements, then talk about some of its major (and widely differing) forms, together with some suggested works from the past and present. We will look as well at music from other cultures that may offer us a richer musical life. As in any introductory text, the process is necessarily selective. We attempt to open the door of musical recognition a little wider.

The Basic Elements of Music

Most ancient cultures shared the belief that music was a vital component of the natural world, a gift from heavenly beings. One theory is that for very early people, natural sounds were the voices of the gods, and human song was developed to imitate their voices. We still often hear comments such as "She sings like an angel."

Credit for the development of formal music goes to the ancient Egyptians and their belief that the god Thoth gave humanity seven basic sounds, perhaps much like the seven-tone scale that would come later. Along with laying the foundations of Western thought, art, and literature, the Greeks also created a profound theory of music. The Greek term *armonia*, which became the English word **harmony**, indicates a connection between music and the structure of the universe. Religions of the world have long believed that through music we can achieve union with the divine. Ancient Chinese philosophers, for example, who believed all nature was ruled by a divine principle of order, saw music as the human connection to that order.

Even before it was thought to be the sound of the gods, music must already have existed. It may have originated in human imitation of pleasing sounds, such as birdsongs or raindrop patters or animal noises, in the same way that visual art may have begun as the human need to imitate the familiar world. Perhaps music began from the need for better communication, with rudimentary musical sounds an integral part of early language. Or there may have been a long ago moment when someone thought, *Why wait for the soothing call of a morning bird when I can make that sound myself?*

Tone

The basic element of music is the **tone**, or note, a sound produced by the human voice or by musical instrument that maintains the same frequency of vibration regardless of duration. Perhaps the imitation of a natural sound was then shaped to become pure and sweet. Or perhaps that pure and sweet tone just came from someone's imagination, and people nearby were astounded when they heard it. However it happened, the discovery of tones marked the beginning of the human victory over the unplanned audio environment. True music began when someone experimented with a variety of tones, some higher, some lower.

The Scale

People in the ancient world who discovered different tones could not have known that they were caused by the frequency of sound-wave vibrations: the higher the frequency, the higher the tone. After a time, someone must have happened upon a distinct progression of individual tones from low to high, and that was the beginning of music as *we* know it. This orderly progression of frequencies from low to high is the **scale**. All cultures that developed music used a scale, though they did not necessarily happen upon the same sequence of tones.

At first, the dominant scale in both non-Western and Western music consisted of five tones, known as a **pentatonic scale**. It remains the basis for most traditional Asian music. The Western scale was expanded to six tones by the sixth century C.E. and was first written down (or notated) by an Italian monk. With the later addition of a seventh tone, the Western **diatonic scale** was complete. Notes were also given letter designations—ABCDEFG—and each sequence of seven would constitute a scale. The addition of sharps and flats—or **half-tones**—expanded the number of scales possible. Over time, the first note of each scale became the identifying **key** in which a given piece of music was composed. The basic scale in Western music begins with the note C—hence CDEFGAB, and these notes acquired the names *do, re, mi, fa, so, la, ti*.

Imagine that you are sitting at a piano. Beginning with C, your finger travels up the seven-tone progression, using only the white keys. You are therefore in the key of C, which many singers find most comfortable. But there are also the five black keys, or half-tones, such as C-sharp and E-flat. When you play the white keys plus the black keys, you are now using the twelve-tone **chromatic scale**. To the list of musical keys we may thus include C-sharp, B-flat, and so on.

When we play or sing a seven whole-tone progression, except for that which starts with A, we are using a *major scale*. A *minor scale* is more complicated. The *natural* minor scale begins with A and goes up seven whole tones. The *melodic* minor scale substitutes G-sharp going up but the whole-tone G coming down. The *harmonic* minor scale substitutes G-sharp going up and also coming down. Though the verbal definitions are complex, music in minor keys is easily recognized. Many songs of heartbreak and loss are written in minor keys, as is instrumental music that seeks to create a somber mood.

Traditional symphonic music is usually identified in terms of the key and type of scale in which it begins (composers can change either or both within a given work) and the *opus* number (that is, where the piece occurs in the composer's repertoire). Thus one might see this on a program: Beethoven, Symphony No. 9 in D Minor, Op. 125.

Combined major and minor keys can be found in blues music (discussed later in the chapter). Composers of classic popular songs have had great success in switching from one scale to another as the lyrics dictate. For example, in the song "Every Time We Say Goodbye," the composer/lyricist Cole Porter

I know that the twelve in each octave and the varieties of rhythm offer me opportunities that all human genius will never exhaust.

—**Igor Stravinsky**

enumerates the emotions he feels at parting from his beloved. In one line he says that, when she is gone, all the joy goes out of his life and "how strange the change from major to minor." The key changes to match the lyrics, creating an unusual and moving effect.

The music of most non-Western cultures is based on a scale of five tones that do not necessarily correspond to Western sounds. The Western preference for seven tones may have to do with the fact that Western listeners are accustomed to the narrower frequency intervals between the seven tones of the familiar scale. Hearing traditional Asian music for the first time and expecting the familiar scale, Western listeners are likely to find the sounds quite strange. But the music can be hypnotic. It places great reliance on the purity of musical line, made possible by the greater distinctness of the tones. There is often less complexity than in music composed using the seven-tone scale.

In contrast, Africa has a long musical tradition without a formalized scale at all. Tones were fundamental, as in other cultures, but these could change to suit the emotion of the musician or singer. Traditional African music has always made strong use of the human voice, and when the voice is the primary way of preserving melody, much variation is the rule. Musical notation is possible, but this doesn't mean performers feel obligated to repeat what others have played or sung. The music of Africa, brought to these shores by slaves and later by those who migrated here, has made possible the evolution of jazz and blues, two art forms that allow for maximum freedom of expression.

Rhythm

Early music throughout the world was probably monophonic: limited to just the melodic line and sung or played without harmony. But rhythmic accompaniment would have been provided when appropriate, such as at ritual events like a funeral or a rite of passage celebrating the arrival of puberty.

We know rhythm was the underlying factor in early Greek ceremonies because we have written accounts of it. Certain rhythms were held appropriate for inspirational ceremonies because of their uplifting effect on the soul, while other rhythms—certainly those involved in the orgies held annually in honor of Dionysus—were deemed conducive to uncontrolled, licentious behavior.

Formal music may have begun with the discovery of tones, but rhythm by itself might well have preceded tone, scale, and the earliest instruments. Most likely, a rat-a-tat pounding of sticks and stones was an early factor in human development, used to mark occasions of great joy or solemnity. The early instincts are still with us. We often see very young children rat-a-tatting with blocks or just with their hands, the beat becoming more pronounced and regular as they grow older. Rap and hip-hop forms of today clearly indicate that we are just as attracted to the hypnotic effect of steady rhythm as our ancestors were.

Moving to a beat—better known as dancing—may be even older than singing, though the two may spontaneously have erupted together on many occasions. Even without specific tones to sing, people must have found pleasure in letting out their feelings at the insistence of loud beats from any number and kinds of sources. Recall that Chapter 2 analyzed contrasting aspects of human culture and human personality: the Apollonian and the Dionysian. The Apollonian half of human beings enjoys order; the Dionysian half exults in unrestrained expressions of feeling. Neither side is sufficient by itself. Civilization advances with Apollonian order, but without Dionysian spontaneity, it can become rigid and uncreative. Dancing to Dionysian rhythms puts Apollonian control temporarily to sleep. Inspired by the rhythm, dancers can shut down their rational side and be driven by forces buried deep in the human unconscious.

Rhythm in music, as in poetry, is an alternation between stress and unstress. It acquires its different forms according to the pattern of alternation used. A familiar rhythm is that of the waltz, created from a stressed beat followed by two unstressed beats. Also described as a "stately" rhythm, it is far more Apollonian than it is Dionysian, and was thus suitable for the aristocrats of nineteenth-century ballrooms, though it had its Dionysian side in an era when touching the opposite sex in public was otherwise frowned upon. Popular among aristocrats of the eighteenth century, the minuet was also based on Apollonian (that is, rigid and repetitive) rhythms. So are the marches used for funeral and graduation processions. Plato approved of stately rhythms, which for him lent gravity to public occasions, affirming order in the state. He disapproved strongly of rhythms that were there only to excite the emotions.

People of today who enjoy letting go on a dance floor to the beat of rock bands evidently find Dionysian liberation a satisfying escape from the Apollonian demands of household duties, jobs, or schoolwork. The rhythms of rock and hip-hop probably date back to the dawn of humanity, and may well have bonded groups together in a collective, joyous release of pent-up energy. Dionysian rhythms have kept us in touch with our deeper self, our wild natures. If not expressed through art, they might find less appropriate means of escape.

In formal musical art, including concert pieces, standard popular songs, country, traditional dance music, and at least the beginning stages of rock, the rhythmic underpinning is often pronounced and unchanged either for the whole work or for specific portions of it. We can say that rhythm is the mortar that holds a work together, that gives coherence to a collection of sounds. A change in rhythm can be a major event, often very exciting to the listener. It opens up new possibilities, new directions, but then the new rhythm must continue the job of holding the piece together.

A conceivable theory of formal musical origins can be expressed as follows: When musical tones joined the ancient human passion for rhythm, a new force was born that provided a way for emotions to be expressed, released, and controlled. Once rhythm was discovered, it never left musical art. Even the plainsong, a chant sung by medieval monks and clerics, has a rhythm, though it is hard to detect because there are so many stressed tones, and those not stressed tend to be delicately sung. If we think the music of Impressionist composer Claude Debussy seems to be lacking in rhythm, perhaps our untrained ears cannot detect the subtle changes in stress marked by a subdued percussion section. In the famous *Bolero* by Debussy's compatriot

Archetypes in This Chapter	
Blues	more than just a musical genre, this term also refers to a feeling of sadness and frustration that accompanies life and especially love.
Hip	originated before the popularity of hip-hop music; suggests people who shake their hips in a confident, carefree way and has come to mean that one is on top of things and very up to date.
Jazz	has come to define much that is non-musical, as in "jazz it up," which means "give it style"; can also refer to "a whole bunch of stuff too complicated to go into at the moment," as in "all that jazz."
Rock	can now mean anything from "We're going to win this game" to "We're going to make our presence felt at the zoning-board meeting."
Roll	has the connotation of having things go smoothly, as in "on a roll," or springing into action, as in the military's "Let's roll!"
Scoundrel	roguish male who embodies a Dionysian approach to life, forever seeking pleasure and shunning responsibility. Many contemporary rock and hip-hop musicians consciously or unconsciously emulate this archetype.

and fellow Impressionist Maurice Ravel, the underlying rhythm is so pronounced that it takes over the entire piece.

Desiring to free themselves from the restraints that traditional rhythms impose, some composers attempt to be totally arrhythmic; that is, they avoid all regular alternations of stress and unstress, seldom repeating a pattern. The listener is kept off guard, presumably on edge, and the piece aspires to create a mood of agitation and emotional instability. Whether this is done because the composer wishes to be "different" or to make some kind of statement through the music, the reality is that non-rhythm is a kind of rhythm. Even if every tone were stressed, the result would be a kind of rhythm.

Thus the issue is not what does or does not constitute rhythm but why music cannot exist without it. What is the magic that rhythm weaves inside us? We can speculate at great length, of course. Children are conceived in rhythm, born in rhythm; parents clap their hands in rhythm to keep children from crying. The universe itself throbs with rhythms: the rotation of the planet, the alternation of the seasons, incoming and outgoing tides, birth and death. How about order and disorder, Apollo and Dionysus, belief and doubt, joy and sorrow? Anthropologists studying early rituals have suggested that rhythmic effects were used to express the heartbeat of Mother Earth.

Rock percussionist Mickey Hart of the Grateful Dead once said, "Rhythm is at the very center of our lives." If you were to ask a number of people which musical element they could most easily dispense with, rhythm would most probably not be the answer.

Melody

The art of music began with differentiated tones played or sung in certain patterns that might or might not have been repeated. One might have flowed into another. These patterns were melodies. **Melody** is the part we remember of a song or a symphonic movement. If we remember nothing beyond a "babble" of instruments and a great deal of percussion, chances are many of us would ask, "What happened to the melody?"

Music was my refuge. I could crawl into the place between the notes and curl my back to loneliness.

—**Maya Angelou**

The discovery of tone made melody possible. Melody can be defined in two ways: one, most familiar to Western ears, as *a significant sequence of musical tones that form a unity, like a sentence of prose, and are usually repeated later in the exact order or as a recognizable variation of the original*; or two, as found in many non-Western cultures, *an arrangement of tones in a flowing sequence that may or may not have a definite end*. Certain melodies were used over and over because they were pleasing, and a method was needed for preserving them. Musical instruments may have been invented for this purpose.

Opera-goers listening to a new work in its premiere performance may at first find that "there are no melodies in it." Someone accustomed to only Western symphonic music may wonder why, at first hearing, there is no beautiful melody in sitar music from India, or may denounce a rock band for pounding out "just noise." But with any new work, we should try to hear what the composer wants us to hear, and *then* we can decide whether we want to hear it again.

Many are understandably drawn to what may be termed *romantic* melody, the melodic line that falls soothingly on the ears and is usually repeated. Much of its emotional impact has to do with the instruments that play it: often the violin, piano, guitar, and flute—instruments that produce delicate sounds. Romantic melody tends to be "gentle," befitting the tender emotions it calls up. It is almost always slow. Popular classics like "Smoke Gets in Your Eyes" and "Melancholy Baby" are said to be melodious for these reasons and, when sung today, are usually accompanied by delicate, as opposed to brassy and percussive, instruments.

A romantic musical style was dominant during the nineteenth and early twentieth centuries. Composers such as Brahms and Tchaikovsky provide lush sequences of tones that are easily recalled and that evoke emotions within the listener. Brahms's "Cradle Song," or "Lullaby," is known throughout the world and has become almost synonymous with treasured memories of an infant's earliest days. The main theme in Tchaikovsky's *Romeo and Juliet* overture reminds people of the joys of first love. Translated into a popular song called "Our Love," it contributed to Tchaikovsky's reputation as a king of melody.

Rhapsody on a Theme of Paganini by Sergei Rachmaninoff (1873–1943) offers excellent examples of romantic melody. The main theme is introduced at the beginning—a sprightly and graceful melody written by Nicolò Paganini, an Italian violinist and composer who lived a century earlier. Though Paganini's work has long been popular with violinists because of its intricate challenges to the instrument, Rachmaninoff's variations on the theme have become immensely more popular with audiences than the original—especially his Seventeenth Variation, in which, after a dramatic silence, the piano enters and plays a melody that is Paganini's lively theme turned around and performed at a much slower tempo. When the string section passionately repeats the theme, the listener cannot help experiencing a surge of emotion.

The world of art has its visual equivalents of familiar and unfamiliar melodies. It too experienced the romanticism of the nineteenth century, producing the calm of peaceful country scenes as well as the majesty of natural forces such as the ocean and towering mountains. Modern artists who wanted to break away from romanticism found support in new and unfamiliar styles of music, while their colleagues in the visual arts attempted to capture musical sound on canvas. Georges Braque, the Cubist painter discussed in Chapter 5, gave us *The Musician*, with Cubist images that parallel the breaking up of the romantic melodic line, as Cubism breaks up visual experience into fragments instead of continuous vision (Color Plate 17).

Among jazz musicians, melody usually means the theme that begins their performance and on which the remainder of it is based. By the conclusion of the piece, the original theme is usually different from the melody we heard at the outset —*very* different. Jazz is complex, requiring an initial willingness to devote the time needed to explore its many treasures. Many of us, at least in the beginning, become confused or bored when the melody disappears and is replaced by varied tones of varied instruments.

An effective way to increase your appreciation for what is often considered non-melody is to become a more attentive listener to jazz. In doing so, you will find variations on a melody performed by different instruments throughout a piece. From jazz move on to **chamber music** (concert music written for a few instruments rather than a symphony orchestra). Once again you will hear clearly defined themes that are then developed through variations into ever more complex patterns of sounds. By extending your definition of melody, you will find yourself enjoying a broader range of musical experience.

Sometimes melody is a sequence of tones that seems to go on indefinitely without repeating. During the rebellion of the 1960s against "the establishment,"

Music is the arithmetic of sounds as optics is the geometry of light.
—**Claude Debussy**

sitar music achieved popularity in the West, partly because of its extended melodic lines and its clearly non-Western sound. Some modern composers are drawn to non-Western sound in an effort to break away from the traditional. Philip Glass, a contemporary American composer, writes melodic lines that keep repeating a single pattern. Some have called his work monotonous and endlessly repetitive, while others find it pleasantly hypnotic. Director Martin Scorsese (to be discussed in Chapter 10) recruited Glass to write the Asian-sounding score for the film *Kundun* (1997), the story of the Dalai Lama. Although Glass is Western, the music was authentically Tibetan, and therefore unfamiliar to most Western ears. Listening to this music is a good way to explore alternative kinds of melody. We should remember that the so-called "beauty of melody" is a matter of historical period and cultural heritage. Not that all melody is beautiful—or that no melody is beautiful; rather, beauty in music has a lot to do with familiarity and the kind of instruments popular within a given cultural tradition.

Extreme departures from tradition have characterized modern Western music since the earliest years of the twentieth century, when composers reacted strongly against the romantic conception of melody. The aggressive **dissonance** in their music has had much to do with its deliberate lack of appeal to those who want music to sound romantic.

Throughout the twentieth century, composers kept experimenting with non-traditional scales and sounds. Sometimes they invented new kinds of musical notes that were not in any scale anyone knew but had to be half-sung and half-spoken. Sometimes composers even have long stretches of silence in their music. In recent years a significant number of composers have reacted against *modernism*, especially what they consider "noisy jangling and crashing," a fierce determination to sound like nothing that ever came before. The new music is called, like the new in visual art, *postmodern*. The most frequently performed works of this genre come from a group of composers calling themselves **minimalists**. Their goal is to divest music of modernism's unnecessary trappings and return to the basic elements, particularly rhythm. Minimalist music, such as that by Philip Glass and John Adams, is sometimes dismissed as coldly formal and unemotional, as well as monotonous, by unsympathetic listeners who also find it unmelodic. But like all unfamiliar music, minimalist compositions can reward those willing to take the time to listen.

It has been said that music is what emotion sounds like. And the emotional life of an individual is exceedingly complex. To insist that music sound only a certain way is like saying that people should feel only a certain way. We can turn away from strange-sounding music, just as we don't have to welcome any stranger we think we don't want to know. But we also have the freedom to make friends.

Harmony and the Orchestra

In Asian music, tones are usually played by themselves, that is, without *harmony*, which is the simultaneous production of tones by voices or instruments. So accustomed are Westerners to hearing simultaneous tones that they tend to take harmony for granted. But like melody, harmony has historical and cultural roots.

During the first millennium, Christian churches incorporated music into the private services of monks and priests as well as public masses. Emphasis was placed on song as a means of communicating with God. Greatly influenced by ancient Hebrew chants, these sung prayers became known as *plainsong*. They were performed in unison by clerics, acting as one voice praising God's glory and asking for mercy and forgiveness. Harmony created by units of voices singing different tones would have been out of place, a violation of the belief that all people were the same in the eyes of God.

During the sixteenth century, as the Renaissance, with its rebirth of classical culture, moved from one European country to another, bringing with it a celebration of life on earth, music—secular music—was eagerly sought. Since the Renaissance emphasized enjoyment during one's brief stay on earth, music could fill leisure hours with many pleasures. The royal courts all had musicians on hand, and new instruments were invented to explore the richness and sensuality of secular music. In these venues scarcely an hour of the day went by without the sounds of lute, recorder, or oboe, playing sometimes alone but often in small groups. Renaissance composers explored the harmonious interweaving of instruments and voices, as if to say that music should be the contribution of a number of individuals, each adding to life's enjoyment, each with a musical statement to make.

The Renaissance also celebrated the uniqueness of each human being. No longer need music be limited to plainsong, delivered in unison to obscure the differences among the singers. Harmony allowed for a variety of interweaving musical themes, each with its own melody, played or sung by individualized instruments or voices. Eventually the development of harmony would lead to the complexities of the *baroque* style in music, art, and architecture, a style that flourished in Europe during the seventeenth century.

The invention of harmony also made possible an innovative art form known as *opera*, a collaboration of many distinct individuals: composers, orchestras, singers, poets who wrote the words, dancers, and that new species of artist, the scenic designer, the whole becoming a rich and complex visual tapestry and festival of sound, all working together to give added meaning to the concept of harmony.

Orchestras grew in size and complexity, and as they did, composers eagerly explored the range of the new instruments. By the eighteenth century the **symphony**, a musical form in separate units, or movements, became a concert staple. Major aggregations of musicians became known as symphony orchestras; these steadily increased in numbers as Haydn, Mozart, Beethoven, Brahms, and Mahler wrote works that required more and more instruments. One of Mahler's major works late in the nineteenth century is titled *The Symphony of a Thousand* because it involves literally that many musicians and singers. Tchaikovsky's *1812 Overture* needs, in addition to a massive orchestra, numerous cannons that are fired as the music reaches its climax. Beethoven's Ninth Symphony is now performed by an enormous orchestra of at least 150 musicians in addition to a chorus of perhaps 200 voices.

In 1990 Leonard Bernstein, an American composer and conductor, was invited to present the Ninth Symphony at the site of the newly fallen Berlin Wall, which had, since the ending of World War II, separated East and West Berlin. On this occasion *more* than 200 musicians and singers from the United States, the Soviet Union, Great Britain, and France participated. The theme of the final movement, a choral setting of the poet Schiller's "Ode to Joy," was an anthem heralding a new dawn of freedom and friendship between the previously separated citizens of Berlin, as well as the ringing hope that all oppressed peoples would triumph in their struggle against tyranny.

To open the 1998 winter Olympics in Nagano, Japan, conductor Seiji Ozawa performed the "Ode to Joy" using choruses from four locations around the globe,

Music provides a kind of pleasure which human nature cannot do without.

—Confucius

Track 5

joined together by satellite. This time the music represented global unity, as athletes from diverse nations, unable to communicate with each other through words, could find in Beethoven's music a common bond.

Musical harmony, especially in the glorious complexities of the great symphony orchestras, has become a model of human society at its most ideal. It requires every musician to pull together for one common purpose. No one sound can be any more important than another, yet each one has its moment of prominence. If one tone is flat, the entire enterprise suffers. The ultimate product is a testimony to the genius of the individual.

Silence

After silence, that which comes nearest to expressing the inexpressible is music.

—**Aldous Huxley**

Silence is the unpublicized ingredient that makes music possible in the same way that the empty space around a sculpture makes the sculpture possible, or the judicious use of wall space can make or break an art exhibit. Just imagine twenty-five original van Goghs crammed together: "Where is *The Starry Night*? Oh, there it is. I almost missed it. Funny, but somehow it's not as exciting as I thought it would be." Fast-forwarding a DVD destroys all dramatic value. The acceleration erases the pauses, which are as significant as the words themselves. After all, if characters talk non-stop, how can a dramatic situation develop? In music, the spaces—or silences—between notes can be equally important.

To deepen an appreciation of music, it is necessary to hear and enjoy silence. Silence has been an integral part of many works. The pauses in the second movement, the "Funeral March," of Beethoven's Third Symphony are as famous as the themes that precede and follow them. They make possible the dramatic effect when the main theme of the movement returns for the last time. There is silence, then part of the theme, then more silence, then more of the theme. The effect reminds the listener of someone trying valiantly to hold back tears.

Think of the last time you were in the presence of someone struggling for self-control while overcome by a powerful surge of emotion. Weren't the silences full of meaning? Great composers handle silences in the same way that great artists like Leonardo da Vinci handle shadows. Great stage actors owe something of their greatness to the mastery they have achieved over the words that they do *not* speak and to the silences before and after the words they do speak.

A famous solo theme for French horn occurs soon after the opening of the fourth movement of Brahms's First Symphony. The moment is heralded by a timpani roll, which is followed by the introduction of the French horn theme. Some conductors, recognizing the musical benefits of silence, make the orchestra pause for several measures before the theme is heard. This silence dramatically intensifies the significance of what follows. The French horn enters like an actor at long last making an appearance for which the audience has been eagerly waiting. In some interpretations, however, there is almost no pause at all, perhaps losing an opportunity for creating a thrilling moment.

The composer John Cage (1912–1992) is famous for having incorporated silence into his work and making it as important as the actual notes he wrote down for musicians to play. One of his compositions, *4′33″*, named for the four and a half minutes it takes to perform it, asks the artist to sit at the piano for that length of time and, with his gestures, maintain the required tempo. Cage insisted that the "notes are silent," but that they are there all the same. One of his longer pieces for the piano combines both played and silent notes, and in yet another, the pianist performs a series of complex chords and difficult "runs" up and down the keyboard, and then sits perfectly still for about fifteen minutes. Audiences, according to one critic, seem "almost afraid to cough." A strong influence on Cage's work was Zen Buddhism, an extremely austere and disciplined form of Buddhism, demanding long hours of meditation in absolute silence.

What ultimately distinguishes one musician from another is not only the ability to play the notes as written and at the proper tempo, but the musical intuition that manifests itself. One way the professional ear can detect the presence of this intuition, or this "feeling for the music," is to listen to how the performer manipulates the silences that surround the tones. Three world-class pianists might record Beethoven's *Pathetique Sonata*, each playing exactly the same notes and giving proper attention to the tempo indicated by the composer, but the interpretation by each will have subtle touches unique to that musician. In almost every instance the telling factor is the handling of silence. Here a pause is elongated, there foreshortened. As with the space surrounding a sculpture, silence in music helps to define, to single out, to create individuality.

The most evident gift from great music is its sound. The subtlest, least publicized gift is the very absence of sound. The definition in the Overview of this chapter was: *Music is the shaped sound between silences.*

The Varieties of Musical Experience

We would have to write a book several times this size to do justice to the multitude of musical experiences available in the humanities. There are so many styles, so many musical forms, that singling out a few is difficult indeed. Within those parameters, however, certain kinds of musical experience—musical genres of the past and present—illustrate what music has to offer and help to explain why the humanities are indispensable to a well-lived, happy life.

A Bach Fugue

Johann Sebastian Bach (1685–1750) was born in a Germany that did not regard music as an art form, that did not recognize what music could do for the human spirit, that viewed music either as court entertainment, composed and performed for upper-class amusement by hirelings paid to do a job, or else as a subordinate adjunct to religious services. The music with which Bach is associated, which indeed he came to epitomize, grew out of religion but went beyond religion in its impact and influence on the future of music as an art. It became the very epitome of the **baroque**, a highly complex style not only of music but of art and architecture as well. Historians of the humanities usually date the baroque period from the middle of the seventeenth century to 1750, which happens to be the very year in which Bach died.

Johann Sebastian Bach, considered a mere employee hired to play the church organ and compose a few hymns, ended up revolutionizing the art of music.

Source: The Granger Collection.

The baroque period was characterized by architectural grandeur and an elaborate use of color and ornamentation. Civic buildings, such as those that still line the Ringstrasse, the main street of Vienna, were adorned with gilt, statuary, and other forms of embellishment, none of which was intended to be purely functional. The term *baroque* was taken from French and Portuguese words that meant "imperfect pearl" and applied to the new style, which was far from classical simplicity. Architecture made abundant use of curved rather than straight lines. And baroque music is exceptionally intricate.

Catholicism found in baroque architectural splendor one means of bringing people back to the fold. The German monk Martin Luther (1483–1546) had rebelled against Catholicism for what he considered its moral corruption, including the fact that the laws of celibacy were regularly broken, even by church leaders. With other reformers, he had started a revolutionary movement known as the Protestant Reformation, which aimed to divest religion of its Catholic sensuality. In sharp contrast to the stark, wooden churches of the Protestant Reformation, the Catholic baroque houses of worship, especially in Italy and Poland, reintroduced marble, brilliant colors, and statues, perhaps in an effort to encourage defectors to return to a reinvented religion with an appeal to both the spirit and the senses. These churches dating from the seventeenth century are adorned with flying angels suspended from brightly painted ceilings and smiling gold cherubs resting near the tops of marble columns. They were for their time the epitome of opulence, offering both dramatic and aesthetic appeal without apology.

Despite the many reforms instituted by Luther and his followers, Lutheranism remained closer to Catholicism than would be true of the multiple Protestant sects which were to develop. While Lutherans generally shunned the impetus toward elaborate visual ornamentation of the churches, they felt differently about ornamentation of their music. Music became especially important in the Lutheran service, for which Bach composed many of his works. As the era progressed, composers, both religious and secular, sought to outdo one another in the intricacy of their compositions. They made strong use of **counterpoint**, playing one melodic line against another, both melodic lines being given equal value and dominance.

Harmony, of course, had been standard in music since the early Renaissance, but Bach's counterpoint carried complexity a step further. Nonetheless, even though he had achieved considerable recognition for his music during his lifetime, after his death his church still considered him as primarily a great organist rather than a composer. When they first began to hear his compositions, congregations may have been slightly confused, if not overwhelmed by what they heard.

When Bach was hired to play the organ—and, if he wished, to compose little pieces to accompany the service—church music in early eighteenth-century Germany was hardly a recognized form of high art. Bach's appetite for experimenting with organ sound was insatiable. Seeking to expand his musical horizons, Bach took a leave of absence and went in 1705 to study with the famous Swedish organist and composer Dietrich Buxtehude, returning with new works of such intricacy and virtuosity that the church choir often could not sing them. By this time, however, word of the new music began to spread. Eventually he became musical director and choir director at St. Thomas's Church in Leipzig, where he remained for most of his productive life, scarcely traveling more than a few miles from the city.

His reputation expanded and blossomed, then began to fade as he grew older, even though the complexity of his work deepened. In some quarters he began to be called old-fashioned. He had almost single-handedly brought baroque music to its pinnacle and then was accused of not being modern enough. By midcentury Franz Josef Haydn (1732–1809) was learning his craft and soon would give birth to 104 symphonies, earning him the reputation he still enjoys as father of that musical genre. Haydn returned to the relative simplicity of classicism, and his tremendous influence helped to make baroque complexity obsolete. But even in Bach's declining years, younger composers were already experimenting with the style that Haydn would make famous.

Through the new works, German music was attaining stature as an art form, and thus the great repertoire of Bach—the cantatas, oratorios, and magnificent displays of counterpoint known as **fugues**—was considered dated even before it was ever really discovered. Bach's music would have to wait a full century before it would take its place among acknowledged masterworks.

Confined both geographically and professionally, Bach found liberation in exploring the possibilities of musical language. The baroque style required not only long, highly fluid melodies and countermelodies, but also **improvisation**—a spontaneous variation or set of variations on a given theme. Through improvisation he could take wings and soar into the endless skies of inner space.

Music in the time of both Bach and Haydn was not expected to express a composer's innermost emotions; and indeed Bach's music is frequently labeled *intellectual*. It is, for example, greatly admired by mathematicians, who see in it a musical parallel to higher calculus. Nonetheless, there is indeed an emotional side to it. Bach's great Toccata and Fugue in D Minor draws the listener into a vortex of sensations that are almost indescribable. The ear discerns the many melodic strands that play against each other, and the inner eye translates the sounds into patterns of light and lines that crisscross, engulf each other, and continually change into shapes never before seen or imagined. Surrendering to this music, we find ourselves visiting strange inner landscapes flooded with both thoughts and feelings.

Track 6

A **toccata** is a freestyle musical form designed to allow the performer to display virtuosity; it is frequently, as in the case of the D Minor work, followed by a fugue, which is more strictly controlled by established musical laws. In a toccata the composer or performer may improvise on the stated themes, taking them in a variety of directions.

We need only listen to the D Minor performed on an organ to be astounded that one pair of hands could master so difficult a composition.

This practice has definite counterparts in jazz. It is no coincidence that jazz players often acknowledge a strong debt to Bach, particularly for his genius at improvisation, and often include variations on Bach melodies in their repertoire. The fugue allows for the simultaneous hearing of different melodies played or sung; it is a swift-moving form, stabilized by the laws of counterpoint—the melodic lines heard simultaneously must complement, not conflict with, each other.

We need only listen to the D Minor performed on an organ to be astounded that one pair of hands could master so difficult a composition. The idea behind the fugue is to demonstrate that what for the average person would be an impossibility is indeed well within the capabilities of the performer. It allows both composer and performer to display their virtuosity. At the same time, the intricacies of the form require strong guidelines as well as enormous technical skills, developed over long years of practice. The result may sound as though the composer were allowing imagination free reign, but in actuality the music is rigorously disciplined. The major jazz composers and performers of our time are often highly trained musicians whose flights of improvisation follow definite rules, even as do the fugues of Bach.

The linear form of Bach's music allows us to experience its complexities little by little, note by note, rather than have them overwhelm us all at once, as baroque architectural interiors can do.

A Beethoven Symphony

Sometimes the history of the humanities lopes along for many years, even decades, without producing an artist who rises to the highest level of creative achievement. It can also happen that many artistic geniuses appear around the same time. The late fifteenth century in Italy, for example, produced three visual artists, acknowledged to be perhaps the world's greatest, all contemporary with each other: Leonardo, Michelangelo, and Raphael. Germany can boast that it gave the world Mozart and Beethoven during the late eighteenth century.

In the baroque musical tradition, which Bach epitomized, composers worked in a limited range of musical forms to find their own way through the music. Bach achieved greatness by making the forms accommodate his tremendous musical intellect and imagination. Mozart easily rivaled Bach with his phenomenal output—and in a much shorter lifespan (1756–1791)—composing not only operas but symphonies, chamber music for inexhaustible combinations of instruments, several huge masses, a long list of songs, and concerti for both violin and piano. Mozart expanded the capabilities of the symphony orchestra, thus preparing the way for Beethoven, who would take it to new heights. In order to provide emotional release from a tormented life in which he gradually lost his hearing, Beethoven composed in new or greatly expanded musical forms. It is not an exaggeration to say he reinvented the music of the West.

I heard one evening a symphony of Beethoven's. I thereupon fell ill of fever; and when recovered I was—a musician.

—Richard Wagner

Whereas Bach was primarily a church composer/ performer, Beethoven composed for churches, concert halls, small salons, private performances, royal chambers, but above all for himself. When he lost his hearing during the peak of his musical career, Beethoven turned inward, and out of his complex and anguished soul came sounds no one had ever heard. Even today, more than a century and a half after the composer's death, when every note written by him has been played and interpreted by thousands upon thousands of musicians and heard by millions, new listeners and performers can find in the music some as yet undisclosed aspect of Beethoven's gigantic personality as well as some unexplored region of their own inner space.

Beethoven built on the new tradition in music established before him by Haydn and Mozart. This tradition combined secular, religious, and nationalistic trends into one. It declared that the music of northern Europe was every bit the equal of Italian music, which had been for centuries the dominant musical tradition of the West. In particular, it created and then quickly broadened the scope of the symphony, which became for Germany what the opera was for Italy.

The development of the symphony cannot be measured in terms of quantity alone. Haydn wrote 104 symphonies, Mozart forty-one, and Beethoven "just" nine. (Later, Johannes Brahms, intimidated by the majestic symphonic creations of Beethoven,

Ludwig van Beethoven expanded the range of many musical forms, including the symphony.

Source: Culver Pictures, Inc.

would spend twenty years working on his first symphony and would ultimately leave the world "just" four!)

In 1804, after having given the world two symphonies in the tradition of Mozart (who had already stretched the limits of the form beyond anything yet known) Beethoven came forth with his Third or E-flat Major Symphony, which he named *Eroica* ("heroic"). The premiere proved to be an occasion for which the music world was still not completely prepared, even though the work had been preceded by Mozart's last symphony, the titanic *Jupiter*. After all, a symphony was originally a twenty-minute concert diversion, consisting of four movements: the first moderately paced, the second slow and lyrical, the third rapid and light-hearted, and the fourth rousing and climactic. The four movements were related only in terms of a composer's characteristic style; they were not expected to make a unified statement of any kind.

The *Eroica* was twice the length of the *Jupiter*. It was a work so huge in conception, so complex in execution, and so overwhelming in impact that by all rights it should have invited immediate comparison with Michelangelo's *David*, the Sistine Chapel ceiling, or the great tragedies of Shakespeare. Unfortunately, many of the first listeners could not accommodate the work's heroic dimensions or its daring innovations, particularly its heavy use of seventh chords, up to that time a musical taboo, considered barbarically dissonant, unfit for civilized ears.

In the opinion of music historians, the most astonishing aspect of the *Eroica* is that it is not just big for the sake of bigness. One critic sums up the matter: "We are used to the scale of the *Eroica*, but what is forever new is a musical substance which requires every second of the vast time expanse which Beethoven organized to contain it. In its size it is wholly efficient, as fine an example of economy of structure as any four-minute Bach fugue."[1] In the *Eroica*, not only do the four movements constitute a unity, but each succeeding movement sounds like a perfect complement to the one before it. It is clear that Beethoven did not finish one movement and then tack on another as though the preceding one had not existed.

The first movement is on a grand, heroic scale, an epic style with noble themes and huge orchestration to be rivaled only by the composer's own fifth and ninth symphonies. The story is that Beethoven, like a number of artists such as Jacques Louis David (1748–1825), was inspired by the heroic image of Napoleon as the liberator of Europe. He thus created, in the opening movement, music that paralleled his feelings and then dedicated the entire work to the man he perceived as savior of the free world. When word reached the composer that his hero had demanded to be crowned emperor, Beethoven apparently rescinded the dedication.

Beethoven is believed to have dedicated his Third Symphony to Napoleon, depicted in this famous portrait, then rescinded the dedication when word reached the composer that Napoleon had declared himself emperor.

Source: Jacques Louis David, *Napoleon Crossing the St. Bernard Pass*, 1800. Credit: © Erich Lessing/Art Resource, NY.

One is tempted to hear in the second movement a musical parallel to Beethoven's profound disillusionment with Napoleon.

The *Eroica*, for many, came to embody the "common man" movement, even if Napoleon did not. In fact, much of Beethoven's music has the same fist-shaking thunder we find in the work of Michelangelo. A musical rebel, defying all tradition, plagued by illness that would eventually rob him of his hearing, misunderstood and criticized by many, he could readily identify with revolutionary movements in his native Germany, as well as in America and France.

One is tempted to hear in the second movement a musical parallel to Beethoven's profound disillusionment with Napoleon. Profound sorrow is certainly there, as indicated by the tempo notation: *marcia funebre* (funeral march). It is the slowest of all slow movements, dirgelike and heartbroken. We have already spoken of it in the section on silence as a musical element. Whether Napoleon was the direct cause of the sorrow or whether Beethoven, having exhausted the range of noble emotions, found himself exploring the depths of sadness, we cannot know. But we can say that the first two movements of the *Eroica* strongly suggest an experience common to nearly everyone: the passage from heroic, idealistic youth to maturity and its awareness of tragedy.

The third movement, by contrast, is almost shocking, with its galloping pace and precise horns, all of it sounding like nothing so much as a hunting party. Out of place? Surely not. Listening carefully to every note of the funeral march shows that there is only so much emotional wrenching one can sustain. Life must go on. The depressed spirit must pull itself up from despair.

The finale begins with a graceful, dancelike melody suggestive of polite society: civilization restored, so to speak. This leads through an intricate development back into the same heroic mood that opened the symphony. We have passed from romantic illusion to the depths of tragedy and, through struggle, upward again to a more mature, sober, and deliberate affirmation. The composer of the *Eroica* captures the human soul in full range. It would not mark Beethoven's last glimpse of paradise.

Track 10

Beethoven's Ninth Symphony was composed around 1818, when he was totally deaf. It is easily four times the length of a late Mozart symphony, and twice that of even the *Eroica*. Not the journey of a young man's soul coping with the sobering realities of life, the Ninth Symphony is rather the final statement of a gigantic mentality that has struggled for years with both physical and creative suffering—of a person who has labored to find and capture it all, as Michelangelo, two centuries earlier, had sought perfection in marble, and as Einstein, a century later, would seek the ultimate equation for unifying the interactions among all the forces in the universe.

During the first three movements of the Ninth, Beethoven gives us one haunting melody after another, complex rhythms, intricate harmonies, and bold dissonance. He seems to be striving to find a musical equivalent to every feeling that can be experienced. By the fourth movement he appears to have concluded that the orchestra alone was not enough to express the sounds he must have heard in the far recesses of his silent world. He needed human voices.

Other composers before him had written large choral works: Bach's *Passion According to Saint Matthew*, Haydn's *Creation*, and Mozart's *Requiem*, to name three supreme examples. But Beethoven pushes the human voice farther than many have believed possible.

There remains considerable controversy about the final movement of the Ninth. Some critics say it takes us as close to the gates of heaven as we can get in this earthly lifetime. Some have called it a musical embarrassment, totally unsingable. One soprano, after attempting it, vehemently declared that Beethoven had no respect whatever for the female voice. Others have suggested that in his deafness Beethoven heard extraordinary sounds that were not contained within the boundaries of music and for which there were no known instruments, not even the human voice. Perhaps such sentiments overromanticize the work. But perhaps not. No one will ever know what Beethoven was hearing.

The musical setting for Friedrich von Schiller's "Ode to Joy," the main theme of the fourth movement, has attained the stature of an international hymn. By far, the majority opinion about this music is that it transcends its own "unsingability" and any breach of musical taste it may commit. Asking whether one "likes it" seems beside the point. One can only feel humbled by its majesty. Listening to Beethoven's Ninth Symphony is discovering what human creativity really means.

The premiere performance of the work in Vienna, at that time the capital of European music, was attended by every Viennese musical luminary. By now fully convinced of the composer's genius, they were eager to discover what new sounds the great man could possibly bring forth from an inner world that was barred forever from the real sounds of humanity and nature. Beethoven was the co-conductor.

Witnesses to the event have left behind stories of the performance, especially of how the maestro conducted with sustained vigor, hearing his own orchestra no doubt, for when the "other" orchestra had finished the work and the enthusiastic applause began, Beethoven had not yet put down his baton. When at last he realized what was happening, he started to walk from the stage, perhaps feeling his music had not communicated. But the other conductor caught up with him and turned him around to see the people on their feet, shouting "Bravissimo!" Beethoven simply bowed his head. No one will ever know what it was he had heard, just as he could not have known what *they* had heard. Nonetheless, that moment lives on in the history of the humanities as a rare meeting of souls in that strange space where the spirit of art lives.

Art Songs

So far we have discussed possible origins of music, the basic elements of music, and two major musical forms and composers who achieved distinction through making glorious musical history. For many of us, however, everyday musical experience comes from *songs*, much shorter compositions with easily remembered melodies and rhythms.

An art song is written as part of the concert repertoire of great singers.

We had nursery songs to teach us and lullabies to soothe us. Most of us learned the alphabet by singing a song about the letters. Nonsense songs with refrains like *Nikkity Nakkity Noo Noo Noo* gave us an outlet for feelings we could not always understand or find words for. Some kind of song-making—if only the spontaneous chanting of a child—is innate to the growing-up process at every time and in every place. Like poetry and the other arts, song evolved into ever more sophisticated styles. Eventually it reached a point at which the composer's choices were rigidly defined by the rules of music.

The birth of song as art probably dates back to the classical period when epic poems like *The Iliad* (see Chapter 4) were sung by minstrels as a means of being more easily remembered. In the early Middle Ages monks sang their prayers as a regular part of the worship service. By the later Middle Ages, however, wealthy aristocrats demanded song as part of court entertainment, and the subject almost always was love. By the time of the great composers we have discussed, song was a recognized art form, expected in concert programs, and performed by highly trained professionals. These works have come to be known as art songs, as distinct from popular songs, which are not originally written as concert pieces.

Mozart and Beethoven wrote art songs in addition to their innumerable other works. Much of the time they supplied musical settings for the poetry of their day. With their prodigious genius they could create these shorter forms fast enough to fulfill the growing demand from well-known singers who needed to extend their repertoires. It was also a way to earn money.

A genius of the art song was Franz Schubert, who in his tragically brief life (1797–1828) composed more than 600! He wrote painstakingly for both singer and accompanist, his musical settings precisely suiting the words and fitting the mood of a poem. An excellent introduction to Schubert is "The Trout," with its sprightly melodic line and rippling fishlike accompaniment, and also "Death and the Maiden," with its agitated melodies and strangely peaceful accompaniment. The maiden of the title sees Death, a savage-looking skeleton, approaching and pleads with him to pass by and not touch her. But Death turns out to be friendly and promises that she will sleep gently in his arms.

Among Schubert's most famous works is the musical setting he gave to "Ave Maria." There is a legend that the composer, chronically poor, wrote the piece rapidly on a napkin or tablecloth and sold it to someone for the equivalent of fifteen cents. True or not, the story does suggest what we know about Schubert: namely, that he was unsuccessful in his lifetime, though, unlike van Gogh, he had a small circle of friends who recognized his genius.

Our sweetest songs are those that tell the saddest thoughts.

—**Percy Bysshe Shelley**

Folk Songs

Unlike many art forms that have established traditions within the humanities, the folk song has followed few aesthetic rules. Some folk songs originated centuries ago, perhaps as a way of spreading news in isolated areas, perhaps as musical improvisations by people who had little else to entertain them. Folk songs didn't require expert musical accompaniment or trained voices. They were likely to be handed down from generation to generation and changed every time they were sung. That's why you'll find many versions of the same song. Often the dedicated concert-goer considers folk music too haphazard in its origins and careless in its execution to warrant serious consideration. Folk songs, however, do indeed fulfill a major requirement of art: *they endure.*

Folk music in recent times has often attained the status of the art song, especially when sung by accomplished singers like Joan Baez, Joni Mitchell, Bob Dylan, Willie Nelson, Ani Difranco, and Ferraby Lionheart. Yet it can still be a participants' art, an affirmation of group identity. In certain parts of the country, let a fiddler introduce the first few notes of "Turkey in the Straw," and almost immediately people are clapping their hands or dancing. During the civil rights movement of the 1960s, the song "We Shall Overcome" created—and even now can create—instant bonding among people who may never have seen each other before. Surely there is a place in the humanities for music that can bring groups together as nothing else can.

Songs sung spontaneously at rallies or sporting events are not exactly folk music, but they fulfill a similar purpose in promoting group solidarity. For example, during the 1980s a widely popular rock group called *Queen* released an album containing the song "We Will Rock You" that is now sung by students all over the country, especially during football games.

The history of folk music includes the *commemorative song*, which derives from times before people had written records of important events. During the Middle Ages, for example, troubadours kept people informed of heroic actions in battles and skirmishes by traveling around and singing songs about them. Maritime lore abounds with songs commemorating events that took place at sea, such as atrocities committed by a pirate captain or the sinking of a ship to its lonely, watery grave. The narrator of the commemorative song is never identified. A typical opening line is: "My name is nothin' extra / So that I will not tell." One song winds up in this self-effacing manner: "Now to conclude and finish / Too far my lines have run." The group and the event are always more important than the singer/reporter.

The commemorative song does not belong just to the past. A modern American folk classic is Don McLean's "Bye, Bye, Miss American Pie," composed in 1971. Its mystifying refrain following the singing of the title, tells how the narrator drove his "Chevy to the levee / But the levee was dry." Like all folk music that continues to be sung, its tune is infectious, even though the meaning of the lyrics is not clear. A popular interpretation is that McLean wrote the song to commemorate the deaths of pop stars Buddy Holly and Richie Valens in a 1959 plane crash. That it does indeed make reference to a disaster is suggested by the final line, which speaks of "the day the music died."

The *work song* is also highly durable, for it is hard to imagine a time when work will not be central to most people's lives. In some cases the work song reflects great hardship and a state of tension between management and labor. Often, however, the music is jolly and full of bounce and joy, as though to help the original creator forget tired limbs and meager salary.

> *I've been workin' on the railroad*
> *All the livelong day;*
> *I've been workin' on the railroad*
> *Just to pass the time away.*

The nineteenth-century folk ballad "John Henry" reflects the conflict between worker and machine at a time when the steam drill was about to replace hammers swung by human arms. John Henry became a folk hero, mythologized as a superhuman individual who was stronger than a machine, at least for a while: in his effort to beat the steam drill through the mountain with his hammer and steel pike, John Henry's great heart finally failed him.

> *He hammered so hard*
> *He burst his poor heart*
> *And he laid down his hammer and he died.*
> *Lord! Lord!*
> *He laid down his hammer and he died.*

In the past, management and labor disputes frequently erupted into violence before they could be settled by the two parties sitting around a table in the presence of a federal arbitrator. All too often workers had little power against corporate ownership. Songs memorializing those who had given their lives in the name of workers' rights no doubt kept up the spirits of many who might otherwise have resigned themselves to defeat.

One such worker was Joe Hill, a Swedish-born immigrant who, like so many others, came to the United States in the early twentieth century with dreams of success, only to be swallowed into a vast labor force, toiling for forty or more hours a week and trying to survive on a minimum wage. A born folk poet and singer, Hill began to compose songs about the hardships endured by the workers and the obstinate refusal of management to meet their demands or even to offer a compromise. He became a modern folk minstrel, and his songs—simple, easily sung and remembered—soon spread from union hall to union hall, adapted to many kinds of labor problems.

Action is the antidote to despair.
—**Joan Baez**

Hill was also an activist, traveling throughout the country, speaking to larger and larger gatherings of workers, and he inevitably acquired the reputation of troublemaker and rabble rouser. While he was in Salt Lake City to address a union meeting, a murder took place, and Hill was arrested and charged with the crime. In a still famous trial, the prosecution produced witnesses who placed Hill at the scene of the crime. After a short jury deliberation he was found guilty and sentenced to die by firing squad. Awaiting his execution, he wrote his final song, in which he said that some people could find justice in Salt Lake City "but not Joe Hill."

Joan Baez, a folk singer who epitomized the human rights movement of the 1960s and 1970s, wrote a commemorative ballad about Joe Hill, one that has already achieved the status of genuine folk art.

> *From San Diego up to Maine,*
> *in every mine and mill,*
> *where working-men defend their rights,*
> *it's there you find Joe Hill,*
> *it's there you find Joe Hill!*[2]

Whether written a century ago or just last week, folk music is easily recognized. It does not evolve in sophistication. It does not acquire subtle rhythms. Its rhymes are always simple, making the words easy to remember. Though "Joe Hill" was written by a seasoned professional who is a master of the guitar and possesses a voice of exquisite control, it has no professional "polish." It could have erupted spontaneously—always the mark of a real folk song.

The *accumulation song* is deliberately drawn out, with verse after verse and a refrain repeated after each one. Songs like "The Twelve Days of Christmas" and "Old MacDonald" start off with one detail (one gift, one animal) and then add more and more as the song continues. Accumulation songs extend group solidarity for longer periods, prolong the high spirits of the gathering, and keep loneliness at bay.

The *scoundrel song* celebrates the Dionysian personality—the perennial favorite of our hidden selves—the lawless, irresponsible, but charming rogue you couldn't trust or marry or put in charge of an important operation but who is always fun. An Irish favorite is "The Wild Rover," which upholds a life of drinking, carousing, gambling, and avoiding work. The narrator proudly sings that "if you don't like me, you can leave me alone." Who can argue with that premise? He intends to

> *eat when I'm hungry and drink when I'm dry,*
> *And if moonshine don't kill me,*
> *I'll live till I die.*

To be sure, society would perish if it depended upon wild rovers. But the subject of a scoundrel song is usually a loner who could not, *would* not adapt easily to the demands of organized society and so could hardly be expected to celebrate the morally upright, the hard working, and the pious.

The *narrative song*, as its label implies, tells a tale, often at great length, answering, like the accumulation song, the need of listeners to stay together as long as possible. It was the folk version of the epic, usually filled with accounts of wondrous and miraculous events. The Scottish ballad "Binorie" recounts the sad story of a miraculous harp that was fashioned from the breastplate of a murdered young woman and that sings as it plays. The harp reveals the events leading up to the woman's murder, then comes to the shocking climax: "My sister it was who did me slay." Quite possibly the song, like many others, was based on an actual event.

Country and western music has carried on the narrative tradition of folk music, adding its own unique tales to the repertoire. During the late 1960s "Ode to Billy Joe" was popular as a crossover, topping country charts as well as the Top 40. Fans listened intently to the tragic story of a teenage boy who jumped to his death from the Tallahatchee Bridge. What was unique about the song was that it gave subtle suggestions about the "why" of the incident but never actually told us in so many words. Radio talk shows had hundreds of callers who gave their opinions, but the composer, Bobbie Gentry, refused to divulge the secret.

The 1960s, a period of widespread alienation in the United States, saw a significant revival of folk music. Young people, often far from home, got together for the night in hastily improvised camps or in communes with ever changing members and became instant—if temporary—friends through the common bond of singing. Joan Baez and Judy Collins attained huge popularity by reviving old songs, particularly those that still spoke to the rebellious spirit seeking freedom from restraint. But the main thrust of the folk revival was the tightness of the group. It could have a distinctly spiritual side. At concerts Judy Collins sang the old hymn "Amazing Grace" and soon had 10,000 voices joining in with hands interlocked in a show of community. The hymn, once revived, has remained an integral part of our culture; it was sung during the funeral of President Ronald Reagan at the National Cathedral in 2004.

New folk minstrels emerged, using *protest songs* to make statements against war, pollution, inequality, and the corruption of the establishment. Bob Dylan's "A Hard Rain's Gonna Fall" and John Lennon's "Give Peace a Chance" were written and sung in protest, originally against the Vietnam War, but since then they have been used to protest other wars, or all wars. They are modern folk songs that attain the level of art. Lennon summed up the dream of a world without war, hunger, and hatred in what may be the most important folk song of the last century: "Imagine." Though composed and sung by a master musician, "Imagine" has all the simplicity and the passionate honesty of the folk tradition. These three songs will probably endure as long as there are troubled times.

A more recent folk minstrel is Ferraby Lionheart, who was raised in the Korea Town section of Nashville and whose songs, especially the words, show considerable Asian influence. Some of them faintly resemble haiku (discussed in Chapter 4) in their deceptive simplicity. "The Octopus and the Ambulance," for example, begins with the admonition to escape from worry and stress by riding in an ambulance and, while there, hear somebody tell a joke about an octopus that made "an awful mess." Listening to the joke, you can "give yourself a break and laugh a while."

These are not songs about the deterioration of nature or about war. They aren't protesting anything but seem to be saying love may be all we need—and maybe some laughter. Lionheart's sound is definitely unlike that of any other Western pop singer around. But as it becomes more well known, critics may label it *folk pop* or *folk rock*. His rhythms are steady and insistent, and he sometimes sings in falsetto. The difference between this and most rock music, however, is that for Lionheart, the words are

Believe it or not, there are places in the world where music is important. There are places in the world where all the arts are a matter of national pride.

—**Frank Zappa**

Bob Dylan and John Lennon are two of the great folk minstrels to protest the war in Vietnam.

as important as the rhythm. His lyrics are a blend of sophisticated poetry and what an idealistic schoolboy might write to the girl he loves.

The protest song, however, is very much alive, especially in the work of Ani Difranco, who began playing the guitar when she was nine years old. By the time she was twenty she had released her first CD, which instantly established her prominence in the field of folk rock. She has since sung in venues ranging from small clubs to Carnegie Hall. Difranco's songs are socially oriented and deal with a wide variety of issues, especially sexism, racism, domestic abuse, homophobia, the rights of people to determine whether they want to reproduce, the plight of the poor and homeless—and most particularly, the idiocy of fighting wars to solve problems. She has campaigned for independent presidential candidates, insisting that what America needs is a leader who is not tied to the philosophy of a particular party.

Difranco is a superb musician. Her guitar work is characterized by staccato rhythms, rapid fingerpicking, and constant changes in tuning. Her lyrics are those of a poet, using complex metaphors, alliteration, and irony. She delivers her words in a half-spoken intonation, with heavy rhythmic stress. With her, folk music has traveled a long road from its grass roots in work songs and nonsense songs intended for community bonding, yet Difranco never forgets that her sophistication ultimately springs from the same heart that produced "Joe Hill."

Ani Difranco and Ferraby Lionheart, two modern folk minstrels who also have rock credentials.

Source: Left: © Andrewe Goetz/Corbis. Right: Photo by R. E. Barbash.

Folk music has inspired concert composers of the past and present. Beethoven was charmed by the Gaelic folk tradition and composed song cycles based on both Irish and Scottish melodic patterns. The American composer Aaron Copland (1900–1990) was so delighted by the country's folk music, especially songs of the old West, that his music has come to define America in sound. *Billy the Kid*, one of Copland's many ballet scores, uses the folk song "Goodbye, Old Paint" (sung by a cowboy to his horse) in a stirring theme and variations. *Rodeo* interweaves themes and rhythms from Saturday-night barn dances. *El Salón México* is an orchestral suite woven out of traditional Mexican folk material and exuberant Latin rhythms, set against Copland's unique dissonance. Perhaps the composer's most famous score was written for the ballet *Appalachian Spring*, which employs a number of folk themes, notably the old Shaker hymn "Simple Gifts." The ballet itself celebrates time-honored rituals like the raising of a barn by everyone in the community.

Folk themes such as those incorporated into this ballet often came from other cultures. Appalachian music, for example, has deep roots in the Gaelic folk music of Ireland and Scotland as well as the British folk tradition. The Israeli *hora* and the Italian *tarantella* are folk dances known throughout the world. *Polka* music was originally derived from Polish folk themes. We encourage you to pay attention to the many folk cultures brought to these shores from other countries and the rich musical experiences they provide.

American folk themes found their way into the concert hall in the symphonic music of Aaron Copland.

The Spiritual

The spiritual had its beginnings in the need of African Americans to articulate and preserve, to give meaning to their suffering, and to demand a rightful place in society. Taken—stolen—away from their homeland as far back as the seventeenth century, with no future except slavery, pain, and death, they took comfort in their relationship with God and an ultimate reward in a paradise where everyone was free.

> *Deep river,*
> *My home lies over Jordan.*
> *Deep river,*
> *I want to cross over into campground.*

Spirituals emphasize God's personal concern for each person, however obscure that person may be in the eyes of other mortals. For instance:

> *I sing because I'm happy,*
> *I sing because I'm free,*
> *For His eye is on the sparrow,*
> *And I know He watches me.*

If all music does not have to express or appeal to the emotions, the spiritual is one kind that exists to make emotional release possible. We cannot imagine what life would have been like for slaves, or what it would be like today in the impoverished sections of inner cities, without this profound music of earthly sorrow and religious hope.

As the spiritual genre grew and developed, it was made more and more complex by church choirs and soloists, each of whom would add the mark of their individual interpretations. Often transported by religious ecstasy, they created the new genre of *gospel* music. Over the years this genre, while remaining as an indigenous part of church services, has also moved into the arena of popular music. It is characterized by giving the singer free reign to add enough notes to allow a fuller emotional expression.

Gospel singer Mahalia Jackson (1911–1972) became the best-known and highly influential exponent of the genre. Born in New Orleans, when that city was bursting at the seams with new music—ragtime, jazz, and blues—she grew up next door to a church in which music played a vital role. She heard traditional hymns played and sung with many rhythmic variations. In addition, the sounds of Mardi Gras music, street vendors, and the songs belted out from the barrooms with wide open doors and windows seeped into her blood. Devoutly religious, Jackson blended spirituals and aspects of the New Orleans secular style into religious songs that became nationally famous when she moved to Chicago and married a businessman who recognized her potential and launched her career. In 1954 Columbia Records signed her to a long-term contract, and gospel music was soon on the charts.

A civil rights activist, Jackson took part in the historic March on Washington in 1963, singing before thousands assembled on the Mall to hear Martin Luther King Jr.'s epoch-making "I Have a Dream" speech.

Blues are songs of despair, but gospel songs are the songs of hope.
—**Mahalia Jackson**

Ragtime

Ragtime dates back to the turn of the twentieth century, to a period when the legendary fortunes of the Rockefellers, Vanderbilts, Goulds, and Astors were being amassed and when the American moneyed aristocracy, their acquaintances, and all those who emulated their Victorian manners were entertaining guests with salon orchestras playing stately waltzes. Their aim was to establish European elegance on this side of the Atlantic.

Some of the less privileged were eager to take advantage of the freedom to pursue upward mobility. They wanted to gain the social recognition already enjoyed by wealthy families, and they wanted to show everyone they were capable of creating elegance of their own. Ragtime emerged from the African American community and its musical traditions, transformed by the influence of European styles. African American musicians wanted to do more than play the minstrel-show type music with which white audiences had come to identify them. Ragtime came along at just the right moment. The acknowledged master of the new genre was Scott Joplin (1868–1917), who began his career in backrooms and honky-tonks but became a national celebrity with the publication of "Maple Leaf Rag" in 1899.

Joplin heard the original ragtime tunes frequently played by small African American combos on riverboats. They may have been variations on old plantation songs, minstrel-show cakewalks, and banjo melodies, usually played at lively tempos. White audiences expected African American music to be high-spirited. The label **ragtime** was coined to identify the syncopation that was the trademark of the new genre. **Syncopation** occurs when the melodic line of a piece is played against, not with, the accented beats of the rhythm accompaniment. Syncopated pieces are usually difficult to play because the left hand and the right hand follow different beats. (For a perfect example of syncopation, listen to George Gershwin's "Fascinatin' Rhythm.")

Joplin was captivated by the new sounds, but he wanted to turn them into a legitimate, recognized genre that would be associated with African Americans but also prove the equal of the foreign imports. This meant imitating or at least

Do not play this piece fast. It is never right to play Ragtime fast."
—**Scott Joplin**

Track 7

coming close to European rhythm. Joplin slowed down the pace to make the music even more stately. On the sheet music of his "rags" he would write: "Do not play this piece fast. It is never right to play Ragtime fast."

The waltz is played in three-quarter time, a tempo that is never varied. Ragtime, played almost exclusively on the piano, is written in *two*-quarter time, its tempo also never changing. The primary influences on Joplin's music, in addition to riverboat songs, were the popular European marches as well as the waltz and the quadrille, a dignified French square dance.

The enormous popularity of "Maple Leaf Rag" and the other Joplin hits that quickly followed made African American musicians sit up and take notice, especially in New Orleans, which was a stronghold for the liberal acceptance of new music. Jelly Roll Morton (1885–1941) introduced Joplin's music to New Orleans but played it at a faster tempo, an innovation that would be integrated into yet another American musical genre.

Jazz

The musical roots of jazz were African, brought to this country by slaves, and the music was marked by what is known as a "call and response" pattern. Participants would sing or play a particular combination of tones, and this would be answered by singing or playing a variation on it. The original purpose was similar to that of the folk song: community bonding.

Jazz came to America 300 years ago in chains.

—Paul Whiteman

During the late nineteenth century, African American musicians went to New Orleans and studied European genres and rhythmic patterns. But they brought with them a knowledge of their own traditional sounds, derived from what were called "field hollers" as well as rhythmic songs sung by slaves as they rowed, and the spirituals that were a profound part of African American religious life.

The typical scale used in African music contains five tones instead of the European scale of seven. New Orleans musicians tried to combine the two without sacrificing the African scale. The result was that they added half-tones, called *blue notes*, to the five-tone scale. From ragtime, they borrowed syncopation. The synthesis of all these strains made possible the evolution of jazz.

As the decades of the twentieth century rolled by, the form attracted a range of musical geniuses, some self-taught, some classically trained. They had—and continue to have—one thing in common: knowing how to maintain a balance between control and the need for soaring release. The call and response form had required that the responders change the original theme, adding their own variation. Even when jazz became a sophisticated art form, improvisation continued to be its major characteristic.

Whatever their training, jazz instrumentalists and composers admire Bach because he more or less invented improvisation, the art of taking flight from a set theme. A typical jazz piece follows a disciplined pattern. The group, or the soloist backed by the group, will play the main theme once through, sometimes a well-known song, sometimes an original tune composed for the group. Then one instrument after another performs a variation of the theme.

Original jazz works have deliberately offbeat titles, like "Take the A Train," "One O'Clock Jump," and "Stompin' at the Savoy"—titles that generally do not relate to anything beyond themselves. Jazz often shapes and defines the "cool scene"—a late-night coming together of sophisticated people who want to lose themselves in the music and escape, if only briefly, from their problems, just as the performers seek to lose themselves in the music.

Duke Ellington did the most to bridge the gap between the concert hall and the intimate jazz club.

Following in the footsteps of Jelly Roll Morton, great jazz soloists like Charlie Parker and Louis Armstrong became famous for going off on lengthy variations, often improvising for ten or fifteen minutes before returning to the theme. One motive behind jazz improvisation was to explore the potential of one's instrument and take it to places that no one else had ever found. In a life tragically interrupted when he was only twenty-eight, a phenomenal cornet player named Bix Beiderbecke is said to have been obsessed with the desire to find the perfect note, beyond the normal range of other players. Presumably, he did not live long enough to reach his goal. Some who were fortunate enough to hear him report that, as he pushed his instrument beyond the ordinary limits of its capabilities, his face turned almost scarlet and all of his facial muscles threatened to break loose from his skin.

Musical histories that deal with jazz as a serious and major art form give preeminence to Edward Kennedy Ellington—known universally as Duke (1899–1974)—the person who did the most to bridge the gap between the concert hall and the intimate jazz club. A bandleader who had Manhattan society driving to the Cotton Club in Harlem during the late 1920s, Ellington sought to expand the range of jazz through continual experimentation "with what he called his 'jungle effects.' When the sounds of 'growling' trumpets and trombones, sinuous clarinets and eerie percussion were recorded, the originality of the orchestration was immediately grasped internationally by music critics and record buyers. . . . As a jazz arranger his great gift was in balancing orchestration and improvisation."[3]

Ellington brought jazz to Carnegie Hall, where it could be played and evaluated in a setting built for the performance of classical concert music. In so doing,

Duke Ellington brought jazz to Carnegie Hall, every piece carefully orchestrated.

Source: © Bettmann Archives/Corbis.

he wrote out elaborate and complex orchestrations—something no one had done before him. He did leave room for solo flights (or else it would not have been jazz), but his own compositions, like "Mood Indigo," "Satin Doll," and "Sophisticated Lady," display a classic sense of discipline and musicianship.

Another major American composer who brought jazz to Carnegie Hall in the early years was George Gershwin (1898–1937). He started his career as a Tin Pan Alley songwriter, then moved on to compose the scores for Broadway musicals of the 1920s and the opera *Porgy and Bess* (fully discussed in Chapter 8). Yet Gershwin, who had been classically trained and could have been a world-class concert pianist had he chosen that path, was hungry for greater things.

In 1924 he found his chance. Paul Whiteman, a bandleader also hungry for serious recognition, commissioned him to write a concert jazz piece. The result was *Rhapsody in Blue*, which combined the textures of romantic works for piano and symphony orchestra with the pulsations, dissonance, and syncopated rhythms of jazz. Gershwin put an American art form on the international musical map. *Rhapsody* became an overnight success and has sold millions of recordings. It remains in the standard concert repertoire of nearly every major orchestra.

Jazz has remained a major art form, studied in every major music school and performed regularly in concert halls throughout the world as well as in annual festivals devoted exclusively to both jazz classics and the very newest styles and performers. The Newport Jazz Festival in Rhode Island and Jazz at Lincoln Center in New York are two notable examples. The genre has produced important artists who are at ease in both the classical and jazz scenes.

One such performer was trumpeter and pianist Miles Davis (1926–1991), whose versatility led him to the forefront of innovators in many subgenres of jazz, including *bebop* and *cool jazz*. By the time he was eighteen, Davis had shown so much talent that the Juilliard School offered him a scholarship, but he proved too impatient to wait for graduation. When he was nineteen, he made his first recording and joined the jazz quintet of Charlie Parker, the premier saxophonist of the period. Because of his youth and lack of professional experience, Davis was used as a *sideman*—a non-soloist who played backup to the stars. It was not very long before he stepped into the solo spotlight. In 1955 he created the Miles Davis Quintet, which took jazz to new heights.

In his earlier work, Davis experimented with bebop, which had become the rage in the 1940s. Bebop was almost totally improvised and therefore greatly favored by soloists who wanted music to serve their unique showcase needs. The more mature Davis of the Quintet gradually eased away from the eccentricities of bebop and moved toward what became known as cool jazz, more disciplined, more faithful to the music, and less given to wild flights of musical fancy. By the late 1950s Davis, who also played Carnegie Hall, was presenting jazz versions of concert music. One of his classic albums is *Sketches of Spain*, featuring works by Joaquin Rodrigo and Manuel de Falla.

George Gershwin's *Rhapsody in Blue* put jazz on the international musical map.

Source: Culver Pictures, Inc.

His [Gershwin's] genius, like all genius, was unique, but his all embracing artistic vision still resonates powerfully today in a world where music is sometimes the only benign avenue of communication between antagonists.

—**Paul Simon**

Miles Davis, the preeminent creator of cool jazz.

Source: Hulton Archive/Getty Images.

Track 8

I've been told that nobody sings the word "hunger" like I do.

—**Billie Holliday**

If it wasn't for bad luck, I wouldn't have no luck at all.

—**Bessie Smith**

Since the early 1980s, trumpeter Wynton Marsalis has distinguished himself as a performer and a composer, crossing over freely from jazz to symphonic music. Classically trained at the Juilliard School, he earned a reputation as its outstanding trumpeter. When he was barely seventeen, Marsalis was playing with the Jazz Messengers, a prestigious band that helped him develop his skills. He has released forty albums and won nine Grammy awards. In 1983 he won in both the symphonic and jazz categories, the first artist ever to do so. In 1997 he became the first jazz composer to win the Pulitzer Prize for music. The prize-winning work was *Blood on the Fields*, commissioned by Jazz at Lincoln Center, which has an international reputation as an outstanding venue in which the finest jazz musicians in the world perform. Marsalis is currently its artistic director.

Like many of the art forms we have studied thus far, jazz has evolved from humble beginnings to a position of glittering importance in the world of the humanities.

Blues

The term *blues* derives from the melancholy mood produced by music that made liberal use of the half-tones in the African American scale, the so-called blue notes. The genre has permeated our vocabulary to such an extent that "blue" seems always to have meant "down in the dumps." Many jazz tunes are bouncy and lively, uplifting the spirit, but the jazz repertoire includes its share of blues.

The genre had its origins, as did ragtime and jazz, in the songs sung by slaves after a grueling day in the fields. While they sometimes desired an upbeat mood, the workers must have, just as often, sought an outlet for depression. As the form became caught up in the entertainment industry of jazz, sophisticated composers and singers turned the old songs into haunting expressions of sadness that found ready listeners among audiences of varied backgrounds. The blue notes helped.

Blues music is almost always about the empty aftermath of a once burning passion. The songs are written from either a male or a female point of view. Men sing of the faithlessness of woman, and women return the compliment about men. Probably the most famous of all the blues songs is "St. Louis Blues" by W. C. Handy (1873–1958), who also composed "Beale Street Blues." If jazz is strongly associated with New Orleans, the headquarters of blues was Memphis, and it was on Beale Street that many of the great blues clubs were located, attracting visitors from all over the world.

Many of the soloists who elevated the form to a high status had tragic lives caused by bad relationships, social discrimination, or substance addiction—in some cases, all three. Outstanding was Bessie Smith (1894–1937), who many believe developed the blues style that was imitated by countless others. She has immortalized many lines from blues lyrics, including "If it wasn't for bad luck, I wouldn't have no luck at all." She achieved considerable renown before the automobile accident that claimed her life at the age of forty-three.

Pop Music

The songs performed by contemporary singers such as Justin Timberlake, Kanye West, and Martina McBride are generally designated *pop music*. If they are still played and sung in the future, they may have attained the stature of popular classics, and a notable few have earned a place in the humanities.

During the 1930s through the early 1950s, big bands were all the fashion, each with at least one big-name singer who needed a constant supply of new songs to please a public eager to buy records and sheet music. Many, many of these songs have become classics, performed by stars such as Tony Bennett, Barbra Streisand, Barbara Cook, and Harry Connick Jr. Until he was close to eighty, vocal stylist Frank Sinatra attracted huge crowds with songs he helped become classics.

The big-band song had a very specific pattern. A song, usually around three minutes in length, would be played once by the orchestra; then a soloist—or a backup group—would sing it through once. The orchestra might or might not follow the vocal by playing another complete chorus. Thus the time allotted for each song was either six or nine minutes. The big-band orchestra played primarily so that couples could dance. Frequently the rhythm would change from song to song, going from a slow fox trot (which would draw most of the audience out to the floor) to a fast jitterbug number (older dancers would sit down) or a Latin American mambo or rumba (attracting the dancers who could execute the required steps in time to the demanding rhythm).

Though this pattern imposed stiff restraints upon lyricists, who had to develop and conclude an idea in a few minutes, the rules are no doubt responsible for the imaginative brilliance of the best songs, such as Jerome Kern's "Smoke Gets in Your Eyes." Otto Harbach, who wrote the lyrics to the song, really deserves the label *poet*. He develops a very common theme, dating at least as far back as Roman poetry: the theme of love lost. At first, the narrator of the song believes the beloved is faithful, though friends think otherwise, saying that when "your heart's on fire" you will realize that "smoke gets in your eyes." The narrator scoffs, only to discover in the next few lines that the beloved has gone. The friends are now the ones who scoff, but the narrator, in an absolutely brilliant repetition of the song title in a totally different context, points out that tears come when the flame of a beautiful romance is dying out and "smoke gets in your eyes."

Irving Berlin (1888–1989), composer of "God Bless America," could not read a note of music but compiled perhaps the largest repertoire of any twentieth-century songwriter. All of his songs express simple, honest, and universal emotions. While Berlin could define the everlasting joys of love, he was at his best when providing the bittersweet happiness of nostalgia. It's all over, but one is left with fond memories all the same. And the nostalgia of the lyric "I'm dreaming of a white Christmas" elevated a popular song written for a sequence in a forgotten movie to the status of a Christmas carol. This and other songs of the period were treasured by millions, who could listen to the words, close their eyes, and relive their past.

Bessie Smith, the great blues singer, sang deeply felt songs about the aftermath of once burning passion.

Source: The Granger Collection.

Through songs we find out things about ourselves. We say, "Oh yeah. I've felt that way."

—Lois Walder

In 1938 the popular singer Kate Smith asked Berlin to compose a patriotic song with which she could end her broadcast celebrating the twentieth anniversary of the armistice that ended World War I. After several attempts proved futile, he remembered a song he had written for an army camp show during that war, a song that was rejected for being "too jingoistic." He found "God Bless America" buried in an old trunk, polished it a bit, and then offered it to Smith. Its first performance on the broadcast of November 20, 1938, electrified both the studio and the vast national audience. The song contains ten short lines and probably takes less than three minutes to sing. No one has to be told about the song's impact in all times and on countless occasions since. When Jerome Kern was asked to indicate Berlin's place in American music, he answered tersely: "Irving Berlin *is* American music."

There is still an audience for the popular song that strikes at the heart, and perhaps that explains why a piece like Joni Mitchell's "Both Sides Now," first heard in the 1960s, is a continuing favorite. Mitchell (b. 1943), who writes both music and lyrics, is as adept at metaphor as the lyricist of "Smoke Gets in Your Eyes." In "Both Sides Now" she writes of coping with disillusionment, and she does so in a series of symbolic images. As a very young girl, she loved to lie back and look up at clouds, which she saw as "ice cream castles" and "feathered canyons." Now that she is an adult, she sees that clouds just "rain and snow on everyone." She has looked at clouds "from both sides now," but refuses to take on adult cynicism about life. She continues to cling to "clouds' illusions" just as she continues to believe in love's and finally *life's* illusions. The song parallels a listener's own process of maturation, and will probably be a favorite for as long as ideals are held and then shattered.

One of the great stylists of popular music was Frank Sinatra (1915–1998), who virtually owned the song of past love now sadly remembered. Composers and lyricists jumped at the chance to write for him, because he was without peer in delivering the song's message through his vocal flexibilities and his acting talent. Many of the songs with which he was associated are permanent classics. They crystallize emotions all of us share and give us comfort in knowing we are not alone.

A typical Sinatra classic is "One for My Baby," in which the narrator can be imagined as sitting at a bar very late at night, with no one around except a bartender who may or may not be listening as he pours out his heart. He has been abandoned by his one true love, though he does not deny having been responsible for the breakup; now there is only the effort to escape the pain through drink. The refrain to which he keeps returning asks the bartender to give him two more drinks: one "for my baby" and "one more for the road." As both songs and poems should do when they achieve art, this one captures a certain moment, an image in the flow of time: here, that of a loner in a bar late at night with no clear future and obviously no one to comfort him.

Frank Sinatra was responsible for turning many songs into enduring classics.

Source: © Hulton Archive/Corbis.

Rock

A pervasive phenomenon ever since it made the scene in the 1950s, rock music has become a major way of defining the present era in sound. **Rock** is a fusion of rhythm and blues, gospel, and country and western styles, and it has many complex facets, ranging from the conscious artistry of trained musicians to the out-of-control bellowing of unintelligible lyrics by performers prancing around a stage. But rock is first and foremost a celebration of the joy of life, sexual release, and often a total disregard for social rules.

As a contemporary musical form, rock realizes its full potential in the rock concert, in a given totality of work presented in a unique program that is almost never repeated after a particular performance or tour. The most famous rock concert ever held took place in Woodstock, New York, in 1970, when bands and performers from all over the world gathered in one place to celebrate togetherness and protest the war in Vietnam. Monsoon rains found thousands of participants rolling around in mud, their enthusiasm undiminished by the hardships and indignities they endured. Not only was there memorable music performed, but the collective experience made the powerful statement that war as a means of settling human problems could no longer be tolerated. Generally speaking, in the history of the humanities there are few works that drive the audience into a frenzy the way a rock concert can. Concerts can take hold of thousands at the same moment, going beyond music altogether, to become a social event.

Rock has undergone many changes since 1955, the year in which the movie *Blackboard Jungle* leaped onto the screen in a flash of music titled "Rock around the Clock." With its overly pronounced and rapid beat, the music had film audiences jumping in the aisles and dancing—even as the rock concert would be doing in a few years. The band that arranged and played this piece was Bill Haley and the Comets, and to them is given the credit for popularizing the musical movement first called **rock 'n' roll**.

The incessant rhythmic beat of "Rock around the Clock" was derived from the rhythm and blues music of small African American dance clubs in the South. Because of their confined spaces, they could only accommodate small combos, which had to make a big sound to compensate. Besides, the polite dances of the big bands no longer suited a postwar generation bogged down in academic studies and office jobs and in need of weekend release. The beat of rock 'n' roll, accentuated by the strings of a twirling bass fiddle, met the new needs.

One year after "Rock around the Clock" spread the new sound nationwide, a young singer from Mississippi named Elvis Presley appeared on television's *Ed Sullivan Show*, the premier venue for showcasing new musical talent. Elvis (1935–1977) quickly became a cultural phenomenon, scandalizing older audiences with the gyrating of his pelvis while simultaneously making rock wildly popular with younger audiences. The immediate musical influence on Elvis was gospel, particularly its exuberance. He added the beat and chord progressions of the rhythm and blues being played in Memphis, where he had gotten his professional start. Finally, Elvis incorporated elements from country-western music, injecting them with a high-powered aggressiveness that remains the signature of rock. In some circles, his music became known as *country rock* or *rockabilly*.

> *. . .we note the glazed stares and numb, expressionless faces of youthful dancers at the great rock auditoriums where light shows, split screen movies, high decibel screams, shouts and moans. . . create a sensory environment characterized by. . . extreme unpredictability."*
>
> —**Alvin Toffler**

Often hailed as the King of Rock, Elvis Presley fused musical elements from rhythm and blues, gospel, and country-western traditions to create his own brand of rock 'n' roll, a style that remains popular decades after his death.

Source: S.S. Archives/Shooting Star International.

In the opinion of rock historian Charlie Gillett, Elvis's peak as an artist was reached in the early days when his work related to the passionate themes of the country rock tradition—usually heartbreak with a strong rhythm, as in his first hit song "Heartbreak Hotel." In Gillett's opinion, becoming a superstar in record-breaking time was the worst thing that could have happened to Elvis. He signed a multimillion-dollar contract with RCA, which promptly put a high-powered gloss on the new music. The singer's former emotional directness became lost against a background of "vocal groups, heavily electrified guitars, and drums . . . more theatrical and self-conscious as he sought to contrive excitement and emotion," formerly generated "without any evident forethought."[4] Other singers and combos followed the trend, and the simple term *rock* was given to a variety of styles, many with the amplification of the later Presley work.

The excitement generated within audiences by rock had been foreshadowed in the frenetic energy of Little Richard, one of early rock's most outrageous performers, who set the style for later acts that would go even further in free-spiritedness. Rock historian Nik Cohn considers Little Richard to have been the true father of rock: "Dressed in shimmering suits with long drape jackets and baggy pants, his hair grown long and straight, white teeth and gold rings flashing in the spotlights, he stood up at, and sometimes on, the piano, hammering boogie chords as he screamed messages of celebration and self-centered pleasure."[5]

By the early 1960s, rock 'n' roll had become popular throughout the Western world. It became so pervasive in England in particular that young musicians began imitating the music they were hearing from across the Atlantic. Ironically, what music historians and fans alike consider rock's most important band emerged not in the United States, where the genre was born, but in the economically depressed northern English port city of Liverpool. In 1964 the Beatles made an indelible mark on American consciousness the moment they were introduced on *The Ed Sullivan Show*, which had showcased Elvis Presley eight years earlier. Their name was whimsical and their hair longer than the short standards of the time. As their fame increased, so did the length of their hair, in what appeared to be defiance of convention. For some performances, they even wore eighteenth-century clothes, including knee breeches, doublets, and waistcoats. Older people shook their heads in despair over the decline of not only music but an entire generation. For it was the young who embraced the bizarre foursome, imitating their hair styles and turning John, Paul, George, and Ringo into icons of cultural revolution. The Beatles appealed to a rising subculture of "hippies," young people who championed freedom from all social and moral restraints. In all of its phases since the 1950s, rock has retained its revolutionary social battle cry, becoming the ultimate form of Dionysian music in our time.

The Beatles were admired for their honesty and a certain purity of heart. Their physical presence was so powerful that they would have attained enormous popularity even if their music had been second-rate. Of course, it was not. Paul McCartney and John Lennon created songs of such originality and beauty that some are considered among the best popular songs in Western culture. Songs like "Yesterday," "Eleanor Rigby" (also a model of syncopation), and "Michelle" have been performed by major symphony orchestras.

Both Lennon, whose life was cut short in 1980 by a deranged fan's bullet, and George Harrison, who played guitar for the group and who died in 2001, were strongly influenced by Indian culture and religion. All four of the Beatles briefly studied meditation at an ashram in India. Harrison studied the sitar, an ancient Indian instrument, with Ravi Shankar, a master Indian musician. Harrison's own

A hundred years from now, people will listen to the Beatles the same way we listen to Mozart.

—Sir Paul McCartney

The Beatles—honesty and an off-center purity of heart.

Source: AP/Wide World Photos.

songs are less well-known than those of Lennon and McCartney, but many of them are deeply felt poems set to high spiritual music.

In 1965 another British combo, the Rolling Stones, came onto the scene, combining the exuberant defiance of the early Beatles with the free-spiritedness of a Little Richard. In the words of rock singer, critic, and poet Patti Smith: "By 1967 they all but eliminated the word guilt from our vocabulary . . . I never considered the Stones drug music . . . they were the drug itself . . . thru demon genius they hit that chord . . . as primitive as a western man could stand. Find the beat and you dance all night."[6]

To the Stones must go the credit for having originated the big-time rock concert, which could fill Yankee Stadium or the Los Angeles Coliseum. Enthusiastic fans were known to camp out for days in advance in order to buy tickets, and that ritual continues undiminished. The rock concert seemed to begin where "primitive" beings left off thousands of years ago. It cut through the many layers of civilized behavior that had evolved to put a lid on the untrammeled expression of freedom, and it demanded from the audience shouting, stamping, cries of ecstasy—a return to the enjoyment of the sheer act of living, unverbalized, unanalyzed, uncensored. Smith describes the historic Madison Square Garden concert of July 25, 1972, as a ritual "like any ancient ceremony," adding, "pass the sacred wafer."

In 1980 another of the great rock bands achieved world prominence with their debut album *Boy*. They were four musicians from Dublin who grew up nestled in the strong Celtic tradition in which people learned to sing when they were old enough to leave the cradle. In keeping with the customary practice of using offbeat names, they discarded their first two, Feedback and The Hype, before settling on U2, and the group arguably remains the premier rock band of the world. U2 became best known for their political and social themes, exemplified by their 2006 Grammy-winning album *How to Dismantle an Atomic Bomb*. For three

U2—rock music with Celtic roots and a peace-driven conscience.

Source: © Mike Blake/Reuters/Corbis.

Track 9

decades now, the band has toured the world, driving home their pleas for peace, equality, and tolerance. The lead singer, Bono, has even been nominated for the Nobel Peace Prize.

Over the sixty years of its existence, rock has, understandably, gone through many changes. Progressive rock, now coming into its own, relies less on individual performances (such as those associated with the Stones' Mick Jagger) and more on the complexity and strength of the music. Many of the newer bands began as regional groups, and their music often reflects their cultural and gender background.

This diversification has given us many intriguing new sounds, including the contributions of female rock groups, which have survived and flourished despite early difficulties in being recognized as the equal of their male colleagues. The Temple of Rain, an all-female band, originated in lower Manhattan's small **avant-garde** clubs. The group, reflecting the sophistication of the New York scene, writes and performs songs protesting racism and gender discrimination.

Mama's Pit, an Italian rock band, combines the exuberant rhythms of folk dances with the darker themes of much progressive rock. Hubris originated in what they describe as Manila's "alternative scene." Like many of the newer ensembles, they write to express themselves, not to win over their audiences. In fact, they proclaim proudly that at first "we did not really catch on," though eventually "we were recognized for our instrumental prowess, challenging music, and thought-provoking lyrics."

Many progressive rock groups say they are happy they have not yet attained widespread recognition. They attract smaller legions of devoted fans, and they do not have to write for the sales charts, thus freeing themselves to go in many new directions.

Miami has recently given rise to The Green Room, named for the topmost part of a wave that enfolds the surfer. Its founder and sole composer/performer is poet Jorge Mejia (b. 1973), whose songs, like a good deal of progressive rock, demand close listening. Mejia, classically trained, orchestrates his music, using a highly advanced synthesizer. Though he incorporates audience-pleasing rhythms, he can change tempo suddenly, darken his mood, and end a song on a note of melancholy alienation. Some of his songs reflect the serenity he says surfers feel when they suddenly find themselves gliding along through the protective green room.

Like Mejia's wave, rock continues to crest. There have already been highly successful rock operas, such as The Who's *Tommy*. The musical *Rent* (discussed in Chapter 2) is a rock updating of the opera *La Bohème*. There have been ballets set to rock beats. In all probability a rock symphony is on the way, perhaps even a rock cantata for a chorus of a hundred singers. The musical form that so many people predicted would soon die a natural death is very much alive and has already contributed much to the humanities.

Hip-Hop

While it is still too early to say whether hip-hop will last as long as rock has, the genre has become a significant part of contemporary society, especially among younger audiences, always seeking new ways to express their identity. **Hip-hop** is a broad term that defines an entire lifestyle, with different musical expressions as integral components. It "encompasses rap, baggy clothing, break-dancing, graffiti, vocabulary, and a general life style."[7] The latter can be described as free-wheeling and centered on the rights of individuals to declare their identity in any way they choose.

Rap, perhaps the most important contribution of the hip-hop culture thus far, is half-sung, half-spoken music with a pronounced and steady beat supporting rapid-fire rhyming words performed by singers with great verbal dexterity and often with extensive vocabularies. The subject matter is frequently social protest, but it can also range from philosophical cynicism about life to frank descriptions of sexual encounters.

Rap had its origins in the urban setting of the Bronx in the late 1970s with toasts, dub talk, and improvisational poetry delivered over music at weddings, proms, and other celebrations. Reminiscent of the call-and-response characteristic of the plantation songs, it would begin with a DJ, band leader, or master of ceremonies shouting in rhythm something like "Now throw your hands in the air / And wave 'em like you just don't care / And if you got on clean underwear / Let me hear you say 'Oh yeah!'" The excited crowd would then scream: "Oh yeah!"[8] The first rap album, *Rapper's Delight*, performed by the Sugarhill Gang, appeared in 1979.

Rap has evolved into what many believe is an art form, and some of its leading exponents have been called modern folk poets. One such is Eminem (b. 1972), whose often cynical lyrics incite fierce controversy wherever they are heard, but they have also won thousands of loyal fans. One rock musician said of Eminem: "He's not a very nice person, but you can't deny the brilliance of his songs."

It is doubtful that rappers are asking to be considered nice. They believe they can best express themselves creatively through their chosen musical form. Rap has also been criticized for glorifying violence and drugs and expressing intolerance toward women and homosexuals. Defenders counter that these charges can also be leveled at some types of rock and that rap music does not promote antisocial values but instead honestly depicts the realities of urban life.

At its best, rap is virtuoso language and a spontaneous kind of poetry, an exercise in exciting creativity.

We're all spokes in a wheel, going to the point, getting the ball rolling. Have you ever seen a wheel with one spoke? It's not a wheel. You got to come from different directions to get to the same point. And roll.

—**Ice Cube**

World Music

The diverse contemporary musical scene also includes contributions from many other cultures. A Chinese composer may be experimenting with new scales and new sounds on a synthesizer; a Cambodian equivalent of Celine Dión may be recording her first CD with a silky voice but in melodic terms that are not based on notes familiar to the West; an Islamic pop singer may be thrilling a cafe audience with a love song in a plaintive trembling vibrato to the accompaniment of an instrument that is akin to but not the same as a mandolin or guitar; a singing group in Zimbabwe may be swaying as they chant an updated version of a much older song of welcome. The majority of these non-Western sounds can be heard via the Internet, and because of today's rapid-fire communication, they will influence tomorrow's musical styles.

In China, music is no longer limited to the marches and patriotic songs approved by the communist government before it opened its doors to the outside world. Western musical influences were there during the earlier twentieth century, but some forms, including hard rock, judged a threat to government or society, were banned. A singer/composer named Cui Jian emerged during the student demonstrations of 1989 with daring lyrics denouncing government tyranny. Defecting to the West, where he found a strong welcome, he performed his new music before thousands in a 1999 Central Park concert. Almost as popular in both East and West is the Tang Dynasty, a Beijing rock band that blends the sounds of the Asian five-note scale with the more familiar diatonic, or seven-note, Western scale.

Traditional Chinese music is still prevalent, making liberal use of percussion, especially drums, timpani, gongs, cymbals, bells, xylophones, and triangles. Percussion has long been a major component of the classical Chinese style. String sections of traditional Chinese concert orchestras include the two-stringed violin, the dulcimer, the lute, and the harp. The woodwind section comprises flutes, pipes, and Chinese trumpets, which look but do not sound like oboes.

An afternoon can be well spent in the exploration of these sounds, now so profusely available on the Web.

Avant-Garde Music

I love the development of our music. How we've tried to develop, y'know? It grows. That is why everyday people come forward with new songs. Music goes on forever.

—**Bob Marley**

Like their counterparts in visual arts, innovators in concert music do not want to sound like anything or anyone that has gone before them; they do not wish to be confined by accepted conventions, but seek to forge new directions. The need to be free from restraints has been a key factor in past works of genius. Beethoven, for example, expanded the range of music in creating his Third Symphony, forcing the music to accommodate his mighty passions. Gershwin, commissioned to write a concert jazz piece, found he could not work within the traditional limits of either jazz or concert music. *Rhapsody in Blue* combined jazz and symphonic music as had never been done before, and there were probably many who doubted it could be done successfully. The Beatles knew the rock music that preceded them, but too many pieces were alike in rhythm and subject matter. Fans were not prepared for the style and the depth of musical expertise the Beatles brought to the form. The four young men with long hair probably did not suspect, at least in the beginning, that they were lifting rock to the level of art. All of these composers did what they had to do: *express themselves in ways congenial to their temperaments regardless of convention.*

Track 4

The need to rebel is felt not just in popular music circles. Today there are composers of concert music who denounce even the diatonic scale and most of the traditional instruments. They may belong to the West, but they do not want to sound connected to any national identity or style. Some have discovered in the synthesizer the key to uncharted inner worlds with sounds that no one has yet heard.

Igor Stravinsky (1882–1971) is for many the father of the modern avant-garde in music. His revolutionary score for the 1913 ballet *The Rite of Spring* introduced sounds so unfamiliar that they, combined with the daring movements of the dancers, sparked a riot at the Paris premiere. Denounced by audiences and critics alike, Stravinsky would win the day, and his **atonality**—music with less regard for key—encouraged composers who followed him to break away from bondage to familiar harmonies and structures.

Another modern music pioneer of the avant-garde was Arnold Schoenberg (1874–1951), born in Berlin and musically educated in Vienna. For his large-scale concert works, he is known to have reduced the size of the symphony orchestra to fifteen instruments, for which he provided dissonant, contrapuntal music and bizarre harmonic progressions. Embracing the Stravinsky atonality, he abandoned key altogether in many of his early works, such as *Pierrot Lunaire*, which was intended as a musical equivalent of mental disturbance. In this work Schoenberg also replaced musical notes with notations requiring the singers to speak, but not always in familiar prose. At times they sound like lost souls crying out for release from solitary confinement. In 1925 Schoenberg moved back to Berlin, where he came under the influence of the growing avant-garde movement in German art and music. It was there that he composed his opera *Moses and Aron*, in which the characters sing-speak of their inability to communicate with each other. Both of these works remain stern tests of one's willingness to entertain the very unfamiliar in sound.

Much of today's music, both popular and concert, comes from sounds created on the synthesizer. Leading the way in the concert use of electronic technology was the French avant-garde composer Edgard Varèse (1883–1965). Starting out as a student of mathematics but unable to resist the excitement of the new music, he utilized his training to study the science of sound. Armed with his experiments in producing unfamiliar sounds using both machines and traditional instruments (though seldom as they were intended to be played), Varèse declared boldly: "I refuse to submit to sounds that have already been heard." He added, "Rules do not make a work of art. You have the right to compose what you want to." Encouraged by his friend and admirer the Impressionist composer Claude Debussy, he explored non-Western music, eventually combining it with his own reconfiguration of Western scales and tonal patterns. In 1923 his work *Hyperprism* premiered, and like Stravinsky's *Rite of Spring*, it caused a riot in the theater. Some of the instruments he employed were sleigh bells, rattles, crash cymbals, an anvil, Chinese blocks, Indian drums, and a washtub with a hole in the bottom, which allowed the player to create the sound of a lion's roar.

When he was seventy-one, Varèse created *Deserts*, his response to atomic energy and the dangers it posed for the world. The piece, which used both taped and synthesized sounds, drove the audience into a frenzy and nearly led to another riot. One critic observed that Varèse deserved the electric chair for composing such noise.

Another dedicated user of the synthesizer to enhance the possibilities of musical sound is Karlheinz Stockhausen (b. 1928), noted for extremely long works, including an orchestral poem called *Light*, which celebrates the seven days of the week. If all seven movements were played non-stop, the audience would find themselves sitting in their chairs continuously for twenty-nine hours. One of his most remarkable—and *truly* avant-garde—achievements was his design of a sphere-shaped auditorium built for the 1970 World's Fair in Osaka, Japan. Within this sphere, an orchestra and chorus performed all of Stockhausen's works five and a half hours daily for 183 days.

Stockhausen is most identified with *serialism*, a musical technique by which the composer disregards all theories of pitch, harmony, and key, creating his own version of musical notes and writing them down in quite non-traditional ways. Those who specialize in the critical analysis of Stockhausen's work insist that his structures, while strange at first to the ear, are geometric and logical within their own set of rules.

Cathy Berberian, Joan La Barbara, and Greetje Bijma are highly productive in their unique innovative styles, much of their work created for female singers. Laurie Anderson and Meredith Monk have also achieved considerable renown. They and their sister composers, using a variety of electronic as well as traditional instruments, dispense not only with ordinary musical notes but, in their songs, with ordinary words. Often they are intent on converting into sound the experience of childbirth and the mother's bond with the newborn, employing a collage of baby talk, distorted nursery rhymes, and unexpected outbreaks of laughter, indicative of both the baby's and the mother's sudden spurts of joy.

In this chapter our goal has been to suggest how your life can be infinitely enriched if you are willing to listen—listen to the great classics of the past and the perhaps great-one-day experiments of the present. Don't forget, Beethoven was often considered too "modern" by some of his contemporaries.

But with all the sound that is there for you to hear, don't forget to spend a little time with your silences.

Key Terms

atonality a characteristic of much avant-garde music, composed without regard for key.

avant-garde art that defies traditional forms; contemporary avant-garde music uses much dissonance and atonality.

baroque label applied to the artistic style of the mid-seventeenth to mid-eighteenth centuries; marked by elaborate ornamentation and complexity; original meaning irregular pearl.

chamber music composition for small ensembles, such as a trio or quartet.

chromatic scale consists of twelve tones; if played on the piano, a consecutive run using both white and black keys.

counterpoint two melodic lines played against each other; characteristic of Bach's compositions.

diatonic scale consists of seven tones; white piano keys only; the fundamental but not the only scale of Western music.

dissonance in music, two or more uncongenial notes sounded or sung at the same time, producing an unfamiliar and, for some, unpleasant effect.

fugue lengthy musical composition, or section within a larger composition, in which two or more melodic lines are played against each other.

half-tone half of one interval between two notes in the diatonic scale; on a piano, half-tones are produced by the black keys.

harmony two or more tones, congenial or otherwise, sounded or sung at the same time.

hip-hop contemporary style of music that includes rap; a lifestyle marked by baggy clothes, idiomatic speech, graffiti, and break-dancing.

improvisation a spontaneous variation or set of variations on a stated musical theme; once performed, it may be written down and repeated by other performers.

key a particular scale that dominates in a musical composition; labeled according to the first note of that scale and whether it is major or minor: e.g., C major; F-sharp minor.

melody either any arrangement of tones in a flowing sequence, or a significant sequence of musical tones that form a unity and are usually meant to be distinguished from what comes before and what follows.

minimalism style of music that rebels against excesses such as overdone orchestrations or use of objects like washboards and garbage can lids; goal is a return to fundamental principles of composition.

pentatonic scale five-tone musical scale that preceded the familiar seven-tone scale dominant in the West; still the basic scale of much non-Western music.

ragtime musical genre, forerunner of jazz, invented in the late 1890s by African American composers, notably Scott Joplin; strongly influenced by slow and stately European dances.

rap major subgenre of hip-hop in which rhyming lyrics are half-sung, half-spoken rapidly.

rhythm alternation of stress and unstress in music, usually created by a percussion instrument.

rock generic name covering a variety of styles that have a loud and insistent beat.

rock 'n' roll style of music introduced in the 1950s and popularized by Elvis Presley; it grew out of a fusion of rhythm and blues, gospel, and country and western styles.

scale the orderly progression of sound-wave frequencies from low to high.

symphony a major orchestral form from the late eighteenth century to the present, usually consisting of four separate sections, or movements, with contrasting tempos, sometimes constituting a unity, often not.

syncopation a form in which the melodic line of a piece is played against, not with, the accented beats of the rhythm accompaniment, as in George Gershwin's "Fascinatin' Rhythm" and the Beatles' "Eleanor Rigby."

toccata musical form perfected by Johann Sebastian Bach, making liberal use of improvisation and allowing for an overpowering display of musical virtuosity by the performer.

tone a single sound produced by a human voice or a musical instrument; also called a note.

Topics for
Writing and Discussion

1. "Background music" is not intended to encourage close attention. It's the music played in stores, restaurants, waiting rooms, and elevators. Become a "foreground" listener. Visit several places in which you expect to hear background music. Write a report on the kinds of music heard in different places. Speculate on why a particular style of music is chosen for a particular location.

2. Attend a concert of music often called "classical." There may be one on campus or in a concert hall conveniently located or on television (the public broadcasting stations have any number). Libraries usually have CDs and DVDs that you can borrow. In a report, describe the program. Indicate which selections pleased you the most, which the least. Explain your reasons for liking some and disliking others. Or even liking or disliking all of them.

3. Explore the connection between music and emotion in your own life. For example: what songs do you sing on long road trips? What music reminds you of incidents in your past? Do you tend to associate certain music with pleasant or unpleasant times? What do you play if you need to relax after a day of disappointment and frustration? What music can you hear over and over, without tiring of it? Can you say why?

4. Many people wear earphones on public transportation, while waiting on line, jogging, or just sitting on a park bench. Go to some place in which you expect to find people with earphones. As politely as possible, ask them what kind of music they are listening to and why. Make a report to the class in which you not only indicate which music you discovered was most popular with earphone people, but offer your opinion on whether earphone music is there for aesthetic reasons—or something else.

5. Write a report taking the form of an imaginary speech made to a friend in which you describe a concert you have just attended, one that featured five selections, all from different periods and representing very different styles of music. Make sure your vocabulary contains musical terms you have gleaned from this chapter.

6. Elvis Presley, Little Richard, and the Beatles represent classics of rock. Name a current hip-hop (including rap) performer or group you believe will achieve similar status. Explain why.

7. Find a CD containing ragtime music (libraries usually have a lot of Scott Joplin). Listen to a number of selections. Write a report presenting (and backing up) your opinion on why ragtime is no longer being written today.

8. Wynton Marsalis is the first composer to win a Pulitzer Prize for a jazz composition. He also serves as chief artistic director for the prestigious Jazz at Lincoln Center series. In your opinion, does jazz belong in a place like Lincoln Center, which also houses Avery Fisher Hall, home of the New York Philharmonic Orchestra and the Metropolitan Opera House? Explain.

9. Bach and Beethoven are frequently found at the top of World's Greatest Composers rankings. Since their time, many composers have attained considerable distinction, yet the two giants remain at the top. What did you learn about their musical accomplishments that might justify their hold on the title "the greatest"? If you think they no longer deserve the honor, explain why.

10. Female rock groups have had a tough time gaining recognition, except in certain places and among smaller contingents of loyal fans. Listen to the music of one such group and discuss the kind of music it plays. Extra credit: Explain why you think female rock bands are having trouble competing in what is still a male-dominated scene. Is it their brand of music? Or a form of sexism? Alternative extra credit: Ask a number of women who say they like rock whether they prefer male to female bands, or vice versa. Report to the class on reasons given.

7 Cinema

Overview

The motion picture, like other arts, is a vehicle of creative expression, and no study of the humanities is complete without including it. Even though it is a most collaborative art form, involving many contributors (think of those closing credits!), genius can be found throughout its history.

After each weekend, the box-office rankings of current films are reported in newspapers and on television, information seldom given concerning art gallery openings or the premiere performance of a new musical composition. Further evidence of public attachment to film can be found each year when nominations and awards are announced. At the Academy Awards telecast, the public is aware at least for one night that film is indeed the most collaborative of all the arts. When all of the participants somehow blend their talents, the result may be a film classic, with a wide following for years to come.

Through the many extra features of a DVD version, we can follow scene by scene the choices made by directors in achieving an effect. We are thus able to understand the reasoning behind camera angles, music or its lack, and the compromises between the final product as shown on the screen and what the director may have originally intended. Documentaries about the making of a film encourage critical analysis, allowing viewers behind the scenes, becoming part of the creative process itself.

This chapter begins with a discussion of the various elements, or *conventions*, of the cinema, for only by understanding their function can we view a film more critically and, if all goes well, with greater enjoyment. Next come milestones in early film history, followed by an analysis of some popular film *genres*, and finally some prominent directors whose work is so completely identified with their personalities and philosophy that they can be called *auteurs*: that is, authors of the film.

● The hard-to-please food critic in *Ratatouille*, an animated film for both children and adults, centering on the mature subject of what constitutes critical taste.

Source: The Everett Collection.

Conventions of Film

In film, as on the stage, **conventions** are the conditions of a genre that audiences agree to accept. They include the rules or the grammar of seeing a film.

Beginning readers learn the rules for print—left to right, top to bottom, capital letters, periods, etc. Rules for film begin with a darkened theater, a screen, and a projector causing light to appear on the screen.

The *camera* is a major convention of film, though audiences don't always "see" it there. But the critical viewer is acutely aware at all times of what the camera is up to. The objects on the screen appear distant or close because the camera can change their size at will. Looking at a **close-up**, we take for granted that the face on the screen will not always be that large. The expression on the face will not always be crucial to the action taking place. Sometimes the camera will focus on a letter lying on a desk, and the close-up signals that this item is going to play an important part in what is to come. In the early days of film, when cameras were much less sophisticated than they are now and directors may have had only one camera to work with, a film was often like a photographed play, lacking in close-ups. This lack was also a convention of its time. Nowadays a director who chooses not to employ close-ups would be considered highly experimental.

Cinematography is the appropriate term for the camera work. Though we are meant to forget the unseen presence of those doing the filming, the critical viewer can find much pleasure in observing whether the camera work adds to film artistry or is simply using tried-and-true techniques, such as the intercut, which is quick back-and-forth images of characters confronting each other, or the **establishing shot**, a scene that identifies where the action is to take place.

Color—or the lack of it—is an important element in cinematography. Before 1936, when the first major Technicolor movie appeared (*The Trail of the Lonesome Pine*), all films were shot in black and white, a convention that is not necessarily an old-fashioned relic to be patiently endured when you are watching an older movie. Some of the best films ever made, such as *Citizen Kane* in 1941, analyzed later in the chapter, derive much of their power from the contrast between light and shadow that black-and-white film makes possible. Although some contemporary filmmakers might still prefer to film in black and white, they rarely do so, because color is demanded by audiences and those purchasing television rights to a film. When a film classic such as *Casablanca* is colorized, however, there is generally an outcry from loyal fans, as if an artist's original had been defaced.

Before the introduction of sound in the talkies, there were silent pictures, with printed cards inserted to indicate necessary dialogue or information. But many of the early films could be understood without such aids. The fact that sound was not possible led to the development of wonderful screen pantomime, such as that epitomized in the work of Buster Keaton or Charlie Chaplin, also discussed later in the chapter.

Background music guided audience reactions in the days of silent films. Rescuers on horseback required one kind of music, a tender love scene another. Music continues to be a major convention of film. Like the camera, it is always there, and we are meant to forget that in real life music does not suddenly come out of nowhere. Pounding rock music adds excitement to scenes of brutality among criminals on city streets. The Simon and Garfunkel song "The Sounds of Silence" underscored the bewildered search of the alienated young hero of Mike Nichols's *The Graduate* (1968). Sometimes music is used as ironic counterpoint to what is being shown, as in Oliver Stone's 1978 antiwar film *Platoon*, in which a scene of violence and atrocities is played against the slow and melodious sounds of Samuel Barber's "Adagio for Strings." The actual sound of silence is so unnatural to a movie audience accustomed to music that it calls attention to itself and seems experimental.

To be an artist means never to avert one's eyes.

—**Akira Kurosawa**

As with the convention of the close-up, the director who chooses not to use music may limit to a smaller audience the appeal of the resulting film.

Point of view is the way the camera is positioned in any given scene so it is clear which character or which mind is experiencing the action. In a murder mystery, for example, the detective's consciousness may be pivotal, and scenes are shot from his or her viewpoint. If all of the other characters are suspects, we should not be allowed to see things from their perspective. On the other hand, if the central character is a clever thief whom we really don't want to see caught, the camera might keep us in that character's mind.

Sometimes the point of view is that of the omniscient director, and the camera will focus on first one, then another character, according to the core of a given scene, but we are not asked to follow the fortunes of one particular character. A sign that the director is shifting into a character's point of view is a close-up of that character.

The same scene can be shown from more than one point of view. In Akira Kurosawa's *Rashomon* (1950), each witness to a crime describes the events in a different way. A film may also begin with confusing dialogue and action that seem to spring from no point of view. The Mexican film *Amores Perros* (2000) begins with a car chase and frantic dialogue by the occupants of one car about the effort to stop the bleeding of a dog. The audience doesn't know the identity of the occupants or why they are being chased. Then there is a crash, and the first of three stories begins, each from a different point of view, showing the varied impact of the crash on the lives of the characters. By the end of the film, the three stories come together, and the importance of the accident is revealed in the line "God laughs at those who make plans." We finally understand why there is no focus on one character throughout the film. The director has become a philosophical observer.

The convention of *time* is as flexible as the director chooses to make it. An action meant to last a minute can be prolonged on screen for several minutes, as the camera focuses on separate objects or people and returns to them again and again. A 1925 film about a massacre, Sergei Eisenstein's *The Battleship Potemkin*, shows the brutality of soldiers firing on civilians. Details—a horrified face, a baby carriage careening out of control, shattered eyeglasses—are shown more than once in a scene lasting far longer than its action in real time. Eisenstein is credited with pioneering in the convention of the **elongated moment**, or the slowing down of time.

D. W. Griffith (1875–1948), often considered the first giant of film art, created a new convention called the **lingering take** for his three-hour epic *The Birth of a Nation* (1915). This kind of shot remains on the screen for a longer interval than the plot requires. It is still used in cinema and television when the director wants to arouse the audience's curiosity. In a mystery, for example, the camera may move, or **pan**, from one suspect to another, pausing on one of them to make the audience think they have seen the guilty person. Usually they haven't.

The opposite is the convention of *compressed time*. In some early movies, the passage of time could be shown by the riffling of calendar pages, or even an insert card with the words "That evening" or simply "Later." A common time-compression device is to show, for example, a tree with bare branches, which then dissolves into a tree covered with blossoms, and the audience knows at once that the season has changed. A more sophisticated technique is to use a close-up of an object in the hands of a child, for example, and then the camera pulls back to show that the object is now in the hands of a different actor playing the same character as an adult. In Joseph Strick's *A Portrait of the Artist as a Young Man* (1977), a pair of eyeglasses worn by one character serves this purpose.

A **dissolve** occurs when one scene fades into another, a technique that replaced the older fading to black to mark the end of a scene. The dissolve often marks a transition in time or place. One scene is fading out as another is superimposed. In one of the cinema masterpieces of the twentieth century, *Casablanca* (discussed later in the chapter), the protagonist, Rick, sits alone in his café late at night while the room in back of him slowly changes into a scene in Paris, the subject of his thoughts.

Deliberately *slowing down* the film signals a lyrical, dreamlike scene, perhaps a beautiful memory or fantasy. Shutting it down completely results in a series of still photographs or **freeze frames**, a technique used by François Truffaut at the beginning of *Jules and Jim* (1961) and later by Martin Scorsese in his gangster film *Goodfellas* (1990).

Deliberately *speeding up* the film makes the characters either comical, like Mack Sennett's Keystone Cops of the 1920s, or surreal and mechanical, like the thugs in *A Clockwork Orange* (1971) fighting each other in fast, jerky movements—all to the music of the equally fast Rossini overture to *The Thieving Magpie*. The unnatural speed produces a sense of machines rather than human beings, with no more lasting effects than the violence in an animated cartoon.

Just as time can expand or contract, so too can space. An example of the **tracking shot** is found in the 1939 *Gone with the Wind*, when Scarlett O'Hara (Vivien Leigh) rushes wildly into the street to find the family doctor. Blundering onto a scene of unburied corpses, and in her dazed condition at first unaware of where she is, Scarlett slowly perceives she is in the midst of death on a scale she has never dreamed of. As the camera slowly backs away, the scene opens wider and wider to reveal hundreds upon hundreds of bodies. The tracking shot is achieved by placing the camera on rollers or a slowly moving platform so that it can track inward or outward, or even complete a circle around characters, as in the famous kissing scene in the 1959 film *On the Beach*, which also involved the elongation of real time. Tracking involves the continuous movement of the camera, without pausing for individual shots. Robert Altman's film *about* film, *The Player* (1992), opens with an eight-minute tracking shot that moves through a film studio and introduces the main characters in the various buildings on the lot, with one of them mentioning the very tracking shot as it is taking place.

The **cut** may be the most familiar convention. In this context, the word has two meanings. As a command from the director, it means "stop." As a technical term, it signifies the movement of the camera from one character or scene to another. If the director does not fade the camera from one scene to the next, he or she will use the cut, sometimes a *quick cut*, so the audience finds itself in another place before it even realizes that the preceding scene is over. The quick cut accelerates the rhythm of a fast-action film. On rare occasions in film, but more frequently on television, the **flip** changes the scene as rapidly as one can turn a coin from one side to another.

Film monsters have frightened audiences ever since the giant ape King Kong overwhelmed the comparatively tiny human object of his love. Building the figure of Kong and manipulating his movements in the jungle and on the side of the Empire State Building required ingenious use of animation techniques. Modern filmmakers can use computers to whip up a storm or devise a creature threatening the planet. We are living at a time when filmmakers are like guests at a buffet table filled with a wide array of *special effects*.

These conventions of film are so familiar that to audiences caught up in the story, there might seem to be no other way to tell it. Yet they have been challenged by a manifesto called "Dogma 9" written by Danish film director Lars von Trier, that demands "pure cinema" from directors who agree to make pictures look and sound as natural as possible. Films are to be photographed with handheld cameras, without using artificial light, optical effects, filters, special effects, or speeding up or slowing down of the camera to alter time. The length of each film is the time needed for the events to take place, as was the case in von Trier's *The Celebration* (1998), about adult children marking the birthday of their father and revealing some unpleasant secrets as they do.

More recently, in *Dogville* (2003), von Trier used even more experimental techniques to tell an even more unpleasant story. Ridding the film of all artificial aids, in a manner reminiscent of Thornton Wilder's play *Our Town*, von Trier shot the film within an almost bare studio, with a minimum of props and with actors using pantomime to tell the story of a refuge-seeking woman (played by Nicole Kidman) who agrees to work for her benefactors but who then becomes the victim of their greed and sadism. Von Trier insists on making films that are the opposite of escapist, and to do so, he doesn't mind doing away with the conventions audiences have come to expect.

Some Early Milestones

The origin of motion pictures can be traced as far back as 1824, when Peter Mark Roget, creator of the popular *Thesaurus*, formulated a theory called "The Persistence of Vision with Regard to Moving Objects." Roget gave some thought to something we all do thousands of times every day: *We blink our eyes.* He realized that when the eyes are momentarily covered as we blink, vision should be interrupted by intervals of blackness, but vision is continuous. The reason, he determined, is the eye's ability to retain an image for a split second after vision is stopped: that is, during the time it takes for the eyelid to close and reopen. Though the eyes keep blinking, the images retained keep overlapping each other, producing an *illusion* of continuous vision. If the object of vision is in motion, the eye is actually absorbing a series of individual "frames," though it sees fluid movement.

Soon after the publication of Roget's theory, entertainers developed the trick of showing an audience drawings of a figure in successive states of motion. The individual drawings were stacked together and held firmly so that the pages could be flipped through rapidly. The figure actually appeared to move. During the mid-nineteenth century, the development of photography made people hungry for tricks in which pictures of actual people replaced drawings. Inventors on both sides of the Atlantic began to develop mechanisms to move the pictures faster and create an ever better illusion of motion. One such mechanism was a circular drum with slits through which the eye peered. Inside the drum, still images were fastened, and when the contraption spun around, the eye saw fluid motion.

The invention of the motion picture camera and projector is attributed to Thomas Edison (1847–1931), who had made the first "peep show," a machine with a slot to look through and a crank handle for turning the pictures inside. This led to the building of penny arcades, where the public could play with the new technology. But Edison, at first more concerned with reproducing sound, concentrated on

Photography is truth. And cinema is truth twenty-four times a second.

—**Jean-Luc Godard**

Thomas Edison invented the movie projector, but it was his assistant who made the first movie, which lasted ten seconds.

the earliest phonograph, and he put aside his work on simulated motion. One day in 1889, his assistant amazed him by putting sound and sight together in a ten-second movie of a person who seemed actually to move and speak.

By 1896 projection technology had advanced to a point at which people could go to the movies to watch extremely brief films presenting one action, such as someone swimming, running, or starting to sneeze. These novelties were presented as interludes in the more important entertainment of the time, live singing and dancing on the vaudeville stage. Full-length films appeared soon after the turn of the century.

Art and Propaganda I: D. W. Griffith

Griffith has been called the father of film because he consolidated and expanded many of the techniques invented by his predecessors and was the first to go beyond gimmickry into the realm of art.
—**Louis Giannetti**

In 1915, when the elegant and huge Strand Theatre opened on Broadway, the director D. W. Griffith gave *The Birth of a Nation*—all three hours of it—to an adoring and dazzled public. This was the same year in which Louis B. Mayer started the company that was to become M.G.M. In that brief span from 1899 to 1915, movies had arrived as a mature form of entertainment, crafted by skilled artists like Griffith.

The film, which dealt with the American Civil War and the Reconstruction period, established movies as a mass medium. Griffith imposed his own point of view on history, one that was sympathetic even to the attacks of the Ku Klux Klan on carpetbaggers, the money-seeking politicians and scam artists from the North who came to the South with false promises of rebuilding shattered homes and cities. Many critics praised the marvelous cinematography and the film's epic sweep, hailing Griffith as the first genius of the new art form, but others denounced the director as a racist who used movies as propaganda. At any rate, the film had everyone talking, and the more intense the controversy, the longer the lines in front of the theater.

The Birth of a Nation was the first film to exhibit a definite directing style. Griffith's camera moves in for a close-up at a climactic moment, then cuts to a scene that moves at a different tempo. His work has been called rhythmic, because of the editing, which does not simply tell a story but controls the pace at which the story is experienced by the audience.

The film also introduced the lingering take, which became Griffith's trademark. During one famous moment, a young Confederate soldier, rushing across a battlefield, stops at the sight of a corpse lying on the ground. He recognizes that this Union soldier had been his closest friend before the war. The grief is short-lived, for he is suddenly pierced by a bullet and falls across his friend's body. Instead of dissolving the scene, Griffith allows the camera to hold the moment silently. There they are, two friends, both dead, two young lives never to realize their human potential.

In summing up the contribution of Griffith to the history of movies, one critic, Gerald Mast, wrote, "The film remains solid as human drama and cinematic excitement, flimsy as social theory."[1]

Art and Propaganda II: Sergei Eisenstein

Propaganda in a different style was offered in 1925 by the Soviet director Sergei Eisenstein (1898–1948). When the Bolsheviks gained power after the overthrow of the Russian czar in 1917, the first leader of the Soviet Union, Vladimir Lenin, recognized the power of film to instruct the public with a message favorable to the

One of the most famous scenes ever filmed, Eisenstein's Odessa steps sequence set a new standard for screen editing technique.

Source: Museum of Modern Art, Film Stills Archive.

state. Eisenstein was chosen to commemorate an unsuccessful Bolshevik uprising against the czarist regime in 1905 in his film *The Battleship Potemkin.* The film features a now famous episode that supposedly recreates a horrifying event in which soldiers loyal to the czar massacre hundreds of innocent civilians on the town steps in the city of Odessa. The massacre apparently never happened, but the film is widely admired for its editing techniques, especially in the famous Odessa steps scene, and is still required viewing in all film schools.

The film was shot on location, using a flight of steps deemed appropriate for the action. The sequence, six and three-quarter minutes long, depicted a minute or two of real time and required the splicing of 157 shots. The sequence begins with 57 shots that show an assortment of happy and unconcerned townspeople on the steps. Most significant of all is a young mother wheeling her baby in a carriage.

Then the soldiers on horseback come thundering to the top of the steps, splattering carnage as they ride. A little boy is separated from his mother and crushed to death in the stampede. The mother, finding her son's body, lifts him as an appeal to the soldiers, who respond by gunning her down. Back to the baby carriage sequence. The mother who had been wheeling the baby carriage is mangled by Cossack sabers. Now there is a close-up of the abandoned carriage, rocking back and forth dangerously on the edge of the steps, pushed ironically over the brink as the mother, bleeding to death, leans against it for support. A close-up

Eisenstein's Odessa Steps sequence in Potemkin *revolutionized the art of film editing.*

shows the innocent child inside the careening vehicle, which is hurtling down the steps, over and around hundreds of corpses. Another character is an apparently cultured woman wearing fragile reading glasses. Throughout the massacre the director returns to her, and each time she is splattered with blood. Finally we see a Cossack rider slashing at something out of our view, followed by a rapid cut to the woman's face. She has been mortally struck in the eye, but we do not actually see the saber strike her. Eisenstein instead gives us a close-up of the glasses lying on the steps, broken.

Although Eisenstein was a loyal Communist Party member and was committed to the Soviet doctrine of art as Communist instruction for the masses, he was also an artist and used film in an innovative way that went far beyond mere propaganda. While using film for Soviet propaganda, Eisenstein nevertheless could not ignore the artist within him.

Major Film Genres

Film genres—for example, a farce or a three-hankie sentimental melodrama—were born almost as soon as movies moved beyond short sequences and began to tell stories. By the mid-1920s, the tastes and preferences of the movie-going public controlled what studios could present. Up until the mid-1930s, when films began to reflect serious social issues brought on by the Great Depression, demand was greatest for formula plots and big-name stars performing in a number of different genres. Popular were westerns and gangster films, with mainly predictable stories designed for quick and easy production to take advantage of public hunger for entertainment. But there was also an audience for language-oriented plays about the marriage problems of those affluent enough to have escaped the widespread poverty of the Depression. This was a genre that can be called the *filmed play*. Directors used stage-trained diction coaches to turn film stars into replicas of British actors, carefully articulating each word and projecting their voices in a manner more suitable for the stage than for screen close-ups. Most of these filmed plays are of interest mainly to film historians, as are the films of one-time screen idols Rudolph Valentino, Clara Bow, and Theda Bara, which seem excessively emotional today, with their broad gestures and exaggerated facial expressions.

In this section we analyze several screen genres that are still prevalent, however much they have changed with the times.

Slapstick Comedy: Sennett and Chaplin

The director Mack Sennett (1884–1960) was known for films filled with **slapstick**, rapid and violent comic action in which people completely lost their dignity, got struck in the face with pies, crashed their cars into each other, and wound up getting doused with water. Sennett's world is one of total chaos, kept in disorder by a band of idiotic, incompetent, bungling policemen known as the Keystone Cops.

Today we tend to think that the speeded-up, jerky movements of the Sennett films were unplanned consequences of early technology. Nothing could be further from the truth! Sennett became obsessed with the sight gag and the potentially unlimited resources of film to provide it. He photographed action at an average of ten frames per second, but he ran the film through the projector at an average of eighteen frames per second—almost twice as fast as it really occurred in the studio. The effect was to dehumanize the characters so that the violent catastrophes—Sennett's stock in trade—could not be taken seriously.

While working for Sennett, an aspiring young comic named Charles Chaplin (1889–1977) happened to put together a funny costume to wear in a crowd scene, probably as a means of getting a little attention. That costume became his signature outfit and would be worn again and again. In baggy trousers and shoes much too big for him, Chaplin became the Little Tramp, the prototype of the social misfit. Chaplin's developing interest in character, not sight gags, as the main source of comedy led him to leave Sennett and strike out on his own. The result: Charlie Chaplin became the first truly big and international star.

The Little Tramp is an incongruity—always out of place wherever he is. Yet he is not completely ridiculous; what humanizes him is the attempt at dignity implicit in both his costume and face. He is also a survivor. In a cruel world he manages to get by. Even though he is thin and weak-looking, he is always able to outwit the villains and bullies who threaten. The ongoing myth in Chaplin films is the eternal triumph of the underdog, a myth with universal appeal.

Chaplin won his reputation during the era of silent films, both short and feature length. Even after the introduction of sound, his films depended largely on his ability to tell a story through mimed actions. He almost always depicted the awkward, inept, and yet lovable underdog who somehow manages to emerge victorious even though the situation nearly overwhelms him. In *The Gold Rush* (1925), the Tramp becomes so hungry he cooks his shoes and eats the shoelaces like spaghetti, delicately twirling them on a fork and dabbing at his mouth to wipe away the imaginary gravy. Though far from nutritious, the shoelaces keep him alive. When his tiny Alaskan cabin is blown to the edge of a cliff during a blizzard, he unknowingly exits through the door—nearly to his doom. Teetering and tottering, he always manages to avoid certain disaster.

Yet his film *Modern Times* (1936) shows Chaplin to have been sensitive to social issues. It is the story of Depression-era society, of a host of workers either being replaced by a machine or treated like one. In the opening shot, the screen is filled with sheep all headed in the same direction. The next shot is of a horde of people coming out of the subway, looking like a herd of human sheep. In a large factory, Chaplin's character works on an assembly line, where his job requires him to tighten the screws on a product ever more quickly, as the boss keeps increasing the speed of the conveyor belt. In an effort to cut time from the workers' lunch break, the boss considers installing an automatic feeding machine so that each worker can keep his hands free. In the most famous scene, Charlie is caught in the gears and becomes part of the machinery. As usual, there is a woman who loves him, as well as an idyllic dream sequence showing how life ought to be, with simplicity, love, and respect for each individual. And as usual, Charlie is ever gallant in ill-fitting but clean clothes.

The Little Tramp becomes part of the machinery in *Modern Times,* a film showing Chaplin's sensitivity to social issues.

Source: S.S. Archives/Shooting Star.

a tramp, a gentleman, a poet, a dreamer, a lonely fellow, always gallant, always hopeful of romance

Farce: The Marx Brothers

The Marx Brothers—Groucho, Chico, and Harpo—dominated the comic scene during the 1930s into the war years of the early 1940s. Usually on the wrong side of rules and regulations, they managed never to be caught, thus delighting those who cheered for the underdog. Whether it was their inability to pay a huge hotel bill or stowing away on ocean liners, they never played it safe, never walked the straight and narrow. Yet audiences always knew that the rules they broke were somehow unfair, or else codes of behavior that only snooty aristocrats would approve.

Their masterpiece, one of the screen's most memorable comedies, is *A Night at the Opera* (1935), where the three try to help a pair of young lovers succeed in the opera world. In an early scene, Groucho, always the suave con man, and Chico, always the seemingly dumb but really clever purveyor of his own brand of common sense, are negotiating a legal contract for the services of an unemployed tenor. The scene is a hilarious satire on legalese language. The two tricksters keep tearing out of the contract whatever they don't understand, until there is nothing left.

One of the most famous scenes takes place in the tiny stateroom in which the three brothers and the tenor, now smuggled on board, are supposed to be living. Into the narrow space pour repairmen as well as maids who are supposed to be making up beds. In addition to the outlandish number of people, there are several huge trunks. Finally, a chambermaid appears and tells Groucho, "I've come to mop up," to which he replies, "You'll have to start on the ceiling." Then someone opens the door from the outside and everyone cascades into the hallway.

The climactic episode of *A Night at the Opera* is the most uproarious in the film. At a performance of Verdi's *Il Trovatore*, both the tenor and the soprano have been unfairly excluded, according to the brothers, who wreak havoc on the opera with their antics. Harpo (a classic mime, never speaking in any of their films) inserts the music of "Take Me out to the Ball Game" as part of the overture, dutifully played by the orchestra. As detectives and police raid the back of the theater, Harpo evades them by climbing up the ropes that change the backdrops. The tenor on stage continues his aria as inappropriate scenes appear and disappear. The villain of the movie is knocked out. The tenor refuses to continue, so the two lovers finish the opera and all ends happily, something that can happen only in a farce.

Though elements of slapstick and farce can be found sporadically in contemporary films, the age of the great comics seems to have passed—or at least to be on hold. Film historians disagree on the cause. Perhaps escapism now takes so many forms—graphic violence, overwhelming special effects, sophisticated editing techniques that make films roar by at dizzying speed—that today's audiences can't be satisfied by the relatively slower pace of the classic comedies.

An all-time classic scene, the packed room in a Marx Brothers farce, about to explode.

Source: The Everett Collection.

Enduring Appeal of the Animated Film

By the early 1930s, the movie-going public was treated to a lengthy evening of film: in addition to an A movie, or feature, and a B or minor movie, there would be a newsreel and a cartoon. Early animated films were black-and-white, carefully drawn cartoons of mischievous animals with high-pitched voices. Invariably, the smaller animals outwitted their larger predators, who met unlikely disasters. In this manner, Disney's Mickey Mouse and Donald Duck achieved international fame. But with Disney's *Snow White and the Seven Dwarfs* (1936), fans were lining up at the box office to see the first full-length animated feature, with color and artwork never before seen, and an unforgettable musical score.

Animation technology has become so sophisticated that the simplicity of *Snow White* makes it appear dated, but the everlasting charm of the story still delights youngsters and gives older adults a brief excursion back to their youth. The Disney group and others who now employ top-notch artists and computer geniuses have developed the means of populating animated films with both human and animal figures that seem almost three-dimensional. The new world of animated film is a virtual universe with its own reality. Contemporary cartoons use dialogue that is frequently sophisticated enough for adults who accompany their small children. In the 1988 film *Who Framed Roger Rabbit?*, for example, the animated seductress calls attention to her own lack of reality by remarking in a sultry voice, "I'm not really bad; I'm just drawn that way."

The new technology has resulted in works that adults can enjoy, with or without children. One such film is Disney's *Ratatouille* (2006), the story of Remy, a gourmet rat who saves the reputation of a fine restaurant and instructs fellow rats to care about what they eat (which should be more than fuel, please, and certainly not garbage). In the process he overcomes his father's opposition and wins the approval of an inordinately hard-to-please food critic.

Remy has read in a cookbook that the right ingredients must be combined, cooked, and then described with just the right words. He becomes the mentor of a young human named Linguine. By hiding under the latter's hat, Remy is able to supervise the composition of dinners that have patrons and eventually the finicky critic clamoring for more. When the human cooks abandon the kitchen, Remy invites his family to help him prepare an exquisite meal. The happy ending finds (as expected) greater understanding between father and son, a budding romance between the inept Linguine and the female chef he has shyly and distantly adored, and the now satisfied food critic remembering with delight the way Remy's food, particularly the vegetable stew of the title, reminds him of his mother's cooking.

Ratatouille enraptured children with its adorable cartoon rodents, but it also pleased adult critical viewers with its theme of what constitutes good taste—rare for any film and heretofore non-existent in an animated one. The work marks a further development of animation as an art form, with a screenplay in which the realistic three-dimensionality of the characters is matched by the intelligence of subject and language.

Film Noir

During the 1920s, after Congress passed legislation prohibiting the sale and consumption of alcohol, illegal drinking establishments called "speakeasies" were supplied by bootleggers with liquor from abroad or else an infamous and potent local concoction referred to as "bathtub gin." The underworld liquor traffic

Film noir makes use of dark, shadowy camerawork to evoke a menacing hostile universe in which nothing is as it appears.

—**Geoff Andrew**

. . . Rather than amorality…[it was] honor among detectives. Find your partner's killer even if it meant breaking your heart. Spade has done the Right Thing and ends up the ultimate cynic.

—**A.M. Sperber and Eric Lax**

triggered the rise of organized crime and in film led to the archetype of the gangster, a cynical antihero who justified his contempt for the law with a belief in a generally corrupt world in which those who followed the rules deserved no mercy.

As appealing as the gangster was the private eye, a pay-for-hire investigator, sometimes a former gangster himself, who knew every dark corner of the city and every murderer lurking in the shadows—someone who shot just as straight as the criminals themselves and who, like them, could kill without a moment's reflection. He operated just outside the law, but was forgiven, even admired, by the audience because he never killed for personal reasons. Identifying with him was easy and unambiguous. He was hired to find the bad guys, and did so, even if his methods were straight out of the gangster's handbook.

Like his gangster counterpart, the private eye projected a deep-rooted cynicism about the corrupt world. Both knew that ruthlessness was necessary for survival. He paved the way for what French critics called **film noir** (literally, "black film"), a new genre "characterized by its dark, somber tone and cynical, pessimistic mood." The term was also used "to describe those Hollywood films of the 40s and early 50s which portrayed the dark and gloomy underworld of crime and corruption, films whose heroes as well as villains are cynical, disillusioned, and often insecure loners." Film noir "characteristically abounds with night scenes . . . with sets that suggest dingy realism, and with lighting that emphasizes deep shadows and accents the mood of fatalism."[2]

The private eye proved an apt hero for *film noir*. He usually worked alone or with one partner, had no family ties, and was good at his trade, operating on the fringes of society, he knew the underworld and could easily pass for a gangster. At the head of the class in this genre stands John Huston's *The Maltese Falcon* (1941), which created the powerful screen persona of Humphrey Bogart (1899–1957). In earlier films, Bogart had often played ruthless gangsters. In *The Maltese Falcon* he was given the opportunity to add a moral streak to his tough-minded realism, and this addition gave depth to his most memorable screen creations.

Here, Bogart plays Sam Spade, who shoots to kill if he has to and has no illusions about the world or the people who inhabit it. Yet he has his own principles, his own code of ethics, even if others have none. The death of his partner involves him in a labyrinth of dangerous intrigue, murder, and deceit as he seeks to solve the murder: "When your partner is killed, you're supposed to do something about it."

Throughout the film, Spade is in trouble with both the police and a conspiracy of international crooks who are seeking the expensive, jeweled bird of the title. Like a warrior of old, Spade is equal to any task, despite being threatened, deceived, cheated, and knocked unconscious. But he has something else: vulnerability. He becomes romantically involved with an attractive woman, a client, who may or may not be worthy of his trust. Yet, love notwithstanding, he never allows emotion to override either his reason or his ethics; instead, he remains a principled realist to the end. In a world like this, he seems to say, you cannot afford to be anything else.

In *Double Indemnity* (1944), by writer-director Billy Wilder, the protagonist (Fred MacMurray) is not a private eye but an insurance investigator, persuaded by a beautiful woman (Barbara Stanwyck) to murder her rich husband and help her collect on a huge policy. The woman pretends to have emotions but is unable to feel either genuine love for the investigator or remorse for the crime they commit. The investigator, recognizing that the woman is not what he had thought, becomes cynical and hard-boiled, the two requirements for a film noir hero. He has seen human nature, including his own, at its worst, but he too achieves a moral vision, confessing to the crime and admitting his corruption.

In film noir, women do not often reach such a vision, nor do the villains ever pretend what they do is morally right—it's only "necessary." Usually absent from the genre are sincere smiles and long discussions of feelings. Typically the point of view is first person, forcing the audience to identify with the hero's dark view of the world.

The genre caught the imagination of European directors such as François Truffaut (1932–1984), whose *Shoot the Piano Player* (1961) was in part a film *about* film, an homage to Alfred Hitchcock (discussed later in this chapter), to the Bogart **persona**, and in particular to film noir. Truffaut was a conscious artist, intrigued by the theme of alienation, strongly suggested by the cynicism of American noir heroes. In *Shoot the Piano Player* the theme of alienation is established in the opening scene. On a shadowy street, one man runs away from another, whom we don't see. He falls and is helped to his feet by a stranger. During their brief walk together, the stranger tells the other man about how he met his wife, about the birth of their first child, how love developed slowly. Will there be a relationship between the two? In other films, the answer is always yes, of course. Here, the two men shake hands and separate. The stranger never appears again. In film noir, that is how the world is.

In another scene, Charlie, the protagonist of the title (Charles Aznavour), hesitates at the door of an impresario who is waiting to hear him audition. Then the door opens and a young woman carrying a violin walks out. There is only the slightest meeting of their eyes, something that in most films suggests that more will come of this encounter. Instead, the camera follows the violinist down a long hallway, down the stairs, and into the street. We never see her again, either.

Resistance to human contact is the core of Charlie's character. He really wants to be left alone to play a tinny piano in a bar and not become involved with the people who need him: his brothers, who are smalltime crooks, the men who are chasing his brothers, and the women who keep being attracted to him. Cynical, philosophical, Charlie remains untouched, almost numb. And yet, before the film is over, he has been forced by circumstances to take part in extortion, kidnapping, suicide, and murder. Like Bogart's character in *The Maltese Falcon*, he cannot remain uninvolved with others. Life doesn't let the loner remain alone, but it doesn't give him much in return.

Romantic Comedy

A movie theater used to be the perfect place for romance, on screen and off, perfect for a Saturday-night date, when couples sitting in the dark could look at other couples on the screen, secure in the knowledge that, no matter what has kept them apart for most of the film, they will surely end in each other's arms.

The man and woman on the screen were apt to be better looking, better dressed, and richer than the couple on a date. For Depression-era audiences, looking at the luxury in a film offered welcome, if temporary, escape. The sets were authentic recreations of Art Deco, and the costumes worn by the actresses were products of world-famous designers. The characters—often a man and woman who love each other—become enmeshed in a ridiculous disarray of circumstances that very nearly but not quite terminate the relationship. After all, if boy meets girl and soon boy gets girl, the film would not be feature length. Instead, boy loses girl through misunderstandings, jumping to conclusions, refusing to listen to facts. Wisecracks substitute for sentimental admissions of affection. True love is hidden rather than spoken, until the end. Audiences knew the admission was coming, even if it didn't turn out that way in real life. But then, who needed a reminder of what real life was like in those hard times?

A classic romantic comedy, *It Happened One Night* (1934) concerns an extraordinarily wealthy young woman (Claudette Colbert) and her attempts to find true love. At the beginning of the picture, the audience knows immediately that she is making a mistake in her choice of mates, but the runaway heiress is so determined to marry a fortune-hunting playboy against her father's wishes that she escapes from the family yacht by swimming to shore. She avoids her father's detectives by taking a bus on which, in the destined-for-each-other world of romantic comedy, she meets a charismatic reporter (played by Clark Gable, the reigning matinee idol of the period), who will, of course, be the true love for which she longs.

As a formerly spoiled and protected but now penniless heiress, she lacks survival skills, but these are quickly furnished by the hero, who intervenes to protect her from a lecherous man in the adjoining seat and offers her the seat next to his. As is customary in the genre, the heroine at first resents the help offered by the reporter.

After a flash flood stops the bus, the heiress and reporter are forced to share the last remaining motel room. The hero, bound by the motion picture moral code of the period, constructs a clothesline with a blanket thrown over it to separate the twin beds, dubbing the divider "the Walls of Jericho." At breakfast he shows her how to dunk a doughnut, a talent her upbringing has never before required. When bus travel is no longer possible, he attempts to explain the technique of hitchhiking. In the film's most famous scene, her provocatively lifted skirt and revelation of a shapely leg prove more effective than the reporter's confident waving of his thumb. In fact, the heiress gradually proves to be the reporter's equal. The romantic comedy heralded the liberation of film women from earlier stereotyping.

The heiress and reporter of course fall in love, and of course are driven apart by circumstances. The heiress seems destined for the playboy. In the romantic comedies of the Great Depression, audiences loved to be reminded that money cannot buy happiness. As the heiress and her father are walking down the aisle toward the altar at her wedding ceremony, her father tells her she is marrying the wrong groom. At the crucial "Do you take this man?" question, the heroine flees the church and dashes to a car conveniently waiting outside—a motif repeated in other films.

The finale, naturally, has to be the return of the heiress and the reporter, now married, to the same motel room, but this time the blanket on the clothesline will come down like the biblical

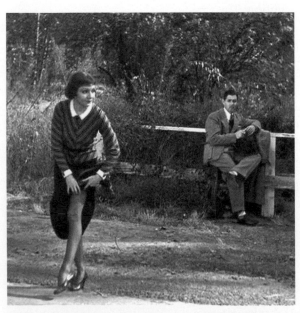

A classic romantic comedy of the 1930s, *It Happened One Night* delivered the popular message that love is more important than money.

Source: Photofest, Inc.

"Walls of Jericho." The reporter has been so sincerely in love, he has been able to bridge class differences and earn the right to marry the rich man's daughter, to the delight of the audience who may have decided the moral of the film was *love is greater than money*. In point of fact, however, the woman remains an heiress, and her approving father will always be there.

As the shadow of war became more ominous and the effects of the Depression lingered in many segments of the country, the movies continued to provide much needed escape. The difference is that audience tastes had grown more sophisticated. In George Cukor's *The Philadelphia Story* (1939), romantic comedy borrowed elements of the *comedy of manners* from the stages of Broadway and London. With elegant and witty dialogue, the genre purported to show the audience how truly educated and articulate people spoke and behaved. But behavior was often scandalous, a clear violation of manners, and therefore hilarious.

In *The Philadelphia Story*, the heroine (played by Katharine Hepburn, an icon of good breeding and intelligence), engaged to marry a wealthy, respectable, and dull second husband, is still in love with her divorced husband (played by Cary Grant, the most dapper leading man in Hollywood), who shows up at the coming nuptials. Class difference, a common theme in comedy of manners, is evident in the film. The heroine's choice of second husband is a self-made man. Obviously proud to be forming an alliance with Old Money, he believes the marriage will advance his career in business and politics. But he doesn't fit in (as her first husband had indeed). Brash and nouveau riche, he doesn't realize, for example, that his brand-new riding clothes mark him as a newcomer, uncomfortable around horses. Nor does he see anything wrong with the newspaper attention and photographs that will accompany his union with a publicity-hating bride-to-be. He is stuffy, overly earnest, and ill at ease as he tries too hard in an alien world. Worst of all, he lacks wit, a cardinal sin in this genre.

The clever lines belong to Hepburn and Grant. They argue throughout the film (which opens with a famous scene in which she breaks his expensive golf club over her knee, after which he reciprocates by pushing her backwards to the floor) and say unpleasant things to each other, but their obvious elegance, pitted against the boorishness of the would-be-groom, inevitably wins the day. They were born for each other. In comedy of manners, the "right" people always triumph.

The heyday of brilliant dialogue and romantic sparring continued into the postwar years when parents of baby boomers, facing inevitable domestic complexities, flocked to movie houses to watch the problems of other married couples that were inevitably resolved satisfyingly. George Cukor's *Adam's Rib* (1949) starred the now legendary Hepburn with the sparring partner with whom she would make eight films, Spencer Tracy. Less overtly comedic than Grant, Tracy usually projected an inner wisdom that Hepburn's characters always recognized and could never resist. Not that they didn't bicker as expected. In the film, Hepburn and Tracy are two attorneys married to each other. Hepburn is defending an abused wife who has shot and seriously wounded her husband, whom she discovered in the arms of another woman. The plot gains its sparkle from the fact that Tracy is the prosecuting attorney.

What sets *Adam's Rib* apart from other romantic comedies is that, despite the undercurrent of true love that persists behind the often bitter clash of wills and opinions, there is a strong theme of gender discrimination, which threatens to tear the lawyers' marriage apart. Hepburn argues that the law has always been tilted in favor of men and unfair to women who refuse to play meek, subservient roles. Her

Screen writers had to invent dialogue that was rich and colorful, pungent and amusing, but also stripped of inessentials.

—**Arthur Knight**

courtroom speeches cause her to realize that in her own marriage she has been expected to bow before her husband's superior knowledge of the law.

The abused wife is exonerated after Hepburn nearly reduces the jury to tears, but Tracy is furious, accusing her of making a mockery of the law. He then reverts to crocodile tears in an effort to win her sympathy—and is successful at it. The traditional happy ending is there, of course. The marriage is saved, but the film leaves us with much to think about. How deeply rooted are gender roles? Doesn't everyone at one time or another make use of them for personal gain? Will there ever be true equality?

Thus far, in this section, we have seen the evolution of a major film genre from breezy, witty entertainment to comedy with a serious undercurrent. The romantic comedy has proved to be an enduringly popular genre, always changing to meet the challenge of new times. By the late 1980s, the movement encouraging sexual equality was in full swing. Both men and women found themselves trying to cope with shifting gender roles. But changes in both society and romantic comedy were on the horizon.

In the groundbreaking *When Harry Met Sally* (1989), independent woman Meg Ryan encounters traditionally disposed man Billy Crystal. Although they barely know each other, the plot sends them driving together cross-country. Along the way, casual conversation turns to sharp repartee, a battle of wits between a woman who believes a non-sexual, friendly relationship can exist between two people and a man who argues that sex will always be the main issue, whether talked about or not. She adds that women aren't nearly as interested in sex as he believes but often pretend to be enjoying it, which she demonstrates by imitating the sounds of orgasm while they sit in a restaurant. Through their developing relationship, the film shows two equal partners.

In the two decades following *When Harry Met Sally*, according to some film historians, gender equality in films began to erode. Women continued to make strides in society, often occupying positions of authority over male workers. The male, in films and on television, was frequently depicted as hapless and very much in need of female guidance. It became difficult to find those elements that made earlier romantic comedies so appealing. In a *New Yorker* article, film critic David Denby analyzes possible reasons. Using the 2007 comedy *Knocked Up* as a contemporary example, he contrasts the squabbling lovers in the old films with their modern-day counterparts and finds that today's are no longer equal partners. "There they are, the young man and young woman of the dominant romantic comedy trend of the past several years—the slovenly hipster and the female straight arrow. The movies form a genre of sorts: the slacker-striver romance. . . . For almost a decade, Hollywood has pulled jokes and romance out of the struggle between male infantilism and female ambition."[3]

Where the genre is headed is as yet unclear. The slacker-achiever couple may prove to be a passing trend. Will there ever be another Hepburn-Tracy partnership? Will witty repartee once again replace run-of-the-mill dialogue? One trend that deserves to be mentioned is the recent emergence of romantic comedies that end in *bittersweet compromise* between the traditional happy ending after a long verbal battle and something that perhaps comes closer to reality.

In the aptly titled *As Good as It Gets* (1997), Helen Hunt plays a struggling single mother working as a waitress trying to bring up an asthmatic son. She attracts the attention of a cranky older man played by Jack Nicholson. The Nicholson character, a successful writer, is extremely demanding, with excessive

By the 1980s romantic comedy was beginning to reflect the change in gender roles. In 1934, Claudette Colbert willingly surrendered her independence to masculine Clark Gable. In 1989, Meg Ryan is self-assured and can get along without male guidance.

compulsions about order and neatness. The couple has little in common. Still, he is able to get good medical help for her son, and he does modify his behavior enough to become a little more romantic. When he proposes marriage, the heroine's mother reminds her that this is "as good as it gets," and the embrace in the final scene suggests that a workable compromise has been reached. Neither character has changed all that much. People usually don't, says the film, but isn't it better to be with someone who has come to understand you than to spend your life dreaming of a perfect relationship?

In *Monsoon Wedding* (2001), a romantic comedy from India, the heroine is a young woman whose parents have arranged a marriage for her. With the approval of both families, the groom is due to arrive soon for an elaborate Punjabi wedding. But the heroine must first determine what her former lover, a married man, plans to do about their secret affair. The questions are old and familiar: Will he divorce his wife? Will the affair continue? Will the bride call off the wedding? Will the groom reject the bride when he learns the truth?

Old-fashioned melodramas would have had loud denunciations and possible disaster. But *Monsoon Wedding* is far more modern than that. When the heroine recognizes that nothing about her affair will change and that the man she is slated to marry is at least a suitable mate, she tells him about her affair. Sobered by the confession but respectful of his bride's honesty, the groom proves to be understanding as they move toward a new definition of love. The result is a film filled with color—the saris, the henna-painted skin, the captivating music—all underscoring a marriage seemingly destined for happiness by blending the modern and the traditional. Again, we are shown a world that's "as good as it gets."

Tokyo is the setting for Sofia Coppola's *Lost in Translation* (2003) starring Bill Murray as an aging actor, Bob Harris, reduced to shooting a whisky commercial in a city filled with bewildering sights and sounds. Staying in the same hotel is Charlotte, a bored young wife (Scarlett Johannsen) whose photographer husband is often absent on business. She and the Bill Murray character meet and share their loneliness. A critic describes their growing intimacy as they explore karaoke bars, talk, and come close to each other before going their separate ways: "In the early hours of the morning, Harris puts his suit jacket around Charlotte's shoulders. The tails reach her knees; the sleeves submerge her hands. The odd couple wander back through the alien city streets. . . . The moment marks a change in their relationship, as it shifts from friendship into an emotional bond. The sight of Charlotte's figure drowned by the jacket is as painful (their relationship is a nonstarter) as it is heart-warming."[4]

Murray, whose career is built on comedy, makes disillusion and apathy as believable as his attraction to the young woman who obviously cares for him. But the ending is realistic and right. They do not have enough in common to sustain a lasting relationship. Perhaps not enough people really do. Yet the need for contact, if only fleeting, is always there. The comedies of compromise refuse to perpetuate mythology.

The new romantic comedy of bittersweet compromise, showing that a less than perfect relationship may be as good as it gets.

Source: Mirabli Films/Delhi Dot Com/The Kobal Collection.

I just put my feet in the air and move them around.

—**Fred Astaire**

The Screen Musical

The stories in musical films, hugely popular in the 1930s into the 1950s, were often similar to those in romantic comedies of the period. The couple was kept apart until the final embrace, except when they sang and danced together. This formula was especially true for Fred Astaire and Ginger Rogers, who essentially played the same people from one film to the next. The clothing and sets in Astaire-Rogers films were lavish. Impeccably garbed Fred, with top hat and tails, and satin-gowned Ginger, with sequins and feathers, dance up and down stairs, on table tops, and even on miraculously cleared dance floors in intricately choreographed routines, even though the script may indicate they have just met and obviously had no time to rehearse. No matter what minor misunderstanding may have separated them, when the band begins to play, the logic of the story disappears as they tapdance, waltz, swirl, and introduce new rhythms.

Dancing at any moment was a convention of musical film, as was singing that could occur anywhere: on the deck of a ship or in a moonlit garden. Anytime a lover wanted to woo, romantic feelings could be described in song. An unseen orchestra offered accompaniment, as the singing and dancing that brought them together offered a preview of a future of harmony. Opera had long had sung dialogue and orchestral accompaniment, but musical comedy songs offered more spoken dialogue and songs that could be sung by the untrained voices of a public expected to buy the records.

The major choreographer of Hollywood musicals in the 1930s was Busby Berkeley (1895–1976), who placed beautiful women in designs that would have been impossible on the stage. Audiences loved synchronized dancing, like that of Radio City Music Hall's high-kicking, long-legged Rockettes (still packing them in), a tradition carried on by the top-hatted ensemble in the finale of *A Chorus Line* and the Irish Step Dancers of *Riverdance*. The screen musical provided effects Broadway could not match. Berkeley was able to arrange his dancers in intricate configurations, photographed from above, with some of them in the dark and others in the light as they swirled into kaleidoscopic patterns.

Singin' in the Rain (1952), directed by Stanley Donen and Gene Kelly, is generally considered the greatest musical Hollywood has ever made. For a change, the plot is believable and deals not with the usual banter between hero and heroine but with what really happened when movies first acquired sound. Gene Kelly, who also stars in the film, dances in joyous abandon on every kind of surface, including a rain-soaked street. In the famous title number, Kelly sings about the happiness of being in love, as he splashes and dances through puddles, umbrella in hand—a scene that can be separated from the story and viewed with delight as an expression of pure joy. *Singin' in the Rain* was glorious escapist entertainment for the public without sacrificing integrity of plot and characterization.

In what has been called the greatest movie musical ever made, there are joyous singing, dancing, and a believable plot.

Source: The Everett Collection, Inc.

As films became more special-effects oriented during the 1980s, the screen musical tried, usually without success, to adapt to the changing fashions by venturing into unexplored territory. *Dirty Dancing*, in 1987, however, was a huge success, largely because it featured spectacular dance routines and the disappearance of by now hackneyed elements. There isn't even any singing by the characters in the film, and we never hear an orchestra suddenly and mysteriously present as a lead-in to a romantic duet.

The female protagonist, Baby, is a young woman who is insecure and seems to have two left feet. She is of course drawn to the male protagonist, a dance instructor at the lake resort where she is staying with her family. Through a plot twist, Baby must learn how to do a professional-level dance routine, and as she rehearses with the dance instructor, they grow romantically involved. He is accused of fraternizing with a guest and of stealing but redeems himself, then rescues the hotel from the lackluster entertainment it has been providing. In the thirty-minute finale not only the performers but the guests do the "dirty dancing" of the title, with its lifts, leaps, bends, and embraces. The resort owner is delighted to see his guests so happy, and he knows they will return the following year, thus saving the enterprise from bankruptcy. Baby's parents, who had opposed her relationship with the seemingly irresponsible dance instructor, are delighted to see that their daughter has so much dancing talent. In fact, *everyone* is delighted, including the filmmakers, who created a modest musical with no special effects that has become a film classic.

Characters and plot are even more believable in the Japanese film *Shall We Dance?* (Masayuki Suo, 1996) in which an affluent businessman, mired in a boring routine life, happens to look out of a commuter train window and see into a room where an attractive woman is giving dance lessons. Acting uncharacteristically, on impulse, he signs up for lessons and finds that learning dance steps shakes him out of the predictability of his life. The core of the film, however, revolves around the intricacies and shifting dynamics of real human relationships, explored in ways rarely found in musicals of yesterday.

In some respects, Rob Marshall's 2002 Oscar-winning *Chicago* is like earlier musicals in its lavish, glitzy production numbers, but unlike them in the seriousness of its cynical satire on ambition, crime, tabloid journalism, and public celebrity worship that exceeds all bounds of reason. It also follows in the wake of Baz Luhrmann's *Moulin Rouge* in its use of what has been described as "pure cinema," using the quick cut in ways undreamed of in years past.

The show-stopper here is the soft-shoe dance by the attorney (Richard Gere), who is defending an accused and apparently guilty murderess (Renée Zellweger). He musically describes how clever lawyers hoodwink and outthink gullible juries. "Give 'em the old razzle-dazzle," he sings. As he goes into his dance, the camera keeps cutting to scenes of an actual court trial, then back to Gere's glittering showmanship. Both *Moulin Rouge* and *Chicago* epitomize the *new* musical, combining traditional elements, dazzling camera work, and serious themes.

The Western

No film genre is more historically associated with Hollywood than the western tale of good and evil. In one film after another, bad guys menace the decent folks in a town that is often the same studio back-lot set, complete with horses, a stagecoach, the jail, the general store, the saloon, and a dusty main street, scene of a thousand shootouts. Actors embody the time-honored personae of cowboys, sheriffs, outlaws, schoolmarms, and dance-hall girls, to the delight of loyal fans. Some of the characters had recognizable historical names, such as Wyatt Earp, Doc Holliday, Jesse and Frank James, and Billy the Kid. Others were purely fictional. All became part of an American morality myth, so much so that children continue to play the parts and tourists continue to visit the Ghost Towns where scenes from a basic western are reenacted in an authentic setting.

In 1939, as Americans were heatedly debating how much the country should be involved in the war that had already begun in Europe, *Destry Rides Again* was a satiric version of the traditional western. In the film, the popular actor James Stewart plays a newly appointed sheriff who refuses to carry a gun! The bad guys are the usual ones who drive law-abiding farmers from their lands, after which they gamble and drink at the local saloon, where the main entertainment is provided by the husky-voiced, scantily clad Frenchy (Marlene Dietrich), the ungenteel costume always a sign that this woman will not win the heart of the good guy, even though she has the traditional heart of gold.

Two other important characters, indispensable in the western, are the good woman, in this case a teacher who is worthy of Destry's affections, and the sheriff's sidekick, a lovable drunk whose irresponsibility immediately wins the audience's affection. The non-violent sheriff manages to maintain order until the lovable sidekick is shot and dies in his arms. At this point, he stands up, straps on his gunbelt (to the cheers of the audience), and goes off to avenge the death and clear the town of evil. During the gun battle in the classic western finale, Frenchy deliberately sacrifices herself by shielding Destry and taking the bullet meant for him. The heart of gold comes through but is not allowed—ever—to end happily.

With decency restored, the farmers can safely return home and Destry can marry his refined lady. Students of contemporary history will find a possible connection between the 1939 date of the film and Destry's realization that pacifism in the long run is ineffective against strong opponents.

In Fred Zinnemann's *High Noon* (1952), Will Kane (Gary Cooper) is retiring from the office of marshal, with his replacement due to arrive the following day. Kane plans to leave the town and open a store with his bride (Grace Kelly), whose Quaker religion opposes the use of firearms. But on Kane's last day, the town is facing the reappearance of a deranged killer who, with his brothers, has vowed revenge against the marshal responsible for his prison sentence. The film examines a legitimate moral dilemma. Kane must decide whether to stay and defend both himself and the law-abiding citizens of the town, who will be in danger should the menacing gang triumph, or to accompany his wife away from violence, to a life of peace. The French film *Shoot the Piano Player*, already discussed, would have a similar theme: is it possible to detach oneself from involvement in violence and moral corruption?

The plot continues to darken in this complex—and, to many, greatest ever—western. As the clock approaches high noon, when the train carrying the villains is due to arrive, Kane seeks help from the townsfolk. Though the town has seemed united in its moral denunciation of the bad men, no one else is willing to fight. After all, it isn't their problem. Kane's pacifist wife begs him to leave, with an ultimatum threatening their brief marriage, but his integrity and loyalty to his duty as marshal cause him to stay. He is left alone to decide whether to fight against overwhelming odds or flee, knowing none would blame him.

Talk low, talk slow, and don't say too much.

—John Wayne

The film has been called the *Hamlet* of the western genre. Like Shakespeare's Prince of Denmark, Will Kane continually asks himself why he should be the one to carry out a dreadful task (in Hamlet's case, the murder of his uncle), why he should have to die for a town that has betrayed him. Yet the film was obliged to abide by *some* of the rules governing the western. The noble marshal simply could not be allowed to die. On the other hand, the creators of this film were not about to turn their believable protagonist into an improbable superman.

In the famous climactic shootout, Kane manages to do away with two of the four villains. As one of the remaining killers is about to blast the unsuspecting Kane, a shot is fired by an unseen gun and the villain falls. The camera then shows us Kane's Quaker wife, who had picked up a gun and sent the killer to his death, but she is then taken captive by the last vengeance-seeking killer. Both Kane and his wife survive and the villain is killed. But the couple now feel alienated from the townsfolk.

Much has been made of the fact that the appearance of *High Noon* coincided with the start of the Korean War. Is this film also saying that pacifism is not a valid position? At the eleventh hour, doesn't the wife recognize that preserving justice at all costs is everyone's obligation? In the tradition of much high art, *High Noon* is content to remain ambiguous, perhaps understanding that it has posed questions for which there are no easy answers. If nothing else, in the manner of the very best myths, it tells us that, when a hero is needed, a hero will be there, because *somebody has to be there*. It doesn't guarantee that "being there" is necessarily its own reward. In the famous last scene, as the townspeople suddenly reappear to congratulate him, Kane bitterly removes his badge and drops it in the dust.

One popular 1969 western boasted two heroes who were on the wrong side of the law. They were a charming pair of bank robbers (Paul Newman and Robert Redford) whose names gave the film its title, *Butch Cassidy and the Sundance Kid*. Throughout George Roy Hill's brand of western, the rogue protagonists commit one crime after another, almost always managing to escape—and, in the true tradition of the rogue hero, with audience approval. (It is much easier to identify with a handsome, smart-talking Dionysian duo than with their humorless pursuers.)

Chased to the edge of a very high cliff, Butch (Newman) urges Sundance (Redford) to jump into the river below, only to learn that his partner can't swim. After he encourages his friend by telling him the fall will probably kill them, they do jump. Hill makes use of the *freeze frame*, at the time a new convention in which the camera stops an action suddenly. The lovable crooks are stranded in midair, bringing unexpected whimsy into a story that is moving toward an inevitable tragic ending. Yet the director's smile never entirely disappears, even when Butch and Sundance are ultimately riddled with bullets by Bolivian police. They die without a shred of remorse or self-pity.

The Old West has been the setting for more recent films, but the old mythology is no longer there. These are not black-and-white tales of good and evil. A significant modern western is Kevin Costner's 1990 *Dances with Wolves*, in which Native Americans are treated more sympathetically than when they were shown as stereotyped menaces to white settlers, who killed them one by one as audiences cheered. *Dances with Wolves* views Native Americans as victims of white oppression, and clearly belongs to the serious tradition of film as something more than popular entertainment. It is also a classic example of revisiting a film genre in a new context.

It is easy enough to guess why American presidents like [High Noon] so much. The man with the nuclear gun who thinks to himself that he often must do the hard thing, the unpopular thing, would also like to think of himself as spiritually resembling Gary Cooper.

—Paul Buhle and David Wagner

Horror and Suspense Films

Even though the sights and sounds of screened horror may cause some to close their eyes and cover their ears, audiences keep coming back for more. The desire to be thrilled in the theater is very old. Long before the invention of motion pictures, audiences watched terrible things happen to actors on stage, safe in the realization that the mutilations and executions were make believe. Shakespeare and his contemporaries showed scenes of eye gouging, amputations, and other forms of torture, sometimes right in front of the audience. In Greek tragedy, horror and violence happened offstage but was reported in often frightening detail by an onstage messenger, whose job was to make audiences shudder as their imaginations filled in the details.

Films can show the gory details magnified, and creepy background music makes certain that viewers are kept on the edge of their seats. Look! There goes the innocent victim down the dark street where the killer waits. Suspense builds as the camera zooms in on an ominous object, such as a pair of shoes walking along a deserted pavement. Or just the fierce eyes of an obsessed murderer—even better, a mask.

In 1929, Spanish director Luis Buñuel captured a horrifying moment, what seemed to be the slitting of an eyeball, in *Un Chien Andalou*. It remains shocking today, as this and other special effects allow us to see blood-spattered mutilations, or smooth, youthful skin peeled from a face that suddenly becomes too horrifying to look at. (Of course, we *do*!)

Social Issues

Beginning with Mr. Deeds Goes to Town. . .*with Gary Cooper as the small-town man who triumphs over city slickers, Capra's work emphasized the common-sense skills and leadership qualities of little people.*

—**Robert Sklar**

From its beginning, some directors recognized the power of film as a medium for social criticism. Such works make a statement about institutions and economic policies that are the root causes of human problems. A very early (1909) one-reel silent movie, *A Corner in Wheat*, took on the stock market and the tragic results of human greed. Like most early films, it exaggerated its case. The discrepancy between the haves and have-nots could not be missed. In one scene, newly made millionaires lift champagne glasses in celebration; a quick cut shows miserable-looking crowds on a bread line.

During the Depression of the 1930s, issue-oriented films became more sophisticated and were almost as popular as the escapist musicals and romantic comedies. Audiences who shared the deprivations experienced by the characters easily identified with real social problems and derived a measure of comfort by realizing that many others were in the same predicaments. Movie screens offered a balance between stories set in elegant drawing rooms and stories set in ill-heated shacks. And though audiences were not afraid to confront grim realities, some films were successful because they combined social realism with contrived happy endings.

Frank Capra (1897–1991) created films about bigotry, political corruption, and the abuse of workers' rights, with attractive, plain-talking heroes. An immigrant himself, the son of a fruit-picker, he had firsthand knowledge of poverty, but he also had profound respect for America, the land of opportunity. The optimism with which he ended his films worked box-office magic, although he has been criticized for providing easy solutions that could never happen in reality.

In *Mr. Deeds Goes to Town* (1936), Gary Cooper (the ideal Capra down-to-earth hero) tries to distribute an inheritance of $20 million to the poor and, as a result, must fight a legal battle to prove his sanity. Goodness once again prevails, and the Depression is over for a lucky few. In the 1939 *Mr. Smith Goes to Washington*, the hero, played by James Stewart, another Capra stalwart, is an idealistic junior senator, unaware that a political machine has sponsored him because of his boyish appeal to voters. Gradually learning that his sponsors are ruthless and willing to do anything to control him, he engages in a marathon filibuster to block the passage of a bill he was supposed to support. Capra provides a by-now-expected happy conclusion in which the forces of righteousness, led by his appealingly innocent hero, are eventually (temporarily?) triumphant.

In Capra's most popular film, *It's a Wonderful Life* (1947), a desperate, bankrupt hero (James Stewart again) is saved at the last minute (and, not coincidentally, on Christmas Eve) by the contributions of grateful townspeople whose homes were spared by his bank. He had contemplated suicide, believing that he was a total failure in life. The film's message—that people's worth is measured by the amount of good they do—has elevated the movie to almost mythic status. Alternately condemned as unabashed sentimentality and praised as a welcome addition to the Christmas spirit, *It's a Wonderful Life* is revived every year during the holiday season.

John Ford (1895–1973), like Capra the son of immigrants, was another director who grew up knowing the underprivileged side of life. He developed a special fondness for that American symbol of rugged individualism, the cowboy. When he became a film director (as early as 1917), he was attracted to scripts about the struggles of the poor to retain their integrity against the encroachments of the wealthy and powerful. The central characters in *The Grapes of Wrath* (1940), adapted from the John Steinbeck novel mentioned in Chapter 4, are the poor Joad family, forced to leave their farm after a bank foreclosure.

The land, unable to sustain them, has become part of the Dust Bowl, and the only opportunity appears to be in California, where they have heard fruit pickers are desperately needed. Ma Joad (Jane Darwell in an Oscar-winning performance) is a resource of quiet wisdom. Her son Tom (Henry Fonda, who brought naturalistic acting to a new level) is an impatient rebel. When they manage to drive their rickety old car to California, they learn that the rule of supply and demand is in full force. So many would-be farm workers have arrived that the advertised wages have been slashed. Tom Joad sees that the struggle for justice must transcend his own family and his own self-interest. He will dedicate his life to the cause of saving all of humanity.

A very different approach to the plight of the poor in the Depression was taken by Preston Sturges (1898–1959) in *Sullivan's Travels* (1941). Sturges, usually a writer-director of lighthearted, clever romantic comedies, seems to have questioned the tired formula that made him a success. His new film was a clearly personal one about a writer-director who decides to abandon comedy and deal with the problems of the poor and homeless. Disguising himself as a vagrant and living under bridges in squatters' camps, he is horrified when he unexpectedly finds himself a real victim of inequality. He is thrown in jail for a crime he didn't commit and sentenced to hard labor on a chain gang. The experience sobers him, but his confrontation with reality leads to an unexpected conclusion. The hero realizes that people need the gift of comedy more than they need to be reminded that they are poor. There is no $20 million to give away—only what Sturges himself possessed in abundance: humor plus a keen awareness of social realities.

The contemporary writer-director Spike Lee (b. 1957) is in the tradition of those who, like Ford, use the medium of film to confront real social problems. Early on, he decided he would devote his life to making films about oppressed minorities and enrolled at NYU. One of Lee's first assignments was to make a short film. His was short enough—ten minutes—but its subject matter was startling. Lee ridiculed the stereotypes of African Americans found in films like *The Birth of a Nation*, substituting *white* stereotypes.

Lee survived criticism of his irreverent school exercise, but the desire to shock by shaking up cherished beliefs has not left him. He has remained socially oriented, tackling such themes as racial and ethnic prejudice (*Do the Right Thing*, 1989), interracial romance (*Jungle Fever*, 1991), the seemingly irreversible poverty of African Americans (*Tales from the Hood*, 1995), and the biography of *Malcolm X* (1992), considered by many critics to be his finest film so far.

Lee has never been afraid to take a stand, both on and off screen. In making *Malcolm X*, he battled against a studio decision to allow a white director to make a film about the hero, and when he was finally given the job, he refused to be constrained by what he regarded as an inadequate budget. Instead he went out and raised private funds. In *Do the Right Thing*, he won critical acclaim for his use of an unusual film convention—a revival of the Greek Chorus—in this case a group of men sitting on the front steps of a house and commenting on what is happening in the neighborhood. Lee remains controversial, a director whose films continue to stimulate debate about whether he exaggerates or is delivering a needed message; whether audiences will imitate violence seen on the screen, and whether he himself is using damaging stereotypes.

There will never be an end of social problems, and films about social issues will always be produced, not only in the United States but all over the world. German director Florian Henckel von Donnersmarck's *The Lives of Others* won the Academy Award for best foreign film of 2006. Though it deals with the government-backed eavesdropping on private citizens that was prevalent in East Berlin before the destruction of the wall separating it from West Berlin, the film has obvious relevance to similar practices in other places and more recent times.

In the film, Captain Gerd Wiesler, with the East German spy organization Stasi, a master of surveillance and interrogation techniques, is assigned to test the loyalty of a gifted playwright and pianist Georg Dreyman. So above-board is Dreyman's behavior that Wiesler believes something must be wrong. He is "too good to be true" and therefore must be investigated.

The artist's apartment is subjected to thorough wire-tapping. In shifts, the captain and a subordinate eavesdrop on every conversation, knowing every detail of the subject's parties, his music, and even his lovemaking. The contrast between the artist and the captain becomes increasingly clear, and is the central core of the

Government-backed spying on the lives of others in a 2007 German thriller with a strong social conscience.

Source: © Lara Tomlin. Originally published in *The New Yorker*.

film. As he eavesdrops, he hears music unfamiliar to him, and as he searches the apartment, he finds poetry he has never read.

A crisis is reached when Dreyman's girlfriend, also a spy, discovers where he has hidden papers that are contrary to the official policies of the regime in power. Yet the conscience of Wiesler is troubled. Should he advance his own career by using the newfound information to indict Dreyman or allow a genuine artist the freedom to be himself? By the end of the film, the Wall has been destroyed, but so has Wiesler. *The Lives of Others* has its share of thrills, stalking, suspense, and betrayal. Unlike most spy films, however, it delivers a subject central to the humanities: the suppression of artistic freedom.

Documentaries and Docudramas

Nonfiction films, or **documentaries**, are often respected for their efforts to tell the truth about an important issue or segment of the population. At the same time, films claiming to be documentaries have aroused opposition because of the possibility that truth has been doctored in order to make a case.

One of the outstanding and influential exponents of this genre is Frederick Wiseman (b. 1938), who specializes in showing familiar institutions in unique ways. Over the years he has made films whose titles hint at their content: *Hospital, Welfare, Racetrack, The Store, High School, Meat*. Unlike some documentary makers who add biting social and political commentaries to their work, Wiseman refrains from making comments or using interviews. He allows what is being filmed to speak for itself.

His best known work, *Titicut Follies* (1967), exposes the brutal treatment of inmates in a Massachusetts hospital for people labeled "criminally insane." The work was banned in that state until just recently. *High School* (1968) uncovers what really happens on a typical day: the bells, the regimentation, the strict enforcement of institutional rules. "Where's your pass?" snaps a hall monitor to a student. A dean is overheard telling another student, "We are out to establish that you are a man and that you can take orders."

An extraordinarily beautiful documentary with minimal narration is *Winged Migration* (2001), photographed by five film crews under the direction of Jacques Perrin. It shows birds—all kinds of birds—in flight, in long journeys marking the seasons as they search for food and nesting places. The film is totally descriptive and impartial. The screen is simply filled with birds endlessly moving, accompanied by music, but with rare commentary demanding any certain response from the viewer beyond recognition of rhythmic beauty. At one point, as a ship containing caged exotic birds makes its way up the Amazon River, one parrot thrusts its head through the bars and reaches down to lift the latch locking the cage. When the wooden door opens and the bird escapes, viewers are tempted to applaud, just as they wince at the sight of birds being shot down by hunters. But the main reaction is probably amazement that filmmakers were able to get so close to their subjects at the right time.

The documentaries of Michael Moore (b. 1954) leave no doubt about his sympathies. His *Roger and Me* (1989) attacked the closing of Flint, Michigan's main industry when General Motors moved its factories out of the country. The "Roger" of the title was the CEO whom Moore pursued throughout the film in an effort to get answers about the corporate decision. *Bowling for Columbine* (2002),

A film is a petrified fountain of thought.

—Jean Cocteau

about the murderous rampage of two Colorado high school students in 1994, made a plea for tough gun control laws. *Fahrenheit 9/11* (2004), which was selected as the best film shown at the Cannes Film Festival in that year, gathered an enormous amount of footage to demonstrate what Moore considered the government's lax handling of the World Trade Center attacks as well as the wars in Afghanistan and Iraq. In 2007, *Sicko* investigated health care in the United States and other countries. As always, Moore's narrative voice guides the way audiences are meant to view the film.

A compromise between documentary and drama is the **docudrama**, which provides narration in addition to Wiseman-style objectivity. It generally focuses on a sympathetic protagonist, who is faced with very real problems. But instead of simply being shown the facts or being guided toward a particular point of view, audiences identify with and root for an oppressed individual, whose misfortunes represent a much larger social problem. Directors of docudramas have built modest careers on the desire to tell a story that would otherwise be overlooked in an industry aiming for blockbuster thrills.

One such director is Ken Loach (b. 1936), who, in *Ladybird, Ladybird*, tells the true story of a woman whose children are taken away after authorities decide she is an unfit mother. They contend that she has never married, that each of her children has a different father, and that she sometimes leaves them alone to go to bars, at one point abandoning them in an apartment that caught fire. When she and a man who wants to marry her try to regain custody rights, they encounter hostility from officials claiming it would not be in the best interests of the children.

Loach's film does not tack on a happy ending. Instead, audiences have an opportunity to meet a woman they would otherwise not know and to decide for themselves whether her suffering was reason enough to claim the children. At its best, docudrama is as inconclusive as reality—and as provocative.

One very successful documentary in recent years has been Al Gore's *An Inconvenient Truth* (2006), a film about global warming that aims to stir audiences up to demand action from governments and industries. Gore's thesis is stated simply but toughly: "Humanity is sitting on a time bomb." The movie won the Academy Award in 2006 for Best Documentary, and in 2007 Gore shared the Nobel Peace Prize for his untiring efforts on behalf of the environment, which the Nobel committee said were directly related to peace in the world. They argued that if Gore's thesis is as accurate as both he and many scientists believe, and if nothing is done to control the warming of Earth and the melting of the ice caps, there will be unceasing violence and warfare as nations struggle for food and water.

Like most works with explosive, disturbing themes, *An Inconvenient Truth* has its share of foes. A judge in Great Britain ruled that scientists in his country had found nine errors in Gore's reasoning. He condemned the apocalyptic alarmism of the film and ruled that it could not be shown in British schools. Other detractors accused Gore of forsaking pure science for partisan politics. But any work that arouses such a storm of controversy, say others, should not be dismissed lightly.

Fictionalized Biography

Films that claim to be about actual people do not always stay close to the facts, and ironically, many of the films that bend the truth are about people with famous names. Fictionalized biographies often seem to do whatever they like with their

Humanity is sitting on a time bomb.

—Al Gore

subjects, and audiences are often misled. The very quality that makes film unique—its ability to put striking images on the screen—is also the quality that can make a film biography lack a major element: fidelity to the facts. Producers of biographical cinema have to make sure their products will sell. They want screenwriters and directors to focus on exciting moments in a real person's life and generally don't mind if these moments never happened or are highly exaggerated.

Lincoln, Gandhi, Lawrence of Arabia, Richard Nixon, Queen Victoria, Thomas Jefferson, John F. Kennedy, not to mention Chopin, Beethoven, van Gogh, and many others, have all been subjects of full-length screen biographies. When people attend these films, what do they expect to see? Do they want to come away with actual knowledge of these personalities? Or do they want to see an absorbing film? Filmmakers have no desire to present a history lesson about important legislation, so when they make a film about an American president, for example, they want to show him as a hero or a lover or, in the case of Nixon, as a fascinating psychological study. Lincoln's log cabin is part of his myth, as is the rail-splitting, the lanky, bearded figure with the sad eyes, who was assassinated while watching a comedy at Ford's Theater. In filmed biographies of him, these elements are usually given greater prominence than his wrestling with the overwhelming complexities of trying to govern a bitterly divided nation.

Omissions and even distortions affect audience perceptions and often create highly inaccurate national memories. One critic, commenting on a 1991 "filmography" of the late President John F. Kennedy, writes rather scathingly: "More than a century before the advent of the Hollywood pseudodocumentary Karl Marx suggested that all great events and personalities in world history happen twice: 'the first time as tragedy, the second as farce.' Oliver Stone's film *JFK* is a case in point."[5] Challenged later about the accuracy of his film, Stone responded with the recommendation that people who want to know what really happened should go to the library and do some research.

Films about artists encounter another problem: how to make the creation of a painting, a novel, or a musical composition as interesting as the wild antics of the creator who lives on the edge of normal behavior. To the credit of writers and directors of the past, some of the films about visual artists have actually left audiences with memories of the art as well as the artist's temper tantrums and mental illness.

Michelangelo, Vincent van Gogh, and Paul Gauguin have all become known to a wider public because of film biographies. In *The Agony and the Ecstasy* (1965), audiences saw Michelangelo cramped and strained as he heroically paints the ceiling of the Sistine Chapel (in fact, the artist had a number of assistants who did their share of the work). They also saw fictionalized bitter and tension-filled confrontations between Michelangelo and Pope Julius II.

In *Lust for Life* (1956), they saw van Gogh and Gauguin arguing violently in the tiny house they shared, so violently that, on one occasion, van Gogh is shown rushing upstairs to cut off his ear (a response with no basis in fact). All the while they are fighting, the two men continue to generate great paintings. Despite some overacting in the scenes depicting the madness that led van Gogh to suicide, the final moments of the film are impressive indeed as the camera slowly pans along a wall on which hang the artist's greatest works. For many, this art show may have been an extraordinary introduction to the genius of a tragic artist—and more than enough justification for the filmography genre.

Composers have suffered their share of inaccuracies. The Mozart in the movie version of Peter Shaffer's play *Amadeus* (1984) was flamboyantly portrayed

Historical accuracy has seldom been the goal of the fictionalized biography. If the subject's life is not as interesting or dramatic as filmmakers would like, they go ahead and change it.

as a giggling, childlike man given to bawdy jokes, uncouth gestures, and continual flirtations. How he found time to compose was a mystery. The film also dramatized the totally unfounded legend that Mozart was poisoned by Antonio Salieri, a court composer who is supposed to have been obsessed with jealousy. According to the script, Salieri paid Mozart to compose a Requiem Mass he intended to pass off as his own work after the poison took effect. In real life, someone else commissioned Mozart to write the Requiem, and the composer died before completing it, possibly from typhoid fever. Less dramatic than attempting to appropriate another man's work after poisoning him is the question of the real-life Salieri's relations with Mozart. The film shows him burning with hatred of his rival. History shows him as an admired musician willing to help the younger man.

Lovers of Edith Piaf's songs have no doubt been delighted to see *La Vie en Rose* (2006), the film based on her life of both success and inner pain. The soundtrack features old favorites such as the title song as well as the passionate and highly personal "Non, Je Ne Regrette Rien" (No, I regret nothing), and Marion Cotillard (winner of the Best Actress Oscar for her performance in the film) convincingly portrays the singer as tormented. Yet those who thrilled to the music may still be wondering whether Piaf was really abandoned by a parent, lived on the street, or had a child out of wedlock. Those who head for the library can at least still have the wonderful music to remember.

Loosely Based on the Original: Film Adaptations

A film made from a popular literary work is under no obligation to follow the book, though sometimes controversies arise concerning the advisability of transferring a work to a different medium. Early on, Hollywood snapped up the work of important writers, promising more money than they hoped to earn from publishing alone.

The Hemingway short story "The Killers," hailed by some literary critics as a nearly perfect example of the genre, became a two-hour routine 1946 gangster movie that bore little relationship to the original. The original was about the sudden appearance of two hit-men in a sleepy middle American town that has been remote from any real contact with evil. Their mission is to kill a fighter who did not "throw" a championship match. Hemingway knew that for most ordinary people, direct confrontation with genuine evil is unthinkable. Nick Adams, the coming-of-age protagonist from whose point of view we perceive the story, has never experienced such a confrontation. When he does, all he can say is, "It's awful." The older and wiser man who owns the diner in which Nick works, responds, in typically laconic Hemingway fashion: "Well, you'd better not think about it." We are never told whether the fighter is eventually killed. It doesn't matter. What does matter is that most of us are powerless to do much about evil in the world. Whether not thinking about it is the best course to take is, of course, open to question. But great literature does nothing if not make us ask questions. In the film, Nick Adams is relegated to a minor role as the movie focuses on the prize fighter and his impressive biceps, displayed prominently enough to make a star of Burt Lancaster. In the story, the fighter never appears. It is all about what it means to come of age.

Even when some fidelity to the original is attempted, Hollywood has often tacked on an ending totally at odds with the author's obvious intention. In Thomas Hardy's novel *Tess of the D'Urbervilles* the protagonist, having killed the man who seduced and deserted her, is sent to the gallows without mercy, an ending consistent with the author's generally pessimistic view of life. In an early film version, the film-makers, believing the public needed a happy ending, twisted the plot so that Tess could be rescued. Hardy, outraged at what had been done to his work, sadly observed, "I am an old man and have no defense against this sort of thing."

In *The Player* (1992), Robert Altman satirized the sugarcoating of serious works in a story about a director who had insisted on preserving the integrity of a novel but who submits to pressure and allows a ludicrous, last-minute happy ending. The director is rewarded with a beautiful wife as well as limitless wealth.

Troy (2004), starring Brad Pitt as Achilles in a film "loosely based" on Homer's *The Iliad*, has been praised for its realistic war scenes, but there were major changes in plot, theme, and important details that seem to go beyond artistic license. Agamemnon is depicted as a liar, really after power though he uses the abduction of Helen as a pretext for war. In the film, he is killed before the end of the war, thus making it impossible for him to return home to face the revenge of his wife and her lover—an outcome well-known to students of mythology as well as the thousands familiar with *The Oresteia* of Aeschylus, one of the landmarks in the history of theater.

Critic Edward Rothstein comments on what he calls director Wolfgang Petersen's "spear and sandal epic" with an imposed theme and overly obvious nod to the growing public disapproval of the war in Iraq: "A latent antiwar message also peeks through, here and there, with a directorial wink. 'If we leave now,' the wise general Nestor says in the film after a few days of fighting, 'we lose all credibility.' This is not quite what Homer had in mind."[6]

Two American Film Classics

On almost everyone's list of classic American films are two masterpieces that appeared within a year of each other: *Citizen Kane* (1941) and *Casablanca* (1942). The history of the humanities is filled with such chronologies. Masterpieces, as well as the artists who produced them, have a way of appearing close together. Perhaps creativity is highly contagious. Remember that three of the greatest artists of all time—Leonardo, Michelangelo, and Raphael—all lived and worked at the same time in Florence.

Citizen Kane

Here was a relatively low-budget film, consigned to an amazing twenty-six-year-old named Orson Welles. Several years before, he had done the radio adaptation of H. G. Wells's *The War of the Worlds* that created panic throughout the United States. After the furor and subsequent notoriety for Welles, Hollywood gave him free reign within the confines of a modest budget. The resulting film, *Citizen Kane*, was far from a box-office sensation, but its reputation as screen art has grown steadily with each passing decade. Like many another artist, Welles died without ever quite knowing the full extent of his achievements. During his lifetime, he was admired for his courage to do what his taste compelled him to do, but studios feared him as one who could be counted on to lose their money.

To be acclaimed "the best" is to challenge other aspirants to the title. Why *Kane*? Why not any one of the other films that have lasted long enough to

I don't say we all ought to behave, but we ought to look as if we could.
—**Orson Welles**

deserve to be called classics? Is it one of the film's major themes—the question of whether money can buy happiness? Then again, other films have dealt with that theme. We don't really attend movies in order to learn lessons about happiness, or pride, or whether crime "pays." It must be something else—something bigger. In its exposure of the hollowness of the American Dream, it has been compared to Fitzgerald's masterpiece, *The Great Gatsby* (Chapter 4).

The plot, which centers on one reporter's attempt to unravel the mystery of Kane's unexplained dying word, "Rosebud," unfolds in a technique innovative for its time and part of the reason for the film's acclaim. The story is told from several points of view. One is the director's objective presentation of the facts, such as the opening: Charles Foster Kane, a man who has interested the public for decades, is on his death bed in his legendary mansion, Xanadu. We hear the unseen protagonist whisper his final word, then we see his hand drop to the side of the bed.

The retrospective of Kane's life begins as a voice-over narration by the reporter who is investigating the meaning of the word. Knowing that the camera cannot photograph what is inside a human being and that the audience can only guess at what lies hidden, Welles makes the investigating reporter the central character. The camera becomes his (and our) eyes.

Testimony comes from several sources, as the reporter interviews everyone who knew Kane. In the shadowy catacombs of the public library, he studies old newspapers in an attempt to recreate every incident in the life of a famous and incredibly wealthy man who starting out as a carefree little boy inherits a great

Citizen Kane was not a box-office sensation when it opened; its techniques were too unfamiliar for too many viewers.

Citizen Kane reveals the hollowness of the American Dream, much like *The Great Gatsby*, with which it has been compared.

Source: Museum of Modern Art/Film Stills Archive.

deal of money and must leave home to collect his fortune. The investigation centers on documents and eyewitness accounts that can assist the search. One sequence is told from the point of view of the man who knew Kane as a boy, one from a longtime associate in the newspaper business, another from his best friend who became disillusioned by Kane's unethical behavior, and the last sequence by the woman who became Kane's mistress and then his second wife. Some incidents appear more than once, but they are told in different versions.

As the reporter pieces together the fragments, we follow the success of Kane's first newspaper venture, the opening of his vast chain, his increasingly gaudy lifestyle, his developing megalomania—the total self-absorption of someone who has everything but is never satisfied. Kane wants to be governor, then perhaps president, but with enough money and power one can become almost royal. His political progress is stopped by scandal when, as a married man, he is shown to be having an affair with a young woman. He then employs his great wealth and influence in an unsuccessful attempt to make his mistress into a star of Grand Opera. Eventually, he and the woman retreat to a mansion surrounded by statues and other art objects Kane has imported. The woman, bored, does jigsaw puzzles, complains, and abandons him. Kane dies, alone.

Individual scenes are as compelling as the innovative structure. In one, the disintegration of Kane's first marriage is indicated in a rapid montage of the couple at the breakfast table, at first sitting next to each other, then sitting farther and farther apart until, in a few seconds of screen time, the wife is shown at the opposite end of a very long table reading a newspaper published by Kane's rival. In another scene, Kane's second wife Susan, the would-be opera star, is shown on the stage, shrieking an aria for the small audience of Kane's friends and employees. As she trills on, the camera slowly ascends from stage level, up through the massive riggings that raise and lower the backdrops, finally coming to rest on a gridwalk hundreds of feet above the appalling recital below. As one stagehand looks on in amusement, the other pinches his nose with two fingers to signify his critique of the performance. The scene is now studied in film schools as a supreme example of the tracking shot.

Another shot illustrates an innovative technique known as *depth focus*, made possible by the wizardry of Welles's cinematographer Greg Toland, who subsequently became a star in his own field. In the scene, Kane's friend Jed, the music critic for Kane's paper, is sitting at his typewriter, finishing a scathing review of the performance. He is shown in the foreground as Kane enters the large room and stands in the background. An obvious rift is implied by the relationship of the figures. Kane is kept in the background so that we can only guess at what he is thinking.

The passion that once drew him to Susan wanes. He continues to purchase more treasures to fill the vast salons of the mansion, ultimately not able to find room for any more. They must remain in their crates. He is a lonely, lost old man, dying with none by his side. The mystery of "Rosebud" is finally understood by the audience in the famous final sequence, which opens with an epic-scale image of thousands of boxes containing Kane's treasures, using an innovative twist on the tracking shot. Instead of widening the shot so that the huge material empire is slowly revealed, the camera shows the whole thing at once, then slowly tracks in toward a distant flickering light, which is discovered to be a furnace into which a workman is tossing the "junk" nobody wants—and, finally, the camera zeros in for a close-up of a seemingly worthless remnant of Kane's lost childhood, a small sled

In Citizen Kane *Orson Welles did not romanticize the American Dream. His film ultimately reveals the hollowness behind the dream and the tragedy of those whose only concerns are money and power.*

The final scene of Citizen Kane *reverses the famous tracking shot of the train station in* Gone with the Wind. *The camera starts wide, without focus, then finally comes to rest on a trivial object: Rosebud.*

containing the word "Rosebud." Even so, neither we nor the reporter ever learns the complete truth about the man. The film captures the ambiguities in human nature and offers as profound an analysis of power-seeking as Hollywood has ever achieved.

Citizen Kane was widely believed to be based on the career of the real-life William Randolph Hearst, a newspaper publisher famous for manipulating the news and sensationalizing events that might otherwise have gone unnoticed. Hearst even tried to prevent the studio from advertising and distributing the work. The character of Susan was said to be based on Hearst's long affair with movie actress Marion Davies. Yet Hearst's California mansion in San Simeon, although filled with treasures like Kane's Xanadu, was also filled with interesting guests who reported that Hearst's hospitality was genuine and knew no bounds. Unlike Susan, Marion Davies remained faithful to the end and seems not to have needed to depend on jigsaw puzzles to pass the time. Reality, however, would have suited Orson Welles much less than the opportunity to create a film of vast, shadowy complexity that continues to fascinate. What he created was not at all the same as a deliberate distortion of historical fact, nor a Hollywoodized decimation of a great literary work. It is a great work of cinema, standing entirely on its own.

Casablanca

Casablanca (1942) became immortal almost in spite of itself. Each day the scriptwriters would give revised scenes to the cast. None of them knew how the film would end, and almost everyone thought it would be a disastrous failure. The United States had just entered World War II, the outcome of which was by no means certain. War movies abounded in Hollywood, most of them filled with multiple scenes of artillery fire, bombings, and mine explosions. Audiences were given Allied successes on the battlefield and reason to cheer. Yet *Casablanca*, despite its wartime background, lacked the expected kind of action scenes. Somehow, through revision after revision, it became a powerful story about ordinary people's ethical dilemmas at a time of conflicting moral values.

Today young people, who may lack full knowledge of the period, are attracted to the film for its powerful love story, but there have been other powerful love stories. Chances are the appeal of *Casablanca* springs from its film noir hero, the hard-boiled but idealistic Rick Blaine, who transcends the stereotype, becoming a three-dimensional, fully realized human being who learns to conceal a broken heart with a facade of toughness that ensures he will never be hurt again. The song from the film, "As Time Goes By," has become a classic in its own right, as has the image of Sam, sitting at the piano, being commanded to "Play it." One of the immortal lines in screen history is Bogart's trademark, "Here's looking at you, kid"—a line that seems to express love quite as much as Romeo's great speeches do. If Juliet is the "sun," Rick's lost love is the "kid."

Because the Hollywood studio system of the 1930s and 1940s had the big stars tied up with long-term contracts, film executives had to commission screenplays tailor-made for the stars' on-camera personalities. Humphrey Bogart became such a star after *The Maltese Falcon*. He was perceived as specializing in the film noir hero: a tough, unflinching man of steel with a susceptible heart and an uncanny ability to survive both danger and personal tragedy.

The studio thought it had found just what it was looking for in the story of an expatriate American who operates an illegal gambling casino in the capital of

French Morocco, neutral territory during World War II. French and German police prowled the streets on the lookout for people trying to buy exit visas, which would allow them to escape. The basically tender-hearted Rick helped them—by letting them gamble for the money. Yet there was always a gun in his pocket, just in case his business was threatened.

As the rewriting continued, Bogart's character apparently took center stage. He is shown as an unemotional realist, at heart concerned about the refugees, but unwilling to become involved in their lives. He cannot afford to. With the apparent blessing of Louis, the police chief who would like nothing better than to crack his veneer, he maintains a well-run establishment in the well-ordered world he has created for himself. Basic to his philosophy of uninvolvement—his defense against the hurt he experienced in Paris when the love of his life left him—is his refusal to take sides in the war, despite the fact that his country is fighting against the Nazis. He shares nothing with anyone about his private life. When the police chief attempts coyly to find out what he is doing in Casablanca, Rick answers in his typical deadpan that he came for the waters. Reminded that they are in a desert and there are no waters in Casablanca, he replies calmly, "I was misinformed."

In one early scene his tough exterior softens just a bit when he counsels a desperate young wife who has come to him for advice. The police chief has offered her enough money for a letter of transit if she agrees to sleep with him. She doesn't want to be disloyal to her husband, but does Rick think she would be wrong to accept the offer? He advises her, instead, to gamble at the roulette wheel and covertly directs the croupier to let her win. The police chief knows what has happened and smilingly accuses Rick of being "a sentimentalist" at heart. But Rick is careful not to show this side of him. He is a loner, just supervising the club, refusing to drink or make friends with the patrons.

Inevitably his armor is pierced. The lost love, Ilse, walks in one night with her husband, Victor Laszlo, a leading Resistance fighter against the Nazis and, for them, the top of the Most Wanted list. Later, after everyone else has left, Rick sits at a table with a drink and a cigarette. The shape of the doorway in back of the room dissolves into a similar shape, that of the Arc de Triomphe in Paris, as the flashback shows him remembering the joy of his passionate love affair with Ilse and their mutual determination to escape the approaching German troops. Ilse has agreed to leave with him on the last train, but he waits at the railway station in vain. Only when she reenters his life does he learn that she was married all the time they were together in Paris but that she had believed that she was a widow. When she discovered at the last minute that her husband was alive, she decided she had to return to him rather than leave with Rick.

Now Rick, still hurt and angry, is nevertheless forced to abandon his neutral stand. When Ilse's husband asks the club's orchestra to play the French national anthem to drown out the singing of Nazi soldiers at a nearby table, the orchestra leader looks to Rick for permission. He nods. The refugees stand, joining Laszlo in an emotional singing of *La Marseillaise*. From that point on, it will be difficult for Rick to remain uninvolved.

The Nazi major seems ready to capture Laszlo, who knows he and Ilse must find a way to escape from Casablanca. Ilse confronts Rick with a gun to get the exit visas, but she cannot shoot. The flame of passion has reignited. He will get the visas for Lazlo if she will stay behind with him. Unable to resist for a second time, she agrees. A plane to freedom awaits at the airport, a plane that Laszlo and Ilse are

The world's favorite Hollywood love story is all the more romantic because it doesn't exalt romantic love above all.

—Stephen D. Greydanes

One of the most famous decisions in the history of film: "Here's looking at you, kid."

Source: The Museum of Modern Art, Film Stills Archive, New York.

After Rick kills the Nazi commander, the French captain shields him by ordering his men to "round up the usual suspects."

supposed to board. Laszlo does not know that Ilse has agreed to stay with Rick. Legend has it that the scriptwriters did not know what they were going to do with the scene. Through the mysterious, often chaotic labyrinth known as the creative process, their dilemma suddenly turned into Rick's famous moral choice.

The choice in that scene (which should be obvious from what we have told you about Rick), a scene that was not written until the final day of shooting, has made film history. Call him a "sentimentalist." Say that what he chose no red-blooded man would ever choose in real life. Or call him a moral role model for all time. Like all great films, *Casablanca* offers its audiences a very complex set of options.

Citizen Kane and *Casablanca* have much in common. Both begin with exposition provided by a news broadcast. Both films employ dialogue sparingly. Neither central character reveals himself through what he says. Both use the screen medium to create a complex reality that we must interpret because neither makes a direct, easily phrased statement about people or existence. Yet the two films are different in that *Citizen Kane* was consciously designed to be a quality film made by an independent young director with no ties to Hollywood, while *Casablanca* was the product of a studio paying high prices to its stars and directed by a man who specialized in action adventure movies rather than artistic masterpieces. Two opposite roads led to the same destination: a secure niche in the history of classic films.

The Film Auteur

The French word **auteur**, or "author," has been applied to the most significant directors, those whose special style and themes are so evident that their work is instantly recognizable. "A film by . . ." usually means the director rather than the scriptwriter (unless they are the same person). The work of the auteur bears signs of individual technique—like an author's unique way of using language or an artist's unique brushstrokes. It can be recognized in camera angles, overlapping dialogue, swift transitions, and a personal view of reality.

Directors who attain auteur status choose the material, write the script or collaborate with the screenwriter, and have total control over the plot and characters. Their situation is unlike that of most of the directors in the old studio system who were simply handed a script that their contracts called for them to accept without question. *Final cut*, that is, the right to decide when the work was indeed completed, was a rare privilege for them. Response cards from preview audiences were read carefully, and contract directors often were forced to make unwanted changes based on those responses. Or an all-powerful producer might decide he didn't like what he saw and demand that the film not be released until it met with his satisfaction. Response cards and powerful producers are still around. Even today, when some directors are honored as never before, the Academy Award for Best Picture is handed to a producer. But it is the great director who is most likely to be remembered, not the producer. This section describes the work of some prominent auteurs.

Ingmar Bergman

Swedish director Ingmar Bergman (1918–2007) did not come to film because of its glamour and the promise of quick wealth. He was a serious theater director intent on creating art, and he saw in film a challenging medium offering him great freedom to explore his subjects. For a decade he studied the techniques of cinema, and by the mid-1950s he had made Sweden very nearly the art film capital of the world. Two of his masterworks, *The Seventh Seal* (1956) and *Wild Strawberries* (1957), are so typically Bergman that they could not have been made by anyone else. Both films are intensely philosophical, concerned about the human place in existence. Both have central characters who wonder whether they are in this world for some reason. They feel themselves alienated from others, meaningless entities walking around on the earth for a few years and then vanishing into endless night.

The Seventh Seal is a medieval fable about a knight who has survived the Crusades, then ironically finds Death waiting for him when he returns home. He challenges the Grim Reaper to a game of chess, the contract being that he can stay alive until Death achieves victory. The knight is determined to delay the inevitable until he discovers the meaning of his life. While the fantasy game proceeds, the knight is also journeying about the countryside in search of something—a person, a cause, a religion—that will convince him that existence has not been an absurd waste of time. The knight's quest very likely paralleled Bergman's own philosophical journey.

In the great tradition of the mythic journey (Chapter 3), the knight has many adventures and interacts with many people along the way, including his former teacher, a brutal hypocrite who had urged him to join the Crusades, and a young woman being tortured and finally burned at the stake as a witch.

In Bergman's great film *The Seventh Seal*, Max von Sydow, left, is the knight who challenges Death to a game of chess in order to gain enough time to seek the meaning of life.

Source: Topham/The Image Works.

The Knight, challenging Death to a chess match in The Seventh Seal, *learns that death is nothing to fear if one has found meaning in life.*

Various penitents thrash each other and themselves as signs of penance for sin and as a means of getting rid of a virulent plague. Organized religion, he finds, does not make existence seem valuable. He discovers the fullness of life only when he meets a young married couple named Joseph and Mary who have one child. In the loving warmth of the family circle, where members support and nurture each other, life begins to make sense. Contrasted with one dark scene after another is the scene in which he and the family share strawberries and fresh milk in the sunlight. Not to have known love and joy is, he realizes, not to have lived.

Bergman's message is simple but not simplistic. He finds it only after struggling with utter nihilism (the belief that all comes to nothing in the end). With the knight's help, the young family escapes Death. Though he himself will die, his final vision is a joyous one, and the film ends with the happy family standing by the sea as the knight joins a joyful procession silhouetted against the sky and led by the figure of Death. There is nothing mournful here. Death is not to be feared if one has lived for something.

In *Wild Strawberries* Bergman shapes an identical vision in contemporary terms. It is the story of an aging doctor facing death, not in allegorical but in a very real, biological way. The film blends reality, dreams, and memories of the past with sophisticated editing techniques, taking advantage of the storytelling economy allowed by the medium. As in *The Seventh Seal*, the author-director uses a journey for his plot structure. Isak Borg must travel to a great university in order to receive an award for distinguished scientific achievement. While he is traveling, he looks closely at his life and asks whether it has really amounted to something. Unlike the knight in *The Seventh Seal*, who has no family in the beginning, Isak Borg has a son and daughter-in-law with whom he shares only a strained relationship lacking in warmth and spontaneity.

The travelers stop to pick up some hitchhikers, two young men and a woman, cheerful, casually dressed, and quite different from the stiff academics he has always known. The young woman looks exactly like the sweetheart Borg loved long ago and begins now to remember, the same actress playing both roles. Though he has no intellectual rapport with his passengers, they help to free him from the emotional repression that has destroyed his family. Gradually he relives the summers in the country when he was a free-spirited youth, long before he became a victim of the codified adult world—a time when he was as spontaneous as he now feels when he stops with the hitchhikers to pick and eat wild strawberries by the roadside. (The fruit becomes symbolic in both films of the sweetness of present existence, all we can know for sure.) Bergman asks why ruin existence with rigid norms of civilized behavior and high intellectual standards that imprison the multidimensional human being within each of us? *Wild Strawberries* is a timeless, poetic plea for humanity to hold fast to youth, to love, and to caring—treasures the world will always need.

Federico Fellini

The young Federico Fellini (1920–1993) learned his craft from the Italian neorealistic directors who, in the aftermath of World War II, had little money to work with and often used untrained actors to tell stories of ordinary people amid the streets and buildings bombed out during that war. Fellini, however, dissatisfied with the limitations of using the camera to photograph only external reality as it unfolded, saw other possibilities. He wanted to be a true artist, using the camera for the haunting imagery it could film. He sought to combine realism with poetry. To retain control of his vision, he became his own screenwriter and, eventually, an *auteur*.

In *La Strada* (1955) Fellini tells the story of Gelsomina, a simple-minded young woman (Giulietta Massina) working in a traveling carnival as assistant to Zampano (Anthony Quinn), billed as the world's strongest man. Secretly in love with him, she becomes his virtual slave, although his enormous ego doesn't allow him to treat her like a fellow human being. He rebukes her for every little mistake and eventually deserts her altogether, leaving her penniless in a world she can never hope to comprehend. The only tenderness she is ever shown comes from a musician, also a victim of Zampano's brutality, who teaches her to play a simple tune on a trumpet. In the final scene, as Zampano sits on the sand near the water and recognizes that for all his strength he is nothing, he begins to recall Gelsomina's devoted smile and the sound of her music. He weeps.

La Dolce Vita (The Good Life), which appeared in 1959, was a three-hour film, shot in color, about the moral decadence of postwar Rome, a gathering place for the rich and the bored. It established Fellini's worldwide reputation among audiences seeking an artistic alternative to commercial movies. The images and camera wizardry are unforgettable. The opening shot has become classic in film history, an example of what would be Fellini's trademark: the bold, fantastic, and symbolic image that stimulates both the eye and the mind. A helicopter is carrying a statue of Jesus to a new location. As it flies over a city of shiny modern hotels and aqua-blue swimming pools, over bikini-clad bathers and merry-makers clinking glasses in sidewalk cafes, the shadow of Jesus is unnoticed by the self-centered, vain, bored, hopelessly materialistic people below.

Fellini's symbolism is not as easy to fathom as one might think. The helicopter image could be interpreted as the need for Christian belief, but it could also be saying something about the decline of the church, powerless against the forces of moral decay in the "new" Italy. The film's climactic image is even more ambiguous. As an assortment of scantily clad sunbathers lazily stretch out on the beach, a huge, unidentifiable dead fish is washed ashore, its still-open eye terrifyingly staring. Is this a message from an angry God? Or is Fellini saying that God is dead, that there is little hope for the redemption of this "good life" because there is no redeemer?

Even *La Strada* had left an ambiguous message. Is love the answer? To what question? The young woman's love for Zampano bore no fruit, and the strongman is left with no one to love him. Is love just another illusion, sweet and poetic but, sadly, non-existent?

As he continued to experiment, Fellini became more and more complex. He turned inward upon himself and concentrated on the often tragic waning of the artist's creativity (perhaps fearing that it was happening to him?). In what many consider Fellini's masterpiece, *8 1/2* (1963), the protagonist is a film director who, like Fellini, has made eight films and is now seeking to finish his ninth, except that he never quite gets there. Early commercial success, fame, a restless sexual

There was in Fellini a joy in images, a sad flavor of life, a something of Cervantes and Rabelais that somehow makes us finally shout "Yes but" to all criticism.

—Donald Lyons

appetite, and the continual pressures exerted by Hollywood-influenced studio executives all conspire to keep him from focusing sharply on his goal.

Again the opening shot is memorable. The protagonist is inside an automobile on a ferry, windows shut tightly so that sounds of reveling passengers cannot be heard. It is the artist alienated within his environment. Yet there is no comfort in that inner space, only more confusion. Fellini in a few breathtaking seconds has summed up the plight of the artist in an indifferent world. The fantastic final scene, in which various kinds of artists are shown dancing in a ring, gives hope that somehow the creative imagination will survive, but it might also mean that true art is simply going in circles within itself unable to reach an audience.

Some have said that Fellini would have reached more people if he had used his genius to good commercial effect, but it is his very need to use film as a vehicle of self-expression that makes him an auteur, one who had to tell his own story whether anyone liked it or not.

Alfred Hitchcock

Unlike Orson Welles, who came to Hollywood determined to create film art, British-born Alfred Hitchcock (1899–1980) was imported to make scary melodramas and only gradually acquired the critical reputation his work continues to merit. Known first as a man who made thrillers about spies and murders among highly civilized people, he was dubbed the "master of suspense" in the late 1930s. The plots in his films were filled with unexpected twists, and always there was a breathtaking and surprising finale with an always new and ingenious kind of danger, as in the 1942 spy film *Saboteur*, when hero and villain have their showdown fight to the death on the torch of the Statue of Liberty.

Hitchcock, however, soon tired of exploiting in obvious ways the audience's love of terror. His work acquired greater subtlety. His evildoers were generally suave, sophisticated beings on the surface, but underneath they were inhuman, disordered, and dangerously antisocial. In films like *Shadow of a Doubt* (1943) and *Strangers on a Train* (1951), evil enters the lives of ordinary, decent people, whom we get to know and like, and only then does Hitchcock, the master craftsman, put them in danger, causing the viewer's heart to pound a little faster.

His greatest early success was the 1946 *Notorious*. In a South American country, a Nazi spy lives in luxurious surroundings with his beautiful wife, who has been manipulated into the marriage by a handsome U.S. intelligence agent seeking to trap the husband. The agent is played by the dapper Cary Grant, whom we have met before, and the wife by Ingrid Bergman, who had been Bogart's beloved Ilse in *Casablanca*. The wife, of course, loves the agent, but his feelings for her are ambiguous until he fully recognizes her perilous circumstances. Then it becomes a matter of rescuing her—certainly a Hollywood cliché. But in Hitchcock's hands, the tired old plot is revitalized, mainly because the director avoids obvious devices, once again imposing evil on an otherwise civilized and ordered world.

The most suspenseful moments in the film occur during an elegant party at the spy's mansion, when the agent and the wife, searching in the wine cellar for a vital message hidden there, are startled to hear the husband coming down the steps. They hide behind a row of shelves. While the husband quietly searches for a certain vintage, a bottle of wine on a shelf next to them perches dangerously on the edge. If it falls, the agent will be exposed, and both he and the wife may die. Without relying on creepy background music, Hitchcock instead gives us a close-up

Drama is life with the dull bits cut out.

—**Alfred Hitchcock**

of the bottle. We keep expecting the bottle to crash and the deadly silence to be shattered. Hitchcock understood that real terror comes from what is imagined by the audience before anything is shown.

Of course, the spy is ultimately foiled, and the wife ends up in the arms of the agent. Hitchcock, with his cynical view of the world, also had a wonderful sense of humor. We can feel him smiling behind the fade-out. The director's personal philosophy, however, had no humor in it. He believed implicitly that we live in a fundamentally amoral universe in which good triumphs only by accident, in which, despite the civilized façade we erect, chaos is the law of nature.

In *The Birds* (1963) that chaos comes frighteningly to life in a formerly peaceful northern California village. Without warning and without any known motives, birds gang up on the town' inhabitants, killing some, injuring others. The most memorable scene is typically Hitchcock: the juxtaposition of danger and normal activity. A woman sits outside an elementary school, enjoying a cigarette as she waits, totally unmindful of a grim scene taking place behind her, where hundreds of blackbirds are massing in the schoolyard. From inside the schoolhouse comes the joyful sound of innocent young voices singing. Suddenly the calm erupts into a scene reminiscent of the elongated moment in Eisenstein's Odessa steps sequence in *The Battleship Potemkin*. The woman, the children, and the teacher are running down a steep hill, holding up their arms to shield themselves from the shrieking onslaught. Hitchcock cuts from one fleeing person to another in a montage so rapid that we actually *see* very little of the devastation but *think* we see it all.

Hitchcock had already used this technique in *Psycho* (1960), considered by many critics to be his masterwork. The film, which remains popular, is one of the scariest movies of all time. Here evil assumes the form of an apparently sweet, shy, and lonely young man who so yearns to be reunited with his dead mother that he sometimes wears her clothes and assumes her identity. In this guise he is capable of committing brutal acts without knowing what he is doing.

In *Psycho*, the Hitchcock vision of the world is fully realized. His philosophy of evil provides him with a signature technique for terrifying the audience. As usual, he places a twisted individual next to people who are unaware they are living in a dangerous world. An attractive young woman who has embezzled a huge sum of money is driving away from the scene of her crime but finds herself caught in a blinding rainstorm. Seeking shelter for the night in a motel where she is the only guest, she is relieved to be the recipient of warm hospitality by the shy young owner. As the woman prepares for bed, feeling snug and cozy and happy that she has evaded pursuit, she steps into an invitingly hot shower, apparently safe.

The shower scene is one of the most admired ever filmed. We do not expect terrible things to happen in such a usually safe place. What surroundings could be more conventional and uncharacteristic of a horror film? As the woman lathers herself generously, washing away her guilt, enjoying the warm stream of water caressing her face, suddenly there appears a silhouette of someone who seems to be holding a knife. Against a score of violins imitating the sounds of a scream, the woman is repeatedly stabbed. We think we are seeing every moment of her agony, but in fact the scene moves so quickly that we are actually watching only a collage of camera shots: the water, the shower head, the woman's hands to her face, blood swirling into the drain; finally there is only an ominous silence as we are shown a close-up of a dead face, eyes still open in horror. We have not seen the murderer, nor have we seen any actual stabbing. The scene, which lasts only 45 seconds, was composed of 78 distinct shots, edited to move so rapidly through the projector that the effect is one of subliminal horror.

In the shower scene of Psycho *we think we are seeing every moment of gruesome horror, but in fact the scene moves so quickly that we actually see only a collage of camera shots. We have not witnessed the actual stabbing.*

Hitchcock combined a civilized directing style with a zest for the bizarre and frightening. The real irony, of course, is that here was a screen auteur who believed that disorder and chaos were found in both human nature and the natural world, yet who communicated his belief in a very planned, meticulously ordered way, with the intricate details of every shot set down in writing before the camera was ever turned on. Perhaps Hitchcock is ultimately saying that art is the only compensation for evil.

Akira Kurosawa

We have already mentioned the Japanese film *Rashomon* as an example of how the cinema is able to show the same scene from different points of view. That film catapulted its director, Akira Kurosawa (1910–1998), into the forefront of internationally recognized filmmakers and brought new audiences to an appreciation of the non-Western cinema. Though he had studied Western techniques very carefully, learning the wizardry of the camera, Kurosawa was also dedicated to recreating his country's past and bringing it to the attention of a worldwide audience. His masterpiece, *The Seven Samurai* (1954), introduced that audience to the

Kurosawa is a man if all genres, all periods, bridging in his work the traditional and the modern, the old and the new, the cutures of the East and the West.

—Ephraim Katz

Kurosawa's masterpiece introduced Western audiences to Japan's noble warrior class.

Source: Courtesy Everett Collection.

code of feudal Japan's warrior class, their nobility, their sense of honor and decency, and their swordsmanship, which samurai were always prepared to demonstrate for a good cause. In some sense, the samurai were the equivalents of King Arthur's Round Table knights.

The Seven Samurai strengthened Kurosawa's already growing reputation and caught the attention of Hollywood, always eager to jump on a new bandwagon. In 1960 director John Sturges brought forth *The Magnificent Seven*, an unabashed westernization of feudal Japan, in which a band of roaming gunfighters with no allegiances fight against an army of bandits terrorizing the innocent inhabitants of a Mexican village. The blazing and dangerous shootout turns the previously lawless bunch into righteous crusaders. The film, which owes everything to Kurosawa, was hailed by critics as an ethical western with a solid sense of values.

Kurosawa always recognized his own debt to Western culture, and one of his most distinctive achievements was the Asianization of Shakespeare. *Throne of Blood* (1957) was his version of *Macbeth*, and *Ran* (1983) was his version of *King Lear*.

Like Chaplin before him, Kurosawa worked in black and white longer than Western directors did, preferring it for the *chiaroscuro* contrast between shadow and light that had distinguished *Citizen Kane* and the major film noir movies. In *Ran*, however, he capitulated to the public—both East and West—in their preference for Technicolor; the result was, in the opinion of many critics, color cinematography that rivals Impressionist art.

Kurosawa is also noted for his meticulous approach to filmmaking, often holding up production if something about the set was not quite right. On one occasion, during the filming of *The Seven Samurai*, he insisted that the painstakingly constructed sixteenth-century fortress—a set costing over a million dollars—be completely torn down and rebuilt because the carpenters had used steel nails that didn't exist at the time in which the film was set. When someone objected "Who'll know there are steel nails holding up the set?" he answered, "I will."

Ironically, as Kurosawa's reputation began to grow in the West, he steadily lost favor in Japan, especially among younger audiences and filmmakers, who thought his historical epics were too old-fashioned. Late in life he was reduced to begging for money to make a film. He even tried to commit suicide. The world of art was grateful that he failed.

Stanley Kubrick

An American director whose films were sometimes funny, even when his themes were death and the destruction of the planet and the cosmos, Stanley Kubrick (1928–1999), in the best tradition of satire, lashed out at self-deception and hypocrisy. He always did the unexpected, refusing to turn out formula work designed for the "blockbuster" market. He used a lot of music in his films, but never as an obvious parallel to emotion. He took many chances in an industry where risk-taking has become increasingly expensive. Very much in the tradition of Orson Welles, the earlier bad boy of Hollywood, Kubrick attained worldwide recognition as a true auteur.

Paths of Glory (1957) is an early, straightforward narrative film based on an incident that struck Kubrick as too bitter for satire. It denounces officials who save themselves at the expense of those serving under them. In World War I an ethical French Army colonel (Kirk Douglas) finds himself at odds with some generals who he believes are attempting to conceal their responsibility for a mistaken strategy that has resulted in unnecessary bloodshed. In an effort to prevent the remaining soldiers from resisting their next order, the generals have decided to make an example of

I think clearly that there's a basic problem with people who are not paying attention with their eyes. They're listening. And they don't get much from listening...

—**Stanley Kubrick**

three soldiers chosen at random and convicted of cowardice. They are to be given a speedy trial with a foregone conclusion—conviction and death by firing squad.

The colonel is assigned to defend them but refuses to just go through the motions and play the generals' game. Instead, he investigates and learns the truth, including the fact that a lieutenant chose one of the men for death not randomly, but for personal reasons.

Despite the eloquence of the colonel in defending them, the men, as expected, are condemned to die. On the night before the execution, they face the prospect in different ways. One becomes so hysterical he needs to be drugged into insensibility. When another points out that a cockroach in the cell will continue to live after they have died, the third man matter-of-factly steps on it and remarks, "Now he won't." The third condemned man has suffered so many injuries during the fighting that he cannot walk. Nevertheless, at dawn he is carried outside on a stretcher that is placed upright in range of the firing squad.

After the execution is duly carried out, the colonel is congratulated for dispatching his assignment so well. He knows that if he remains silent about the costly errors of the generals, he is sure to earn a promotion. To their astonishment, he insists on telling the truth, then walks out of the meeting after hearing that the next morning the troops will once again be commanded to suffer more bloodshed in a hopeless cause. In a moving final scene, he passes a tavern where a young German woman, a prisoner of war, is singing a plaintive song for the entertainment of happily drunken soldiers. He decides to delay telling them the grim news about what awaits them the next day. Released during the Korean War that many were protesting as immoral, *Paths of Glory* was readily seen as its own kind of protest, from a director who was not afraid to use the film medium as an agent of change.

Dr. Strangelove, or How I Learned to Stop Worrying and Love the Bomb (1963) continued Kubrick's interest in antiwar, antihypocrisy themes, but in a blatantly satiric style. It was made just when America was becoming involved in Vietnam and some legislators as well as many in the Pentagon were considering an all-out nuclear war against the communist world.

The film concerns the effort of a general named Jack D. Ripper to start a war by ordering American pilots to drop a nuclear bomb on the Soviet Union. When word reaches the Pentagon, the president and his staff are able to rescind the order, but one bomber crew continues flying. Kubrick parodies World War II movies by making the bomber crew the customary cross-section of geographic and ethnic backgrounds. The music accompanying the bomber as it flies over Soviet territory is the Civil War song "When Johnny Comes Marching Home Again." The pilot, wearing a ten-gallon hat, discovers that the bomb bay door will not open; undaunted, he climbs on the bomb himself and, uttering a triumphant "Yee-haw," rides it gleefully to the destruction of both himself and thousands of civilians below.

The president of the United States puts in a call to the leader of the Soviet Union. In an effort to be fair, he suggests that, since an American plane has bombed Soviet territory, perhaps the Soviet leader would like to retaliate by bombing "only" one place in America. But that solution would not work. He learns that a Doomsday Machine designed by the Soviets to rid the planet of all life for the next ninety-nine years has started its countdown. Nothing can stop it. As politicians and military strategists on both sides prepare to take shelter deep underground (accompanied by lovely young women who will breed future generations), they look forward to a time when their descendants will be able to continue the hostilities, once Earth has breathable air again. The final scene shows an airplane being refueled by another plane in midair, to the tune of "We'll Meet Again."

Kubrick showed himself consistently concerned about cruelty, whether it stems from corruption in high places or the dehumanizing effects of technology, or—as in *A Clockwork Orange* (1971)—from a ruthless penal system that tames a violent central character, using methods that are as sadistic as he is. The film's protagonist is Alex, a violent criminal so passionately in love with Beethoven's Ninth Symphony that his sexuality becomes uncontrollably stimulated when he hears it and he commits one violent rape after another. When he is finally captured and sent to prison, Alex is offered a chance for early parole, but only if he is willing to submit to behavior modification to ensure that he will never commit another crime. He agrees and is strapped to a machine, his eyes taped open, while being forced to look at films of brutality. Simultaneously, he is given sickening drugs and forced to listen to the final movement of the Ninth Symphony. This aversive conditioning will, according to the theory, safeguard society. From that time forward, the music as well as thoughts of crime will cause Alex excruciating pain. In this sci-fi treatment of a serious theme, Kubrick continued his imaginative examination of contemporary problems for which we human beings as yet have found no solution. In this case, the problem was the question of whether "justice" may be as bad as the crimes it seeks to punish.

Riding the atom bomb happily to the earth in Kubrick's vicious satire on presidential and military mentality.

Source: The Everett Collection.

Francis Ford Coppola

If Francis Ford Coppola (b. 1939) had directed only *The Godfather* trilogy beginning in 1972, he might still lay claim to being an acknowledged American film auteur. He took the popular theme of rival Mafia families and, especially in the first two films of the trilogy, transcended Hollywood formula to achieve works of Greek-like tragic dimensions, the dream of many an artist working in both theater and film.

In Mario Puzo's powerful novel of a Mafia empire and its ruling patriarch, respectfully known as "godfather" to the extended Mafia family (Color Plate 28), Coppola saw the stuff of which great tragedy is made: a proud family dynasty in which the sins of the father condemn the next generations to repeat the same crimes of extortion and brutal murder and to suffer the vengeance of their enemies. The protagonist of the saga is the eldest son of the patriarch, a young man of basic moral decency who, like Hamlet, is forced into upholding his murdered father's honor, though he lacks the tough-mindedness for the job.

Coppola brought other riches to the project besides co-authorship of the screenplay and a director's keen sense of rhythm. He possessed the stage director's ability to extract performances of sustained psychological realism and subtlety (still rare in the film medium) and the film director's ability to tell a story in image, sound, and quick cuts, always in control of a pace that kept audiences on the edge of their seats. In one memorable and representative scene, the idyll of a Sicilian wedding, filmed against a glorious background of mountains, olive trees, and azure sky, with a lilting Italian melody playing off in the distance, is abruptly interrupted by a car bombing. *The Godfather* renders themes of family tragedy, violence, and betrayal with a haunting visual lyricism never before achieved in a gangster film.

Like many others who score a tremendous box-office success, win awards, and earn lavish praise from critics and peers, Coppola seemed to believe he had

A belief in a supernatural source of evil is not necessary; man alone is quite capable of every wickedness.

—Joseph Conrad

been handed a blank check and could proceed to go his independent way. He established his own company and embarked on projects that took no notice of current public tastes. In 1979 he engineered one of the most controversial film projects of all time: *Apocalypse Now*, loosely based on Joseph Conrad's great novel *Heart of Darkness*, which dealt with the search through a dense jungle for a missing white trader, finally discovered to be a mad tyrant ruling an African tribe.

Coppola's film sets the story in Cambodia during the Vietnam War, and it involves the search for a missing U.S. military officer, who is eventually revealed as a cruel overlord. A box-office disappointment in 1975, it was released in a restored version in 2001, but critical reaction has always been decidedly mixed. Many critics place it up there with *Citizen Kane*; others see it as an ambitious failure. Keep in mind, however, that even the failures of an artist are worth our time.

Martin Scorsese

Let me put it this way: I'm always questioning…You save a man on one corner and on the next corner a man dies…It begs the question, the constant question of what our existence is, the 'Who-are-we? Why are we here?' kind of thing.

—**Martin Scorsese**

Unlike other auteurs who announced early on that they were walking a different path, Martin Scorsese (b. 1942) reached his present status after initially turning out low-grade formula stuff. Perhaps the reason was that this son of Sicilian immigrants, raised on the crime-ridden streets of New York City, was a product of a professional school of film from which he earned two degrees and at which he wrote and directed several prize-winning short films, leading almost automatically to a job in Hollywood. He paid his dues by working on projects that did nothing for his artistic reputation but caused studio bigwigs to take notice of a talented young filmmaker eager to operate within the system.

Scorsese, armed with studio backing, wasted no time creating a major effort: *Mean Streets* (1973) set in the Little Italy of his adolescent years. It was a moody piece about a young man (the director himself?) alienated from and bitter within a bad environment. The handheld camera, moving along actual locations, made the film seem almost like a home movie and lent further authenticity to it. Whether entertaining or not, it dazzled may critics with its honesty and its performances that in no way resembled traditional acting. Much of the public, however, stayed away.

Scorsese bounced back with a feminist film, *Alice Doesn't Live Here Anymore* (1975), which appeared at just the right time, when critics and public alike were clamoring for movies with strong heroines. The success of *Alice* enabled him to go off on his own once again, and the result was *Taxi Driver* (1976), in which he returned to his favorite subject: the dangerous streets of New York and the angry sensibilities of those who are trapped there. The protagonist is a Vietnam veteran, already scarred psychologically by the war, now driving a cab and turning nearly psychotic from the environment and the frantic pace of city life. The film won the Grand Prize at the Cannes Film Festival, and its star, Robert De Niro, would begin a long partnership with Scorsese. The team paired again in *Raging Bull* (1980), a biography of one-time boxing champion Jake La Motta. Unlike some other filmographies, this portrait, shot in black and white, is brutally realistic and, according to reliable reports, psychologically accurate. There's no denying that Scorsese has been heavily influenced by the film noir tradition, and once again we observe that this genre often transcends escapist formula and becomes screen art.

Emboldened by awards and critical praise, Scorsese, like most auteurs, took a bold chance. In 1988 he filmed an adaptation of Nikos Kazantzakis's highly controversial novel *The Last Temptation of Christ*, seeking to show Jesus as a human being with human doubts and fears. The film was condemned not only by many religious groups, but also by the very critics who had praised Scorsese's earlier work. Some complained that the director soft-pedaled much of the psychological torment Jesus undergoes in the novel.

Changing course again, Scorsese made an uncharacteristically genteel film, *The Age of Innocence*, in 1993. Scorsese seems to have wanted to show what he could do in an entirely unexpected style. The movie, based on Edith Wharton's classic American novel about the moneyed aristocracy of a century ago and its rigid code of manners, moves slowly, relying on many close-ups of expressionless faces, belonging to characters unable to express their true feelings. The plot centers on the love of a married man for a wealthy widow at a time when upper-class marriages did *not* end in divorce. All three characters in the triangle are unhappy: the widow, because she knows she will never have the man she loves; the husband, who knows he must, with feelings of guilt, endure a loveless marriage to a woman who has done him no wrong; and the wife, who knows her husband's anguish but is powerless to help. Very possibly Scorsese was drawn to Wharton's novel because he was looking for a different kind of dramatic tension, one that could not be verbalized by the characters. The material provided a stirring context for a drama of exquisite subtlety.

The Age of Innocence is worth revisiting if only for its lush set decorations, for its gracious music, for its costumes, and for the high style with which the actors move and speak. It features one memorable camera sequence in which a host of New York businessmen in their bowler hats are shown walking briskly along Madison Avenue, while in the background we hear the traditional ballad *I Dreamt I Dwelt in Marble Halls*—cinematic irony at its very best. The slow and melodious music played against the rapid strides of the hundreds of extras makes a powerful statement about corporate culture.

Having become a Hollywood icon, Scorsese somehow never won an Academy Award for Best Picture, until *The Departed* in 2006. Some critics maintained that the celebrated director and acknowledged auteur had sold out to studio bosses who wanted him to take advantage of the public's craving for extreme violence and bloodshed. But others found in this movie, about an Irish mob boss and his two young protégés who are working on both sides of the law (one has infiltrated the police department, and the other is actually an undercover police officer spying on the mob boss), a reaffirmation of Scorsese's patented cynicism, working now with all of his camera skills and mastery of pacing. The finale, in which all three of its stars, Leonardo Di Caprio, Matt Damon, and Jack Nicholson, die in graphic shootouts, has caused many film-goers to turn away from the screen. *The Departed* is a triumph of film realism, if nothing else. Whether one prefers the more subtle Scorsese of *The Age of Innocence* is a matter of taste.

Pedro Almodóvar

A master of startling narratives and a unique cinematic style, Spanish film director Pedro Almodóvar (b. 1949) creates films with the recurrent themes of loneliness and the need people have to connect with each other. The work that helped establish his fame with

With *The Departed*, Scorsese uses all of his directing skills to create his most violent film, reaffirming the cynicism in much of his work.

Source: The Everett Collection.

American audiences was *To sobre mi madre* (*All About My Mother*, 1999), which won the Academy Award for Best Foreign Language film. The plot centers on a single mother in Madrid who sees her teenage son killed by a speeding car and her subsequent journey to Barcelona in quest of the father, a transvestite who has had no previous knowledge of the son's existence. The son's death is used as a device to bring the mother to a city foreign to her and to show her interactions with a variety of striking and memorable characters, including yet another transvestite and a pregnant nun, whom she takes care of. Each character, in typically Almodóvar fashion, needs a human connection and understanding, sometimes there, sometimes not there. The uniqueness of his work, however, is the result not so much of his themes but of his characters, none of whom is stereotyped, all of whom are three-dimensional human beings with different behavioral characteristics.

Hable con ella (*Talk to Her*, 2002) has been hailed by critics in many countries as a masterpiece. A technicality kept it from Oscar consideration, though it was allowed to be cited for its screenplay. The film's central location is a hospital, one of Almodóvar's favorite settings, for a hospital is a place in which the need for connection is acute. In the film, two men visit two comatose women and talk to them, returning again and again in hopes of waking them from what they fear will be a permanent sleep. One of the comatose patients had been a dancer, and her devoted bedside companion becomes the film's hero, a hospital worker who has had no previous encounters with her.

Lonely, as is usual in an Almodóvar film, and desperate for love (also usual), Benigno tries to inhabit the dancer's life by visiting her favorite haunts: a dance studio; a movie house that shows only subtle, uncommercial films; and a theater where he watches ballets and dance revues. The dancer has been in a deep coma for four years. Benigno understands that she will probably never recover, but going through a day in her life is the only way this poignant and pathetically comic individual can make the connection.

The other man, Marco, has found love with a former female bullfighter plunged into a coma after being gored nearly to death. Since she too is unresponsive as he talks to her, and since he therefore shares the same feelings as Benigno, the two men form their own connection, one that subtly suggests the possibility of homosexual attraction, except that nothing comes of it. But that is very much at the core of Almodóvar's work. Often the chance for a deeper connection suddenly appears, only to remain unacknowledged.

Audiences who hunger for challenging screen fare rallied around *Talk to Her*. It is a film without closure, without a climax in any traditional sense. Yet it is not slice-of-life either. Almodóvar uses flashbacks and fantasy, often slipping inside the mind of a character without warning. He will even change the style abruptly, as when he introduces a seven-minute, silent-film sequence in the middle of *Talk to Her* that only in retrospect seems to have a connection with the theme of lost and unfound human connections.

Quite clearly, Pedro Almodóvar doesn't mind mystifying audiences and making them lean into a film that they must watch with an intense focus not usually demanded in a movie theater. His work cannot be viewed passively or for brief relaxation. You can't get up to visit the refreshment counter—at least not without becoming disoriented when you return. It is pure cinema that makes no compromises. And if it doesn't necessarily gel into a neatly shaped whole, the strange journey is eminently worth the time to broaden your toleration and eventual enjoyment of the unfamiliar and the unexpected.

Notes on Critical Viewing

Throughout this book so far, we have stressed the primacy of critical thinking in your life and the role played by the humanities in helping you to develop the skill. The critical viewing of films is a way to bring the pleasure of movie-going to a new and higher level. Recognizing the choices made by filmmakers is akin to learning more about the craft of a poem or a painting. Films come in a variety of themes and styles. Here are some criteria that will help you determine the merit of a film:

Use of a style unique to cinema. No other medium can so skillfully show quick cuts, overlapping dialogue, in contrast to the long speeches of many stage plays, and powerful imagery that needs no words. (In Buñuel's *Viridiana*, an imperious employer reaches out to seduce a frightened servant. Instead of showing the human attack, the camera shifts to a cat pouncing on a mouse.)

Characters with complex inner lives. The best films, like the best novels and plays, reward close attention of viewers willing to listen carefully and concentrate. (There is nothing wrong with casual entertainment, but you tend to forget it once you leave the theater.) For example, Rick Blaine in *Casablanca* is both the hard-boiled realist of film noir and a tender-hearted romantic who would like the world to be a better place.

Relevance to the times. Both documentary and fictional films are sometimes responses to social conditions in need of reform. Ford's *The Grapes of Wrath*, which dealt with displaced farmers forced to become ill-paid migrant workers, and Chaplin's *Modern Times*, which showed the dehumanization of the working class during the Depression, are good examples.

Integrity. Films that present serious problems should respect their audiences enough not to hand them unbelievable solutions. The hero of Coppola's *Godfather* films would rather not become a ruthless killer expected to vindicate the family honor. Coppola might have distorted Mario Puzo's novel by having the hero's moral sense triumph, but he did not. He remained faithful to the novel's recognition that, in Mafia culture, family honor supersedes all else.

Avoidance of stereotypes. Films, past or present, that depict minorities as adorable but unsophisticated, and foreign characters as people wearing strange clothes and following strange customs, may seek to entertain but do little to widen our perspective. For example, both *The Godfather* films and *The Departed* have three-dimensional characters who may be law-defying but are not portrayed as being rotten and soulless and nothing more.

Gravity of theme. If a film deals with a timeless subject, it is usually a sign that the writer or director is reaching for art. *Citizen Kane* concerns the moral decline of a person who values wealth and fame above all else. Both *Wild Strawberries* and *The Seventh Seal* are concerned with the search for the meaning and purpose of life. But a big theme does not guarantee an artistic result. Two-dimensional characters and stilted dialogue can doom even the most high-minded film.

No violations of probability. Distortion of the events in the biography of a public figure is inexcusable, as are tacked-on happy endings not justified by the events leading up to them. Cinema announced early in its history that anything could be fair game when pleasing an audience was at stake, and Hollywood has always been cynical about audience willingness to face reality. In the 1940 stage play *Our Town*, the heroine dies in childbirth, and the implied statement is that birth and death are natural to the life cycle; people have to live with that. It would have been dishonest for the playwright, Thornton Wilder, to ignore death, nor should death have come only to old people. Wilder knows that life does not follow an expected scenario. In the screen version, however, the heroine is brought back from near death, apparently through the strength of love. The film distorted the author's intention. It lied about life. To lie when a film promises to be true to life is to cheat those in the audience who appreciate screen art and do not require a sugar-coated myth.

Realistic depiction of gender. In many films the stereotypical woman has been a decorative "handmaiden" whose happiness depends on victory in the mating game. Typically she is well groomed and well dressed (though never seen at an ironing board) and will encounter a powerful man who by the end of the picture will be convinced that happiness for him will mean marriage to her. Being blonde was helpful, as was living in a society with lots of discretionary income to lavish on jewels and other gifts, supposedly what women really want. Fortunately, Hollywood has broken the mold in the past (Ma Joad was poor but strong-willed and independent) and continues to do so. Films from abroad, especially countries with serious problems of gender inequality, are giving audiences realistic, often painful, insights into women's lives. And many Hollywood and independent films now offer women as capable, multifaceted protagonists, like Frances McDormand's pregnant police chief in *Fargo* (1996).

This chapter has discussed many films, and if you have viewed the ones we singled out for praise, you may disagree with our assessment. Nothing could be more harmonious with the spirit of the humanities than disputes among critical thinkers giving serious consideration to a work that aspires to be art. Often the dispute itself is more important than the work. If you disagree, you are expressing your precious rights of free thought and free speech. What is crucial is the willingness to consider, the openness to possibility, the intelligence to choose.

Key Terms

auteur French term for "author," used in reference to certain film directors whose imprint is found in almost every film they make, because of recognizable camera styles, rhythms, themes, and symbols.

cinematography the way the camera tells a story.

close-up film technique in which the camera moves in to enlarge the image of one character or object on the screen.

conventions elements of filmmaking often unnoticed by audiences, e.g., the presence of the camera and its variety of shots.

cut film technique in which the camera moves from one character to another or from one scene to another; also, a director's command that the shooting of a scene must stop.

dissolve film technique in which one scene fades out, to be replaced by another, or the camera superimposes the next scene on the present one, which then gradually fades out.

docudrama nonfiction film that has not only a narrator but characters, either real people or actors, and a story line.

documentary nonfiction film that usually has a narrator but not a structured story line.

elongated moment film technique associated with Eisenstein, in which an action that may be brief in real time is broken into component details and thus lasts longer in screen time.

establishing shot camera shot used to identify the location of a scene, such as the exterior of a house, which is then followed by an interior scene; sometimes dialogue from the interior scene is heard behind the establishing shot, before we see who is talking.

film noir a genre of film known for dark settings, cynicism, and emphasis on the seamy side of human nature; the story usually centers on crime in the city, investigated by an alienated hero.

flip a cut in which a screen image is turned over quickly like a coin, becoming something else; may still be found in comedies.

freeze frame film technique in which the camera suddenly stops the action and the image becomes a photograph.

genre a category of film, such as romantic comedy, western, or film noir; recognizing genre helps film-goers know what to expect about style and content.

lingering take film technique associated with Griffith, in which the camera lingers on a face or an object to underscore a dramatic effect or a significant moment.

pan film technique in which the camera travels from one character to another, or from one object in a room to another, without pausing on anyone or anything.

persona a characterization identified with a certain actor, such as Humphrey Bogart, often to the point where the public comes to believe the actor and the character are the same person.

point of view the vantage from which the camera is filming a scene so the audience knows whether it is supposed to be inside a character's consciousness or sharing the director's objectivity.

slapstick an enduring comic style in which characters are totally dehumanized, fall down, get hit repeatedly, or flattened against a wall when a door violently opens; the term comes from the sound made by two sticks being slapped together, a sound often used in old films and plays to make a slap or a punch in the nose seem more violent.

tracking shot film technique in which the camera, on rollers or rails, moves in for a close-up or moves outward to display a wider area, such as the gradual revelation of the hundreds of dead in the railway depot scene from *Gone with the Wind*.

Topics for
Writing and Discussion

1. Some of the films mentioned in the chapter—*Citizen Kane*, for example—did not fare well at the box office, though they were critically acclaimed. Others were poorly reviewed yet showed soaring box-office receipts. Some critics look with disfavor on the blockbuster, implying that a broad segment of the public is lacking in taste and patronizes bad films. Identify a film you have seen recently that did well at the box office but not with critics and that you consider cinema art. Or identify a film you have seen recently that did not fare well at the box office but that you consider a work of art. Explain why in either case.

2. Write a short paper on a director not mentioned in the chapter whom you consider a film auteur.

3. Chaplin and Bogart were discussed in the chapter as having a screen persona. Write a short paper on a contemporary screen figure who, in your opinion, projects a specific persona, playing the same sort of role in every film. Give specific examples.

4. Does it make any difference that the famous Odessa steps incident depicted in Eisenstein's *Battleship Potemkin* may never have happened? In other words, if a film pretends to be history, is it able to stray from the facts? Does historical accuracy add to a film's value as entertainment?

5. Women and minorities did not fare well in many earlier films. Has the situation improved? Does more need to be done? If so, suggest some remedies.

6. Almost every film today is shot in color. Earlier masterpieces such as *Citizen Kane* and *Casablanca* are in black and white. In the case of both of these films, color was available but not chosen. Why do you think the directors preferred black and white?

7. Reread the section on Alfred Hitchcock's techniques for creating horror scenes. (Or better still, rent *Psycho*.) Compare these techniques with those found in a contemporary horror film. Which do you prefer—the old or the new? Why?

8. Special effects, such as those in the *Spiderman* mega-hits, are hugely popular with audiences. What is *your* opinion? Do you prefer a lot of special effects, or a straightforward story with no special effects? Explain.

9. Look over the section on Major Genres of Film. Which are rarely seen anymore? Why do you think this is the case? Which remain popular? Again, why do you think so?

10. Discuss a film genre that has been overhauled, restyled to fit contemporary tastes. Cite an example of a recent film in the genre and compare it with one you learned about in the chapter.

8 Morality

Overview

Because **moral** problems arise almost every day of our lives and because artists and philosophers are so often concerned with right and wrong, morality is a major theme in the humanities. It is strongly present in much fiction, poetry, drama, television, and film, and can be indirectly found in the visual arts and music. It is, of course, central in religious thought, philosophy, and law.

Morality can be defined as *the basis for a choice among significant options*. That definition eliminates a host of ordinary decisions and trivial differences of opinion. What is required is a "significant" option. This chapter is about significant moral problems that have concerned thoughtful people through the ages and continue to concern us today. These options can be put in the form of questions that seem universal, not tied to specific cultures or time. Here are five questions that have stirred debate among moral philosophers.

1. *Does the end ever justify the means?* If the goal is considered beneficial, is it morally right to do *anything*—including individual acts that on their own would be considered wrong or even criminal to achieve that goal? Machiavelli, one of the philosophers discussed in this chapter, would say yes. Others would say that any moral transgression, even telling a lie, is wrong under any circumstances.

2. *Are punishment and the fear of punishment the only things that keep a person from doing wrong?* The question of whether to obey the law when we can get away with breaking it is at the heart of a famous debate between Glaucon and Socrates in Plato's *Republic*, discussed in this chapter in the section on self-interest.

3. *Do the needs of society outweigh the needs of the individual?* Several philosophers have argued that the individual always come first. John Rawls, in the section on altruism, has a different idea.

4. *Should economic resources be owned and controlled by individuals or by communities?* Some political and economic leaders defend the free market, as described by Adam Smith, and others argue that the free market system does not work in quite the way

An American artist shows scorn for corrupt power. The police officer is being bribed in return for silence and protection. The title ironically echoes that of Kant's major work: *The Critique of Pure Reason*.

Source: Jack Levine, *Feast of Pure Reason* (1937). Credit: On extended loan from the United States WPA Art Program. Museum of Modern Art, NY. Reprinted with permission of VAGA, New York, NY.

Smith described. Some say that the perception of free enterprise as moral or not depends on whether one has an unlimited or rigidly fixed income.

5. *Are results all that matter, or do intentions also count?* The philosopher Jeremy Bentham favors results, but the philosopher Immanuel Kant and many religious thinkers believe it is important to consider motive as well as actions when deciding whether a certain action is or is not moral.

How We Arrive at Moral Decisions

Some philosophers argue that the knowledge of right and wrong is with us from birth. Others believe that we are *taught* the difference between the two. Sometimes we may know what is right, but we do the opposite and then try to justify our actions in some way. Sometimes we say we *used* to know what is right, but now experience has made us less certain. One way or another, we cannot escape *having* to choose.

Moral Systems

Elevation of morality over other goods in human life has been honored, wherever it has been achieved, as a tempering of the otherwise unquenchable human appetite for power, wealth, pleasure, and the rest.

—Jack Miles

Morals are an acquirement—like music, like a foreign language, like poetry, poker, piety, paralysis—no one is born with them.

—Mark Twain

A network of related values on which moral choices are based is called a **moral system.** Most religions, for example, share the belief that certain rules must be followed whether or not they interfere with an individual's personal desires, and often these rules are found in a sacred book. Accepting these rules thus involves (1) faith in the existence of the divinity making the rules, and (2) faith that the sacred book was written by those in a position to record correctly the words of that divinity.

Another moral system is based on reason. One does what is right because reason determines it to be right and therefore doing wrong is irrational. This view in turn depends on faith in reason as the ultimate decision maker in all matters.

Those who have a hard time making up their minds when faced with a difficult choice might wish to consult a moral authority, such as a well-known philosopher, a religious leader, or even a close friend with a reputation for making intelligent decisions. Yet another question immediately pops up: *In the event that two sources offer sharply divergent opinions—or absolute rules—about making a moral decision, which one do we follow?* Will we follow our gut feeling? Will the decision, in the end, come down to self-interest? Will we lack confidence in our own reasoning? Will it simply be easier to follow a moral authority than to wrestle with the problem and agonize over our decision?

You may have some thoughtful answers to moral questions. If so, and if you know the source of your answers, you may already understand a great deal of moral philosophy. By the end of this chapter you may not have definite answers to all of the questions, but you will have been introduced to some theories and some thinkers who have thought long and hard about them. Then it will be up to you to decide which to follow—or, if you prefer, which is right.

The words *should* and *should not* appearing in comments on morality seem appropriate for people who approach the subject with a desire to measure an action based on a particular text as interpreted by a specially trained or consecrated leader. Most religions are guided by commandments, but the *shoulds* and *should nots* can be found in rules of the military and other institutions as well.

People who feel uncomfortable with an absolute *should* are apt to reject the word in favor of *moral relativism* (discussed more fully later in the chapter). "Who's to say what's right?" "People are different. What's good for one may not be good for someone else." "Times change; there are no universals." All of us know of instances in which people who thought differently have been damaged by those who believed there was only one right way. Or one may reject *should* in favor of a simpler rule: "As long as no one is hurt, and if it makes you happy, do it."

Most of us derive some or all parts of a moral system from a variety of sources. Family, education, and society are all influential; so are fairy tales, literature, plays, movies, and television. No matter what the source, there are common taboos against killing, stealing, adultery, lying, and so on, and common beliefs about what constitutes praiseworthy behavior. Some people in totalitarian societies protest against the imposition of what seem to be arbitrary moral rules by a rigid governing body. Yet if you could travel from place to place, interviewing people at random, people not actively engaged in governing, you would probably discover a large body of moral principles that *are* universally accepted.

Nonetheless, sometimes these principles and their sources can be at odds with each other. Your rational assessment of a situation may lead you in one direction, religion in another, and family tradition in still another. Life pushes us into so many quandaries that doing the right thing in every instance is exceedingly difficult. That is why the humanities are sensitive to the pain and suffering that can be caused by moral dilemmas and the tragic results that often result from our choices. The humanities may also be the source of hidden moral beliefs and assumptions that underlie stories or characterizations. In the discussion of critical thinking in Chapter 2, we pointed out that the ability to discover hidden assumptions is an invaluable tool for the person who wishes to lead a rational life. Such a discovery is especially vital if we are to put our moral houses in order—if we are to take control of our lives and fully understand what makes us act as we do.

Conscience is the inner voice that tells us someone may be looking.

—H.L. Mencken

Morality in the Arts

If moral themes were removed from literature, what remained would be scanty indeed. Nathaniel Hawthorne's *The Scarlet Letter* (1850) ultimately wonders whether the individual citizen should be bound by the moral rules of the community. Hester Prynne, the protagonist, a member of Boston's austere Puritan community, is trapped in a loveless marriage. While her husband is away, she succumbs against her better judgment to her passion for a handsome young pastor who cares for her in a tender way she has never known. When a child is born and Hester refuses to name the father, the outraged community, led by the elders of the church, force her to wear a scarlet "A" (for adulteress) on her clothing and to endure the scorn of all the citizens. Though Hawthorne was raised as a strict Puritan, the democratic side of him began to see that an inflexible moral code, imposed by both religion and the community, was more sinful than the adulterous relationship, which had, after all, grown out of a sincere love. Even though *The Scarlet Letter* was written a century and a half ago, the question of whether genuine love supersedes a rigid moral code is still with us.

Hamlet deals with many issues, but perhaps most strongly with the question of whether the need to avenge the wrong done to one's father outweighs the need to follow one's own moral path. *The Godfather* restates the question in a tragic film. The issue of whether duty to one's family outweighs all other considerations, including personal preferences, remains as crucial today as it was in Shakespeare's time. By extension, we can add the conflict that erupts when the family disapproves of a son's or daughter's marital choice, and the inner turmoil when a son or daughter agonizes over whether to tell parents about a sexual preference they adamantly oppose.

Visual artists often concern themselves with moral wrongs. Picasso's *Guernica* remains one of the most potent statements ever made about the horror of attacking an enemy city and killing hundreds of innocent people. The atomic bombing of Hiroshima and Nagasaki, which destroyed thousands of civilians, the burning of Vietnamese villages (made unforgettable in Oliver Stone's 1978 film *Platoon*), and the deaths of non-combatants in the U.S.-led invasion of Iraq, which will inevitably be the subject of many novels and films . . . all of these descendants of *Guernica* keep the wheels of our mind spinning. Does even a just cause excuse acts of inhumanity? When is inhumanity humane?

Even music can be born from a moral stance. Music that is explicitly religious, such as Bach's *Passion According to Saint Matthew*, is a translation into sound of humanity's closeness to God. By contrast, a work such as Ravel's *La Valse* (The Waltz) has been interpreted as a musical vision of the chaos of Europe after the devastation of World War I. The work begins as a disciplined waltz, then gradually reflects chaos with crashing dissonance and electrifying rhythmic changes. It may be the product of an artist who mourns the passing of an age in which values were clear and straightforward. The moral dimension of a given work can lead to as much discussion and analysis as its form.

The relationship between morality and the law has raised problems that underlie many works of literature, stage, and screen. In the 1957 film *Twelve Angry Men*, eleven members of a sequestered jury are in favor of finding the defendant guilty of murder, but one person is not so sure and insists on closer analysis. As the intensity builds, we begin to see that some of the jurors simply want to go home and others had their minds made up from the beginning. The juror who opposes their decision finally wins them over, but we are left with an uncertainty. We don't know whether justice has been done.

The television series *Law and Order* frequently ends ambiguously, as police investigations followed by courtroom verdicts or plea-bargaining call into question the gulf between crime and punishment, let alone justice. The public remains fascinated, as shown by the continued popularity of the series and its spin-offs.

The need to make a choice among significant options cannot be overstated. In George Bernard Shaw's play *The Doctor's Dilemma* (1906), an expensive cure for a previously fatal disease has been found, but it is so rare and so expensive that a physician in the play must choose between two applicants. One is a decent, hard-working doctor who has helped many patients; the other is an artist, a man of genius but a scoundrel, apparently interested only in himself and his work.

Shaw's play The Doctor's Dilemma *illustrates how painful a moral choice between two compelling options can be.*

The play gives the audience a chance to debate the issue of how much selfishness or selflessness is involved in evaluating human life. The caring doctor, who devotes his entire life to others, ultimately is given the cure, while the artist must die. In his typically ironic ending, Shaw makes us realize that the self-interest of the artist has enriched the lives of thousands and we must be careful before we jump to hasty moral judgments.

Such dilemmas have inspired innumerable discussion groups, some of which, for example, have argued over which survivor of a shipwreck should be allowed into an overcrowded lifeboat that has space for only one more. In actual cases, medical transplant teams must choose between patients desperately in need of a scarce liver, kidney, or some other organ. Who goes to the head of the line while others wait their turn with the likelihood of more pain and death?

Shaw's play thus continues to have relevance. Consider the cost of health care in a large corporation. Management must choose an insurance plan with benefits that are either equal for all employees or different according to an employee's rank, usefulness to the organization, or citizenship. For example, would the dental care available to the company's chief executive officer be the same as that available to the cafeteria worker here on a temporary work visa? Minimum dental care is cheap: numb the area around the problem tooth and extract it. Making impressions of the area and fitting a crown in order to save the tooth can cost thousands of dollars. Does the morality of self-interest give management the right to make these distinctions? Yes, say many who argue that, in doing so, the company stays profitable, secure in the knowledge that an almost unlimited supply of applicants for the job of kitchen help is available.

There is really nothing more to say–except why. But since why is difficult to handle, one must take refuge in how.

—Toni Morrison

The Morality of Self-Interest

When young siblings angrily dispute who owns what, a parent will remind them not to fight. Instead, they are urged to share. In school, children are taught to obey rules, not to be selfish, and to cooperate with other members of a team. Public praise for philanthropists reminds us that charity is good, that acting out of self-interest is wrong (except when it was the way the donor's fortune was amassed). Yet free societies are also based on the principle that free enterprise, which benefits the entrepreneur first, also helps employees and their families. Getting ahead is a recognized goal, with its implied corollary that some must win while others lose.

The moral sentiment is the drop that balances the sea.

—Ralph Waldo Emerson

Is acting out of self-interest a bad thing? Is selflessness necessarily good? If everyone acted our of self-interest, would it breed a self-reliance that is better for society as a whole? During a sweeping nineteenth-century movement, self-interest came to the fore as the most desirable characteristic of a human being. The term was often preceded by the adjective *enlightened*. It was believed that self-reliant people, realizing their full potential as human beings, would enrich, not damage, society. Other theories, however, still popular today, tell us that, in a choice between self-interest and the general good, self-interest would prevail. That is the position taken by Glaucon in his classic debate with Socrates.

Glaucon versus Socrates

Early in *The Republic*, a series of philosophical dialogues between Socrates and his students, as chronicled by Plato, a confrontation occurs between Socrates, who is always on the side of reason, and Glaucon, a student described by Plato as "that most pugnacious of men" and a firm believer that everyone does the right thing out of motives that have nothing to do with reason or innate goodness. To strengthen his case, Glaucon tells the tale of a shepherd named Gyges, who discovers that a ring he has removed from a corpse has the power to make him invisible. (Think Frodo in *Lord of the Rings*.) Taking full advantage of his newfound power "he contrived to be chosen one of the messengers who were sent to the court; where as soon as he arrived he seduced the queen, and with her help conspired against the king and slew him, and took the kingdom."[1]

An argument then ensues in the class over whether a basically honest and just man would do the same thing. For all his "pugnaciousness," Glaucon is made to be ingenious as well. Glaucon continues: "Suppose now that there were two such magic rings, and the just [man] put on one of them and the unjust the other; no man can be imagined to be of such an iron nature that he would stand fast in justice. No man could keep his hands off what was not his own when he could safely take what he liked out of the market, or go into houses and lie with any one at his pleasure, or kill or release from prison whom he would, and in all respects be like a God among men."[2]

Socrates argues that, if the just man decided not to take advantage of the magic ring, he would die in peace, content that his had been a good life. Glaucon quickly counters by asking the group to suppose that somehow the just man had developed a reputation for being unjust, while the unjust man enjoyed the opposite reputation. Would the just man not decide he would be a fool not to use the powers of the ring? What would be the satisfaction of doing the right thing if nobody knew it? Furthermore, what if he was made to suffer excruciating torture because of his supposed lack of goodness? (Socrates, of course, is famous for teaching that nothing bad can happen to good people.) It will not be long, concludes Glaucon, before the just man realizes that the *appearance* of goodness is all that matters.

Having a reputation for being truthful, hence trustworthy, the unjust man goes on to enjoy all the benefits that come with social approval. "With his reputation of virtue, he will hold offices of state, ally himself by marriage to any family he may choose, become a partner in any business, and having no scruples about being dishonest, turn all these disadvantages to profit."[3] Society, so goes Glaucon's argument, expects virtue to be only an appearance. Virtue is the result of pressure brought to bear upon each of us, not of the human capacity to determine, through reason, what is right and what is wrong.

Yet reason is precisely what Socrates relies on, and his counterargument is one that has stirred up as much controversy as his opponent's. He maintains that the virtuous act is done *for its own sake*. Rational humans live according to the law, even if the law is harmful to them. Periclean democracy, or the direct rule of citizens, was still very new in the world, and Socrates firmly believed that rationality would give rise to laws that were fair, just, and moral. Plato attributes to Socrates one of the most ringing (and still controversial) declarations in all of philosophy: "To know the good is to do the good."

Socrates' meaning, which at first seems naive, is actually awesome in its simplicity and ultimately hard to refute. What he says is that people cannot claim to be deliberately choosing the wrong action despite knowing the right one. If you do the wrong thing, then that is what you know. *Acting is part of knowing*. In other words, anyone can pretend to know something, but the *only* possible proof of that knowledge is through actions. If your deeds are bad, then there is no evidence that you knew what was right. We may disagree, but the force of the argument is powerful.

Socrates paid with his life for his trust in reason. After being found guilty of trumped-up charges, he was sentenced to death. He refused to bargain for a lighter sentence, which would have required him to agree never to teach again. That would have meant no longer seeking the truth, and without possessing the truth, he would be no better than Glaucon's shepherd.

He does observe, however, that the opinion of others is important, but the opinion of good people *only*. Why should one care what bad people think? If one

Truth has no special time of its own. Its hour is now–always.

—**Albert Schweitzer**

lives so as to win the respect of the good, then obviously one has led a good life. Then he gives one of his final lessons before drinking the hemlock that will end his days: "*not life, but a good life, is to be chiefly valued.*"

Nowadays it is not hard to find people who admire billionaire tycoons because they succeed so well without even the advantage of a magic ring. Their success is perhaps equivalent to Glaucon's idea of a good reputation, even though hordes of people know that the methods for achieving that success have not always been admirable. Also in the Glaucon camp are those who quote with admiration the cynical adage attributed to baseball manager Leo Durocher: "Nice guys finish last."

Yet, we may ask, what guided the Athenians who voted for the death sentence? Socrates was convicted not by a jury as we know it today, but rather, by an assembly of all the citizens. Reason may not, after all, have been *their* guiding principle. Political factors appear to have been involved. The philosopher's teachings sometimes challenged the state. Did the self-interest of the state finally triumph? And should it have? Even today, we might well inquire whether any governing body can totally sacrifice its well-being, its power, its political future in the name of reason alone.

Later in *The Republic*, Plato admits that the majority of people—both the governing and the governed—will generally be driven by self-interest unless both are held in check by one supreme ruler, a man like Socrates, motivated solely by what reason advises in every instance; a man not out for himself, ruling because he has a clear vision of a state in which justice prevails. He called this ruler the *philosopher-king*. Whether such a being has ever existed or *could* ever exist has long been debated. A number of rulers have made claims about their wisdom, and millions have had faith that their rulers were wise and good, but are such a claim and a people's faith the deciding factors?

Plato's plan has a major problem: who would decide on the identity of the philosopher-king? Reason says only the wisest would be qualified to make the decision. Since there can be only one "wisest person," who could decide that the right choice had been made? What would prevent *anyone* from claiming to be that person? Glaucon would probably say that the struggle for the power of being such a supreme ruler would result in all manner of underhanded magic-ring ploys on the part of ambitious people who would cheat, even kill, to win the position.

In the long history of the humanities, works abound that deal with the theme of self-interest, clearly a problem that has preyed on the conscience of a good many people. In the theater, a discipline that thrives on plots of conflict, the repertoire of important plays would be considerably shorter without that theme.

A play by the French existential philosopher Jean-Paul Sartre (1905–1980) examines the choice made by a young white woman whose testimony could save a black man from death. *The Respectful Prostitute* (1947) is based on an actual event involving two prostitutes who were urged by a judge and a sheriff to accuse two black men of rape, so that

They deem him their worst enemy who tells them the truth.

—Plato

Archetypes in This Chapter

Glaucon	a figure in Plato's *Republic* who has come to symbolize the hard-nosed realist always ready to challenge the lofty principles of idealists.
Greed	developed from various moral denunciations of hedonism and later of capitalist theories based on Adam Smith, but also praised as one of life's goods by supporters of the Smith theory that amassing wealth out of self-interest also benefits others.
Kindness	popular version of altruism, a quality we seek and admire whether we embody it or not.
Morals	for many, proper and acceptable conduct in all matters and not open to discussion; usually based on religious, family, and societal requirements that nonetheless can conflict with each other, causing much confusion.
Philosopher-king	the ideal of the totally rational ruler who puts aside all self-interest.
Puritan	broad term for a morally rigid person.
Ten Commandments	the archetypal set of moral laws for all cultures influenced by Judaism, Christianity, and Islam. Ingrained in most people born within such cultures whether or not they are religious.

the mob would feel justified in lynching them. One of the prostitutes agreed to lie. Sartre's drama focuses on just one prostitute, Lizzie. The play begins after the accusation of rape has been made. The men are being hunted by dozens of armed deputies and police bloodhounds. One of them seeks out Lizzie and begs her to tell police the truth. His passionate entreaties convince her that she cannot lie, not even in a racist community that wants to find and execute the fugitives. She resolves to save the men.

Later, however, she learns that one of her customers, a racist young man, is the son of a powerful senator. He and his father urge Lizzie to go ahead with the false accusation, because social stability requires certain sacrifices, one of which she must now make. Their argument is that the example of these two black men, if convicted, will guarantee that the area will be much safer in the future for decent, law-abiding citizens. Sartre's heroine experiences much inner torment before finally relenting and changing her story, inventing a harrowing account of how she was violently attacked. In a society clearly based on class and skin color, Sartre is saying, words like "reason," "virtue," and "the good" become subordinated to the majority will, and this becomes a major cause of injustice. Or rather, those words are used by the privileged class to justify their power. "Inferiors," or so they believe, could not be expected to understand the terms.

In real life we have all heard and read about the importance of testifying under oath to determine guilt or confirm an alibi. Perhaps lynch mobs are no longer prevalent, but threats to witnesses and the establishment of witness protection programs attest to the dangers that sometimes accompany telling the truth.

In Robert Bolt's 1960 Pulitzer Prize play *A Man for All Seasons*, the issue is religious conviction versus self-preservation. Based on historical events, the play concerns the dilemma and subsequent martyrdom faced by the writer and philosopher Thomas More. Widely admired in his native England and often honored by his once close friend King Henry VIII, More was eventually placed in a position of having to give his approval to the king's pending divorce or risk execution by upholding church doctrine. More, a faithful Catholic, believed so implicitly in the laws of the church that he could not do as the king demanded, not even to save his own life. In Socratic terms, More was objecting to Henry's efforts to rewrite church doctrine to suit his own needs, and thus assenting to the divorce would have amounted to a betrayal of reason. Although the king privately pleads with his friend not to die for his belief, More's obstinate refusal to sanction the divorce publicly leaves Henry no choice. More is beheaded. He was eventually canonized by the Catholic church.

The works of nineteenth-century novelists teem with male characters obsessed with moving to higher levels of society by making advantageous deals that injure the naive and benefit the shrewd, while poor but ambitious women use their charms to win proposals of marriage from good providers whom they do not and never will love. William Thackeray's Becky Sharp, heroine of the aptly titled *Vanity Fair*, is, like her American counterpart Scarlett O'Hara, the lasting symbol of the woman who uses her charm to get what she wants but inevitably finds herself alone and unloved.

In the short story "The Idealist," by Irish writer Frank O'Connor (1903–1966), a Protestant student in an Irish school is profoundly influenced by inspirational books about boys in such schools for whom honor and tradition are all-important. The student notes that, whenever Catholic classmates are late for school, they lie to the headmaster, saying they have been to Mass and thus escape punishment. The young hero, however, is so conditioned by his reading to believe in telling the truth at all costs that he is severely beaten every time he is late without offering an excuse. At length, broken in spirit (and nearly in body!), he lies like all the others. The story ends with the headmaster smiling to himself in triumph. The last holdout has finally come into the fold.

There are also cynical writers who tell us that acting solely according to virtuous principles may *sound* praiseworthy but is in the end foolish and self-defeating. Often the cynicism is couched in humor. James Thurber, the *New Yorker* cartoonist and writer who specialized in making people laugh, dealt with righteousness as a futile enterprise in his *Fables for Our Time*. In these short stories, the humorist takes a second look at some time-honored tales and nursery rhymes that preach the value of honesty at all costs. One tells the story of a good, clean-living citizen whose life is one of strict moral and physical discipline, who is so predictable in all his opinions and actions that his wife knows she can take advantage of his clockwork bedtime habits by sneaking out to meet her lover. Then the pair decide to do away with him. Waiting until the appointed hour when the husband always falls asleep, the lover steals into the house and strangles him. Thurber concludes with an updated version of the old nursery rhyme, changing it to say that "early to rise, early to bed makes a man healthy, wealthy, and dead."

Following World War II, America emerged from the Great Depression and new moneyed classes came upon the scene. A good many people had amassed huge sums in the war effort and were often viewed with distrust. The evil of greed reared its head once more, supplying literature, drama, and cinema with abundant plot material. John Huston's *The Treasure of the Sierra Madre*, a 1948 film starring Humphrey Bogart in another of his memorable roles (see Chapter 7), was a cinematic updating of the classic fable about three partners who reap a great fortune—in this case, gold from an abandoned mine—only to destroy each other because each one wants the fortune for himself. In the humanities, extreme self-interest has seldom been applauded and is shown as the force that drives people to commit evil acts.

Frank O'Connor's short story "The Idealist" shows the terrible things that happen to a schoolboy who always believes in telling the truth.

Enlightened Self-Interest

The Renaissance philosopher Niccoló Machiavelli (1469–1527) argued in favor of political self-interest as the only possible means to a stable and harmonious society. His most famous work, *The Prince*, contains advice to all aspiring rulers. Effective leaders, he claims, must never assume their followers would seek a justice inconvenient to themselves. He therefore concludes that the wisest course for a true leader is to gain respect and obedience by creating a sense of awe. Leaders must present an intimidating appearance, letting the populace know that someone regal is in charge. They should dress well and be surrounded by signs of power, such as riding in magnificent carriages followed by a large retinue of influential friends, security personnel, and important local politicians. This advice has been followed by modern leaders, who fly from country to country in gigantic, official planes and are escorted to their destinations in stretch limousines, long motorcades, and a parade of bodyguards.

Machiavelli's political philosophy may well have been inspired by Plato and Aristotle, neither of whom accepted wholeheartedly the democratic state installed by Pericles. The latter believed that all laws and court decisions should be made by the private citizens (even though citizens constituted only about 5 percent of the

The end may justify the means as long as there's something that justifies the end.

—Leon Trotsky

total population, the other 95 percent being slaves and women). Plato and Aristotle did not trust even this small percentage to be rational enough to make fair decisions. Both demanded strong rule from the top in order to guarantee stability and justice. Plato created the philosopher-king; Aristotle advanced the theory that the ideal government had three major components: the king, the aristocrats, and groups of outstanding citizens known for their wisdom and fair dealings.

All three philosophers—Machiavelli, Plato, and Aristotle—were against ruthless, self-interested dictatorship and the whimsical rule of people whose wealth enabled them to buy their way to power. All three were concerned for the welfare of the total society, but they stopped short of recommending direct rule of the populace. Instead, wise rulers best served the interest of their country by imposing, for unselfish reasons, their own, carefully considered political philosophy. This idea can be called **enlightened self-interest**: serving the self in order to have an effective government that provides for people better than they could provide for themselves.

Machiavelli believed that, by acting in his own self-interest, the wise ruler was better for the state than one who was permissive.

The term **Machiavellian** has unfortunately become a reference to cynical individuals who exert power over others by manipulating them through duplicity. Literature offers a gallery of characters that critics have labeled—and always negatively—Machiavellian, such as Iago in Shakespeare's *Othello*. They are usually the villains, preying upon unsuspecting goodness. The true philosophy behind *The Prince* emerged from the Renaissance focus on individualism. In a sense, Machiavelli's ideal ruler typified the new age, for such a ruler was unencumbered by the restraints of the Christlike existence demanded of (but not necessarily realized by) rulers in the Middle Ages. The book was dedicated to Lorenzo de Medici, an aristocrat of Florence, a powerful political figure and patron of the arts, credited by Machiavelli with being the fully realized human being that was the Renaissance ideal, a man whose enlightened self-interest had helped make Florence a great city.

Thomas Hobbes (1588–1679) was a political philosopher who believed that tight autocratic control was necessary because the masses of people, *not* their rulers, were out for themselves. He believed that egoism was the natural condition of humanity. He described human beings as basically "nasty" and "brutish" and denied that such a thing as a noble purpose could exist. With this pessimistic view of the individual, Hobbes wrote *Leviathan* (1651), recommending a political system based on absolute monarchy. He employed the term *commonwealth* to describe the ideal state, one in which each subject must willingly turn over his rights to the sovereign for the mutual protection of all people from each other. He advised that "every man should say to every man, *I authorize and give up my right of governing myself, to this man* [i.e., the Leader], *or to this assembly of men, on this condition, that thou give up thy right to him, and authorize all his actions in like manner.*"[4]

Although this may sound like a democratic kind of social contract whereby each person willingly gives up individual rights for the good of all, Hobbes makes no pretense of democracy. Reason told him that, once power is invested in the monarch, that ruler could not, by definition, be answerable to the people. If he were, he would not be feared, and if he were not feared, order would disintegrate. The monarch, backed by an invincible army, would protect his subjects from each other as well as from attacks from other nations. Hence the term *Leviathan*, which for Hobbes meant "*mortal god*, to which we owe under the *immortal God*, our peace and defense." The commonwealth would then flourish peacefully—an impossibility if each citizen were allowed to think and act for himself. Without the Leviathan, every person would distrust every other person, with the result that no person or property would be safe. Without the absolute strength of the leader, "every man has a right to every thing; even to one another's body. And therefore, as long as this natural right of every man endureth, there can be no security to any man."[5]

We can see that Hobbes and Machiavelli both favor non-democratic government as the only means to prevent self-interest from destroying society. Hobbes, further influenced by the rise of rational philosophy during the seventeenth century in reaction to the other-worldliness of the Middle Ages, maintained that reason alone, not a sentimental faith in human nature, could allow humanity to live in peace and harmony. Tough-minded as his political philosophy was, he insisted that it represented the only *rational* course if the human race were to survive its own cutthroat instincts.

Economics and Self-Interest

The economic philosopher Adam Smith (1723–1790) believed that the perfect society was one in which all people were free to pursue self-interest. Like Karl Marx, who would come later (see Chapter 10), he observed that economic well-being was the guiding force in human life. People were interested in making money, getting ahead, providing the most comfortable standard of living for themselves and their families. Greed itself was not necessarily a bad thing, as long as one did not break the law or harm others in the process of accumulating wealth. Greed in itself was thus not immoral. It was the natural condition of humanity.

Smith's theory that people should have the freedom to pursue wealth became the basis for the capitalist system of today. To those who argued that unlimited freedom of economic activity would yield a society of constant conflict and dangerous competition, Smith's answer was that *without* such freedom only those in power would enjoy the pleasures that rightfully belong to everyone.

His policy is called **laissez-faire** (a French phrase meaning "allow to do") and is based on the principle that businesses should be free to charge whatever they want for their goods and services. The public's response, not government controls, will regulate the process. Smith's ideal society has a built-in system of checks and balances that prevent the accumulation of wealth in just a few corporations.

Manufacturers, or *entrepreneurs*, as they are called in economic theory, perform a service for the public by seeking to make a profit for themselves. The salaries paid to employees increase the money supply, which keeps circulating throughout the economy, guaranteeing more employment for everyone. Without their being aware of it, says Smith, all people who live in a free-market system are joined together "as by an invisible hand."

It is in the best interest of the entrepreneur to manufacture products that people actually need. To continue to make an unneeded product would result in bankruptcy. (Once the automobile displaced the horse and carriage as the primary means of transportation, who would have wanted to buy buggy whips?)

Problems develop when entrepreneurs become *too* greedy. If a product is successful and large numbers of people buy it, chances are the price will go up. But, Smith adds, if costs get too high, people will stop buying; companies will be forced to lower prices—or go out of business. He is also in favor of unlimited, unrestricted competition as a market stabilizer. If one person charges too much, another will seize the chance to become rich by manufacturing the same product at a lower price. Demanding more and more money in exchange for goods is not immoral in

Adam Smith correctly observed that it is from the self-interest of the butcher, the baker and brewer that we expect our dinner, not from their benevolence.

—Donald Livingston

Without civic morality communities perish; without personal morality their survival has no value.

—Bertrand Russell

People create their own questions because they're afraid to look straight. All you have to do is look straight and see the road, and when you see it, don't sit looking at it–walk.

—Ayn Rand

Smith's philosophy. The consumer inevitably benefits as public response exercises control over wanton enterprises.

Critics of Smith's version of **capitalism** sometimes point out that he lacked the foresight to see that entrepreneurs could collaborate and secretly agree not to undersell each other. In this way, prices remain stable, and everyone profits except the consumer. Smith also did not predict our present era of large aggregates, supercompanies formed from merger after merger until they all but monopolize the market for thousands of products under their control. One vestige of Smith's invisible hand (maybe one finger of it), however, remains strong, and that is the slowing down of sales when prices go too high. Yet, even at that, critics add, entrepreneurs can mutually agree to cut down on production in order to bolster prices, as the Organization of Petroleum Export Countries (OPEC) frequently does.

Smith's laissez-faire policy is predicated on the assumption that the laws of supply and demand will apply in every instance. The price goes up; nobody buys; the price goes down; the cycle repeats itself. When products are cheap, everyone starts buying them again, so the price goes up and the cycle repeats itself. But economists tell us that resources are not unlimited and may not always be available. Crude oil, for example, is non-renewable, no matter what OPEC does. The most pessimistic projections say that eventually there will be none left. The invisible hand in this case will totally vanish.

Nor could Smith have predicted the global economy that exists today, in which there are a few separate nations fending for themselves, but mainly an intricate network of mutual dependence. A bank collapse in a powerful country that previously attracted much foreign investment can cause chaos all over the world. Economists tend to agree that there is no such thing as a global self-regulating market. In any case, Smith's theory that self-interest is in the best interest of humanity continues to be debated. Recent world problems have only added to the controversy. We cannot make the blanket statement that economic self-interest is not moral. We still depend on a free market and faith in Adam Smith's theory of the invisible hand. But we have to admit that it poses problems that may never be resolved.

For novelist Ayn Rand (1905–1982), however, capitalism was close to divine. She preached complete reliance on the free market, which she believed encourages the strong and self-reliant to make the most of their own talents, without having to spend a lifetime helping others, who would only grow weaker and lose the incentive to help themselves. Born in pre-revolutionary Russia, Rand as a teenager witnessed the sweeping changes and promise of a glorious future in a classless society. She resisted indoctrination after analyzing communist ideology, rejecting Karl Marx's claims about the benefits society would receive once the bourgeoisie had been eliminated.

Rand defected to the West and started writing. In the work that brought her fame in the United States, *The Fountainhead* (1943), she became a spokesperson for rugged, uncompromising individualism. The hero of the novel is a celebrated architect, known for his daring designs and fierce integrity, who refuses to lower his standards and turn out mediocre work for a muddled committee totally lacking in his vision and genius. Howard Roark is a descendant of the epic heroes of old, a strident loner, equal to any challenge.

In one of her famous essays, *The Virtue of Selfishness*, she says that people of foresight and vision should have unlimited opportunities to follow their own laws. In her version of the invisible hand, the strident loner does help others, but not out of the belief that it is moral and honorable to make sacrifices for them. Rand believed society profits because superior people such as Howard Roark build great cities and make the world a better place. But they must be left alone. Roark proudly asserts: "No man is worth five minutes of my time."

Rand's *Atlas Shrugged* (1957) presents a group of high-powered achievers who, tired of mass culture and socialist policies, create a utopian society high on a mountaintop, from which the lazy masses are excluded. At one point Rand makes a scathing denunciation of the Marxist dictum "From each according to his ability, to each according to his need." She has one of the characters, who had been a dedicated worker, finally express his disillusionment with socialist demands that he work for the desperately poor.

> the harder you work the more is demanded of you, and you stand slinging buckets forty hours a week, then forty-eight, then fifty-six—for your neighbor's supper—for his wife's operation—for his child's measles—for his mother's wheel chair—for his uncle's shirt—for his nephew's schooling—for the baby next door—for the baby to be born—for anyone anywhere around you—it's theirs to receive, from diapers to dentures—and yours to work, from sunup to sundown[6]

Ayn Rand believed society profits from the genius of strong people, who must be left alone.

Source: Warner Bros./The Kobal Collection.

Transcending Self-Interest: Altruism

Self-interest is sometimes necessary. We recognize that in politics those who are called public servants serve their own interests, at least to an extent. Being elected to office brings fulfillment to their lives, as well as recognition and notoriety. Political self-interest can cause pessimists to assume that all politicians are out for wealth and power, that they take advantage of their position and cheat wherever possible. No one will deny that political corruption has always existed and will no doubt continue to exist, but American democracy is built on the principle of representative government. This means that we will always have to elect certain people willing to represent us. It would be depressing indeed to believe that in serving their own needs, the majority of them were not also serving *us*. Yet this brand of self-interest is not exactly the same thing as devoting one's life or risking all in the interest of others.

Can there be a place for **altruism**, or greater concern for the welfare of others more than for oneself? Some would say no, arguing that, even if reason in the Socratic sense requires us to place others before ourselves, what *appears* to be an altruistic, or selfless, act really springs from secret motives of self-interest.

To be sure, many examples of altruistic acts require no questioning of motives. During a shooting incident at an elementary school, for example, a teacher shielded the body of a child and received a fatal bullet instead. In such instances, the cynics are quiet, but they may later observe that the number of people willing to practice altruism is trivially small. The death of 300 firefighters in the disaster of September 11, 2001, may have changed many attitudes. Nor can we ever know how many of the thousands who perished that day did so because they stayed to help others.

When a blind man carries a lame man, both go forward.

—**Swedish proverb**

Detractors might argue that the heroism displayed on September 11 was only a temporary interlude in the ongoing drama of self-interest. They might concede that at times of extreme disaster, the urge to suppress self-interest is strong, but they would argue that at most other times, altruism disappears.

In the everyday world, altruism *does* exist: in volunteers comforting the sick, youth groups devoted to getting rid of their town's litter, and in advocacy for any cause from which one stands to gain nothing tangible. Lifeguards swim out to answer a distress call without thinking twice. Passersby find lost wallets and mail them back untouched, without their own return address. In the Sudan, where millions of innocent women, men, and children were being slaughtered in acts of "ethnic cleansing" or were dying from malnutrition and disease, members of the group Doctors without Borders, humanitarian medical personnel, worked tirelessly to save as many lives as they could, even though they faced the possibility of being shot for their efforts or being infected with disease themselves.

In the corporate world of today, where workers may become aware of defective auto parts, unsanitary food preparations, or the deliberate advertising of products that are dangerous to health, cases of altruistic "whistle-blowing" exist. Michael Mann's 1999 film *The Insider*, based on an actual case, deals with a conflict between the need to transcend self-interest and the knowledge that doing so could result in not only the loss of a very comfortable income but even physical harm. It poses a question that all too frequently must be asked. Does an employee

Al Pacino, left, and Russell Crowe in *The Insider*. Crowe plays a man forced to decide between providing a comfortable life for his family and blowing the whistle on a tobacco company.

Source: The Everett Collection, Inc.

have a moral responsibility to blow the whistle when it is perceived that a product is harmful and often deadly?

In the film, a tobacco company scientist finally decides to appear on television to reveal information about chemical additives in cigarettes that he believes make smoking more addictive. The decision does not come easily. His contract with the tobacco company had specifically stated that he must never reveal the truth to the public, and he realizes his high income allows him to provide handsomely for his family in a well-appointed home. When he finally places moral responsibility before his own and his family's interest and agrees to testify in court, he is threatened, placed under surveillance, and grilled on the witness stand. His personal reputation and his marriage are destroyed.

Still he persists and agrees to appear on the television program *60 Minutes*, but the producers of the show are told by their superiors it would be best not to air the interview. The *Wall Street Journal*, however, prints the hero's story, and *60 Minutes* is finally willing to run it. There is a singular lack of triumph after the truth is revealed and the protagonist has acted righteously. He has indeed lost everything, and his future seems bleak. We are left to wonder whether his tragic losses are offset by the moral integrity of his actions. In the most notable works, there are no easy moral victories. If nothing else, we learn from them that doing the right thing takes not only courage but the willingness to stand quite alone.

Though much literature reflects the belief that self-interest is stronger than altruism, many major works can be found in which characters perform noble deeds that in no way benefit themselves. A famous example is *A Tale of Two Cities* (1859) by Charles Dickens (1812–1870). The hero, Sydney Carton, is a well-educated but essentially unfulfilled gentleman, with little taste for causes and allegiances. And the woman he loves, Lucy, has married Charles Darnay, an expatriate French aristocrat who bears a strong resemblance to Carton. When the French Revolution breaks out, Darnay returns to Paris in order to save the life of one of his servants but is apprehended by the revolutionists and sentenced to die on the guillotine. Aware of the deep love between Lucy and Darnay, the heretofore detached Carton engineers a plot to smuggle Darnay out of the Bastille by taking his place. As he awaits the guillotine, Carton silently thinks, "This is a far far better thing I do than I have ever done. It's a far far better rest I go to than I have ever known." Millions of readers have wept over this ending, though some critics have dismissed the novel for being overly sentimental. Not only does nobility of purpose carry a high price, but it is frequently subject to critical scorn.

People are naturally suspicious when they hear that someone has committed a purely altruistic act. Often they will seek out hidden motives of self-interest.

Altruism, the extreme opposite of self-interest, comes from the Latin *alter*, meaning "other." The word does not occur often in ordinary conversation. Hearing that an "altruist" has done something considered noble for others, we might look for a motive arising out of self-interest. Was the act truly unselfish, or was it done for the sake of a handsome tax reduction, favorable publicity, or even the pleasure of self-satisfaction? Was the self more involved than the "other"?

Yet the altruistic behavior of some people is above question. We've all heard inspiring declarations like "There is no greater love than to die for another." During times of war there are reports of soldiers who sacrifice themselves for others in their platoon. The stirring words of the seventeenth-century Anglican priest and poet John Donne (see Chapter 4) have become emblazoned in the history of the humanities: "No man is an island entire of itself; every man is a piece of the continent, a part of the main. If a clod be washed away by the sea, Europe is the less, as well as if a promontory were. . . . Any man's death diminishes me, because I am involved in mankind. And therefore never send to know for whom the bell tolls; it tolls for thee."[7] Ernest Hemingway took the title of his 1940 novel *For Whom the Bell Tolls* from this passage. The novel centers on an American who takes part in the Spanish Civil War and gives up his life to save others.

Steven Pinker, a Harvard psychology professor, writes that some moral philosophers and scientists are trying to validate what many still think may be the case—namely, that the moral instinct, the tendency to do what is right regardless of personal gain, is inborn in the species. "Though no one has identified genes for morality," he says, "there is circumstantial evidence they exist." Paraphrasing Richard Dawkins's contention that altruism has evolved in our species, Pinker explains: "Fairness is very close to what scientists call reciprocal altruism, where a willingness to be nice to others can evolve as long as the favor helps the recipient more than it costs the giver and the recipient returns the favor when fortunes reverse."[8]

Far from altruistic are the business executives involved in scandals, indictments, and imprisonments for dubious accounting practices, insider trading, and excessive bonuses unconnected to prudent business practices. The injured have included stockholders, employees, and the occasional whistle-blower who has notified the authorities about alleged crimes. Although three whistle-blowers were once honored by being pictured on the cover of a news magazine, most have not benefited in the least. Being known as the guardian of moral behavior does not enhance the résumé of a job-seeker!

Finding a job becomes even harder in these days of newer practices such as "outsourcing" that are said to benefit the disadvantaged in countries with lower standards of living than ours. When calling about a hotel room or how to solve a computer problem, one may be talking to someone in a far distant location, working for much less than employers would have to pay in America for the same job. Or one may be wearing a dress or shirt that has been manufactured in a factory thousands of miles away, in which workers toil for long hours and low pay in less than ideal conditions. Charity toward the underprivileged, or a new means of amassing huge profits? Would anyone step forward and refuse to work for an outsourcing company on the grounds that it is exploiting the downtrodden?

Moral Authorities

For centuries philosophers have been debating which source of moral values is most defensible, and as the world's population has increased along with a multiplicity of cultural and religious traditions, the need has arisen to find a stabilizing force acceptable to all. So far this force has not been discovered, at least to the satisfaction of everyone. In this section we will consider some of the major kinds of moral authorities that have put forth guidelines from which we can choose.

A Philosophical Defense of Altruism

American philosopher John Rawls (1921–2002), having thought deeply about whether altruism truly exists, agrees with Socrates that reason does not support self-interest. The way he does it is to propose that each of us pretend to be wearing a "Veil of Ignorance," which wipes out all awareness of who we are and where we came from. Starting from Square Zero, so to speak, we then list the requirements for an ideal society. That is, if you didn't *know* you were rich or would be someday or if you didn't *know* you came from a poor background, what would be on your list? Rawls lists two requirements he thinks everyone would cite:

1. Equal and maximum liberty (political, intellectual, and religious) for each person consistent with equal liberty for others.

2. Wealth and power to be distributed equally except where inequalities would work to the advantage of all and where there would be equal opportunity to achieve advantageous positions of equality.[9]

As we can see from this ingenious argument, the "Veil of Ignorance" puts everyone on an equal plane, and from this there would have to be general agreement about the just and fair society. What if you put "equal distribution of wealth" on your list and then found out you were going to be fabulously wealthy some day? You might then reconsider your choices. However, if you were honest, you would recognize that your self-interest was getting in the way of your reasoning. You would in fact be saying: "I believe in unequal distribution of wealth because I'm going to be rich." Similarly, if you discovered that you were poor and would always be so, you might change "equal distribution of wealth" to "tax the rich and give it to the poor." Rawls is not saying the reconsidered concepts are wrong. He is merely pointing out that self-interest usually colors our attitudes toward what is right or just.

The Moral Mathematics of Jeremy Bentham

Born into a well-established, conservative English family, Jeremy Bentham (1748–1832) was confirmed at the age of thirteen in the Episcopal (Church of England) faith. The ceremony required him to follow the absolute moral laws of his religion. As he matured and observed the world around him, he came to the conclusion that most people neither abided by these laws nor practiced any sort of other-directed morality. He saw humankind as a society of animals all driven by the need to gratify their basic (and often base) desires: in short, the need to serve only themselves.

On the other hand, he was unwilling to say that self-interest was wrong, though the pursuit of it might be contrary to the rigid morality taught to him as a child. Why must moral laws be so contrary to human nature? Accordingly, he became a philosopher and formulated the theory that, since self-serving pleasure was the natural condition sought by everyone, all people must have an equal chance of attaining it. He rebelled against the moral codes set forth by religion and traditional philosophy as well as those that became laws binding on an entire population. What, he asked, gave anyone the right to tell anyone else which pleasures to enjoy and which to avoid? But must there not be guidelines? Surely *everyone* could not wantonly pursue pleasure if this meant interfering with the right of others to do the same. *Unrestricted* self-interest made no sense to him.

As a philosopher he was attracted to science and mathematics, for these fields offered methods of achieving certainty. Accordingly, mathematics became the basis for a moral system that allowed self-interest to be both defended and restricted.

The greatest happiness of the greatest number is the foundation of morals and legislation.

—Jeremy Bentham

Numbers. Bentham declared that numbers were the key to moral certainty: finding a formula that would decide the right course of action in every instance. For him, the goal was a society in which the maximum number of people achieved the maximum amount of pleasure *without* impinging on the rights of others. He denied the validity of **moral absolutism**, defining the good as *the greatest good for the greatest number.*

In Bentham's system, before you decide upon an action with consequences that will affect others, you assign a plus or minus numerical value to the degree of pleasure or pain that action might cause for the most people. Let us say that, in a modern example, the question is whether to allow a giant resort complex to be built along a lakefront. So many plus points go to the builders, construction workers, and service personnel, all of whom stand to profit from the enterprise. Additional plus points are awarded to vacationers, who will surely benefit from having a place in which to relax and relieve stress. Minus points, however, come from environmentalists concerned about the inevitable pollution and the extermination of fish and waterfowl and from nearby residents who see the resort as destroying the neighborhood and bringing down the resale value of their property. The calculator (an invention Bentham would have loved) will tell the story. Plus points for those who benefit, minus points for those who don't. You do the simple arithmetic and get the moral answer.

Bentham's **moral mathematics** also adds or subtracts points based on "intensity" and "duration." In the example of the resort, we must consider the annoying sounds and air pollution of road expansion and the possibly permanent damage to wildlife. What do you think? Which side would get the most points? May points be determined strictly by the number of individuals involved? If so, the residents might outnumber the owners and the contractors. But what if the builders insist that the number of possible vacationers is almost infinite?

Results and Motives. For Bentham, measurable results tell all. The number of people benefiting is proof of moral rightness. But critics of Bentham's morality see many problems. Suppose the builder of the proposed resort has had a longstanding feud with the head of the environmental committee, a feud stemming from personal differences that have nothing to do with business or pollution. What if anger and revenge are his motives? He has proposed the entire scheme just to embarrass environmentalists in front of their supporters. The calculation yields only external results and pays no attention to motives *unless* there is the chance that a motive, once discovered, might cause pain to a lot of people, but that is unlikely to happen in this hypothetical case.

Another numerical question sidesteps motive. Is it better to give $10 to a cause because you believe it is the right thing to do or $1,000 to the same cause because you want to see your picture in the paper along with a caption praising your philanthropy? For Bentham (and probably for the fund-raisers) the larger amount would be preferable and morally approved.

What might be Bentham's mathematical calculations for a decision on abortion? Homosexuality? Abortion might be considered right or wrong depending on whether an underpopulated country needs more pregnancies carried to completion. As for homosexuality, the question would be whether it harms the general population. Would there be fewer babies born in a society that looked favorably on homosexual activity between consenting adults? Despite the fact that Bentham was essentially a political radical, he would have to approve of a ban on homosexuality if the greatest number in a given society decided that the practice would lessen the population and deprive the future of artists, philanthropists, scientists, and so on. In such a society homosexuality would be mathematically immoral, yet moral in a society that placed the highest priority on, for example, human rights.

In his famous essay satirizing the British treatment of the Irish poor, Jonathan Swift (1667–1745) almost seems to have had prophetic insight into Bentham's **utilitarianism**, which would emerge a century later. Swift launches his devastating attack on British arrogance by reducing the problem of the poor to a game of numbers in "A Modest Proposal," with the subtitle "For Preventing the Children of Poor People in Ireland from Becoming a Burden to Their Parents and Country and for Making Them Beneficial to the Public."

Adopting the persona of a country gentleman without personal knowledge of poverty, he begins by stating his concern about the number of beggars on the street, as well as mothers followed by "three, four or six children, *all in rags*." Instead of pleading for charity, Swift's narrator reverses the usual argument and takes the approach of a practical businessman, calculating the value of turning the youngest Irish children into dinner entrées for the wealthy: "I have been assured by a very knowing American of my acquaintance in London, that a young healthy child well nursed is at a year, delicious, nourishing and wholesome food, whether stewed, roasted, baked or boiled, and I make no doubt that it will equally serve in a fricassee or ragout."

The narrator then calmly computes the figures: 20,000 for breeding, only one-fourth males, more than usual, he points out, than for "other livestock." The one-year-old child "will make two dishes as an entrée entertainment for friends, and when the family dines alone the fore or hind quarter will make a reasonable dish . . . seasoned with a little pepper or salt." The consequences of the new industry, in addition to reducing the number of poor children who die from malnutrition, will be that the breeders are rid of needless expenses; taverns will have a new dish, and "a skillful cook, who understands how to please his guests will contrive to make it as expensive as they please"; marriages will increase; and mothers will be treated more tenderly as they fatten up their children. Moreover, his proposal is not based on any desire for personal profit, because he has "no children by which I can propose to get a single penny, my youngest being nine years old and my wife past child-bearing."

As can be imagined, "A Modest Proposal" aroused indignation among readers who failed to understand Swift's purpose. Some literalists took him at his word, denouncing "his savagery," not recognizing that he was creating what remains as a masterfully vicious satire on cold calculations as a solution to human issues.

Bentham believed in various definitions of the good, depending on particular circumstances. The lakeside resort, for example, might bring wealth to the town nearby, but it might also draw tourists away from another resort twenty miles away. Back to the calculator. "The greatest good for the greatest number" may have to be redefined. What happens when mathematical calculations do not agree with each other? My pleasure, in other words, is your pain—and vice versa.

Bentham decided therefore that the government would have to step in and be responsible for providing the greatest good for the greatest number. He organized a political party called the Philosophical Radicals in order to campaign for moral reform based on his mathematical system. The name was eventually changed to the Utilitarian Party, suggesting a practical approach to moral philosophy, basically democratic in that it recognized the equality of all individuals in the matter of decision making, with majority rule holding sway.

Swift might almost be said to be anticipating making fun of Bentham's moral mathematics when he attacked the shocking treatment of the Irish poor by the British. He made it seem like a game of numbers devoid of humanity.

Utilitarianism Modified: John Stuart Mill

Also designated as a Utilitarian, John Stuart Mill (1806–1873) came a half-century after Bentham. His father, James Mill, a close friend of Bentham, had assisted the philosopher in the development of his political party. James Mill was an elitist when it came to the education of his son, who was allowed to associate only with friends of whose intellectual capacities the father approved. But he was also taught a Socratic brand of rational liberalism: that is, almost unlimited freedom for those responsible enough to use it for purposes other than the gratification of selfish desires.

As Mill matured and became a philosopher and writer, he expressed approval of Bentham's views on government's responsibility to guard the rights of the private citizen, but he disagreed that majority rule is always the proper course. Bentham's mathematics had implied that decisions were quantifiable, but what about matters of taste? Followers of Mill continue to question the wisdom of the majority in all decisions. What if, for example, a proposal to erect a new museum or an opera house were put to a popular vote, and it had to compete with a new sports stadium? The "greatest number" might well opt for "low art" instead of "high art," thus depriving those with educated tastes of the pleasures that ought to be available to them. Imposing low art on everyone regardless of preference was, for Mill, as immoral as imposing absolute standards that had to apply in every situation. Mill questioned whether the rule of the majority may not in fact deprive many people of their own moral rights.

Our society's preoccupation with winners—with blockbusters, sports rankings, runs batted in, bestsellers, awards, scorekeeping of every kind—has caused regret in critics, concerned that numbers may overlook quality. Think back to the debate between the public building of a sports stadium or an opera house. A more subtle distinction has been made in a recent debate by two individuals who love opera but are divided on the question of whether the public should be asked to support it.

Mitchell Cohen is concerned about the availability of the art to the general public. If opera is not subsidized, will only the rich be able to enjoy it? "One consideration should surely be inequality in cultural opportunities . . . no important domain of culture should be accessible chiefly to social elites. So I offer a social democratic precept: in access to culture, no citizen should be more equal than others. Public funding for arts (opera among them) ought to help make varied forms of culture available in a fair manner to all citizens."[10]

Bruce Ackerman, on the other hand, argues that if society is neutral and fair, without preference for one form of art over another, and if we truly respect each other, we would recognize that "the Met merely provides another form of entertainment no different from skateboarding or hula-hooping. I myself do not hold this view—but for those who do, the case for selective subsidy vanishes immediately: why subsidize opera, and not skateboarding, if they are simply rival entertainments struggling for the consumer dollar?"[11]

Mill recognized that government was needed to balance irresponsibility on the part of the general population. But this did not give government the right to legislate morality for the responsible few. In the matter of the opera house, the equitable course would be for a committee of acknowledged patrons of the arts to decide that the aesthetic needs of society were more important than a sports stadium, and this committee would have the backing of the local government. In defending the rights of enlightened citizens, Mill proved to be more radical than Bentham.

We can never be sure that the opinion we are endeavoring to stifle is a false opinion, and if we were sure, stifling it would be an evil still.

—John Stuart Mill

One of Mill's most famous essays, *The Tyranny of the Majority*, maintains that letting the majority rule in all decisions is just as bad as the autocratic rule of monarchs in previous centuries. Mill writes that his objective "is to assert one very simple principle" regarding how societies may deal with an individual, "whether the means used be physical force in the form of legal penalties, or the moral coercion of public opinion." According to Mill, "the sole end for which mankind are warranted, individually or collectively, in interfering with the liberty of action of any of their number, is self-protection. That is, the only purpose for which power can be rightfully exercised over any member of a civilized community, against his will, is to prevent harm to others. His own good, either physical or moral, is not a sufficient warrant."[12] Mill's writings greatly influenced American democratic thought, especially that of Thomas Jefferson.

The English artist William Hogarth (1697–1764), famous for paintings and engravings that poke fun at all levels of English society, gave us *The Enraged Musician*, showing both sides of the conflict. The musician in question sits by his open window, his work interrupted by an extremely noisy crowd. What if the musician were to call the police on the grounds that his right to work in privacy has been violated? What if the case ended up in court? Would the judge rule that the crowd has a right to cavort as it pleases as long as no one is being physically

What is morality in any given time or place? It is what the majority then and there happen to like, and immorality is what they dislike.
—**Alfred North Whitehead**

Hogarth was probably the leading satiric artist of the eighteenth century in England. The question here is: what is Hogarth poking fun at?

Source: William Hogarth, *The Enraged Musician* (1741). Credit: Max A. Polster Archive.

harmed? Or that the musician is right in objecting to the crowd on the grounds that his work is more important than their fun? What do you think Mill would say?

A contemporary political scientist, Hans J. Morgenthau (1904–1980), echoes Mill's brand of liberalism: "Civilized man shares with the barbarian the faculty of making moral judgments, but excels over him in knowing why he makes them. He knows—as Socrates, the Greek tragedians . . . the Biblical prophets and the great moralists and tragedians of all ages know—what is meant by the sanctity of the moral law. The moral law is not made for the convenience of man, rather it is an indispensable precondition for his civilized existence."[13] The key word for both Mill and Morgenthau is "civilized." Both philosophers champion the maximum freedom for all persons of intelligence, good will, and objectivity, but they recognize that reason sometimes imposes limitations.

The Moral Imperative of Immanuel Kant

Born in East Prussia and a resident there for most of his life, the German philosopher Immanuel Kant (1724–1804) was, like Bentham, impressed with the certainties that science was able to achieve. As a member of the faculty at the University of Königsberg, he read insatiably in a number of fields, becoming so adept that he was given courses to teach in mathematics, physics, anthropology, logic, metaphysics, and ethics. This impressive background made Kant feel comfortable with both science and philosophy, and he would merge the two into one of the most influential systems of thought ever devised.

The various branches of his philosophy are like the spokes of a wheel, all radiating from a central belief, adopted from science, that truth is arrived at through experience. He differed, however, from kindred philosophers who took the extreme position that experience is strictly what our senses tell us.

Kant's view is that the input of the senses does not constitute experience until it is *interpreted* by our inborn rational capacity. He believes that we are born with mental **categories** into which sensory data are filed, much as a postal worker takes an armful of random mail and flips each letter into an appropriate box. We know, for example, that the chair is "next to" the table because we understand "nextness." If we did not, the spatial relationship would be meaningless. In such a case, if someone asked us to go fetch the chair next to the table, we would return a blank stare.

Kant then turns his attention to moral concerns. His theory is that the sense of right and wrong is also inborn. True, we come to understand "yes" or "no" from our parents, but no learning can take place unless we are able to attach approval and disapproval, first to specific actions, then to the abstract concepts of right and wrong. For Kant, the average person has no trouble reaching these abstractions because a moral sense, again inborn, gradually unfolds in the same way that a bud gradually opens into a flower. He calls this inborn faculty the **moral imperative**, or *sense of ought*: an intuitive classification of actions and choices as morally acceptable or unacceptable. Experience teaches us which specific actions are right and which are not, but "rightness" and "wrongness," like "nextness," cannot be taught.

Take, for example, the principle of honesty. Without a universal recognition of what it means, we could never ask "What time is it?" We rely on the honesty of the answer, or we would not have asked the question. People depend on a promise to keep an appointment or return borrowed money. If the promise is not kept, we

Morality is not properly the doctrine of how we make ourselves happy, but how we make ourselves worthy of happiness.

—**Immanuel Kant**

say "That person has not been honest." If the breaker of the promise is not mentally disturbed, he or she would also recognize that the principle of honesty has been violated.

For Kant, slavery, which he was firmly against, was a particularly illuminating example. Kant argued that, regardless of the number of people who held slaves and justified their actions for a variety of reasons, even including religious ones, the fact remained that slavery was morally wrong. That slave-holders had to search around for justifications clearly indicated a secret knowledge that what they were doing was reprehensible. Socrates had said, "To know the good is to do the good." Kant did not believe this was necessarily true. Each of us is born with a knowledge of the good, whether or not we disregard it later. He admitted that self-interest all too often suppressed the moral imperative.

Kantian ethical philosophy has given us a powerful way of knowing in advance whether a proposed action is morally right. It does not depend upon consequences, and it is not relative to varying circumstances. It is a very simple procedure. All it demands is that we hesitate before we act and ask ourselves one vital question: *Would it be all right for everyone else to do this?*

A person temporarily poor sees a drunken man weaving his way down the street. A wallet falls out of the man's pocket without his noticing. He continues on his way. The poor observer immediately picks it up and sees that it contains a considerable amount of money. The drunken man cannot walk very fast, so it would be a simple matter to catch up with him and return the wallet.

The finder of the wallet is now like Glaucon's shepherd, invisible as far as the owner of the wallet is concerned. The temptation is great to wait until the owner is well out of sight and then to disappear with the money. Why not? Who would return the money under those circumstances? Suppose now that the finder of the wallet is convinced that the money is compensation for unjust treatment, and that people deserve what they can get. It's a dog-eat-dog world, is it not?

If faced with this example, Kant would surely not assume that this person, knowing deep down inside that keeping the wallet is wrong, would shout for the owner to stop so it could be returned. Keeping the wallet would in fact be making a definite choice between two options, deliberately choosing the immoral one.

But, you ask, how can we be certain that it *is* immoral? Just because the person has been taught that keeping what belongs to someone else is the same as stealing? Suppose the finder does not accept this view and believes that the world is really amoral, and so the wallet is not returned. And so no one is the wiser for it.

The story, however, does not end there. Having decided to use some of the money for a sumptuous dinner and later a comfortable hotel room, the finder is walking down a deserted street and is accosted by a thief who, brandishing a weapon, demands and gets money. The thief disappears, and the new victim is left once more homeless and hungry. Would the thought arise: "It serves you right"?

In Kantian terms, the latter response is indeed possible, but not very probable. The chances are good that the finder of the wallet would be exceedingly angry about the theft. Translating the anger into philosophical terms, the principle would be: *It was all right for me to keep the wallet, but wrong for the thief to steal it from me.*

If we agree that keeping the wallet is stealing, then what is the difference between the first and second thefts? The answer: NONE. Kant tells us that, before we commit any act, we should stop to ask ourselves: *Can we will that this act be universally acceptable?* Anyone who took the wallet but cannot do this, is actually saying: *It's all right for a particular person to steal, but not for everyone.* Such reasoning immediately strikes us as absurd. Accepting it is tantamount to saying that one person is the sole exception to a universal moral law. Stealing is universally wrong, except when I do it.

Kant's theory is ingenious, we must admit. In all probability none of us will lead morally perfect lives, but that does not excuse us from differentiating between the right and the wrong. It is a strong argument against a moral code that begins and ends with the self. His logic is impeccable, but one could only wish that every member of society were endowed with Kantian rationality.

Religion and Morality

Kant's parents were deeply religious, teaching that moral laws were set forth by God and could not be altered. As Kant grew older and learned about new theories in science and philosophy, he used reason rather than religion to justify absolute moral principles. For many however, religion itself remains a strong moral force. Though some of us may have subsequently entertained moral alternatives, we probably hear the whispers of those early teachings whenever we are faced with a moral evaluation of an action.

Remember, "action," either taken or avoided, is at the heart of significant moral choice, sometimes at odds with religious belief. A number of years ago the parents of an infant born with an abnormal heart were faced with an agonizing choice when a physician at Johns Hopkins University offered to perform the world's first heart surgery. Admittedly experimental at the time, the operation would, if successful, rescue a "blue baby" from respiratory problems that would surely result in imminent death. The parents had a short time to consider whether to allow the surgery. One argument against the surgery was the possible interpretation that "God's will" had created the baby with the disability and that it was meant to be. The doctor countered with another interpretation: it was "God's will" that he had been experimenting in the laboratory on a technique that would bypass the damaged artery and save the child. The parents gave their consent, the baby survived, and a medical breakthrough was hailed.

If the parents had followed a religion that strictly forbade tampering with God's will, their decision in favor of the doctor would have been against their moral code. Would their loved ones—the baby's siblings, aunts, and uncles—have been united in denouncing the successful surgery as immoral? Or would all of them ultimately decide that it was all right to question God's will under certain circumstances? Which ones? Does the list go on indefinitely? What then happens to the concept of God's will? Does it become meaningless?

Moral choices based on religious laws frequently clash with other options. Throughout history, religion has strongly influenced concepts not only of honoring the family but almost every kind of acceptable human behavior, often with harsh treatment for offenders.

The major world religions—Hinduism, Judaism, Christianity, and Islam—provide moral orientation for most of the world's population. They differ in many respects, and wars are still being fought in the name of some religious teachings.

Ritual is the basis of some of the conflict: dietary restrictions, clothing, methods and frequency of prayer, who belongs within a particular sect and who is outside it (and what to name the baby). Some conflict is theological: the true path to salvation, which leader warrants being called "divine," even the nature of deity itself. These concerns constitute traditions—often one opposed to another. They may include daily activities based on rankings within the family and what constitutes an appropriate role according to age and gender.

All of the major religions, however, show great similarities in their moral precepts. They share the belief that the world was not created for human beings to do with as they please. They all believe that human beings owe an obligation to either a personal God or to the moral order governing the universe. They believe no one is free to behave irresponsibly toward themselves (since *they* did not create themselves), toward others, or toward the earth (which they did not create either).

Basic moral codes for Western societies derive, wholly or partly, from the precepts expressed in the Ten Commandments, recorded in the Hebrew Bible as having been delivered by God to Moses after leading his people out of slavery in Egypt. These commandments

Good laws lead to the making of better ones; bad ones bring about worse.

—**Jean-Jacques Rousseau**

1. require people to recognize only one God.
2. forbid the making and worshiping of any graven image.
3. forbid the taking of the Lord's name in vain.
4. require that the Sabbath be kept holy.
5. require that people honor their parents.
6. forbid killing.
7. forbid adultery.
8. forbid stealing.
9. forbid the bearing of false witness against another.
10. forbid the coveting of another's wife and of another's goods.

Most of the commandments have parallels all over the world. Rules against killing and stealing are part of a universal criminal code. It is taken for granted that everyone tells lies for one reason or another, but it is hard to imagine any society in which lying is not condemned. Rules against adultery are either approved by the community or are legally enforced—sometimes with the death penalty.

The first four commandments will not be found in law books, although some communities have *blue laws* requiring businesses to be closed on Sunday, or at least preventing the sale of liquor on the morning when people are expected to worship. Nor are there universal rules for how to honor one's parents.

From its beginning, Hebrew moral law served to remind the powerful they were not exempt from obeying God's commands. Biblical prophets were not afraid to confront sinners no matter how exalted their rank, as when Nathan denounced King David for doing away with the husband of Bathsheba, whom David wished to marry. Biblical scholar Huston Smith describes the democratizing effect of the Ten Commandments:

> *Social as well as individual transgressions were denounced by the prophets. The prerequisite of political stability is social justice . . . Stated theologically the point reads: God has high standards. Divinity will not put up forever with exploitation, corruption, and mediocrity . . . One thing is common to all [the prophets]: the conviction that*

every human being, simply by virtue of his or her humanity, is a child of God and therefore in possession of rights that even kings must respect.[14]

Hebrew moral law is concerned primarily with actions based on principles. It places limitations, for example, on what an injured party may demand for revenge. "An eye for an eye and a tooth for a tooth" prevents restitution from being more than what was lost in the original crime. The Sermon on the Mount tells us: "Ye have heard that it hath been said, an eye for an eye and a tooth for a tooth: But I say unto you, That ye resist not evil: but whosoever shall smite thee on thy right cheek, turn to him the other also" (Matthew 5:38–39).

The commandment to turn the other cheek was already foreshadowed in the Buddhist moral treatise *Dhammapada*: " 'He abused me, he beat me, he defeated me, he robbed me'—in those who harbor such thoughts hatred will never cease. For hatred does not cease by hatred at any time; hatred ceases by love—this is an old rule."[15]

In general, Islam requires its followers to observe the biblical laws, for Mohammed declared that both Moses and Jesus were true prophets (see Chapter 10). He stressed especially the doctrines of brotherhood and placing the interests of others before one's own. But he also warned enemies of God not to attack or persecute the devout.

Punishment for disobedience to scriptural laws varies from religion to religion, as do promised rewards for leading a virtuous existence. Hebrew morality focuses on family and community. Disobedience can result in ostracism. Leading an exemplary life brings inner peace as well as good repute in the community. After death, the good person lives on in the happy memories of friends and family or, for some believers, in the world to come.

Islam fosters the belief that after death the virtuous children of Allah will be with him in paradise, a sentiment echoed in Christianity. Christian concepts of heaven for the blessed and hell for the damned evolved slowly. The Christian Bible's Gospel of Luke reports the dialogue between Jesus and one of the thieves who were also being crucified. The thief refers to the "kingdom" to which Jesus will go after death: "And he said unto Jesus, Lord, remember me when thou comest into thy kingdom. And Jesus said unto him, Verily I say unto thee, Today shalt thou be with me in paradise" (Luke 23:42–43).

"Paradise" is variously interpreted. Does it mean a state of freedom from pain, similar to the Hindu *moksha* and the Buddhist *nirvana*? The promise that the thief would be "with" Jesus, however, may indicate that the reference is to continuing life in a definite *place*. Both Christians and Muslims for the most part believe in an afterlife.

As Christianity developed and spread, the promise of joy for the virtuous in heaven and eternal torment in hell for the damned became increasingly ingrained in religious minds. The vivid images of heaven and hell in *The Divine Comedy* by Italian poet Dante Alighieri (1265–1321) have strongly influenced how many think of rewards and punishment after death. (The term *comedy* is used in the sense of "not tragic"; the work ends on a note of joy when the poet finally sees God.)

Dante pictures hell or the Inferno as a deep pit in which sinners endure degrees of endless pain, depending on the gravity of the offense. Punishment takes

The vivid images of heaven and hell in Dante's Divine Comedy *have strongly influenced how many think of rewards and punishments after death.*

place on seven separate circles, not all of which are fiery. Though in the popular mind hell is associated with flames, in actuality the lowest circle of hell, home of Satan—the worst offender of all—is described by Dante as a lake of thick ice, representing a total lack of feeling and a total absence of love.

Purgatory is a mountain on which live those guilty of less grievous sins who will eventually ascend to paradise, the abode of God, the angels, and the souls of the righteous. Paradise consists of nine circles of heaven arranged in a hierarchy of blessedness—from ordinary good people to martyrs and saints. The abode of God is in a tenth heaven (10 being considered a perfect number), only briefly glimpsed by the poet, who is unable to describe in detail his mystic vision.

Naturally enough, the drama of sin, punishment, and redemption has inspired writers, artists, and philosophers for centuries. The thought of hell's torments has incited as much anger as fear and given rise to the age-old question of why humankind must be punished for sins that were predestined. In addition, the sinner has proved to be a more durable figure for writers than the virtuous person, even as in popular entertainment in film and television the characters who are bad tend to be more interesting than the characters who are good.

The classic example of moral ambiguity is the treatment of Lucifer in John Milton's epic poem *Paradise Lost* (1667). Milton declares at the outset that his purpose in writing the poem is to "justify the ways of God to men." Like Hawthorne after him, he was raised in the strict Puritan faith, which required a belief in predestination. The three main characters are Adam, Eve, and Lucifer. We learn that, before creation, Lucifer had been one of the angels closest in attendance to God, that he was jealous of God's power and organized an unsuccessful rebellion. He and his cohorts were banished from heaven and allowed to live in a dark palace called Pandemonium. There Lucifer becomes a powerful ruler, exulting in his authority and ostensibly embodying many admirable traits of the defiant individualist. Shaking his fist toward heaven, he cries out that he "would rather reign in Hell than serve in Heaven." Scholars and historians of the humanities have long debated the issue of whether Lucifer is really the hero of the poem.

The argument that Milton intended Lucifer to be despicable has not convinced everyone, even though, as the serpent in the garden, he eventually loses his heroic qualities. Nor is everyone convinced that the poet entirely makes his point when he tells us that God allowed Lucifer free access to human beings in order to tempt them. In the poem, God says he wants no more rebellion in heaven and so creates the race of mortals, capable of either sinning or choosing virtue. In this way only the good would be with God. Milton describes the fall of humankind as "fortunate," for the disobeying of divine law required the sacrifice of Jesus. Without sin, in other words, the path to redemption would never have been revealed.

The morality set forth by religion is exceedingly complex, open to much question, yet still a powerful force that helps us to understand many of the agonizing problems in the world today.

The Morality of Work

In the Western world, most of us are taught religious moral codes as we grow up; when we go to work for a living, we come under the influence of still other kinds of rules. By the time we leave school—or even before we do—we have learned the importance of work. Relatives ask, "What are you going to be when you grow up?" Before we know it, we *have* grown up to face the second question asked at introductions: "What do you do?" With rare exceptions, we tend to be defined according to the answer. Thus "good" and "bad" also have connotations of important versus unimportant jobs.

Western society accords honor to some and amusement toward other kinds of work, and scorn for no work. One of the most poignant reminders of work's fierce hold on us is contained in this passage from a 1987 novel, *Of Love and Shadows*, by Chilean author Isabel Allende (b. 1942): "He remembered his father's lesson: work as a source of pride. Idleness was foreign to the family. In the Leal household, holidays and even vacations were spent in some worthwhile undertaking. The family had had its difficult moments, but they had never dreamed of accepting charity, even from those who had previously helped."[16]

The viewpoint is that of Javier, a biologist who lost his job because of his political views and is trying to find any kind of work for fear of being disgraced. But the authorities block his efforts. Hours of waiting and frequent rejections result in humiliation and sleeplessness.

> *Without a job, he gradually lost his identity. He would have accepted any offers, however mean the pay, because he desperately needed to feel useful. As a man without employment, he was an outsider, anonymous, ignored by all because he was no longer productive, and that was the measure of a man in the world he lived in . . . The day his youngest son put on the kitchen table the few coins he had earned walking rich men's dogs, Javier cringed like a cornered animal. Since that moment he never looked anyone in the eyes; he sank into total despair.*[17]

The despair led to suicide.

The workplace is for many people the means to the good life. As they describe their work, people reveal cherished values, which also become the basis for making decisions. In his book *Working* (1974), Studs Terkel (b. 1912) includes interviews with a variety of workers. The driver of a city garbage truck observes, "It's not like years ago, where people used everything. They're not too economy-wise today. They'll throw anything away." He speaks with approval of people who take care of their property and disapproval of those who throw garbage out the window. He doesn't approve of rules and the "spotters" who enforce them:

> *They'll turn you in for stopping for coffee. I can't see that. If you have a coffee break in the alley it's just using a little psychology. You'll get more out of them. But if you're watched continually, you're gonna lay down . . ." He is concerned with public disregard for his job, with jokes like "How's business, picking up?" and he knows, "My kids would just love to see me doing something else. I tell 'em, 'Honey, this is a good job. There's nothing to be ashamed of. We're not stealin' the money. You have everything you need.' "*[18]

A professional hockey player describes for Terkel the thrill of being on the ice when an audience of 20,000 gave the team an ovation, and the disappointment of being fired at age twenty-two. He describes how his teammates respond to injury:

> *"If you get hurt, the other players switch off. Nobody's sympathetic. When you get hurt, they don't look at you, even players on your own*

A work life that denies our individuality, our creativity, our moral and aesthetic sensibility is one that denies our dignity as human beings.

—**Jerome M. Egal**

*team. The curtain comes down 'cause it could have been me. . . . You
don't want to think too much about it." He knows that to the team
owners "You're a piece of property" and cynically observes that the
team doctor says he is ready to play even though his shoulder has not
yet healed. When the shoulder rips during play, the owner "shrugs his
shoulders, walks away. He doesn't really hate me. He's impersonal."*[19]

Yet the owners have not acted immorally according to the rules of that particular workplace.

All of the people interviewed for Terkel's book envision an ideal world of friendship, trust, and security—qualities associated with altruism. In an altruistic world, Isabel Allende's Javier would not be denied employment because of his politics; the sanitation truck driver would be credited with good judgment about when to stop for a break; hockey club owners would indicate genuine sympathy for the injuries of their players.

Firm believers in the morality of self-interest argue that economics is at the heart of all speculation about work. When unemployment is low, people are needed and are treated better because the law of supply and demand rules here as it does everywhere else. Others who look beyond self-interest would claim that respect, creativity, and idealism are not isolated examples but that they can be found in places never dreamed of by the realists—even in the workplace. Believers in altruism conceive of workers who take pride in doing the best possible job and in helping their fellow employees to do *their* best.

Be forewarned. Just as virtuous people are not always the most interesting to the makers of the humanities, so too people who love their jobs are usually not elevated to the status of heroes. In fiction and in film, a widespread assumption is that work is one thing and true freedom quite another. One of the themes in John Steinbeck's *The Grapes of Wrath* is the tragic separation of workers from the products of their labor. In following the misfortunes of the Joad family after they are dispossessed of their farm during the Great Depression, Steinbeck points out that, as long as they worked their land, they were content and had a sense of dignity. They lived the good life, being identified with their work, in the best sense. They were what they did. After they are forced to pack up their old truck and head into parts unknown in search of jobs, life holds no joy for them. They have lost their dignity.

Menial, routine, assembly-line jobs that require little or no thought are the subject of much literature, as well as visual art. *Bus Riders*, a 1962 sculpture by the American artist George Segal, shown here, clearly depicts a group of people who have become dehumanized by their work.

Much creative expression focuses on the tragedy of workers' loss of identity. What effect do you think the artist wanted this sculpture to have on viewers?

Source: George Segal, *Bus Riders* (1962). Credit: VAGA, New York, NY, Hirshorn Museum and Sculpture Garden.

Work is essential for most of us, and we defeat ourselves by starting out with the attitude that work is an unfortunate necessity that keeps us from what we *really* would like to do. The rules of any given workplace are external authorities in that they cannot accommodate the self-interest of each employee. Employee morale may improve if the Suggestion Box is more than a prop; nevertheless, a company can't function efficiently by allowing its workers unlimited freedom of when to show up, when to leave, and what needs to be accomplished each day. What would happen if someone, asked by a superior when a certain task would be completed, sat back in a chair, feet up on the desk, and said, "Whenever I feel like doing it"?

The moral authority in the workplace can be two-sided. Sometimes employees find company demands unreasonable. Differences can be resolved through negotiation, but often not until a lengthy strike has brought business to a halt. In rare cases they are never resolved, and the company has to shut down.

Moral Relativism

Morality consists of suspecting other people of not being legally married.
—**George Bernard Shaw**

If the opposite of "relative" is "absolute," it is easy to understand the appeal of the former, a term that promises flexibility and tolerance versus the latter, which connotes uncompromising rigidity. Moral relativists point out that prison, torture, war, and genocide have been inflicted by those certain there is only one truth and they know what it is. The temptation is great to reject all theories that place unwavering restrictions on us. According to **moral relativism**, beliefs about right and wrong have no universal meaning. It is therefore possible to make (and to hear) remarks like these:

> "Well, who has the right to tell another person what to do? A lot of trouble has been caused by people who were sure they were right."
>
> "It all depends . . ." (on the situation, the culture, the time a choice was made).
>
> "As long as they're happy" (a criterion that ignores those who aren't).

Many of the moral philosophers build a case for absolutism. After all, Socrates believed right and wrong were the same for all people, Kant believed in an inborn moral imperative, and Bentham said the right thing is that which provides the greatest good for the greatest number. Moral relativism, on the other hand, is the belief that right and wrong must be defined within a given context.

That context is not limited to the workplace. It can also be the culture, the community, the family, and religion. Each of these areas governing human behavior may impose absolute moral standards, but the standards are not always harmonious with each other. Bitter clashes result when two absolutes refuse to give ground: religious laws and those of the community, for example.

The Global View

A major factor in the rise of moral relativism is the globalized concept of human society. New communication technologies have made it easy for the world's various cultures to be in contact with each other, and exposure to the customs and values of different cultures has inevitably widened the issue of morality. Many cultural observers now argue that the appeal to absolute reason by Socrates and Kant, among others, was narrowly Western. It isn't that other cultures are thought of as not being rational; rather, it is the recognition that, while the capacity to reason may be universally shared, ideas and values arrived at rationally are influenced by culture, traditions, and circumstances.

Still, there are those who argue that aboriginal natives, for example, would be better off learning to succeed in the dominant culture, learning its ways and following its rules of behavior. The relativist, on the other hand, likes to point out that the imposition of dominant-culture values has caused breakdowns in both individuals and families. James Michener's 1959 novel *Hawaii* offered a fictionalized account of what happened when missionaries from the United States told native Polynesians their sexual morality was unacceptable to civilized people. In particular, they condemned the practice of marriage between siblings, assuring those who were "guilty" that they were damned. One "guilty" man felt such shame that he took his own life.

In 2000, a Cree Indian argued against what she considered cultural abuse in a church-run boarding school supported by the Canadian government. "The schools took us from our parents and taught us that the ways of our people were shameful and wrong," she said. She argued that efforts to make natives assimilate into "white" Canada were wrong, that being forced to learn English, adopt Christianity, and acquire "suitable" job skills led to "heavy drinking and domestic disharmony" and to the loss of her native tongue and traditions.[20]

Everybody always did our thinking for us.

—Winifred Jourdain

The problem offers no easy solutions. Some principles, taught in early childhood, are so deeply ingrained that they motivate actions throughout life and conflict with those of a different society. When an American living in Japan once held a birthday party for his five-year-old son, many of the invited children were Japanese. During a game of musical chairs, the father noticed that, when the music stopped, one of the Japanese children stood next to the chair but did not sit down.

> So Gregory scrambled into her seat, and Chitose-chan beamed proudly at her own good manners. Then I walked over and told her that she had just lost the game and would have to sit out. She gazed up at me, her luminous eyes full of shocked disbelief, looking like Bambi might after a discussion of venison burgers. "You mean I lose because I'm polite?" Chitose-chan's eyes asked. "You mean the point of the game is to be rude? Well now that I think of it, I guess that is the point. American kids are taught to be winners, to seize their opportunities and maybe the next kid's as well. Japanese children are taught to be good citizens, to be team players, to obey rules, to be a mosaic tile in some larger design.[21]

Sui Sin Far (1867–1914), a writer born to a Chinese mother and an English father, offers further evidence of how values are culturally created and how deep cultural misunderstandings are inevitable. In her story "The Americanizing of Pau Tsu," the difference in cultural practices ultimately leads to confusion in principles of etiquette, which are, after all, a form of morality—and relative at that, though not always acknowledged as such. The author describes how an eighteen-year-old Chinese bride is startled by the many new customs in her American husband's country.

> *It puzzled her to be always seeing this and hearing that—sights and sounds which as yet had no meaning for her. Why was it necessary to receive visitors nearly every evening?—visitors who could neither understand nor make themselves understood, by her, for all their curious smiles and stares . . . And why, oh! Why should she be constrained to eat her food with clumsy murderous looking American implements instead of with her own elegant and easily manipulated ivory chopsticks?*[22]

The young woman is particularly embarrassed when she becomes ill and is examined by an American doctor, a male, for she believes it is wrong for a man to look upon the flesh of any woman who is not his wife.

In a real-life incident, also involving the moral gulf between cultures, the mother of an Asian visual arts student in an American school of the arts refused to give permission for her son to attend a life-drawing class in which nude female models would pose. The department head later reported that he attempted to "reason" with the woman, who obstinately held her ground, insisting that her son was being unfairly forced to violate a strict moral principle. Given the ultimatum that her son take the required course or leave the school, she withdrew the boy and enrolled him the next day in a neighborhood school that offered no arts courses.

Another source of dispute has been school bans on students wearing head coverings that indicate religious affiliation. In order to have a cohesive student body, school officials in some European countries have forbidden the distinctive head coverings of certain religions but have often not been consistent about other religious symbols, such as those worn as jewelry. Immigrant students who abandon public school secularism for religious school may be encouraged to accept further separation from the dominant culture of the host country through a different set of heroes, villains, and causes of historical events. Objectivity is indeed an elusive goal.

Cultural traditions and generational differences uneasily exist side by side: an "assimilated" child impatient with a grandparent's old-world cooking; young people unwilling to accept traditional matchmaking; a religious teenager clashing with atheistic parents. Can the relativist position solve all conflicts by claiming that universal right and wrong are always outmoded concepts? Or are some issues simply a matter of taste, similar to one's preference for an ice cream flavor, while other things, like genocide, are to be considered absolutely wrong? Yet even genocide will be defended by those who commit atrocities in retaliation for past wrongs.

Almost every part of the world is now available to travelers and Internet users, and it seems inevitable that many will reject the idea that morality is the exclusive property of one group and all other traditions should be changed. An offshoot of cultural relativism, however, is that what used to be respect for the ideas of others can turn into the belief that no absolute values can ever exist. Or that there are no truths that can be accepted the world over. In our own lives, we can see how we view events differently as we age. What frightens children seems benign to adults, just as scandals seem harmless at a later date. If a good many moral viewpoints inevitably change, must we abandon the idea of universal, unchanging values?

Travelers may be delighted to observe cultures different from those in their home country. Seeing something truly different makes one more story to tell when they return home, whether it is the taste of an unfamiliar food or an exuberant wedding dance. One may be charmed by unexpected hospitality or by a gift offered by a merchant at a bazaar or by the appearance of a man accompanied by more than one wife. One is less charmed by the appearance of brutality and abuse, no matter how traditional the custom is said to be. Child prostitution, genital mutilation, and abandonment of unwanted family members are among the practices that horrify observers suddenly unwilling to be moral relativists.

An example of moral relativism in action is found in a prize-winning film from Iceland, *The Seagull's Laughter* (2003). The main character is Agga, a teenager and amateur sleuth who suspects that an abused wife has murdered her brutal husband, assisted in the crime by family members. Agga goes to the police and tells them about all of the clues she has gathered to confirm her suspicions. They agree to investigate. Agga then has a change of heart, realizing what would happen after the arrest. Money would be lost, a disabled family member would be institutionalized, there would be hardship all around. She returns to the police department and announces that she has made up the stories. In her case, the end—peace and prosperity in a poor household—justifies the means: letting the murderer get away with her crime. Bentham's judgment of "the greatest good for the greatest number" might also be applied here. The absolutist position is that justice must be served by punishment of all murderers regardless of extenuating circumstances.

Feminist Morality

Moral relativism of a different form has arisen during the past three decades from philosophers and cultural historians all over the world who point out that cultural, religious, and literary traditions have been dominated by the male viewpoint. In some cases, this coincides with the female viewpoint, but all too often it does not. The discrepancy, they say, is especially obvious in the formulation and application of moral principles—a consequence of the low esteem in which women have been held in many areas of the world. Restrictions on dress, education, travel, and even expression of personal feelings continue to exist in some areas, though old rules are gradually eroding in many cultures.

Traditional philosophical debates over morality seem unsatisfactory to this relatively new branch of philosophy that has adopted the label *feminist ethics*, emphasizing the special circumstances surrounding half the world's population. The contemporary philosopher Rosemarie Tong (b. 1947) takes issue with schools of ethics that seek absolute moral principles. She is particularly critical of Kant's belief that we can test the validity (or lack of it) of a moral decision by deciding whether it would be right for everyone. Tong's contention is that, for Kant as well as many other male philosophers, "universal" means *men only*. Feminist ethics maintains that universal and impartial standards are difficult to apply when gender differences are ignored. Women's ways of feeling and women's needs may alter the moral nature of given circumstances.

Women have served all these centuries as looking glasses possessing the magic and delicious power of reflecting the figure of man as twice its natural size.

—Virginia Woolf

Philosophers like Tong ask that we consider all relevant circumstances—especially the relevance of gender needs and differences—before we make a moral decision or evaluate somebody else's moral decision. A target of feminist criticism is the popular six-step approach to morality devised by developmental psychologist Lawrence Kohlberg, according to which the enlightened human being ascends from the most basic guidelines for behavior to the universal perspective found in Socrates and Kant:

Stage One: strict reward and punishment.

Stage Two: reciprocity (you hurt me, I hurt you).

Stage Three: the need for approval.

Stage Four: duty for the sake of social order.

Stage Five: the desire to avoid harming others.

Stage Six: universal ethics binding on all.

To test his theory, Kohlberg asked people how they would judge the case of a man, desperately in need of pain medicine for his terminally ill wife, who was being overcharged by the only pharmacist in his remote town. Should the man steal the medicine? If he did, would he be guilty of an immoral act or a justifiable one? If he did not steal the medicine, on the grounds that he could not will that stealing is universally acceptable, would he have reached Stage Six? One man answered that stealing would be morally permissible because the wife's need was greater than the pharmacist's (pure Bentham). A woman concentrated on the relationship between the man and the wife. She was concerned that, if the man were sent to jail, the wife's condition would worsen; hence, the man should somehow find the money and pay the exorbitant price. There is some Bentham in this view, but Rosemarie Tong points out that, because the woman questioned did not indicate how the husband could "somehow" find the money, she would not have fit into one of Kohlberg's levels. Yet her answer *was* a moral one, according to Tong, because feelings (fear that the wife's illness would take a turn for the worse) *are* crucial in moral evaluations.

Feminist philosophers are also suspicious of the absolutes in ethics derived from major religions on the grounds that they were set down by men without consulting women. To the objection that God communicated only to men, Elisabeth Schussler Fiorenza of the Harvard Divinity School faculty asks whether Jesus, who delivered the Beatitudes to a vast audience of oppressed people, would have been likely to ignore women, all of whom, the world over, occupied second-rate status.

She also finds that the "figure of Wisdom in the Hebrew Bible is almost always cast in female form or invoked with female imagery, and in the Gospels, Jesus too speaks with Wisdom's voice" In addition, "After the crucifixion, the women of Galilee helped hold together the Jesus movement in Jerusalem as other disciples fled. Women were the first to discover the empty tomb and the first to experience a vision of the resurrected Jesus."[23]

Paul, a Hebrew originally named Saul, who represents a bridge between Judaism and Christianity, wrote in one of his epistles that there "is neither Jew nor Greek, there is neither slave nor free, there is neither male nor female, for you are all one." Schussler Fiorenza contends that, following in Paul's footsteps, women were full participants in, and often leaders of, the early missionary movement.

Yet somehow women have been blamed for all the world's ills, have been stoned for immorality (despite the admonition of Christ, who prevented the crowd from stoning a prostitute), and have traditionally been told to "love, honor, and obey" their husbands, while men have been allowed plenty of license in their own conduct as long as they were caretakers of their wives. Women have traditionally found themselves forced into the worst types of employment. During the Industrial Revolution in America, poor women, often newly arrived immigrants who spoke very little English, were hardly recognized as human beings. Desperate for any job they could find, they were packed into sweatshops, toiling long hours over sewing machines or ironing boards in rooms without windows or any safety devices. Disasters like that at the Triangle Shirt Company—one of the most notorious sweatshops, which burst into flames trapping over 500 employees, most of them women and underage children—did lead to some improvement in working conditions but did little to improve the status of working-class women. As late as 1963, the United States had to pass a law to require that women and men be paid equally for doing the same job. Before the law passed (and unfortunately still in the minds of many employers), it was assumed that women should naturally make less money than men did—after all, they were *just* women. And women still fight to break through the "glass ceiling," which prevents them from attaining high-level positions in many sectors of the economy.

Feminine ethicists of today believe serious injustices and inequalities persist. Advances in medical technology now allow for gender selection in fetuses. Protests have been raised that, if prospective parents can control the sex of their children, preference will be overwhelmingly in favor of boys, especially in those areas where males are needed for their physical prowess. The preferred sex is also apt to be male in countries where, as Matt Ridley, points out, "a rich son has a chance of having more than one wife or more than one sex partner, and a polygamous son can have more offspring than any daughter," and that "even in monogamous societies sons inherit wealth and status, but daughters leave home when they marry."[24]

Feminine ethicists worry that, if the dominant population is male, the plight of women can only worsen, and right and wrong will be subject more than ever to male definition. If Bentham's numbers are used to decide moral issues, will they be determined by "male math"? If morality is based on duty, may *duty* be defined as "obligation to abide by male standards"?

Answers to these complex questions do not come easily. Yet feminist moral philosophy has already enhanced awareness that women's thoughts and feelings have been largely ignored over the centuries. Perhaps that philosophy will effect a change in universal moral standards.

We have said from the outset that being human is an art, and nowhere is that assumption more crucial than in moral matters. You can decide that you are a fully realized human being if you get everything you can from life regardless of how others are affected. You can also decide that moral integrity—doing what you know to be right regardless of profit—is the mark of a fully realized human being. There are risks involved, to be sure. The risk of running afoul of someone else's moral code, enforced by bully tactics, is and always has been there. But a ringing declaration in the humanities is that moral integrity is worth the risk. Gambling on integrity may be basic to the human condition in its finest hour.

I have yet to hear a man ask for advice on how to combine marriage and a career.

—Gloria Steinem

When a woman tells the truth she is creating the possibility for more truth around her.

—Adrienne Rich

Key Terms

altruism the quality of acting out of concern for the welfare of others rather than one's own.

capitalism economic system based on Adam Smith's philosophy that if people are allowed to make as much money as they can, others will profit also.

categories according to Immanuel Kant, mental "compartments" that we are born with, which allow us to interpret data from the senses; an inborn sense of reason allows us to understand spatial relationships ("nextness") as well as moral or immoral actions.

enlightened self-interest condition in which wise rulers impose, for unselfish reasons, their own political philosophy in order to have an effective government that provides for people better than those people could provide for themselves.

laissez-faire French phrase meaning "allow to do"; an economic policy of allowing businesses the freedom to operate with little or no government control.

Machiavellian pertains to the manipulation of others through duplicity; derived from Machiavelli's theory of government that advocates a powerful leader who exerts power over others.

moral an adjective indicating a choice between significant options, based on principles derived from reason, family teachings, education, religion, or law.

moral absolutism belief that a given set of moral standards, derived from reason, religion, or culture, is universally binding.

moral imperative in Kantian philosophy, the inborn capacity to understand what is right when we are faced with moral decisions; one of the Kantian categories, or mental "compartments."

moral mathematics a scientific system of making choices between options based on projected quantifiable positive or negative effects.

moral relativism the belief that moral standards are not universal but, rather, vary depending on time, culture, and situation.

moral system a network of beliefs that can form the basis on which a moral choice is made: e.g., religious laws or Socratic reasoning.

morality the study of moral systems by which significant choices are made; in popular usage, the user's sense of right conduct, so that a given person is said to be or not be "moral."

utilitarianism belief founded on Bentham's moral mathematics that, because moral choices have a scientific basis, they should not be made for the individual by any rulers espousing any particular moral system but should be the result of logical analysis of the number of people who could benefit from a given choice: "the greatest good for the greatest number."

Topics for
Writing and Discussion

1. If morality begins in the home, what happens to someone who has been given a strong moral upbringing only to go out into the world and find that it is the clever, not the good, who generally succeed?

2. A dramatic example of the conflict between the law and differing moral systems is the issue of the death penalty. Write a short paper in which you: (1) summarize the rationale behind the death penalty as held by its proponents; (2) summarize a major argument that has been advanced in opposition to it; and (3) present as well as defend your own view.

3. After Socrates was sentenced to death, his followers told him how easy it would be to simply walk out of his minimum security prison and pleaded with him to do so. Pretend that he agonizes over the choice and asks first Bentham, then Kant for advice. Indicate what each philosopher would have recommended. Then present and defend your own view.

4. The arts were discussed as one of the sources of moral values. Cite a movie or television show you have seen recently that you believe suggests a recommended moral choice. How convincing do you think it was?

5. Reread the description of Shaw's play *The Doctor's Dilemma*. What *was* that dilemma? What was the doctor's decision? Was Shaw in support or opposition to the decision? What would *your* decision have been?

6. You are the mayor of a local government that has commissioners split evenly on the question of how a large amount of tax money should be spent. You listen

to the arguments of citizens who urge you to vote in favor of a new arts center, one with space for rehearsals and performances of dance, theater, and music of all kinds. Other citizens point to a survey which shows that the majority prefers a new sports arena. You have studied and been impressed by Mill's support of the rugged individualist. The commissioners are tied. You have the tie-breaking vote. What is it? Why?

7. Which character in which book said, "No man is worth five minutes of my time"? Why did the book's author consider that character heroic? How do you think that book should be received in today's world?

8. Look again at Hogarth's picture of *The Enraged Musician*. Why is it placed in this chapter? Whose side do you think Hogarth is on: the noisy crowd's or the musician's? Whose side would Bentham be on? John Stuart Mill? In each case, explain your answer.

9. You go to a supermarket with friends, who begin to remove the price labels fastened to the shelf under some items, replacing them with lower-priced labels taken from other items. They intend to tell the cashier that they want the price on the shelf, not in the computer, and urge you to help them. You are torn between group loyalty and the conviction that what they are doing is morally wrong. You have a hard time making up your mind, but fortunately you have read this chapter and know something about various options offered by moral philosophers. (1) What would Socrates do and why would he do it? (2) What would Glaucon do and why? (3) What would Rosemarie Tong do and why?

10. Imagine that a close friend is considering blowing the whistle on the manager of the drugstore in which she works part-time. Write a dialogue between the two of you in which (1) she explains what the manager is doing wrong; (2) she tells you the risks she would be taking, including jeopardizing her job; (3) you set forth the advice that you have for your friend; and (4) you present the final decision and the reason for it.

9 Happiness

Overview

The search for happiness is high up on the list of themes in the humanities. Consider how many novels and plays deal with unhappy people and either end sadly, all happiness denied, or somehow manage to conclude with a "happy ending." Think of how many poems, how many songs express the intricacies of joy or despair. Some of the world's greatest artworks capture human faces in moments made significant by what we take to be the presence or absence of happiness.

Small wonder that moral philosophy, in addition to its concerns for defining good and bad actions, also engages in exhaustive analysis of what makes life itself good and therefore happy. Few of us would deny that a good life is a happy one, for who would deliberately seek to be unhappy? So there would seem to be no need for analysis. What more is there to say? Happiness is good, and everyone wants it. But how easy is it to attain that thing called happiness? And what is it, anyway?

Happy, a word from our earliest memories, is written in cake frosting, shouted at midnight on New Year's Eve, and invoked by well-wishers during wedding receptions and ship sailings. It crops up automatically in everyday conversation. Good news is greeted with the congratulatory "I'm so happy for you." The word is even used to cover disappointment upon hearing of a friend's surprising decision to leave school in the middle of the semester, or to reject a long-awaited promotion, or to cancel a wedding even after the caterer has been chosen and the invitations mailed. We say, "Oh well, as long as she's happy." It's like breathing. We never think about it.

The need to find happiness becomes acute when it appears to have vanished. There is a sense of something missing, something lost, and then comes the desperate search for the elusive prize. People go to psychiatrists; they write or read any number of books on the subject of being happy.

Moral philosophy tells us that the problem becomes complex when we try to spell out what is meant by the good life. Is it one that is pleasurable, regardless of how pleasure is obtained? Is it one based on strict moral principles, obeyed even if it means a loss of pleasure? Or is that life happiest when it achieves something praised by others?

An Italian baroque artist visualizes the complexities of that thing we call happiness.

Source: Galleria e Museo Estense, Modena, Italy/The Bridgeman Art Library.

O happiness! Our being's end and
aim!
Good, pleasure, ease, content!
Whate'ver thy name:
That something still which prompts
the eternal sigh,
For which we bear to live or dare to
die.

—Alexander Pope

Joy is an emotion we have all experienced. Is joy equivalent to happiness? Most of us have experienced the release that comes from dancing—the easing of tension, the welcome break from worry, the relaxation of the thought process. No one would deny that letting oneself go in this manner is joyful. Yet we all know that joy is not an emotion we can feel continuously. Is joy an *ingredient* of happiness, or a by-product of it? Do we always feel joy when we think we are being happy? Can we be happy *without* joy? Is happiness a purely subjective state? Can our life be happy without our knowing it?

The humanities provide us with many interesting possibilities. As you study the subject, one of them may strike a responsive chord in you. You may even find you are happier than you knew.

Hedonism: Happiness as Pleasure

The Greek philosopher Aristippus (435–356 B.C.E.) declared happiness to be the *sum total of pleasures experienced during one's lifetime.* He thought of pleasure in purely physical terms: taste, sexual excitement, touch, and so on. He admits that a certain amount of satisfaction comes with the knowledge, for example, that one's country is faring well, but nothing mental compares with physical comfort. Bodily pain is far worse than mental pain, and therefore bodily pleasure is better than mental pleasure. People, he said, are by nature selfish animals, concerned solely with their own comforts. He asked the question that has been asked for centuries: *Is anything greater than being happy?* He said no, and added that, if it were not for pleasure, saying you were happy would mean nothing.

The writings of Aristippus have not survived, but a historian named Diogenes Laertius, living in the third century C.E., has provided a detailed summary of his philosophy of pleasure. He pointed out that Aristippus proved his argument by noting that, from the time they were capable of making choices between available options, people always selected what provided the most pleasure and the least amount of pain. Home and society might try to teach less selfish values, but instinct prevailed in the end.

Thus, if Aristippus is right, people prefer not to work, but do so only because what they earn will provide them with pleasure. There is no satisfaction in work for its own sake. As a matter of fact, Aristippus believed there was no satisfaction in even the memory or anticipation of pleasure. Nothing counted except what could be experienced at the moment.

Hedonism (from the Greek for "delight") is the name given to the philosophy that happiness is equivalent to physical pleasure and to the possession of things that provide us with pleasure. Hedonism has survived for thousands of years, substantially unchanged from its inception.

The artist Diego Velázquez (1599–1660) has given us one of the best visual representations of hedonism in *Los Borrachos* (The Drunkards), reproduced on the next page. The laughing figure on the left is Bacchus, the god of wine, whose associate is bestowing a garland of grape leaves on the kneeling figure. The work seems to give a comic reference to the traditional honoring of a hero with a laurel wreath. Velázquez may be spoofing the purely hedonistic life, but the painting allows viewers to place their own interpretation on the scene. To the dedicated hedonist, the

To the dedicated hedonist, the pleasure experienced by these drunken men may be all that is necessary for pure happiness.

Source: Diego Velázquez, *Los Borrachos* (1629). Credit: Alinari/Art Resource, NY.

pleasure obviously being experienced by the men may be all that is necessary for the highest state of happiness.

The Greek society in which Aristippus lived may have produced Socrates, Plato, and Aristotle, who spent their lives in thought, but it was also highly receptive to the idea that hedonism was basic to human nature. In fact, both Plato and Aristotle addressed themselves to the subject, disagreeing with the views of Aristippus but acknowledging the popular appeal of his ideas. In his famous analysis of love, Plato does not discredit the pleasures of sex but elevates nonphysical love to a position of greater importance. While Aristippus excludes the idea of intellectual pleasure, Plato and Aristotle believe it is one of the defining graces of a fully realized life. Aristotle developed a philosophy of happiness vastly different from that of Aristippus, as we shall see later in this chapter.

Between the austere Middle Ages and the time of the militantly rigid Puritans—both periods of strict moral codes—poets, including Shakespeare, celebrated the "eat, drink, and be merry" slogan of hedonism. One of the most famous declarations comes in this widely welcomed piece of poetic advice from Robert Herrick (1591–1674):

> *Gather ye rose-buds while ye may,*
> *Old time is still a-flying:*

Regardless of time and place human beings cherish a common desire for happiness and a wish to avert suffering.

—**The Dalai Lama**

And this same flower that smiles today
Tomorrow may be dying.

Track 16

Another name given to this hedonist view is **carpe diem** (from the Latin "seize the day"). While this advice is rooted in Aristippus, it has had numerous applications through the ages. For some, it means doing the most with their potential; it means reaching for the stars. For others, such as Omar Khayyám in *The Rubáiyát*, it means, as it does in Herrick, have all you can during your brief lifetime.

A contemporary of Herrick, Andrew Marvell (1621–1678), makes a similar plea, this time to one special person in a poem called "To His Coy Mistress."

> *Had we but world enough, and time,*
> *This coyness, lady, were no crime.*
> *We would sit down, and think which way*
> *To walk, and pass our long love's day.*

If he had forever to woo her, the poet adds, he would spend a hundred years praising her eyes, two hundred for each breast and "thirty thousand to the rest."

> *But at my back I always hear*
> *Time's winged chariot hurrying near:*
> *And yonder all before us lie*
> *Deserts of vast eternity.*
> *Thy beauty shall no more be found,*
> *Nor, in thy marble vault, shall sound*
> *My echoing song: then worms shall try*
> *That long preserv'd virginity:*
> *And your quaint honour turn to dust,*
> *And into ashes all my lust.*
> *The grave's a fine and private place,*
> *But none I think do there embrace.*

Can it be that there was only one summer that I was ten?

—May Swenson

Many people are proud to call themselves hedonists. They openly boast of their income and possessions. They assert that with only one chance to live, they should deny themselves nothing and try to have it all. A bumper sticker proclaims: "He who dies with the most toys wins." Another boasts: "We're spending our grandchildren's inheritance." A current restatement of *carpe diem* is "Life is not a rehearsal. This is it!"

Still, hedonism does carry with it the reputation for reckless excess; therefore, many try to avoid applying the label to themselves. While they may admit they seek comfort and avoid discomfort as often as possible, they do not like to be considered selfish. Their priorities are giving and receiving love (sometimes more than in a physical sense), raising a family, finding an occupation both useful and satisfying, having security, pursuing intellectual stimulation, and expressing themselves creatively. Aristippus would contend that such persons are secret hedonists afraid to admit they are—but that they *ought* to! They seek pleasure but deny themselves too much. They sacrifice everything for their children, only to be confronted later with a thankless "What did you ever do for me?" They live frugally and work hard so their retirement years will be golden yet risk dying just before their pension comes due.

Hedonist Assumptions

For a hedonist, there never seems to be enough pleasurable moments in life. There seems to be so much undeserved pain. "Why me?" is a frequent question both openly and silently asked. When am I going to get *my* chance to be happy?"

So the first hedonist assumption is that *everyone deserves as much pleasure as possible.* A variant of this assumption is that *people never really get as much pleasure as they deserve.* Other people always appear to have more. Those believed to have more may communicate—even exaggerate—their pleasures, especially unexpected bonuses, which point out how truly deserving they really are. Those without bonuses perpetuate the myth that the undeserving are getting more from life.

A second assumption, vitally related to the first, is that *pleasure is automatically good.* In unprosperous times, when some are barely eating enough to get by, those who are able to eat anything they want are undoubtedly envied. No one feels sorry for the affluent people who might overeat and overdrink!

Hedonists recognize that people cannot possibly have pleasure every moment of their lives, but still, they think they should. A third assumption, therefore, is that *no amount of pleasure is ever too much.* There may be a submerged feeling of guilt about gorging oneself in an "All U Can Eat" restaurant or downing one drink after another at somebody's open house, but the typical hedonist response is, "There will be time enough to cut down; don't bother me now." Besides, overindulgence in moments of plenty supposedly means making up for past disappointments.

A fourth hedonist assumption is that *the absence of pleasure is a misfortune for which compensation is due.* Many who attempt robbery believe they are only getting even with society. Those who carry the hedonist viewpoint through life find themselves plotting continually: "Just wait until *I* have the upper hand!" Since moments without definite feelings of pleasure are an abomination, they entertain themselves by thinking of the moment when they will finally gain "rightful" pleasures.

This particular mindset stems from the **big-earnings theory**. An *earning* is considered the pleasure owed to a deserving person for services rendered or unpleasant chores completed. In the ledger that many hedonists carry inside themselves, there is a strict accounting of pleasures owed them; eventually a vast number may accumulate. Unless something happens to change their philosophy of happiness, these hedonists may become obsessed with thinking about pleasures due. If they are paid off, life is good; if not, life is bad. Life is evaluated strictly in terms of total payments received. An excellent life is one in which no big earning is left unrewarded.

> *I fear not the uncleanness of meat but the uncleanness of desire.*
> —**Augustine**

Hedonism Reconsidered

Since it is one of the oldest known theories of happiness, hedonism has been subjected to ongoing critical appraisal by philosophers and cultural historians alike. Hedonism has inspired three major critical questions: first, whether this philosophy is based on an accurate view of human nature; second, whether people are pleasure-loving at all times and in all places; and third, whether the idea that happiness is the sum total of all possible pleasures is self-defeating.

Too much of a good thing can be wonderful.

—**Mae West**

The crux of the arguments may be how limited or unlimited is our definition of *pleasure*. Fundamental hedonism is clear: pleasure is experienced through the five senses. People who spend time in thought are denying themselves that much pleasure and, we assume, that much happiness. People who devote their lives to working in a clinic a thousand miles from civilization, who expose themselves daily to the risk of disease without even the reward of outside recognition, are supposedly doing without pleasure. But how can we assume such people are deliberately perverting their own natures to follow a calling that requires them to labor in the interest of others? Are those whose happiness is not derived from hedonism wasting their time or being cheated of the pleasure they secretly desire?

In describing a conversation with noted writer Joseph Heller, the late novelist Kurt Vonnegut (1922–2007) reconsiders hedonism powerfully.

> *True story. Word of Honor.*
>
> *Joseph Heller, an important and funny writer now dead, and I were at a party given by a billionaire on Shelter Island. I said, "Joe, how does it make you feel to know that our host only yesterday may have made more money than your novel* Catch-22 *has earned in its entire history?"*
>
> *And Joe said, "I've got something he can never have."*
>
> *And I said, "What on earth could that be, Joe?"*
>
> *And Joe said, "The knowledge that I've got enough."*[1]

Buddhist monks sitting alone in silent meditation for hours, even days, at a time lose contact with the self in ways that the hedonist could never understand. Are they robbing themselves of the pleasure that their natures crave? Is it accurate to say that celibacy is necessarily a sublimation of normal sexual passion, as many contend? Or is human nature such that it cannot be narrowly defined? May sensory pleasure be all-sufficing for some and less fulfilling to others?

If, as existentialists (discussed in Chapter 10) maintain, no such thing as human nature exists at all and humanity is indeed a self-defining, self-determining species, then there is ample room for alternate ways of defining pleasure. In fact, those who choose to do so can relegate physical pleasure to a low priority without being unnatural.

Epicureanism: Happiness Is Avoiding Pain

In a musical comedy some years back, the heroine, trying to explain to the audience in song why she adores the hero, compares her love to a number of familiar pleasures. She includes the smell of bread baking and the feeling she has when a tooth stops hurting. In the first instance, she is a hedonist, directly sensuous in her values. In the second, however, she turns to a different philosophy of happiness: **epicureanism**. The sudden cessation of a toothache is not directly pleasurable in itself, but it *brings* happiness, according to that philosophy: the happiness of not being in pain.

Epicureanism is named for the Greek thinker Epicurus (c. 341–270 B.C.E.), who first formulated its precepts. Aware of Aristippus and his beliefs, Epicurus was highly critical of a philosophy he believed weak in logic and, more than that, impossible to follow.

Epicurean Assumptions

Epicurus indirectly accepted the initial premise of hedonism, that pleasure is a great good, but he added that it was not the *only* good. He refused to say with the hedonists that the more pleasure we have, the happier we are: "And since pleasure is the first good and natural to us, for this very reason we do not choose every pleasure, but sometimes we pass over many pleasures, when greater discomfort accrues to us as a result of them."[2]

Epicurus was particularly critical of those who recommended pleasures in excess, for these, he knew, would always be followed by both physical and moral pain. "For from prudence are sprung all the other virtues, and it teaches us that it is not possible to live pleasantly without living prudently and honourably and justly."[3]

For Epicurus, hedonism was a time-conscious, death-ridden philosophy. If happiness increased with the quantity of physical pleasures, then logically no life could ever be long enough. We are here for an uncertain amount of time, true, but all of us are subject to the gradual infirmities that come with age—if indeed we do not burn ourselves out before age ever becomes a problem. Therefore hedonists are fundamentally insecure and unhappy, unable to accept the inevitability of age and death, always worried about the loss of pleasure. Thus the major assumption of epicureanism is that nothing lasts forever and we must accept this fact cheerfully. If we are to define the good life, it is the wiser course of action not to believe that it consists only of pleasure.

Archibald MacLeish, whose poem "Ars Poetica" we studied in Chapter 4, accuses the hedonist Andrew Marvell of being so obsessed with the brevity of life and the thought of death that he could not enjoy life while he had it. MacLeish's "You, Andrew Marvell" begins with these lines:

> And here face down beneath the sun
> And here upon earth's noonward height
> To feel the always coming on
> The always rising of the night.

Pleasure is the beginning and end of living happily.

—**Epicurus**

Another epicurean assumption is that no one can sustain pleasure over prolonged periods of time. We cannot indefinitely gorge ourselves on delicious food, indulge in sex, stay drunk. Why, then, saddle ourselves with a philosophy of life that is so limiting from the very outset? Unable to satisfy our pleasure- seeking instincts perpetually, we do the next best thing: seek material possessions or fame, both of which symbolize happiness without *bringing* happiness. Money and fame are constantly in the hedonist's thoughts. They are the compensations for having to die. They are the only possible tangible embodiments of a successful life. When age makes physical pleasure less attainable, people turn to the accumulation of wealth. But Epicurus also recognized that the pursuit of wealth was self- defeating, futile. The same is true of insisting on fame. The wealthy or the famous person feels insecure and distrustful of others, certain that others are envious and scheming.

Why, asked Epicurus, burden ourselves with a philosophy with built-in disappointments, frustrations, and inevitable pain? Why not, rather, change the *requirements* for the good life? He assumed people of reason had free will and could control their desire for pleasure, and therefore they could reduce the amount of pain that always follows pleasure. Complete happiness is a moderate amount of pleasure with complete freedom from pain—an unlikely scenario for most people, but one that can be more nearly realized as we exert our will not to suffer. To those who would ask "Why may I not agree to the suffering as long as I have the pleasure?" epicureanism answers, "The anticipation of pain, if it is intense, detracts from the pleasure."

In "What Makes a Happy Life," Martial (c. 40–104 C.E.), a Roman poet born in Spain, offers epicurean advice:

> *What makes a happy life, dear friend,*
> *If thou wouldst briefly learn, attend—*
> *An income left, not earned by toil;*
> *Some acres of a kindly soil;*
> *The pot unfailing on the fire;*
> *No lawsuits, seldom town attire;*
> *Health, strength with grace; a peaceful mind;*
> *Shrewdness with honesty combined;*
> *Plain living, equal friends and free;*
> *Evenings of temperate gaiety;*
> *A wife discreet yet blithe and bright;*
> *Sound slumber that lends wings to night.*
> *With all thy heart embrace thy lot,*
> *Wish not for death, and fear it not.*

Hedonists might find that prescription lacking in excitement. They might say it is based on being satisfied with whatever one has, and they might ask: is ambition so bad? Health is fine, but who wants to go through life with just "plain living?" And what is "temperate gaiety"? Isn't it leaving the party just when the fun is getting started? What satisfaction would there be in that? Even the "pot unfailing on the fire," though probably filled with nourishing and sustaining food, cannot really compete with gourmet delights. Being able to afford nothing else is one thing, but that doesn't mean we wouldn't *long* for a better life.

Insofar as it recognizes the importance of pleasure in our lives, epicureanism is not so much an all-out attack on hedonism as a modification of it. Unpleasantness is part of life, the epicurean admits and therefore plans strategies to ward it off as much as possible rather than march forward in the blind hope that things are going to be fine. The worst that can happen when you anticipate pain is that you will not be disappointed. But clearly, you have a good chance of doing something about much of life's pain before it occurs *if* you apply yourself conscientiously to the task.

Exerting control and enjoying pleasure in moderation, epicureans share with hedonists delight in the taste of exquisite food—but epicureans, anticipating the pain of overindulgence, stop themselves before reaching their limit. They will drink, but never to the point of drunkenness, and not at all if they are certain their health would suffer.

Hedonism is particularly hard to resist for people who become multimillionaires. They may become extravagant, self-indulgent, and for a time at least, totally hedonistic. Hollywood abounds with tragic stories of gifted actors, directors, and writers who were unable to resist the luxuries bought through stardom and found

A real obstacle to happiness is to expect too much happiness.
—Fontenelle

themselves suddenly out of popularity and out of work. Some, however, read the danger signs and left before being completely swept up in the excitement of possessing whatever they want. Ernest Hemingway sold many of his works to the movies for comfortable amounts that gave promise of an extravagant lifestyle. But unable to watch what had been done to them, he denounced Hollywood, its elaborate homes, its desperate thirst for celebrity, and its utter lack of interest in anything that could not make money.

At the peak of his career, however, Hemingway was as exciting and dramatic a figure as any of his heroes: the envy of men and the fantasy figure of women. Famous as a womanizer and a hard-drinker, he seems to have mellowed over the years and either adopted an epicurean outlook or at least admired those who did. A character in Hemingway's story "In Another Country" fully illustrates the epicurean outlook. Before going off to war, a major in the Italian army married a beautiful woman considerably younger than he. He discovers she was unfaithful while he was fighting. Now, injured and confined to a hospital, he learns his wife has died of pneumonia. "She had been sick only a few days. No one expected her to die." The lesson he gleans from the tragedy is a lesson about how best to live. A man, he explains, should not marry.

> *"He cannot marry. He cannot marry," he said angrily. "If he is to lose everything, he should not place himself in a position to lose that. He should not place himself in a position to lose. He should find things he cannot lose."*[4]

A hedonist reading this account might argue that it does not show epicurean control and discipline as much as a weary response to a world that has lost its luster, and this only proves that pleasure is the only thing worth living for. The question is worth pondering.

Confirmed epicureans avoid excess, seeking out many non-physical pleasures that are less likely to be affected by the aging process. They are lovers of art, theater, books, and music, perhaps realizing that the humanities represent treasures one "cannot lose." After all, intellectual and aesthetic pleasures seldom lead to pain. Epicureans are typically lean and trim, exercising their bodies to keep in the best possible shape. They are mentally agile and aware of the latest developments in many fields. They are good workers, and the one who finds a marital partner with a similar outlook is likely to build a reasonably happy relationship.

Pure hedonists, however, warn epicureans that they sell themselves too short and may often settle for less than they have a right to expect from life. The hedonist maintains that, unless you work aggressively at being happy, you will give up too easily, spending too much time running away from pain that might not be there. Why not go for all you can and take your chances? The pure epicurean, however, might well answer with an old French song that says "the joys of love are but a moment long; the pain of love endures forever."

Epicureanism Reconsidered

One objection that can be raised to epicureanism is that it is as firmly rooted in self-interest as the philosophy from which it departs. It has been accused of being

He should not place himself in a position to lose. He should find things he cannot lose.

—**Ernest Hemingway**

Epicureans are typically lean and trim, exercising their bodies to keep in the best possible shape. They are mentally agile and aware of the latest developments in many fields.

hedonism in a disguised form. In seeking to avoid pain, it may be saying indirectly that pleasure really is the goal. Does it merely redefine pleasure? In addition to the good feeling one gets from the absence of pain, are not the pleasures of reading and spending one's life with the arts ultimately *selfish*?

Thus another objection is that epicureans are more interested in their own peace of mind than in social causes. If not wishing to lose means detaching oneself from life as much as possible, any form of activism becomes off limits. We may question how profound or lasting would be the peace of mind that comes from the careful control of one's own life if such were achieved at the cost of worrying about the pain of others. Concern for one's neighbor, stressed in all of the world's major religions, is generally absent from the traditional epicurean outlook. To be sure, Aristippus and Epicurus belonged to the classical world, and most classical theories of happiness focus on the individual, as though happiness *by definition* were a matter of how one's own life is faring.

In at least one of his novels, *For Whom the Bell Tolls* (1940), Hemingway does exhibit a strong social consciousness. The hero, Robert Jordan, is like the author, a rugged individualist who is used to dictating his own terms to life. But he becomes so involved with the anti-fascist cause in the Spanish Civil War of the 1930s that he gives up his life to save a band of guerrillas. Jordan is the complete opposite of Frederic Henry, the hero of Hemingway's youthful novel *A Farewell to Arms* (1929), who deserts the army and runs away with the woman he loves. Perhaps being unable to turn his back on a social cause became part of Hemingway's well-lighted place: self-satisfaction gained through self-sacrifice.

We cannot rule out the possibility that happiness can be achieved only by working to combat pain wherever it is found, and sometimes the battle incurs personal suffering, which is accepted as the high price of success. After all, there are people, seldom mentioned in history books, who have voluntarily spent their shortened lives nursing the sick in parts of the world ravaged by plagues of one kind or another. Maybe the new epicureanism seeks not only to avoid pain oneself but to do everything possible to help *others* avoid pain.

The disaster that befell New York and Washington on September 11, 2001, a cataclysmic event that took almost 3,000 lives, had an effect quite different from the total chaos the terrorists may have planned. Instead of scattering to the winds in a "Save yourself" mode, hundreds of police and firefighters gave up their own lives in an attempt to rescue as many victims as they could. It is now apparent from cellphone calls made to loved ones before the collapse of the towers that a number of those who might have escaped stayed to help others, forfeiting their lives to do so. There are further indications that some of the passengers aboard Flight 93, which crashed in a Pennsylvania meadow, may have overpowered the hijackers in order to save perhaps thousands who might have died had the deadly mission been completed. Who is to say that dedicated epicureans would not, in moments of extreme crisis, forgo self-interest? After all, if someone survived by not trying to save another, would that individual lead a peaceful and contented life from that day on? Would it be said that it was a good life, exemplifying happiness?

The cynic might say that social consciousness is only an extension of a principle stated by Epicurus: "The just man is most free from trouble." That is, happiness consists of an undisturbed conscience; if you want tranquility, you must sometimes labor in the interest of others. After all, can you sit down to relish a

Wisdom consists of the anticipation of consequences.

—**Norman Cousins**

gourmet meal with three ragged and starving children pressing their noses against the restaurant window? But it seems unfair to assume that, given the dimensions of the September 11th catastrophe, all apparently selfless work is ultimately rooted in the effort to reach inner peace.

Stoicism: Happiness as a Strategy for Survival

A famous poster shows a cat holding tightly to the knotted end of a rope and just hanging there in empty black space. The caption reads: *When you come to the end of your rope, tie a knot and hang on.* This, in capsule form, is the philosophy of **stoicism**. It operates under even fewer illusions about life than does epicureanism. It tells us neither to plan ahead for a lifetime of unlimited pleasure nor to expect to avoid pain through discipline and moderation. Stoicism asserts pain is intrinsic to living. Even the most dedicated epicureans will feel a certain amount of frustration when their disciplined approach to living goes awry. The best possible course is to be prepared for the worst and to develop a technique for dealing with it. *Epicureans avoid; stoics cope.*

The art of life is more like the wrestler's art than the dancer's. It should stand ready and firm to meet onsets which are sudden and unexpected.

—Marcus Aurelius

Stoic Assumptions

Stoicism sees the will as the means through which each of us can control our response to external events. Despite the disasters that may befall us, stoics believe in human reason. They believe it is reasonable to know that disasters—natural, social, personal—inevitably happen. Life just occurs. We make our plans, but we cannot include life in those plans. As one philosopher put it: "Life is what happens to us while we are making other plans." But we shouldn't believe that all is chaos in the universe. If there is order within the human mind, there may be order in the universe as well, and the unpredictable things that happen may be *part* of that order. Understanding this, we can see to it that the will is in tune with events as they occur. The sometimes despairing question "How can terrible things be part of any order?" may be irrelevant. Stoics contend disasters are possible to accept without emotion.

Stoicism was born over 2,000 years ago. Like hedonism and its modified offspring epicureanism, it is the product of Greek intellect; it lays heavy stress on human reason and the belief that humankind is a superior form of animal life. The philosophy of Zeno, its first major advocate (335–264 B.C.E.), is therefore close in spirit to that of Plato and Aristotle.

The school founded by Zeno was located in a columned portico called a *stoa*—hence the name of the philosophy. Central to stoicism is the belief that true happiness is not a matter of circumstance, of good fortune, or of what happens to us, but rather a matter of *how we respond to what happens.* Happiness, like sorrow, is an idea, an attitude, not an object or an event. If no one welcomes the first day of spring, how can it be said that spring is a time of hope and joy? If in some remote civilization with unusual customs and mores the birth of a child were considered a dreadful curse, then the inability to produce offspring might be regarded as a happy stroke of luck.

To find the roots of unhappiness, we must look inward. Nothing is under our control except the way we think about things. Natural disasters, social upheavals, wars, revolutions, outbreaks of disease, rising crime rates—all happen as a result of either accidental or highly complicated causes. Our happiness should not depend on their *not* taking place. We cannot alter external circumstances, but we can decide not to feel negatively toward them.

"How do you expect me to feel?" is a common response when we are asked why we are so glum about a certain outcome—say, not being promoted to a higher position. Stoics cite habit as the guilty culprit, contending that people are conditioned by the values their society puts on what happens to or around them. This is acceptable; that is not. This is cause for joy; that is cause for tears. Reactions become automatic after a while. People come to *think* they are unhappy; hence they *are* unhappy. But typical responses can be altered. We can refuse to be affected in customary ways or as others tend to be affected.

One of the best-known stoic teachers was a Greek named Epictetus (50–130 C.E.), who was captured and enslaved by the Romans. His brilliance was eventually recognized, and he was allowed to conduct classes. But prior to that, Epictetus was tortured and oppressed in his captivity. On one occasion his leg was broken on a whim of his master's. During this period of extreme suffering, Epictetus was faced with the choice of surrendering to despair or finding some means of enduring. He chose the latter course, recognizing that nothing, not even torture, was unbearable unless one wished to find it so. After his liberation, he dedicated his life to spreading the stoic creed, which had preserved his spirit intact for so many years.

Stoicism later found ready acceptance among the Romans and became a sort of unofficial state philosophy. Its emphasis on reason and the control of negative emotions accorded well with the Roman ideal of the perfect human being. Besides, Rome was an empire-building civilization, requiring a superbly disciplined military machine to carry out its conquests. It therefore found a meaningful application of stoic teachings: the rigors of military training as well as the hardships of war itself must never depress the human spirit. Good soldiers, with feelings well under their control, must become indifferent to their own suffering.

When Christianity began to spread throughout the Roman Empire, many of the converts had, naturally enough, already been exposed to stoic beliefs. The by-then ancient and honorable philosophy accorded well with the outlook and needs of Christians. After all, they had to face untold sufferings—continual persecution, torture, flight, starvation, separation from loved ones. The stoic doctrine of inner control blended perfectly with the Christian belief that only the soul, not the body, mattered. One could endure all manner of pain and remain serene.

Christian martyrdom was deeply rooted in stoic principles. After all, the teachings of Jesus had strongly illustrated those principles, especially the directives to love one's enemies and to turn the other cheek. A famous martyrdom is that of Thomas á Becket (1118–1170), the archbishop of Canterbury and, as such, the pope's representative in England, sworn to carry out papal decrees and to uphold church dogma. By the twelfth century, however, England was becoming a major world power, and the English monarchy assumed more and more authority, even in matters of religion. King Henry II, once Becket's friend, had laws passed that were in direct violation of church canon. The pope was displeased, and Becket, of course, sided with him, causing a dangerous rift between monarch and prelate. Late in 1170 Becket urged the pope to dismiss several bishops known to be politically on the king's side. The king then sent four knights to Canterbury with the

True instruction is this: to learn to wish that each thing should come to pass as it does.

—**Epictetus**

king's command for Becket to restore the deposed bishops, but Becket refused. Knowing that he had probably signed his own death warrant, the archbishop went into the cathedral to pray.

While he was there, the knights returned, this time with an armed band. Becket's attendants saw them coming, shut the heavy doors, and were about to lock them when the archbishop cried out: "God's house must be closed against no man." The assassins, thus given unchallenged entry, rushed to the altar, whereupon Becket made a ringing stoic declaration: "For the name of Jesus and for the defense of the Church I am ready to embrace death." They fell upon him with their swords, and he was murdered on the altar. The scene was memorably recorded in the verse play *Murder in the Cathedral* (1935) by the American poet T. S. Eliot and later in the film *Becket* (1964).

Whether religiously oriented or not, stoicism remains as pervasive as ever and offers to many a genuine alternative to hedonism. In a period of ever accelerating change, of being wary of possible violence as a condition of life, of the realization that prosperity may not last forever, it is small wonder that many are asking less for pleasure than for inner peace. Although weekly pilgrimages to analysts continue, some principles of stoicism may be at work here also. After all, self-knowledge is vital to psychoanalysis. Analysts contend that people will be able to transcend negative feelings once they understand what is making them unhappy or ineffective. This may be the same thing as saying that happiness is really within our own power to create and preserve. Not everyone agrees.

Success is getting what you want; happiness is wanting what you get.

—**Anonymous**

Stoicism Reconsidered

Stoicism in modern dress is, for its advocates, still a viable theory of happiness. Its basic assumption remains much the same as always: tranquility is worth any price. Stoicism has something to offer the chronically poor and dispossessed, who also suffer from low self-esteem and cannot see that they deserve any better fate. Even the most zealous social worker might agree that in some cases a stoic attitude is better than false hope for a better tomorrow.

One negative aspect of stoicism is its convenience. If you're down and out, abandoned by family and friends, with no prospects that things will turn around for you, why not become a stoic? Surely the distance is short from "Things are pretty bleak" to "There is no reason to believe things should be otherwise." Does this view mean simply coping but *doing* nothing?

Suppose, however, that the ad hoc stoic—the person who adopts this philosophy out of sheer desperation—suddenly experiences an unexpected reversal of fortune. Say he or she wins $5 million in the state lottery or, more modestly, finds a good-paying job. Or suppose, as actually happened in the wake of a TV newscaster's human-interest documentary about the homeless in New York, a couple randomly singled out for an interview found themselves swamped with offers of money, jobs, shelter—even a film contract! What happens to stoic doctrines then? Can one embrace stoicism one day and abandon it for hedonism the next?

Some might respond "Why not?" If adversity can be endured because the rational control of emotion makes endurance possible, dropping stoicism when it is no longer working or necessary is not necessarily *un*reasonable. Others could

The stoical scheme of supplying our wants by topping off our desires is like cutting off our feet when we want shoes.

—**Jonathan Swift**

object to this line of thought, claiming that reason, which justified the initial adoption of the stoic philosophy during bad times, also requires us to believe that good fortune is not likely to be permanent.

There is an old fable about a tyrannical king who, finding himself plagued by bad fortune, kept asking various wise men to give him grounds for hope. If they could not, their heads were chopped off. Finally, one clever sage gave him a plaque to hang on his bedroom wall: *These Things Shall Pass*. The king, deriving much comfort from the plaque, rewarded the sage handsomely, until the king's fortunes took a turn for the better. The maxim, which had once buoyed up his spirits, now angered him, and he ordered the once-favored philosopher to be beheaded.

A frequently raised objection to stoicism is that its advocates secretly want everyone else to be as miserable as they are, yet they don't realize it. Is adversity more bearable when no one around you is having a run of good luck? Loving the company of the miserable may be a fundamental human trait. Enjoying nothing so much as the sad tales of others may be as universal as secretly resenting a friend's prosperity. The German word **schadenfreude** describes the pleasure derived from the misfortunes of others. Radio and television programmers assume there's a smaller audience for good news than for accounts of grisly murders and natural disasters that kill thousands.

Yet another objection is that what passes for reason in stoicism should really be called rationalizing, a process by which we find satisfying rather than logical reasons for believing something. The possibility exists that control for the stoic actually means manipulating thoughts so that reality becomes bearable. When loved ones stop calling, do we endure the absence by admitting the possibility that they have transferred their affections or have ceased to be interested in us for this or that reason? Or do we more likely find reasons that make us feel good, such as the loved one's responding to a job interview? The interview may well turn out to be the actual reason, but the point is that we pick and choose among comfortable versions of reality. In this way, say the detractors, what masquerades as stoic acceptance is a false sense that reality is being fearlessly confronted. We accept what we *want* to accept, rejecting everything else. The trouble, they warn, is that rejected reality can strike back at any time, delivering a crushing blow.

Classical stoicism emerged from two cultures, the Greek and the Roman, with their strong belief in fate. The universe was run by all-powerful deities who intervened in human affairs whenever they chose. The gods and goddesses were capricious and unpredictable, but human reason could counteract heavenly whimsy by expecting ill times before they occurred. In other words, the universe of the Greeks and Romans was predictably full of disaster. But perhaps the universe really does not make even that much sense. Perhaps disasters are no less certain than continual success. A very strong criticism of stoicism is thus a recognition that it can inspire debilitating passivity. Expecting to fail has kept many a potential winner from even getting started.

There is also the passivity of the fortunate, especially when it comes to turning away from the fact that people the world over are suffering and that much could be done to help. "I'm a stoic and believe those who suffer from poverty or the ravages of war would be happier if they would only follow my example" can be an excuse for enjoying a comfortable existence without the nagging of conscience.

Joy is a net of love by which you can catch souls.

—**Mother Teresa**

Harriet Beecher Stowe's novel *Uncle Tom's Cabin* (1852) opened the eyes of many who were unaware of the wretched poverty in which slaves were forced to live without hope of liberation. The title character, however, adopts a stoic acceptance of his lot and has since lent his name as the very icon of non-resistance. Looking at the novel from our century and a half remove, one might become infuriated by conditions that force those without hope to embrace stoicism. In contrast, one character, Eliza, also a slave, is indeed desperate enough to endanger her life in a flight from the plantation. Modern readers often criticize the passivity of Tom and praise the courage of Eliza.

Aristotelianism: Happiness as the Quality of a Whole Lifetime

For Aristotle, Plato's famous pupil and founder of the Lyceum, an early version of the liberal arts college, happiness is the purpose for which we live. In analyzing this most complex of phenomena, Aristotle concludes that happiness is not a moment-to-moment experience of pleasurable things but a way of characterizing how one's life is being conducted. Happiness is living and having lived a good life. It is not measured in momentary eruptions of joy. *Complete* happiness comes with the final summing up of one's life. But if we are leading a good life along the way, we can know that we are on the right path. Then the philosopher goes on to investigate what *makes* life good, therefore happy.

Pleasure a Limited Goal; Happiness a Complete Goal

In his great work on the conduct of living, *The Nicomachean Ethics* (named for his son Nichomachus), Aristotle makes a list of the things that can be said to make life good. What he wants to determine is the nature of the *highest* good, the one that is valued for its own sake, the one that, when (or if) reached, leaves nothing else to be desired.

If you asked passersby what makes them happy, you would probably hear "money," "health," "love," "a good job with a good future," "a house in a good neighborhood," and so on. No one can deny these are to be counted as among the goods that life can offer. As each one is named, you could continue, "Yes, and is that all?" Chances are that the other goods would be named in succession. That is, is money enough? Well no, not if my heath is bad. Is health then enough? Well, no, not if I hate my job. Is a good job enough? Well, no, not if I haven't found someone to share my life.

If someone were to ask you whether it would be enough if you were completely happy, you would have to think a minute, wouldn't you? You couldn't say, "Not if I didn't have money," because, logically, if money were important to your happiness and you didn't have any, you couldn't be *completely* happy then.

Aristotle concludes that the reason we want money, health, love, and all the other things that seem to be worth striving for is that they *provide* happiness. Therefore they cannot *be* happiness. The person who delivers your mail is not the mail. Individual goods, in other words, are means to the end, which is happiness. None of them can be the end in itself, though some people often make the mistake of believing that is possible. For example, a poor person might dream of someday

When a small child...I thought success spelled happiness. I was wrong, happiness is like a butterfly which appears and delights us for one brief moment, but soon flies away.

—**Anna Pavlova**

winning the lottery and suddenly having millions. "If I had all that money, I wouldn't ask for anything more." Want to bet? In identifying happiness with any particular state or possession, we can *always* think of something else that would be better and therefore our life could be *more* happy at that moment. Just as Einstein told the world that at the speed of light time stops, so too can it be said that in a state of complete happiness, desire and need stop. But *only* then.

Aristotle therefore defines happiness as the highest, or final, good. Since nearly all of us continually strive for greater goods than we have at any particular time, it follows that achieving complete happiness, reaching the final good, *must* be the goal, the purpose of life. It also follows that what affords us pleasure or joy at any given moment cannot be the same thing as happiness, because it is always possible to think of something that would be better. Winning gold medals in the Olympics leaves athletes in a state of extreme joy, often identified as *euphoria*, yet two medals are better than one, and three even better than that. Aristotle, who probably attended Olympic games too, might have told the rejoicing athletes that winning games is among the things that make life good, but when complete happiness is achieved, they would not need to compete ever again.

Aristotle's theory has enormous implications for how we can best live. It assures us that life can still be good without our having everything we thought we wanted. Every so often we can stop and take inventory and then decide how our life is going. Is it headed in a direction that can be summed up as "Yes, this is a good life—so far"?

Further, *do we want things that make happiness more difficult to attain than need be?* The answer, according to Aristotle, is staring us in the face: if happiness is the same as the good life, why not simply *live* the good life? He believed there was one good which stood out above all, one good that was better than all the others that promote happiness, and that was *reason*. If we allow reason to be our guide in making all decisions, we will always do the right thing. By doing the right thing in every circumstance—not the most profitable or immediately pleasurable—one can be sure that the summing up will be on the side of the good life.

Aristotle, very much like Socrates before him, equated reason with virtue. The virtuous course is also the perfection of a particular action. To act out of self-interest, ignoring others, can never be excellence. Too many others can be hurt by the action, and pardoning oneself to avoid guilt means lying. Of what action is *lying* the perfection? Do we judge a lie to be a perfect action if nobody finds out? Or if we believe no one has been hurt? How can we know? And even if we could be assured that the lie is a harmless one, might we not be encouraged to choose lying over the truth in another, or perhaps even *every*, case? A life built on lies is bound to crumble like a house of cards.

Aristotle believed that the path to happiness was a life lived in accordance with reason and virtue. This cannot be said for a life that achieves only *some* of the goods that are possible: recognition without love, for example, or money without health, or health without fulfilling any other purpose. A life that has displayed reason and virtue in all actions and decisions can be one that is free of care, free of guilt, free from wishing that much more could have been done.

But it may *not* be. A person who has lived a totally virtuous life may, in the end, regret that all goals had not been reached: the promised pay hike never received; the novel never written; a reconciliation never reached. But—and this is crucial—such regret is not a sign that the life was not a good one. In other words, according to Aristotle's theory, life can be good even though you are not always

Aristotle believed happiness was not the same as goods we desire in hopes they will make us happy. It was a state, a condition, the satisfaction of knowing that one has lived a good life, dominated by reason and virtue.

Happiness arises from awareness of being.

—**Trich Nhat Hahn**

aware of it. Of course, the secret is to *become* aware of it by asking every so often *What am I doing that makes my life good?* Not: what is missing in my life? If the "missing" is also the unattainable, then you have willfully blocked the road to happiness. Whatever happens, if you can look in the mirror and say you are a good person, and you are smart enough to know that everything cannot be attained, your life is proceeding happily.

Providing Happiness: A Government's Responsibility?

Aristotle proposed that the *only* purpose of a government was to see to it that the citizens were happy. Having deduced that the purpose of living is the attainment of the happy life, the philosopher believed that nothing should be allowed to hinder the quest. The institutions of society exist for no reason other than to promote the happiness of all and therefore the means to that end.

Law and order in the well-regulated state are necessary; otherwise the happiness of all cannot be guaranteed. People must be protected against their own baser natures, as well as against those who wish them harm, in order that their higher potential may be realized. For many critics of this theory, questions remain: How much power should the state be given before it contradicts its avowed purpose, which is to promote the happiness of all? Will not some harm inevitably be done to the innocent? In this age of DNA testing, many of those executed for high crimes have later been found not to have been guilty. The justification "Yes, but look how many killers the death penalty has kept off the streets" does not satisfy those who would support the view that the happiness—and therefore the rights—of all must come first. How, they ask, can happiness be guaranteed when freedom is denied?

Aristotle held fast to the belief that the road to happiness was through the exercise of virtue and reason and that the government must not stand in the way of reason. This would imply that the government itself should be a model of rationality. And therein lies the great dilemma. How can government *reasonably* protect the state if it sometimes has to use *unreasonable* methods?

There is a further dilemma. What happens when the ruler's rational view of happiness differs from the people's? In *The Republic* Plato reports a famous debate over whether the best interests of the government can coincide with the best interests of the governed. Socrates believed that there was only one rational course in every decision that had to be made and that, if the government truly followed reason, then it would automatically serve the interests of the people. That belief was the foundation of his decision not to escape from prison, though he had questioned the justice that brought him there. What he did *not* question was the logic of having law itself. He was found guilty, however unjustly, and therefore the law required a penalty, which in his case was death by drinking hemlock. He argued it was unreasonable to assume that everyone who thought he had been unjustly imprisoned had the right to escape if he could. Aristotle had less faith in the power of the ordinary citizen to be rational, but that only made him insist that those who governed *must* be capable of using reason at all times. Whether that has ever happened is open to endless debate.

Aristotle Reconsidered

There are always going to be limitations on happiness. Many millions have no choice but to wait and hope for a miraculous change of fortune: people who live under oppressive governments or in places where drought or other natural disasters create famine and the spread of fatal disease; people who cannot be said to have had or maybe never *will* have anything that can be called a good. It is almost impossible to tell them that their lives are good, that they are happy without knowing it. Aristotle would probably not have even tried. Recognizing when one is fortunate in comparison to many others can be a limitation on one's own progress toward happiness, and helping those in need might be the only way to find the path again. Until one does find it and until no further help is necessary (an unimaginable condition), complete happiness is unreachable.

The economic disaster of the Great Depression was addressed by the administration of Franklin D. Roosevelt, which began in 1933, promising what it called a "New Deal." Based on the theories of John Maynard Keynes, an English economist, the New Deal was to stimulate economic growth—hence the expansion of the job market—through government spending on a vast array of new social programs. Financed by the government, the Works Projects Administration (WPA) and the Civilian Conservation Corps (CCC) put the unemployed to work building roads, laying railroad tracks, cleaning up the cities and the countryside, and building dams to supply electrical power for new homes and factories. The New Deal proclaimed that the government's responsibility was to look out for the welfare of all citizens. In theory, everyone capable of working would have a job; and also in theory, making a fair wage and putting food on the table equated with happiness.

Aristotle's theory assumed an open society with citizens' welfare as the major concern of government. Since his time, it is clear, all societies have become much more complex and the role of government tangled in webs of red tape. Can anyone in any society rely solely on government to provide happiness? Is happiness unattainable under a *repressive* government? Does it follow that no one can ever be happy in Aristotle's sense of the word?

No, no, we are not satisfied, and we will not be satisfied until justice rolls down like waters and righteousness like a mighty stream.
—**Martin Luther King, Jr.**

Aristotle believed the function of government was to provide for the happiness of each citizen.

The Humanities and Unhappiness

Any theory of happiness is just that: a theory. People whose circumstances are deplorable, who live in fear, hunger, and ill health, whose lifespan is often considerably shorter than it could be, who can rightly say that they never did harm to another person yet they suffer, cannot be blamed for feeling they deserve a better fate. Misfortune is, unfortunately, inherent in this business of living. The amount of suffering in the world is for many a permanent roadblock to the happy life.

The humanities have not turned a deaf ear to human misery. The sometimes futile attempt to escape from poverty, for example, is the subject of much great art and literature. For example, Victor Hugo's *Les Misérables* (1862) called powerful attention to the plight of the poor in France. The hero, Jean Valjean, steals a loaf of bread for his hungry family, is sent to prison, and after his release gets into trouble again. He is then relentlessly pursued by Javert, a police inspector obsessed with punishing anyone who breaks a law regardless of the reason. The pursuit continues for hundreds of pages, resulting in Javert's suicide because he cannot capture Valjean and the latter's reunion with his family now as an old man near death—and all because of a loaf of bread!

The master novelist of the truly desperate is Charles Dickens (1812–1870), some of whose memorable characters are children near starvation and working for corrupt taskmasters. In a memorable scene from the novel *Oliver Twist*, the poor, starving orphan of the title holds out his little bowl and timidly asks the head of the wretched workhouse whether he could have a bit more gruel—a request which brings down as fearful a display of wrath as exists in all of literature. Later, Oliver is taken in by the villainous Fagin, who controls a band of boy pickpockets. The "happy ending," in which Oliver is discovered to be the long-lost grandson of a wealthy man, was not available to Fagin's other slaves. Nor does it disguise Dickens's real subject: society's indifference to poverty.

In Dickens's popular seasonal treat *A Christmas Carol*, there is, again, a happy ending, this time with an entire family rescued from dire poverty by the once miserly skinflint Ebenezer Scrooge, whose supernatural visitors effect his change of heart. But happy endings were demanded by nineteenth-century readers, most of them members of the comfortable middle class, who didn't mind confronting the cold and hunger of the poor as long as they could anticipate joy on the final page, casting a golden glow of unreality over the truth. One suspects, however, that Dickens was confident discerning readers would see through the sham and recognize that real poverty wasn't going away.

Following the Depression years of the 1930s, American writers and artists were preoccupied with the bitter realism of characters suffering from hunger, disease, and isolation. Edward Hopper's art (discussed in Chapter 5) specialized in loneliness and the despair of life in urban America, just emerging from the

I simplified the scene and made the restaurant bigger. I was painting the loneliness of a large city.

—**Edward Hopper**

Edward Hopper specialized in painting lonely, despairing people and the limitations of the American Dream.

Source: Edward Hopper, American, 1882–1967, *Nighthawks*, 1942, oil on canvas, 84.1 × 152.4 cm. Friends of the American Art Collection/The Art Institute of Chicago.

most severe economic depression in its history. Hopper's works show the limitations of the American Dream, of believing that in a free society anybody can reach the top. How many people continue to base their idea of happiness on how successful they can be? How often do they make unrealistic lists of the goods they *must* have before they can even consider whether they are happy? The irony is that those who have almost nothing and have therefore shorter lists probably stand a better chance at happiness than the more fortunate and perennially dissatisfied.

Conditions in the modern world have not conspired to bring about rosier views in the literary depiction of life. The victims of desperate economic times and the daily threat of violence figure in the work of writers surrounded by bitterness and death in many parts of the world. A popular Egyptian novel in recent years, Alaa Al Aswany's *The Yacoubian Building* (2002), revolves around the tenants of an apartment house in Cairo. To one extent or another, all long for prosperity. The central character is Taha, son of the building's janitor, who has aspirations to become a policeman and then marry the woman he loves. When he is turned away from the police academy even after scoring high on the entrance examination, he enrolls in college, where he is snubbed by the wealthier, better-dressed students but welcomed by those as poor as he. They introduce Taha to a charismatic leader promising change and declaring the way to bring it about is to disrupt the status quo through well-placed bombs. What stands out in the novel is the fact that this solution is not described as a misfortune or the tragedy of modern times, but simply as a sad commentary on the way things are.

One might ask, how is it possible to be truly happy in a world where we are so often faced with the continued suffering of the less fortunate? Before we try to answer that question, let us look at a few inspiring examples of people whose lives—and, unfortunately, deaths—exemplify how life *can* be good even under the most trying of circumstances.

Models of the Happy Life

History is filled with remarkable examples of how good lives managed to overcome horrible barriers. Consider this remarkable passage by Austrian psychiatrist Viktor Frankl, held in a Nazi concentration camp. It illustrates how life can be good, even in the shadow of death.

> *The size of human suffering is absolutely relative. . . . It also follows that a very trifling thing can cause the greatest of joys. Take as an example something that happened on our journey from Auschwitz to the camp affiliated with Dachau. We had all been afraid that our transport was heading for the Mauthausen camp. We became more and more tense as we approached a certain bridge over the Danube which the train would have to cross in order to reach Mauthausen. . . . Those who have never seen anything similar cannot possibly imagine the dance of joy performed in the carriage by the prisoners when they saw that our transport was not crossing the bridge and was instead heading "only" for Dachau.[5]*

The Aristotelian moral of this story is that the rational course was for the prisoners to put themselves into the hands of a two-pronged fate: Mauthausen or Dachau—certain death or a chance to live, even if imprisoned. Knowing the two possibilities in advance, it was rational to be prepared for either eventuality, not to wish for luck. Had liberation been the only possible good that would have satisfied them, the fact that the transport did not cross the Danube would not have been enough to fill them with optimism. Instead, they made their own "luck."

Another inspiring example of Aristotelian happiness is that of Anne Frank (1929–1945), a Jewish girl who, with her parents and others, was hidden in the attic of an Amsterdam office building during the Nazi occupation. To occupy her time and possibly leave something of value behind, she began writing a diary of her thoughts and feelings, a work that was subsequently found, published, and read by millions.

Not the dewy-eyed idealist portrayed on stage, film, and television, Anne Frank was a girl with an adult mind that knew what it was doing at each moment. In 1944 she wrote: "I have made up my mind now to lead a different life from other girls and, later on, different from ordinary housewives." The "different life" was that of the calm, reflective writer. "I can shake off everything if I write, my sorrows disappear, my courage is reborn." After the war, she hoped to write and publish a work of great significance, but if this goal were denied, "my diary will be a great help."[6]

Anne Frank never knew she would become a legendary figure, an icon who continues to teach us the way to be happy under the most appalling circumstances.

Source: Handout/Reuters/Corbis.

Remarkably able to transcend what would have been an understandable fear for her own safety and that of her family and friends, Frank takes the larger view, thinking sadly of those who have already been captured and sent to camps. "If it is as bad as this in Holland, whatever will it be like in the distant and barbarous regions they are sent to? We assume that most of them are murdered. The English radio speaks of their being gassed; perhaps that is the quickest way to die."[7]

Anne Frank's strength may have come from the fact that she knew herself to be innocent of any wrongdoing, and also from an acceptance of the conditions under which she and the others hiding in the attic had to live. She became the mainstay of the entire group. On the occasion of Hanukkah, she made presents for everyone out of old materials she found in the attic.

Her writing consistently reveals a person of resolve, one who has her emotions generally under control, and like the stoics, one whose spirit refuses to be broken. She admits to being afraid of death, but can that be called irrational? At the same time, she is not obsessed with fear. "When I sat in front of the window this morning I suddenly realized that we have had a great, great many compensations. I mean inward compensation."[8]

She proudly admits to believing nobody is all bad, despite the suffering she and her family have had to bear and the possibility of even more dreadful consequences to come. In the context of her brief but intensely rational life, her forgiving attitude seems more the triumph of the happy person (in Aristotle's sense) than the sentimentality of a young romantic. Observations like hers are not the result of a momentary, on-the-spot impulse, sudden flurries of passing joy unjustified by the circumstances; rather, they persist in one form or another

Whosoever is happy will make others happy too.

—**Anne Frank**

Aristotle would agree that Martin Luther King Jr. was a tragic victim, but would add that his was the very archetype of the happy life.

Source: Steve Schapiro/Corbis.

Considered by many to be the greatest orator since Abraham Lincoln, he gave hope to millions with his "I Have a Dream" speech on August 28, 1963.

throughout the diary, evidence of a mature mind that knows intuitively what Aristotle had reasoned thousands of years ago: *life is good for one who is good.* Though Anne Frank was eventually captured and killed in a concentration camp, we can say, in Aristotelian terms, that hers was a happy life tragically foreshortened.

Martin Luther King Jr. (1929–1968), winner of the Nobel Peace Prize in 1964, devoted his own foreshortened life to non-violent protest against racism and the denial of civil rights to African Americans. An ordained Baptist minister, King was often in the midst of police brutality, urging victims to stay calm and not to reciprocate in kind when force was used. Considered by many as the greatest American orator since Abraham Lincoln, he gave hope with his stirring rhetoric to millions of the poor. He made numerous memorable speeches, but the most memorable of all was his "I Have a Dream" oration, delivered on the Washington Mall on August 28, 1963.

In this oration, heard by the many thousands assembled for the March on Washington, King confronted the bitter truths of injustice, discrimination, school and housing segregation, and widespread joblessness. Without giving hollow protestations of hope, he gave what he surely must have considered rational reasons for hope, but always stressing non-violence.

> *Let us not seek to satisfy our thirst for freedom by drinking from the cup of bitterness and hatred. We must ever conduct our struggle on the high plane of dignity and discipline. We must not allow our creative protest to degenerate into physical violence. Again and again we must rise to the majestic heights of meeting physical force with soul force.*

Later in the speech, King introduced the now famous motif of "I have a dream," a statement that begins eight paragraphs. One is a poignant personal reference that is at the same time universal:

> *I have a dream that my four little children will one day live in a nation where they will not be judged by the color of their skin but by the content of their character.*

It is impossible to think that Dr. King was unaware of how dangerous it was to stand by his uncompromising principles and to take his powers of oratory into the most segregated parts of the country, knowing full well how many enemies were lying in wait. Five years after giving this speech that now belongs in the history of the humanities, he was assassinated by a man who spent the remainder of his life in prison, never admitting guilt or showing remorse.

Now, would Aristotle say Martin Luther King's life was a happy one? The answer is very probably *yes*. Aristotle would argue that he was a good man in the highest sense of that word, preaching a non-violent creed. His was a life extraordinarily characterized by virtue and reason, and although he was a tragic victim, his was the very archetype of a happy life.

Eastern Philosophy of Happiness

In the West, as we have abundantly seen, happiness is often regarded as an entity, almost like an object that is to be sought, possessed, and cherished. To the non-Western mind what we call happiness is often called *bliss*, and it is a state, a condition. It is nothing that is ever owned. It is very like what is meant when someone remarks, "My head is in a good place today." It is somewhere to go, not something to hold. It is a place occupied sometimes, but not always. It is close to the stoicism of Western philosophy in that the state is one in which we cope with life's inevitable pain. For those who heed its call, bliss is the serenity that carries us through life.

The Eastern religions of Hinduism and Buddhism. Though they differ on many points, both stress the attainment of total release from suffering as the goal of living and the thing that makes life good—and, we would say, *happy*.

Learn to be calm and you will always be happy.

—Paramhansa Yogananda

Gandhi

A sterling example of the Hindu path to bliss, or **moksha**, is provided by the life and death of Mohandas Gandhi (1869–1948), who spent his life preaching a gospel of non-violence. He attained a huge following, who anointed him with the title **Mahatma**, meaning "one who is wise and good." The word itself derives from two Sanskrit terms: *maha*, which means "great," and *atman*, which means "soul."

Like Siddhartha, Gandhi wanted to do more than simply save himself by becoming detached from all participation in the world. He wanted to save the world by persuading all those who would listen that a serene and therefore happy existence could come about only through non-violence and love.

Hindu doctrine teaches that the divine spirit dwells inside each person, that the soul of each person is part of *brahman*, the great soul, and therefore is fundamentally good. Unfortunately, the world is filled with luxuries, in plentiful supply to the rich, and with handsome and beautiful human beings who arouse sexual longings that must be fulfilled. The desire to possess both objects (including land) and other people leads to frustration and despair, because, as epicureans well know, there can never be enough pleasure if pleasure is the only goal. The thwarting of burning desire causes people to become violent, to seize what they want by any means.

Gandhi realized that when frustration was multiplied by the entire population of an oppressed land or by an ethnic group subjugated by a stronger power, then revolutionary uprisings were inevitable. The endless cycle of violence, war, and death (often of the most innocent) made life bitter. He knew that, for many, the only way to reach serenity was to back off and do nothing. But for himself, there could be no bliss, no serenity, in a world ruled by hate. Thus he became, as King would become, an activist, determined to make non-violence a potent counterforce.

As a native of India, Gandhi lived under British colonial rule and suffered the pain of discrimination. Speaking out against British imperialism, he acquired considerable notoriety and was frequently denounced in churches and meeting halls, but he also attracted many followers, including foreigners sympathetic to his cause. He carried his message to South Africa, where he found the same sort of prejudice and resistance to change. Exhausted and frequently ill from hunger strikes, he persisted, obsessed with the need to convince those who gathered to hear his speeches that there was only one way for people to live a good life in a good world: to lay down all weapons and talk to each other. He was convinced that through dialogue everyone would discover the basic oneness of all humanity. How could you hate someone who was really *you*?

Gandhi was painfully aware that the greatest threat to peace in India, even more than British sovereignty, was the irreconcilable divide between Hindus and Muslims—each practicing a different religion: the Hindus with their *brahman*, the soul of the world but not a personal god, and the Muslims with their father god, Allah. Hindus had no sacred books like the Qur'an, the word of God as delivered to the prophet Mohammed. To the Muslims, the Hindus were godless infidels. But often, the Hindus held the upper hand. This, after all, was their country.

Even under adversity, Mahatma Gandhi exemplified Aristotle's happy life.

Source: Bettman Corbis.

Gandhi stepped into this bitter conflict and sought to convince each side they could live in peace, that they must tolerate their differences and respect the rights of each to believe as they wished and practice religion as they saw fit. In 1947 India became an independent nation with self-rule, a tremendous step forward for which Gandhi was partly responsible. Yet he was not satisfied. The internal conflicts might never be resolved.

Gandhi's dream, like that of Martin Luther King Jr. decades later, would remain unrealized. On January 30, 1948, as he was about to enter a temple for a period of meditation, he was shot and killed by a Hindu fundamentalist, who apparently hated Muslims and could not tolerate the idea of universal love and peaceful coexistence.

Once again we have evidence that if perfect happiness is to be anything more than momentary joy, it has to be recognized as a distant goal that can probably never be reached but can be *approached* through unceasing effort. One can only conclude that Gandhi was one of the few really happy people. He may not have known he was or have even taken the time to think about the matter. If Aristotle's spirit had followed him about, much like a guardian angel, the Greek philosopher might have decided that his was a shining example of the happy life. He did not have health or wealth, two of the components of (but not the equivalents of) Aristotelian happiness, but he surely possessed the two most important ones: reason and virtue.

Gandhi's is an extreme, actually an archetypal, example of the good life. We should not expect it to demonstrate how the average citizen of India or any non-Western country views happiness, any more than we should expect the average citizen of the West to agree with Socrates or Epicurus or Epictetus. Perhaps happiness is a gossamer thing that we can ascribe to certain lives, while we wish that *ours* could be better.

Buddhist Paths to Happiness: Hinayana and Mahayana

For Buddhists, bliss, or **nirvana**, has a twofold nature. Historians of Buddhism explain that over the centuries the religion divided into two schools, both leading to nirvana. One is **Hinayana**, which means "little ferry-boat." It developed first, and its job was to formulate the teachings of Siddhartha into a systematic use of the Four Noble Truths, which are: *life is filled with pain; the cause of pain is frustrated desire; there is a way out of pain; the way out is the Eightfold Path.* The latter has to do with how we think, speak, behave toward others, and above all, how we find peace through meditation (see Chapter 10).

While Hinayana Buddhism involves moral conduct, which is automatic if we follow all of the recommended steps, its practice was seen by those who came after Siddhartha as too narrow, too limited. It proved to be a wonderful means of self-help, of lifting the spirits of the depressed and the stressed-out people of the world (as it still is for the many who practice Buddhist meditation in Western societies), but not a way to assist others who may have lost their way.

Gradually the school known as **Mahayana**, "big ferryboat," developed, adding a larger perspective and a more expansive concept of bliss. In Tibetan Buddhism, which continues the lineage of Siddhartha and teaches that nirvana is attainable in one lifetime by those who follow the rigorous discipline of the Eightfold Path, the fully enlightened person now becomes a buddha. In the company of other buddhas, he or she is ready to follow in the footsteps of Siddhartha: that is, renouncing bondage to the illusory pleasures of this world and doing whatever is necessary, wherever it may be. It can mean something as simple as collecting clothes, food, and other supplies for victims of a devastating fire, storm, or earthquake, or joining a corps of volunteers and helping to rebuild damaged homes. Or it can mean becoming a world-renowned person, carrying a message of peace and tolerance to millions. In Buddhism, both choices have equal importance.

There is nothing self-congratulatory about the Mahayana path. One does not pat oneself on the back and bask in the glow of satisfaction that comes from knowing one has done a good deed or made a tremendous sacrifice. Mahayana Buddhism says it is the logical next step after one has practiced the

---

Archetypes in This Chapter

Deserving	from earliest childhood we are conditioned to expect praise or material rewards; this has an impact later on our sense of how happy we are or are not.
Failure	inability to live up to standards imposed by society and its institutions, especially family, education, and workplace.
Happy	what we are brought up to believe we are supposed to be and, as we grow, what we deserve to be.
Ownership	one of the most important of all icons; what we learn to desire; what we come to think we deserve, the maximum of which we often equate with total happiness.
Peace	state or condition of being without personal stress; state of coexistence in which there is mutual understanding and no hostility, working toward which is the fundamental quality of the happy life for a good many persons, past and present.
Sad	exceedingly complex icon; a condition we are led to believe no one deserves and often assumed by those who enjoy self-pity or who desperately need compassion from others.
Success	often believed to be a tangible entity we must seek, or an inner self-congratulatory sensation, especially when it is achieved at the expense of someone else's failure.

We have no more right to consume happiness without producing it than to consume wealth without producing it.

—**George Bernard Shaw**

Hinayana, or narrow, way. The idea is that, having reached enlightenment after long years of meditation, one has no choice but to live in and through others, just as Siddhartha, having reached enlightenment after forty days and forty nights of sitting under the *bodhi* tree, declined to enter nirvana, feeling he must share his bliss with everyone else: he must teach them how to be as serene as he has become.

Many thousands in the East and the West do not practice Buddhism as such, nor do they nor can they take the extreme steps of Gandhi or King, but they nonetheless care deeply about social issues, such as poverty or the environment. These people find they cannot be personally—or at least not entirely—happy in the midst of so much that is going wrong. Then there are people who, though comfortable in their own fortunate lives, feel guilty when they see photographs of hungry children in war-torn countries or the homeless in any major city anywhere. They can't shrug it off with a "Well, they're not people I know, and what can *I* do?" Whether they know it or not, they have already taken a few steps on the Mahayana, or wider, path.

In the time of Siddhartha the world had many troubles, but there were no global conflicts of today's dimensions, no continual outbreaks of terrorism, no everyday fears that disaster is omnipresent and waiting to happen anywhere, anytime, to anyone. Were he alive today, he would very likely have been at Ground Zero on September 12, 2001, asking what he could do to help. For most of the rest of us, doing what is necessary may have an understandably narrower definition. There are obligations to family, to work, to our circle of friends. There are children to meet at the corner where the school bus leaves them off, an aging parent or other relative to care for, and a host of personal tasks to be done, such as pursuing a degree, learning a trade or profession, supporting a family. Most of us cannot become buddhas or live as Siddhartha did, wandering from place to place without a family, eating very little, paying scant attention to our other wants. Yet Mahayana Buddhism does not expect quite this much. However far you go on the Path is better than not taking that first step. This is the Buddhist view of happiness.

The Dalai Lama

The Dalai Lama, the acknowledged leader of Tibetan Buddhism, is a role model for thousands who seek to emulate his serenity as well as his Mahayana efforts on behalf of world peace. Those who admire him and flock to his lectures often are curious about what it means to do without many of the pleasures that a others of his stature and following usually enjoy—particularly pleasures of the flesh.

> *I am sometimes asked whether this vow of celibacy is really desirable and indeed whether it is really possible. Suffice to say that its practice is not simply a matter of suppressing sexual desires. On the contrary, it is necessary to fully accept the existence of those desires and to transcend them by the power of reasoning. When successful, the result of the mind can be very beneficial. The trouble with sexual desire is that it is a blind desire and can only give temporary satisfaction. Thus, as Nagarjuna said: "When you*

*have an itch, you scratch. But not to itch at all is better than
any amount of scratching."*[9]

His writings are full of wise sayings and aphorisms in short entries that
remind one of the *Tao Te Ching* of Lao-tzu. And with their publication and dis-
semination throughout the globe, the Dalai Lama must, of course, hope that he
will lead thousands, even millions, to the path of serenity. Knowing how to live
a serene existence would make a good many people desist from doing their
utmost to spread terror and hatred and continually renew the cycle of war
and broken peace accords. He cannot, however, wish that the peace (and hope
for happiness) of the entire world would come about only when all sides are of
one mind.

> *All the waters and rivers of different lands and climes have their
> ultimate meeting point in the ocean. So, too, the differing viewpoints
> on society, the variety of economic theories, and the means to their
> attainment benefit mankind itself. There is no point in indulging in
> dissension-creating discussions on differing ideologies. No positive
> result has accrued from attempting to convert all men of different
> temperaments and likings into one common ideology and mode
> of behavior.*[10]

In his view, serenity—or, as he calls it, tranquility—has to be achieved through
acceptance of, not the burning need to change, everyone else.

> *The essence of all spiritual life is your emotion, your attitude
> toward others. Once you have pure and sincere motivation, all the
> rest follows. You can develop this right attitude toward others on
> the basis of kindness, love, and respect, and on the clear realization
> of the oneness of all human beings.*[11]

Whether we call it *bliss*, *moksha*, or *nirvana*, or go with the hedonists and
insist that it is having as much as possible of life's pleasures—plenty of money, sex,
fast cars, a showcase for a home—the nature of the good life remains open to
debate. This chapter has not promised an easy resolution, a neat summing up.
Happiness is but one of the colors we apply to the canvas of "human."

The terms *winner* and *loser* are strong in our vocabularies. Frequently they
drive us to an either-or approach to living. Blithely we describe someone as a loser
and resolve that only *winner* will ever apply to *us*. But if a loser is someone who
fails at everything, must a winner be the exact opposite? Is it possible to win continually? Do we always know what it *means* to win? And what is *loss*? The absence
of money, health, love? Can these be absent continually?

We do not wish to leave you with the impression that Aristippus, Epicurus,
Aristotle, or Siddhartha discovered the best and only road to happiness. Our
advice is to carefully map out your requirements for the good life, bearing in
mind some of the options discussed in this chapter. Once you recognize that *you*
are in control of defining happiness and can make it mean what is possible for
you, not what you can never hope to achieve, then you may experience a measure
of contentment.

If you want to be happy, be.
—**Leo Tolstoy**

Key Terms

big-earnings theory from the hedonist view that people who work hard or who make sacrifices for others deserve material rewards.

carpe diem Latin phrase meaning "seize the day"; a major hedonist creed which advises us to live for the moment and amass all the pleasures we can.

epicureanism based on teachings of Epicurus, the belief that happiness is freedom from pain.

hedonism from the Greek for "delight," the belief that happiness consists of the sum of all the pleasures we can experience.

Hinayana one of the two major schools of Buddhism; from the Sanskrit meaning "little ferryboat," also called the "narrow path," the personal attainment of serenity through meditation.

Mahatma from Sanskrit words meaning "great" and "soul," a title of love and respect for one who is known to be wise and good; applied to Gandhi.

Mahayana one of the two major schools of Buddhism; from Sanskrit meaning "big ferryboat," the wider path to happiness, attainable by helping others find the way.

moksha early Hindu term for the highest state of happiness possible, a condition of pure bliss in which one is free from all desire.

nirvana Buddhist term for the highest state of happiness possible, akin to the Hindu concept of *moksha*.

schadenfreude German term for the experience of joy in the misfortunes of others.

stoicism named for the *stoa* (porch) where Zeno taught the philosophy of curbing desire to cope with the inevitability of pain.

Topics for
Writing and Discussion

1. If you had to choose one theory of happiness discussed in this chapter as dominant in our society, which would it be? Explain. Then indicate whether it represents your own view.

2. Create and then describe three television commercials for the same product, each directed toward a different audience: (a) a hedonist, (b) an epicurean, and (c) a Buddhist.

3. Choose one of the following options for discussion or a short paper:
   a. A gambler who has lost all evening makes one last bet with money that has been saved for the down payment on a house and wins back twice the sum. Could you justify the risk? Or take the gambler to task regardless of the win? Is life a matter of taking risks anyway? Is it worth playing close to the vest?
   b. In a children's game of musical chairs, one child is clearly the winner. Should the organizers of the game give each child the same prize in order not to hurt anyone's feelings? Or should children be taught at an early age how the world usually works? Which of these two approaches is likely to produce the happier child?
   c. The big-earnings theory, discussed in the chapter, maintains that people who work hard or sacrifice

for each other deserve substantial rewards. Pretend you have found somebody's wallet containing $1,000 as well as the name and phone number of the owner. You return it and receive a "thank you very much" and that's all. You ask Aristippus, Epicurus, and Aristotle how you should feel. What do they answer?

4. Write a toast you would make for a newly married couple, as if you were (a) a stoic and then (b) the Dalai Lama.

5. Andrew Carnegie wrote: "While the law of competition may be sometimes hard for the individual, it is best for each race, because it insures the survival of the fittest. We accept and therefore welcome great inequality of environment, the concentration of business in the hands of a few, and the law of competition between them as being essential for the future progress of the race." On which theory of happiness is this idea based? Do you agree with it? Why or why not?

6. Which theory of happiness in your opinion is most helpful to the world and which the least? Explain your answers.

7. The mother in a very poor family once made fried dough with powdered sugar for Thanksgiving dinner

and told everyone they were going to have a real treat. Which philosophy of happiness would be most likely to say this was a lie? Which would be most likely to agree with the mother? Think carefully before you answer, then explain your choices.

8. Go back to the opening page of this chapter and look carefully at the illustration. The artist called it "Good Fortune." Do the people in the drawing exemplify that title? Is something else going on?

9. The English philosopher Bertrand Russell said work is a major component of happiness. Which kind of work do you anticipate doing? Which kind of work do you think offers the best chance of leading you to happiness? Are they the same?

10. A philosopher said, "Take care that your happiness does not depend on what happens to you." To which theory of happiness is this statement most closely related? Is it, in your opinion, a reasonable or even possible approach to living? What can be said in favor of and against it?

10 Freedom

Overview

Like love and happiness, freedom is a desirable commodity. The fundamental belief of our society is that everyone is equal at birth, entitled to life, liberty, and the pursuit of happiness. Freedom is vital to the art of being human: the freedom to create and to enjoy what others create; the freedom to think and listen to the thoughts of others, whether in agreement or not; the freedom to examine one's options and then decide on the wisest course of action.

Yet like love and happiness, freedom has not had the same meaning in every historical context. The Greeks, for example, invented the concept of democracy and passed on as their legacy the model of the democratic state, in which citizens are free to think, to question, and to speak out. At the same time, free citizens comprised only about 5 percent of the population. The rest were slaves and women, whom the citizens generally deemed too irrational and irresponsible to be trusted with political decisions. Similarly, the Roman state also denied freedom to the majority of the population and held many thousands in slavery, believing that it had the right to enslave the conquered in the name of civilization, which it was bringing to the barbarian world. But Rome also had its famous Forum, where duly qualified citizens had the right to exchange ideas and debate the laws, even if an emperor such as Caligula ruled with an iron hand.

Christianity struggled for centuries with the complexity of freedom. Like most monotheistic religions, Christianity demanded obedience to the one, all-knowing God. The idea that God was necessarily omnipotent implied, however, that God had to know the result of every human choice before the choice was made. Whether or not the potential thief was inwardly torn between desiring to steal and realizing it was wrong, God could not be imagined as looking down in suspense, wondering what the person was going to do. In the mind of an all-knowing God, the deed was already accomplished. If indeed the choice, known by God in advance, was to go ahead and steal, how then, asked many, could the thief be held accountable for an act he could not avoid committing? To solve the problem, the Christian theologian Augustine, as we pointed out in Chapter 10, said that God gave humanity free will as a gift. To say that the result of choice is known to God does not mean that God *demanded* a certain outcome. Humanity is both free by God's grace and predestined because of God's

Man is free. This at once a heady luxury and also the source of his discontent.

—**Carlton Beck**

◔ An artist's whimsical drawing suggesting the forces that control our actions.

Source: Fineart America.

In all this he always acts according to necessary laws, from which he has no means of emancipating himself.

—Baron d'Holbach

foreknowledge. Detractors argue that Augustine cannot have it both ways. We are either free or we are not free.

The Augustine problem is only one of many recognized by the humanities in relation to that highly valued human state—being able to do what one feels like doing. It seems clear that, before we can insist on freedom, we need to understand just what we are talking about. A close look at the subject raises a very important question: *How free are we?* Can we really do what we please?

Another question: *When we argue that we should be free to do what we really want to do, how do we know what we really want?* Perhaps many forces are pushing us in one direction or another. How much of what we are, what we think, and what we do was determined long before we ever entered this world? A great many scientists, philosophers, sociologists, economists, and psychologists maintain that total freedom is an impossibility, even in a free society.

This chapter focuses on *whether or not the will is truly free.* It also asks *what does it mean to be a truly free individual?* We will look into two major aspects of the debate. **Determinism** is the philosophical belief that complete freedom of the will does not exist, that there are too many factors governing our choices. Its opposite is **indeterminism**, the belief that our actions are not necessarily determined by a prior cause, and therefore we have free will to make choices. Determinist arguments outnumber indeterminist arguments, but readers must resolve the issue for themselves. Besides the philosophical speculation about whether or not we have free will, there is also the political issue of *freedom.* **Libertarianism** holds that one's free will should be unrestricted. Most governments, however, impose some curbs on human freedom.

Determinism: People Are Limited in Their Choices

First, we will consider the many arguments claiming that we are not, or at least not completely, free. Only when we offer a meaningful challenge to these arguments do the words *I am free* acquire true and powerful significance. Growing up and constantly hearing the phrase *free country* is likely to put our rational faculties to sleep, to lull us into the unexamined assumption that, because we are told we live in a free country, we must obviously be free.

We think of freedom as the ability to choose between alternatives, particularly those that strongly oppose each other: obeying the speed limit or driving faster than we should down the highway; spending an entire paycheck for a night on the town or saving a substantial portion; deciding on marriage or staying single. Listing the number of options with which we are faced each day might cause us to think we are indeed free.

Yet stop a moment and reflect on even one of these options. Without an automobile, the first alternatives are reduced to just words. There is a limitation right off. Without the money or adequate credit, we cannot buy the automobile—another limitation. Without a job, we cannot have either money or credit. What kind of job? It has to be a good one if we seek a certain kind of automobile. If we do not have sufficient training, many jobs are out of the question. Of course, money to buy ten cars can be inherited or left by a benefactor, but to qualify, we have to be born in the right circumstances.

Economic considerations encompass only one class of limitations. Suppose one is born without the coordination that makes driving possible: a genetic limitation. In order to go 50 miles per hour in a 40 mile zone, one must be willing to risk being stopped by the police. Even if this were a first offense, one would be forever deprived of the opportunity to commit a first offense again—a legal limitation. As the offenses mount, the limitations on choice become imposing.

Rigid determinists believe the limitations that are integral to our lives are too numerous for there to be any question of making a *free* choice, ever. We are free to vote for whomever we like *from a given list of candidates*. Our social class lays down the parameters of our lifestyle. Responsibilities incurred by marriage and family tell some they must continue reporting to jobs they may not like, or tell others they must put a career on hold in order to care for children. Switching roles results not in greater freedom but in different limitations.

Augustine's concept of predestination Chapter 10) would have qualified him as a determinist were it not for his counter belief in God's *gift* of free will. Had they known the term, the Puritans of the early American colonies would have denied that they were determinists even though they believed in predestination. The reason? They argued that, though people's choices were already known to the all-knowing God, ordinary mortals could know if they were saved or damned by performing good deeds, reading their Bible, and appearing in church—signs they would be welcomed into heaven. And in this way, the good Puritans believed, they were directing their own destinies.

Determinism proper emerged from the eighteenth-century revolution in philosophy, triggered by science—in particular, the impact of the view that every effect must have a cause. Taking this scientific law and applying it to human behavior, some philosophers argued that all choice is limited by a prior condition, limited so severely that it cannot be considered a free choice. Each of us is in fact the product of a chain of cause and effect stretching back to the very dawn of existence.

Let us examine a few major arguments against the existence or exercise of free will: limitations on freedom of action, past and present; institutional determinism; economic determinism; character consistency; behaviorism; genetics; and sociobiology.

Despite his own widely publicized life of personal indulgence, the artist Picasso is here drawn to a condition that limits free choice in this portrait of a woman who is enslaved by her designated role either as housewife or employee.

Source: Pablo Picasso, *Woman Ironing* (1904). Credit: © 2003 Estate of Pablo Picasso. Artists Rights Society (ARS), New York/ The Solomon R. Guggenheim Museum, New York, Thannhauser Collection, gift, Justin K. Thannhauser. 1978 Photo David Heald at The Solomon R. Guggenheim Foundation, New York, NY.

The issue of freedom has haunted philosophers for a long time, and it appears there are more arguments against freedom than for it.

Past and Present Limitations on Free Action

The most evident obstacles to freedom of choice and action are the restrictions imposed on the individual by groups in power. Enforced slavery is, regrettably, not a thing of the past. In far too many places, for example, young children are either sold to or kidnapped by underground organizations reaping huge profits from offering their services for a price. When driving in certain parts of the United States, one can see prisoners in their orange uniforms hacking away at underbrush under the broiling sun.

The independent film *Chinese Dreams* (2004) deals with uneducated, poverty-stricken young men in China who are lured into signing up for work in the United States with promises of unlimited opportunities but who are smuggled into the country, brought to New York without being told where they are, forced into menial labor for long hours every day in the stifling heat of a restaurant kitchen, and made to live in dirty, crowded, airless dormitories, never seeing sunlight. When the sensitive young protagonist finally escapes one night, he is penniless and bewildered by the roaring traffic and frenetic pace of the big city, a vast neon wasteland in which he will never be free to create his own destiny.

Millions exist in countries that deny freedom to all but a privileged few. Azar Nafisi, now a professor at Johns Hopkins University and author of *Reading Lolita in Tehran*, formerly taught in Iran at a university held to be the most liberal in that country. It did admit some women, but they were not treated as the equals of the male students. "I felt helpless as I listened to their endless tales of woe. Female students were being penalized for running up the stairs when they were late for classes, for laughing in the hallways, for talking to members of the opposite sex."[1]

Thwarted in her attempts to enlarge the scope of her students' reading background and their critical thinking skills, Nafisi decides she will never be allowed to teach books that invite a free exchange of ideas and so offers her resignation, which is promptly refused on the grounds that only the university has the right to decide when employment is to be terminated. At length she does manage to leave, but not without a feeling of regret that she has been unable to fulfill her mission as a teacher, one dedicated to opening the minds of her students so that they might think for themselves.

Facing up to the reality that freedom is denied to a large portion of the world's population can be unpleasant. We may be tempted to just shrug our shoulders, as if to say, "But what can I do about it? Let's just be glad *we're* free." Yet understanding that *free* is not a word to be tossed about lightly or to be simply *assumed* is the first, absolutely essential step we must take. Even if we are lucky enough not to be penalized for laughing in the hallway, so goes the determinist argument, too many other forces must at some point be recognized, all the more frightening because they have no human face.

Institutional Determinism

Though he is known as one of the staunchest advocates of freedom from oppression, Jean-Jacques Rousseau (1712–1778), whom many consider the major architect of the French Revolution, is also famous for his analysis of the forces that limit freedom. Since these forces are still at work, he must be considered, in part at least, a determinist. If he could be asked, his answer might well be: "I wish I were not, but the conditions under which we live require me to adopt this belief."

Rousseau's thinking was as radical as that of any activist of the modern era. He was vehemently against any repressive government with the power to limit human choices. The ideal form of government, he reasoned, is something we *should* be free to create. Total freedom, however, was for him impossible, given the uncontrollable forces stacked against everyone. But to take what freedom remained and surrender it to one human being or group of human beings was an affront to all civilized people. He believed the ideal government was answerable to the entire population rather than existing for personal power or prestige.

In fanning the revolutionary flames beginning to sweep through a France increasingly outraged at the decadence of the aristocracy and the injustices suffered by the common people, Rousseau constructed a mythical account of the origin of the human species to back up his claim that freedom was both a natural condition and a natural right. Called *A Discourse on the Origins of Inequality*, the myth draws a romantic picture of a lost age of innocence, when early people lived in peace and harmony, sharing the fruits of the earth through a common realization that nature provided equal bounty for everyone. In this age of innocence, no laws or government existed because, obviously, law and government are not necessary when everyone is happy and there is no crime. In and of itself, the idea of a lost age of innocence was not new. Judaism, Christianity, and Islam all share the belief that our earliest ancestors lived in the Garden of Eden before their fall from God's grace. In Color Plate 40, you will find one of the most famous depictions of the Garden paintings: *The Garden of Eden* by the Flemish artist Jan Brueghel (1568–1625).

In the Rousseau myth, there came one day *the man with the stick*, the first person to take it into his head to grab more than his natural share of things, the first person to *abuse* nature's gift of freedom by putting it to his own advantage. With his stick he carved out a private piece of territory for himself: "The first man, who, after enclosing a piece of ground, took it into his head to say, 'This is mine,' and found people simple enough to believe him, was the true founder of civil society."

The man with the stick was the founder of society as Rousseau knew it because, by creating the model of the exploiter (the inhuman alternative to natural freedom), he and his followers became an ever present threat to the rights of the others. The exploiters therefore had to be suppressed by the gradual development of law, government, and all other institutions dedicated to the curtailment, or the limitation, of natural rights. But these safeguards of liberty, once in place, become despotic. It is here that Rousseau's position truly becomes revolutionary—literally. Rousseau asserted that revolution, even if violent, is a genuine alternative to exploitation and in many cases may be the only means by which to deal with it.

Rousseau explains and justifies revolution in the name of natural rights belonging to all, but he fails to account for the *origin* of the man with the stick in his myth. What made this one man decide to become possessive while the others were joyously bobbing for golden apples in an age of sun and fun? Or was he merely the first to manifest himself? Did the potential for exploitation lie deep within *every* member of that "innocent" society? If so, when were institutional safeguards ever *not* needed?

Rousseau's anti-institutional bias is based on the assumption that in the *state of nature* (a phrase hotly debated then and since), humankind is decent, tame, moral, and benevolent. Only when held in check, only when threatened with punishment for disobedient acts, do people become hateful, aggressive, and violent— except for periods of rebelling in a just cause. But what Rousseau did not know, because he died a decade before the revolution he predicted, was that Napoleon Bonaparte would rise from the ashes of France and, sword in hand, create a new

I am as free as Nature first made man,
Ere the base laws of servitude began,
When wild in woods the noble savage ran.

—**John Dryden**

The man with the stick was the founder of society as Rousseau knew it because, by creating the model of the exploiter, he and his followers became an ever present threat to the rights of others.

Rousseau justifies revolution in the name of natural rights but fails to account for the origin of the man with the stick.

age of exploitation, perhaps even more oppressive than the one it supplanted. History shows us that this cycle of oppression, liberation, and further oppression has been repeated many times over.

How shall we ever put Rousseau's assumption to the test? How shall we ever know whether most people, left on their own without law or government, would remain peaceful and willing to share the fruits of the earth with each other, or whether the *people with sticks* would come along and start once again the cycle of exploitation and revolution? What *does* appear certain is that few revolutions within human memory have been without their exploiters, often the revolutionary leaders themselves.

A tragic example of a revolutionary cause turned lethal occurred on November 18, 1978, when over 900 members of a religious sect called People's Temple were ordered to commit suicide by drinking cyanide-laced Kool-Aid. From all accounts, their leader, Jim Jones, was in the beginning earnest about establishing a communal agricultural society, which, had it come to pass, would have resembled Rousseau's free and benevolent community. But when many became disillusioned and tried to defect, the community turned into a prison. One member was able in secret to contact outside sources, describing Jones's manic, self-absorbed leadership, forced sexual intercourse, and brutal beatings administered to those who disobeyed his rules. Four Americans, including U.S. Representative Leo Ryan and several relatives of Jones's prisoners, visited the camp but were gunned down before they could reboard their plane. Facing exposure and the end of his control over the group, Jones ordered the mass suicide. Among the dead were 270 children. A memorial service was held, and one speaker said: "Remember the people of Jonestown, not for their horrible deaths, but for who they were—people in search of a better world."

If a strong-willed person leads a benevolent cause, Rousseau might have said, does it sometimes lead to "forced benevolence," which then must be autocratically monitored? Is the stick inborn in certain people, who become a menace to civilized life and must in turn be controlled? Are the institutions of control inevitable? And can *they* in turn become oppressive, acting as curtailments on everyone's freedom?

Rousseau believed he had solved the problem when he advanced the theory of the *social contract*. By this he meant that the only way to guarantee the protection of human rights was not through unlimited freedom but through each citizen's willingness to hand over some rights to institutions dedicated to the maintenance of order within society. The social contract is a cornerstone of **institutional determinism**, which holds that government controls are needed to protect people from other people.

The problem, unfortunately, did not end there. What happens when institutions insist they must have more and more power in order to do their job? Are they then challenged by those who insist on unlimited freedom? And if unlimited freedom should ever be realized, will a person with a stick suddenly appear? Does the whole cycle begin again?

> *If you ask me what I came to do in this world, I, an artist, will answer you, "I am here to live out loud."*
>
> —**Emile Zola**

Economic Determinism

The philosophy of Karl Marx (1818–1883) profoundly influenced the Bolshevik Revolution of 1917 in Russia and the subsequent spread of socialism and communism throughout the world. Despite the failure of the socialist experiment in the Soviet Union and its satellite nations, Marxism continues to be strong in other countries, notably China, North Korea, and Cuba.

Marx believed that money was the key influence in all of our choices. As an economist, he developed a theory explaining that our behavior, our hopes and aspirations, our career choices are all determined by the social class into which we are born. The rich want to hold onto their money and tend to favor legislation designed to keep their holdings intact. The poor desire to better themselves, and in some cases, this desire becomes an obsession, eclipsing everything else in their lives. Lacking money, some who are driven to a life of crime might otherwise have been decent neighbors. If we are middle class, we want to climb to the top, while making sure that those below are not following too closely.

Marx believed that **economic determinism**—which holds that the quest for money and property controls our thinking and dictates our actions—inevitably led to a society divided into two classes: the affluent **bourgeoisie**, or middle class that controls means of production, and the **proletariat**, or workers. Sooner or later the proletariat, made furious by the unfair distribution of wealth, would unite, rise up, and seize the means of production for themselves. Marx envisioned this demand taking place naturally and without violence.

His theory was influenced by the thinking of an earlier German philosopher, Georg Wilhelm Friedrich Hegel (1770–1831), who had developed the theory that we reach philosophical certainty through a method he called the **dialectic**, which involves analyzing opposing views and combining them into a *synthesis*. Marx took Hegel's abstractions and applied them to the concrete realities of the class struggle. The opposition of the bourgeoisie, who want to hold onto money and power, and the proletariat, bent on seizing some of it, would lead to a synthesis Marx called the *classless society*.

Communism, a social system based on the idea of the classless society, was the banner of the 1917 revolution in Russia. The Communists disagreed with Marx, however, in the matter of non-violence. They had grown tired of waiting for the *natural* coming of what was described as a workers' paradise. Their leader, Vladimir Lenin (1870–1924), extended Marxism to include the idea that a one-class society might have to be reached through violent revolution. With "The ends justify the means!" as their battle cry, the Communist Party overthrew the czar (eventually executing him and his family) and established a new order whereby all property would be state owned. There would be no private sector, no capitalism with its assumption that clever entrepreneurs had the right to exploit others and get as far ahead as possible.

Communism entails complete state ownership, usually referred to as *public* ownership. Socialism is nearly the same thing but holds that a limited amount of private business is a necessity. For example, the Soviet Union soon realized that public ownership of all farm lands was not practical. Could farmers be induced to raise crops and livestock for society as a whole rather than for themselves and their families? Since the answer seemed to be no, the agricultural workers were given small farms (about one acre) and told they could answer their own needs first and then sell what was left over. As a result, they were better off than factory workers in the city. The vast majority of the population under communism were given assigned jobs, and everybody was paid what was considered a modest, but decent, wage. The housing program was administered by the state under the strictest of guidelines: so many square feet per person.

As time went on, more and more capitalism became necessary. The classless society never really materialized, and because the private sector grew, a few people prospered while the mass of workers looked on with envy. Propaganda was strong,

. . . only romantic fools and children of affluence can suppose that being poor is anything but hard.

—Irving Howe

We don't allow our enemies to have guns. Why should we allow them to have ideas?

—Joseph Stalin

The freedom and independence of the worker during the labor process do not exist.

—Karl Marx

constantly assuring the people that their sacrifices were for the good of all. But as time went by, workers began to wonder when the "paradise" was coming. It began to look as though the separation of the rich and the poor was still there. Without being able to satisfy their self-interest, most workers could not be motivated to produce more goods or provide more efficient service.

A serious consequence of the communist experiment was that the majority of workers were unable to see the products of their labor, unlike the farmers. (Much the same is true of assembly-line workers everywhere.) Salespeople in department stores, without the incentive of commissions, failed to go out of their way to sell goods.

The coming of television was a boon to bored Soviet workers crammed into tiny apartments. They scrimped to buy even the tiniest set, but this enabled them to see how their counterparts in the West were supposedly living. Many of the viewers probably did not realize the sitcoms were not telling the whole truth. The illusion must have been powerful indeed: Workers in a free society, with the help of labor unions, were more than comfortable. Viewers under communism might have seen the American sitcom *Julia*, starring an African American. The series centered on the romantic relationships of Julia, a nurse, presumed to be middle-class, except that she lived in a multiroom apartment that did not seem to reflect a nurse's salary. Modest, but decent, wages eventually did not suffice for a population tired of scrounging around in grocery stores for a few vegetables and the limited supply of meat farmers were able to provide.

Whether or not the classless society could ever exist, Marxist theory is still invoked by many as a way of explaining, at least partly, what motivates human behavior. The free world has seen the failure of Soviet communism, but we must remember that economic determinism is a major philosophy and *not* the same thing as the failed system instituted by the Soviet Union and its allies. There remains the question: *To what extent do economic needs control us and therefore set limits on freedom?*

In Chapter 8 we discussed Adam Smith's theory that capitalism is the natural driving force behind human life. Smith argues that greed, natural to humanity, is good because it ensures a free market system. If businesses are allowed the freedom to do what they like, they will provide employment, which in turn gives people disposable income, which in turn moves the economy upward. When there is too much money to spend, businesses raise prices, until a point is reached at which buying slows down and prices began to fall.

Marxism and capitalism share a common underlying assumption: economic needs dominate. Others believe both systems are flawed, because there are never enough material resources to satisfy everybody. In a communist society, workers may not be motivated to produce abundantly. In a capitalist society, the affluent can afford to buy whatever they want regardless of price, but inflated costs eventually harm those less fortunate. The case for determinism at this point becomes very strong. Can anybody escape the desire for more money? The more one has, the less one is likely to be satisfied. The less one has, the need for more becomes obsessive. According to economic determinists, all human behavior can be understood in terms of how much money is or is not available.

Traditional humanists object. They find it degrading to suppose that money should be a paramount concern. After all, are not philosophy, literature, and music supposed to be *alternatives* to the accumulation of wealth? Still, finding pleasure in other than material resources is one thing; denying that economic motivation drives enlightened people is quite another.

There remains the question: To what extent do economic needs control us and therefore set limits on freedom?

When the state exists, there is no freedom. When there is freedom, there will be no state.

—Vladimir Lenin

The art of being human does not entail making a choice between the humanities and money. It *does* require that we observe ourselves in action. If economic motives are not the sole reasons that we do what we do, they *are* sometimes the major ones. Common sense tells us that the poorer we are, the more we look for opportunities to advance.

Theoretically, the chronically poor, those who barely survive on the fringes of society, always have the option of giving up thoughts of advancement and deciding instead to enjoy music and art. Yet museums have entrance fees, galleries charge sometimes exorbitant amounts for original paintings, concerts are expensive, and even CDs can strain a modest budget.

Creative artists, once romantically thought to be "above" the vulgarity of seeking money, retain agents, negotiate contracts, charge high fees for television interviews and college lectures, and go on promotional tours to boost the sales of their latest film or publication.

We never know when economics will suddenly assume the dominant role in our life. We are often constrained by economics, such as when our only options are staying in a job we hate or not being able to make our car payments. Still, to be economically determined is not the same as being either a Marxist or a crass materialist. The important thing is at all times to recognize the roots of our behavior (or try to, anyway). We are chronically unfree the more we remain blind to reality when it confronts us. We take a step on the path to freedom when we begin to see the things that limit us—or when we impose the limitations on ourselves.

Character Consistency

Enduring characters in memorable works of fiction—Don Quixote, Becky Sharp, Huckleberry Finn, and Scarlett O'Hara, for example—stay in our minds not because they are amorphous, fluid, and unpredictable, but because they have specific character traits that can be summarized and that readily explain what they do. If they were real people, the determinist would say they lack free will, that they are bound by the very traits that make them come alive to us.

We think of each other as we think of literary characters. We characterize our family, friends, and associates as we interpret what they say and do. This person is witty and intelligent; that person is arrogant and pretentious; another is totally amoral. Of course, due reflection tells us that real-life people, unlike many characters in books, are unfairly placed in rigid categories. At the same time, when someone does something unexpected and atypical, we are likely to say, "He isn't himself" or "That is so unlike her." We expect predictability. We expect consistency. A determinist argument often advanced is that, the more people are consistent and predictable, the less they are free. A frequently heard determinist pronouncement is that, because insane people are totally unpredictable, *only the insane are totally free.*

Suppose someone stops a stranger in the street and strikes that person in the face. Imagine a panel of experts on human behavior being told this story and asked to predict what the response of the stricken person would be. Their predictions would surely be based on some cause-and-effect view of human interaction, which they would call *rational behavior.* But what does this mean? Does it not mean that the stricken person is expected to respond in one of certain ways that are accepted and shared by all "rational" persons? Thus, the assaulted person may be projected as (1) striking back out of righteous anger; (2) not striking back, because of pacifist beliefs, but attempting to leave without undergoing further

The inherent vice of capitalism is the unequal sharing of blessings; the inherent virtue of socialism is the equal sharing of miseries.

—**Winston Churchill**

A foolish consistency is the hobgoblin of little minds.

—**Ralph Waldo Emerson**

Nothing that is not a real crime makes a man appear so contemptible in the eyes of the world as inconsistency.

—**Joseph Addison**

harm; (3) voluntarily deciding against the use of force on his or her own, preferring to call a police officer; (4) turning the other cheek, because of a strong religious upbringing; or perhaps (5) simply staring in disbelief at the assailant, not quite knowing what to do.

But now suppose the victim does not respond in any of these predicted ways but, instead, suddenly produces a sword and bids the attacker kneel down and be knighted. There is a good chance that not the assailant but the assailed would be hauled away for observation. Such a response would not fall within any *meaningful* category of behavior. The determinist is likely to argue that, of the responses considered, the King Arthur action is the only one rightfully labeled *free*. Under these circumstances, how many of us live in a free world? Or would *want* to if everyone were unpredictable?

Some indeterminists and libertarians not only criticize the character-consistency argument but urge us not to be bound by the character traits instilled in us during the so-called acculturation process. They tell us we can be rational without being continuously predictable. If such were not the case, how could we explain the creative and the imaginative, the divergent thinkers whose oddball notions have in one way or another altered the shape of human experience? Are all of them insane? And, come to think of it, do any of us want to acquire a hard-and-fast reputation for being always and tiresomely the same?

Behaviorism

Founded on the work of B. F. Skinner (1904–1991), **behaviorism** is a school of thought that says we are what we do, and how we behave is determined by a series of rewards and punishments that begins to weave its web as soon as we are born.

If, says Skinner, humanity has a nature, it lies in *the capacity to be conditioned.* Everything we do is the result of a reinforcement of behavior. Those actions that are followed by pleasant consequences tend to be repeated; those followed by unpleasant or painful consequences tend to be avoided. Behaviorism is both a philosophy and a method used by some psychologists to alter patterns of human behavior that need to be changed, according to individual wishes or institutional commands. In both theory and practice, behaviorism believes that what people do is determined by responses to the consequences of their actions. The child who repeatedly drops dishes on the floor is scolded or otherwise punished until the unacceptable behavior is at last avoided.

According to Skinner, freedom is nothing but the effort to escape from the unpleasant consequences of certain actions. We slap at a mosquito that's about to attack to prevent the itching that will follow if we don't. A child who throws a tantrum and is sent to bed without supper may cry so loudly that the parents will change their minds in order that *they* in turn may escape the sound of the crying. Whatever the motive for escape, says behaviorism, the fact remains that the *desir* to escape is a determining force; moreover, if freedom is defined as escape, no such thing as pure and absolute freedom exists because freeing oneself from all unpleasantness is impossible.

People, says Skinner, identify the state of absolute freedom as one in which "aversive control" is absent: that is, if there is no apparent oppression, then people imagine themselves to be free. Skinner calls such people "happy slaves." They are molded by hidden controls and don't know it. Their freedom is an illusion. Victims of oppression are in a sense better off. At least they know where they stand.

Comments like "He isn't himself" or "That is so unlike her" indicate how predictable people are expected to be.

The determinist would argue that only the insane are truly free, because their behavior can't be predicted.

Physics does not change the nature of the world it studies, and no science of behavior can change the essential nature of man, even though both sciences yield technology with a vast power to manipulate their subject matters.

—B. F. Skinner

Skinner adds that "the literature of freedom has been designed to make men 'conscious' of aversive control, but in its choice of methods it has failed to rescue the happy slave."[2] Activists who fight against oppression are concerned solely with obvious victims, not enlightening those who believe they are free.

Behaviorism is often rejected by those who believe that human beings are distinguished from other animals, and that, while animal behavior can be molded through rewards and punishments, human beings have intellect and free will. Skinner's position is that the desire to hold fast to the ancient and honorable abstraction "freedom" is tied in with the belief that human dignity is lost if it is shown that humanity is not nor ever can be considered free. What happens to the great artists, writers, and philosophers if they are considered only products of conditioning forces? "We are not inclined to give a person credit for achievements which are in fact due to forces over which he has no control," says Skinner."[3]

But, he argues further, *dignity* has no meaning as an absolute abstraction. People do not vibrantly experience an inner something called "dignity" at the thought of being free. Like every other human condition, dignity is a very specific response to a particular kind of stimulus: it is the positive reinforcement given to one who has behaved properly or who has performed some achievement deemed notable. Dignity equals praise. Dignity equals recognition. Robbing people of their dignity is taking away recognition they believe they have rightfully earned. It is their reward, much as we give our pets a treat when they show they have learned the trick we taught them.

Praise and recognition represent very positive reinforcements and, as such, are among the most pervasive of conditioning forces. Moreover, we may push Skinner's idea even further and point out that to win praise and recognition, some people would do just about anything required of them. Many forgive their own lapses of artistic or intellectual integrity when the stakes are high enough. How many writers and composers have said a fond farewell to the novel in the desk drawer or the sonata in the piano bench in exchange for fame and fortune in the world of popular entertainment?

Some believe dignity is personal integrity, and that those who hold fast to their dignity, in this sense of the word, are indeed free. For them, the tortured van Gogh possessed *both* dignity and creative freedom.

Skinner would not agree. The title he gave to one of his most influential works is, in fact, *Beyond Freedom and Dignity*. We need, says Skinner, to take broad terms that mean very little in themselves—like "freedom" and "dignity"—and redefine them in strictly behavioral language. We need to concentrate on creating what Skinner calls a "technology of behavior." Since people are going to be conditioned anyway, the focus should be on the good controls that *can* exist. He maintains that "the problem is to free men, not from control, but from certain kinds of control, and it can be solved only if our analysis takes all consequences into account."[4]

Skinner is also a modern utopian thinker, believing that eventually an ideal society can be designed in which people develop their abilities to the maximum through carefully preplanned reinforcements. In such a society there would be no crime, no aggression, no exploitation. *But would we want such a society?*

Anti-Skinnerians argue that a "technology of behavior" sounds too threatening to all hope of freedom. When "behavioral technicians," as he calls the conditioners, realize how much power they have, what will stop them from using those identical controls that Skinner wants to eliminate? What if van Gogh had lived in a

Science can point out dangers, but science cannot turn the direction of minds and hearts. That is the province of spiritual powers within and without our very beings–powers that are the mysteries of life itself.

—Chief Oren Lyons
Faithkeeper of the Turtle Clan
of the Onondaga Iroquois

behaviorally engineered community, one in which the residents were rewarded with candy for going to art galleries displaying his work and with free vacations if they bought it? Suppose those who publicly denounced his work were carted off to jail. Suppose further that as an artist, he had the right to file a petition against those who scoffed at him and was rewarded by having the governing body take money from his detractors and give it to him. Would he then have been truly free? If the detractors who lost their money appealed the ruling on the grounds that van Gogh's work was a hodgepodge, totally lacking in artistic value, perhaps the next step would be that the governing body would reexamine the work and inform van Gogh that, if he wished to continue exhibiting, he would henceforth have to paint in an approved style. Once conditioning becomes institutionalized, how long before *it* becomes aversive control?

Genetics

The sequence:
> *two genomes in each cell (one from each parent)*
> *chromosomes–transmitters of genetic instructions*
> *genes (inside chromosomes)*
> *DNA molecules (inside genes)*

Perhaps the major medical science of the future, *genetics* developed from a study of the role played by biological factors in determining how plants, animals, and human beings develop their characteristics. Exhaustive research has found the way to look inside the infinitesimal cells that compose the various forms of life, discovering what they in turn are made of.

There are an estimated 3 trillion cells in a human body. Within each cell are two **genomes** (one from each parent), which are sets of genetic instructions that determine gender, hair and eye coloring, height, and certain tendencies, such as susceptibility to a disease that runs in the family. These instructions are transmitted through **chromosomes**, long stringy bodies in the cell's nucleus, inside which are the **genes**, granular substances containing the **DNA** molecules, long strands of sugar and sulphate that are the actual carriers of the genetic code determining how we will look and how we will sound.

We now know that diabetes, Alzheimer's disease, cystic fibrosis, and certain forms of cancer can be inherited. Arguments have been advanced that one can inherit alcoholism and other dependencies once thought to have been socially acquired. Advances in genetic research can come almost weekly. Now that the strands of DNA (deoxyribonucleic acid) have all been identified and labeled, gene replacement therapy has become a major goal in medical science. The time may not be far off when an inherited birth defect can be stopped in its tracks by locating and replacing the gene responsible.

Opinions are sharply divided about the advisability and the ethics of investing in medical science the power to use such therapy. Many are afraid of where it could lead. Suppose a gene is discovered that governs intelligence. Will science be able to produce a "super" child? Some say that nothing is wrong with making smarter humans. Others say that gene specialists would have too much power.

On the other hand, what happens if society demands that genes must be left alone to do whatever they are biologically suited to do? Preventable birth defects and inherited diseases would continue unchecked. Yet some are disturbed by the idea of interfering with nature or producing a super race. For certain religious sects, such practices substitute the will of science for the will of God.

In the social sciences, the role of genetics becomes intertwined with the long debate about heredity versus environment, also known as the nature versus nurture dispute. Do we owe our personalities and behavioral patterns to our genetic makeup, or to the influence of family, peers, education, and the social structure around us? Replacing a faulty gene is one thing; replacing external influences at will is quite another.

In addition, no one can say for sure how much of what we are is determined by more than the DNA molecule or by the nurturers. Other factors, including—yes!—a person's will can affect even one's genetic destiny. There are documented cases of people with supposedly incurable diseases who have refused to accept a death verdict and whose determination to live has thwarted medical predictions.

Still, despite all the debates, genetic science continues to make powerful strides and seeks to probe ever deeper into once unimagined possibilities for assuring the human species of a brighter and longer future. Gene replacement has already been amazingly successful, particularly in mice and chimpanzees. Using their knowledge of genetic codes, scientists have cloned animals. This means they already have in their hands the process of bringing about pre-arranged genetic results. Many medical researchers want unrestricted access to stem cells that may, as the technology develops, grow healthier hearts and organs and eliminate diabetes as well as various genetically transmitted diseases. Powerful religious groups lobby against the use of human embryos for the research, but recently a way has been found to extricate stem cells from skin alone. Yet even so, debates over the ethics of interfering with natural processes are likely to continue.

Literature has long been concerned with the danger inherent in out-of-control scientific experiments. One of the earliest literary works to sound a warning was *Frankenstein*, a novel written in 1818 by Mary Wollstonecraft Shelley (1797–1851). The book has become a classic anti-science fable, lending its two central figures—the scientist who creates a live being from sundry body parts and the creature itself—to countless film versions and even comic books, not to mention Broadway musicals.

The subtitle of the novel is *A Modern Prometheus*, from the ancient Greek myth about a man who was half-human and half-god. The human side of his nature caused him to seek liberty and self-determination, to become, in short, as powerful as the gods. In the novel, Victor Frankenstein, the Promethean figure, is a sensitive, gentle person intrigued from childhood by science (then called natural philosophy) and eager to learn everything possible in order to improve the lives of all people, even as his mythological ancestor sought to aid humankind by stealing fire from the gods. As he matures, he finds himself particularly concerned with the way the body functions.

> *Wealth was an inferior object; but what glory would attend the discovery, if I could but banish disease from the human frame, and render man invulnerable to any but a violent death.*

Archetypes in This Chapter

Age of innocence	mythical long-ago when people were happier and life was simpler.
Frankenstein	originally the name of the experimenting doctor in Mary Shelley's famous novel but now used to designate an experiment gone terribly wrong; also a reference to a protégé who turns out to be the opposite of what the mentor intended.
Freedom	can mean liberation from prison, a relationship, or any kind of oppression; also used to mean the major characteristic of democratic societies.
Natural	derived from Rousseau's idea of whatever belongs to the perfect state of nature; now loosely employed to describe such things as food that has not been treated with additives and the sexual orientation deemed acceptable by mainstream society.
Prometheus	in Greek mythology, the titan who stole fire from the gods and gave it to humankind, and was thereafter punished by being chained to a rock where each day an eagle would devour his liver. The myth of Prometheus has had such great influence on the humanities that it gave rise to the adjective "promethean," which signifies a person who is boldly original in thinking or creativity.
Sisyphus	in Greek mythology, a king who was punished for stealing a secret from Zeus by being forever forced to push a huge stone up a hill in Hades only to have it roll down to the bottom every time he neared the top; the adjective derived from this influential myth describes any futile or endlessly laborious action.

Frankenstein is the archetype of a scientific experiment gone terribly wrong.

Yet how is he to find the secret of immortality unless he first learns where life comes from? For Mary Shelley, wife of the famous Romantic poet Percy Bysshe Shelley, nature was to be admired, adored, glorified, but not analyzed—and certainly no human being had the right to tamper with its workings. The tragic flaw of Victor Frankenstein is that he wants to be more than a part of nature, existing harmoniously with the rest. Not content with merely understanding how the spark of life enters lifeless matter—from electricity, he is convinced—he must go further. He must assemble parts of cadavers into an eight-foot superman who will represent the perfection of the species and live forever. The outcome of his experiment is not what he expects.

> *I had selected his features as beautiful. Beautiful! Great God! His yellow skin scarcely covered the work of muscles and arteries beneath; his hair was of a lustrous black, and flowing; his teeth of a pearly whiteness, but these luxuriances only formed a more horrid contrast with his watery eyes, and seemed almost of the same colour as the dun white sockets in which they were set, his shriveled complexion, and straight black lips.*

The Creature, as he is called in the novel once he comes to life, is not the scary ogre of movie fame. Instead, he is an innocent, who kills because his ugly appearance causes him to be persecuted. Not understanding his superhuman strength, he defends himself in the only way he can. Nonetheless, he has become an archetype of an experiment gone terribly wrong.

The work seems surprisingly relevant today, and we may not be far from having yet another version, this time about a geneticist who seeks to create a perfect human being only to . . . well, you can fill in the rest. Meanwhile, comic writer Mel Brooks has had fun writing *Young Frankenstein*, first as a 1974 film and then a 2007 Broadway musical, both about Victor's heir, who wants to recreate the experiment and get it right this time. The new monster sings and dances—if this can be called getting it right. Few novelists have given the future public so enduring (and changeable) an icon as Mary Shelley did in creating Frankenstein.

Manipulation of genes in the sports world is already taking place. Some athletes have been using "gene doping." Foreign genes are injected into cells of the muscles; they carry a "growth code," and the muscles become strengthened. Theodore Friedman, director of the human gene therapy program at the University of California at San Diego, told the National Institute of Health that those "intent on subverting the gene therapy will do so. The technology is too easy."

On the other hand, successful gene therapy, performed with the intention of curing once fatal illness or prolonging human life, may silence those who denounce genetic science. If people can live longer, healthier lives, may not they be free to maximize their potential?

Sociobiology

A discipline combining biology and social science, **sociobiology** assumes the absence of free will and studies human behavior in terms of *genetic investment*. Its beliefs are closely related to those of the self-interest philosophies. The basic assumption is that everything we do pertains to our genetic strain. Love between two people is a matter of genes. If a single male wants unlimited sex with different partners, he is showing that he is not ready to make a genetic investment; he has no immediate need to continue his genetic line. A single female may also want unlimited sex, but even with birth-control devices, she has to think about the possibility that she is making more of a genetic investment than her partner. Marriage and family are viewed as a mutual agreement to make the investment. Married people who do not wish to have children are showing that genetic investment is not necessary for their happiness. Everyone is not the same, but everyone can be studied in relation to a "genetic attitude." How we feel about genetic propagation determines everything we do.

Traditional definitions of love are thus displaced. People who share the same genetic attitudes are likely to attract each other. Even family ties result from sharing a similar gene pool. Altruism, or self-sacrifice, is also redefined. A mother sacrifices for her children, because they represent the continuing life of her own genes. She would face death to save her own child, but not someone else's—unless she has become so close to another's child that she considers the child part of her family, or unless she imagines the child in danger is her own. Soldiers who die to save their battalion do so because the battalion has become a substitute family.

Sociobiologists contend that not just romantic but *all* decisions—political, religious, educational, financial—relate in one way or another to genetics. If nothing else, genes determine *who* we are, and who we are determines what we stand for, and apparently we cannot decide to walk a different path.

But all of this is only half the story. There are many who advance contrary arguments, many for whom freedom is a reality that can be attained.

Sociobiology redefines love in terms of how much genetic investment people are willing to make.

Possibilities for Freedom

This chapter has reviewed a great many determinist views, extending far back into the past and continuing strongly into the present. One reason is that determinist arguments are too powerful to be ignored. Another is that, when the summing up is made, we shall find that much of what they say does indeed apply to many, but perhaps not all, people. The state of being a free person may well be a gift not equally shared. Perhaps the art of being human includes the art of being free, where that is possible. Yet like any art, freedom needs to be very delicately and carefully fashioned and preserved.

Even in free societies, there are many who choose a determinist path. Jeremy Rifkin, in his 2004 book *The European Dream: How Europe's Vision of the Future Is Eclipsing the American Dream*, maintains that Americans in general define freedom in terms of "autonomy and mobility, which requires amassing wealth." We may be free to choose between living for or scorning the pursuit of wealth, but, Rifkin argues, most Americans never feel that they have enough money. By contrast, he finds that "Europeans define freedom in community—in belonging, not belongings." Whether or not this definition is an overgeneralization, we probably need to begin our investigation into possibilities for freedom on a cautionary note, reminding ourselves that we cannot simply *assume* we have a free will or are free.

I have no friends
I make my mind my friend
I have no enemy
I make carelessness my enemy
I have no armor
I make benevolence my armor
—14th century Japanese samurai

A Pessimist's Definition of the Will

Many have argued that the phrase "free will" is redundant, that in fact, if one *has* a will at all, it must be free. The existence of will implies freedom. But! Is there in fact such a thing as the will? Or is what some philosophers have called "will" nothing but causation working through our conscious level, making us *think* we are doing what we want, not what we must? B. F. Skinner, for example, argues that the will can-

Schopenhauer believed that free will was the will to live and could be used for selfish purposes.

not be detected, cannot be felt. We cannot say "I have free will" with reference to a specific sensation or emotion. So *where* is will? Not everyone agrees on an answer.

The German philosopher Arthur Schopenhauer (1788–1860) had no doubt that the will existed, but the fact did not fill him with unmixed feelings of joy. First, he tells us how to *see* the will objectified in an action. Stand in front of a mirror. Observe yourself. Think you would like to raise your left arm. Then do it. One instant the desire to raise the arm is locked inside the mind, the consciousness. The next instant, it is visibly present in the action perceived in the mirror.

Whereas many have thought that having discovered the will is enough to dignify the human condition, Schopenhauer went on to ask: *What is the will for?* It is obvious, one might respond. The will makes free choices among available options.

> *Schopenhauer: Indeed, but is that enough to justify optimism about the human condition? (We say we do not understand.)*
> *Schopenhauer: Is a free choice always a good choice? Suppose the choice is to kill someone. Does the fact that it was a free choice in any way soften the horror of the crime? Do we take a measure of comfort in knowing that the decision to murder was determined solely by the will of the murderer? Would it not be far better had the potential killer been conditioned by a religious upbringing that taught benevolence towards one's fellows?*

Schopenhauer believed the will is actually the will *to live*. The will drives us to actions that we think will benefit us, will ensure our survival. Often these are downright evil.

> *Unjust or wicked actions are, in regard to him who performs them, signs of the strength of his affirmation of the will to live, and thus how far he still is from true salvation, which is denial of this will.*[5]

In other words, while not denying our freedom to act, Schopenhauer is also saying that everyone is constrained, is *forced*, to use the power of will to further their own cause, even if that means harm to others. The freedom of not acting also exists, but too often this results from the fear of being caught—or at least, of not profiting from the act—and cannot be construed as a true denial of will.

Yet, if salvation lies in this very denial, Schopenhauer must believe such a thing is possible. While remaining pessimistic about human nature in general, he would not have written his books if he had not entertained the hope that a rare few would understand and would curb their own aggressive drives.

In a dialogue between Man and the World Spirit, Schopenhauer thinks of what he might say to the Spirit: "Should I tell him that the value of life lies precisely in this, that it teaches him not to want it?"[6] The philosopher is not recommending suicide here. He is talking about willfully turning aside from the pleasures and successes life appears to offer, because the free pursuit of them only makes us evil in our intentions: that is, solely self-centered. Yet, he believed, few were capable of abandoning the pursuit of success-regardless-of-cost. A disillusioned idealist, Schopenhauer longed for a world of peace and *good* will, but he saw little chance that it would ever come about.

Feminists disapprove of Schopenhauer's seemingly blatant put-down of women. In truth, much of what he said about women tends to be condescending and insulting. He called them "incurable philistines." He said "the entire sex have proved incapable of a single truly great, genuine and original achievement in art, or indeed of creating anything of lasting value."[7] He also believed, however, that their will to power is much less aggressive and destructive than that of men, and that, while fathers train their children to exercise their wills for evil purposes, mothers impart softer values. For Schopenhauer, in a sense, women are more apt to deny their wills, and by his own definition, are better for the world than men.

Regret and Relief

The American philosopher William James (1842–1910) reviewed the case for pure determinism as set forth by European philosophers and concluded they were wrong. In fact, James developed the theory he pointedly called *indeterminism*, with a specific meaning that presents the world as a random collection of chance happenings. Determinism, for James, was too coldly logical: cause A leads to effect B. Determinism made people seem like well-run, well-oiled machines. James said, on the contrary, people were indecisive and unpredictable, exactly the opposite of machines.

> *If everything were predetermined, we would not be able to look back and see that genuine alternatives existed, but we were not aware of them at the time.*

Take regret, he said. Regret is a universal phenomenon. At any given moment people are able to think back over a hundred choices they wish they had not made. But at the same time, regret cannot be meaningfully experienced unless there exists an opposite—satisfaction—that gives regret its identity. In other words, within the random collection of happenings, people sometimes make what they consider the right move and many times make what they consider the wrong move. If everything were predetermined—that is, if the will were not free—looking backward could not reveal missed chances. We could not see them unless they had existed, though we may have been blind to them at the moment of choice. How often do murderers think back and realize that they did not *have* to carry a pistol when confronting their eventual victim? For James, hindsight is proof that genuine alternatives always exist. The determinist would reply that alternatives not chosen have no real existence. Something always makes us choose one—and only one.

If we were to extend his philosophy of indeterminism, we could say that another revealing exercise is to sit back and think of all of the terrible things we might have done last week but refrained from doing, such as

Having a confrontation with a friend that could have threatened the relationship.

Lying about something that would have involved a whole series of other lies.

Dropping a course in an impulsive moment, a course required for graduation.

Taking a chance and driving the old car with two bald tires.

We would probably feel relieved we had not done these things. Thus the experience of *relief* is another sign of freedom of will. When we consider the wrong moves that might have been made but were not, we are aware of having chosen wisely. We were free to do so, because we *could* have made the wrong decision. Nothing except our own intelligence determined the choice.

Our lives are probably split down the middle, with good moves on one side and bad moves on the other. That we can say we have made many mistakes is an admission that we know ourselves to be free agents. That we have sometimes chosen wisely may cause us to think, " If the good choice was predetermined, then I freely embrace determinism!"

Psychoanalysis: Freedom through the Conscious Ego

Certain schools of psychology are based on the premise that whatever we think or do is impelled by a previous cause which is not always of our own choosing. **Psychoanalysis**, in examining a patient's dreams, the thought processes evidenced in their conversation, and their free association of ideas, seeks to free people from acting without the knowledge of why they do what they do. It aims to lead people to a rational state of mind in which free choice is possible, to help people integrate their behavior by learning the causes of deviant, antisocial, or uncharacteristic actions. The theory is that, once a cause is discovered, the subterranean forces driving actions can be fully or at least partially controlled. Therapists hold out the hope that, through understanding and proper guidance, people who undergo treatment because they don't like who they are, or what they do, can change and become less "determined" than they were before.

Psychoanalysis and **psychotherapy**, invented by Sigmund Freud (1856–1939) to assist people toward mental health, are based on the assumption that, because of painful events in the past hidden away in our unconscious minds, many of us have bizarre dreams, make odd statements, and perform actions we cannot comprehend. In other words, our lives are determined by unconscious prior causes: sometimes by guilt-ridden emotions we have refused to deal with; often by desires of the *id*, that primitive, animal self human beings possessed long before they developed the rational *ego*.

Psychoanalysis has had a tremendous influence on theater, films, television, and literature. It has replaced the "who done it?" with the "what made him do it?"

In the Freudian view, the ego is the Apollonian conscious mind, and the id is the Dionysian self. In the id are sexual and aggressive drives that society has urged us to suppress. The values imposed on us by family, education, religion, the law, and the opinions of others he called the *superego*, the voice inside that tells us what we may or may not do. Yes, the will is free to disobey this voice, but chances are those who do so will be plagued by guilt. And yes, we are free *not* to think about our guilt, but, for Freud, denying it only makes matters worse.

The aim of the Freudian therapist is to analyze the patient's dreams, characteristic use of language, and free associations, to uncover the hidden self responsible for neurotic—that is, disordered—behavior, and to lead the patient to a happier life dominated by the ego. Presumably the successfully psychoanalyzed patient comes to possess freedom of the will, having been released from the determining phantoms of the past. Will thus resides in the fully conscious ego.

In recent years Freud's theories have been reevaluated. There is growing skepticism about two of his basic assumptions: the first, that all behavior can sooner or later be traced back to significant early experiences, often in childhood; and the second, that the ego, or the conscious self, is capable of rational, sustained thought once the suppressed secrets of the past are brought to light. For many, human behavior is far more complex than Freud suggests, and freedom is not attainable in the therapist's office.

Another objection is that the role of the superego, as defined by Freud, is far less pronounced than it was in his day. Sexual mores, in particular, are far less rigid, violations less apt to instill guilt. Today's therapists often take on the role of friends and counselors, willing to listen when close acquaintances and, especially, family members do not; but they are less apt to search for dreadful skeletons in the closet.

Nevertheless, Freud has received much recognition in the study of the humanities for having created one of the most prominent and influential myths of the twentieth century: *the myth of the liberated self*. Novels, plays, and films, especially in the first half of the twentieth century, display the overwhelming impact of Freud. The

An eighteenth-century painting, uncharacteristic of its time, amazingly anticipates the Freudian view that dreams have a powerful hold on our unconscious.

Source: John Henry Fuseli, *The Nightmare* (1781). Credit: The Detroit Institute of Arts, USA/Founders Society purchase with Mr. and Mrs. Bert L. Smokler and Mr. and Mrs. Lawrence A. Fleischman funds/The Bridgeman Art Library.

most popular plot centers on a man or a woman haunted by nightmarish dreams and held prisoner by past guilt, which the conscious mind refuses to confront. He or she then meets a benevolent, wise (and often attractive) analyst, who forsakes all personal concerns and works solely to free the prisoner from the shackles of tormenting guilt.

The structure of this generic therapy plot is usually that of a detective story. The old question "Who done it?" is replaced by "Why was it done?" or "What is someone afraid to face?" Sometimes (indeed very often) we learn that the victim was responsible for the death of a sibling, as in Alfred Hitchcock's popular 1945 film *Spellbound*. In the film, the victim of suppressed guilt is troubled by nightmarish dreams involving snowstorms. At lunch one day, another therapist, a beautiful woman of course, observes him using a fork to make parallel lines on a white tablecloth. Through therapy, she forces him to confront his buried past, in which he had slid down the wrought-iron railing on his parents' front steps, unaware that his younger brother was perched at the bottom. An inevitable collision caused the boy to be impaled on a spear-like post, a trauma that he has locked deep in his unconscious for many years. As expected, the recognition liberates him from guilt and steers him straight into the waiting arms of the beautiful therapist.

Psychoanalytic films, with their familiar plot structure and predictably happy endings, were extremely popular during and just after World War II. Interestingly enough, the emergence of Freudian-based entertainment coincided not only with the recovery of the American economy from the dismal depression of the 1930s but also with the recognition that the United States had to enter World War II to help free those overrun by fascist forces. The need for the literature and drama of freedom was apparently an insatiable one. Whether on the battlefield or in the therapist's office, characters struggled against overwhelming odds and in most cases emerged victorious.

Freud-based stories are by no means relegated to the war years, however. Pat Conroy's popular 1988 novel *The Prince of Tides*, which became an equally popular 1991 film, hinges on a disturbed man's complex mental journey back to his childhood, under the guidance of a wise female therapist, who helps him to uncover the suppressed memory of violent rape by an escaped convict long ago. Shame, guilt, and fear of social condemnation have prevented him from being a successful husband and father, but when he finally faces the truth that he is not responsible for the traumatic experience, he is able to return to his family, his rational self completely restored.

Writers who remain unconvinced that anybody can readily be freed from a suppressed past show less optimism, and a few have given us memorable modern tragedies. Tennessee Williams's milestone work *A Streetcar Named Desire* (1947) presented audiences with a harrowing study of mental illness culminating in madness. The heroine, Blanche DuBois, tries to give the impression that she is a genteel Southern belle, carrying on the elegant traditions of the Old South, but as the play deepens, she exhibits unmistakable signs of an unstable mental condition that causes her to denounce her sister's uncouth husband while she is at the same time driven by a fierce sexual attraction to him. Recognizing this attraction and thinking of his own sexual gratification, the husband rapes her. The abuse causes Blanche to retreat into a fantasy world from which she will never escape. The author himself was in therapy for a good part of his life, apparently unable to free himself from the demons of his own past.

Dennis Lehane's novel *Mystic River* (2001) is a dark tale about a troubled man who has attempted all his life to absolve himself of the guilt he suffered when, as an innocent child, he was abused sexually. As is so often the case after such childhood traumas, the boy grows up with feelings of worthlessness and an inability to communicate his feelings, even to his wife. His suppressed passion for revenge becomes his tragic flaw when he murders a man he believes to be a child-molester, an act that leads to his own violent death at the hands of his best friend. In 2003, Clint Eastwood directed a powerful screen adaptation of the novel, which won Oscars for Tim Robbins as the troubled protagonist and Sean Penn as the friend. David Denby in the *New Yorker* magazine declared the film "as close as Hollywood has ever come to creating true Greek tragedy."

Of course, thorough-going determinists can always argue that the liberation of the unconscious and the confrontation with reality may provide the illusion of freedom but only for a time. Stamping a patient's chart CURED does not guarantee that the person who walks out of the office for the last time is free from all determining influences. Just as physicists discovered

Freudian psychology has provided subjects for tragedies of nearly classic dimensions, as in Clint Eastwood's powerful screen adaptation of *Mystic River*, starring Sean Penn and Tim Robbins.

Source: Warner Bros./The Kobal Collection/Wallance, Merie W.J.

that matter is composed of particles within particles within particles, so too may the self be a circular staircase leading down into an infinity of shadows. Freud understood this and was generally cynical about human existence, but his theories provided hope that many could ascend that staircase into the clear light of day.

Studying the humanities of the past century would be difficult indeed without recognition of Freud's role. Many schools of psychotherapy continue to be rooted in his thought, and millions have been restored to mental health through psychoanalytical methods. That Freud's views may not represent an all-inclusive means to human freedom from the determining past should not eclipse the importance of these views to both the arts and to modern psychology.

Existentialism

After the armistice ended World War I in 1918, European countries exhausted from years of turmoil and a staggering loss of life eagerly sought new ways of thinking and living. Then Roman-style nationalism, the belief that one's country was superior to all others and had a right to subjugate the rest of civilization, reared its head once more. A maniacal dictator named Adolf Hitler decided to take advantage of the chaos that usually follows a large-scale conflict. Thousands were enslaved, tortured, and executed. The freedom to be whatever they wished to be was denied to thousands more.

I know of no more encouraging fact than the unquestionable ability of man to elevate his life by a conscious endeavor.

—Henry David Thoreau

After Hitler and his allies were defeated in 1945, there came a call for new approaches, new values, and a new way of defining freedom that, if difficult to attain, was nonetheless within the reach of anyone prepared to work for it. That definition was provided by the philosophy called *existentialism*, born in the middle of the nineteenth century, but little known until postwar cynicism spread throughout Europe. It took an especially strong hold in France, a nation that once prided itself on being the cultural center of Western civilization but had been brought to its knees by Nazi occupation. After the war, France found itself without a guiding philosophy, and its art reflected hopelessness and despair. But then, existentialism was rediscovered, and with it, a strong light that could be seen at the end of a long, dark tunnel. Existentialism taught that people are free to be anything they want—but that freedom comes with a price.

Religious Existentialism

The first official existentialist was a Dane, Søren Kierkegaard (1813–1855), who was raised in an austere religious environment, rebelled against it for a time, then returned to it as a matter of conscious choice, without the need of mystic revelations. For Kierkegaard, religion became a psychological reality freely accepted rather than a revealed truth with required acceptance. When one reached a point of absolute despair (as indeed he did) and felt ready to turn to God, one could take a **leap of faith**.

In that leap, however, lie undeniable anxieties. The leap must be made over many counterarguments, especially scientific evidence that seriously questions religious beliefs. On one's knees in the darkness of a church, one might feel one's prayers soaring heavenward and have a sense of union with God, but one can never *know* if God is listening—or is even there at all.

So long as the heaven of Thou is spread out over me the winds of causality cower at my heels, and the whirlpool of fate stays its course.

—Martin Buber

According to Buber, if you can address someone (including God) they must exist at least for you. Objects have objective reality, but since you don't address them, they have no actual existence.

To dramatize the plight of the believer, Kierkegaard recounts the biblical tale of Abraham and Isaac in his book *Fear and Trembling*. An angel appears to Abraham and tells him God demands the sacrifice of his son Isaac. Abraham is appalled, but what can he do? If God wants the sacrifice and he is God's servant, he must obey. His unquestioning willingness to do as God commands is a leap of faith. And in that leap, in that raising of the knife, must not Abraham experience unutterable anguish? Suppose the message was not really from God—what then? The anguish of Abraham represented for Kierkegaard the existential dilemma of all people. An existential dilemma is knowing that one is free to make a choice, but who knows whether it is the right or even best choice?

The philosopher Martin Buber (1878–1965), like Kierkegaard, found his way to religion through non-traditional means. He is most famous for defining two kinds of relationships a person can have. The first is the "I/it"—the objective relationship with objects and events outside, with concrete reality. Here there is no God, but only the existential moment. The second relationship is "I/Thou," representing a bridge to God. For Buber, an "it" must be defined; it has to be justified as concrete reality, otherwise there can be no relationship. A "Thou" is not defined, but addressed. The difference is clear. If you can address someone (whether a person standing in front of you or God, unseen), objective definition is beside the point. The fact that you are addressing anyone means that for you, at least, they exist. When it comes to "I/it," objective proof is possible. The "it" is out there for all to see. The experience of God comes through feeling, through intuition, through an overpowering sense of God's presence, and is not out there for all to see. Hence there can be no challenging it. Buber and Kierkegaard are very close on this point.

Early in his adult life Buber approached religion intellectually. He was a scholar of sacred Hebrew texts, concerned with the interpretation of traditional religious history as being a matter of myth and legend. Yet he sought the fundamental truth behind them. He did not address God personally. God was not a "Thou" until the reading of one particular text—just a few sentences, really—changed his life forever.

> I opened a little book entitled the *Zervaat Ribesh*—that is the testament of Rabbi Israel Baal-Shem—and the words flashed toward me; "He takes unto himself the quality of fervor, for he is hallowed and become another man and is worthy to create and is become like the Holy One, blessed be He, when he created his world." It was then that, over-powered in an instant, I experienced the Hasidic soul.[8]

In Chapter 2 we would have called this a Dionysian religious experience. Buber discovered that truth in religion comes from irresistible feeling, not analytical thought. From that moment on he became a Hasid—a member of a sect that emphasizes joy in God's closeness to humanity and the warm fellowship with other members of God's family.

He was then led to a passionate concern for the sacredness of human relationships, for in human contact he also found God. Every person with whom one connects was for him a "Thou," and every "Thou" contained the spirit of God. In one of his books he tells of greeting a visitor perfunctorily; though he showed the man ordinary courtesy, he was eager to return to a scholarly manuscript he was editing. Upon learning that his visitor later committed suicide, Buber recognized that human beings are more important than any task.

"I/Thou" created a revolution in modern ethics, for here was a philosopher who dispensed with the rules, who challenged the moral absolutes of both the Socratic and major religious traditions, but still found a way to affirm that moral goodness was there in every human heart, provided it was sought. Not everyone would find it, but each of us was free to search for it.

Secular Existentialism

A different kind of existentialism swept over Europe after World War II. It accorded well with the depressed mood of countries that had been devastated by fighting and loss, but at the same time, its belief in freedom as a natural condition helped to stir up some optimism.

Secular existentialism does not seek to address a God whose existence we cannot prove. Belief in God entails obeying commandments as well as believing that one is put here for the purpose of deserving God's love and mercy. Secular existentialism believes almost all religions erroneously teach that human beings have an *essence* which defines their humanness, but all we can be sure of is *existence*. Once we recognize that fact, we can begin to work our way out of the sense of abandonment that comes with the understanding that human beings are alone in a bewildering universe that exists for no known reason. Of course, this means that each of us is free in the sense of having no obligation to a higher force or indeed to anything else, but this brand of freedom is at first confusing if not terrifying. Most people, say the secular existentialists, choose religion or some other authority that lays down guidelines for them. Even if they don't obey them, they have at least a perspective. They know what they are *supposed* to be doing.

Central to the secular existential movement is the thought of three French philosophers: Jean-Paul Sartre (1905–1980), Simone de Beauvoir (1908–1986), and Albert Camus (1913–1960). Sartre, the most influential of the three, bases his belief in the human right of self-definition on the absolute certainty that God cannot exist. He is opposed to the acceptance of God as a matter of psychological necessity. Deep down we know that each of us is alone in a world that makes no sense—something that must have seemed all too true to many war-weary survivors in Europe.

Sartre maintains there is no such thing as human nature. People *talk* about human nature, but who has ever seen it? We cannot assume people are fundamentally good *or* bad, when in fact they are *neither* at birth. No one comes into this world to serve any purpose whatever or to fulfill some preexisting definition of what it means to be human. "If man, as the existentialist conceives him, is indefinable, it is because at first he is nothing. Only afterward will he be something, and he himself will have made what he will be. Thus, there is no human nature, since there is no God to conceive it."[9]

Saying that humankind is born without any identifying nature is in direct conflict with earlier philosophies that describe everyone as having an essence. In Christianity, for example, that essence is the soul. For Aristotle, it is rationality. In short, existentialism says you have to work at developing an essence that can be defined as human, an essence that for him includes good will and a strong, clear sense of moral responsibility to one's fellows. For the religious existentialist, one creates an essence that is spiritual and longs for union with God. Thus the ringing declaration of both religious and secular existentialism is *Existence precedes essence*.

According to Sartre, only natural phenomena and manufactured objects have essences from the beginning. A paper cutter was "born" to cut paper. If it doesn't cut paper, you have the right to demand your money back. A storm was "born" to bring

Freedom is fragile and must be protected. To sacrifice it, even as a temporary measure, is to betray it.
—**Germaine Greer**

Man is condemned to be free.
—**Jean-Paul Sartre**

wind and rain (or snow) and maybe knock down a few buildings in its path. Even animals have essences, for they too are natural phenomena. A tiger has to growl and be carnivorous. But human beings somehow escaped *having* to be anything.

Ah, but there is a bright side to the picture. We *are* capable of reason, a faculty we develop through experience. Some choose to exploit this capacity more than others do. Some decide they cannot live without an essence, without a purpose, without a way of defining themselves. The bad news is that each person must find the definition all alone. If one borrows an essence from the past, from the traditions and beliefs of one's ancestors, or is influenced by peer pressure or educational or religious institutions, the right to define oneself is forfeited. One's essence has already been predefined.

Once we realize we have no essence, we have to create one freely; or, as Sartre puts it, we are "doomed to freedom." Each of us, having declared our essence, must then take responsibility for it. You cannot decide you are going to be such-and-such, only to deny, when your actions harm someone else, that you ever made that decision. No one is free to be morally unaccountable. True freedom carries a hefty price tag, reason tells us. You cannot argue that reason guarantees the right to behave any way you want to, unless, as Kant (Chapter 8) would say, you can accord that right to everyone else. In that case, you'd have to be careful not to turn your back on anyone. Do we *really* want to live in a society in which no one is responsible for anything?

Many, says Sartre, prefer to believe they serve a purpose and what they do was meant to be. He relates the tale of a young man who could not pass the examinations for various professional careers and decided he was meant to fail because he was truly destined to become a priest. Nonsense! declares Sartre. The young man was always in charge of his own life and should not have turned to the priesthood solely on the hunch that destiny was forcing him into it. Freedom is a painful thing sometimes. If we fail, we try to blame others or circumstances, thus denying the truth of our freedom.

Sartre argues that most people—to avoid difficult choices—prefer to become things and believe they serve a destined purpose, like a paper cutter. Whatever a *thing* does, it must do in order to fulfill its thingness. Things have no moral responsibility. If we cut our finger on the paper cutter, we cannot blame *it* for our clumsiness. People would rather renounce freedom than blame themselves for what happens to them.

The true existentialist—like Abraham—has to make choices, and is always confronted with anguish. An existential ship's officer, faced with the awful decision of having a dangerously overcrowded lifeboat or tossing some of the survivors into the sea, where they will certainly die, might decide to sacrifice certain people to save the others, but he would not be able to argue that he was a victim of circumstances. Of course, he *could* do so, but if he does, he cannot be considered *authentic*. An authentic person is one who defines himself or herself, stands behind the definition, and willingly accepts either praise or blame.

Simone de Beauvoir, a feminist writer and close associate of Sartre, urged women to create bold new essences. Her route to existentialism was the feminist rejection of male rules and the essences males imposed on females.

> By the time humankind reached the stage of written mythology and law, the patriarchate was definitely established: the males were to write the codes. It was natural for them to give woman a subordinate position, yet one could suppose that they would look upon her with the same benevolence as upon children and cattle—but not at all.

While setting up the machinery of woman's oppression, the legislators were afraid of her.[10]

If not the most influential of the French existentialists, Albert Camus has surely been the most poetic—and dramatic. In his three major essays, "An Absurd Reasoning," "The Absurd Man," and "The Myth of Sisyphus," he makes the existential case that rationality is found not in the universe but in the human mind. The intellect, attempting to make sense out of reality, realizes it is not to be understood. Why then are we rational? To what end? Reason leads us to the conclusion that living is absurd, meaningless.

Having said this, he begins "An Absurd Reasoning" with his most often quoted statement: "There is but one truly serious philosophical problem, and that is suicide." Where Sartre believed that abandonment in a meaningless universe opened the door to freedom, Camus goes deeper, analyzing that condition of abandonment and insisting that life is not worth living if we cannot assign a value to it. Yet, if life is absurd, what value *can* it have?

Camus's answer is that it has an absurd value. What we think and do may not make any ultimate sense, but perhaps "ultimate sense" ought never to have been the goal. That there is only this existential moment, this here and now, does not imply that the moment is not worth experiencing. Unlike his colleagues, Camus talks about the colors, the sounds, the continually unfolding wonders of the universe. Absurd, yes, in that they have no meaning beyond themselves, but this fact does not make suicide the inevitable, the *only* recourse.

If we do not, as Hamlet does not, choose suicide, then we must have a purpose. That is, if we *had* chosen suicide, would it not be said that our purpose was to do away with ourselves? People don't kill themselves without reason. Choosing life rather than death is, therefore, purposeful as well. But if the world is absurd and we choose to remain in it, it must follow that we accept the absurdity and move on from there. In that lies our freedom, and with freedom comes an infinite number of possibilities.

To dramatize his point, Camus recounts the Greek myth of Sisyphus, "the wisest and most prudent of mortals," who also questioned the meaning of life. To find the answer, he stole secrets from the gods. They retaliated by condemning him to roll a heavy rock up a steep hill. When, through exhausting labor and physical pain, he reaches the top, the rock rolls back down, and Sisyphus has to start all over again. This is to continue for eternity.

> *I leave Sisyphus at the foot of the mountain! One always finds one's burden again. But Sisyphus teaches the higher fidelity that negates the gods and raises rocks. He too concludes that all is well. This universe henceforth without a master seems to him neither sterile nor futile. Each atom of that stone, each mineral flake of that night-filled mountain, in itself forms a world. The struggle itself toward the heights is enough to fill a man's heart. One must imagine Sisyphus happy.*[11]

There are many American existential writings as well. In *Mother Night* (1972), a novel by Kurt Vonnegut, an American newspaper columnist ostensibly defects to Germany during World War II and gets a job writing anti-Semitic propaganda for a German newspaper. After the conflict is over, he is tried as a war criminal, the charge being that the message of hatred in his inflammatory

Real generosity toward the future lies in giving all to the present.

—**Albert Camus**

columns played a part in the Holocaust. The man's defense is that he was actually an American spy sent on an undercover mission by President Roosevelt himself. Of course, since Roosevelt is dead, the journalist cannot prove what he claims. The author's message is that we are what we say we are and thus we need to be very careful about defining ourselves. In the author's eyes, the journalist was guilty because he had created for himself an essence which led, however indirectly, to the deaths of many innocent people. Whether he was secretly anti-Semitic or merely carrying out orders can never be known. He narrates his story from an Israeli prison, his freedom denied. Had he made a responsible use of freedom before?

The view of freedom expressed in much existential philosophy and literature has been widely questioned. Is it the freedom to behave without regard for others? The Norwegian philosopher Dagfinn Føllesdal asks this ominous question: "Can one who creates his own values do anything that is morally wrong?" True, the existentialists insist that one be held accountable for speech and actions, but are people free to lie? To behave toward others in a way that will draw praise and make it easy to manipulate them? And if people use their freedom for their own profit, are they *really* free, or are they victims of their own selfishness?

Freedom within Limitations

Keep in mind always the present you are constructing. It should be the future you want.
—**Alice Walker**

By now it may have occurred to the reader that the philosophies of freedom we have been discussing were all generated by Western thinkers living in comparatively open societies in which freedom of thought and expression are taken for granted. Even Augustine, within the confines of Christianity, was at liberty to express his doubts. Determinists like Marx and Skinner were not threatened with jail for saying that our choices are not freely made.

Sometimes it happens that a philosopher of freedom is in fact living under an oppressive government: Rousseau, for example, in a rigid monarchy; Sartre, during the Nazi rule in France. Both fought against tyranny: Rousseau through his pen, and Sartre through his work in the French Underground, an organized covert attempt to help those being sought or persecuted by the Nazis. Neither philosopher abandoned his belief that freedom was the natural condition of humanity. That belief tends to be echoed throughout the humanities in different ways.

What does freedom mean to those who grow up in societies which have been embroiled in bitter religious and territorial disputes that severely limit choices? Or do those who are born into centuries-old ways of being human resign themselves to some form of slavery? Is freedom a narrowly Western idea? Or may we now extend its possible meanings?

For the Japanese, strongly influenced as they are by Western capitalism and the urgent need to do well financially, there is as well the strong tradition of family honor. Many of us, accustomed to more open pathways, would see this severe limitation as an impediment to the exercise of will. Succeeding in business is often the way for a Japanese son or daughter to win family approval. But in the West, one may well decide that a business career is not the right choice and embark on another. There is the heartbreaking story of a Japanese student attending an Ivy League university who killed herself when she received less than an "A" grade in one subject and thought her family would be disgraced. She left a note saying that because she had not studied hard enough, there was no other course of action open to her.

Japanese society is nothing if not rule driven, Western influences notwithstanding. We have already studied the principles of Zen Buddhism, a dominant practice in Japan. Zen requires long hours of meditation. To excel in any of the martial arts demands many years of training in body coordination and muscular development. These arts are also products of a civilized society in which ethics and good manners are essential. Opponents must bow to each other as a mark of deep respect. The Japanese love of the beautiful dictates how tea is prepared and served and how flowers are arranged in a vase. All of these requirements might strike some in the West as cumbersome impositions, as jailers imprisoning the will. Yet it is doubtful that the Japanese would agree.

One of the foremost modern spokespersons for Buddhist thought and practice was Chögyam Trungpa (1939–1987), a monk who fled Chinese persecution in his native Tibet and founded a still-thriving American Buddhist community in Boulder, Colorado. Among those who came there to absorb his teachings was the poet Allen Ginsberg, a major voice of the Beat Generation, post–World War II writers, artists, and composers who found themselves disillusioned with the greed they saw on all sides and what they took to be the goal of rebuilding America as a more materialistic version of what it had once been. The Beats proclaimed themselves social dropouts, adrift in a land that called itself the cradle of liberty where people could be whatever they wanted to be yet were really slaves to its shoddy values.

Many, like Ginsberg, saw in Buddhism the one true path to freeing themselves from this enslavement; and the road to true freedom was through the discipline of meditation and the renunciation of materialistic desires. One of Trungpa's major works is in fact titled *The Myth of Freedom* (1976), by which he means that Western definitions of the word often require an absence of external control and the right to disobey the rules whenever it suits—or, better yet, the right to become the boss and impose whatever rules one wants. Trungpa would perhaps have agreed with behaviorists that, for most people, freedom meant getting out from under aversive controls—that is, from all those authorities that wish to shape our lives.

Trungpa maintains such freedom is impossible to achieve. One must first wake up to the reality of pain and suffering. It is absurd to suppose that following the American Dream and striving for wealth and the pleasures it can buy will avoid pain and suffering. If anything, wealth and pleasure only add to the pain because, as Epicurus points out (Chapter 12), there is never enough pleasure to satisfy us. And even if we had all the money we could ever want and spent our life doing whatever we pleased, there would be the excruciating pain of recognizing that death will bring an end to our holiday. According to Trungpa:

> *we must begin by seeing the experience of life as it is. We must see the truth of suffering, the reality of dissatisfaction. We cannot ignore it and attempt to examine only the glorious pleasurable aspects of life. If one searches for a promised land, a Treasure Island, then the search only leads to more pain. We cannot reach such islands, we cannot attain enlightenment in such a manner. So all sects and schools of Buddhism agree that we must begin by facing the reality of our living situations. We cannot begin by dreaming.*[12]

Trungpa defines true freedom as surrendering to reality and, by accepting things as they are, to liberate oneself from pain, which is, after all, the goal of the free person. In his view, one can be free though tightly shackled. Even in a narrow prison cell, freedom is possible, because no one can put chains on our thoughts and feelings. This doctrine of freedom through personal choice despite limitations has inspired hundreds of Trungpa's followers. However, a critic has said it is doubtful that it would bring solace to the many who still live in slavery or under severe autocratic rule.

Perhaps all one can say at this point in time is that there are many paths to freedom and that some of them still have impassable barriers. All the more reason to be grateful if you have the right to choose.

It seems appropriate to close this book with a theory—and it is just that—by means of which we can apply the word *free* to ourselves. According to this theory, derived from a number of sources, freedom is achieved *only* when we place limits on our options.

People who jog know all about the relationship between freedom and limits. They will tell you about a consciousness of freedom in running, pushing against the wind and feeling their arms and legs equal to the demands made by the will— for runners, in contrast to what Skinner has said, *do* feel their will. When there is a sharp incline, runners must draw upon reserve strength. On the downward slope, they know that power needs to be conserved. If they run flat out, they may not have enough left for the final mile. If they are running against others and there is a need to win, they accelerate; if all they want to do is complete the course, they adopt a more leisurely pace.

But the vivid experience of will does not happen all of a sudden. In the beginning, jogging is a distinct effort accompanied by pain and soreness. There is the inevitable pulling of muscles, the labored breathing, the tendency to overheat rapidly. In the beginning, joggers often stop running for the slightest excuse. After a time they set a goal: to the end of the road and then back; one mile; two miles; down to the county line. Self-imposed limits are crucial. The goal must be met. Even wind and rain are not likely to keep the determined runner at home. The ultimate feeling of liberation—the sense of floating, the runner's high—occurs when the runner's body is equal to the task set by the will. And the will is experienced when runners feel at ease within the limitations they impose on themselves.

In Chapter 4, we talked about the sonnet form in which the poet's choices are determined by the number of required lines: fourteen. It would be easy for the poet to complain that the length limitation prevents the free expression of an idea, and indeed, many poets have chosen to write in "free" verse for which no restrictions exist. Yet the Romantic poet William Wordsworth does not see the rigid sonnet rules as constraints upon freedom.

He who bears in his heart a cathedral to be built is already victorious. He who seeks to become sexton of a finished cathedral is already defeated.

—**Antoine de Saint-Exupery**

> *Nuns fret not at their convent's narrow room;*
> *And hermits are contented with their cells;*
> *And students with their pensive citadels;*
> *Maids at the wheel, the weaver at his loom*
> *Sit blithe and happy; bees that soar for bloom,*
> *High as the highest Peak of Furness-fells,*
> *Will murmur by the hour in foxglove bells:*
> *In truth the prison unto which we doom*
> *Ourselves, no prison is: and hence for me,*
> *In sundry moods, 'twas pastime to be bound*
> *Within the Sonnet's scanty plot of ground;*
> *Pleased if some Souls (for such there needs must be)*
> *Who have felt the weight of too much liberty,*
> *Should find brief solace there, as I have found.*

There is in the poem an implied comparison between *liberty* and *freedom*. Liberty means going anywhere one wants and doing anything one wants. Liberty means that any door can be opened. Yet if we have all possible doors to choose from, would we ever open even one?

Why, one asks, is freedom so vital? If Sartre is right in saying that most people prefer not to be free, why should we *have* to be free? Or if freedom and liberty are not the same thing, what's wrong with seeking liberty for its own sake? What's wrong with going through life unfettered by rules and behaving in any way one desires? Why need we define ourselves at all and then be responsible for what we do?

When you put a tight lid on a pan of boiling water, the energy inside will become intense. So too will the joy of living be intense to the degree that we face a limited number of choices. Liberty is bewildering. Liberty does not know what to choose. Defining oneself as a certain kind of person is the first limitation. Unless we can do that, we become scattered to the winds, at the mercy of every gust. Narrowing the range of possibilities and *then finding the best way to work within that range*—this might, after all, be the answer. And what is the question? It is: *How can I do the most with the one life I have after I take inventory of how much freedom of choice is available to me?*

Of course, determinist arguments are powerful, and one has the right to believe there is no free will and thus one cannot be held responsible for anything. If one adopts that view, one must accept the fact that no one else is responsible either. Determinism is the only logical course for some. Many artists and philosophers do not agree. If a painting is decried by those who fund the exhibit, we don't hear the artist saying, "But I came from a bad environment that forced me to paint that way." Instead, the artist defends the work and decries the funders. Without *this* kind of freedom, there can be no pride in any accomplishment.

If determinism is chosen, is the chooser forced to do it? Surprisingly enough, many *do* choose determinism without realizing it. How many people do we know who seem to be happy only when they find someone who will listen to their tragic tales of victimization—by other people, by the law, by the government, by their parents, and on and on? Never by themselves. As Sartre continually reminds us, the only way to be an authentic person is to admit that you are free and to take responsibility for the bad choices you make. We have conceded many times that not everyone is lucky enough to have the right to choose. Those who do and who prefer to see themselves as helpless victims without responsibility would do well to recognize that they were nonetheless free to reject that responsibility.

Authentic people advertise their natures. We always know what to expect from them. Inauthentic people, backed into a corner after being blamed for something, try to plead their innocence by saying something forced them to make a wrongful choice. If free will is a fact of life for many, it cannot be accepted here and rejected there—at their convenience.

In the final analysis, true freedom may reside in the limitations we impose on ourselves freely. To believe that freedom means having unlimited options is to be trapped in infinity. Only by deliberately narrowing our range of options can we experience the exhilarating sense of being truly our own persons. It is freedom to say we can do this or, on the other hand, that. It is not freedom to say we can do this, or that, or perhaps that other thing, or even its opposite, and on and on forever. When we come to this realization, we also see we need not trap ourselves by always choosing the easy way. At a sumptuous buffet we can gorge ourselves or decide to enjoy fully a limited amount of delicious food.

Without freedom, no art; art lives only on the restraints it imposes on itself, and dies of all others.

—**Albert Camus**

Those who achieve the strength of inner control are not only authentic persons, they are *good people*. They never want to harm others, for doing so would mean being at the mercy of uncontrollable passions, becoming the victims they choose not to be.

A study of the humanities, looking into the minds and hearts of creative and thoughtful human beings, reveals many, many innovations in art and philosophy. Many, many artists and philosophers have changed the course of human consciousness and given us options our ancient ancestors could not have dreamed of: options for experiencing the beautiful, the different, even sometimes the shocking, and of course the thought-provoking. How predetermined were *they*, when the greatest of them did what nobody else had ever done? If they were predetermined, why was there not more than one Beethoven or Shakespeare, people who might have been similarly directed? The humanities would seem to be the study of the free spirit, and from this each of us can know that more can be done with our lives. It is your birthright as a human being to reach up and mentally redo the Sistine Chapel ceiling if you don't happen to like it. Once you have investigated the past, it is your birthright to let go of it, but knowingly and with full awareness of what you want the present to be. It is your birthright to reach into the darkness and from it pull forth a new lantern, however unfamiliar the shape, however irregular the beam of light.

Reaching beyond ourselves is a natural right. Without the risk of failure, there can be no possibility of success. The American novelist and poet Stephen Crane sums it all up:

> I saw a man pursuing the horizon;
> Round and round they sped.
> I was disturbed at this;
> I accosted the man.
> "It is futile," I said,
> "You can never—"
> "You lie," he cried
> And ran on.[13]

Key Terms

behaviorism both a philosophy and a school of psychology that believes people are what they do and what they do is determined by systems of rewards and punishments.

bourgeoisie the middle classes; in Marxism, those who control capital and the means of production and exploit the proletariat.

chromosomes long stringy bodies in the nucleus of the cell, containing the genes made of DNA.

determinism the philosophical belief that everything has a prior cause and consequently absolute free will cannot exist.

dialectic the philosophical method of Hegel, involving the presentation of one idea, followed by an analysis of its opposite, and then arriving at a truth that combines the two; adopted by Marx to describe the conflict between the proletariat and the bourgeoisie and

the eventual establishment of a classless society.

DNA abbreviation for *deoxyribonucleic acid*, which forms long strands of sugar and sulphate within the gene and carries the genetic codes throughout the body.

economic determinism another name for the philosophy of Karl Marx, maintaining that our behavior is controlled by the need for money.

genes granular substances within the chromosome that contain the DNA molecules.

genome the genetic blueprint of a living being, contained within each of its cells.

indeterminism the philosophy expounded by William James, that whatever happens does so randomly, without a clear prior cause, and therefore we have free will to make choices.

institutional determinism name given to Rousseau's belief that the will is governed by restrictive forces of law, education, and religion, all necessary because of the inborn depravity of a few people.

leap of faith phrase used by Kierkegaard to indicate that religion can be freely chosen, but to do so, one must bypass reason and thus can never be sure if the choice was right.

libertarianism a political and philosophical belief in unrestricted free will.

proletariat in Marxism, the working classes who will eventually rise up against the affluent bourgeoisie, leading to the classless society.

psychoanalysis a technique developed by Sigmund Freud that examines a patient's dreams and patterns of free association of ideas in an effort to diagnosis the causes of neurotic behavior and mental illness.

psychotherapy clinical treatments of mental disorders based on the findings of the psychoanalysis, usually involving discussion sessions in which the patient is encouraged to talk openly about his or her dreams and to go from one subject to another without being interrupted or "kept to task."

sociobiology a social science that believes human behavior can be analyzed in terms of genetic investment or the lack of it—that is, the extent to which one is motivated by the need to propagate one's genes, either directly, through a sexual relationship, or indirectly, through the need to survive physically, socially, or economically.

Topics for
Writing and Discussion

1. Though the chapter is titled "Freedom," you didn't find anywhere in it a succinct definition of the term. The reason is that the word is used in many different contexts and often quite vaguely. From having read the chapter, give as many versions of "freedom" as you can.

2. Define and describe determinism. Do the same for two philosophies that oppose it.

3. Of the determinist philosophies discussed in the chapter, which ones do you believe have the most bearing on your life? Which the least? In view of your answer, would you call yourself a complete determinist? Partial? Not at all? Explain.

4. Whether or not people agree with B. F. Skinner, most do concur that all of us are subject to a certain amount of aversive control. Describe one or two aversive controls in your own life, present or past.

5. Great strides have been taken in the science of genetics and genetic research, especially in the use of stem cells for the treatment of conditions such as diabetes and Parkinson's disease. Opponents of even limited federal funding maintain that dissecting the cells to learn more about genetic diseases is tantamount to murder. Advocates of funding say the research will result in extraordinary medical breakthroughs. Support your argument for or against federal funding.

6. Rousseau's famous position was that, if it were not for the necessary but oppressive limitations imposed by social institutions, people would be naturally benevolent toward each other. Do you agree that in a state of nature, without any limitations, people would get along? Or is aggression inherent in human nature and must be controlled?

7. On what does William James base his argument to support free will? We can't deny that the conditions he cites actually exist, but do they prove we act freely?

8. The gist of Schopenhauer's free-will theory is that it would probably be better if the will were not free. Why does he believe this?

9. The chapter discusses two schools of existentialism. On what do they agree? Where do they disagree?

10. The chapter discusses a number of religious and philosophical beliefs that say freedom comes only within limitations. Discuss at least two of these limitations. Do they apply to your life at present? If not, would you be willing to try them?

Endnotes

Chapter 2

1. William Wharton, *Dad* (New York: Avon, 1981), 419–420.
2. e.e.cummings, "may my heart always be open to little birds," *Poems 1929–1954* (New York: Harcourt Brace, 1954).
3. Anthony Lane, "Review: A Mighty Heart," *New Yorker*, June 25, 2007, 131.
4. Howard Cohen, *Miami Herald Weekend*, July 3, 2007, 28.
5. Alex Ross, "Review: La Pasión Según San Marcos," *New Yorker*, March 5, 2001, 100–101.
6. William Wordsworth, "The world is too much with us," *The Major Poets, English and American* (New York: Harcourt Brace, 1954), 257.

Chapter 3

1. Anthony Lane, "Review: Eternal Sunshine of the Spotless Mind," *New Yorker*, March 22, 2004, 103.
2. June Singer, *Boundaries of the Soul: The Practice of Jung's Psychology* (New York: Doubleday, 1972), 79.
3. Singer, *Boundaries of the Soul*.
4. Joseph Campbell, *The Myths of God: Oriental Mythology* (New York: Viking Penguin, 1976), 243.
5. Campbell, *The Myths of God*, 342.
6. Campbell, *The Myths of God*, 9–10.
7. Edith Hamilton, *Mythology* (New York: New American Library, 1969), 63.
8. *Paradise Lost*, Book VII, ll. 211–217.
9. Hamilton, *Mythology*, 89.
10. Rose Anna Mueller, "La Llorona, The Weeping Woman," *Community College Humanities Review* 20, no. 1 (1999): 28–33.
11. J.R.R. Tolkien, *The Return of the King* (New York: Ballantine, 1966), 384.
12. Paraphrased from R. H. Blythe, *Zen and Zen Classics* (Tokyo: Hokuseido, 1960–1970).

Chapter 4

1. John Steinbeck, *The Grapes of Wrath* (1940; reprint, New York: Penguin, 1992).
2. *The Iliad of Homer*, trans. Robert Fitzgerald (Garden City, NY: Doubleday Anchor, 1975).
3. Sappho, "Ode to Aphrodite," trans. J. Addington Symonds, in *Our Heritage of World Literature*, ed. Stith Thompson and John Gassner (New York: Dryden Press, 1942), 258.
4. Catullus, trans. Walter Savage Landor, *Our Heritage of World Literature*, 268.
5. "Llagas de Amor," trans. John K. Wilde and Francisco Aragon, in *Federico Garcia Lorca: Selected Verse*, ed. Christopher Maurer (New York: Farrar, Straus and Giroux, 1989–1994).
6. Jaron Lanier, "Jaron's World: The Meaning of Metaphor," *Discovery*, February 2007.
7. *Collected Sonnets of Edna St. Vincent Millay*, ed. Ruth Bornschlegel and Norma Millay (New York: Harper and Row, 1987).
8. *Red Dragonfly on My Shoulder*, trans. Stkvua Cassedy amd Kunihiro Sustake (New York: HarperCollins, 1992).
9. *Red Dragonfly on My Shoulder*.
10. Attributed to Isabel Crawford (1865–1961), a Baptist missionary to the Plains Indians.
11. Emily Dickinson, *Complete Poems*, ed. Thomas H. Johnson (Boston: Little Brown, 1966).
12. Georgia Douglas Johnson, "Black Woman," in *The Portable Harlem Renaissance*, ed. Daniel Levering Lewis (New York: Penguin, 1995).
13. *The Collected Poems of Archibald MacLeish, 1917–1982* (Boston: Houghton Mifflin, 1995).
14. Billy Collins, *Sailing Alone around the Room* (New York: Random House, 2001).
15. *The Bread Loaf Anthology of Contemporary American Poetry* (Hanover, NH: University Press of New England, 1985).

16. F. Scott Fitzgerald, *The Great Gatsby* (New York: Scribner Paperback, 1995), 160–161.
17. Khaled Hosseini, *The Kite Runner* (New York: Riverhead, 2003), 324.
18. Nadine Gordimer, "A Beneficiary," *New Yorker*, May 21, 2007, 66–73.

Chapter 5

1. Walt Whitman, "There Was a Child Went Forth," *Leaves of Grass* (New York: Barnes and Noble, 1993), 305.
2. William Fleming, *Art and Ideas* (New York: Henry Holt, 1959), 307–308.
3. Bruce Cole and Adelheid Gealt, *Art of the Western World* (New York: Summit, 1985), 271.
4. Jan Garden Castro, *The Art and Life of Georgia O'Keeffe* (New York: Crown, 1985), 25.
5. Amy Helene Kirshke, *Aaron Douglas: Art, Race, and the Harlem Renaissance* (Jackson: University Press of Mississippi, 1995), 10, 77.
6. John Perrault, "Forging Ahead: A Sculpture Conference Diary," *Village Voice*, September 21, 1982, 84.
7. Jonathan Lipman, *Frank Lloyd Wright and the Johnson Wax Building* (New York: Rizzoli, 1986), xii.

Chapter 6

1. Abraham Veinus, Syracuse University, line notes for Ludwig van Beethoven, Symphony No. 3 in E Flat Major, *Eroica*, Philharmonic Promenade Orchestra of London, Adrian Boult cond., Vanguard.
2. Joan Baez, "Joe Hill," http://www.ilyric.net/Lyrics/J/Joan-Baez/Joe-Hill.html/.
3. Alan Bullock and R. B. Woodings, eds., *20th Century Culture* (New York: Harper and Row, 1983), 212.
4. Charlie Gillett, *The Penguin Book of Rock and Roll Writing*, ed. Clinton Haydin (London: Penguin, 1992), 14.
5. Gillett, 11.
6. Gillett 212.
7. J. Decibel.
8. Decibel.

Chapter 7

1. Gerald Mast, *A Short History of the Movies* (New York: Macmillan, 1986), 68.
2. Ephraim Katz, *The Film Encyclopedia*, 3rd ed. (New York: Harper Perennial, 1998), 121.
3. David Denby, *New Yorker*, July 23, 2007.
4. Harriet Quick, "Review: Lost in Translation," *British Vogue*, January 2004, 101.
5. Edward Jay Epstein, "The Second Coming of Jim Garrison," *Atlantic Monthly*, March 1993, 89.
6. Edward Rothstein, "Connections: To Homer Iraq Would Be More of Same," *New York Times*, June 5, 2004, A17.

Chapter 8

1. Plato, *The Republic*, trans. Benjamin Jowett (New York: Doubleday, 1973), 44.
2. Plato, *The Republic*, 44.
3. Plato, *The Republic*, 46.
4. Thomas Hobbes, *Leviathan*, in *Basic Problems of Philosophy*, ed. Daniel Bronstein, Yervant Kriokorian, and Philip Weiner (Englewood Cliffs, NJ: Prentice Hall, 1964), 155.
5. Thomas Hobbes, *Leviathan*, 159.
6. Ayn Rand, *Atlas Shrugged* (New York: Dutton, 1957), 661.
7. John Donne, *The College Survey of English Literature*, ed. Alexander M. Witherspoon et al. (New York: Harcourt Brace and World, 1947), 340–341.
8. Steven Pinker, "The Moral Instinct," *New York Times Magazine*, January 27, 2008, 36–37.
9. John Rawls, quoted in Donald Palmer, *Does the Center Hold?* (Mountain View, CA: Mayfield, 1996), 262.
10. "Arguments: Should Opera Be Subsidized?" *Dissent*, Summer 1999, 96.
11. "Arguments," 98.
12. In Palmer, *Does the Center Hold?* 342.
13. Hans J. Morgenthau, "The Sanctity of Moral Law," *New Republic*, December 2, 1959.
14. Huston Smith, *The World's Religions* (San Francisco: Harper, 1991), 290–291.
15. John A. Hutchinson, *Paths of Faith*, 2nd ed. (New York: McGraw-Hill, 1973), 121–122.
16. Isabel Allende, *Of Love and Shadows*, trans. Margaret Sayers Pedern (New York: Knopf, 1987), 115.
17. Allende, *Of Love and Shadows*.
18. Studs Terkel, *Working* (New York: Pantheon, 1974), 48.
19. Terkel, *Working*.
20. From an article by Colin Nickerson, which appeared originally in the *Boston Globe* and was reprinted in the *Miami Herald*, September 17, 2000.
21. Nicholas D. Kristof, "In Japan Nice Guys (and Girls) Finish Together," *New York Times*, April 12, 1998.
22. Sui Sin Far, "The Americanizing of Pau Tsu," in *Asian American Literature*, ed. Shawn Wong (New York: HarperCollins Literary Mosaic Series, 1996), 68–69.
23. Cullen Murphy, "Was Jesus a Feminist?" *Harvard Magazine*, September/October 1998.
24. Matt Ridley, "A Boy or a Girl," *Smithsonian*, June 1993.

Chapter 9

1. Kurt Vonnegut, "Joe Heller," *New Yorker*, May 10, 2005.
2. Epicurus, *The Extant Remains*, trans. Cyril Bailey (London: Oxford University Press, 1926), 64.
3. Epicurus, *The Extant Remains*, 65.
4. *The Complete Short Stories of Ernest Hemingway* (New York: Scribners, 1982), 289–290.
5. Viktor Frankl, *Man's Search for Meaning: An Introduction to Logotherapy*, preface by Gordon W. Allport (New York: Washington Square, 1998), 90.

6. Anne Frank, *The Diary of a Young Girl*, ed. Otto J. Frank and Miriam Pressler, trans. Susan Massotty (New York: Doubleday, 1991), 281.
7. Frank, *The Diary of a Young Girl*, 54.
8. Frank, *The Diary of a Young Girl*, 190.
9. Dalai Lama, *The Path to Tranquility* (New York: Viking Arcana, 1999), 163.
10. Dalai Lama, *The Path to Tranquility*, 303.
11. Dalai Lama, *The Path to Tranquility*, 395.

Chapter 10

1. Azar Nafisi, *Reading* Lolita *in Tehran* (New York: Random House, 2004), 9.
2. B. F. Skinner, *Beyond Freedom and Dignity* (New York: Bantam, 1972), 37.
3. Skinner, *Beyond Freedom and Dignity*, 41.
4. Skinner, *Beyond Freedom and Dignity*, 39.
5. Arthur Schopenhauer, *Esssays and Aphorisms*, ed. and trans. R. J. Hollingdale (London: Penguin, 1970), 65.
6. Schopenhauer, *Esssays and Aphorisms*, 65.
7. Schopenhauer, *Esssays and Aphorisms*, 86.
8. Martin Buber, *Tales of the Hasidim* (New York: Schoken, 1992), viii.
9. Jean-Paul Sartre, *Existentialism and Human Emotions*, trans. Bernard Frechtman (New York: Philosophical Library, 1947), 15.
10. Simone de Beauvoir, *The Second Sex*, ed. and trans. H. M. Parchley (New York: Knopf, 1969), 79.
11. Albert Camus, *The Myth of Sisyphus and Other Essays*, trans. Justin O'Brien (New York: Vintage, 1995), 123.
12. Chögyam Trungpa, *The Myth of Freedom* (Berkeley, CA: Shambhala, 1976), 1–2.
13. Stephen Crane, "I Saw a Man," *Readings in Stephen Crane*, ed. Bonnie Szumski (San Diego, CA: Green Haven, 1998), 194.

Index

SOUND OF THE HUMANITIES

Track Listing for Enclosed Audio CD

TRACK 1
Claude Debussy, "Clair de Lune"   4:25

Debussy's "Clair de Lune" or "Moonlight" could be called a poem in music. It belongs to a musical school known as Impressionism, one that closely parallels the art movement of that name. Its purpose is to create visual images in the mind as listeners close their eyes and listen.

TRACK 2
Homer, from *The Iliad*   3:15

In this excerpt of Homer's epic, which is an account of a war strategy meeting in the Greek camp, the leaders of the war against Troy remind each other that their army is invincible and should be able to master the "illustrious" Hector.

TRACK 3
William Shakespeare, Sonnet XXIX   0:55

One of the great sonnets, this is typical of the love poems of the Elizabethan Age—with one exception: Shakespeare did it better than his contemporaries. The discussion in chapter 4 explains the rigors of iambic pentameter, but notice how the sonnet's leader manages to make clear the meaning, not the rhythm.

TRACK 4
Igor Stravinsky, from *Rite of Spring*   2:41

This excerpt illustrates how Stravinsky changed the direction of modern music. It uses dissonance, abrupt rhythmic changes, and "unmelodic" melodic lines underscoring the revolutionary dance movements of this modern ballet.

TRACK 5
Pyotr Il'yich Tchaikovsky, from *1812 Overture*   3:42

The finale, with its cannon fire added to the resounding orchestration, illustrates the Dionysian element in music. Tchaikovsky was noted for frequently stretching the bounds of musical form.

TRACK 6
Johann Sebastian Bach, from "Toccata and Fugue in D Minor"   2:58

One of Bach's greatest organ works, this piece illustrates the complex interweaving of melodic lines characteristic of baroque music.

TRACK 7
Scott Joplin, "Maple Leaf Rag"   3:08

One of Joplin's best loved and frequently played rags, the "Maple Leaf Rag" demonstrates the composer's virtuosity and absolute mastery of the piano even though it ironically has a much faster tempo than is generally characteristic of ragtime.

TRACK 8
W.C. Handy, "St. Louis Blues"   2:57

Handy's piece did for the blues what Joplin's "Maple Leaf Rag" did the ragtime—established the musical genre in the American consciousness. As was often true of the blues, the jaunty style of the music plays against the lyrics (not sung here), which tell the classic tale of a heartbroken women deserted by her man—in this case, lured away by a flashy St. Louis woman "with her diamond rings."

TRACK 9
The Green Room, "Alive"   3:31

The unfamiliar musical patterns of the track, from the progressive rock band The Green Room's first CD, point to the composer Jorge Meija's classical musical training.

TRACK 10
Ludwig von Beethoven, from Symphony No. 9, 4th Movement   4:39

To find a musical parallel to the final chapter, Freedom, we turned to Beethoven's setting of Schiller's "Ode to Joy," expressing gratitude for the heaven-sent gift: joyous recognition of life's goodness as well as of human equality and brother-hood. It has become, fittingly, the anthem of freedom.

TRACK 11
Sophocles, from *Oedipus Rex*   3:21
This excerpt of the great classical tragedy is from a scene near the end, after Oedipus has blinded himself rather than face the four children he has unknowingly sired by his wife/mother. The actor illustrates the extreme emotions that great tragic moments contain.

TRACK 12
William Shakespeare, from *Othello:* Act V, Scene ii   2:28
Othello's final speech, ending in his death from a self-inflicted dagger thrust. It is one of the finest examples of a recognition scene in tragedy, that is, a sequence near the end of a play in which the protagonist recognizes the flaw that brought about his downfall. Othello's is that he loved "not wisely, but too well."

TRACK 13
Wolfgang Amadeus Mozart, from *The Marriage of Figaro*   5:00
The famous aria "Dove sono (Where have they gone?)" is sung by the Countess, alone on stage, as she sadly remembers her younger day, when she and her now philandering husband were newly and happily married. She asks the question that millions have asked: why does time erase our joys?

TRACK 14
from *The Dhammapada:* "Mindfulness is the Way to the Immortal"   2:40
The twelve teachings in this excerpt are centered on defining and recommending the state of mindfulness, which, in the Buddhist philosophy, means being totally awake and able to view things as they are—without interference from the self or ego. Mindfulness is achieved through long hours of meditation.

TRACK 15
from *The Bible:* "The Book of Job"   2:38
After the long-suffering Job has finally decided to ask God why he has had to undergo so many tribulations, the voice of God is heard coming from a whirlwind. The deity's declaration of absolute power and not being answerable to mortals, who have no right to question him, is deeply embedded in not only Judaic but also Christian and Islamic doctrine.

TRACK 16
Omar Khayyam, from *The Rubaiyat*   3:12
The "carpe diem" (seize the day) philosophy, central to the philosophy of hedonism, is here given one of is most enduring expressions. Khayyam urges us to "take the cash" and "forget the credit," meaning that there is little point in foregoing immediate pleasures in hopes that one will be rewarded in an afterlife.

TRACK 17
William Shakespeare, from *Romeo and Juliet:* Act II, Scene ii   6:42
In the famous balcony scene, Romeo has seen Juliet from a distance at a masked ball, goes to her home, where he hides below in the shadows, hoping for a glimpse of his beloved. She finally appears, and what follows is an exchange of words that constitute the language of true love for thousands the world over.

TRACK 18
Richard Strauss, from *Death and Transfiguration*   3:58
The excerpt presents the final four minutes from the Strauss tone poem that translates into music the stages of dying. Earlier in the piece there are restless throes that signal the oncoming of the final moment, and here the music softens into a theme of majestic beauty that builds in intensity to represent the transfiguration: the passing of the soul into a state of peace and bliss.

TRACK 19
James Joyce, from *Ulysses:* "Molly Bloom's Soliloquy"   3:49
This interior monologue, which shocked so many of its first readers, runs 45 pages at the end of Joyce's novel. It presents the thoughts and emotions—often quite erotic—running through the mind of Molly Bloom as the remembers her first meeting with her husband, Leopold Bloom, who has just tumbled into bed after spending the day wandering Dublin.

TOTAL TIME   66:08

Plate 1 Leonardo da Vinci, Mona Lisa. Louvre, Paris, France. Credit: Réunion des Musées Nationaux/Art Resource, NY.

The complexity of her expression has made this the most famous work of art in the world.

Plate 2 Romare Bearden, *Mississippi Monday* (1941). Credit: Copyright © Romare Bearden Foundation/Licensed by VAGA, New York, NY.

Bearden claimed he was more concerned with aesthetics than with social commentary. What do you think engaged him aesthetically about this scene?

Plate 3 Norman Rockwell, Marine Homecoming (1945). Credit: Printed by permission of the Norman Rockwell Family Agency Copyright ©1945 The Norman Rockwell Family Entities. Photo: The Curtis Publishing Company.

To see Rockwell's work is to gain invaluable knowledge of how a large segment of the population lived in the early twentieth century and to recognize the importance of historical context.

Plate 4 Dante Gabriel Rossetti, *Pandora Holding Her Box* (1869). Credit: AFP/Getty Images.

Two depictions of how the world's troubles began. Above, Dante Gabriel Rossetti's *Pandora* shows the moment just as the mythical woman opens the box releasing evil into the world. Below, Gabriel Alix's *Food for the Spirit* portrays the biblical first man and woman in the Garden of Eden prior to the Fall.

Plate 5 Gabriel Alix, *Food for the Spirit* (1992). Credit: Courtesy of Macondo.

Plate 6 Leonardo da Vinci, *The Last Supper* (1495–1498).
Credit: © Superstock, Inc.

Two renditions of the same subject. Da Vinci's (above) has won
universal acceptance for its reverential treatment of Jesus and
the disciples. Van der Woestyne's modern rendering of the scene
seems primarily concerned with its bold technique.

Plate 7 Gustave van der Woestyne, *The Last Supper* (1927).
Credit: Photographic Service City of Bruges, Jan Termont - Dirk Van
der Borght. Groeninge Museum, Bruges, Belgium.

Plate 8 Wassily Kandinsky, *Composition VII.* (1913).
Tretyakov Gallery, Moscow. Copyright © 2003 Artists Rights Society [ARS], New York/ADAGP,
Paris. Credit: Bridgeman Art Library.

An abstractionist, Kandinsky believed that what mattered is form, not meaning—a
pleasing arrangement of lines and color existing for no purpose other than aesthetic
experience.

Plate 9 Raphael, *The School of Athens*
(1510). Stanza della Segnatura, Stanze di
Raffaello, Vatican Palace. Credit: Scala/Art
Resource, NY.

The two figures in the center, top level,
are Plato (left) and Aristotle, his pupil.

Plate 10 Artemisia Gentileschi, *Judith Beheading Holofernes* (1620). Uffizi, Florence, Italy. Credit: Scala/Art Resource, NY.

Example of late Renaissance realism by a feminine artist scandalous in her own time.

Plate 11 Francisco Goya, *Family of Charles IV* (1800). Museo del Prado, Madrid, Spain. Credit: Erich Lessing/Art Resource, NY.

This painting is far from the idealization of royalty found in traditional portraits, but the royal family didn't seem to notice.

Plate 12 Francisco Goya, *Saturn Devouring His Children* (1819–1823). Museo del Prado, Madrid. Credit: Scala/Art Resource, NY.

Paintings such as this one raise questions about the meaning of art that is intended to provoke revulsion and horror. Does art have to be beautiful to command our respect?

Plate 13 Claude Monet, *Impression: Sunrise* (1872; Musée Marmottan, Paris). Credit: Museé Marmottan, Paris. Photo: A.K.G., Berlin/Superstock.

The painting that gave Impressionism its name. Monet avoids photographic realism in favor of depicting his personal experience of light and color.

Plate 14 Berthe Morisot, *The Psyche* (1876).
Fundacion Coleccion Thyssen-Bornemisza, Madrid.
Credit: Copyright © Nimatallah/Art Resource, NY.

Only partially influenced by Impressionism, Morisot combines
light and color with domestic realism.

Plate 15 Mary Cassatt, *Mother and Child Against a Green
Background* (1897). Museé d'Orsay, Paris. Credit: Erich
Lessing/Art Resource, NY.

American Impressionist Cassatt uses her subjects as
designs and events of light and color. The background is
more important for its color than its detail.

● **Plate 16** Vincent van Gogh, *The Starry Night* (1889).
The Museum of Modern Art, New York. Acquired through the Lillie P. Bliss Bequest, [472.19]. Credit: Digital Image © The Museum of Modern Art/Licensed by SCALA/Art Resource, NY.

The artist's most famous work, illustrating his love of color and his fierce, stabbing brushstrokes. Van Gogh is often called a post-Impressionist. Looking at this painting, can you think of any reason why it does not fit within the Impressionist school?

● **Plate 17** Georges Braque, *The Musician* (c. 1914). Kunstmuseum, Basel, Switzerland. Credit: Bridgeman-Giraudon/ Art Resource, NY © 2008 Estate on Georges Braque/Artists Rights Society (ARS), NY.

The Cubist equivalent of the unfamiliar in modern music.

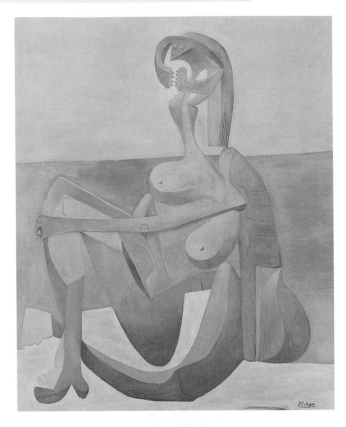

Plate 18 Pablo Picasso, Seated Bather (1930). The Museum of Modern Art, New York. Mrs. Simon Guggenheim Fund, [82.50]. Credit: © 2005 Estate of Pablo Picasso/Artists Rights Society (ARS), New York/Digital Image © The Museum of Modern Art/Licensed by SCALA/Art Resource, NY.

A prime example of Cubism. The figure is somewhat recognizable, but Picasso composed it out of geometric blocks.

Plate 19 Salvador Dalí, *Invention of the Monsters* (1937). Art Institute of Chicago. Credit: Salvador Dalí, Spanish, 1904–1989, *Inventions of the Monsters,* 1937, oil on canvas, 51.2 x 78.4 cm, Joseph Winterbotham Collection, 1943.798 Reproduction, The Art Institute of Chicago. © 2008 Gala-Salvador Dali Foundation/Artists Rights Society (ARS), NY.

Freudian elements in a surrealist painting suggesting wicked thoughts and death longings repressed and filed away in the unconscious.

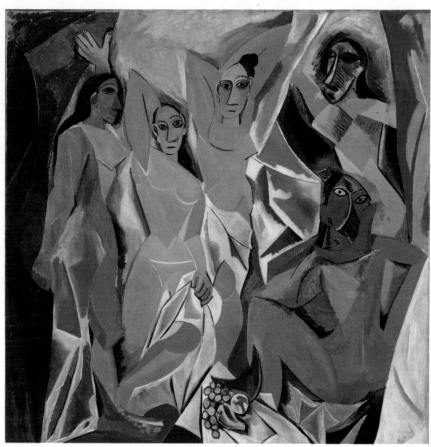

Plate 20 (Left) African mask, Lega culture. Democratic Republic of the Congo. Credit: University of Iowa Museum of Art, Stanley Collection. (Right) Pablo Picasso, *Les Demoiselles d'Avignon*, June-July 1907. Credit: Acquired through the Lille P. Bliss Bequest, The Museum of Modern Art, New York, NY. Digital Image © The Museum of Modern Art/Licensed by SCALA/Art Resource, NY. © 1999 Estate of Pablo Picasso/Artists Rights Society (ARS), New York.

When you look at the mask and at Picasso's famous painting side by side, you can see a major influence on the development of the artist's work.

Plate 21 Ogata Korin, *Azaleas* (late seventeenth century). Credit: The Hatakeyama Memorial Museum of Fine Art, Tokyo.

Korin's work exemplifies the simplicity of Japanese and Chinese art that so intrigued Western artists such as Georgia O'Keeffe.

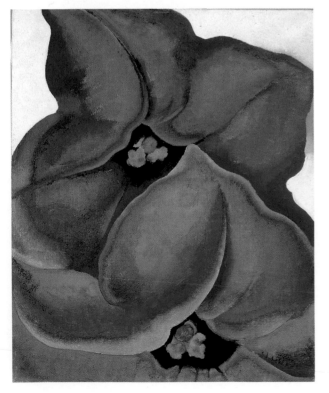

Plate 22 Georgia O'Keeffe, *Purple Petunias* (1925). Credit: Collection of the Newark Museum, New Jersey. Bequest of Miss Cora Louise Hartshorn, 1958. [Inv.58.167]. Copyright © 2003 The Georgia O'Keeffe Foundation/Artists Rights Society [ARS], New York. Photo: Copyright The Newark Museum/Art Resource, NY.

Like the Japanese artist Korin, O'Keeffe simplified the natural world by focusing on the beauty of a single subject.

● **Plate 23** R.C. Gorman, *Navajo Dawn* (1989).
Credit: R.C. Gorman's Navajo Gallery.

Gorman, an artist of the Southwest, who may
have been influenced by O'Keeffe, simplifies
this desert scene to a point of near abstraction.

● **Plate 24** Maggie Taylor, *The Philosopher's Daughter*
(2000). Credit: Courtesy of Maggie Taylor.

Computer art using images from scanners and
cameras to create an entirely imagined scene.

Plate 25 Andy Warhol, *Marilyn Monroe* (1962).
Credit: Phillips, The International Fine Art Auctioneers, UK. Copyright © 2003 Andy Warhol Foundation for the Visual Arts/Artists Rights Society [ARS], New York. TM 2002 Marilyn Monroe LLC by CMG Worldwide Inc. http://www.MarilynMonroe.com. Photo: Bridgeman Art Library.

Warhol's celebrity portraits, such as this one of the screen goddess Marilyn Monroe, suggest tacky movie magazines, but they are more than that. They make serious comments on our culture, Hollywood celebrities and their fans, and the individuals they depict.

Plate 26 Sydney Opera House. Credit: © L. Clarke/Corbis.

Like many architectural works, the Sydney Opera House is meant to provide aesthetic pleasure as well as to fill citizens with pride. Now a favorite landmark, the opera house was not warmly embraced by all citizens when first completed in 1973.

Plate 27 Finale from *A Chorus Line* (1975). Credit: Everett Collection.

This photograph depicts the musical's famous finale, in which those driven and skilled enough to make the show's final cut lose their individuality and meld into " One,"a chorus line.

 Plate 28 Scene from *The Godfather* (1973). Credit: Photofest, Inc.

A scene from the famous wedding sequence that opens Francis Ford Coppola's film. On the surface, *The Godfather* is an intimate exploration of honor, revenge, and betrayal in the Mafia. The film's deeper themes, however, point to the relationship of crime, power, and the American Dream.

● **Plate 29** Chagall, *Job in Despair*. Credit: Image courtesy of goldmarkart.com. © 2008 Estate of Marc Chagall, Artists Rights Society (ARS), NY.

The Book of Job faces one of the most challenging questions for religious writers: why do disasters befall the innocent?